HEALTHCARE:
THE IMPACT OF THE
HUMAN RIGHTS ACT 1998

HEALTHCARE: THE IMPACT OF THE HUMAN RIGHTS ACT 1998

Austen Garwood-Gowers, LLB (Hons), Cert Couns, PhD
Senior Lecturer in Law
Nottingham Law School, The Nottingham Trent University
Formerly of Middlesex University Business School, London

John Tingle, BA (Law Hons), Cert Ed, MEd, Barrister
Reader in Health Law and Director of the Centre for Health Law
Department of Academic Legal Studies
Nottingham Law School
The Nottingham Trent University

Tom Lewis, BA (Hons) (Oxon), Solicitor
Senior Lecturer in Law, Nottingham Law School
The Nottingham Trent University

Cavendish
Publishing
Limited

London • Sydney

First published in Great Britain 2001 by Cavendish Publishing Limited,
The Glass House, Wharton Street, London WC1X 9PX, United Kingdom
Telephone: +44 (0)20 7278 8000   Facsimile: +44 (0)20 7278 8080
Email: info@cavendishpublishing.com
Website: www.cavendishpublishing.com

British Library Cataloguing in Publication Data

Garwood-Gowers, Austen –
Healthcare law: the impact of the Human Rights Act 1998
1 Great Britain. Human Rights Act 1998 2 Medical care – Law and
legislation 3 Human rights – Great Britain
I Title II Tingle, John, 1954 III Lewis, Tom
344.4'1'04

ISBN 1 85941 670 5

Printed and bound in Great Britain

CONTRIBUTORS

The Editors

Austen Garwood-Gowers, LLB, PhD, is Senior Lecturer in Law Nottingham Law School, The Nottingham Trent University. He was previously at Middlesex University Business School, specialising in civil liberties and human rights, tort and medical law and ethics. He has written extensively on healthcare law issues.

John Tingle, BA, Cert Ed, MEd, Barrister, Reader in Health Care Law and Director of the Centre for Health Law, Department of Academic Legal Studies, The Nottingham Trent University has written extensively in the field of health law and was editor of *Health Care Risk Report* from 1995 until May 2001.

Tom Lewis, BA (Oxon), Solicitor, is Senior Lecturer in Law at The Nottingham Trent University.

Contributors

Laura Davidson, MA, LLM (Cantab), is a Barrister at the Chambers of Kieran Coonan QC, 6 Pump Court, Temple, EC4, with a particular interest in mental health and medical law, human rights and criminal law. She holds the Nightingale Research Studentship in mental health at Trinity Hall, the University of Cambridge, where she is currently completing a doctorate. She has lectured at various special units, as well as having spoken at numerous conferences in the UK and overseas. She is an honorary Senior Research Fellow at the University of Florida. An additional interest in international crime has led to her contribution of two chapters on international mutual assistance to the next edition of *Jones on Extradition* (2001, London: Sweet & Maxwell).

Rod Edmunds, BA, LLB, is Senior Lecturer in Law at the University of Sussex. He has an active research interest in the property and succession rights of people who lack mental capacity.

Charles Foster, Barrister, practises from the Chambers of Kieran Coonan QC, 6 Pump Court, Temple, EC4. He read law and veterinary medicine at Cambridge University, following which he researched wild animal immobilisation in Saudi Arabia and comparative anatomy at the Royal College of Surgeons. He later became a Research Fellow at the Faculty of Law, Hebrew University, Jerusalem, and Research Assistant to Aharon Barak, Judge of the Supreme Court of Israel. Charles is the author of *Civil Advocacy* (2001, London: Cavendish Publishing), *Clinical Confidentiality* (2000, Sudbury: Monitor Press), *Drafting* (2001, London: Cavendish Publishing), *Personal Injury Toolkit* (1997), *Disclosure and Confidentiality* (1996), *Tripping and Slipping Cases* (1994 and 1996, London: Sweet & Maxwell), and editor (with John Tingle) of *Clinical Guidelines: Law, Policy and Practice* (2001, London: Cavendish Publishing), as well as having contributed chapters in other legal and non-legal works. A regular contributor to the *Solicitors' Journal, Health Care Risk Report* and other legal journals, he also writes for a number of non-legal publications and is a member of the Bar of Ireland.

John Hodgson, MA, LLM, Solicitor, Principal Lecturer Department of Professional Legal Studies, The Nottingham Trent University.

Melanie Latham, BSc, PhD, is Senior Lecturer in Law at the Manchester Metropolitan University School of Law. Her research interests are multidisciplinary and comparative, but largely centre on the study of medical law, health politics, bioethics and rights in European States, particularly Britain and France. Her book, *Regulating Reproduction: A Century of Conflict in Britain and France* (Manchester: Manchester UP), is due to be published in January 2002 and examines reproductive law and politics in the 20th century in both countries.

Siobhan Leonard is Senior Lecturer at the School of Law, Manchester Metropolitan University. She specialises in European law and human rights law and is editor of *Human Rights in the 21st Century* (with Angela Hegarty, 1999, London: Cavendish Publishing).

Alasdair Maclean, BSc, MBBS, PG Dip Law, M Jur, is a Lecturer in Law at the University of Southampton. He is the author of *Briefcase on Medical Law* (2001, London: Cavendish Publishing).

Sabine Michalowski, PhD, is Lecturer in Law, at the University of Essex, where specialises in medical law. She is the author of *German Constitutional Law – The Protection of Civil Liberties* (1999, Aldershot: Ashgate, with Lorna Woods), and has written several articles on medical ethics, confidentiality and medical privilege.

Wendy Outhwaite is a barrister at 2 Harcourt Buildings, London, specialising in clinical negligence, personal injury, human rights and judicial review.

Gerard Panting, MA, DMJ, MRCGP, is Head of Policy and External Relations at the Medical Protection Society. He formerly headed up the UK Division, having moved to the Society in 1987. He was previously a trainer and course organiser for a six-man partnership in St Albans, Hertfordshire, and a Deputy Police Surgeon for Hemel Hempstead and St Albans, the latter post having undoubtedly kindled his interest in the law. Gerard's special interests include consent law, complaints procedures and the development of risk management.

Aurora Plomer is a Lecturer in Law at the University of Leeds. She is an associate partner in the EU funded project EURICON on the regulation of clinical trials on neonates. She has conducted research for the Council of Europe and directed a major study on the funding of IVF in the NHS. She has published several articles on medical law and ethics.

Jeff Sapiro, MA, PG Dip, RGN, RMN, is Senior Lecturer in medical ethics and law in the School of Health, Biological and Environmental Science, Middlesex University.

Marc Stauch, MA (Oxon), Solicitor, is Lecturer in Law at the University of Leicester. He was formerly at The Nottingham Trent University. He has published widely in the fields of medical and tort law and is a co-author, with Kay Wheat and John Tingle, of *Sourcebook on Medical Law* (1998, London: Cavendish Publishing).

David Stone, BA, MA, Solicitor, formerly partner in Bird & Bird, London, is currently Partner in Hempsons, London. He has been Deputy District Judge, South Eastern Circuit since 1999. David Stone has many years' experience advising NHS and private sector organisations on health care law, clinical negligence litigation, professional regulation, commercial disputes, data protection, defamation, and the impact of information technology. He contributed to *Cook and Jabbari on Pharmaceuticals, Biotechnology and the Law* (1991, London: Macmillan); *The Lawyer's Factbook* (London: Gee); numerous articles for health care journals, and frequent lectures to healthcare professionals and managers. He is on the editorial board of *Health Care Risk Report*.

Teresa Sutton, LLB, MPhil is Lecturer in Law at the School of Legal Studies, University of Sussex.

Anjilay Ungoed-Thomas, MA, PG Dip Law, BA, RNT, RCNT, RN, is Principal Lecturer in medical ethics and law in the School of Health, Biological and Environmental Science, Middlesex University.

Steven Wheatley, LLB, LLM, is Lecturer in Law at the Liverpool Law School, University of Liverpool.

John Williams, LLB (Wales), LLB (Cantab), is Professor of Law and Head of Department of Law at the University of Wales, Aberystwyth. He recently authored 'The inappropriate adult' (2000) 22 Journal of Social Welfare and Family Law 43, 'The Crime and Disorder Act 1998: conflicting roles for the appropriate adult' [2000] Crim LR 911 and 'Hunger strikes: a prisoner's right or a "wicked folly"?' (2001) 40(3) Howard Journal 285. His research interests include the law relating to vulnerable adults, especially the abuse of older people. His current project is research is into the impact of the Human Rights Act 1998 on the law and procedures relating to vulnerable adult protection.

Katherine S Williams, LLB (Wales), LLB (Cantab), is Lecturer in Law at the University of Wales, Aberystwyth. She is the author of *Textbook on Criminology* (3rd edn, 1997, London: Blackstone) and articles on CCTV and e-commerce. Her research interests include the impact of the Human Rights Act 1998 on various aspects of law and social interaction, in particular as it relates to vulnerable adults, education and criminal justice. She is also analysing the effects of devolution in Wales, often analysing the dual effects of devolution and human rights

Peteris Zilgalvis, JD, is Deputy Head of the Bioethics Division at the Council of Europe, and is Secretary of the Working Parties on Biomedical research and Biotechnology. A member of the California State Bar since 1990, he was formerly at the World Bank. He has published articles and chapters of books on bioethics, environmental law, and economic reform.

ACKNOWLEDGMENTS

The idea for this book came out of a conference entitled 'The Human Rights Act 1998 and Healthcare'. This was a dynamic event held run by the Centre of Health Law at The Nottingham Trent University on 10 May 2000 and we are indebted to all of those who helped John Tingle facilitate it.

For help in the initial stages of developing the book we would like to thank Jonathon Griffiths, formerly of The Nottingham Trent University Law School and now at Queen Mary, University of London. That the book came together in such a short time is due to a large degree to the contributors who turned conference presentations or, in some cases, blank 'Word documents' (few people these days start with a blank sheet of paper!) into well reasoned and detailed chapters within a few months. Tom Lewis of The Nottingham Trent University Department of Academic Legal Studies assisted us greatly in the editorial process by editing the chapters on Human Rights Act points. He also produced a quick guide to some 'Convention terms and concepts' which is included below. Kay Wheat of the same department also kindly helped out by editing the chapters on the medical law points.

As editors we have enjoyed investing our time bringing together a work which deals with such cutting-edge issues. We hope you benefit from reading it.

CONTENTS

Contributors		*v*
Acknowledgments		*ix*
Table of Cases		*xv*
Table of Legislation		*xxxiii*
Table of Statutory Instruments		*xxxvii*
Table of International Instruments		*xxxix*
Convention Terms and Concepts		*xlv*
Table of Abbreviations		*li*

1   **The Human Rights Act 1998: A Potent Tool for Changing Healthcare Law and Practice**   **1**

Austen Garwood-Gowers and John Tingle

2   **The Human Rights Act 1998 and the Common Law, a Healthcare Law Perspective**   **13**

John Hodgson

3   **The European Convention on Human Rights and Biomedicine: Its Past, Present and Future**   **31**

Peteris Zilgalvis

4   **The Scope of Impact of the Human Rights Act 1998 on Healthcare and NHS Resource Allocation**   **49**

Wendy Outhwaite

5   **Litigating Bioethics: The Role of Autonomy and Dignity**   **67**

Steven Wheatley

6   **The Individual's Right to Treatment under the Human Rights Act 1998**   **81**

Alasdair Maclean

7   **Access, Procedure and the Human Rights Act 1998 in Medical Cases**   **99**

Charles Foster

8   **Medical Complaints, Discipline and the Human Rights Act 1998**   **113**

Gerard Panting

9   **Confidentiality, Access to Health Records and the Human Rights Act 1998**   **127**

David Stone

10 Vulnerable Adults – Confidentiality and
    Inter-disciplinary Working   147
    Kate S Williams and John Williams

11 The Impact of the Human Rights Act 1998 on Mental Health
    Law and Practice: Part I   163
    Laura Davidson

12 The Impact of the Human Rights Act 1998 on Mental Health
    Law: Part II   181
    Laura Davidson

13 The Human Rights Act 1998 and Private Property Rights in the
    Context of Community Care   201
    Rod Edmunds and Teresa Sutton

14 Time for Competent Minors to Have the Same Right of Self-
    Determination as Competent Adults with Respect to Medical
    Intervention?   225
    Austen Garwood-Gowers

15 Young Children, Best Interests and the Human Rights Act 1998   243
    Sabine Michalowski

16 Pregnancy and the Human Rights Act 1998   259
    Marc Stauch

17 Euthanasia and the Human Rights Act 1998   273
    Jeff Sapiro and Angie Ungoed-Thomas

18 Extraction and Use of Body Materials for Transplantation and
    Research Purposes: The Impact of the Human Rights Act 1998   295
    Austen Garwood-Gowers

19 Medical Research, Consent and the European Convention on
    Human Rights and Biomedicine   313
    Aurora Plomer

20 The European Convention on Biomedicine and the Human
    Rights Act 1998: Grasping the Nettle of Biomedicine?   331
    Melanie Latham and Siobhan Leonard

Contents

Appendix 1:   The Human Rights Act 1998   347

Appendix 2:   Convention for the Protection of Human Rights and
              Dignity of the Human Being with Regard to the
              Application of Biology and Medicine: The European
              Convention on Human Rights and Biomedicine   375

Bibliography   387
Index   401

TABLE OF CASES

A (Children) (Conjoined Twins: Medical
 Treatment), Re [2001] 1 FLR 1; [2000] All ER (D) 1211;
 (2000) The Times, 10 October 9, 51, 57, 58, 245, 256, 258, 285

A, Re [1992] 3 Med LR 303 Fam Div 279, 303

A v United Kingdom, Reports 1998-VI, para 22;
 (1998) 27 EHRR 611. . . . . .71, 192, 292

A NHS Trust v D [2000] 2 FCR 577; [2000] TLR 552 . . . . .58, 250, 251, 258

ADT v UK, App No 35765/97,
 Case Decided 31 July 2000 79

Abdulaziz, Cabales and Balkandali v United
 Kingdom, Judgment 28 May 1985,
 Series A, No 94; (1985) 7 EHRR 471 . . . . .73, 286, 317

Acmanne v Belgium, App No 10435/83;
 (1984) 40 DR 251 . . . . .59, 72

Aerts v Belgium, *See* R v Secretary of State for the
 Home Office ex p Gilkes; Aerts v Belgium—

Ahmed v Austria, Reports 1996-VI, para 40 71

Airedale NHS Trust v Bland [1993] AC 789;
 [1993] 1 All ER 821 . . . . .23, 55, 97, 274, 275,
 278–85, 294, 302

Airey v Ireland (1979) 2 EHRR 305 112

Albert and Le Compte v Belgium (1983) 5 EHRR 533 . . . . .100, 101

Alkmaar, Nederlands Jurisprudentie 1985, No 106
 Supreme Court, 27 November 1984 275

Alliance and Leicester plc v Slayford, 2000 WL 1280058 216

Alsterland v Sweden (1988) 56 DR 229 E Comm HR 102

Anderson v The Scottish Ministers and Another,
 Inner House, 16 June 2000 . . . . .168, 173

Andreucci v Italy, Series A, No 228-G (1992) 110

Argyll v Argyll [1967] Ch 302 130

Artico v Italy (1981) 3 EHRR 1 162

Ashingdane v UK (1985) 7 EHRR 528 . . . . .164–66, 170, 172, 174, 180, 191

Associated Provincial Picture House
 v Wednesbury Corporation [1948] 1 KB 223 82

Association X v UK, App No 7154/75;
 (1978) 14 DR 31 . . . . .56, 90–92, 244

AG's Reference (No 3 of 1994)
 [1998] AC 245 . . . . .259, 265

AG's Reference (No 34 of 1992)
 (1993) 15 Cr App R(S) 167 195

AG v Able [1984] 1 All ER 277 276
AG v Guardian Newspapers
    [1988] 3 All ER 545 . . . . .152, 153
AG v Guardian Newspapers (No 2)
    (Spycatcher case) [1990] 1 AC 109 130
AG v X and Others [1992] 1 IR 1 261
Auckland AHB v AG [1993] 1 NZLR 235 (NZ) 283
Axen v Germany (1983) 6 EHRR 195 . . . . .108, 109

B (A Minor) (Wardship: Medical Treatment), Re
    [1981] 1 WLR 1421 CA 281
Balfour v United Kingdom [1997] EHRLR 665 101
Barker v Barking, Havering and Brentwood
    Community Healthcare NHS Trust (Warley
    Hospital) and Dr Jason Taylor
    [1999] Lloyd's Rep Med 101 CA 165
Barrett v Enfield LBC [1999] 3 WLR 79 103
Barrett v United Kingdom (1997) 23 EHRR CD 185 286
Beard v UK, App No 24882/94 214
Benham v United Kingdom, Judgment 10 June 1996;
    Reports 1996-III 18
Biggin Hill Airport Ltd v Bromley LBC
    (2001) 98 LSG 42 211
Bolam v Friern Hospital Management Committee
    [1957] 1 WLR 582 . . . . .23, 99, 104, 283, 321–23
Bolitho v City and Hackney HA
    [1997] 4 All ER 771 . . . . .321, 322
Botta v Italy Reports (1998) 26 EHRR 241 . . . . .72, 73, 209, 267
Boughanemi v France (1996) 22 EHRR 228 200
Boumar v Belgium, Judgment 28 November 1988,
    Series A, No 129; (1989) 11 EHRR 1 . . . . .237, 298
British Railways Board v Pickin
    [1974] AC 765 HL 1
Brown v Heathlands Mental Health Services Trust
    [1996] 1 All ER 133 203
Brüggemann and Scheuten v Federal Republic of
    Germany, App No 6959/75;
    (1981) 3 EHRR 244; (1978) 10 DR 100 . . . . .76, 95, 263
Bucholz v Germany (1981) 3 EHRR 597 110

Burton v Islington HA and de Martell v Merton and
Sutton HA [1992] 3 All ER 833. 265
Burton v UK (1996) 22 EHRR CD 134 . . . . .213, 214

C (A Baby), Re (1996) 32 BMLR 44 281
C (A Minor) (Medical Treatment), Re
[1998] 1 Lloyd's Rep Med 1 Fam Div 85, 282
C (A Minor) (Wardship: Medical Treatment), Re
[1989] 2 All ER 782 CA 281
C (Adult: Refusal of Medical Treatment), Re
[1994] 1 All ER 819 . . . . .148, 279
C (Courts' Inherent Jurisdiction) (Child: Detention
and Treatment), Re (1998) 40 BMLR 31 . . . . .230, 249, 251
C (HIV Test), Re [1999] 2 FLR 1004 . . . . .254, 256, 258
C (Medical Treatment), Re [1998] 1 FLR 384 248
C & G Homes v Secretary of State for Health
[1991] Ch 365 . . . . .204, 205, 208
C v S [1988] QB 135 262
CR v UK, Case 20190/92, Judgment 22 November 1995 . . . . .16, 22
Camitta v Fager, Eq No 73-171 (Mass, 5 September 1973) 300
Caradon DC v Paton [2000] 3 EGLR 57 204
Cayouette v Mathieu [1987] RJQ 2230 Sup Ct 300
Central Control Board (Liquor Traffic)
v Cannon Brewery Co Ltd [1919] AC 742 HL 1
Chapman v UK, App No 27238/95,
Judgment 18 January 2001 214
Chatterton v Gerson [19081] QB 432 312
Chorherr v Austria, Judgment 25 August 1993,
Series A, No 266-B 21
Ciliz v Netherlands, App No 29192/95,
Case Decided 11 July 2000 . . . . .73, 74
Claire Conroy, In the Matter of
486 2d 1209 (1985) NJ Sup Ct 280
Cleburne Living Centre Inc v City of Cleburne
437 US 432 (1985) 221
Coco v AN Clark (Engineers) Ltd [1969] RPC 41 . . . . .129, 133
Commission v Germany, App No 10565/83;
(1984) 7 EHRR 152 . . . . .244, 250
Costello-Roberts v UK, Series A, No 247 (1993) 71

Coster v UK, App No 24976/94 214

Council of Civil Service Unions v Minister of the
    Civil Service [1985] AC 374 HL 2

Crane Neck Association v New York/Long Island
    County Services Group 460 NE 2d 1336 (NY 1984) 222

Cruzan v Director, Missouri Department of Health
    497 US 261 (1990) US Sup Ct 283

Curley v United Kingdom, App No 32340/96,
    28 March 2000; (2000) The Times, 5 April 188, 193

D v United Kingdom (1997) 24 EHRR 423 ....52, 56, 72, 245, 251, 293

D, Re (1997) 41 BMLR 81 282

Daniels v Walker [2000] 1 WLR 1382 29

De Wilde, Ooms and Versyp v Netherlands
    (1971) 1 EHRR 373 167

Denmark, Norway, Sweden and the Netherlands
    v Greece (1969) 12 Yearbook 186 93

Douglas v Hello! Ltd [2001] 2 WLR 992 216

Dr Barnardo's Homes National Incorporated
    Association's Application, Re (1955) 7 P & CR 176 203–05

Dr Bonham's Case (1610) 8 Co Rep 114a 1

Dudgeon v UK, Series A, No 45 (1982);
    (1982) 4 EHRR 149 ....79, 240, 270, 290

E v Norway (1990) 17 EHRR 30. 186–88

E (A Minor) (Wardship: Medical Treatment), Re
    [1993] 1 FLR 386 ....226, 227

ELH and PBH v UK, App Nos 32094/96 and
    32568/96; (1997) 91A DR 61 75

East African Asians v UK, App No 4403/70;
    (1981) 3 EHRR 76 93

Eckle v Germany (1982) 5 EHRR 1 110

Edmonds v Armstrong Funeral Home Ltd
    (1931) 1 DLR 676 308

Engel v Netherlands (1976) 1 EHRR 647 ....165, 166, 170

F v West Berkshire AHA [1989] 2 All ER 545 ....99, 104, 325, 326

F (Mental Patient: Sterilisation), Re
    [1990] 2 AC 1; [1989] 2 All ER 545 ....26, 28, 148, 159, 280, 297, 329

F (In Utero), Re [1988] Fam 122. ....262, 266

FC v UK, App 37344/97, 30 March 1999 197
Factortame v Secretary of State for Transport (No 2)
    [1991] All ER 70 CJEC and HL 2
Family T v Austria, App No 14013/88,
    14 December 1989; (1990) 64 DR 176 ....236, 298
Fey v Austria (1993) 16 EHRR 387 111
Finlayson v HM Advocate [1979] JC 33 279
Fischer v Austria (1995) 20 EHRR 349 108
Frenchay Healthcare NHS Trust v S
    [1994] 2 All ER 403; (1994) 17 BMLR 156 CA 86, 283

G v Italy Series A, No 228-F (1992) 110
G (A Minor), Re [1996] 2 All ER 65 151
G (Persistent Vegetative State), Re
    [1995] 2 FCR 46 Fam Div 86, 283
Gaskin v United Kingdom (1989) 12 EHRR 36 ....135, 196
Gautrin v France (1998) 28 EHRR 196 111
Gillick v West Norfolk and Wisbech AHA
    [1985] 3 All ER 402 ....148, 152, 226–28, 237,
                                       242, 248, 301, 325
Gillow v UK (1986) 11 EHRR 335 ....166, 196, 213
Gold v Haringey HA
    [1987] 2 All ER 888 ....314, 321
Golder v UK (1975) 1 EHRR 524 ....5, 102, 316
Grare v France (1992) 15 EHRR CD 100 ....192, 193
Guenoun v France (1990) 66 DR 181 E Comm HR 108
Guerra v Baptiste [1996] 1 AC 397 195
Guerra v Italy (1998) 26 EHRR 357 56
Guzzardi v Italy (1980) 3 EHRR 333 ....166, 173, 175, 178, 237, 238, 317

H v Mental Health Review Tribunal, North and East
    London Region (2001) The Times, 2 April 172, 182, 183
H v Norway (1990), App No 17004/90;
    (1992) 73 DE 155 ....51, 262, 340
H (Adult: Incompetent), Re
    (1997) 38 BMLR 11 Fam Div 283
H, Re; M, Re (2000) unreported,
    6 October Fam Div 23
Hackethal case (1988) G Sup Ct 278

Hakansson and Sturesson
  v Sweden (1990) 13 EHRR 1 109
Halford v UK, Judgment 25 June 1997,
  (1997) 24 EHRR 523 . . . . .18, 157
Handyside v UK, Series A, No 24;
  (1979–80) 1 EHRR 737 . . . . .160, 198, 239, 246, 315
Hardman v Amin [2000] Lloyd's Rep Med 498 66
Hart v Brown 289 2 Ad 386 (1972) 300
Hashman & Harrup v United Kingdom, Case 25594/94,
  Judgment 25 November 1999 . . . . .20, 22, 27
Hellewell v Chief Constable of Derbyshire
  [1995] 4 All ER 473 130
Herczegfalvy v Austria, Series A, No 244 (1992);
  (1992) 15 EHRR 437 . . . . .52, 61, 71, 163, 164, 192, 193,
                                                           239, 244, 245, 251, 254, 292, 298, 341
Hill v Chief Constable of West Yorkshire [1989] AC 53 . . . . .103, 284
Hill v Community of Damien of Molokia
  911 P 2d 861 (NM 1996) 222, 223
HIV Haemophiliac Litigation, Re [1990] NLJR 1349 284
Hornsby v Greece (1997) 24 EHRR 250 102
Houston, Applicant (1997) 5 Med LR 237 229
Huber v France (1998) 26 EHRR 457 101
Hurtado v Switzerland, Series A, No 280-A (1994) 52, 60, 72, 93, 244, 293
Hussain v United Kingdom (1996) 22 EHRR 1 189

Ireland v UK (1978) 2 EHRR 25 . . . . .52, 191, 192, 291
Iskon v UK (1994) 76A D & R 90 211

J (A Minor) (Child in Care) (Medical Treatment), Re
  [1992] 4 All ER 614 . . . . .81, 85
J (A Minor) (Consent to Medical Treatment), Re;
  sub nom W (A Minor) (Medical Treatment:
  Courts' Jurisdiction), Re [1992] 4 All ER 627;
  [1993] Fam 64; [1992] 3 WLR 758;
  [1992] 2 FCR 785 . . . . .4, 10, 148, 226–32, 242, 301, 325
J (A Minor) (Wardship: Medical Treatment), Re
  [1991] Fam 33; [1990] 3 All ER 930;
  [1991] 1 FLR 366 . . . . .55, 81, 84, 85, 249, 279, 281
J (Specific Issue Orders: Muslim Upbringing and
  Circumcision), Re [1999] 2 FLR 678 Fam Div 258

JA Pye (Oxford) Ltd and Another
    v Graham and Another [2001] 2 WLR 1293 ....212, 216
JT v UK, App 26494/95, 30 March 2000 196
James v UK (1986) 8 EHRR 123 ....210, 211
Jane Smith v UK, App No 25154/94 214
Johansen v Norway (1996) 23 EHRR 33 ....53, 246, 255
Johnson v United Kingdom (1997) EHRR 296 182
Jullien v France (1991) 71 DR 141 156

K (A Minor) (Abortion), Re (1993) unreported 260
K v Austria Series A, No 255-B (1993) 182
K v UK, App No 11468/85 (1991), 15 April 1988 ....180, 188
Kaye v Robertson [1991] FSR 62 129
Keegan v Ireland (1994) 18 EHRR 342 200
Keenan v UK, App No 27229/95, 3 April 2001;
    (2001) The Times, 18 April 191
Kiliç v Turkey, App No 22492/93,
    Case Decided 28 March 2000 70
Koendjbiharie v Netherlands (1990) 13 EHRR 820 ....187, 188
Kokkinakis v Greece, Judgment 25 May 1993,
    Series A, No 260-A 17
Konig v Germany (1978) 2 EHRR 170 110
Kopp v Switzerland, Judgment 25 March 1998 19
Kosiek v Germany (1986) 9 EHRR 328 101
Krippendorf v GMC [2000] TLR 29 119
Kruslin v France (1990) 12 EHRR 547 158

L v Bournewood [1998] 3 All ER 289 ....22, 25, 28
L (Medical Treatment: Gillick Competency), Re
    [1998] 2 FLR 810 230
LCB v United Kingdom (1998) 27 EHRR 212;
    [1998] TLR 381 ....56, 61, 92, 244, 284, 285, 292
Labita v Italy, App No 26772/95,
    Case Decided 6 April 2000 71
Lamy v Belgium (1989) 11 EHRR 529 183
Larissis and Others v Greece, Judgment of
    24 February 1998; Reports 1997-III 18
Laskey, Jaggard and Brown v United Kingdom,
    Reports 1997-I; (1997) 24 EHRR 39 ....74, 79, 160, 287

Law Hospital NHS Trust v Lord Advocate
(1996) 39 BMLR 166 283
Lawless v Ireland (Merits), Judgment of 1 July 1961, Series A,
Vol 3; (1979–80) 1 EHRR 15 ECtHR 2
Le Compte, Van Leuven and De Meyere
v Belgium (1981) 4 EHRR 1 . . . . .101, 111
Lee v UK, App No 25289/94 214
Litwa v Poland (2000) unreported, 4 April 173, 175, 178
Lloyd's Application, Re (1993) 66 P & CR 112 . . . . .207, 208
Luberti v Italy (1984) 6 EHRR 440 . . . . .171, 193

M, Re (Child: Refusal of Medical Treatment)
[1999] 2 FCR 29 . . . . .228, 230
MB, Re (An Adult: Medical Treatment)
(1997) 38 BMLR 175; [1997] 2 FLR 426;
[1997] 2 FCR 541 CA 81, 148, 225, 262, 266, 269
MS v Sweden [1998] EHRLR 115 53
McCormick v Lord Advocate 1953 SC 39 2
McFall v Shimp (1978) 10 Pa D & C (3d) 90
Ct Comm Pl, Pa 269, 296
McGinley and Egan v United Kingdom
(1998) 27 EHRR 1 143
McKay v Essex AHA [1982] QB 1166 . . . . .58, 266
McLeod v United Kingdom, Case 24755/94,
Judgment 23 September 1998 19
Mains Farm v Worthington 854 P 2d 1072 (Wash 1993) 223
Malone v UK (1984) 7 EHRR 14 . . . . .157, 158
Manieri v Italy Series A, No 229-D (1992) 110
Marckx v Belgium (1979) 2 EHRR 300 .200, 210, 211, 255, 267, 286
Margareta and Roger Andersson v Sweden,
Case 24755/94, Judgment 25 February 1992 19
Matznetter v Austria (1969) 1 EHRR 198 183
Maynard v West Midlands RHA [1984] 1 WLR 634 23
Meering v Grahame-White Aviation (1919) 122 LT 44 24
Megyeri v Germany (1992) 15 EHRR 584 . . . . .112, 183
Mentes v Turkey (1998) 26 EHRR 595 213
Milbury Care Services Limited's Application, Re,
1999/LP/78/95; transcript 30 April 1999 . . . . .203, 206, 212, 219, 221
Mitchigan Protection and Advocacy Service
v Babin 18 F 3d 337 (6th Cir 1994) 223

Munro v United Kingdom (1987) 52 DR 158 112
Muti v Italy Series A, No 281-C (1994) 110

NHS Trust A v Mrs M and NHS Trust B v Mrs H
   [2000] All ER 1522; [2000] EWHC 29;
   (2000) The Times, 29 November 9, 11, 51, 56, 58, 97, 250,
                                                          283, 293, 294
Nancy B v Hotel Dieu de Quebec
   (1992) 86 DLR (4th) 385 Can 280, 286
National & Provincial Building Society,
   Cases 117/1996/736/933–35,
   Judgment 23 October 1997 28
National Schizophrenia Fellowship
   v Ribble Estates SA [1994] 1 EGLR 181 . . . . .203, 205
Nationwide News Pty Ltd v Wills
   (1992) 177 CLR 1 FC 92/032 323
Neigel v France [1997] EHRLR 424 101
Neumeister v Austria (1968) 1 EHRR 91 183
Nielson v Denmark (1988) 11 EHRR 175 . . . . .54, 236, 237, 298
Niemetz v Germany (1992) 16 EHRR 97 . . . . .145, 156, 198
North West Lancashire HA v A, D and G
   [1999] Lloyd's Rep Med 399 . . . . .88, 93, 264
Nwabueze v GMC [2000] 1 WLR 1760; (2000) 56 BMLR 106;
   (2000) The Times, 11 April PC 122

Obermeier v Austria (1990) 13 EHRR 290 102
Observer and Guardian v UK (1992) 14 EHRR 153 315
Open Door Counselling and Dublin Well Woman
   Clinic v Ireland, Series A, No 246-A (1993);
   (1992) 15 EHRR 244 . . . . .79, 161, 262, 287–89, 315
Osman v UK, App No 23452/94; (2000) 29 EHRR 245;
   [1999] 1 FLR 193; (1998) 5 BHRC 293 . . . . .56, 63, 70, 90, 91, 103,
                                                     217, 268, 285
Oxford v Moss (1979) 68 Cr App R 183 129

Parliamentary Assembly Opinion No 184,
   2 February 1995, Doc 7210 34
Parliamentary Assembly Opinion No 198,
   26 September 1996, Doc 7622 34
Paschim Banga Khet Mazdoor Samity
   v State of West Bengal [1996] 4 SCC 37 . . . . .57, 64

Passannante v Italy (1998) 26 EHRR CD 153 . . . . .52, 60

Paton v Trustees of BPAS [1979] QB 276 262

Paton v UK (1981) 3 EHRR 408; (1980) 19 DR 244 . . . . .51, 95, 259, 261, 262, 289

Pauger v Austria (1998) 25 EHRR 105 109

Pearce v United Bristol Healthcare NHS Trust
   [1999] PIQR 53 321

Percy v Director of Public Prosecutions
   [1995] 1 WLR 1382 21

Peter Smallwood v UK, App No 29779/96;
   [1999] EHRLR 221 247

Peters v Netherlands (1994) (1994) 77A DR 75 . . . . .53, 198

Piersack v Belgium (1986) B 47 23 111

Porter v United Kingdom (1987) 54 DR 207 E Comm HR 102

Pratt v AG for Jamaica [1993] 4 All ER 769 195

Preto v Italy (1983) 6 EHRR 182 109

Queen, the, on the Application of 'H' v MHRT, North and East London
   Region (2000) unreported, 15 November QBD 176

Quinlan, Re 70 NJ 10 (1976); 355 A 2d 647 (1976) 280, 283

R, Re [1991] 3 WLR 592 148

R v Blogg (1981) 3 Cr App R(S) 114 195

R v Bournewood Community and Mental Health
   NHS Trust ex p L [1998] 3 All ER 289 . . . . .165, 167, 171, 180, 184, 186, 196

R v Brent LBC ex p D (1998) 1 CCLR 234 56

R v Cambridge DHA ex p B
   [1995] 1 WLR 898; [1995] 1 FLR 1055 . . . . .63, 81, 82

R v Canons Park MHRT ex p A [1995] QB 60 . . . . .176, 177

R v Central Birmingham HA
   ex p Collier (1988) LEXIS, 6 January 62, 64

R v Chard (1993) The Times, 23 September 277

R v Chief Immigration Officer, Heathrow Airport and
   Another ex p Salamat Bibi [1976] 1 WLR 979 25

R v Civil Service Appeal Board
   ex p Cunningham [1992] ICR 816. 115

R v Collins ex p S [1998] 3 All ER 673 81

R v Department of Health
   ex p Source Informatics Ltd [2000] Lloyd's Rep 76 . . . . .133, 143

R v DPP ex p Kebeline and Others [1999] 3 WLR 972 28

R v Egdell [1990] 2 WLR 471 ....153, 154

R v Etchells [1996] 1 Cr App R(S) CA 194

R v Fawcett (Lynne) (1994) 16 Cr App R(S) 55;
   [1994] Crim LR(S) 704 CA 194

R v Fernhill Manor School
   ex p Brown (1993) 5 Admin LR 159 4

R v Fox (1841) 2 QB 246 308

R v General Medical Council ex p Richards
   (2001) The Times, 24 January QBD Administrative Court 117

R v General Medical Council ex p Toth [2000] Lloyd's Rep Med 368;
   [2000] 1 WLR 2209; (2000) The Times, 29 June 116, 120

R v Gibbins and Proctor (1918) 13 Cr App Rep 134. 282

R v Halliday [1917] AC 260 HL 1

R v Hallstrom ex p W [1986] QB 1090 1

R v Hodgson (1967) 52 Cr App R 113 ....194, 195

R v Horseferry Road Justices ex p Independent
   Broadcasting Authority [1987] QB 54;
   [1986] 2 All ER 666 307

R v Human Fertilisation and Embryology Authority
   ex p Blood [1997] 2 FLR 742 QBD and CA 342

R v Kitching and Adams [1976] 6 WWR 697 (Manitoba) 279

R v London South and South West Region MHRT ex p Moyle
   [2000] Lloyd's Rep Med 143 ....176, 178, 179

R v Lyons, 15 Cr App R(S) 765 CA 194

R v Malcherek [1981] 2 All ER 422 279

R v MHRT and Others ex p Russell Hall
   [1999] 2 All ER 132 189

R v MHRT ex p Secretary of State
   (2000) unreported, 15 December (CO/1928/2000) 171, 185

R v MHRT for the South
   Thames Region ex p Smith (Anthony David)
   (1999) 47 BMLR 104 QBD 173, 176, 178

R v MHRT, North and East London Region and Another ex p H
   [2001] EWCA Civ 415; (2001) The Times, 2 April 178, 185

R v Mersey MHRT ex p D
   [1987] CLY 2420 174

R v Mid Glamorgan Family Health Services
   ex p Martin [1995] 1 All ER 356 134

R v Ministry of Defence ex p Smith [1996] QB 517 65

R v Moore (1986) 8 Cr App R(S) 376 194

R v North and East Devon HA ex p Coughlan
   [2000] 2 WLR 622; [1999] Lloyd's Rep 306;
   [1999] BLGR 703 . . . . .60, 65, 145, 165

R v North West Lancashire HA ex p A and Others
   [1999] TLR 622; [1999] LLR 399 . . . . .64, 145

R v Portsmouth Hospitals NHS Trust
   ex p Carol Glass [1999] Lloyd's Rep Med 367;
   [1999] 2 FLR 905; [1999] All ER (D) 836 . . . . .29, 83

R v R [1992] 2 AC 599 16

R v Richmond LBC ex p W [2000] BLGR 318 QBD 165

R v Royal Borough of Kensington and Chelsea
   ex p Grillo [1996] 28 HLR 94. 115

R v Secretary of State for Health ex p ML [2001] 1 FLR 406 199

R v Secretary of State for the Home Department
   ex p Bradley [1991] 1 WLR 134 186

R v Secretary of State for the Home Department
   ex p M (1999) Imm AR 548; [2000] COD 49 56

R v Secretary of State for the Home Office
   ex p Gilkes; Aerts v Belgium [1998] EHRLR 777 . . . . .112, 170, 172, 174, 190, 193

R v Smith [1974] 1 All ER 376 263

R v Spear (John) [2001] 2 WLR 1692;
   [2001] EWCA Crim 2 182

R v Stone [1977] 2 All ER 341; [1977] QB 354. 282

R v UK, Series A, No 121-C,
   Decision 8 July 1987 246

R v United Kingdom, App No 25949/94; (1983) 33 DR 270 . . . . .287, 288, 290

R v United Kingdom, Judgment 28 November 1988,
   Series A, No 144; (1988) 10 EHRR 74 236

R v Wilson ex p Williamson [1996] COD 42 168

R v Young (1784) 4 Wentworth's System of
   Pleading 219 307

R v Zacharcko [1988] Crim LR 546 194

R (A Minor) (Wardship: Consent to Treatment), Re
   [1991] 4 All ER 177; [1992] Fam 11 . . . . .4, 10, 85, 226–29, 232, 301, 325

R v Cox (1992) 12 BMLR 38 274

R (On the Application of C) v Mental Health Review
   Tribunal, London South and South West Regions
   (2001) The Times, 3 July 186

Rasmussen v Denmark, Judgment 28 November
    1984, Series A, No 87; (1985) 7 EHRR 372 317

Raymond v Honey [1983] 1 AC 1 HL 1

Reeve v UK (1994) 79A D & R 147 266

Reibl v Hughes (1980) 114 DLR (3d) 646
    Sup Ct of Canada 312

Reid v Secretary of State for Scotland
    1997 SLT 555 OH; [1999] 2 AC 512 CA 174, 176, 178

Rekvényi v Hungary, Judgment 20 May 1999 20

Rex v Coate (1772) Lofft 73 26

Ribitsch v Austria, Series A, No 336 (1995) 71

Richard and Others v Surrey Hampshire
    Boarders NHS Trust 203

Robins v United Kingdom
    (1997) 26 EHRR 527 E Comm HR 102

Rodriguez v AG of British Columbia
    (1993) 82 BCLR (2d) 273 Sup Ct of Canada 278

Rose v Bouchet [1999] IRLR 463 219

Roux v UK [1997] EHRLR 102 180

Rowe and Davies v UK, App 28901/95 (1998) 183

S (Adult: Refusal of Medical Treatment), Re
    [1992] 4 All ER 671 225

SL, Re [2000] 2 FLR 452 104

S v UK, App No 10741/84 (1984) 211, 212

SW v UK, Judgment 22 November 1995,
    Series A, No 335-B 18

Salabiaku v France (1988) 13 EHRR 379 ....178, 185, 186

Schiesser v Switzerland (1979) 2 EHRR 417 182

Schloendorff v Society of New York Hospital
    105 NE 92 (1914); 211 NY 125 ....225, 280

Schuler-Zgraggen v Switzerland (1993) 16 EHRR 405 109

Scialacqua v Italy (1998) 26 EHRR CD 164 64

Scott v Wakem (1862) 3 F & F 328 26

Selmouni v France (2000) 29 EHRR 403 292

Shaw v DPP [1962] AC 220 16

Sheffield and Horsham v UK (1998) 27 EHHR 163 ....88, 245, 264

Sidaway v Bethlem Royal and Maudsley Hospital
    Governors [1985] 1 All ER 643; [1985] AC 871 ....23, 225, 321, 322

Silva Pontes v Portugal (1994) 18 EHRR 156 102

Silver v UK (A/161) (1983) 5 EHRR 347 157

Singh v UK (1967) 10 YB 478 189

Smith v Smith (1958) 317 SW 2d (275) Sup Ct Ark 279

Smith v Tunbridge Wells HA [1994] 5 Med LR 334 321

Soering v United Kingdom (1989) 11 EHRR 439 ....161, 169, 175, 178, 195

Sanchez-Reisse v Switzerland (1986) 9 EHRR 71 183

Spadeo and Scalabrino, Judgment
   28 September 1995, Series A, No 315-B 240

Spencer v United Kingdom [1998] EHRLR 348 142

Sporrong and Lonnroth v Sweden (1982) 5 EHRR 35 210

St George's Healthcare NHS Trust v S [1999] Fam 26;
   [1998] 3 All ER 673 CA 262, 269, 279

Stanley Johnson v United Kingdom
   (1999) 27 EHRR 296 ....171, 172, 184, 189, 191–93

Starrs v Ruxton [2000] JC 208 182

Steel and Others v United Kingdom, Case 24838/94,
   Judgment 23 September 1998 ....17, 20–22

Stefan v GMC [1999] Lloyd's Rep Med 90 115

Stewart v United Kingdom,
   App No 10044/82; 7 EHRR 457 ....156, 284

Strunk v Strunk 445 SW 2d 145 (Ky 1969) 299

Stubbings *et al* v UK (1997) 23 EHRR 213 102

Stubbings v Webb [2000] UKHRR 684 106

Sunday Times v United Kingdom (No 1),
   Case 6538/74, Judgment 26 April 1979,
   Series A, No 226; (1979) 2 EHRR 245 ....15–19, 22, 158, 160, 169, 198

Sunday Times v United Kingdom (No 2),
   Judgment 26 November 1991, Series A, No 217 ....20, 22

Sutherland v United Kingdom 24 EHRR CD 22 ....240, 309

Swindon and Marlborough NHS Trust
   v S [1995] 3 Med LR 84. 283

Symm v Fraser (1863) 3 F & F 859 26

T (A Minor) (Wardship: Medical Treatment), Re
   [1997] 1 All ER 906; (1996) 35 BMLR 63 CA 86, 280, 282

T (Adult) (Refusal of Treatment), Re
   [1992] 4 All ER 649 ....148, 279, 286

T (Wardship: Medical Treatment), Re
   [1997] 1 FLR 502; (1997) 9 CFLQ 179 252–58

TP and KM v United Kingdom,
  App No 28945/95, 26 May 1998 103
Tanko v Finland, Case 23634/94 (1994) unreported 52, 60
Taylors and Others
  v UK, App No 23412/94 (1994) unreported 63
Thynne, Wilson and Gunnell
  v UK (1990) 13 EHRR 666 194
Tod-Heatley v Benham (1880) 40 Ch D 80 ....207, 219
Tolstoy Miloslavsky v the United Kingdom,
  13 July 1995, Series A, No 316-B 17
Toth v Austria (1991) 14 EHRR 551 ....182, 183
Tyrer, Judgment 25 April 1978, Series A, No 26;
  (1978) 2 EHRR 1 ....71, 233

US v Scott 788 F Supp 1555 (D Kan 1992) 222
US v Wagner 940 F Supp 972 (ND Tex 1996) 222

V v UK and T v UK (1999) EHRR 121 ....189, 195
Vacco v Quill 117 S Ct 2293 (1997) US Sup Ct 277
Vallee v France (French AIDS case)
  (1994) 18 EHRR 549 62
Van Droogenbroeck v Belgium (1991) 13 EHRR 546 179
Van Marle v Netherlands (1986) 8 EHRR 483 101
Varey v UK, App No 26662/95 214
Vogt v Germany (1995) 21 EHRR 205 101

W v Edgell [1990] 1 All ER 835 ....130, 131, 133, 142, 197
W v Sweden (1988) 59 DR 158 ....165, 180
W (A Minor) (Medical Treatment), Re
  See J (A Minor) (Consent to Medical Treatment)—
Waddington v Miah [1974] 1 WLR 683 1
Walker v Daniels [2000] UKHRR 648 ....105, 114
Ward of Court, In the Matter of a
  [1995] 2 IRLM 401 Ir Sup Ct 283
Washington v Glucksberg 521 US 702 (1997) 277
Waters v Commissioner of Police for the Metropolis
  (2000) unreported 103
Weeks v UK (1987) 10 EHRR 293 ....179, 188, 194, 197
Wemhoff v Germany (1968) 1 EHRR 55 110

Whitehouse v Jordan [1981] 1 WLR 246 .... .23

Whiteside v UK (1994) 76A DR 80 .... .213

Wickramsinghe v United Kingdom [1998] EHRLR 338 .... .101

Widmer v Switzerland, App No 20527/92
    (1993) unreported 51, 290, 293, 340

Wingrove v UK (1997) 24 EHRR 1 .... .159

Winnipeg Child and Family Services (Northwest Area)
    v G (DF) [1997] 2 SCR 925 .... .270

Winterwerp v Netherlands (1979) 2 EHRR 387 .... 163, 164, 168, 176, 178, 183

Wittig case (1984) G Sup Ct .... .278

Woolgar v Chief Constable of the Sussex Police
    [1999] 3 All ER 604 CA .... .131

X v Austria, App No 8278/78; (1979) 18 DR 154 .... 53, 198, 239, 245, 286, 298

X v Bedfordshire CC [1995] 2 AC 633 .... .104

X v Denmark (1983) 32 DR 282 .... 52, 61, 234, 244

X v France (French AIDS case) (1992) 14 EHRR 483 .... .62

X v Federal Republic of Germany,
    App No 1056/83; (1985) 7 EHRR 15 .... 61, 90, 291, 292

X v Iceland (1976) 5 DR 85 .... .196

X v Ireland, App No 6839/74; (1976) 7 DR 78 .... .90

X v United Kingdom, App No 8416/78; (1980) 9 DR 244 .... 51, 340

X v United Kingdom (1978) 14 DR 31 .... .59

X v United Kingdom
    (1979) 2 Digest 444 E Comm HR .... .108

X v United Kingdom (1981) 24 DR 57;
    (1981) 4 EHRR 181 .... 24, 102, 184

X v United Kingdom (1983) 6 EHRR .... .101

X v United Kingdom, App No 10083/82;
    (1984) 6 EHRR 140 .... .95

X v United Kingdom, Case 24755/94,
    Judgment 23 September 1998 .... 25, 27

X v United Kingdom [1998] EHRR 480,
    2 Digest 444 E Comm HR .... .101

X v Y [1988] 2 All ER 648 .... .153

X and Y v Netherlands Series A, No 91 (1985);
    (1985) 8 EHRR 252 .... 53, 75, 141, 162, 267, 315

X and Y v United Kingdom (1978) 12 DR 32 .... .61

X, Y and Z v United Kingdom (1997) 24 EHRR 143 .... .196

Y v United Kingdom, Edwards v United Kingdom,
  Costello Roberts v United Kingdom, Series A, Vol 247 4
Y (Mental Incapacity: Bone Marrow Transplant), Re
  [1997] 2 WLR 556; (1996) Med L Rev 204 ....231, 300, 330

Z v Finland (1998) 25 EHRR 371 ....142, 156, 157, 197
Zamir v UK (1983) 40 DR 42 ....169, 183
Zumtobel v Austria (1993) 17 EHRR 116 109

TABLE OF LEGISLATION

Abortion Act 1967 (UK) 260, 261, 263, 264
  s 1(1) 260
  s 1(1)(a)–(d) 260
  s 1(1)(a) 264
  s 1(1)(b)–(d) 264
Access to Health Records
  Act 1990 (UK) 135, 137, 143
  ss 4, 5 139
Access to Medical Reports
  Act 1988 (UK) 134
Age of Legal Capacity (Scotland)
  Act 1991—
  s 2(4) 228

Bail Act 1976 (UK)—
  s 3(6A) 175
Basic Law (Grundgesetz) (Germany)—
  Art 97(1) 14
Bill of Rights 1688 (UK) 3
Bill of Rights Ordinance
  1990 (Hong Kong) 2
Burial Act 1991 (Netherlands) 276
Burial Laws Amendment
  Act 1880 (UK)—
  s 7 307

Care Standards Act 2000 (UK) . . .148, 150
  ss 70, 80(6) 148
Charter of Rights and
  Freedoms 1982 (Canada) 2, 278
Children Act 1989 (UK) 232, 325
  s 1 151
  s 1(1) 243, 297
  s 43(8) 232
  s 44(7) 232
  Sched 3, para 4(4) 232
  Sched 3, para 5(5) 232
Civil Liability (Congenital
  Disabilities) Act 1976 (UK) 265
  s 2 265

Claim of Rights 1688 (Scotland) 3
Compulsory Purchase
  Act 1965 (UK) 203
Congenital Disabilities
  (Civil Liability)
  Act 1976 (UK) 267, 268
Constitution of South Africa—
  Arts 21, 27 57
Constitution of Switzerland—
  Art 20 40
Constitution of Trinidad and
  Tobago 195
Constitution of the USA 1, 2
Crime and Disorder Act 1998 (UK)—
  s 115 160
Crime (Sentences) Act 1997 (UK)—
  s 2(2) 175
Criminal Code (Australia, NT) 275
Criminal Code (Belgium)—
  Art 422 278
Criminal Code (Canada)—
  s 241 278
Criminal Code (Netherlands)—
  Art 40 275
  Art 293 .275, 276
Criminal Justice (Northern
  Ireland) Act 1945 (UK)—
  s 25 260
Criminal Justice Act 1991 (UK)—
  s 1(2) 194
  s 2(2)(b) .189, 194
  s 4(1), (2) 175
  s 31(2) 194
  s 33 189
  s 34 185
Criminal Justice Act 1993 (UK) 194
Criminal Justice and Public
  Order Act 1994 (UK) 241

Data Protection Act 1984 (UK) . . .135, 137

Data Protection Act
    1998 (UK) 9, 10, 128,
                135–46, 154, 197
    ss 1(1), 2 137
    s 2(1) 142
    ss 7, 8 139
    s 17 136
    ss 29, 33 139
    ss 68–69 137
    s 68 142
    s 69 139
    Sched 1, Pt 2 138
    Sched 2 . . . . .138, 144
    Sched 3 . . . . .138, 144
    Sched 3, para 8 139
Death with Dignity Act 1994
    (Oregon) 275, 277
    s 3.14 275
Disabilities Act 1990 (USA) 221
Disability Discrimination
    Act 1995 (UK) 10, 94, 202,
                217–22, 224
    Pt III 218–20, 222, 223
    s 22 218
    s 22(1)(a) 218
    s 23 218
    s 24(1) 218
    s 24(3)(a) 219
    ss 25–28 220
    s 25(2), (3) 220
    s 28(1) 220
Disability Rights Commission
    Act 1999 (UK) 218, 220
    ss 3–5, 7, 10 220
    Sched 3, para 23(1) 220

European Communities
    Act 1972 (UK) .2
    s 3 27
Euthanasia Act 2001
    (Netherlands) 276, 288
Euthanasia Laws Act 1997
    (Australia) 275, 278

Fair Housing Act 1968 (USA) 221
Fair Housing Amendments
    Act 1988 (USA) 221–23
    para 3604(f)(1) 221, 222
    para 3604(f)(3)(B) 222
Family Law Reform
    Act 1969 (UK) 232
    s 8 325
    s 8(1) 227
    s 8(3) 227, 232
Fatal Accidents Act 1976 (UK) 59

Health Act 1999 (UK) 113
Health and Social Care
    Act 2001 (UK) 146
    s 60 146
Housing Act 1980 (UK) 204
Human Fertilisation and
    Embryology
    Act 1990 (UK) 75, 336, 342
    s 37 260
Human Organ Transplants
    Act 1989 (UK) 77
    ss 1, 2 77
Human Rights
    Act 1998 (UK) 1–11, 23–25,
          27–29, 49, 51, 55, 58, 59,
    63, 67–69, 74, 75, 79, 81, 82, 84, 87,
    92, 94, 96, 97, 99, 103, 105, 113–15,
    120, 122, 124, 125, 127, 128, 140,
    145, 148–50, 154, 155, 157,
    161–63, 167, 168, 181, 185,
    186, 188, 189, 200–02, 208,
    211, 213–17, 223, 224, 226,
    231, 232, 234, 238, 243,
    247–51, 253–59, 263, 273, 284,
    289, 290, 293–95, 297, 300, 301,
    303, 308, 309, 313, 314, 317,
    331, 332, 341, 344, 346
    s 1 347
    s 2 . . . . .3, 163, 232, 273, 347
    s 2(1) 149

Human Rights Act 1998 (UK) (Contd)—
s 2(1)(a) 27
s 3 ....3, 5, 140, 149, 212,
                    215, 216, 224, 231,
                    273, 348
s 3(1) 68, 212
s 4 ....3, 140, 178, 185, 349
s 4(2) 68
s 5 349
s 6 ....3, 4, 25, 49, 140, 149, 155,
                    212, 215, 216, 308, 350
s 6(1) 68, 82, 150, 214, 216, 243
s 6(2) 68, 214
s 6(3)(a) 25, 75, 243
s 6(3)(b) 150
s 7 ....6, 25, 140, 150, 308,
                    350–52
s 7(1) 216
s 7(3) 289
s 8 ....6, 25, 49, 273, 308, 352
s 8(1) 216
s 8(4) 50
s 9 ....25, 353
s 10 ....141, 273, 353, 354
s 11 354
s 12 ....354, 355
s 13 355
s 14 ....355, 356
s 15 356
s 16 ....356, 357
s 17 357
s 18 ....357, 358
s 19 ....4, 200, 359
s 20 359
s 21 ....360, 361
s 22 362
Sched 1 ....5, 6, 140, 362
Sched 1, Arts 2, 3, 8, 10 273
Sched 1, Pt I, Arts 2–18 362–67
Sched 1, Pt II, Arts 1–3 367
Sched 1, Pt III, Arts 1–2 ......367, 368
Sched 2, paras 1–6 368–70
Sched 3, Pts I, II 370–72
Sched 4, paras 1–4 372–73

Human Tissue Act
1961 (UK) 11, 305–09
s 1 ....305, 309
s 1(1), (2), (7) 306
s 1(8) 307
Infant Life (Preservation)
Act 1929 (UK) 260
s 1(1) 260

Land Registration Act 1925 (UK) 216
Law of Property Act 1925 224
s 84 ....211, 212
s 84(1) 206
Limitation Act 1980 (UK) 106, 212
s 33 106

Magna Carta 1215 (UK) 3
Medical (Professional Performance)
Act 1995 (UK) 118
Medical Act 1983 (UK)—
s 35A 131, 144
Mental Deficiency Act 1959 (UK)—
s 6 188
Mental Health Act
1983 (UK) 10, 22, 23,
                    25–28, 165–69,
                    171, 173, 176, 178, 179,
                    184, 185, 187, 196,
                    200, 226, 302, 326
s 2 ....168, 180
s 2(4) 168
s 3 ....168, 169, 176, 180,
                    186, 187, 196
s 3(1), (2)(a) 173
s 13(2) 169
s 29 168
s 29(3)(c) 181
s 37 ....172, 194
s 42 179
ss 47, 54 175
s 72 ....176, 178, 185
s 72(2)(a) 176

Mental Health Act 1983 (UK) (Contd)—
 s 72(2)(b)(i) 176, 177
 s 72(2)(b)(ii) 177
 s 72(3) 190
 s 73 184
 s 73(1)(b) 177
 s 73(2) 179
 s 73(7) 190
 s 117 165
 s 131(1) 22
 s 135 ....169, 170, 198
 s 135(6) 170
 s 136 ....164, 169, 170, 198
 s 145(1) 173

National Assistance
 Act 1948 (UK) 167
 s 47 ....167, 188, 198
National Assistance Amendment
 Act 1951 (UK)—
 s 1 ....167, 181
National Health Service
 Act 1977 (UK)—
 s 3 62
National Health Service and
 Community Care Act 1990 (UK) 81
 s 46(3) 201

Offences Against the Person
 Act 1861 (UK) 260
 ss 58, 59 260

Patient Self Determination
 Act 1990 (NJ) 280
Penal Code (Netherlands)—
 Art 293 276
Police and Criminal Evidence
 Act 1984 (UK)—
 s 17(6) 19
Public Health (Control of Disease)
 Act 1984 (UK) 131, 144, 199
 ss 35, 37, 67(2) 199

Race Relations Act 1976 (UK) 218
Rehabilitation Act 1973 (USA)—
 s 503 221
Residential Homes Act 1984 (UK) 150
Rights of the Terminally Ill
 Act 1995 (Australia, NT) 275, 278

Scotland Act 1998 (UK) 4
Sex Discrimination Act 1976 (UK) 218
Sexual Offences Act 1956 (UK)—
 s 12(1) 241
Sexual Offences Act 1967 (UK) 16
 s 1 241
Suicide Act 1961 (UK) 277, 286, 287
 s 2 286
 s 2(1) 276
Supreme Court Act 1981 (UK) 134

Treaty of Union between
 England and Scotland 1707 2

TABLE OF STATUTORY INSTRUMENTS

Abortion Regulations 1991 (SI 1991/499) 131

Civil Procedure Rules 1998 ....9, 99, 105, 110, 120, 134
    Pt 1.1 105
    r 6 120

Data Protection (Processing of Sensitive Personal Data)
    Order 2000 (SI 2000/417) 144
Data Protection (Subject Access Modification) (Health)
    Order 2000 (SI 2000/413) 140, 145
Disability Rights Commission Act 1999 (Commencement
    No 1 and Transitional Provision) Order 1999 (SI 1999/2210) 218
Disability Rights Commission Act 1999 (Commencement
    No 2 and Transitional Provision) Order 2000 (SI 2000/880) 218

Human Rights Act (Commencement) Order 1998
    (SI 1998/2882) 6

Mental Health Review Tribunal Rules 1983 (SI 1983/942) 186
    r 11 182
    r 12 ....183, 197
    r 62(3) 196

NHS (General Medical Services) Amendment (No 4)
    Regulations 2000 (SI 2000/2383) 146

Property (NI) Order 1978 (SI 1978/459) (NI 4)—
    Art 5 211
Public Health (Infectious Diseases) Regulations 1988
    (SI 1988/1546)—
    reg 3 199

TABLE OF INTERNATIONAL INSTRUMENTS

Directives

Directive, OJ C306, 18.10.97 (Clinical Trials Directive) 313, 314
 Art 1(1), (4) 314
Directive 95/46/EC (Data Protection Directive) 10, 136

Treaties and Conventions

Amsterdam Treaty 1997 ....334, 335
 Arts 6(1), (2), 152 336
 Arts 152(1), 176 335
 Arts 226, 234 337

Declaration of Helsinki (revised 1975) 317–19, 327
 Ch III, Arts 2, 4 318
Declaration of Helsinki (revised 2000) 317, 327
 Arts 19, 24 327

Treaty Establishing the European Communities (EC Treaty) 342
 Arts 49, 50 342
European Convention for the Prevention of Torture and
 Inhuman or Degrading Treatment or Punishment 1987 338
European Convention for the Protection of Human Rights and
 Dignity of the Human Being with Regard to the
 Application of Biology 1997 (Convention on Human
 Rights and Biomedicine) 9, 11, 31–47, 68, 76, 78, 303, 313,
                                          314, 316, 317, 319, 320, 327–29,
                                          331, 332, 337–46
 Ch VIII 338
 Art 1 ....36, 44, 338
 Arts 2–4 37
 Art 2 ....303, 319, 320, 327
 Art 3 ....319, 327, 337
 Art 4 321
 Arts 5–9 37
 Art 5 ....37, 39, 44, 314, 315, 320–24,
                                          337, 340–42
 Art 6 ....38, 39, 41, 326, 342
 Art 6(1), (2) 323
 Art 6(3) 342
 Art 6(4), (5) 323

European Convention for the Protection of Human Rights and
   Dignity of the Human Being with Regard to the
   Application of Biology 1997 (Contd)—
   Arts 7, 8 ....39, 341
   Art 9 39
   Art 10 40
   Arts 11–13 42
   Art 11 ....320, 337
   Art 12 43
   Art 13 ....43, 44, 320, 337
   Art 14 ....42, 77, 320, 337
   Arts 15–18 40
   Art 16 ....40, 41, 320, 324, 342
   Art 16(ii) 327
   Art 16(iii) 324, 330
   Art 16(v) 324
   Art 17 ....39, 41, 320, 323, 324, 326, 329
   Art 17(1)(iv) 324
   Art 17(1)(ii) 327
   Art 17(2)(i), (ii) 327, 328
   Art 18 ....42, 44, 45, 337, 342
   Art 19 320
   Art 20 ....39, 43, 320, 323
   Art 21 ....43, 44, 77, 320, 337
   Art 22 43
   Art 23 338
   Art 24 ....337, 339
   Art 25 339
   Art 26 320
   Art 26.1 40
   Art 29 ....314, 339
   Art 32 314
   Arts 124, 126 339
   Protocol on the Prohibition of Cloning
     Human Beings 1998 ....36, 44, 45, 77, 78, 375–85
   Protocol on Biomedical Research (draft) 36, 40, 41, 43, 44
   Protocol on Human Genetics (draft) 36, 43
   Protocol on the Protection of the Foetus
     and the Human Embryo (draft) 36, 42, 45
   Protocol on Transplantation of Organs
     and Tissues of Human Origin (draft) 36, 44

European Convention for the Protection of Individuals
with Regard to Automatic Processing of Personal Data .35, 40
European Convention on Data Protection 1981 . . . . .135, 140, 157
European Convention on the Protection of Human Rights
and Fundamental Freedoms 1950 .1–4, 6, 9–11, 13, 17, 24, 25,
27, 28, 32, 35, 49, 55–57, 61, 64, 65, 67,
68, 70, 72, 74, 75, 79, 81, 82, 87, 95, 97,
99, 127, 142, 145, 149, 150, 155, 157,
161–63, 165, 166, 168, 169, 173–75, 178,
184, 190, 191, 196, 197, 200, 208, 212,
214, 215, 217, 231–33, 238, 243, 259,
261, 263, 265, 267, 269–71, 284, 285,
289, 290, 292, 294, 297, 298, 309, 311,
314, 316, 331, 337, 338, 340–44
Art 2 . . . . .6, 9, 29, 50, 51, 55–61, 64, 68–70,
89–92, 94, 95, 181, 191, 235, 250, 251,
261, 262, 265, 284–88, 291–93,
303, 331, 340–42
Art 2(1) 56, 90, 244, 249, 250, 284, 285
Art 2(2) 285
Art 3 . . . . .6, 51, 52, 56, 58–61, 64, 65,
68–72, 89, 90, 92–95, 170, 181,
190–95, 233, 234, 237, 244, 245,
250, 251, 254, 255, 270, 284,
291–93, 303, 331, 340, 341
Art 3(a) 316
Art 4 6
Art 5 . . . . .4, 6, 13, 14, 18, 20, 24, 28, 52, 54,
164, 165, 168, 170–76, 178–81, 183–85,
190, 193, 194, 197, 231, 234–40,
297, 298, 300–04, 309, 310
Art 5(1) 14, 18, 20, 163, 164, 166, 167,
171, 176, 180, 181, 185,
189, 236, 237
Art 5(1)(a) 164, 174, 179, 188
Art 5(1)(e) 24, 164, 167, 168, 170, 172,
174–76, 178, 179, 186, 190
Art 5(4) 24, 25, 180–89, 193, 197, 236
Art 5(5) 24
Art 6 . . . . .6, 9, 13, 53, 99–115, 122,
181–83, 210, 268, 326

European Convention on the Protection of Human Rights
  and Fundamental Freedoms 1950 (Contd)—
  Art 6(1) 14, 27, 53, 62, 100, 102,
                                                    113, 115, 118, 121, 216
  Art 6(2), (3) 114
  Art 6(3)(c) 112
  Art 7 . . . . .6, 16, 17
  Art 7(1) 27
  Arts 8–11 14
  Art 8 . . . . .4, 6, 10, 53, 54, 59, 60, 64–66, 68,
                                                    70, 73–76, 87–89, 92, 94, 95, 127,
                                                    128, 130, 133–35, 141–45, 156,
                                                    157, 162, 168, 181, 196–200,
                                                    210, 212–14, 231, 233, 236, 238–40,
                                                    245, 246, 255, 261–64, 266–68, 270,
                                                    284, 286–90, 293, 297, 298, 300–04,
                                                    308–10, 315, 317, 340, 342
  Art 8(1) 72–74, 76, 77, 155, 156, 160, 195,
                                                    238, 245, 246, 251, 254, 255,
                                                    263, 270, 286
  Art 8(2) 19, 67, 73, 76, 79, 88, 142, 156–58,
                                                    197, 198, 213, 214, 238, 239, 246,
                                                    248, 266, 270, 286, 288, 289,
                                                    298, 303, 308
  Art 9 . . . . .6, 54, 157, 247, 289
  Art 9(1) 251
  Art 10 . . . . .6, 15, 128, 134, 141–43, 145,
                                                    160, 235, 284, 286, 287, 315
  Art 10(2) 20, 21, 67, 142, 160, 197, 287
  Art 11 6
  Art 12 . . . . .6, 54, 61, 75, 342
  Art 13 344
  Art 14 . . . . .4, 6, 10, 54, 62, 89, 93–95, 181,
                                                    209–11, 231, 239–41, 264,
                                                    301, 309, 326, 327
  Art 15 . . . . .2, 16
  Art 16 6
  Art 26 . . . . .3, 232
  Art 27 35
  Art 27(2) 3, 232
  Art 28 6

European Convention on the Protection of Human Rights
   and Fundamental Freedoms 1950 (Contd)—
   Art 29 35
   Art 31 ....3, 232
   Art 32 35
   Art 37(1) 196
   Art 41 50
   Art 46 ....3, 232
   Art 47 339
   Protocol No 1 196
      Arts 1–3 ....5, 6
      Art 1 ....210, 211, 213
   Protocol No 4 317
      Art 2...238
   Protocol No 6 196
      Arts 1, 2 ....5, 6
   Protocol No 12 209
      Art 1...209
European Convention on the Rights of the Child 1989 ....35, 328
   Art 3 ....328, 329
European Social Charter 1961 ....35, 338
   Art 11 69
   Art 13 ....87, 89

International Covenant on Civil and Political Rights 35
International Covenant on Economic, Social,
   and Cultural Rights 35

Maastricht Treaty (Treaty on European Union)—
   Art G, para 38 335

Public Statement on Turkey (adopted 15 December 1992)
   (1993) 14 HRLJ 49 338
Public Statement on Turkey (No 2) (1997) 18 HRLJ 294 338

Recommendation No R (90)3 of the Committee of
   Ministers to Member States on Medical Research
   on the Human Being 40

United Nations Convention on the Elimination of all
Forms of Racial Discrimination 1965 43
United Nations Universal Declaration of
Human Rights 1948 . . . . .13, 35

Vienna Convention on the Law of Treaties of 23 May 1969—
Art 31 316
Art 31(1), (3) 316
Art 31(3)(a), (b) 317
Art 33 316

CONVENTION TERMS AND CONCEPTS

Tom Lewis

Introduction

This glossary is aimed at the Convention neophyte. It is intended to provide a quick guide to terms and concepts commonly referred to in the following chapters. Further explanation and development of these will be found in the chapters themselves.

The European Convention on Human Rights and Fundamental Freedoms

The European Convention on Human Rights (ECHR) is an international human rights treaty drafted and signed in 1950 under the auspices of the Council of Europe. It can be read as a response to the horrors of the Nazi regime and as a statement of Western liberal ideology in the face of Soviet hegemony in Eastern Europe. *Prima facie*, the rights contained within it are predominantly of the 'civil and political' as opposed to 'social and economic' variety. In other words they are, for the most part, freedoms or liberties (albeit expressed in positive terms) – rights which do not require positive action from others in order for them to be enjoyed. Social and economic rights by contrast do require such positive action, for example, the right to housing or the right to social security payments. The following chapters, however, will demonstrate that there is often no easy line to draw between these categories of rights. To take an obvious example, the right to life protected by Art 2 of the ECHR may be seen as having little worth without some level of healthcare provision.

The Strasbourg Institutions

The ECHR is unusual amongst the plethora of international human rights treaties in that it has a mechanism to ensure its own enforcement, the European Court of Human Rights (the Court) based at Strasbourg. This is certainly one of the main reasons for the Convention's success. Individuals who claim that their Convention rights have been violated by a Member State of the Council of Europe can apply to the Court for redress. Until November 1998, there also existed a European Commission of Human Rights which acted primarily as an arbiter of the admissibility of applications and used to provide a preliminary opinion on the merits of applications. Protocol 11 abolished the Commission whose role has now been taken over by a restructured Court.

Absolute rights

Some of the rights contained in the ECHR are expressed in absolute terms. The drafters considered that certain rights were so fundamental that absolutely no countervailing interest could legitimise interference with them. For example, the right not to be 'subjected to torture or to inhuman or degrading treatment or punishment' as enshrined by Art 3. There are absolutely no circumstances which justify a State in perpetrating treatment which would amount to that listed in the Article. Indeed, the Court has gone further than this. The State's responsibility has been held to be engaged where it has failed to provide a sufficient legal framework to protect an individual from such treatment by another individual (*A v UK* (1998) 27 EHRR 611). Thus, there has been a degree of horizontality of application (see below). Furthermore, it has been found to be a breach of Art 3 where a State proposes to deport or extradite an individual to another State in which he or she would face conditions which would be inhuman or degrading (see *Soering v UK* (1989) 11 EHRR 439; *D v UK* (1997) 24 EHRR 423). This demonstrates another Convention principle, that of effectiveness (see below).

Limited and qualified rights

Most of the Convention rights are qualified or limited in some way. Thus, the Article will afford protection for the fundamental right of an individual but there will be specific provision for this to be overridden in some circumstances in the interests of society as a whole. For example, in Art 5 (the right to liberty) and Art 6 (the right to a fair trial) the right is set out in the first part of the Article and there then follow specific limitations on its scope. With Arts 8 (privacy), 9 (thought conscience and religion), 10 (expression), and 11 (assembly and association), the approach is slightly different. Here the right is set out in the first paragraph and the circumstances and conditions under which the right may be restricted are set out in the second. These second paragraphs all have a requirement that, for restrictions to be permissible, they must be in 'accordance with' or 'prescribed by' law, be in pursuit of a 'legitimate aim' and be 'necessary in a democratic society'.

The rule of law

This is a core concept in the ECHR and is stated in the Preamble to be part of the shared 'common heritage' of the European nations. The jurisprudence particularly stresses the benefits of certainty and foreseeability over arbitrariness. In the context of the qualified rights discussed above, the phrases 'in accordance with the law' and 'prescribed by law' mean that there must be an ascertainable legal framework in existence which governs the interference in question.

Legitimate aims

With regard to the qualified rights, the State can only interfere with the exercise of the right if it is in pursuit of one of the 'legitimate aims' set out in the second paragraphs. A brief perusal of these will reveal that they are couched in wide terms and States have not found it difficult to fit their restricting measures within these parameters.

Proportionality

It is a foundational tenet of the whole Convention system that an individual's right may only be restricted to an extent that is proportionate to achieving the aim of protecting the wider public interest. This concept is most obviously conveyed by the phrase 'necessary in a democratic society' in Arts 8, 9, 10 and 11. The State may only take such measures to restrict the exercise of the right as are 'necessary in a democratic society'. Any measures taken must correspond to a 'pressing social need'. Thus, the ECHR seeks to strike the desperately difficult balance between individual human rights and the interests of society at large. This concept is fundamentally different to that of *Wednesbury* unreasonableness by which an administrative decision may only be challenged successfully if it is 'so outrageous in its defiance of logic or accepted moral standards that no sensible person who had applied his mind to the question to be decided could have arrived at it' (Lord Diplock, in *Council of Civil Service Unions v Minister for the Civil Service* [1985] AC 375, p 410). Thus, the level of scrutiny will be much more rigorous under proportionality than under *Wednesbury*.

Margin of appreciation

This is an international law doctrine which enables the Strasbourg Court to afford a degree of latitude to the defendant States coming before it as to their application and interpretation of the Convention rights. The idea is that having regard to national circumstances, morals and other relevant factors States may legitimately take varied approaches and where appropriate should be given some leeway in doing so.

The doctrine has been most commonly cited in cases concerning national emergencies and terrorist situations where the State is commonly left a wide margin of appreciation on the basis that the national authorities are better placed than the international judge to make an assessment of what measures are necessary. The doctrine has, also, commonly been utilised in cases where the State decides to restrict the exercise of a right on the grounds of morality. In such areas, where there is no identifiable European consensus, the Court has been very reluctant to impose its own view and has afforded States a wide margin of appreciation (see *Handyside v UK* (1976) 1 EHRR 737). In such cases, the point at which the doctrine enters the picture is at the proportionality stage. The Court allows a margin of appreciation to the State in assessing what is 'necessary in a democratic society' in the pursuit of one of the legitimate aims. The doctrine is, to say the least, a controversial one. Some see it as a form of insidious cultural relativism which if not reigned in will seriously dilute the protection of rights; others as a necessary aspect of sensitivity to the different democratic traditions across Europe (for contrasting views see Lord Lester of Herne Hill, [1998] EHRLR 73 and Paul Mahoney, [1997] EHRLR 364).

Whilst the doctrine is taken to be applicable to all Articles under the ECHR[1] it was never certain that it would apply under the Human Rights Act (HRA) 1998. Giving it wide scope domestically would contradict with the reality of giving rights full and due recognition in this country which is arguably why the HRA 1998 was put in place. Indeed, Singh, Hunt and Demetriou suggested that excluding the doctrine would not lead to the courts usurping the function of the legislature or the executive with the experience of European Community Law suggesting that the courts:

> ... would be well able to apply ECHR concepts both to provide enhanced protection for fundamental rights and to show due deference to the judgment of other organs of the state in appropriate contexts.[2]

Lord Hope of Craighead in the House of Lords case of *R v DPP ex p Kebeline and Others* [1999] 3 WLR 972 has ended the legal debate by stating the margin of appreciation 'is not available to the national courts when they are considering Convention issues arising within their own countries' (pp 93–94). Clearly, this makes sense; there is no real basis to construe the UK legislature as having intended to give a margin of appreciation to act in conflict with a human rights law it passed to itself, UK courts and public bodies. The doctrine of margin of appreciation is one only makes sense in the context of interpretations of the ECHR in the European Court of Human Rights because it is a doctrine that stems out of the fact of European supervision of a national authority (see *Buckley v United Kingdom* (1996) 23 EHRR 101, p 129, paras 74–75) where, as Lord Hope puts it, 'by reason of their direct and continuous contact with the vital forces of their countries, the national authorities are in principle better placed to evaluate local needs and conditions than an international court'.[3] Of course, in interpreting the HRA, the courts will still be able to balance competing rights and interests using, in particular, the doctrine of proportionality.

Evolutive/dynamic interpretation

This is a key aspect of ECHR jurisprudence. The interpretation given to the rights contained in the Convention by the Strasbourg institutions are not static. The Convention is a 'living instrument'. Interpretations evolve to meet changing social conditions. Hence, for example, while contemporary realities and attitudes in 1950 *might* make judicial corporal punishment of juvenile offenders in the Isle of Man 'acceptable' in 1950 it was not 'acceptable' and infringed Art 3 in 1978 when considered by the Court in the *Tyrer* case.[4] It should be noted that there is no system of binding precedent at Strasbourg

---

1   Macdonald, 1987, p 192.
2   Singh, Hunt and Demetriou, 1999, p 15.
3   *R v DPP ex p Kebeline and Others* [1999] 3 WLR 972, p 973.
4   Judgment 25 April 1978, Series A, No 26, p 15.

and, as a consequence, some of the older decisions need to be read with caution.

Horizontality

The political ideology which fuelled the drafting of the ECHR perceived the main threat to human rights as coming from the State. Reflecting this is the fact that the defendant at Strasbourg is always the State. However, a degree of indirect horizontality of application is evident in the jurisprudence of the European Court and Commission. In other words, there has been a limited and indirect application of Convention rights to protect individuals from actions of *other individuals*. Thus, where a State fails to provide a legal framework to protect an individual's rights from abuse by other individuals the responsibility of the State may be engaged. It is most notable in relation to Arts 3 and 8 (see *A v UK* (1998) 27 EHRR 611 and *X and Y v The Netherlands* (1998) 8 EHRR 235.

Positive obligations

The rights contained in the Convention are predominantly of the 'hands off' variety, not requiring any positive action by the State. However, the Strasbourg organs have, in some circumstances, interpreted what are *prima facie* negative rights necessarily to require positive action on the part of the State. This has been most evident in Arts 8 and 2 (see *Marckx v Belgium* (1979) 2 EHRR 300; *Osman v UK* (1988) 29 EHRR 245).

Effectiveness

Underlying interpretation of all the Convention rights is the effectiveness principle which is to say that the ECHR is concerned with interpreting rights in a manner which is practical and effective. One aspect of this is that the ECHR has stressed the importance of looking beyond appearances and formalities to the realities of the position of the individual.

TABLE OF ABBREVIATIONS

ACHRE	Advisory Committee on Human Radiation Experiments
ASW	Approved social worker
BMA	British Medical Association
CAHBI	Ad Hoc Committee of Experts on Bioethics
CDBI	Steering Committee on Bioethics
CDDH	Steering Committee for Human Rights
CDSP	European Health Committee
CERD	Convention Committee
CJA	Criminal Justice Act
COMETH	Working Parties on Xenotransplantation, Biotechnology and Psychiatry and Human Rights. Standing Conference of European National Ethics Committees
CPP	Committee on Professional Performance
CPR	Civil Procedure Rules
DDA	Disability Discrimination Act
DEBRA	Demo droit Ethical Review of Biomedical Research Activity
DoH	Department of Health
DPA	Data Protection Act
DSPD	Dangerous severe personality disorder
ECHRB	European Convention on Human Rights and Biomedicine
ECHR	European Convention on Human Rights
E Comm	European Commission on Human Rights
ECtHR	European Court of Human Rights
EV	Elective Ventilation
EHR	Electronic health record
EPR	Electronic patient record
EU	European Union

FHAA	Federal Fair Housing Amendments Act
FLRA	Family Law Reform Act
GDC	General Dental Council
GMC	General Medical Council
HC	Health Committee
HFEA	Human Fertilisation and Embryology Authority
HRA	Human Rights Act
ICH	International Committee on Harmonisation
LDT	Living donor transplantation
MHA	Mental Health Act
MHRT	Mental Health Review Tribunal
MREC	Multi-Centre Research Ethics Committee
NHBD	Non-heart beating donor
NHSLA	National Health Service Litigation Authority
NIMBY	Not in my back yard
OECD	Organisation for Economic Co-operation and Development
PCC	Professional Conduct Committee
PPC	Preliminary Proceedings Committee
PVS	Persistent vegetative state
RCGP	Royal College of General Practitioners
REC	Research Ethics Committee

UKCC	United Kingdom Central Council for Nursing, Midwifery and Health Visiting
ULTRA	Unrelated Live Transplant Regulatory Authority
UNESCO	United Nations Educational, Scientific and Cultural Organisation
WHO	World Health Organisation

CHAPTER 1

THE HUMAN RIGHTS ACT 1998:
A POTENT TOOL FOR CHANGING HEALTHCARE
LAW AND PRACTICE

Austen Garwood-Gowers and John Tingle

THE PASSING OF THE HUMAN RIGHTS ACT 1998:
A MONUMENTAL SHIFT IN THE UK CONSTITUTION?

Traditionally, the UK has protected rights in a residual fashion; Parliament would legislate and citizens – or rather subjects – would retain the rights to do whatever Parliament had not prohibited. Under the US Constitution the US courts have been empowered to strike out legislative provisions contrary to the fundamental rights protected under the Constitution. However, in the English system Parliament is omnicompetent; its supremacy or sovereignty can only be challenged in the event of a transfer of power following internal revolution or external invasion. Coke CJ in *Dr Bonham's Case*, stated that: 'When an Act of Parliament is against common right or reason, or repugnant, or impossible to be performed, the common law will control it, and adjudge such Act to be void.'[1] However, no statutory provision has ever been overturned under English law and Coke's approach does not seem to be good law. As Lord Reid put it, in *British Railways Board v Pickin* [1974] AC 765 HL, p 782:

> The idea that a court is entitled to disregard a provision in an Act of Parliament on any ground must seem strange and startling to anyone with any knowledge of the history and law of our constitution ... In early times many learned lawyers seem to have believed that an Act of Parliament could be disregarded in so far as it was contrary to the law of God or the law of nature or natural justice, but since the supremacy of Parliament was fully demonstrated by the Revolution of 1688 any such idea has become obsolete.

The most the courts of England and Wales can do is resolve any uncertainties as to the meaning of legislative provisions in favour of the rights of the citizen[2] and to review administrative action taken by national or local or other

---

1   (1610) 8 Co Rep 114a, p 118.
2   This is done, eg, through the presumptions against the taking of property without compensation (*Central Control Board (Liquor Traffic) v Cannon Brewery Co Ltd* [1919] AC 742 HL, p 752); retrospective effect of legislation (*Waddington v Miah* [1974] 1 WLR 683); denial of access to the courts (*Raymond v Honey* [1983] 1 AC 1 HL); interference with the liberty of the subject (*R v Hallstrom ex p W* [1986] QB 1090) except in wartime (*R v Halliday* [1917] AC 260 HL); non-compliance with international treaty obligations (which include human rights treaties such as the ECHR).

government authorities.[3] On the other hand, when the Treaty of Union was signed between England and Scotland in 1707, the Scottish Court reserved the right to treat an Act of Parliament as void for breaching a fundamental term of the Treaty. Admittedly, in *McCormick v Lord Advocate* 1953 SC 39, it was not foreseen that this was likely ever to happen in practice. An advantage claimed for giving less power to the judges under the English position is one of democratic accountability; namely, that judges who are not chosen by the populus cannot overturn the decisions of a Parliament whose members, in the case of the House of Commons, are chosen by the populace.

Over the last 50 years, Parliament has retained its ultimate sovereignty but lost some control over elements of day to day decision making. The biggest single change in this respect has been membership of the European Union (EU).[4] On the human rights front, the UK has, since 1951, bound itself to accept (subject to 'derogations' made under the Convention in specific cases)[5] the decisions of the European Court of Human Rights as a 'final appeal court' on matters concerning the rights protected under Articles of the European Convention on Human Rights (ECHR) and a number of its protocols, to which it is a signatory. A person in the UK can apply to have his or her case heard by the European Court of Human Rights if (s)he has exhausted the possibilities for getting it overturned within the domestic system of law (that is, the courts and, in criminal cases, the Home Secretary).

Campaigns for a domestic Bill of Rights have been long standing. However, one of the concerns about implementing such a Bill has been the impact on sovereignty of the legislature. In the US system, sovereignty is compromised by the ability of judges to have the ultimate say, using the US Constitution to strike down legislative provisions. The Canadian and Hong Kong solutions avoid this by using a limited form of judicial entrenchment where the courts can override legislative provisions inconsistent with the legitimate protection of rights, subject to the legislature having the ultimate say.[6] The Human Rights Act 1998 (HRA), which brings the ECHR rights more or less wholesale into the fabric of English law, adopts the New Zealand

---

3   Review of statutory and, in some cases, prerogative powers (see *Council of Civil Service Unions v Minister of the Civil Service* [1985] AC 374 HL).

4   The effect of the European Communities Act 1972 is that courts may override any rule of national law found to be in conflict with any directly enforceable rule of Community law – see *Factortame v Secretary of State for Transport (No 2)* [1991] 1 All ER 70 CJEC and HL.

5   When a decision is made against it under the Convention, a State is obligated to change its law so as to remove the possibility of a future violation of the same kind. However, in specific instances the State may not wish to do this and may under Art 15 of the Convention use the power of derogation if it is an emergency. See, eg, *Lawless v Ireland (Merits)*, Judgment 1 July 1961, Series A, Vol 3; (1979–80) 1 EHRR 15 ECtHR.

6   There are different ways in which limited judicial entrenchment can work in practice including the Canadian (Canadian Charter of Rights and Freedoms 1982) and Hong Kong (Bill of Rights Ordinance 1990) models elucidated in detail by the Constitution Unit, 1996, Chapter 2.

stance of being an interpretative tool only. Under s 3 of the HRA, 'primary and subordinate legislation' must be read and given effect in a way which is compatible with the Convention rights. Provisions that cannot be interpreted in a manner consistent with those rights can be declared incompatible by the courts (s 4), but it is left up to Parliament as to whether it does anything about this incompatibility and whether it legislates in future in a manner consistent with rights. Only common law has to come into line with the Convention rights.

Despite this limitation, the Act is likely to go down in history as a monumental shift in the UK Constitution, like the Magna Carta 1215 and the Bill of Rights 1688,[7] but more potent in terms of advancing the legal protection of human rights.

The courts and tribunals will interpret law in a manner more consistent with human rights

The HRA 1998 will result in courts and tribunals interpreting law in a manner more consistent with human rights for a number of reasons:

(a) Its existence will put pressure on Parliament to change legislative provisions so as to be consistent with the Convention rights.

(b) The danger that some of the Articles might be interpreted in a flawed, nonsensical or overly restrictive fashion has been reduced by the presence of s 2 of the Act. Under s 2, a domestic court or tribunal in making decisions about whether one or more of the Articles have been violated has to take into account, in so far as it thinks it relevant to the case at hand, the so called 'Strasbourg jurisprudence' which includes: judgments, decisions, declarations and advisory opinions of the European Court of Human Rights (the Court); opinions of the Commission given in a report adopted under Art 31 of the Convention; decisions of the Commission in connection with Art 26 or 27(2) of the Convention; or decision of the Committee of Ministers taken under Art 46 of the Convention. As will be seen in the course of this book, the 'Strasbourg jurisprudence' includes a number of cases and decisions which are about healthcare law or are of great relevance to it.

(c) Under s 6 of the Act it is unlawful for a public authority (or a private/partly private body exercising a public function) to act in a way which is incompatible with the rights that have been brought into domestic law under the Act. Courts and tribunals are included within the

---

7   The Bill and its Scottish counterpart the Claim of Right were not human rights instruments in the modern sense; they were primarily concerned with the relationship between the Crown and Parliament. However, both did contain some guarantees of personal liberty.

definition of a public authority. Consequently, when cases arise, they have a duty to ensure that existing common law is 'brought into line' with Convention rights as protected under the Act. In Chapter 2, John Hodgson lays out several examples of how common law may be affected in practice. Clearly, some effects are going to be felt in healthcare law and he outlines a few examples. A further example is provided in Chapter 14 where Austen Garwood-Gowers suggests that the common law approach established in *Re W (A Minor) (Medical Treatment)* [1992] 3 WLR 758 and *Re R (A Minor) (Wardship: Consent to Treatment)* [1991] 4 All ER 177 where competent minors can be forced to undergo medical intervention, where consent has been obtained 'on their behalf' may be inconsistent with the right not to be discriminated against (Art 14) in conjunction with the right to privacy (Art 8) or indeed the right to liberty and security (Art 5). Section 6's definition of a public authority would clearly include both NHS-run medical organisations (for example, Hospitals) and non-NHS-run institutions where medical services paid for by the NHS are being provided (for example, NHS patients being catered to in a doctor's surgery). It will probably also include private medicine itself.[8]

The Act will result in Parliament feeling more constrained to exercise its sovereignty in a manner consistent with human rights

Whilst Parliament will, in theory, be able to continue doing what it wants in relation to potential violation of human rights, in practice, violations are likely to decrease. Section 19 of the Act, requiring the minister in charge of a Bill to make a statement about its compatibility with the Convention rights, came into force on 24 November 1988. By the Scotland Act 1998, the main equivalent provisions of the HRA effectively came into force in Scotland in May 1999. This is an important development. In the past, important civil liberties, such as the right to silence, have often been 'damaged' without the media and public paying much attention. Now Parliamentary actions in human rights terms are more firmly in the public eye. Producing legislation in a manner inconsistent with the Convention rights could prove to be a source of significant political embarrassment. Equally, so could refusing to change a legislative provision following a declaration by the courts of its

---

8   In *Y v UK, Edwards v UK, Costello Roberts v UK*, Series A, Vol 247, paras 26–28, the European Court held that the UK Government could be liable for rights violations in the administration of discipline in private schools. The reasoning was that they coexist with a system of public education and that the Convention right to education is guaranteed equally to pupils in State and public schools. This type of argument could be extended to saying private medicine should be covered by the HRA 1998 as a public service running alongside publicly provided medicine. However, in *R v Fernhill Manor School ex p Brown* (1993) 5 Admin LR 159, p 175, Brooke J took the view that the provision of private medicine was purely a private matter (and, hence, in this case, not amenable to judicial review).

incompatibility with the HRA 1998. Our system of rights remains in the strict sense residual. However, it has a 'positive rights protection element' which for day to day purposes of the operation of the constitution may prove more important. That is unless, or perhaps until, a future (almost certainly Conservative) government should decide to change it.

Removing the denial of justice stemming from delays

The principal limitations with the Court is that it can take years to get one's case heard since one must first exhaust domestic possibilities for appeal. For example, in *Golder v United Kingdom* (1975) 1 EHRR 524 the applicant had been released from prison by the time he won his case in the European Court for a violation of his right to privacy in the failure of the prison authorities to allow him to contact a solicitor for the purpose of initiating a libel action. He succeeded in establishing an important legal principle for prisoners in future but achieved nothing for his own situation.

The HRA 1998 includes, with one amendment,[9] a wholesale adoption of the Convention Articles.[10] It provides the opportunity for claims of violation of these Articles to be heard directly in the domestic courts and tribunals and, as such, draws to a close an era of this 'justice delayed is justice denied' situation.[11]

Facilitating an increase in cases brought before the courts

The implementation of the HRA 1998 will inevitably mean that some claims of breaches of human rights that would not have been brought before the European Court because of the delays (and possibly the expense involved in exhausting domestic remedies) will see the light of day in the domestic courts.

---

9   HRA 1998, s 3. The Convention rights are listed under Sched 1 to the Act. As Brazier states (1999, p 5), 'contrary to what is often said in the popular press' the Act did not incorporate the Convention into English law.

10 The Act has also brought Arts 1–3 of the First Protocol and Arts 1 and 2 of the Sixth Protocol into the fabric of domestic law.

11 Nearly all other European countries have signed up to the Convention and all or some of its Protocols and in most of these countries the Convention provisions were long ago embodied by legislation into their domestic law.

Table 1: the Convention (and Protocol) rights protected under the HRA 1998

- Article 2 – the right to life
- Article 3 – prohibition of torture
- Article 4 – prohibition of slavery and forced labour
- Article 5 – right to liberty and security
- Article 6 – right to a fair trial
- Article 7 – no punishment without law (that is, without breaking the criminal law)
- Article 8 – right to respect for private and family life
- Article 9 – freedom of thought, conscience and religion
- Article 10 – freedom of expression
- Article 11 – freedom of assembly and association
- Article 12 – right to marry and found a family
- Article 14 – prohibition of discrimination
- Article 1 of First Protocol – protection of property
- Article 2 of First Protocol – right to education
- Article 3 of First Protocol – right to free elections
- Article 1 of Sixth Protocol – no death penalty (exceptions in time of war/imminent threat of war are laid down in Art 2, Sixth Protocol which is also in Sched 1. Articles 1 and 2 of the Sixth Protocol to be read in conjunction with Arts 16 and 28 of the Convention).

Victims can gain compensation

To bring proceedings you must be (or would be) a victim of the unlawful act (s 7). Relief or remedy can be granted within the powers of the tribunal or court and in civil proceedings it is possible for damages to be awarded where necessary for just satisfaction (s 8).

The Act will stimulate the creation of a consciousness about rights

In signing the Commencement Order for the Act, the Home Secretary, Jack Straw stated that:

The Government's objective is to promote a culture of rights and responsibilities throughout our society.[12]

Perhaps the most important thing that the Act will help bring about is an increased awareness about rights. Rights education is becoming a more important element within schools and the general knowledge of society at large is improving. This will have knock-on effects in terms of people being more aware of the possibilities of taking legal action to defend their rights. It may also result in public bodies and parliament, having less of a tendency to act contrary to rights through being more conscious of their nature and ambit. As the Lord Chancellor, Lord Irvine, commented:

The objective of the Human Rights Act is to promote a culture of respect for human rights and responsibilities which over time will permeate the whole of our institutions and society.[13]

THE IMPACT OF THE ACT ON HEALTHCARE LAW

An increasing rights consciousness in healthcare

The Nation's health is a major priority on the political agenda of the leading political parties. It is also a central concern for most people – hardly surprising when one considers that there is nothing more basic and fundamental than our own health and the health of our families. Recent events, such as Shipman, the Bristol Heart Surgery Scandal and Alder Hay, have rocked public confidence in the NHS. These scandals have also coincided with the implementation of the HRA 1998 and have combined together to reinforce a patient's rights culture in UK society. It is a well known fact that litigation and complaints in healthcare have risen over the last 10 years. The National Audit Office[14] stated that:

... reported liability for clinical negligence continues to increase within the NHS, with total potential liabilities of £2.4 billion disclosed in the accounts at 31 March 1999, an increase of £0.6 billion.

Every year the Health Service Ombudsman reports rises in complaints to his office.[15] This new public appetite for complaining and litigiousness has become a feature of the healthcare environment for all health carers, and they all seem aware of the fact. The public is less tolerant, more demanding with greater expectations.

---

12 'Government to "Bring rights home"' (2000) Press Release, 12 July.
13 *Ibid.*
14 National Audit Office, 2000.
15 Health Service Ombudsman for England, 2000.

Despite the above trends of increasing health litigation and complaints, the Government's view is that the general public needs more formal methods of protection and rights enforcement. Patients are seen as the weaker party in the care equation. The Health and Social Care Act 2001 contains a number of provisions designed to enforce patients' rights, such as the establishment of Patients' Forums, Annual Reports to Patients' Forums and so on. Perhaps these measures are seen as a way of giving some patients a means of satisfactorily resolving their complaints without recourse to legal action.

Health Secretary, Alan Milburn, in a recent address to patient groups at the King's Fund, called for a new bond of trust between patients and the NHS.[16] He expressed a widely held sentiment that the NHS is too much a 1940s system operating in a 21st century world:

> It is too much a system that caters for its own needs – its own convenience – and not enough for the needs and convenience of those who use it.

He called for a patient revolution in the NHS:

> So patients need more information about their service and about their care. But the NHS of the future has to be an NHS where patients have real power too.

Patient empowerment is the latest concept which is permeating the corridors of power in the NHS. Health organisations are being directed to organise services around the needs of their patients and not around their own perceived organisational needs. The NHS is being forced to become patient centred. The next few years will see how well the NHS responds to the new centrally directed patient revolution.

The HRA 1998 is likely to inspire an apparently complimentary revolution in healthcare law and practice. Healthcare organisations as well as the courts will have to cope with what may be major changes over a period of years whilst cases raising HRA 1998 points are brought in a wide variety of healthcare law areas. The Government organisation, which manages litigation in the NHS, the National Health Service Litigation Authority (NHSLA) clearly envisages that the HRA 1998 will have a significant impact on healthcare law. The NHSLA has facilitated education courses on the Act for health organisations and produced a special advisory edition of its journal giving indications of the possible impacts of the HRA 1998 in the healthcare field.[17]

---

16 DoH/King's Fund, 2001.
17 NHSLA, 2000.

Assessing the impact of the Act in different areas

Within the 20 chapters of this book, you will find discussion of the impact of the Act on most of the key areas of healthcare law. In chapter 2, John Hodgson considers how various aspects of the common law, including healthcare related aspects, have already been found by the European Commission or the Court to conflict with various Articles of the Convention. It is trite to say that conflicts will increase now that a claimant can use the Articles more than persuasively in the domestic courts. However, John rightly warns us that: 'While there will be a strong tendency to seek to use the Human Rights Act as a catchall means to put right all previous rules of law which are against the client's case, the courts are unlikely to accept such arguments.' Illustrations in point are the interpretation of the right to life (protected by Art 2) in the Court of Appeal decision of *Re A (Children) (Conjoined Twins: Medical Treatment)* [2001] 1 FLR 1 and the High Court's decision in *NHS Trust A v Mrs M* and *NHS Trust B v Mrs H* [2000] EWHC 29 (25 October 2000).

Steven Wheatley in Chapter 5 analyses how the HRA 1998 would deal with the tensions between the notion of autonomy as self-rule and principles that conflict with self-rule – such as the notion of dignity which is behind the exclusion of whole human cloning found in the European Convention on Human Rights and Biomedicine (ECHRB). With science pushing back the frontiers of medicine into areas considered by many to be 'unnatural', these tensions are likely to become increasingly evident in the coming years.

In Chapter 4, Wendy Outhwaite looks at the scope of impact the HRA 1998 may have on the NHS. In Chapter 6, Alasdair Maclean presents the opposite side by looking at whether the argument that individuals have a right to treatment will gain more legal currency with the passing of the Act, particularly where the treatment is necessary to maintain life and therefore becomes an Art 2 issue.

Gerard Panting notes in Chapter 8 that the Act has already had some impact in the field of medical complaints and discipline with the GMC bringing its procedures more into line with Art 6 which protects the right to a fair trial. Charles Foster, in the preceding chapter, states that the Act is unlikely to have much impact on the availability of funding for litigants in medical cases nor on procedure in civil courts in medical cases since the Civil Procedure Rules were drafted to be compliant with the Act. However, there are a number of caveats with regard to civil procedure and also a possible impact of the Act on other procedures in tribunals in which medical issues are debated

Another area where major changes are not expected from the implementation of the Act is confidentiality and access to medical records, considered by David Stone in Chapter 9. The latest legislation in this area is the Data Protection Act 1998 which, in the main, came into force in March 2000, though some of its provisions will be phased in gradually until 2007. The

Act was a response to the EU Directive of 1995[18] which was principally designed, to protect the fundamental rights and freedoms of natural persons and, in particular, their right to privacy with respect to the processing of personal data.

Since the directive was designed to comply with the ECHR, it would be surprising if the Act's provisions, which were designed to comply with the directive, are significantly out of step with any of the Convention rights. In the following chapter, Kate and John Williams address confidentiality in the more specific context of vulnerable adults receiving medical or social care and inter-disciplinary working. They suggest that the Act will necessitate 'a radical rethink of policies, practices and procedures'.

Traditionally. mental health has been an area where violation of ECHR Articles by Member States is common, with the UK being one of the worst offenders. In Chapters 11 and 12 Laura Davidson shows that: 'There are numerous areas in the present MHA [Mental Health Act 1983] open to challenge under the HRA 1998.'

The degree of success of the public policy shift towards community care for persons with mental disability or illness is partly relative to the provision of suitable accommodation. However, the provision of group homes in the community for such persons raises tensions with the private property rights of the community at large. In Chapter 13, Rod Edmunds and Teresa Sutton express the hope that there will be improvement in the current provision of group homes through favourable interpretation under the HRA 1998 and sympathetic reform of the Disability Discrimination Act 1995.

In Chapter 14, Austen Garwood-Gowers presents the first of two chapters on minors by investigating whether competent minors will be able to gain a complete right of self-determination under the Human Rights Act 1998. Having noted that the Court of Appeal decisions in *Re W (A Minor) (Medical Treatment)* [1992] 3 WLR 758 and *Re R (A Minor) (Wardship: Consent to Treatment)* [1991] 4 All ER 177 held that a medical intervention could be forced upon the competent minor where a parent/guardian had consented, Dr Garwood-Gowers argues that this would very probably be held to conflict with Art 8 in conjunction with Art 14. In the next chapter, Sabine Michalowski looks at young and, therefore, typically incompetent children. She examines how the question of best interests will be reinterpreted in the light of Convention rights. She argues that the rights-based approach does not provide a set solution to every given problem and mainly identifies the competing rights of the child and of each parent, without necessarily giving clear indications as to how to weigh these conflicting rights.[19] The weighing process will be up to the judiciary and Michalowski suggests that whilst some

---

18   95/46/EC.

19   For a critique of the rights-based approach on these grounds, see Herring, 1999a, p 235.

portents of previous precedent are good, but if the poor ones are followed the opportunity presented by the Act could be lost.

It would be surprising if the Human Rights Act had much impact in terms of abortion law. However, as Marc Stauch points out in Chapter 16, it is entirely possible that the Act might have some impact in the area of recklessly causing foetal harm. At the other end of life spectrum is the old human rights chestnut of euthanasia examined in Chapter 17 by Angie Ungoed-Thomas and Jeff Sapiro. They point out that cases heard in Strasbourg could have clearly defined the position of the Convention as regards euthanasia but have largely failed to do so. Whilst the passive euthanasia analysis set out in Bland has been viewed as consistent with the Convention rights,[20] the extent to which English law will prove compatible with the HRA 1998 when it comes to medically-assisted death remains uncertain.

In Chapter 18, Austen Garwood-Gowers explores the use of body materials for research and transplantation purposes from a human rights perspective. The use of materials from dead persons has been the subject of recent scandals at a number of hospitals, most notably Alder Hay. Elective ventilation has been abandoned on the basis of being unlawful but catheters are inserted without consent for the purposes of non-heart beating donation and the UK has a system under the Human Tissue Act 1961 which is partially based on the notion of 'presumed consent'. There have been calls for a more fully 'presumed consent' system of organ procurement. Dr Garwood-Gowers argues that 'presumed consent' is a misnomer and that any system of procurement that violates principles of consent is both unethical and contrary to human rights.

A final important aspect of the book is discussion of the ECHRB which spans three chapters. As Deputy Head of the Bioethics Division of the Council of Europe's Legal Affairs Directorate General, Peteris Zilgalvis is well placed to analyse the development of the ECHRB and chart its future direction which he does in Chapter 3. In Chapter 20, Melanie Latham and Siobhan Leonard expand upon the scientific frontiers theme by looking at biotechnology and its regulation under the Convention. Meanwhile, in Chapter 19, Aurora Plomer of the Department of Law, University of Leeds, looks at the contribution that the ECHRB is making in the regulation of medical research. Her chapter includes analysis of the regulation of research in specific areas such as with regard to minors and incompetent adults.

---

20   Butler-Sloss LJ in *NHS Trust A v M* and *NHS Trust B v H* (2000) *The Times*, 29 November.

CHAPTER 2

THE HUMAN RIGHTS ACT 1998 AND THE COMMON LAW, A HEALTHCARE LAW PERSPECTIVE

John Hodgson

COMMON LAW RULES AND THE EUROPEAN CONVENTION

When the European Convention on Human Rights (ECHR) was drafted in 1949–50, the focus was on human rights writ large. It was part of the general post-war settlement, and was initially conceived as a regional version of the Universal Declaration of Human Rights.[1] It was not until a late stage in the travaux préparatoires that a draft tabled by the UK delegation actually produced an enforcement mechanism.[2] Even so the Preamble clearly indicates the relationship with the Universal Declaration:

> The governments signatory hereto, being members of the Council of Europe
>
> Considering the Universal Declaration of Human Rights proclaimed by the General Assembly of the United Nations on 10 December 1948;
>
> Considering that this Declaration aims at securing the universal and effective recognition and observance of the Rights therein declared;
>
> Considering that the aim of the Council of Europe is the achievement of greater unity between its members and that one of the methods by which that aim is to be pursued is the maintenance and further realisation of human rights and fundamental freedoms;
>
> Reaffirming their profound belief in those fundamental freedoms which are the foundation of justice and peace in the world and are best maintained on the one hand by an effective political democracy and on the other by a common understanding and observance of the human rights upon which they depend;
>
> Being resolved, as the governments of European countries which are like-minded and have a common heritage of political traditions, ideals, freedom and the rule of law, to take the first steps for the collective enforcement of certain of the rights stated in the Universal Declaration.

While there is a specific guarantee of 'due process' in Art 5 (relating to the deprivation of liberty) and Art 6 (relating to trial), it is clear that these were specifically aimed at preventing a repetition of the arbitrary arrests of the GeStapo and other Nazi bodies and the mockery of legality in Freisler's

---

1   See, in particular, Teitgen, 1975, pp 38ff.

2   *Ibid*, Vol III, pp 280ff.

Volksgericht, with obvious reference to similar abuses in the remaining dictatorships of the left and right in Europe at the time.

Article 5(1) states that:

Everyone has the right to liberty and security of person. No one shall be deprived of his liberty save in the following cases and in accordance with a procedure prescribed by law:

a   the lawful detention of a person after conviction by a competent court;

b   the lawful arrest or detention of a person for non-compliance with the lawful order of a court or in order to secure the fulfilment of any obligation prescribed by law;

c   the lawful arrest or detention of a person effected for the purpose of bringing him before the competent legal authority on reasonable suspicion of having committed an offence or when it is reasonably considered necessary to prevent his committing an offence or fleeing after having done so;

d   the detention of a minor by lawful order for the purpose of educational supervision or his lawful detention for the purpose of bringing him before the competent legal authority;

e   the lawful detention of persons for the prevention of the spreading of infectious diseases, of persons of unsound mind, alcoholics or drug addicts or vagrants.

Article 6(1) states that:

In the determination of his civil rights and obligations or of any criminal charge against him, everyone is entitled to a fair and public hearing within a reasonable time by an independent and impartial tribunal established by law.

Articles 8–11 concerning privacy, religious freedom, freedom of expression and of assembly all also contain derogations which must, *inter alia*, be 'prescribed by law', or some similar phrase. Thus in Art 8 interference with privacy must be 'in accordance with the law'. (Interestingly, although the terminology of the English text varies in this way, that of the French text does not.) Clearly these requirements are analogous to that in Art 5 that detention be 'lawful'.

At this time there was no indication that the UK (primarily England) might have difficulty complying with the 'according to/prescribed by law' concept in Arts 5 and 8–11 or the provision of a 'fair hearing' in Art 6 by virtue of the existence and application of the common law. In most signatory nations, the law explicitly derives from a constitutional source and/or a legal code. Individual legislative instruments derive their force from these and the role of the courts is to interpret and apply the law. They are, however, subject to the law, and cannot 'make law': see, for example, the German Basic Law (*Grundgesetz*), Art 97(1):

Die Richter sind unabhängig und nur dem Gesetze unterworfen [Judges are independent and subject only to the law].

In the UK, of course, much of the law is in the form of statutes, statutory instruments and EC legislation, in respect of which the judicial function is the standard one of interpretation and application. However, the rules of the common law are different. Although in theory the immemorial legal customs of England declared and refined by generations of judicial pronouncement, they are in truth judge made law.[3]

THE JURISPRUDENCE

The question of the compatibility of common law rules with the ECHR first arose in the *Sunday Times* case[4] in which the editor of the *Sunday Times* claimed *inter alia* that holding it in contempt of court over its coverage of the Thalidomide case amounted to a breach of Art 10 (freedom of expression) which was not 'prescribed by law' because the law of contempt, at that time a purely common law concept, was insufficiently clear and precise to be lawful.

The Phillimore Committee had considered the issues of contempt in its Report in 1974, and had identified a number of areas of uncertainty and complexity. In the House of Lords, Lord Reid, in particular, agreed that the law was uncertain.

The European Court of Human Rights (the Court) rejected a very broad submission that 'prescribed by law' meant 'prescribed by a legislative instrument':

> The Court observes that the word 'law' in the expression 'prescribed by law' covers not only statute but also unwritten law. Accordingly, the Court does not attach importance here to the fact that contempt of court is a creature of the common law and not of legislation. It would clearly be contrary to the intention of the drafters of the Convention to hold that a restriction imposed by virtue of the common law is not 'prescribed by law' on the sole ground that it is not enunciated in legislation; this would deprive a common law state which is party to the Convention of the protection of Art 10(2) (Art 10-2) and strike at the very roots of that state's legal system [para 47].

Indeed, the basic submission was less broad, merely that 'legislation is required only if – as in the present case – the common law rules are so uncertain that they do not satisfy what the applicants maintain is the concept enshrined in that expression, namely, the principle of legal certainty'. The Court sought to indicate what 'prescribed by law' required by way of certainty in para 49:

---

3   Lord Reid, 1972, p 22.
4   *Sunday Times v UK (No 1)*, Case 6538/74, Judgment 26 April 1979.

In the Court's opinion, the following are two of the requirements that flow from the expression 'prescribed by law'. Firstly, the law must be adequately accessible: the citizen must be able to have an indication that is adequate in the circumstances of the legal rules applicable to a given case. Secondly, a norm cannot be regarded as a 'law' unless it is formulated with sufficient precision to enable the citizen to regulate his conduct: He must be able – if need be with appropriate advice – to foresee, to a degree that is reasonable in the circumstances, the consequences which a given action may entail. Those consequences need not be foreseeable with absolute certainty: experience shows this to be unattainable. Again, whilst certainty is highly desirable, it may bring in its train excessive rigidity and the law must be able to keep pace with changing circumstances. Accordingly, many laws are inevitably couched in terms which, to a greater or lesser extent, are vague and whose interpretation and application are questions of practice.

The *Sunday Times* claimed that two principles of the law of contempt fell foul of this criterion of precision, but the Court found against them, albeit with some reservations in relation to one principle which had a less than impressive pedigree in case law.

The case does, however, recognise that lack of precision may take a particular law (including a rule of the common law) out of the ambit of 'prescribed by law'. Subsequent cases have considered in a range of contexts how far English judicial method secures the necessary degree of precision. There have certainly been instances where judges have exercised their powers very sweepingly. In *Shaw v DPP*[5] the House of Lords in effect invented a new crime. This did not result in an ECHR reference because it predated the conferment of the right of individual petition. In *R v R*,[6] the House of Lords overturned centuries of practice by declaring that a husband could be guilty of rape of his wife. Although this was strictly a case of interpretation of the relevant section of the Sexual Offences Act, it was in large part a classically common law analysis of the pre-statutory history going back to extra-judicial *dicta* of Hale CJ. This did result in a reference under the ECHR: *CR v United Kingdom*.[7] The actual complaint was of retrospective criminality, covered by Art 7. However, the real issue was again the scope of the powers of the judiciary. The Court expressed its view of the principle in issue as follows:

The guarantee enshrined in Art 7,[8] which is an essential element of the rule of law, occupies a prominent place in the Convention system of protection, as is underlined by the fact that no derogation from it is permissible under Art 15 in time of war or other public emergency. It should be construed and applied, as

---

5   [1962] AC 220.

6   [1992] 2 AC 599.

7   Case 20190/92, Judgment 22 November 1995.

8   'No one shall be held guilty of any criminal offence on account of any act or omission which did not constitute a criminal offence under national or international law at the time when it was committed.'

follows from its object and purpose, in such a way as to provide effective safeguards against arbitrary prosecution, conviction and punishment. Accordingly, as the Court held in *Kokkinakis v Greece*, Judgment of 25 May 1993,[9] Art 7 is not confined to prohibiting the retrospective application of the criminal law to an accused's disadvantage: it also embodies, more generally, the principle that only the law can define a crime and prescribe a penalty (*nullum crimen, nulla poena sine lege*) and the principle that the criminal law must not be extensively construed to an accused's detriment, for instance by analogy. From these principles, it follows that an offence must be clearly defined in the law. In its aforementioned judgment, the Court added that this requirement is satisfied where the individual can know from the wording of the relevant provision and, if need be, with the assistance of the courts' interpretation of it, what acts and omissions will make him criminally liable. The Court, thus, indicated that when speaking of 'law' Art 7 alludes to the very same concept as that to which the Convention refers elsewhere when using that term, a concept which comprises written as well as unwritten law and implies qualitative requirements, notably those of accessibility and foreseeability (see, as a recent authority, the judgment of *Tolstoy Miloslavsky v UK*, 13 July 1995).[10] However clearly drafted a legal provision may be, in any system of law, including criminal law, there is an inevitable element of judicial interpretation. There will always be a need for elucidation of doubtful points and for adaptation to changing circumstances. Indeed, in the UK, as in the other Convention States, the progressive development of the criminal law through judicial law-making is a well entrenched and necessary part of legal tradition. Art 7 of the Convention cannot be read as outlawing the gradual clarification of the rules of criminal liability through judicial interpretation from case to case, provided that the resultant development is consistent with the essence of the offence and could reasonably be foreseen.

The Court went on to hold (perhaps surprisingly) that there was a sufficiently clear trend of development in the case law to make this 'development' one which was consistent and foreseeable in this sense. However, again there is recognition that there are criteria which must be met. While neither this case nor the *Sunday Times* one suggests any desire on the part of the Court to intermeddle officiously with the operation of common law principles (indeed, quite the reverse) there is at least the potential for this.

In two cases which concerned the question of whether action taken by the police in purported exercise of powers to prevent a breach of the peace was consistent with the ECHR rights of the complainants, the issue of the certainty or otherwise of the concept of breach of the peace was raised. The Court adopted the same approach as previously. In *Steel and Others v United Kingdom*,[11] the issue was dealt with as follows:

---

9   Series A, No 260-A, p 22, para 52.

10   Series A, No 316-B, pp 71–72, para 37.

11   Case 24838/94, Judgment 23 September 1998.

The applicants contended that their arrests and initial periods of detention had not been 'lawful', since the concept of breach of the peace and the attendant powers of arrest were insufficiently certain under English law.

First, they submitted that if, as appeared from the national case-law ..., an individual committed a breach of the peace when he or she behaved in a manner the natural consequence of which was that others would react violently, it was difficult to judge the extent to which one could engage in protest activity, in the presence of those who might be annoyed, without causing a breach of the peace. Secondly, the power to arrest whenever there were reasonable grounds for apprehending that a breach of the peace was about to take place granted too wide a discretion to the police. Thirdly, there had been conflicting decisions at Court of Appeal level as to the definition of breach of the peace ...

The Court recalls that the expressions 'lawful' and 'in accordance with a procedure prescribed by law' in Art 5(1) stipulate not only full compliance with the procedural and substantive rules of national law, but also that any deprivation of liberty be consistent with the purpose of Art 5 and not arbitrary (see the *Benham v UK*, Judgment of 10 June 1996).[12] In addition, given the importance of personal liberty, it is essential that the applicable national law meet the standard of 'lawfulness' set by the Convention, which requires that all law, whether written or unwritten, be sufficiently precise to allow the citizen – if need be, with appropriate advice – to foresee, to a degree that is reasonable in the circumstances, the consequences which a given action may entail (see *SW v UK*, Judgment of 22 November 1995,[13] and, *mutatis mutandis, Sunday Times v UK (No 1)*, Judgment of 26 April 1979,[14] and *Halford v UK*, Judgment of 25 June 1997).[15]

In this connection, the Court observes that the concept of breach of the peace has been clarified by the English courts over the last two decades, to the extent that it is now sufficiently established that a breach of the peace is committed only when an individual causes harm, or appears likely to cause harm, to persons or property or acts in a manner the natural consequence of which would be to provoke others to violence. It is also clear that a person may be arrested for causing a breach of the peace or where it is reasonably apprehended that he or she is likely to cause a breach of the peace.

Accordingly, the Court considers that the relevant legal rules provided sufficient guidance and were formulated with the degree of precision required by the Convention (see, for example, *Larissis and Others v Greece*, Judgment of 24 February 1998).[16]

---

12 Reports 1996-III, pp 752–53, para 40.
13 Series A, No 335-B, pp 41–42, paras 35–36.
14 Series A, No 30, p 31, para 49.
15 Reports 1997-III, p 1017, para 49.
16 Reports 1998-I, p 377, para 34.

In the simultaneously decided case of *McLeod v United Kingdom*[17] a differently constituted chamber of the Court reached a similar conclusion, although using somewhat different authorities:

> The Court recalls that the expression 'in accordance with the law', within the meaning of Art 8(2), requires firstly that the impugned measures should have a basis in domestic law. It also refers to the quality of the law in question, requiring that it be accessible to the persons concerned and formulated with sufficient precision to enable them – if need be, with appropriate advice – to foresee, to a degree that is reasonable in the circumstances, the consequences which a given action may entail (see, amongst many others, *Margareta and Roger Andersson v Sweden*, Judgment of 25 February 1992).[18] However, those consequences need not be foreseeable with absolute certainty, since such certainty might give rise to excessive rigidity, and the law must be able to keep pace with changing circumstances (see, *mutatis mutandis, Sunday Times v UK (No 1)*, Judgment of 26 April 1979).[19]

> In this connection, the Court observes that the concept of breach of the peace has been clarified by the English courts over the last two decades, to the extent that it is now sufficiently established that a breach of the peace is committed only when an individual causes harm, or appears likely to cause harm, to persons or property, or acts in a manner the natural consequence of which would be to provoke violence in others ...

> Furthermore, the English courts have recognised that the police have a duty to prevent a breach of the peace that they reasonably apprehend will occur and to stop a breach of the peace that is occurring. In the execution of this duty, the police have the power to enter into and remain on private property without the consent of the owner or occupier ... Despite the general abolition of common law powers of entry without warrant, this power was preserved by s 17(6) of PACE 1984 ...

> When considering whether the national law was complied with, the Court recalls that it is primarily for the national authorities, notably the courts, to interpret and apply domestic law (see, as a recent authority, *Kopp v Switzerland*, Judgment of 25 March 1998).[20] In this regard, the Court notes that in its decision the Court of Appeal took into account the criticisms of the common law power of the police to enter private premises to prevent a breach of the peace cited by the applicant in her memorial to the Court, and found that the common law power was applicable in situations involving domestic disturbance ...

> In conclusion, the Court finds that the power of the police to enter private premises without a warrant to deal with or prevent a breach of the peace was defined with sufficient precision for the foreseeability criterion to be satisfied. The interference was, therefore, 'in accordance with the law'.

---

17   Case 24755/94, Judgment 23 September 1998.
18   Series A, No 226-A, p 25, para 75.
19   Series A, No 30, p 31, para 49.
20   Reports of Judgments and Decisions 1998-II, p 541, para 59.

It is to be noted that, in particular in the *Steel* case, considerable stress was laid on relatively recent case-law and other activity as having clarified the law to an acceptable extent.

Finally, in *Hashman & Harrup v United Kingdom*[21] an again largely differently constituted Chamber had to consider whether the common law power to bind over for behaviour that was *contra bonos mores* satisfied the established certainty criteria. The Court concluded that it did not:

> The Court recalls that one of the requirements flowing from the expression 'prescribed by law' is foreseeability. A norm cannot be regarded as a 'law' unless it is formulated with sufficient precision to enable the citizen to regulate his conduct. At the same time, whilst certainty in the law is highly desirable, it may bring in its train excessive rigidity and the law must be able to keep pace with changing circumstances. The level of precision required of domestic legislation – which cannot in any case provide for every eventuality – depends to a considerable degree on the content of the instrument in question, the field it is designed to cover and the number and status of those to whom it is addressed (see generally in this connection, the *Rekvényi v Hungary* judgment of 20 May 1999, para 34).

> The Court further recalls that prior restraint on freedom of expression must call for the most careful scrutiny on its part (see, in the context of the necessity for a prior restraint, *Sunday Times v United Kingdom (No 2)*, Judgment of 26 November 1991).[22]

> The Court has already considered the issue of 'lawfulness' for the purposes of Art 5 of the Convention of orders to be bound over to keep the peace and be of good behaviour (in [the] *Steel and Others* judgment, pp 2738–40, paras 71–77). In that case, the Court found that the elements of breach of the peace were adequately defined by English law (*ibid*, p 2739, para 75) ...

> The Court also noted that the requirement under Art 10(2) that an interference with the exercise of freedom of expression be 'prescribed by law' is similar to that under Art 5(1) that any deprivation of liberty be 'lawful' (*ibid*, p 2742, para 94).

> It is a feature of the present case that it concerns an interference with freedom of expression which was not expressed to be a 'sanction', or punishment, for behaviour of a certain type, but rather an order, imposed on the applicants, not to breach the peace or behave *contra bonos mores* in the future. The binding-over order in the present case thus had purely prospective effect. It did not require a finding that there had been a breach of the peace. The case is thus different from the case of *Steel and Others*, in which the proceedings brought against the first and second applicants were in respect of breaches of the peace which were later found to have been committed.

> The Court must consider the question of whether behaviour *contra bonos mores* is adequately defined for the purposes of Art 10(2) of the Convention.

---

21   Case 25594/94, Judgment 25 November 1999.
22   Series A, No 217, pp 29–30, para 51.

The Court first recalls that in its *Steel and Others* judgment, it noted that the expression 'to be of good behaviour' 'was particularly imprecise and offered little guidance to the person bound over as to the type of conduct which would amount to a breach of the order' (p 2739, para 76). Those considerations apply equally in the present case, where the applicants were not charged with any criminal offence, and were found not to have breached the peace.

The Court next notes that conduct *contra bonos mores* is defined as behaviour which is 'wrong rather than right in the judgment of the majority of contemporary fellow citizens ...'. It cannot agree with the Government that this definition has the same objective element as conduct 'likely to cause annoyance', which was at issue in the case of *Chorherr* [*v Austria*], Judgment of 25 August 1993.[23] The Court considers that the question of whether conduct is 'likely to cause annoyance' is a question which goes to the very heart of the nature of the conduct proscribed: it is conduct whose likely consequence is the annoyance of others. Similarly, the definition of breach of the peace given in the case of *Percy v Director of Public Prosecutions*[24] – that it includes conduct the natural consequences of which would be to provoke others to violence – also describes behaviour by reference to its effects. Conduct which is 'wrong rather than right in the judgment of the majority of contemporary citizens', by contrast, is conduct which is not described at all, but merely expressed to be 'wrong' in the opinion of a majority of citizens ...

With specific reference to the facts of the present case, the Court does not accept that it must have been evident to the applicants what they were being ordered not do for the period of their binding over. Whilst in the case of *Steel and Others* the applicants had been found to have breached the peace, and the Court found that it was apparent that the bind over related to similar behaviour (*ibid*), the present applicants did not breach the peace, and given the lack of precision referred to above, it cannot be said that what they were being bound over not to do must have been apparent to them.

The Court thus finds that the order by which the applicants were bound over to keep the peace and not to behave *contra bonos mores* did not comply with the requirement of Art 10(2) of the Convention that it be 'prescribed by law'.

THE PRESENT POSITION AND THE IMPLICATIONS FOR HEALTHCARE LAW

The effect of this decision is that the incompatibility of a rule of the common law with the ECHR by reason of uncertainty has moved from the realm of theory to that of reality. The next question is, therefore, whether there are other common law rules which fall into the same category and, in particular, whether any of them affect health law.

23   Series A, No 266-B, pp 35–36, para 25.
24   [1995] 1 WLR 1382.

There would seem to be two different sets of circumstances where this might be the case:

(a) Where the existing law is confused and lacks conceptual clarity. The Court clearly had reservations in this respect in both the *Sunday Times* and *Steel and Others* cases, although these doubts did not prevail. The *Hashman & Harrup* case is in this category.

(b) Where the existing law is substantially changed by judicial action. This was a cause of some concern in the *CR* case, although there was held to be a process of change rather than a quantum leap, and again no breach was found.

There is one fairly obvious medico-legally relevant example of the second category. This is the expansion of the doctrine of necessity to authorise the practice of not using Mental Health Act (MHA) 1983 powers to detain compliant but non-competent patients as established in *L v Bournewood*.[25] In this case, an autistic adult, who was incapable of consenting to treatment, was returned to hospital after an incident of self-harming at a day centre. No steps were taken to secure his admission as a compulsory patient, that is, to 'section' him,[26] and he was not subjected to tests or treatment to which he objected. The issue was whether this action was lawful. The interest is primarily aroused by the principal ground for the decision, namely that the common law doctrine of necessity permits doctors to treat incompetent but compliant clients under the provisions of s 131(1) of the MHA 1983. The majority (Lord Goff, with whom Lord Lloyd and Lord Hope agreed) further held that such treatment did not amount to a detention which constituted imprisonment for the purposes of the tort of false imprisonment. The minority (Lords Steyn and Nolan) held that there was a detention which amounted to an imprisonment but found that this detention was justified.

Lord Goff accepted that there were aspects of the handling of Mr L, for instance his removal by ambulance from the day centre to the hospital, which did amount to 'detention', although he considered these to be justified by the doctrine of necessity as being undertaken in Mr L's best interests. It is difficult to quarrel with this analysis so far as such short term measures are concerned. It would appear that Mr L's mental state at that time was such that he could be equated with a severely injured physical trauma victim, who may likewise be lawfully conveyed to hospital although she cannot consent. This aspect of the doctrine of necessity would certainly meet the ECHR certainty test. An alternative analysis is of course that this is not the doctrine of necessity at work, but that those responsible for the initial transfer were acting in L's best interests, although this was not an approach canvassed in the speeches. It is clear that doctors act lawfully when they treat an unconscious or incompetent

---

25 [1998] 3 All ER 289.
26 Under MHA 1983, Pt II.

patient in his best interests and that, where proposed treatment is not in those best interests, it will be unlawful, even when death will result.[27] This particular issue is one of the first to be considered judicially under the Human Rights Act 1998 (HRA). In *Re H, Re M*[28] Butler-Sloss LJ ruled that none of the substantive Convention rights were infringed and that this approach remained the law. As it is not suggested that this area of the law is in anyway uncertain,[29] it is not relevant to this discussion.

So far as the longer term decision to admit Mr L as an informal patient is concerned, the majority seem to have fallen into a very English error, namely to look primarily at what the doctors in the case have done. In English law, there is an all purpose test for medical negligence, the *Bolam*[30] test:

> [N]egligence means failure to act in accordance with the standards of reasonably competent medical men at the time ... I myself would prefer to put it this way, that he is not guilty of negligence if he has acted in accordance with a standard accepted as proper by a responsible body of medical men skilled in that particular art.

This test has been applied to the diagnostic process in *Maynard v West Midlands RHA* [1984] 1 WLR 634, the actual management of the patient in *Whitehouse v Jordan* [1981] 1 WLR 246 and to advice on the risks and benefits of treatment (so called 'informed consent' cases) in *Sidaway v Bethlem Royal and Maudsley Hospital Governors* [1985] 1 All ER 643. The English courts do concede that medical opinion may not be the last word on the subject. Lord Bridge, supported by Lord Keith, said in *Sidaway*:

> [E]ven in a case where ... no expert witness in the relevant medical field condemns the non-disclosure as being in conflict with accepted and responsible medical practice, I am of opinion that the judge might in certain circumstances come to the conclusion that disclosure of a particular risk was so necessary to an informed choice on the part of the patient that no reasonably prudent medical man would fail to make it.

There was no question of the *bona fides* of the doctors treating Mr L and no significant challenge to their clinical decisions. That, traditionally, has been enough for English judges to put aside any reservations in other medico-legal contexts. It seems to have been good enough for the majority in the present case. A patient-centred approach would show us a person incapable of deciding for himself, brought willy-nilly to the hospital and given no option of leaving. The doctors had already considered whether to use the MHA 1983 compulsory powers but decided that it was not necessary as 'he was, as I [Dr Manjubhashini, the consultant psychiatrist] noted at the time, "quite

---

27 *Airedale NHS Trust v Bland* [1993] 1 All ER 821.

28 (2000) unreported, 6 October Fam Div, Butler-Sloss P. See (2000) *The Guardian*, 7 October.

29 As distinct from being ethically contentious.

30 *Bolam v Friern Hospital Management Committee* [1957] 1 WLR 582.

compliant" and "had not attempted to run away". He was therefore admitted as an informal patient.' This seems to be a detention, just as in *Meering v Grahame-White Aviation* (1919) 122 LT 44 where a workman was suspected of theft. He was instructed to go to an office and wait there, which he did. Unbeknown to him at the time a policeman was posted to prevent him leaving. He later learned what had occurred and successfully claimed false imprisonment. The policeman may not be outside the door in L's case, but the decision not to let him leave had been made, it was not a matter of future conjecture as the majority suggest.

The view that informal treatment is in general desirable was derived by the judges from the Percy report.[31] It was clearly recognised that there was a distinction between a patient with capacity to consent and who consented, and a patient who lacked capacity but was compliant. The former were referred to by Mr Pleming QC (counsel for the Secretary of State for Health) as voluntary and the latter as informal patients. Lord Goff adopts this formulation; Lord Steyn refers to them as 'compliant but incapacitated'.

Although the evidence before the House from the Department of Health suggested that 90% of all patients are voluntary or informal, there is no clear breakdown of the split. Indeed, as the two groups have the same legal status it would be difficult to distinguish them. It is, however, suggested that the number of those detained formally would have risen by 22,000 from 11,000, had the decision of the Court of Appeal been upheld, and this suggests in very approximate terms that some 20% of the total come into the 'informal' category. This assumes that there are some 99,000 voluntary and informal patients to 11,000 compulsory ones, of whom 22,000 would be affected.[32]

Liberty of the person is dealt with in Art 5 of the Convention.[33] The provisions of Art 5(1)(e), (4) and (5) clearly apply to compulsory patients.[34] Do they apply to informal patients? This will, in turn, depend on whether such patients have been detained. The majority in the House of Lords found that there had been no detention. While the decision of the national court is not conclusive of the issue under the Convention, it will be taken into account and may be persuasive. If such patients have been detained within the meaning of the Convention, it will be necessary to examine whether that detention satisfies the requirements established by the European Court for lawfulness.[35]

The HRA 1998 provides protection against action by public authorities in contravention of Convention rights, either by way of appeal or judicial

---

31 Royal Commission, 1957.

32 Any calculation is complicated by the fact that much depends on whether the group of patients will typically need short or long term care. This group is likely to require long term care.

33 Set out above.

34 *X v UK* (1981) 4 EHRR 181.

35 These requirements are considered later.

review,[36] but there is no overt reference to the rules of the common law. It is true that much of the litigation before the Commission and Court of Human Rights at Strasbourg has arisen from statute. For example, the issue in *X v United Kingdom*[37] was whether the then provision relating to compulsory detention under the MHA 1983, which vested the ultimate decision on detention in the Secretary of State, was compatible with the Convention right to have detention determined by a 'court'.[38] It was held that it was not, and as a result the status of Mental Health Review Tribunals was changed; from being consultative bodies, they became the actual decision makers.

It is clearly conceptually easier to subject legislation to tests of compliance with the Convention. New legislation is the result of a specific, public and formal process. Existing legislation has a definite meaning and this either is, or is not, compatible with the Convention. Common law rules are less definite, being subject to constant reinterpretation. To some extent the Act does provide safeguards. By s 6, it will be unlawful for any public authority, which includes a court by virtue of s 6(3)(a), to act in a way which is incompatible with a Convention right, unless it is obliged to do so by specific legislation. This would clearly allow someone in the position of Mr L, who argued that a public authority, namely the NHS Trust, was acting inconsistently with the Convention in reliance on the common law either to commence proceedings claiming relief or, if proceedings were brought against him, to rely on the relevant Convention rights.[39] If he considers that the court has not adjudicated in accordance with the Convention, then he may appeal and the appellate court will itself consider the merits of the argument under the Convention.[40] Since, in general, the function of the court is to determine the case by upholding the arguments of one or other party, the majority of these cases will not present conceptual difficulties. The practical effect will be that the court must weigh the actions complained of against the Convention, whereas previously they did not do so.[41]

There will be areas, and *L v Bournewood* appears to be one, where the relevant legal rules are non statutory principles of the common law. What is common to the five speeches in the Lords in the Bournewood case is that the essential justification for the management of Mr L is that it is justified by the doctrine of necessity. This is an entirely judge-made doctrine. Lord Goff, for the majority, simply asserted that it applied, as did Lord Nolan, agreeing with him on this point: 'Furthermore his treatment while in hospital was plainly

---

36   HRA 1998, s 9.

37   Case 24755/94, Judgment 23 September 1998.

38   ECHR, Art 5(4).

39   HRA 1998, s 7.

40   *Ibid*, s 8.

41   *R v Chief Immigration Officer, Heathrow Airport and Another ex p Salamat Bibi* [1976] 1 WLR 979.

justified on the basis of the common law doctrine of necessity.' Lord Goff did say a little about the development of the doctrine:

> The second point relates to the function of the common law doctrine of necessity in justifying actions which might otherwise be tortious, and so has the effect of providing a defence to actions in tort. The importance of this was, I believe, first revealed in the judgments in *In Re F (Mental Patient: Sterilisation)* [1990] 2 AC 1. I wish, however, to express my gratitude to counsel for the appellants, Mr John Grace QC and Mr Andrew Grubb, for drawing to our attention three earlier cases in which the doctrine was invoked, viz *Rex v Coate* (1772) Lofft 73, especially at p 75, *per* Lord Mansfield; *Scott v Wakem* (1862) 3 F & F 328, p 333, *per* Bramwell, B; and *Symm v Fraser* (1863) 3 F & F 859, p 883, *per* Cockburn CJ, all of which provide authority for the proposition that the common law permitted the detention of those who were a danger, or potential danger, to themselves or others, in so far as this was shown to be necessary. I must confess that I was unaware of these authorities though, now that they have been drawn to my attention, I am not surprised that they should exist. The concept of necessity has its role to play in all branches of our law of obligations – in contract (see the cases on agency of necessity), in tort (see *In Re F (Mental Patient: Sterilisation)* [1990] 2 AC 1) and in restitution (see the sections on necessity in the standard books on the subject) – and in our criminal law. It is therefore a concept of great importance. It is perhaps surprising, however, that the significant role it has to play in the law of torts has come to be recognised at so late a stage in the development of our law.[42]

Lord Steyn, also, did not consider the scope of the doctrine of justification in detail, although he did consider how far the statutory framework was consistent with the survival of an independent common law justification for detention.[43] He concluded that there was no incompatibility.

What is completely lacking from the speeches is any suggestion that there is anything untoward about asserting that, what Lord Goff acknowledges to be a somewhat undefined doctrine, can lawfully operate in a field as important as that of the liberty of the subject, even where there is a statutory scheme, the safeguards of which are not available to those in the position of Mr L. Lord Steyn does at least acknowledge that the loss of safeguards is regrettable:

> The general effect of the decision of the House is to leave compliant incapacitated patients without the safeguards enshrined in the 1983 Act. This is an unfortunate result. The Mental Health Act Commission has expressed concern about such informal patients in successive reports. And in a helpful written submission the Commission has again voiced those concerns and explained in detail the beneficial effects of the ruling of the Court of Appeal. The common law principle of necessity is a useful concept, but it contains none of the safeguards of the 1983 Act. It places effective and unqualified control in

---

42 [1998] 3 All ER 289, p 301.

43 *Ibid*, pp 306–07.

the hands of the hospital psychiatrist and other healthcare professionals. It is, of course, true that such professionals owe a duty of care to patients and that they will almost invariably act in what they consider to be the best interests of the patient. But neither habeas corpus nor judicial review are sufficient safeguards against misjudgments and professional lapses in the case of compliant incapacitated patients. Given that such patients are diagnostically indistinguishable from compulsory patients, there is no reason to withhold the specific and effective protections of the 1983 Act from a large class of vulnerable mentally incapacitated individuals. Their moral right to be treated with dignity requires nothing less. The only comfort is that counsel for the Secretary of State has assured the House that reform of the law is under active consideration.[44]

The question which must be posed is: To what extent is the existence of wholly judge-made doctrines such as necessity consistent with the notion of rights enjoyed under law as developed in the jurisprudence of the European Court?

The Convention does provide in Art 7(1) that, in respect of criminal proceedings, there may be no retrospective criminalisation, but there is no explicit provision in relation to retrospective alteration of the law in other respects. However, the Convention does provide in Art 6(1) for a version of 'due process':

In the determination of his civil rights and obligations or of any criminal charge against him, everyone is entitled to a fair and public hearing within a reasonable time by an independent and impartial tribunal established by law.

One the one hand, this provides for judicial as opposed to administrative, control of these matters, as in the case of *X v United Kingdom*. On the other, it may provide for an element of legality or certainty, as in *Hashman & Harrup v United Kingdom*. The 'right to a court' is interpreted as the right to a court which will adjudicate lawfully on the basis of established principles and not capriciously. The overt message of the Government in *Bringing Rights Home* (1997, White Paper) has been that the UK courts will now be able to measure statutes against Convention standards. There is no equivalent overt recognition of the need to do the same for common law rules.

This is an important procedural and substantive protection for the individual. It will become the more so, since the HRA 1998 requires UK courts to 'take into account' decisions of the European Court,[45] although these are persuasive rather than binding, unlike the position in relation to EC law.[46] It, thus, follows that when considering how a particular line of authority is to be developed or applied, at least in contexts in which it has a bearing on the rights protected under the Convention, the court must test its preferred

---

44   *Ibid*, pp 307–08.

45   HRA 1998, s 2(1)(a).

46   European Communities Act 1972, s 3.

conclusion against this requirement of foreseeability, predictability and certainty. This may be a wider field than currently anticipated, as there is an increasing tendency for the Convention and its protocols to be invoked in commercial and property matters.[47] However, there is no doubt that cases involving classic human rights issues, such as the *Bournewood* case itself, will in future be judged against this yardstick. It would be unfair to criticise the speeches in the case for failure to address this issue, since it is clear that, until the Act came into force, the only use which UK courts could make of the Convention was to resolve ambiguities in favour of an interpretation which gives effect to the UK's international law obligations. What is clear is that the doctrine of necessity which was successfully invoked is precisely the sort of common law doctrine which is in danger of infringing the principle of lawfulness because of its uncertain scope and capacity for development. The application of the principle of necessity to treatment of the incompetent, as opposed to emergency treatment of the traumatised only goes back to *In Re F (Mental Patient: Sterilisation)*.

Lord Goff admits and asserts as much in his speech in *Bournewood*. The inescapable conclusion is that, in addition to the much-heralded requirement to examine legislation for its compatibility with the HRA 1998, and the opportunity to subject all public decision making and administration to examination under the Act, it will also be necessary to apply the tests and standards of the Convention to all common law rules.

In *Bournewood*, such an investigation would have led, at a minimum, to a much more rigorous analysis of the scope which the doctrine of necessity had already acquired. The issue of whether L was detained would have been considered from the point of view of Art 5 of the Convention, with appropriate weight being placed on the protection conferred by the MHA 1983 scheme on compulsory patients. In that context, it must surely have followed that the views of the Court of Appeal and of Lord Steyn must have prevailed.

SOME CAVEATS

While there will be a strong tendency to seek to use the HRA 1998 as a catch-all means to put right all previous rules of law which are against the client's case, the courts are unlikely to accept most such arguments. There will need to be a very high degree of uncertainty or unacceptability of a common law rule before the judges are going to accept that their predecessors have created an unlawful rule. In *R v DPP ex p Kebeline and Others* [1999] 3 WLR 972, the House

---

47 Eg, *National & Provincial Building Society*, Case 117/1996/736/933–35, Judgment 23 October 1997.

of Lords warned, albeit in a different context, that it should not be assumed that the judges would rush to declare provisions incompatible with HRA 1998 obligations and would rather be conducting a sophisticated analysis to give effect to the existing rule wherever and so far as possible. In *Daniels v Walker* [2000] 1 WLR 1382, the Court of Appeal similarly discouraged recourse to Art 6 in relation to civil procedural rules.

It has been argued that 'Do Not Resuscitate' orders may fall foul of Art 2 guaranteeing the right to life. It is well established that the law will not require doctors to treat where this is not in accordance with their professional opinion as to the best interests of the patient. The latest example is *R v Portsmouth Hospitals NHS Trust ex p Glass* [1999] 2 FLR 905. However, this area of the law seems to be perfectly clear for ECHR purposes. While there are hotly debated ethical questions over the boundaries of permissible treatment, it is highly unlikely that the HRA 1998 will assist in their resolution.

THE EUROPEAN CONVENTION ON HUMAN RIGHTS AND BIOMEDICINE: ITS PAST, PRESENT AND FUTURE

Peteris Zilgalvis[1]

INTRODUCTION

This chapter is intended to be an introduction to the Convention on Human Rights and Biomedicine (ECHRB), its beginnings, its current status and its possible role in the future European and global legal landscape.

The ECHRB is the first international agreement on the new biomedical technologies. Its full title is the Convention for the Protection of Human Rights and Dignity of the Human Being with regard to the Application of Biology and Medicine. It was opened for signature on 4 April 1997 in Oviedo, Spain and 29 countries[2] have signed to date. It is expected that other States will be signing, and ratifying, the Convention in the future. In addition to the Member States of the Council of Europe, the following States, which took part in the preparation of the Convention may sign: Australia, Canada, the Holy See, Japan and the United States of America.

Seven Member States have ratified and the ECHRB has come into force for these countries.[3] The Convention first came into force on 1 December 1999. It is up to the countries signing and ratifying the Convention to give effect to its provisions in their national legislation. This process is followed up by the Secretariat and the Steering Committee on Bioethics (CDBI) at the Council of Europe. Assistance is provided to signatories to adapt their institutions and legislation to the requirements of the Convention. The preparation of the Convention was an initiative of the Council of Europe in Strasbourg.

---

1   Note that the views expressed are personal and do not necessarily reflect any official position of the Council of Europe.

2   As of 1 January 2001: Croatia, Cyprus, Czech Republic, Denmark, Estonia, Finland, France, Georgia, Greece, Hungary, Iceland, Italy, Latvia, Lithuania, Luxembourg, Moldova, Netherlands, Norway, Poland, Portugal, Romania, San Marino, Slovak Republic, Slovenia, Spain, Sweden, Switzerland, the former Yugoslav Republic of Macedonia and Turkey.

3   Denmark, Georgia, Greece, San Marino, Slovak Republic, Slovenia and Spain.

THE COUNCIL OF EUROPE

Set up in 1949,[4] the Council of Europe is an intergovernmental organisation with a pan-European vocation that fosters political, legal and cultural co-operation between its 41 member European pluralistic democracies. It is quite distinct from the 15 nation European Union (EU), though all of the EU member countries are also members of the Council of Europe. The aims of the Council of Europe, as specified by its Statute, are to protect human rights and strengthen pluralist democracy, to enhance European cultural identity and seek out solutions to the major problems of our time, such as the bioethical problems addressed by the ECHRB. The Council of Europe operates through two principal bodies, the Committee of Ministers (its decision making body) and the Parliamentary Assembly (its deliberative body). A Secretariat General serves these bodies and is headed by a Secretary General elected for five years. The most tangible results of intergovernmental co-operation in the Council are European Conventions, drawn up as a contract between signatory States. Each State accepts a number of obligations in return for acceptance of the same obligations by other States. It is necessary to stress that that the treaties are not legal instruments of the Council of Europe as such, but owe their existence to the Member States that sign and ratify them. Even though the treaties have a life of their own, they are in many cases followed by expert committees set up within the Council of Europe.[5] The Council of Europe has drawn up more than 170 multilateral Conventions,[6] including the European Convention on Human Rights.

---

4   The Statute on the Council of Europe emerged from the Congress of Europe which was convened at the Hague on 7 May 1948 to draw up proposals for European unity in the aftermath of the Second World War. The Congress revealed the differences in opinion between those who were unconditional supporters of a European federation and those who favoured simple intergovernmental co-operation (see Craig and De Búrca, 1998, p 8; and Kapteyn and VerLoren van Themaat, 1989, p 3). On 27 and 28 January 1949, the five Ministers of foreign affairs of the Brussels Treaty countries reached a compromise: a Council of Europe consisting of a ministerial committee, to meet in private; and a consultative body, to meet in public. In order to satisfy the countries supporting co-operation, the Assembly was purely consultative in nature, with decision-making powers vested in the Committee of Ministers. On 5 May 1949, the treaty constituting the Statute of the Council of Europe was signed by 10 countries in London, UK (see www.coe.int, 'A short history').

5   Polakiewicz, 1999, p 10.

6   Further information on the Conventions and agreements in the European Treaty Series (ETS) can be found in English or French at
http://conventions.coe.int/treaty/EN/Menuprincipal.htm.

THE PROCESS OF DEVELOPING THE ECHRB AND ITS RATIONALE

The Ad Hoc Committee of Experts on Bioethics (CAHBI) was set up under the direct authority of the Committee of Ministers in 1985 and, in 1992, became the CDBI. The Committee has addressed the problems confronting mankind as a result of the advances in medicine and biology. The CDBI is responsible for the intergovernmental activities of the Council of Europe in the field of bioethics. These activities have led to the adoption of Recommendations of the Committee of Ministers in the field of bioethics on subjects such as genetic engineering, medical research on human beings, genetic testing, and on the use of human embryos and foetuses in scientific research; and to the preparation of the Convention, which was adopted by the Committee of Ministers on 19 November 1996.

The motivation behind the Convention was provided by the spectacular progress achieved in biology and medicine and the attendant concerns that the rapid pace of this progress has raised. This progress has produced great achievements in matters of health and further achievements can be expected in the future. At the same time, fundamental values concerning the individual, the family, health, privacy, human rights and human dignity must be observed. In regard to the Council of Europe, the fundamental basis for this discussion was, and is, human rights; with human dignity, the equal, inherent dignity of all human beings providing the essential foundation of all human rights philosophy and law.

The Convention's roots can be traced to the 17th Conference of the European Ministers of Justice (Istanbul, Turkey, 5–7 June 1990) which adopted Resolution No 3 on bioethics which recommended that the Committee of Ministers instruct the CAHBI to examine the possibility of preparing a framework Convention 'setting out common general standards for the protection of the human person[7] in the context of the development of the biomedical sciences'. The resolution was based on a proposal by Ms Catherine Lalumiere, Secretary General of the Council of Europe at that time. The Parliamentary Assembly of the Council of Europe recommended in June 1991, in its Recommendation 1160, that the Committee of Ministers 'envisage a framework Convention comprising a main text with general principles and additional protocols on specific aspects'. We will see that this approach, based on a framework Convention with specific protocols, was the one that was eventually adopted.

---

7   It is interesting to note that the term 'human person', utilised in a number of documents proposing the preparation of the Convention, does not appear in the Convention itself. The Convention utilises 'everyone', 'human being' or 'person'.

The support for the proposal continued to grow when in September 1991, the Committee of Ministers instructed the CAHBI to prepare a framework Convention setting out common general standards for the protection of the human person in the context of the biomedical sciences. They included an allusion to protocols to this Convention on organ transplants and the use of substances of human origin, and on biomedical research.

In March 1992, the CAHBI formed a Working Party to prepare the draft Convention. In July 1994, a first version of the draft Convention was opened for public consultation and was submitted to the Parliamentary Assembly for an opinion.[8] The CDBI, which had replaced the CAHBI, took this opinion and others into account in preparing a final draft. The CDBI confirmed this draft on 7 June 1996 and submitted it to the Parliamentary Assembly for an opinion.[9] The Committee of Ministers adopted the Convention on 19 November 1996.[10]

The Convention is structured so as to set out only the important principles in order to provide a common framework for the protection of human rights and human dignity in both longstanding and currently developing areas concerning the application of biology and medicine. It was decided that additional standards and more detailed questions would be dealt with in the five additional protocols.

The Convention gives precedence to the human being over the sole interest of science or society. The aim of the Convention is to protect human rights and dignity and all of its Articles must be interpreted in this light. The main focus of the Convention in regard to biomedical research is specifically this human rights aspect, unlike other legal instruments in the field, which may concentrate, for example, to a large extent on the economic and public health aspects of making new medicines available more quickly. The interests of society and science are not neglected, however, and come immediately after those of the individual. On this basis, it establishes that consent is obligatory for any medical treatment or research and recognises the right of all individuals to have access to information concerning their health. The text also sets out safeguards protecting anyone, of any age, who is unable to give consent.

---

8   Opinion No 184, 2 February 1995, Doc 7210.

9   Opinion No 198, 26 September 1996, Doc 7622.

10 Germany and Belgium requested that their abstention, when the Committee of Ministers voted on the adoption of the Convention and the authorisation of publication of the explanatory report, be recorded.

THE LINK BETWEEN ECHRB AND OTHER HUMAN RIGHTS INSTRUMENTS

The term 'human rights' as used in the title and text of the Convention refers to the principles found in the European Convention for the Protection of Human Rights and Fundamental Freedoms (ECHR) of 4 November 1950, which guarantees the protection of such rights. The ECHRB not only shares the same underlying approach, many ethical principles and legal concepts, but also elaborates on some of the principles found in that Convention.

Additionally, the Preamble to the Convention acknowledges the fundamental nature of the principles of human rights enshrined in: The Universal Declaration of Human Rights; the International Covenant on Civil and Political Rights; the International Covenant on Economic, Social and Cultural Rights; the Convention on the Rights of the Child; the European Social Charter; and, in a more specific instrument, the European Convention for the Protection of Individuals with regard to Automatic Processing of Personal Data. This Convention builds on the principles embodied in these instruments to ensure the protection of human rights in the context of the recent advances in biology and medicine.

While there is no possibility for recourse to the European Court of Human Rights (the Court) at this time in regard to individual cases connected to the Convention, Art 29 of the Convention provides that the Court may give advisory opinions concerning interpretation of the Convention at the request of the Government of a Party or the CDBI (with membership restricted to the parties to the Convention for this question). Additionally, it requires any party to furnish an explanation of the manner in which its internal law ensures the effective implementation of any of the provisions of the Convention, if so requested by the Secretary General of the Council of Europe.

The ECHRB is also like the ECHR in that its existence does not preclude a State from having 'better' protection of human rights; Art 27 states that none of the ECHRB provisions shall be interpreted as limiting the possibility for a party to grant a wider measure of protection with regard to the application of biology and medicine than is stipulated in the Convention. The expression 'wider protection', in the case of a conflict between various rights provided for in the Convention, must be interpreted in the light of the aim of the Convention, the protection of the human being.

Unlike the ECHR, the ECHRB is subject, under Art 32, to re-examination no later than five years from its entry into force (1 December 1999) and afterwards at intervals determined by the Committee in charge of its re-examination. This is a reflection of the fact that, whilst the core human rights dealt with under the ECHR remain constant over time, the ECHRB reflects their application to a rapidly changing field and, thus, it needs regular review.

TYPES OF PROVISION WITHIN THE ECHRB AND PROPOSALS FOR PROTOCOLS

The Convention contains two types of provisions. The first part of the Convention is a codification of the principles of modern medical law in regard to information and consent and to the protection of those unable to consent. The second part contains the provisions addressing biomedical research and the new biomedical technologies. These issues are to be addressed in the additional Protocols to the Convention. Five additional Protocols have been proposed to supplement the Convention. The Protocols are designed to address the ethical and legal issues raised by present or future scientific advances through the further development, in specific fields, of the principles contained in the Convention. The additional Protocol on the Prohibition of Cloning Human Beings and the draft additional Protocol on Transplantation of Organs and Tissues of Human Origin have been completed to date. Any State that is a signatory to the Convention is able to sign a Protocol.

The draft additional Protocols on Biomedical Research, Protection of the Human Embryo and Foetus and on Human Genetics are all currently being developed by working parties made up of high level experts nominated by Council of Europe Member States with the assistance of the Secretariat of the Council of Europe (the Bioethics Section in the Directorate of Legal Affairs). The high level experts take into account the views of non-governmental and professional organisations active in the respective fields in the preparation of the Protocols. This is done through consultations with such organisations between meetings and through consultations with European-wide bodies arranged in Strasbourg during the meetings of the working parties. The working parties also consult with other regional and international bodies that are working with related issues.

The working parties meet at least twice a year in Strasbourg and, between meetings, consult with their own governments and with other national delegations not represented in the particular working party. The progress of work on the Protocols is reviewed at least twice a year by the CDBI plenary. Protocols may be signed by States that have signed the Convention and may be ratified once the Convention has been ratified in that State.

ECHRB ARTICLES

Article 1: ECHRB purpose and object

Returning to the Convention itself, Art 1 sets out its purpose and object, this being the protection of the dignity and identity of all human beings and the guarantee, without discrimination, for everyone of respect for their integrity and other rights and fundamental freedoms with regard to the application of biology and medicine. The drafters preferred the phrase 'application of biology and medicine' to that of 'life sciences', in particular, as they wished to exclude animal and plant biology from the scope of the Convention.

Article 2: Primacy of the human being and health protection of the health of the human being

Article 2 establishes the primacy of the human being over the sole interest of society or science. Article 3 (equitable access to healthcare) states that parties shall take appropriate measures with a view to providing equitable access to healthcare of appropriate quality within their jurisdictions. It is important to note that this requirement is qualified by the following statement: 'taking into account health needs and available resources.' Parties will have to set priorities for their healthcare expenditures themselves and the drafters fully realised that there is a wide income disparity between the most developed and less developed Council of Europe Member States, thereby rendering any attempt at setting some prescribed level of healthcare unsuccessful. The Article requires that access to healthcare be equitable. The Explanatory Report to the Convention notes that in this context, 'equitable' means first and foremost the absence of unjustified discrimination. Although not synonymous with absolute equality, equitable access would imply effectively obtaining a satisfactory degree of healthcare.

Article 4: Professional standards

Article 4 (professional standards) of the Convention requires that any intervention in the health field, including research, must be carried out in accordance with the relevant professional obligations and standards. The term 'intervention' is used here in a broad sense covering all medical activities directed at human beings for preventive care, diagnosis, treatment, rehabilitation, or research. The Article covers both written and unwritten rules.

Articles 5–9: Consent and intervention without consent

The Convention clearly states the general rule that an intervention in the health field may only be carried out after the patient has given free and informed consent to it (Art 5). Consent may be looked at in the ethical sense, as a critical component of the relationship between a physician and his patient within the context of medical, ethical and professional standards that the medical professional has sworn to uphold, while, in the legal sense, it can extend to liability for the physician who does not fulfil the necessary steps of obtaining consent.

Freedom of consent implies that consent may be withdrawn at any time, but does not mean that the withdrawal of consent during an operation, for example, must always be honoured if such an obligation would be contrary to the professional standards and obligations which the physicians must uphold.

The Convention also provides safeguards for persons not able to consent (Art 6), such as: that the intervention only be for that person's direct benefit; that where a minor is involved any intervention is only carried out with the authorisation of the person or body responsible by law for the minor; that the opinion of a minor be taken into consideration as an increasingly determining factor in proportion to his or her age and degree of maturity.

Moreover, it is important to note that a parent, for example, has responsibility for a child, not power over that child. This means that the parent must always act in the interests of the child and must ensure that the decisions taken further the well-being and health of the child. Physicians and other healthcare professionals, under their professional standards, must also act in the interests of the patient (the child in this case).

Similarly, where, according to law, an adult does not have the capacity to consent to an intervention because of a mental disability, disease, or other similar reasons, an intervention may only be carried out with the authorisation of the legally responsible person or body and, as much as possible, the individual concerned should take part in the authorisation procedure. The incapacity to consent referred to in Art 6 must be understood in the context of a given intervention. The diversity of legal systems in Europe has been taken into account. In some countries, a patient's capacity to consent may be verified for each single intervention while other countries base their system on the institution of legal incapacitation under which a person may be declared incapable of giving consent to one or several types of act. Since the Convention does not aim to introduce a single system for Europe but to protect persons who are not able to give their consent, the reference in the text to domestic law seems necessary. It is up to domestic law in each country to determine whether or not a person is capable of consenting to an intervention, taking account of the need to deprive persons of their capacity for autonomy only where it is necessary in their best interests.

In order to safeguard fundamental human rights and, in particular, to avoid the application of discriminatory criteria, para 3 of Art 6 lists the reasons why an adult may be considered incapable of consenting under domestic law, namely a mental disability, a disease or similar reasons. The Explanatory Report to the Convention states that the term 'similar reasons' refers to such situations as accidents or states of coma, for example, where the patient is unable to formulate his or her wishes or to communicate them. If an adult has been declared incapable but at a certain time does not suffer from a reduced mental capacity (if their illness improves favourably as one example), they must, according to Art 5, give consent themselves.

The Explanatory Report to the Convention states that the participation of adults not able to consent in decisions must not be totally ruled out. This is reflected in the obligation found in Art 6, para 3, to involve the adult in the authorisation procedure whenever possible.

Article 6 notes that its requirement is subject to the provisions of Arts 17 (protection of persons undergoing research) and 20 (protection of persons not able to consent to organ removal). The exceptions to Art 6 in these two contexts are addressed below.

The protection of persons who have a mental disorder is addressed in Art 7. It states that subject to protective conditions prescribed by law, a person who has a mental disorder of a serious nature may be subjected, without his or her consent, to an intervention aimed at treating his or her mental disorder only where, without such treatment, serious harm is likely to result to his or her health. The Explanatory Report expands, in para 52, that the refusal to consent to an intervention may only be disregarded under those circumstances prescribed by law and where a failure to intervene would result in serious harm to the health of the individual (or to the health and safety of others).

Medically necessary interventions in the context of emergency situations are also addressed by the Convention. Article 8 requires that, when the appropriate consent cannot be obtained because of an emergency situation, any medically necessary intervention may be carried out immediately for the benefit of the health of the person concerned. It is important to note that this Article addresses specifically interventions for treatment in the context of an emergency situation, not research on emergency medicine, for instance.

Previously expressed wishes of a patient relating to a medical intervention are dealt with in Art 9. This Article states that such wishes shall be taken into account if the patient is not in a state at the time of the intervention to express his or her wishes. The Explanatory Report notes that this Article covers not only the (unforeseeable) emergency situations addressed by Art 8, but also situations where persons have foreseen that they might be unable to give their valid consent in the future. An example could be in the case of a progressive disease such as senile dementia. It should be kept in mind that taking these wishes into account does not mean that they should necessarily be followed. The Explanatory Report gives the example of a wish expressed long before the intervention that it would now be medically and scientifically obsolete to fulfil as a situation where a wish might not be followed.

Article 10: Private life and the right to information

Chapter III and Art 10 deal with private life[11] and the right to information. Article 10 sets out the principle that everyone has the right to respect for private life in relation to information about his or her health. Paragraph 2 states that everyone is entitled to know any information collected about his or her health, but also states that the wishes of individuals not to be informed shall be observed.[12] These rights are qualified by the third paragraph, which states that, in exceptional cases, restrictions may be placed by law on the exercise of the rights contained in para 2 in the interests of the patient. It is also noted in the Explanatory Report that the right to know or not to know may be restricted on the basis of Art 26.1 in order to protect the rights of a third party or of society.

Articles 15–18: Research

Requirements for research to be undertaken on persons in the fields of biology and medicine are set out in the Convention in the Chapter on Scientific Research specifically and in other chapters. The Convention and its draft additional Protocol on Biomedical Research apply to all biomedical research undertaken on human beings. The general rule for scientific research is set out in Art 15. It states that scientific research in biomedicine shall be carried out freely,[13] subject to the provisions of the Convention and the other legal provisions ensuring the protection of the human being. The fundamental principle for research involving human beings, as in the rest of the Convention is the free, informed, express, specific and documented consent of the person(s) taking part.

The Convention also stipulates additionally (in Art 16) that research on a person may only be undertaken if all the following conditions are met:[14]

---

11 This Article reaffirms the principle introduced in Art 8 (right to respect for private and family life) of the ECHR and reiterated in the Convention for the Protection of Individuals with Regard to Automatic Processing of Personal Data. These instruments also give us the term 'private life'. During the drafting of the Convention and its Protocols, several experts commented that 'privacy' would be more appropriate in modern English usage, but the terminology of the aforementioned instruments was retained in order to make clear the links to their enunciated principles and related case law.

12 The Explanatory Report notes that the exercise of the right not to know this or that fact concerning his or her health is not regarded as an impediment to the validity of his or her consent to an intervention. The example is given of a person validly consenting to the removal of a cyst despite not wishing to know its nature.

13 The freedom of scientific research is a constitutionally protected right in some of the Member States, see, eg, Art 20 of the Swiss Constitution.

14 These conditions were largely inspired by Recommendation No R (90)3 of the Committee of Ministers to Member States on medical research on the human being.

(i)   if there is no alternative of comparable effectiveness to research on humans;

(ii) the risks which may be incurred by that person are not disproportionate to the potential benefits of the research;

(iii) the research has been approved by the competent body after independent examination of its scientific merit, including assessment of the importance of the aim of the research, and multidisciplinary review of its ethical acceptability;

(iv) the persons undergoing research have been informed of their rights and the safeguards prescribed by law for their protection;

(v) the necessary consent has been given expressly, specifically and is documented. Such consent may be freely withdrawn at any time.

Particular attention is being paid in the Council of Europe to the fulfilment of the requirement for multidisciplinary review of the ethical acceptability of biomedical research. First of all, this is being done through a more detailed examination of the subject of ethical review and ethics committees in the additional Protocol on Biomedical Research. This will serve to harmonise the principles of ethical review of research involving human beings in Europe. Additionally, the Council is undertaking a program of co-operation in 1997–2001 with its member countries in central and eastern Europe and elsewhere called the Demo Droit Ethical Review of Biomedical Research Activity (DEBRA) consisting of multilateral and bilateral meetings, study visits and informative materials on best practice in this field in Europe. This activity has been supported in the past by the European Commission and Norway.

The Convention pays specific attention to the protection of persons not able to consent to research and of embryos *in vitro*. Article 17 deals with protection of persons not able to consent to research and sets out that research on a person not able to consent to research may only be undertaken if:

(a) the conditions just mentioned from Art 16, which are applicable to all research, are fulfilled;

(b) the persons to undergo research have been informed of their rights and the safeguards prescribed by law for their protection;

(c) the results of the research have the potential to produce real and direct benefit to his or her health;

(d) research of comparable effectiveness cannot be carried out on individuals capable of giving consent;

(e) the necessary authorisation provided for under Art 6 (of the Convention) has been given specifically and in writing; and

(f) the person concerned does not object.

Article 17 also provides, exceptionally and under the protective conditions prescribed by law, that research which does not have the potential to produce results of direct benefit to the health of a person not able to consent to research may be carried out if stringent conditions are fulfilled. In addition to the aforementioned requirements for research on persons not able to consent, it adds that the research has the aim of contributing, through significant improvement to the scientific understanding of the individual's condition, disease, or disorder, to the ultimate attainment of results capable of conferring benefit to the person concerned or to other persons in the same age category or afflicted with the same disease or disorder or having the same condition. Finally, the research must entail only minimal risk and minimal burden for the individual concerned.

A key issue for biomedical researchers in the EU and Council of Europe countries is how to observe ethical review requirements in multi-centre research which may be foreseen in a number of EU and non-EU, party to the Convention and non-party countries without seriously delaying the start of the research due to a multiplicity and diversity of procedures for obtaining opinions from ethics committees in various regions. At the same time, adequate ethical review of such research must be assured. The Working Party preparing the additional Protocol is currently considering this subject as one of the issues that it may address. Other issues under consideration for inclusion in this additional Protocol are risks and benefits of research, scientific quality, independent examination of research by an ethics committee, information to be submitted to the ethics committee, information for research participants, confidentiality and the right to information, dependent persons, undue influence, safety, duty of care, non-interference with necessary clinical interventions, and research during pregnancy or breastfeeding.

Article 18 states that where the law allows research on embryos *in vitro*, it shall ensure adequate protection of the embryo and stipulates that the creation of human embryos for research purposes is prohibited. This does not mean that research on supernumerary embryos created for fertilisation purposes is prohibited by this Article. As noted above, an additional Protocol on the Protection of the Human Embryo and Foetus is under preparation by a working party under the authority of the CDBI.

Articles 11–13: Controls on genetics and prohibition of discrimination

Chapter IV (human genome) is relevant to research and other interventions specifically in the genetic field. This Chapter seeks to prevent the use of genetic tests for purposes that may be selective or discriminatory. Article 11 establishes the principle that any form of discrimination against an individual because of his or her genetic heritage is prohibited. This expands the protections of Art 14 of the ECHR, which states that the enjoyment of the rights and freedoms set forth in the Convention must be secured without discrimination on the basis of sex, race, colour, language, religion, political or other opinion, national or social origin, association with a national minority, property, birth or other status, to include genetic heritage.

The Explanatory Report notes that this prohibition of discrimination applies to all areas included in the field of application of the ECHRB. This notion also includes non-discrimination on grounds of race as understood by the 1965 United Nations Convention on the Elimination of all Forms of Racial Discrimination as it has been interpreted by the Convention Committee. Discrimination must be understood as unfair discrimination. The Explanatory Report states that this prohibition cannot prohibit positive measures implemented with the goal of re-establishing a certain balance in favour of those at a disadvantage because of their genetic inheritance.

Article 12 states that tests which are predictive of genetic diseases or which serve to identify the person being tested as a carrier of a gene responsible for a disease or to detect a genetic predisposition or susceptibility to a disease may be performed only for health purposes or for scientific research linked to health purposes, and subject to additional genetic counselling. Thus, research utilising such tests should be undertaken in the context of developing medical treatment and enhancing the possibility to prevent disease.

Article 13 states that interventions seeking to modify the human genome may only be undertaken for preventive, diagnostic, or therapeutic purposes and only if the aim is not to introduce any modification in the genome of any descendants. The Explanatory Report explains that medical research intending to genetically modify spermatozoa or ova that are not for procreation is only possible *in vitro* with appropriate ethical or regulatory approval. Provisions regarding genetic research are currently being developed further primarily in the additional Protocol on Human Genetics, but also, in a more general sense, including ethical review of research, in the additional Protocol on Biomedical Research. The Working Party preparing the additional Protocol on Human Genetics is also considering issues such as access to genetic services, individual genetic testing, genetic screening programmes, non-stigmatisation, interventions on the human genome, genetic counselling, applications of genetics related to employment, applications of genetics related to insurance, applications of genetics related to identification, and the protection of private life.

Articles 21 and 22: Removal of organs and tissues from living donors for transplantation purposes

Chapter VI addresses organ and tissue removal from living donors for transplantation purposes. Article 20 (protection of persons not able to consent to organ removal) sets out the conditions for such removals from living persons. The protection of persons not able to consent to organ removal is dealt with in Art 21. It states that no organ or tissue removal may be carried out on a person who does not have the capacity to consent under Art 5. Paragraph 2 does provide, exceptionally and under the protective conditions prescribed by law, for the removal of regenerative tissue if the listed, restrictive conditions are met. An additional Protocol on Transplantation of Organs and Tissues of Human Origin has been accepted by the CDBI and has been sent to the Parliamentary Assembly for an opinion, prior to its discussion by the Committee of Ministers.

Article 21 prohibits financial gain from the human body and its parts.[15] The issue of financial gain arising from the human body or its parts will be addressed further in the context of biomedical research in the additional Protocol on Biomedical Research and in a related report addressing research on biological materials.

PROTOCOL ON PROHIBITION OF CLONING HUMAN BEINGS

The additional Protocol to the ECHRB on the Prohibition of Cloning Human Beings opened for signature on 12 January 1998. The Protocol has been signed by 29 Council of Europe Member States[16] and has been ratified by five.[17] The Protocol follows from the principle of protecting human dignity found in Art 1 of the Convention; also from Art 13, which provides that an intervention seeking to modify the human genome may only be undertaken for preventive, diagnostic, or therapeutic purposes, and only if its aim is not to introduce any modification in the genome of any descendants; and from Art 18 which ensures the protection of the embryo *in vitro* in the framework of research and forbids the creation of embryos specifically for use in research.

Article 1 of the Protocol states that any intervention seeking to create a human being identical to another human being, whether living or dead, is prohibited. The next paragraph explains that for the purpose of this Article,

---

15 The Explanatory Report notes that the question of patents was not considered in connection with this provision; accordingly, it was not intended to apply to the issue of the patentability of biotechnological inventions.

16 Croatia, Cyprus, Czech Republic, Denmark, Estonia, Finland, France, Georgia, Greece, Hungary, Iceland, Italy, Latvia, Lithuania, Luxembourg, Moldova, The Netherlands, Norway, Poland, Portugal, Romania, San Marino, Slovak Republic, Slovenia, Spain, Sweden, Switzerland, The Former Yugoslav Republic of Macedonia and Turkey.

17 Georgia, Greece, Slovakia, Slovenia and Spain.

the term human being 'genetically identical' to another human being means a human being sharing with another the same nuclear gene set.

In conformity with the approach followed for the ECHRB, the Protocol leaves it to domestic law to set the scope of the expression 'human being' in regard to the application of the Protocol. The Explanatory Report to the Protocol explains that the term 'nuclear' means only that genes of the nucleus, not the mitochondrial genes, are examined in regard to identity, which is why the prohibition of human cloning also extends to all nuclear transfer methods which seek to create identical human beings. The term used in the additional Protocol, 'the same nuclear gene set', takes into account the fact that some genes may undergo somatic mutation during development. As it is known, monozygotic twins who have developed from a single fertilised egg will share the same nuclear gene set, but may not have genes that are 100% identical.

The Protocol does not intend to discriminate in any way against monozygotic twins occurring naturally. It also does not intend to address hormone stimulation to treat infertility in women, which may result in twins being born.

In regard to biomedical research, cloning cells and tissues is an ethically acceptable and valuable biomedical technique, particularly important for the development of new therapies, and is not addressed by the prohibition in the Protocol. It does not intend to prohibit cloning techniques utilised in cell biology.

There are different points of view, however, regarding the ethical acceptability of cloning undifferentiated cells of embryonic origin. Art 18 of the Convention ensures adequate protection of the embryo *in vitro* in those States in which such research is allowed and it is suspected that this subject will be looked at in the additional Protocol on the Protection of the Human Embryo and Foetus. Thus, it is necessary to distinguish between cloning of cells as a technique, use of embryonic cells in cloning techniques, and human cloning utilising processes such as embryo splitting or nuclear transfer. The first activity is ethically acceptable, the second is under examination and the third falls under the prohibition foreseen by the Protocol.

The ethical rationale behind the prohibition of the third activity, the cloning of human beings, is firstly that deliberately cloning human beings would present a threat to human identity because it would mean giving up the indispensable protection against predetermination of the human genetic constitution by a third party. Secondly, it is reasoned that human dignity would be endangered by instrumentalisation of human beings through artificial human cloning. Thirdly, since it is thought that naturally occurring genetic recombination is likely to create more freedom for the individual than a predetermined genetic make-up, it follows that it is in the interest of defending human rights and dignity to keep the essentially random nature of the composition of an individual's genes.

CONCLUSION

The potential benefits created by technology, science and medicine are vast, but without the adequate supervision that a functioning ethical and legal framework offers, this potential for improvements in health and living standards could be misused to other ends. In conclusion, by protecting human rights and dignity in the context of the new biomedical technologies, the Convention helps to provide assurance that the positive implications of such activities will be appreciated and supported while threatening developments which alarm the people of Europe and the rest of the world are not allowed to blacken the image of biomedicine and biomedical research. The positive appreciation of progress in biology and medicine can only be increased by the guarantee that there is an ethical and legal basis for evaluating such undertakings, rather than deciding on inaction and allowing the public to surmise that the only 'ethical' criteria in this field are 'if it can be done and there is enough money backing it, it will be done'.

The additional Protocols to the Convention, as they are completed and opened for signature and ratification, will give further guidance in their specific fields. Other activities of the CDBI also look to the future, though they are not expected to result in legally binding instruments in the near future. Examples are the Working Parties on Xenotransplantation, Biotechnology and Psychiatry and Human Rights. A different perspective is provided by the Standing Conference of European National Ethics Committees, which is provided secretarial support by the Council of Europe Secretariat and provides an opportunity for the national ethics committees to come together bi-annually to discuss practical and ethical aspects of their work, as well as to extend assistance to Council of Europe Member States wishing to create national ethics bodies. Conferences and symposia, such as the 1999 International Conference of the Council of Europe on ethical issues arising from the application of biotechnology, will continue to be organised.

The Council of Europe seeks to co-operate with other concerned European and international institutions and organisations to ensure that an ethical and legal infrastructure continues to develop and that it reflects the principles and philosophy of our European democratic heritage. In order to reach consensus, the first step that we must take is that of initiating and conducting an open dialogue. It is in the interest of all that ideas be freely exchanged and debated openly.

Further, it is recognised that there is a need for international co-operation in this field to extend the same protections for the individual in this field foreseen in the ECHRB beyond its Member States in Europe. A debate on bioethical issues is ongoing in international organisations such as the World Health Organisation, UNESCO and OECD, among others. It might be presumptuous to offer the solutions agreed upon in Europe for the

Convention as a template for a future international agreement, but the experience of the Convention, being the first legally binding instrument addressing the new biomedical technologies, could certainly be useful for a future, geographically expanded discussion.

THE SCOPE OF IMPACT OF THE HUMAN RIGHTS ACT 1998 ON HEALTHCARE AND NHS RESOURCE ALLOCATION

Wendy Outhwaite

INTRODUCTION

The Human Rights Act 1998 (HRA), which came fully into force on 2 October 2000, will have a significant impact on the practice of medicine in the UK as it brings the Articles of the European Convention on Human Rights and Fundamental Freedoms (ECHR) into domestic law. Inevitably, public authorities involved in healthcare will be faced with new challenges. As the law is in a state of development, it is impossible at this stage to predict the future with certainty. Much will depend on the attitude of the courts. On the one hand, the courts may embrace the existing jurisprudence of the European Court of Human Rights (the Court) with enthusiasm, even if it changes our own domestic law. Alternatively, the courts may attempt to apply the ECHR in such a manner as would inevitably result in the same outcome as under the existing domestic law. Accurate predictions are therefore impossible. Some guidance can be gleaned both from the Convention jurisprudence and the early cases decided by the domestic courts with the Convention in mind.

THE STATUTORY DUTY ON PUBLIC AUTHORITIES

NHS trusts and health authorities are 'public authorities' within the meaning of the HRA 1998. It follows that they have a statutory duty to act in accordance with the Convention pursuant to s 6 of the HRA 1998. Failure to do so risks litigation by individuals wishing to enforce their Convention rights in relation to healthcare. This means that public authorities will face claims for a new and independent cause of action, that is, breach of an individual's Convention right. This may lead to a significant amount of new litigation and, thereby, increase the demands upon the resources of healthcare providers.

Remedies

Pursuant to s 8 of the HRA 1998, a claimant could be awarded both damages and/or declaratory or injunctive relief.

Damages

Damages will be awarded when it is 'necessary to afford just satisfaction' to the person compensated. In determining whether to award damages and/or the amount of the award, the court is required by s 8(4) of the HRA 1998 to take into account the principles applied by the Court in relation to awards of compensation under Art 41 of the ECHR. The English lawyer will be familiar with the concept of damage awards, particularly in personal injury matters, which are made up of pecuniary loss (that is, special damages); non-pecuniary loss (that is, damages to compensate for pain, suffering and loss of amenity) and costs. In the main, if the European Court makes an award of damages, it adopts the same approach. However, the Court often gives only declaratory relief and costs. An award of damages can be presumed to follow once liability has been established, as in the domestic courts. Moreover, when the Court does make an award of damages, its methodology is often inconsistent and, in general, the level of damages awarded is usually low.

Injunctions and declaratory relief

Often, a mere declaration that an individual's human rights have been breached will be sufficient in itself to afford just satisfaction. In such circumstances, the Court will give no further remedy.

In respect of injunctions, it is thought that, in the future, the Court is likely to be more interventionist than it has been in the past. Both mandatory injunctions, compelling a public authority to take positive action, or prohibitory injunctions compelling a public authority to refrain from specific action are likely to become more commonplace.

THE RELEVANT CONVENTION RIGHTS

The following Articles of the ECHR are particularly important to consider when making decisions on healthcare:

Article 2: Right to life

A more detailed analysis of Art 2 will be made below but, in summary, Art 2 provides that: 'Everyone's right to life shall be protected by law ...' There is no absolute 'right to life' itself, merely a right to legal protection of life. The text of Art 2 itself provides for the legal deprivation of life in certain limited circumstances, for example, pursuant to war.

Similarly, even a cursory examination of the ECHR case law shows that there is no absolute right to life under Art 2. 'Preventable deaths' do not always violate the Convention. For example, passive euthanasia (that is, where no positive steps are taken to save a life: *Widmer v Switzerland* No 20527/92 (unreported)) is permissible under certain circumstances.[1] Furthermore, the European Commission/Court of Human Rights has considered abortion to be lawful: *X v United Kingdom* 8416/(UK) 9 DR 244; *Paton v United Kingdom* (1980) 19 DR 244 where abortion was permitted 'for the health of the mother'.[2] The case law of the domestic court permits the withdrawal of treatment resulting in the death of the patient *if* such action is in the interests of the patient: *NHS Trust A v M; NHS Trust B v H* [2000] All ER 1522 and *Re A (Children) (Conjoined Twins: Medical Treatment)* [2000] All ER (D) 1211.

In theory, the duty under Art 2 could, on the one hand, be no more than the prevention of killing and, on the other hand, the positive duty to save life.

The protection afforded by Art 2 is expressed to be for 'everyone' but it is not clear that it extends to the life of a foetus. In the same way that the common law does not protect the sanctity of life of a foetus before it is born and independent of its mother, there are examples of Art 2 not protecting the unborn from the termination of a pregnancy. In *Paton v United Kingdom* an analysis of 'everyone' in Art 2 concluded that:

> In nearly all these instances the use of the word is such that it can apply only post-natally. None indicates clearly that it has any possible prenatal application, although such application in a rare case cannot be entirely excluded. All of the limitations contained in Art 2 by their nature concerned persons already born and cannot be applied to the foetus. Thus, both the general usage of the term 'everyone' ('*toute personne*') of the Convention and the context in which this term is employed in Art 2 tend to support the view that it does not include the unborn.

Nevertheless, in *H v Norway* (1992) 73 DR 155, notwithstanding that an abortion was permitted to prevent a 'difficult situation of life', the European Commission indicated that Art 2 would protect the life of an embryo 'in certain circumstances' which it did not then identify. The precise ambit and degree of protection afforded by Art 2 is therefore unknown.

As will be seen below, the exact nature and extent of the duty under Art 2 is unclear.

Article 3: Freedom from torture and inhuman and degrading treatment

Article 3 provides that:

---

1 For further discussion of euthanasia in relation to the HRA 1998, see Sapiro and Ungoed-Thomas, Chapter 17, below.

2 See, further, Stauch, Chapter 16, below.

No one shall be subject to torture or to inhuman or degrading treatment or punishment.

Treatment could be 'inhuman' if it 'causes intense physical or mental suffering'. Treatment could be 'degrading' if it arouses in the victim a feeling of fear, anguish and inferiority capable of humiliating and debasing the victim and possibly breaking his physical or moral resistance.

Medical treatment, or the lack of it, can breach Art 3 if it constitutes a 'lack of proper medical care' as in *Tanko v Finland* 23634/94 (1994) (unreported). This can include where treatment is unduly delayed as in *Hurtado v Switzerland* (1994) Series A, No 280-A; *D v United Kingdom* (1997) 24 EHRR 423; *Passannante v Italy* (1998) 26 EHRR CD 153. Treatment that has not been consented to can also breach this Article under certain circumstances (see *X v Denmark* (1983) 32 DR 282). Nonetheless, generally, it is difficult to show a breach of Art 3 with regard to medical treatment, because being inhuman or degrading treatment requires a significant level of 'severity'. Medical treatment can often be unpleasant or painful for the patient, but this tends to present no problem where the intervention is in the patient's best interests unless, for example, some of the pain or degradation was unnecessarily inflicted.

In order to determine whether there has been a breach of Art 3 all the circumstances of the case must be considered, pursuant to *Ireland v United Kingdom* (1978) 2 EHRR 25, para 162. In particular, regard should be had to the duration of the treatment; its physical or mental effects and the sex, age and state of health of the victim.

Although treatment which would otherwise breach Art 3 can be justified by the therapeutic need, as it was in *Herczegfalvy v Austria* (1992) 15 EHRR 437, it cannot be justified 'in the public interest'.

4.3.3 Article 5

This protects an individual's right to liberty and security of the person. It is subject to exceptions, so that individuals can legitimately be detained on health grounds. For example, it is permissible to detain 'persons of unsound mind', alcoholics, drug abusers and persons spreading infectious diseases, pursuant to Art 5 of the ECHR. However, such detainees are entitled to procedural safeguards.[3]

3　See Garwood-Gowers' discussion of Art 5 in relation to competent minors, Chapter 14, below.

Article 6(1)

This protects the right of the individual to a fair hearing in the determination of his civil rights and obligations and will be examined further below.[4]

Article 8

This protects the respect for an individual's home, correspondence, and private and family life. The notion of 'private life' includes the right to physical integrity, as is illustrated, for example, in *X and Y v The Netherlands* (1985) 8 EHRR 252. Even a minor compulsory medical intervention, such as a blood test to establish paternity, has been held by the Commission in *X v Austria* (1979) 18 DR 154 to be an interference with the right to respect for private life in breach of Art 8. Similarly, a compulsory urine test breached Art 8 in *Peters v The Netherlands* (1994) 77A DR 75. The notion of 'private life' also includes the right to human dignity (in particular, the right to self-determination) and privacy (in particular, the confidentiality of medical data: *MS v Sweden* [1998] EHRLR 115).

The principle of respect for private life are subject to possible exceptions. However, such exceptions must be 'in accordance with law' and 'necessary in a democratic society' and 'proportionate' in addition to pursuing one of the following legitimate aims: '... in the interests of national security, public safety or the economic well-being of the country, for the prevention of disorder or crime, for the protection of health or morals, or for the protection of the rights and freedoms of others.' These are difficult criteria to satisfy.

Article 8 protects human dignity and the European Court has recognised the right to autonomy of a patient with capacity to consent.[5] Arguably, even patients with an incapacity, for instance, children, ought to be accorded greater autonomy with regard to their healthcare. As will be seen elsewhere in this book,[6] the consent or views of the parents to physical intervention for their children is not necessarily determinative of the legality of the treatment. Even parents are not given *carte blanche* to breach the Convention rights of their children. For example, in *Johansen v Norway* (1996) 23 EHRR 33, para 78, the European Court stated that it would:

> ... attach particular importance to the best interests of the child, which, depending on their nature and seriousness, may override those of the parent. In particular ... the parent cannot be entitled under Art 8 of the Convention to have such measures taken as would harm the child's health and development.

---

4   ECHR, Art 6 is discussed by Foster, Chapter 7, below, in relation to disciplinary procedures.

5   It may well result in competent minors being afforded the legal right to veto interventions they disagree with – a right they do not currently have under English law. See further, Garwood-Gowers, Chapter 14, below.

6   See Michalowski, Chapter 15, below.

Similarly, in *Nielson v Denmark* (1988) 11 EHRR 175 which concerned a mother who put her 12 year old son in a closed psychiatric ward on medical advice and was challenged under Art 8 of the ECHR, the European Court stated that:

> The rights of the holder of parental authority cannot be unlimited and ... it is incumbent on the state to provide safeguards against abuse.

There may be cases where it is arguable that the child's wishes should prevail over wishes of the parents over its medical treatment in reliance on Art 8 and/or Art 14. It is clear that although parental consent and the therapeutic need of the patient will play an important part in deciding what treatment (if any) to administer to a patient, even a patient with an incapacity, nevertheless, NHS Trusts and health authorities will have to pay particular attention to the patient's human dignity and right to autonomy.

Article 9

This protects an individual's 'freedom of thought, conscience and religion' and the freedom to 'manifest his religion or belief in ... practice or observance'. In practice, this reflects the rule under the common law that medical treatment should not be forced on a patient if he refuses consent on the grounds of his religion. For example, a Jehovah's witness is entitled to refuse blood and blood products, even by way of a valid advance directive. By ignoring such a refusal, a medical professional would, risk committing a trespass to the person and may breach Art 9. This right can be over emphasised. For example, in the conjoined twins case the religious objections of the parents to proposed surgery that would result in the death of one of their twins was not enough to prevent the surgery. If an individual objected to medical treatment on religious grounds then such treatment could still be given if it falls within the ECHR exceptions or is justified by another Convention right (for example, the right to life).

Article 12

This protects an individual's 'right to marry and found a family'.

Article 14: Freedom from discrimination

This prohibits discrimination 'on any ground' in the enjoyment of the Convention rights and freedoms. It is not a substantive right but is brought into play when there is discrimination in relation to a matter affecting one of the substantive rights covered by the ECHR. For instance, as Garwood-Gowers suggests, not allowing competent minors the same right to veto unwanted medical interventions as competent adults, could be a breach of Art 14 in conjunction with either Art 5 or 8.[7]

---

7   See Garwood-Gowers, Chapter 14, below.

POTENTIAL CLAIMS BY PATIENTS IN RESPECT OF HEALTHCARE UNDER THE HRA 1998

There are a number of novel potential claims for breach of ECHR rights which may be anticipated. The HRA 1998 imposes the new positive duty on public authorities to comply with the Convention. As a result, numerous patient treatment issues emerge. Moreover, 'courts and tribunals' themselves 'must take into account' the Convention jurisprudence. As a result, patients, or their families, will rely on the HRA 1998 in order to either obtain specific treatment or alternatively to prevent specific treatment being administered or withdrawn. In the past, the nature and degree of the treatment that was given depended largely on the clinical judgment of the medical practitioner acting in the best interests of the patient and the availability (or otherwise) of resources. Now, the medical practitioner must decide on the nature and extent of treatment in consideration of the patient's (and the patient's family's) Convention rights. This can be difficult: often the Convention rights of the patient in themselves conflict. The following sets out some of the claims that can be anticipated. Whether or not they will be successful is much harder to predict.

Potential actions in respect of life-threatening conditions

The ambit of potential actions by claimants in respect of life-threatening conditions depends on the nature and extent of Art 2 of the ECHR. An analysis of the manner in which Art 2 has been applied in the healthcare arena, both in the European Court and the domestic courts, fails to provide a cogent approach. However, the following analysis may be helpful.

The nature of the duty under Art 2

The common law has always recognised the 'sanctity of human life' and, within limits, protected it. The common law 'sanctity of human life' and the Art 2 Convention right to life are obviously similar, but are not the same. Historically, medical practitioners knew the nature and extent of their duty to the patient. For example, in *Airedale NHS Trust v Bland* [1993] AC 789, p 867 it was confirmed that:

> The doctor who is caring for ... a patient cannot ... be under an absolute obligation to prolong his life by any means available to him, regardless of the quality of the patient's life.

At common law, the absolute duty not to kill was different from a duty to maintain life, as was illustrated in *Re J (A Minor) (Wardship: Medical Treatment)* [1991] Fam 33. It followed that, if, in the clinical judgment of the medical practitioner, it was in the 'best interests' of the patient not to have his life prolonged, then the patient could be allowed to die. It was legal, therefore, both to fail to give life-saving treatment and to withdraw such life-saving treatment. Such withdrawal of treatment was classified by the court as an omission to treat, rather than an positive act, principally so that doctors were not vulnerable to a charge of murder. The relevant test was, therefore, the best interests of the patient in the clinical judgment of the medical practitioner.

However, even the domestic court recognised that, in certain circumstances, there was a positive duty to protect life. For example, in *R v Brent LBC ex p D* (1998) 1 CCLR 234, an illegal immigrant, who was an AIDS sufferer, faced deportation. Moses J considered that it was the duty of every civilised nation to safeguard life and health. The applicant's deportation was refused on the basis that it would prejudice his health and perhaps even his life. Similar decisions have been made applying Arts 2 and 3 of the Convention by the domestic and European courts in respect of deportation: *R v Secretary of State for the Home Department ex p M* (1999) Imm AR 548; [2000] COD 49 and *D v United Kingdom* (1997) 24 EHRR 423 (the 'deportation cases'). It is implicit in the judgment in *NHS Trust A v M; NHS Trust B v H* [2000] All ER 1522 that there is a positive duty to promote or safeguard life, but that such duty is qualified.

Similarly, particularly in its recent jurisprudence, the Court and the Commission consider that there is a positive duty arising out of Art 2. For example, in *Association X v United Kingdom* [1978] 14 DR 31 the Commission stated that Art 2(1):

... enjoins the state not only to refrain from taking life intentionally, but, further, to take appropriate steps to safeguard life.

Such words were repeated by the European Court in *LCB v United Kingdom* (1998) 27 EHRR 212, para 36:

The first sentence of Art 2(1) enjoins the state not only to refrain from the intentional and unlawful taking of life, but also to take appropriate steps to safeguard the lives of those within its jurisdiction.

The wider duty to take positive steps to protect life was also acknowledged in *Osman v United Kingdom* (1999) 29 EHRR 245, where the Court stated that a litigant would succeed against a public authority in a claim for breach of Art 2 if:

... the authorities did not do all that could be reasonably expected of them to avoid a real and immediate risk to life of which they have or ought to have knowledge.

Furthermore, Judge Jambrek in *Guerra v Italy* (1998) 26 EHRR 357, para 387 stated that the protection of health and physical integrity was closely associated with the right to life, and that the law in respect of Art 2 was ripe for further development. It should be remembered that any positive duty to promote and safeguard life is owed both to the individual and to the general public.

In other jurisdictions, there is a positive duty to save life, at least in respect of emergency treatment. For example, Art 27 of the South African Constitution provides that: 'No one may be refused emergency medical treatment.' Similarly, in India, in *Paschim Banga Khet Mazdoor Samity v State of West Bengal* [1996] 4 SCC 37, the court found a breach of Art 21 (which is equivalent to Art 2 of the ECHR) in a case where a person with head injury and brain haemorrhage was refused treatment at six successive hospitals because hospitals either had inadequate medical facilities or did not have vacant beds. The court declared:

> Article 21 imposes an obligation on the state to safeguard the right to life of every person. Preservation of human life is thus of paramount importance. The government hospitals run by the state and medical officers employed therein are duty bound to extend medical assistance for preserving human life. Failure on the part of a government hospital to provide timely medical treatment to a person in need of such treatment results in violation of his right to life guaranteed under Art 21.

As yet, there is no English authority stating that there is an absolute duty under the ECHR to provide emergency medical treatment.

The application of Art 2 in the UK courts

In *Re A (Children) (Conjoined Twins: Medical Treatment)* [2000] All ER (D) 1211, a proposed surgical separation of Siamese twins would result in the death of one twin known as M. The Court of Appeal openly acknowledged that the surgery was not an omission to treat (and, therefore, not analogous with the withdrawal of treatment) but instead was an active invasion of M's body that would terminate her life. Nevertheless, having recognised the 'right to life' of each twin, the surgical separation of the Siamese twins was held to be lawful. The killing of one twin was held to be justified by the Court of Appeal in the legitimate defence of the twin known as J, who was in effect being killed by her sister M who was only alive because she 'sucked the lifeblood out of J'. The methodology adopted by the Court was to scrutinise the 'best interests' of each twin and perform a balancing exercise between the welfare of each twin, by considering the worthwhileness of the surgery to each twin, the actual condition of each twin and the manner in which each could exercise her right to life. As M was beyond help, in that she was incapable of independent life from J, and both twins would die unless separated, surgery to save J's life was lawful. The Court of Appeal considered the case to be 'unique' and 'difficult'. Again, it is not clear how far any general principles can be extracted from the decision, given the unusual factual circumstances of the case. What is clear is that the Court adopted a hybrid approach: it considered both the twins' right to life and their 'best interests'.

Similarly, in *A NHS Trust v D* [2000] TLR 552, the court made a declaration that a severely disabled child need not be given artificial ventilation to prolong his life, as it was held by Cazelet J specifically not to be in the child's best interests. Notwithstanding that the child would die, there was held to be no breach of the child's Art 2 right. Again, the Court recognised the importance of the 'right to life' but did not consider it to be the sole consideration. The 'best interests' of the child were determinative. Again, in *NHS Trust A v M; NHS Trust B v H* [2000] All ER 1522, the Court sanctioned the withdrawal of artificial nutrition and hydration from adult patients in PVS resulting in their deaths as being in their 'best interests'.

It is clear, therefore, that the 'best interests of the patient test' survives, subject to the recognition of the importance of the right to life. Potential problems caused by the doctrine of double effect, where treatment improving the quality of life has the additional effect of shortening life, are circumvented. If the 'best interests' of the patient test survives (albeit in an evolved form) then there is no blanket ban on treatment which is beneficial but incidentally shortens life. Alternatively, such treatment may be justified by counterbalancing the patient's Art 2 right to life with his Art 3 right to freedom from inhuman and degrading treatment including unnecessary pain and suffering. The lack of benefit of treatment in the long term coupled with the pain and discomfort of invasive procedures was certainly determinative in *A NHS Trust v D* [2000] TLR 552.

The effect of Art 2 on the common law concept of the quality of life/right to life

In *McKay v Essex AHA* [1982] QB 1166, the Court of Appeal held that a live foetus with severe abnormalities is not worse off than one having no life at all. The right to life of the individual was not invalidated or lessened as a result of a poor quality of life. It is unlikely that this view will change in the light of the HRA 1998. It was reaffirmed by Cazelet J in *A NHS Trust v D* [2000] TLR 552. Similarly, in *Re A (Children) (Conjoined Twins: Medical Treatment)* [2000] All ER (D) 1211, better known as 'the *Siamese twins* case', the Court of Appeal considered that the life of each conjoined twin had an equal value in the eyes of the law. This was so, notwithstanding that one twin had the capacity for independent life and was bright and alert with functioning heart and lungs, whereas the other twin had only a primitive brain, had no effective heart or lung function and was dependent on blood and oxygen from her sister through a shared aorta. The Court does not judge the value of a life by the quality of the life enjoyed. However, the court clearly did carry out a qualitative comparative assessment of each twin in determining the treatment that might lawfully be given by applying the 'best interests' test. Put shortly, although the 'right to life' is acknowledged, nevertheless, a qualitative assessment will determine the nature and extent of the medical treatment to be administered or withheld.

The effect of Art 2 on the common law concept of consent

If there is a positive duty to 'promote and safeguard life' then the patient's consent may not determine of whether treatment can be given, as it does under the common law. A public authority may be required to protect individual members of the public against life-threatening risks, even against the individual's wishes, for example by a compulsory vaccination scheme, as in *X v United Kingdom* (1978) 14 DR 31, or by compulsory testing, for example of tuberculosis as in *Acmanne v Belgium* (1984) 40 DR 251. Perhaps even non-consensual Caesarean operations may be carried out on pregnant women to save the life of the unborn baby, which is the reversal of the present legal position. However, in all these instances, the court would have to weigh up the right to life with other rights such as privacy and liberty and security.

An action to obtain specific life-saving treatment

Often, life-saving treatment will be in the best interests of the patient. In that event, Art 2 of the ECHR may enable a patient to demand particular life-saving treatment as of right. Such life-saving treatment could include surgery (for example, organ transplant surgery) or the provision of a particularly efficient drug (such as cancer drugs). If life-saving treatment is available, then the terminally ill patient will most likely want it. Article 2 may be interpreted by the courts to hold that the public authority's duty to promote and safeguard life, when combined with the patient's best interests, means that such life-saving treatment must be given to the patient. Conceivably the situation might be different and the life-saving treatment might not be demanded by the patient if a breach of Arts 3 and/or 8 of the ECHR come into play.

An action to obtain protection from life-threatening conditions

The positive duty on public authorities under Art 2 to 'promote and safeguard life' may require positive action to prevent life-threatening conditions. For example, vaccination programmes may need to be widened to cover 'killer diseases' which appear to be on the increase such as tuberculosis, meningitis and prostate cancer. Such vaccination programmes may even be made compulsory, as was held in *Acmanne v Belgium* (1984) 40 DR 251. Effective screening programmes (notably for cancers) might be necessary under the HRA 1998. Individuals might bring an action either to oblige the NHS to provide such screening or vaccination programmes, or alternatively to seek compensation for damage which resulted from the lack of such programmes. Typically, if an individual dies as a result of not being diagnosed with a fatal disease because adequate screening was unavailable, the family could claim in the same way as for a Fatal Accident Act 1976 claim.

An action to obtain different or better quality of treatment

This is not restricted to 'life-threatening' conditions, but could apply to all types of medical treatment. In *Tanko v Finland,* Case 23634/94 (1994) (unreported), the European Court has held that a failure to provide 'proper medical treatment' may breach Art 3 of the ECHR. In short, a failure to give proper medical care could constitute 'torture or inhuman or degrading treatment'. Breaches of Art 3 may be more prevalent where emergency medical treatment is not given.

The exact ambit of 'proper medical care' is uncertain: it may simply be synonymous with non-negligent medical care or, alternatively, 'appropriate' or 'best available' medical care. It is anticipated that patients will rely on Art 2 and/or Art 3 of the ECHR in order to obtain costly and effective drugs, rather than the cheaper and less efficient ones more commonly offered. The recommendations or guidance provided by other bodies or institutions does not absolve a public authority of its positive duties under the ECHR. In short, a public authority can still be vulnerable to litigation even if it follows the recommendations of the National Institute for Clinical Excellence.

Similarly, delays in treatment can be 'inhuman' or 'degrading'. In *Hurtado v Switzerland* (1994) Series A, No 280-A, there was a breach of Art 3 in failing to x-ray for a fractured rib timeously, and refusing to let the applicant change his trousers which had been soiled as a result of the arrest involving the use of a stun gun on him. Waiting list delays were held to breach Art 3 in *Passannante v Italy* (1998) 26 EHRR CD 153.

Both Arts 3 and 8 can be used to ensure the respect for human dignity. Potentially, the following are incompatible with a patient's dignity: inadequate pain relief, the circumstances of admission to hospital (for example, being treated on a trolley in a corridor or being left in soiled bedding). Complaint has even been made about mixed gender wards.

An action to preserve particular facilities

Historically, in order to cut costs, services were rationalised, which sometimes involved the closure of residential facilities. The residents of such facilities may now rely on Art 8 of the ECHR in order to prevent the closure. If there is an interference with the patient's 'home', the public authority must justify the closure by using the limited exceptions listed in Art 8. In *R v North and East Devon HA ex p Coughlan* [2000] 2 WLR 622, the closure of Mardon House, a residential facility for the disabled, could not be justified as being for the economic well-being of the country. The absolute discretion on the public authority to administer its finances was subject to restrictions.[8]

---

8   For further discussion of an action to preserve facilities in relation to private property rights in the context of community care, see Edmunds and Sutton, Chapter 13, below.

An action to obtain fertility treatment

The Art 12 'right to found a family', may be used to attempt to obtain fertility treatment, such as IVF, or even impotency drugs, such as Viagra. Such applications are likely to fail. The analogous submission of a right to adopt in order to 'found a family' was rejected by the European Court in *X & Y v United Kingdom* (1978) 12 DR 32 .

An action in respect of experimental and non-consensual medical treatment

Experimental medical treatment may amount to 'torture or inhuman or degrading treatment' in breach of Art 3 of the ECHR, if there is no informed consent: *X v Denmark* (1983) 32 DR 282. Anecdotal evidence suggests that the lack of informed consent is more prevalent than might be thought. For example, premature babies are commonly administered with drugs which have not been tested for use on such babies, similarly novel ventilation systems are applied without the parents being informed that the treatment is experimental in nature. Such treatment could arguably breach Art 3 of the ECHR and damages might be payable.

However, treatment may lawfully be administered where there is a therapeutic need. In *Herczegfalvy v Austria* (1992) 15 EHRR 437, the European Court stated:

> ... a measure which is a therapeutic necessity cannot be regarded as inhuman or degrading. The Court must nevertheless satisfy itself that the medical necessity has been convincingly shown to exist.

Given that *Herczegfalvy* concerned a patient lacking the capacity to consent, it is not entirely clear to what extent medical treatment which is a 'therapeutic necessity' may be administered, notwithstanding the lack of consent of the patient. Cases involving the force-feeding of detainees: *X v Germany* (1985) 7 EHRR 152, suggest that the absence of consent under the ECHR may not be as important as under the common law: it does not necessarily give rise to a successful damages claim under the Convention.

An action to obtain information

Article 2 imposes a duty to warn of known health risks. In *LCB v United Kingdom* [1998] TLR 381, there was a risk of a child developing leukaemia because her soldier father had been exposed to excessive radiation as part of the nuclear testing at Christmas Island. The European Court asserted that, if the State knew or ought to have known of particular life-threatening risks, then it should inform or warn those people who were affected. In the same way, individuals should be given information and warnings by public authorities operating in the health sector in respect of threats to life, for example, epidemics, environmental pollution and food contamination.

An action to obtain non-discriminatory healthcare

Discrimination in health provision is likely to be contrary to Art 14. For example, the minimum and maximum age limits for screening and the exclusion of patients over a particular age from the organ transplant lists are likely to breach Art 14.

In the same way, postcode prescribing is likely to breach Art 14. The treatment to which a patient is entitled should not depend on his place of residence. This is particularly so in relation to emergency healthcare.

Actions in respect of mental patients

These are considered in Chapters 11 and 12 by Laura Davidson. Confidentiality in relation to vulnerable adults is considered in Chapter 10 by Kate and John Williams.

Actions in respect of delays in determining litigation

Article 6(1) provides that there should be a determination of a claim 'within a reasonable time'. The circumstances of each case determines how long is 'reasonable'. Undue delay can lead to an additional award of damages. For example, in the French AIDS cases (*X v France* (1992) 14 EHRR 483; *Vallee v France* (1994) 18 EHRR 549), patients infected by contaminated blood during blood transfusions had not had their applications for compensation determined within two years. The European Court awarded each patient compensation for delay of about £20,000. The litigation of the terminally ill must be expeditious.

The defence of lack of resources

Historically, the court would not dictate to health authorities or NHS trusts the manner in which its resources should be spent. In *R v Central Birmingham HA ex p Collier* (1988) LEXIS, 6 January, the parents of a child needing an urgent heart operation submitted that excessive delay was a breach of the Secretary of State's duty, under s 3 of the National Health Service Act 1977 to provide 'the effective provision of health services'. The Court of Appeal held that it could not 'substitute its own judgment for the judgment of those who are responsible for the allocation of resources'. Stephen Brown LJ declared that it was not 'for the courts of this country to arrange the lists in hospital'. However, the court indicated that it would have intervened if it could be shown that the health authority had acted unreasonably.

Following the judgment of the Court of Appeal in *R v Cambridge DHA ex p B* [1995] 1 WLR 898, an impecunious NHS trust was not obliged to give particular treatment. Jaymee Bowen, then 10 years old, had non-Hodgkin's lymphoma and common acute lymphoblastic leukaemia. She had a relapse and was unsuccessfully treated with chemotherapy and a bone marrow transplant. The health authority, contrary to her father's wishes, considered that further treatment was not in the patient's best interests. The estimated cost of such treatment was £75,000. It had a 10% to 20% chance of success. During the course of his judgment, Sir Thomas Bingham MR stated that:

> It is common knowledge that health authorities of all kinds are constantly pressed to make ends meet ... they cannot provide all the treatments they would like ... Difficult and agonising judgments have to be made as to how a limited budget is best allocated to the maximum advantage of the maximum number of patients.

However, Laws J at first instance (in *R v Cambridgeshire HA* [1995] 1 FLR 1055) considered that, even where treatment was very costly and the chances of success were small, nevertheless, life-saving treatment should be given and that the health authority should, unless it could prove a detriment to another, fund it:

> ... where the question is whether the life of a 10 year old child might be saved by however slim a chance, the responsible authority ... must do more than toll the bell of tight resources.

Under the HRA, it is possible that the duty to promote and safeguard life will outweigh financial considerations, provided that the treatment is in the best interests of the patient. At the very least, NHS Trusts or Health Authorities might be put to proof that it could not afford the treatment in question because it was funding treatment of greater priority elsewhere.

Significantly, in *Osman v United Kingdom* (2000) 29 EHRR 245 the Court stated that the positive obligation to safeguard life:

> ... must be interpreted in a way which does not impose an impossible or disproportionate burden on the authorities. Accordingly, not every claimed risk to life can entail for the authorities a Convention requirement to take operational measures to prevent that risk from materialising.

This suggests that the availability of resources is sometimes a relevant defence. This is a controversial area. (See, also, *Taylors and Others v United Kingdom*, App No 23412/94 (unreported).)

It may be possible to distinguish, on the one hand, emergency and life-saving treatment and, on the other hand, other sorts of treatment.

Lack of resources in relation to life-saving treatment

The duty under Art 2 to 'promote and safeguard life' is a heavy duty, as can be seen in the recent deportation cases. It is implicit in such decisions that there is a duty to provide life-saving medical treatment, or at least, not to withdraw such treatment.

It is not suggested that every patient has an absolute right to life. Nor is it suggested that a patient with a life-threatening condition will invariably be able to demand life-saving treatment as of right. However, given the duty to promote and safeguard life, it is suggested that, where life-saving treatment is held by the medical practitioners and/or the court to be in the 'best interests' of the patient, such life-saving treatment must be given. At first blush, this may not seem very different from the common law duty to act in the patient's 'best interests'. However, the difference may be where the public authority refuses to give life-saving treatment solely because of lack of resources. The court would not interfere with such position under the common law. It might interfere in the light of the Convention duty. In particular, in *Scialacqua v Italy* (1998) 26 EHRR CD 164 the Commission assumed that Art 2 imposed a duty to cover the cost of life-saving medical treatment. The decision is analogous to the Indian case of *Paschim Banga Khet Mazdoor Samity v State of West Bengal* (1996) 4 SCC 37 (considered above) where the lack of beds was not a defence to the breach of a Convention right. A lack of resources was insufficient to avoid liability.

On the one hand, the Court might approach the Convention duty in the same way as it approached the statutory duty in *R v Central Birmingham HA ex p Collier* (1988) LEXIS, 6 January, so that, notwithstanding the statutory duty, the public authority retains a discretion as to whether to fund medical treatment with which the court will not interfere. However, it is more likely that in the light of the Art 2 duty if coupled with the 'best interests' of the patient, then lack of resources will not be a defence to a failure to provide such treatment.

Other treatment

It is even less certain that a patient has a right to medical treatment, which is not emergency or life-saving treatment. The Court of Appeal has already considered such claims.

In *R v North West Lancashire HA ex p A and Others* [1999] TLR 622 which pre-dates the incorporation of Convention rights, the Court of Appeal did not appreciate the 'human rights' submissions being made under Arts 3 and 8 during an application for gender reassignment surgery. Auld LJ criticised such submissions with the words:

Such an unfocused recourse to Strasbourg jurisprudence, whether before or after the incorporation of the Convention into English law, was positively unhelpful, cluttering up the court's consideration of adequate and more precise domestic principles and authorities governing the issues in play.

He concluded that neither Art 8 nor Art 3 imposed a positive obligation on the NHS trust to provide gender reassignment surgery, and continued:

It was plain ... that Art 3 was not designed for circumstances of the sort where the challenge was to a health authority's allocation of finite funds between competing demands.

This case gives a very strong indication that, as in the past, the public authority alone would determine the nature of the treatment to be given with limited resources. If this is so, at least under Art 3, a lack of resources would continue to be a defence. However, it is quite possible that a differently constituted Court might have had a different approach. The logic of this case may be difficult to square with the deportation cases where the lack of access to medical treatment amounted to a breach of Art 3. There was no acknowledgement of the teleological approach to the Convention as a 'living instrument' which is generally accepted. The Art 3 obligation to be given 'proper medical care' may have been underestimated.

Resources for healthcare will always be tight. Demand will always outstrip supply. However, in determining whether or not to give particular treatment, the medical practitioner ought to have regard to the obligations imposed by the Convention. The safety-net defence of 'lack of resources' may not be that safe a net.

Economies

A public authority will not always have an unfettered discretion to do as it wishes with its resources. For example, in *R v North and East Devon HA ex p Coughlan*, the health authority's decision to close Mardon House, a residential facility for the disabled which Miss Coughlan had been promised was a 'home for life', was overturned by the Court. All parties accepted that an enforced move from Mardon House would be, 'emotionally devastating and seriously anti-therapeutic' for Miss Coughlan. Nevertheless, the health authority asserted that the interference with Miss Coughlan's respect to her home was justified under the exceptions in Art 8, namely, 'the economic well being of the country'. In rejecting such argument, the Court of Appeal cited with approval the *dicta* of Sir Thomas Bingham in *R v Ministry of Defence ex p Smith* [1996] QB 517, p 554E:

The more substantial the interference with human rights, the more the court will require by way of justification before it is satisfied that the decision is reasonable ...

The Court of Appeal agreed. It is suggested that a mere assertion that there is an economic need for the closure of a home will be insufficient. The public authority bears a significant evidential burden in order to justify the breach of the patient's Art 8 right. The court will carry out a qualitative assessment on the basis of the evidence in each case.

INCREASED DAMAGES AWARDS

Recently, it has been suggested that the Art 8 right to respect for family life may require a higher level of damages awards in clinical negligence cases. Although the case was decided on the common law, Henriques J in *Hardman v Amin* [2000] Lloyd's Rep Med 498 said that:

> ... throughout my deliberations I have had regard to the Article 8 entitlements to 'respect for his private and family life and his home' ... the consequences of this judgment as it stands will be able to permit the Hardmans as a family unit independent of the state to meet Daniel's needs. A failure to provide adequate compensation would have disrupted and prevented the family leading as 'normal' a life as possible. It would have deprived the family of its autonomy vesting all major decisions as to care in the state.

This reasoning applies equally well to personal injury cases. Article 8 may be used to increase damage awards so that the future care costs are borne by the family rather than discounting the award for care provided by the NHS. This will be expensive for defendants.

CHAPTER 5

LITIGATING BIOETHICS: THE ROLE OF AUTONOMY AND DIGNITY

Steven Wheatley

INTRODUCTION

The amount of impact the Human Rights Act 1998 (HRA) will have on the legal regulation of biomedicine is uncertain. The Act will, though, affect the language deployed in medical litigation. Moreover, it may have the important effect of orienting such litigation around what, at their core, are ethical arguments. This is not just because rights themselves are a matter of ethics, but also because the limits placed on rights under the Convention also involve ethical consideration – such as the the the utilitarian question of 'necessary in a democratic society' (Arts 8(2) and 10(2)) and the deontological question of health and morals (Art 8(2)). Significantly, we might examine the extent to which a regime which seeks to accord (human) rights to individuals in healthcare will accord priority to individual autonomy.

The *Oxford Concise Dictionary* (10th edn) defines 'autonomy' as 'the possession or right of self-government' and/or 'freedom of action'. Autonomy then includes the right to physical and moral integrity; in short, autonomy affords us the right to be ourselves.[1] A regime on the regulation of biomedicine which prioritised autonomy would reject any paternalistic approach to medical treatment; would prohibit interventions against a person's will, even if in 'their best interests'; and provide that the person making treatment and non-treatment decisions would be the patient. It should be noted, however, that a regime which accorded respect for individual autonomy would not view the patient as an atomised individual – separate from their community. In respecting the freely determined decisions of the patient we cannot ignore the interest and rights of other (autonomous) individuals which, where appropriate, would need to be weighed in the balance.

---

1   Loucaides, 1990, p 175.

The legal regime on the regulation of biomedicine has not solely had recourse to the concept of individual autonomy, however. The Convention on Human Rights and Biomedicine (ECHRB) (1997), for example, resolves 'to take such measures as are necessary to safeguard *human dignity and the fundamental rights and freedoms* of the individual with regard to the application of biology and medicine'.[2] We might then have recourse to both individual autonomy and human dignity in determining the outcome of medical litigation, and the resolution of bioethical questions. To illustrate the ways in which bioethical questions may be resolved under the HRA 1998, this chapter examines two scenarios which concern both legal and ethical issues: the allocation of costly medical resources; and the use of assisted reproduction medicine. In the first example – access to expensive medical treatment – the issue of individual autonomy will be dominant in the discussion; in our dealings on the issue of assisted reproductive medicine, a possible role for human dignity in the regime on human rights and biomedicine will be examined.

THE LEGAL REGIME

The HRA 1998 came into force on 2 October 2000. It was introduced to 'give effect' to the European Convention on Human Rights (ECHR) (1950).[3] The Convention provides minimum standards on civil and political rights in Member States. Significantly, for these purposes, it provides for a right to life (Art 2), freedom from 'inhuman and degrading treatment' (Art 3), and the right to respect for 'private life' (Art 8). Following the introduction of the HRA 1998, so far as it is possible to do so, courts are required to read, and give effect to, all primary and subordinate legislation in a way that is compatible with the Convention rights.[4] Further, it is unlawful for a public authority to act in a way that is incompatible with a Convention right,[5] unless as the result of primary legislation, the authority could not have acted differently.[6]

---

2   Preamble, Convention on the Protection of Human Rights and Dignity of the Human Being with Regard to the Application of Biology and Medicine, adopted by the Ministers of the Council at Oviedo, 4 April 1997, ETS No 164 (emphasis added). As of 14 September 2000, 29 States had signed the Convention, and six ratified it (Denmark, Greece, San Marino, Slovakia, Slovenia and Spain); the Convention came into force on 1 December 1999.

3   HRA 1998, Preamble.

4   *Ibid*, s 3(1). Where a statute is incompatible with a Convention right, the statute remains in force with the courts empowered only to issue a 'declaration of incompatibility': s 4(2).

5   *Ibid*, s 6(1).

6   *Ibid*, s 6(2).

National Health trusts, health authorities and regulatory authorities (such as the Human Fertilisation and Embryology Authority (HFEA)) are public authorities for the purposes of the Act. Having outlined, albeit briefly, the applicable legal regime, this chapter will now examine two circumstances in which the HRA 1998 might be deployed to litigate legal and ethical issues relating to medical treatment.

EXAMPLE 1: ACCESS TO EXPENSIVE MEDICAL TREATMENT

There are many expensive drugs or medical treatments which have the capacity to either prolong or improve a sick person's quality of life. It has generally been assumed that governments and health authorities enjoy a right to ration access to such treatments by reference to their duty to achieve the highest attainable standards of healthcare for all.[7] That is, government's may take into account the healthcare needs of all the population and not merely the demands of persons seeking medical treatment. Thus, a decision to either spend half a million pounds on a life-saving procedure for one person, or on drug treatments to dramatically increase the quality of life of 10 people, is one for health authorities alone. The adoption of the HRA 1998, a regime which provides for individual human rights and respect for individual autonomy, might pose a threat to this 'community based' approach to the allocation of healthcare resources. This potential threat will be examined.

We will, in this context, examine the position of a hypothetical patient, Bernard Smith, who suffers from an illness which renders him housebound, which increasingly causes painful episodes and associated nausea, and which, his doctors have informed him, will cause his premature death. A new drug has come onto the market and has been shown both to improve the condition of most patients taking the drug, and to reduce significantly their chances of dying from the illness. The drug costs one million pounds a year and needs to be taken for the remainder of the patient's life. Bernard Smith's health authority has refused him access to the drug on the grounds of cost. In challenging this decision by the health authority, Bernard may make reference to the following 'Convention rights' provided under the HRA 1998:

Article 2

Everyone's life shall be protected by law.

Article 3

No one shall be subjected to torture or to inhuman or degrading treatment or punishment.

---

7   See European Social Charter 1961, Art 11.

Article 8

(1) Everyone has the right to respect for his private and family life, his home and his correspondence.

(2) There shall be no interference by a public authority with the exercise of this right except such as is in accordance with the law and is necessary in a democratic society in the interests of national security, public safety or the economic well-being of the country, for the prevention of disorder or crime, for the protection of health or morals, or for the protection of the rights and freedoms of others.

We will consider their application in turn.

The right to life and access to treatment

The obligation contained in Art 2, on the right to life, is not exclusively concerned with intentional killing by agents of the State, but extends to an obligation 'to take appropriate steps to safeguard the lives of those within its jurisdiction ...'.[8] This (positive) obligation does not require that the authorities take all possible steps to keep a person alive. As the European Court of Human Rights (the Court) in *Kiliç v Turkey* stated:

> Not every claimed risk to life ... can entail for the authorities a Convention requirement to take ... measures to prevent that risk from materialising. For a positive obligation to arise, it must be established that the authorities knew or ought to have known at the time of the existence of a real and immediate risk to the life of an identified individual or individuals ... and that they failed to take measures within the scope of their powers which, judged reasonably, might have been expected to avoid that risk ...[9]

As the Court noted in *Osman v United Kingdom*, the question as to whether the State authorities have failed to Act reasonably can only be answered 'in the light of all the circumstances of any particular case'.[10] Clearly, in the healthcare scenario, there are restrictions on what can reasonably be expected of an authority in terms of financial outlay for one group of patients when this would end up compromising another.[11]

Freedom from inhuman and degrading treatment and access to medical care

Art 3 of the ECHR provides that: 'No one shall be subjected to torture or to inhuman or degrading treatment or punishment.' The Court of Human Rights

---

8 *Osman v UK*, Reports 1998-VIII, para 115.

9 *Kiliç v Turkey*, App No 22492/93, Case Decided 28 March 2000, para 63.

10 *Osman v UK*, Reports 1998-VIII, para 115.

11 For further discussion, see Chapters 6 and 17, below.

confirmed, in *Ahmed v Austria*, that Art 3 'enshrines one of the fundamental values of democratic societies ... [It] prohibits in absolute terms torture or inhuman or degrading treatment or punishment'.[12] It is unlikely that the prohibition on 'torture' will be of significant value in developing a human rights regime on biomedical issues. Of greater value will be the prohibition on both degrading and inhuman treatment. For there to be an ill treatment violating Art 3, the act complained of must attain a minimum level of severity. The assessment of this minimum is relative; it depends on all the circumstances of the case, such as the duration of the treatment, its physical and mental effects and, in some cases, the sex, age and state of health of the victim.[13] As the Court explained in *Labita v Italy*:

> Treatment has been held by the Court to be 'inhuman' because, *inter alia*, it was premeditated, was applied for hours at a stretch and caused either actual bodily injury or intense physical and mental suffering, and also 'degrading' because it was such as to arouse in its victims feelings of fear, anguish and inferiority capable of humiliating and debasing them.[14]

It does not matter that the treatment is carried out in a private place, or by persons unaware of the humiliating nature of the procedure; it may be sufficient that the person is 'humiliated in his own eyes, even if not in the eyes of others'.[15] This sense of degradation and humiliation would not include such procedures as those associated with the treatment of a seriously or terminally ill patient. For a treatment to occasion a violation of Art 3, it 'must attain a particular level of severity, and ... be other than the usual element of humiliation inherent in any [treatment]'.[16]

Famously, in *Herczegfalvy v Austria*, the Court determined that as 'a general rule, a measure which is a therapeutic necessity cannot be regarded as inhuman or degrading'.[17] Standard medical procedure will not then be considered a violation of Art 3. The medical patient is not, however, excluded from the protection of the provision. Any inhuman or degrading procedure or treatment not made strictly necessary by the person's condition 'diminishes human dignity and is in principle an infringements of the rights set forth in Art 3'.[18] Consequently, a medical intervention which might be considered inhuman or degrading, and which is not necessitated by medical requirements, is prohibited under the ECHR.

There is no claim here, however, that Bernard Smith is being subjected – in a positive sense – to inhuman or degrading treatment. His claim relates to an

---

12 *Ahmed v Austria*, Reports 1996-VI, para 40.
13 *A v UK*, Reports 1998-VI, para 22.
14 *Labita v Italy*, App No 26772/95, Case Decided 6 April 2000, para 120.
15 *Tyrer*, Series A, No 26 (1979–80), para 32.
16 *Costello-Roberts v UK*, Series A, No 247 (1993), at para 30.
17 Series A, No 244 (1992), para 82.
18 *Ribitsch v Austria*, Series A, No 336 (1995), para 38.

absence of treatment, which leads him to suffer (arguably) in an inhuman and degrading way. Article 3 does not, though, only protect the individual from deliberate interventions which are inhuman and degrading. It also protects against the withdrawal of medical treatment where the consequences of that withdrawal are that the person suffers in an 'inhuman or degrading' way.[19] Further, it may be that the failure of public authorities to provide effective medical care results in a patient suffering an 'inhuman and degrading' treatment sufficient to violate Art 3.[20]

Article 3 provides the most potentially significant ground for challenging allocation decisions relating to medical resources. No exceptions are admitted and there is no defence available in cases of a breach of the provision. Treatment not rendered necessary by the patient's condition, and which degrades or humiliates is absolutely prohibited. Further, it is at least arguable that where the withdrawal of treatment, or its non-provision (in circumstances where treatment is requested or possible) results in suffering that might be considered inhuman or degrading, there exists a violation of Art 3. To avoid this significant breach of the Convention, the public authorities must provide the relevant medical treatment – irrespective of cost, or other considerations. To avail himself of the protection afforded by Art 3, however, Bernard Smith would have to show that his (preventable) condition causes inhuman and/or degrading suffering. Article 3 is absolute. There are, however, clear policy reasons why the courts will be reluctant to recognise all but the most extreme of suffering to be 'inhuman' or 'degrading' and, thus, covered by Art 3. Consequently, the provision may be of less value than first inspection might suggest.

Effective respect for private life and access to medical treatment

Article 8(1) provides that: 'Everyone has the right to respect for his private and family life ...' The protection afforded by the Article extends beyond physical integrity.[21] In *Botta v Italy*, the European Court accepted that private life:

> ... includes a person's physical and psychological integrity; the guarantee afforded by Art 8 of the Convention is primarily intended to ensure the development, without outside interference, of the personality of each individual in his relations with other human beings.[22]

---

19 In *D v UK*, the Court concluded that the withdrawal of treatment, and the manner of its withdrawal (in the deportation of an AIDS sufferer to St Kitts), would, if carried out, occasion a violation of Art 3 as it 'would expose him to a real risk of dying under most distressing circumstances and would thus amount to inhuman treatment' (1997) 24 EHRR 423, para 53.

20 *Hurtado v Switzerland*, Series A, No 280-A (1994).

21 *Acmanne v Belgium*, App No 10435/83; (1985) 40 DR 251, p 255.

22 *Botta v Italy*, Reports 1998-I, para 32.

Further, the Court accepted that Art 8 may 'in certain cases, impose positive obligations inherent in an effective respect for private life'.[23] Public authorities must not only, therefore, refrain from interfering in the private life of persons; they are required, in certain circumstances, to take positive measures to ensure an effective respect for private life. In determining when such positive measures are required, the State must have recourse to both the interests of the individual and of the community as a whole, and it will, under Art 8(2), enjoy a certain margin of appreciation in deciding when to act.[24] On questions of medical treatment and allocation of resources, the State may take into account the interests of the general population, as well as those of the individuals concerned. This may include the cost of any proposed treatment.

It is evident that many illnesses and conditions impede the ability of the human person to develop in community with others. This is certainly the case with Bernard Smith, who might justifiably claim that his condition prevents him from living a 'full' life in community with others. For Art 8 to be applicable, the applicant must demonstrate 'a direct and immediate link between the measures sought by an applicant and the latter's private and/or family life'.[25] That is, the treatment must have the possibility of removing the debilitating condition or illness that impedes the development of the human person, and not simply improving his conditions of living, or lifestyle.[26] Once this is established, it is at least arguable that a refusal to provide relevant medical treatment raises a claim of failure to ensure the effective respect for private life, required by Art 8(1). This is, however, an area in which states enjoy a wide margin of appreciation in determining the steps to be taken to ensure compliance with the Convention – and they may do this 'with due regard to the needs and resources of the community and of individuals'.[27]

Even if a violation of Art 8(1) were to be found, it would be open to the public authority to defend the interference under Art 8(2). If we assume that the prohibition is 'in accordance with the law', the courts would then be required to ascertain whether the interference in respect for private life came under one of the legitimate headings – national security, public safety or the economic well-being of the country, for the prevention of disorder or crime, for the protection of health or morals, or for the protection of the rights and freedoms of others – and crucially was 'necessary in a democratic society'. The most likely ground for restricting access to medical treatment in the NHS would be the cost of treatment: in Art 8(2) terms – the 'economic well-being of the country'. An example of this justification was seen in *Ciliz v The Netherlands*. Here, the Court was required to determine whether the

---

23   *Botta v Italy*, Reports 1998-I, para 33.
24   *Ciliz v The Netherlands*, App No 29192/95, Case Decided 11 July 2000, para 61.
25   *Botta v Italy*, Reports 1998-I, para 33.
26   *Ibid*, para 35.
27   *Abdulaziz, Cabales and Balkandali v UK*, Series A, No 94 (1985), para 67.

deportation of an illegal immigrant constituted a violation of Art 8 – 'right to respect for his private and family life' – given that the applicant had a child in The Netherlands. The Court accepted that the deportation of illegal immigrants was a legitimate aim within Art 8(2): '... the economic well-being of the country',[28] and did not enquire further into the veracity of the claim. The main consideration before the Court was whether the action could be considered 'necessary in a democratic society'. In *Laskey, Jaggard and Brown v United Kingdom*, the Court confirmed that the notion of 'necessary in a democratic society' implies that the interference corresponds to a pressing social need and, in particular, that it is proportionate to the legitimate aim pursued. The State's margin of appreciation in determining the existence of a pressing social need, and the question of proportionality:

> ... is not identical in each case but will vary according to the context. Relevant factors include the nature of the Convention right in issue, its importance for the individual ...[29]

Hence, the State is permitted to take into account the interests of the wider community but must, under the principle of proportionality, show itself to have appropriately weighed these relative to the impact on the individual. Clearly, a patient with a severely disabling condition would have a stronger claim than one whose condition simply made life more difficult, but not impossible to live.

In examining the value of the HRA 1998 to Bernard Smith, as he seeks to challenge the refusal of the health authority to authorise the expensive treatment he requires, it is not clear that Bernard will obtain that which he wants: access to the treatment. What is clear, however, is that he will be recognised as an autonomous person, whose expressed wishes are to be taken into account – although the authorities may balance his demands with the interests of other (autonomous) persons within society. In the following section, we will examine a restriction on the rights of persons to make choices – and have those choices respected – even where it is not clear that the rights of others would, in any way, be affected by the exercise of those choices.

EXAMPLE 2: DESIGNING BABIES

In 1999, Alan and Louise Masterton lost their daughter in a bonfire accident. They have made repeated requests to be allowed to use sex selection techniques made available by assisted reproduction medicine to have another

---

28 *Ciliz v The Netherlands*, App No 29192/95, Case Decided 11 July 2000, para 63.
29 *Laskey, Jaggard and Brown v UK*, Reports 1997-I, para 42.

daughter (they already have three sons and do not want another boy).[30] Should the Mastertons be allowed to employ assisted reproduction medicine to have the child they want? The case illustrates the evident tensions, in the deployment of assisted reproduction medicine, between the understandable desires of people to have children for their own reasons, and the views of wider society which might want to restrict the use of the technology; further, it raises both legal and ethical questions as to the extent of our ability to 'design' our children.

The legal regulation of assisted reproduction medicine in the UK is, in the main, the responsibility of the HFEA. The Authority operates by licensing clinics to carry out relevant treatments.[31] Clinics are required to comply with both the Human Fertilisation and Embryology Act 1990 and the Code of Practice issued by the HFEA. Ultimately, it is for the clinician to make the decision as to whether a particular treatment is offered to a particular patient. Failure by the clinic to follow the Code of Practice would expose it to the risk of losing its licence. The HFEA Code of Practice provides that centres for assisted reproduction medicine should not select the sex of embryos for social reasons,[32] nor use sperm sorting techniques in sex selection.[33] This prohibition would clearly impact upon people like the Mastertons. This section will examine the grounds for any challenge to the prohibition under the HRA 1998 – either directly against the centre refusing treatment[34] or, more likely, against the HFEA, whose guidelines led to that refusal.

In this instance, the relevant Convention rights are Art 8 (right to respect for private life) and Art 12: 'Men and women of marriageable age have the right to marry and to found a family, according to the national laws governing the exercise of this right.' The most relevant Convention right would appear to be Art 12, which provides, without exception, a right for persons of marriageable age 'to marry and found a family'. The right is not, though, absolute and the provision must be read in conjunction with Art 8.[35] A married couple may not, then, demand, as of right, that the State provides assisted reproduction treatment – or provide, as in this case, a particular treatment. The claim here is not a right to have a child, but a right to have a child of a particular type: female.

---

30   (2000) *The Guardian*, 13 March.

31   See generally, Brazier, 1999.

32   HFEA Code of Practice, 4th edn, 1998, para 7.2.

33   *Ibid*, para 7.21.

34   See, *X and Y v The Netherlands*, Series A, No 91 (1985). Under the HRA 1998, there exists the possibility, given s 6(3)(a), that Convention rights might enjoy 'horizontal effect' and apply to private law. If this is accepted, Convention rights will apply to the patient/physician relationships in the private sector.

35   *ELH and PBH v UK*, App Nos 32094/96 and 32568/96; (1997) 91A DR 61, p 64.

The law recognises a certain amount of choice in the kind of children we have. It is now possible to identify, with much greater precision, those foetuses likely to develop into persons with certain debilitating illnesses or conditions, such as cystic fibrosis and Huntington's disease. Couples, or individuals, are then presented with the possibility of terminating a pregnancy, or deciding not to implant embryos created *in vitro*. We can, as a result of this technology, to a limited extent, 'design' our prospective children – or at least 'design out' serious faults. In the case of sex selection, parents are permitted to select the sex of the embryo, or use sperm sorting techniques in sex selection, where serious hereditary sex-related disease can be avoided. What they are not permitted to do, under the present regulations, is select the sex of their child for social reasons.

The right to make choices as to the kind of children we want is protected by Art 8. Support for this view may be found in *Brüggemann and Scheuten v Federal Republic of Germany*, and, in particular, the dissenting opinion of James Fawcett.[36] Interferences by the State in individual decisions on pregnancy (and medical treatment relating to pregnancy) must constitute an infringement of the right protected under Art 8(1) – and must be justified. Restrictions on assisted reproduction treatment within the NHS are likely on the grounds of cost. This is an issue we have previously examined. Assuming that there are no implications to the health of any persons involved, the only grounds for restricting access to assisted reproduction medicine in the private sector are the protection of morals and the protection of the rights and freedoms of others (Art 8(2)).

In relation to the rights of others, the HFEA Code of Practice requires that the interests of the child be taken into account when determining access to assisted reproduction medicine. Consequently, we might talk of the 'right' of the child not to have a central aspect of its identity predetermined by its parents: its gender. There are clear philosophical and practical problems in affording rights to those not yet conceived; further, there are ethical difficulties in protecting a person's human rights by preventing them from being born. It is submitted, therefore, that the strongest ground upon which such a restriction might legitimately be justified is the 'protection of morals'.

LITIGATING BIOETHICS: THE ROLE OF AUTONOMY AND DIGNITY

The restriction on sex selection for social reasons contained in the HFEA Code of Practice is replicated in the Council of Europe's ECHRB (1997). According

---

36 *Brüggemann and Scheuten v Federal Republic of Germany,* App No 6959/74; (1978) 10 DR 100.

to Art 14 of that Convention, techniques of medically assisted procreation for choosing a future child's sex are prohibited, except where serious hereditary sex-related disease is to be avoided. The prohibition provides for a clear limit on individual autonomy; it restricts the choices persons might make in respect of their prospective children. There are two further, similar, limitations on individual autonomy in the regime on human rights and biomedicine adopted by the Council of Europe. First, a prohibition on the commercialisation of the human body,[37] in particular the sale of (live) human body parts, which is considered 'an affront to human dignity'.[38] Secondly, and of more relevance to the issue of sex selection for social reasons, a prohibition on human cloning. This is dealt with in a separate Protocol to the ECHRB, on the Prohibition on Cloning Human Beings (1998). The Protocol considers that the 'instrumentalisation of human beings through the *deliberate* creation of genetically identical human beings is contrary to human dignity' and constitutes a misuse of biology and medicine.[39] The Explanatory Report to the Additional Protocol makes clear that the deliberate cloning of humans constitutes 'a threat to human identity, as it would give up the indispensable protection against the predetermination of the human genetic constitution by a third party'.[40] The Protocol prohibits any 'intervention seeking to create a human being genetically identical to another human being, whether living or dead'.[41] A similar argument may be made in relation to sex selection for social reasons: medicine should not be deployed to predetermine artificially, for social reasons, a potential human.

Whatever the prohibitions on human cloning and sex selection within the Council of Europe regime, any such prohibition must be considered to constitute an interference by the State in the right to respect for private life (Art 8(1)). We must then consider the possible justification for such an interference. We might refer to the rights of other persons – the prospective children. Indeed, the Preamble to the Protocol on the Prohibition on Cloning Human Beings notes the 'serious difficulties of a medical, psychological and social nature' that might result for the cloned individual. The main concern of the Protocol on Human Cloning is, though, as noted, the protection of human

---

37 The 'human body and its parts shall not, as such, give rise to financial gain': Art 21.

38 Explanatory Report to the ECHRB, Council of Europe Document DIR/JUR (97) 5, para 131. The provision does not apply to such products as hair and nails, which are discarded tissues, and the sale of which is not an affront to human dignity: para 133. The Human Organ Transplants Act 1989 provides that live organ donation between unrelated persons must only be undertaken with the prior agreement of the Unrelated Live Transplant Regulatory Authority (ULTRA): s 2. The Act prohibits financial payment in return for the donation of a live organ: s 1.

39 Preamble, Protocol on the Prohibition on Cloning Human Beings (1998) ETS No 168 (emphasis added).

40 Council of Europe Document DIR/JUR (98) 7, para 3.

41 Protocol on the Prohibition on Cloning Human Beings, Art 1.

dignity. As with the prohibition on sex selection, the use of medicine for human reproductive cloning is prohibited because it allows us artificially to predetermine crucial aspects of a person's identity. This, according to the Protocol on Human Cloning (1998), violates our concept of human dignity. Consequently, the justification for the interference in the right to private and family life in prohibiting the use of assisted reproduction technology for these reasons, is 'the protection of morals'. In this context, human dignity 'trumps' the rights of individuals to have their decisions respected.

CONCLUSION

The recognition that human dignity might be capable of overriding individual autonomy is significant. Traditionally, the right to individual autonomy has been central to legal and ethical discourse in issues relating to biomedicine. As noted, autonomy includes both physical and moral integrity and the right to make decisions about our own lives. In *Life's Dominion*, Dworkin argues that the value we ascribe to autonomy derives from the capacity it protects, 'the capacity to express one's own character ... in the life one leads'. He continues by noting that recognition of a right of autonomy 'makes self-creation possible'.[42] There exist, however, within the posited regime on biomedicine, significant limitations on a right to make choices in respect of the kinds of children we wish to conceive: we can neither clone ourselves (or others), nor decide for ourselves the sex of our children (unless there are good medical reasons). This limitation is justified, within the Council of Europe regime, by reference to 'human dignity'. The prohibitions on sex selection and human cloning are not justified by the need to protect the human dignity of those individuals who wish to select the sex of their children, or even those who might wish to have children that are a clone of themselves (or others). The prohibitions are justified by reference to the need to protect the value of human dignity; that is, the value we accord all human persons by virtue of their membership of the human species. As the ECHRB (1997) makes clear: we need to respect the human being 'both as an individual and as a member of the human species'.[43] Thus, certain choices should not be respected because they violate our concept of human dignity; dignity trumps autonomy.

We must be careful, however. Feldman describes this aspect of human dignity – 'the dignity of the species as a whole' – as the 'objective aspect' of

---

42 Dworkin, 1993, pp 223–24.
43 ECHRB 1997, Preamble.

human dignity.[44] Despite the nomenclature employed, there is nothing objective about this concept of human dignity; it is highly contingent. The recognition of human dignity as a legal value, capable of trumping individual autonomy, raises the possibility of the legal regulation of biomedicine by public sentiment, and the public's (adverse) reaction to novel medical practices and procedures. This is clearly unacceptable, and will not be permitted under the HRA 1998. The European Court has previously determined that practices may not be prohibited because the general public are 'shocked, offended or disturbed by [them]'.[45] That is not to suggest that public morality may not be used to justify limits on individual autonomy. The European Court has confirmed, in *Laskey, Jaggard and Brown v United Kingdom*, what Art 8(2) itself says – that the State maintains the 'prerogative ... on moral grounds to seek to deter [certain] acts'.[46] Moreover, in *Open Door and Dublin Well Woman v Ireland*, it acknowledged that national authorities enjoy a wide margin of appreciation in questions of morality, particularly in area of 'belief concerning the nature of human life'.[47] The margin of appreciation is not, however, unlimited, and the State must demonstrate the existence of a pressing social need for the measures in question and, in particular, that the restriction is 'proportionate to the legitimate aim pursued'.[48] Even where there exists a 'pressing social need', the justifications for the limitation must not be outweighed by the detrimental effects on the life of the applicant.[49] Restrictions on access to medical treatment and technology, on grounds of morality may not be introduced without regard to their impact on the individuals concerned.

This chapter has examined the ways in which the Convention rights – to life, to freedom from degrading and inhuman treatment and to respect for private life – may be deployed in litigating two bioethical questions: the allocation of medical resources and issues surrounding assisted reproduction. The work has noted that the regime adopted in the HRA 1998 era will accord priority to the autonomy of the individual patient. No invasive procedure will be permitted without the consent of the patient – recourse to the concept of human dignity will not, for example, justify the forced feeding of anorexic patients. Further, the expressed wishes of the competent patient to access

---

44 Feldman, 1999, p 684.

45 *Dudgeon*, Series A, No 45 (1982), para 60.

46 *Laskey, Jaggard and Brown v UK*, Reports 1997-I, para 50. Cf *ADT v UK*, App No 35765/97, Case Decided 31 July 2000, paras 37–39.

47 *Open Door and Dublin Well Woman v Ireland*, Series A, No 246-A (1993), para 68.

48 *Ibid*, para 70.

49 *ADT v UK*, App No 35765/97, Case Decided 31 July 2000, para 32.

certain forms of treatment are to be respected – if not always recognised and acted upon. Those wishes must be balanced with the rights of other persons in the society, for example, those who may be denied treatment as a consequence of the first receiving it, or members of the wider society who might be expected to pay for the treatment. Significantly, this work has shown that certain decisions to access particular forms of medical treatment are not to be respected because they offend against the society's concept of human dignity. The regime on human rights and biomedicine will, therefore, respect both the autonomy of the individual and the inherent dignity of members of the human species. Crucially, where these aspects are incompatible, the courts will be required to develop and elucidate criteria for the resolution of conflict between autonomy and dignity – and individual rights to autonomy will not always 'trump' the collective rights of the society to have its concept of human dignity, in the uniqueness and value of the human person, respected.

CHAPTER 6

THE INDIVIDUAL'S RIGHT TO TREATMENT UNDER THE HUMAN RIGHTS ACT 1998

Alasdair Maclean

INTRODUCTION

The rise of consumerism, feminism and the discipline of bioethics have all contributed to an increasing demand from individuals to be involved in healthcare decisions that affect themselves, their children and other relatives. The executive has, to a limited extent, supported this movement for greater involvement in our own healthcare. Documents such as the *Patient's Charter* and *Changing Childbirth* (DoH, 1993) bear witness to this trend, as does the Lord Chancellor's report, *Making Decisions* (1999), which deals with the power to make decisions for incompetent adults. Legislation moving in this direction, though perhaps not far enough, includes the NHS and Community Care Act 1990 and the Disability Discrimination Act 1995.[1] Despite these moves towards increasing patient choice, the individual's legally protected rights regarding treatment choices remain largely negative in character. Thus, while the courts have affirmed the right of the individual to refuse treatment,[2] the right to demand treatment has been consistently denied.[3]

Of all the right to treatment cases, it was only in the first instance hearing of *Ex p B* that the court based its ruling on human rights. Laws J stated:

> ... certain rights, broadly those occupying a central place in the European Convention on Human Rights (ECHR) and obviously including the right to life, are not to be perceived merely as moral or political aspirations nor as enjoying a legal status only upon the international plane of this country's Convention obligations. They are to be vindicated as sharing with other principles the substance of the English common law. Concretely, the law requires that where a public body enjoys a discretion whose exercise may infringe such a right, it is not to be permitted to perpetrate any such infringement unless it can show a substantial objective justification on public interest grounds.[4]

---

1   Smith, 1997.

2   *R v Collins ex p S* [1998] 3 All ER 673; *Re MB (An Adult: Medical Treatment)* (1997) 38 BMLR 175 CA; [1997] 2 FLR 426.

3   *Re J (A Minor) (Wardship: Medical Treatment)* [1990] 3 All ER 930; *Re J (A Minor) (Consent to Medical Treatment)* [1992] 4 All ER 614; *R v Cambridge DHA ex p B* [1995] 1 FLR 1055 CA.

4   *R v Cambridge DHA ex p B* [1995] 1 FLR 1055 QBD, p 1060.

In the Court of Appeal, however, Law J's decision was reversed without even a mention of human rights.[5] This neglect of rights arguments can no longer continue now that the Human Rights Act 1998 (HRA) is in force. The Lord Chancellor, Lord Irvine notes:

> A major change which the Act will bring flows from the shift to a right based system. Under this system a citizen's right is asserted as a positive entitlement expressed in clear and principled terms.[6]

The Act requires that public authorities and their agents – which will include healthcare professionals – comply with the Convention rights.[7] Furthermore, where the common law and the Convention rights clash, the common law will have to adapt so as to protect those rights.[8] These changes, along with the move from *Wednesbury* irrationality to proportionality and the greater transparency that will be required, will make it easier for the individual to challenge the decisions of public bodies.[9]

Clearly individuals are going to attempt to use the Act to demand a right to treatment.

THE *DAVID GLASS* CASE: AN ILLUSTRATION

David Glass was born severely disabled. He is almost blind, suffers from epilepsy, has spastic quadriplegia and severe learning disabilities. He is not, however, terminally ill. Nor is he without cognitive function since he turns his head towards sounds, smiles, laughs and registers likes and dislikes by facial expressions. Following a tonsillectomy, David – who was then 12 years old – developed diarrhoea, exacerbation of his epilepsy and a life-threatening septicaemia.[10]

The medical staff decided that, rather than attempt to treat the septicaemia, it was in David's best interests to be allowed to die. Without consulting David's mother, a 'Do Not Resuscitate' order was placed in David's notes and, against her expressed wishes, the doctors began a morphine infusion. There was a breakdown in trust between the hospital staff and the Glass family and, on 21 October 1999, a violent altercation erupted. David's family decided to take matters into their own hands and they attempted to resuscitate David themselves. According to one of the consultant

---

5   *R v Cambridge* [1995] 1 FLR 1055 CA, p 1066.

6   Lord Irvine of Lairg, 1998, p 224.

7   HRA 1998, s 6(1).

8   Lord Cooke of Thorndon, 1999, p 257.

9   O'Sullivan, 1998; Supperstone and Coppell, 1999.

10 Septicaemia is an infection of blood that may cause failure of any or all organs such as the kidneys, liver and lungs. It is treatable with antibiotics but may still be fatal.

paediatricians, they began 'blowing raspberries in his ears, banging his chest and rubbing his arms and legs very vigorously despite being asked not to'.[11]

Contrary to the doctor's predictions, David survived and has since celebrated his 14th birthday. Mrs Glass sought a judicial review of the decisions made by the medical staff. At first instance, the judge held that: 'Judicial review is too blunt a tool for the sensitive and ongoing problems of the type thrown up in David's case.'[12] The Court of Appeal also rejected the application. Lord Woolf MR stated:

> There can be no doubt that the best course is for a parent of a child to agree on the course which the doctors are proposing to take, having fully consulted the parent and for the parent to fully understand what is involved. That is the course which should always be adopted in a case of this nature. If that is not possible and there is a conflict, and if the conflict is of a grave nature, the matter must then be brought before the court so the court can decide what is in the best interests of the child concerned. Faced with a particular problem, the courts will answer that problem.[13]

By the time that David's case had reached court, he had been successfully treated with antibiotics by the family's general practitioner. Neither the High Court nor the Court of Appeal was called upon to make a life and death decision. Furthermore, the question of David's future care had already been determined. However, despite this, the Court of Appeal detailed the principles that would be applied in decisions of this nature:

(1) the sanctity of life;

(2) the non-interference by the courts in areas of clinical judgment in the treatment of patients ... where this can be avoided ...;

(3) the refusal of the courts to dictate appropriate treatment to a medical practitioner ... subject to the power which the courts always have to take decisions in relation to the child's best interests. In doing so, the court takes fully into account the attitude of medical practitioners;

(4) that treatment without consent save in an emergency is trespass to the person;

(5) that the courts will interfere to protect the interests of a minor or a person under a disability.[14]

The principles, as described by Lord Woolf MR, are those used by the judiciary in deciding common law conflicts over life-determining (non) treatment decisions. These principles contain two potentially important

---

11 Mark Ashton, quoted by Dyer, 1999.
12 *R v Portsmouth Hospitals NHS Trust ex p Carol Glass* [1999] Lloyd's Rep Med 367, p 368.
13 *Ibid*, p 376.
14 *Ibid*, p 374–75, *per* Lord Woolf MR.

variations on the existing common law judgments.[15] First, Lord Woolf varied the second principle by adding the caveat 'where this can be avoided'. This suggests that there may be occasions where the court will interfere with clinical judgment. Second, Lord Woolf MR constrained the third principle by noting that the courts must always, 'take decisions in relation to the child's best interests'. This constraint, however, is significantly weakened by the condition that the courts will take 'fully into account' the doctor's opinions. It is suggested that the HRA 1998 may provide the meat to flesh out the bones of these constraints. To assess the potential for these two caveats, it is first necessary to consider the pre-existing common law.

THE COMMON LAW

The question of whether a patient should be treated against the wishes and advice of the medical staff arose in *Re J (A Minor) (Wardship: Medical Treatment)*.[16] J was a ward of court with very severe mental and physical disabilities. He was not terminally ill but equally was not expected to live much beyond early adolescence. He had been ventilated on two previous occasions and the doctors believed that he would be unlikely to survive another collapse. The Court of Appeal held that reventilation was not in J's best interests and could lawfully be withheld by the doctors. Lord Donaldson MR made a number of statements that arguably conflict with Lord Woolf MR's constraints. First, he stated:

> A child who is a ward of court should be treated medically in exactly the same way as one who is not, the only difference being that the doctors will be looking to the court rather than to the parents for any necessary consents.[17]

He continued:

> No one can *dictate* the treatment to be given to the child, neither court, parents nor doctors. There are checks and balances. The doctors can recommend treatment A in preference to treatment B. They can also refuse to adopt treatment C on the grounds that it is medically contra-indicated or for some other reason is a treatment which they could not conscientiously administer. The court or parents for their part can refuse to consent to treatment A or B or both, but cannot insist on treatment C.[18]

Finally, he also added that: 'What the court can do is to withhold consent to treatment of which it disapproves and it can express its approval of other

---

15 Fennell, 2000, p 128.

16 *Re J (A Minor) (Wardship: Medical Treatment)* [1990] 3 All ER 930.

17 *Ibid*, p 934.

18 *Ibid*.

treatment proposed by the authority and its doctors.'[19] Lord Donaldson MR repeated his opinion in *Re R (A Minor) (Wardship: Medical Treatment)* when he stated:

> No doctor can be required to treat a child, whether by the court in the exercise of its wardship jurisdiction, by the parents, by the child or by anyone else. The decisions whether to treat is dependent upon an exercise of his own professional judgment ...[20]

Subsequently, the question arose again in *Re J (A Minor) (Consent to Medical Treatment)*.[21] J was severely mentally disabled and suffered from cerebral palsy, blindness and epilepsy. His doctor suggested that, should the need arise, it would be medically inappropriate, cruel and futile to mechanically ventilate J. At first instance, the judge made an interim order requiring the health authority to provide all available treatment to J including 'intensive resuscitation'. The health authority appealed against the order. J's mother sought to uphold the order and relied on a report by an expert in child health from a different London teaching hospital who took the opposite view to J's own doctor.

The Court of Appeal allowed the appeal and set aside the order 'leaving the health authority and its medical staff free, subject to those with parental responsibilities for J consenting to him being treated by the medical staff ... to treat J in accordance with their best clinical judgment'. Lord Donaldson MR stated that:

> The fundamental issue in this appeal is whether the court in the exercise of its inherent power to protect the interests of minors should ever require a medical practitioner or health authority acting by a medical practitioner to adopt a course of treatment which in the *bona fide* clinical judgment of the practitioner concerned is contra-indicated as not being in the best interests of the patients. I have to say that I cannot at present conceive of any circumstances in which this would be other than an abuse of power as directly or indirectly requiring the practitioner to act contrary to the fundamental duty to which he owes his patient.[22]

In a similar vein, Balcombe LJ stated that: 'If the court orders a doctor to treat a child in a manner contrary to his or her clinical judgment it would place a conscientious doctor in an impossible position.'[23] This viewpoint has been subsequently confirmed.[24]

---

19 *Re J (A Minor) (Wardship: Medical Treatment)* [1990] 3 All ER 930, p 939.

20 *Re R (A Minor) (Wardship: Medical Treatment)* [1991] 4 All ER 177, p 187.

21 *Re J (A Minor) (Consent to Medical Treatment)* [1992] 4 All ER 614.

22 *Ibid*, p 622.

23 *Ibid*, p 625.

24 *Re C (A Minor) (Medical Treatment)* [1998] 1 Lloyd's Rep Med 1.

A crucial point and a potential area of conflict in these cases is who decides what are the 'best interests' of the patient. In *Frenchay v S*, Sir Thomas Bingham MR stated:

> It is I think, important that there should not be a belief that what the doctor says is in the patient's best interest is the patient's best interest. For my part I would certainly reserve to the court the ultimate power and duty to review the doctors' decision in the light of all the facts.[25]

However, he went on to consider the doctors' position if their opinion was not accepted. He stated:

> ... either they [the doctors] would feel obliged to embark upon the surgical procedure necessary ... which the consultant has made quite clear is contrary in a profound sense to his judgment of what is in the patient's best interests, and which he is himself unwilling to authorise ... That may sometimes be the right course for the court to adopt, but it seems to me a highly unsatisfactory position into which one should be reluctant to lead doctors unless the court has real doubt about the reliability, or *bona fides*, or correctness of the medical opinion in question.[26]

In *Re G (Persistent Vegetative State)*, Sir Stephen Brown P went one step further and stated: 'I have no doubt that the law requires, as the BMA guidelines indicate, that treatment decisions must be based upon the doctor's assessment of the patient's best interests.'[27] This requires that, 'the responsibility must ultimately remain with the doctors in charge of the case, albeit taking fully into account views of the relatives'.[28]

Although Lord Woolf has reasserted the court's right – at least in regard to minors – to determine the best interests of the patient, his comments were *obiter* and largely academic since no life was at stake. In practice, it was only in *Re T* that the courts sided with the parents' view of the child's best interests and, in that case, the parents rejected the offer of treatment so there was no question of the court being faced with the necessity of dictating that the doctors treat the patient in accordance with his best interests as determined by the court.[29] What the courts say is not necessarily what they do.

It appears, then, that had Mrs Glass approached the High Court at the time of the conflict, the judge would probably have accepted the doctors' opinion that not treating David was in his 'best interests'. One of the difficulties for patients, such as David Glass, is that the common law approaches this type of conflict from the perspective of the doctor's duty. As

---

25 *Frenchay Healthcare NHS Trust v S* [1994] 2 All ER 403, p 411.

26 *Ibid*, pp 411–12.

27 *Re G (Persistent Vegetative State)* [1995] 2 FCR 46, p 50.

28 *Ibid*.

29 *Re T (A Minor) (Wardship: Medical Treatment)* [1997] 1 All ER 906.

Lord Irvine noted (see above, p 82), the HRA 1998 will bring a change in emphasis such that the correct approach for the courts, and any other public body, will be from the perspective of the individual's rights and not the doctor's duty. Will this change in emphasis allow the patient more scope for ensuring that a request for treatment is granted?

THE RIGHT TO DEMAND
TREATMENT AND THE HRA 1998

There are three possibilities that arise with the advent of the HRA 1998: first, that there is a general right to treatment; second, that there is a right to treatment only in certain limited circumstances; and third, that the HRA 1998 does not support a right to demand medical treatment.

A general right to treatment

It is unlikely that a general right to treatment could be made out under the HRA 1998. It should be remembered that, unlike education, the ECHR does not specifically refer to medical treatment. Instead, the government's responsibility for the provision of healthcare arises from the European Social Charter 1961 (revised 1966). Article 13 of the Social Charter provides:

> With a view to ensuring the effective exercise of the right to social and medical assistance, the parties undertake: (1) to ensure that any person who is without adequate resources and who is unable to secure such resources either by his own efforts or from other sources ... be granted adequate assistance, and, in case of sickness, the care necessitated by his condition.

It is important to note that this is only politically persuasive rather than legally binding. In any event, even if the courts were to consider its provisions, it is implausible that, 'adequate assistance ... necessitated by his condition' would give the individual the right to demand treatment that his physician did not consider a suitable option. Given that Europe has specifically considered the provision of healthcare to be an issue for the social charter rather than the Convention, the courts would be reluctant to find a stronger right to treatment within the Convention rights. Any claim for a right to treatment would need to be made under Art 8, which states that:

> Everyone has the right to respect for his private and family life, his home and his correspondence.

The argument would be that the government has a positive obligation to provide treatment that is necessary for the individual to pursue his life goals. Any failure to provide this treatment would be failing to respect those autonomously chosen goals and hence would demonstrate a lack of respect for his private life. The same argument would follow under the right to respect for family life when the patient is the individual's child or close relative. Thus, Feldman notes that: 'The state's positive obligation of respect increases protection for people's implementation of private choices.'[30] He later suggests that an extension of the State's obligation under Art 8, 'could compel the state to give practical assistance to those who lack the physical (or, perhaps financial) capacity to give effect to their moral choices'.[31] Since health can be seen as a moral value, from both an individual and social perspective, the individual's choice of what constitutes health should be respected by the State.[32] It follows that a particular choice of treatment should be respected if it is capable of achieving the health end sought by the patient. Similarly, the actual choice of treatment also has a moral value, for example, the choice by Jehovah's Witnesses to have a non-blood volume expander to replace blood loss.

This argument suggests that there may be potential for a claim under Art 8. However, the State is allowed a number of grounds for derogation including:

> ... the economic well-being of the country ... for the protection of health or morals, or for the protection of the rights and freedoms of others.[33]

Although their arguments may be open to criticism, the court will invariably be able to deny the positive obligation based on one of these grounds. Thus, in *North West Lancashire HA v A, D & G*, three transsexuals challenged the decision of the health authority to refuse them gender reassignment surgery. Although the health authority's decision was quashed as being irrational, the judgment was based on domestic legal principles. Regarding the question of whether the refusal to fund the treatment could amount to a breach of Art 8, Auld LJ stated:

> In any event, Art 8 imposes no positive obligations to provide treatment. The ECHR in *Sheffield and Horsham v UK* (1998) 27 EHRR 163, which concerned post-operative refusal to accord legal status as a woman, said at 191, para 52: The Court reiterates that the notion of 'respect' is not clear-cut, especially as far as the positive obligations inherent in that concept are concerned: having regard to the diversity of the practices followed and the situation obtaining in the contracting states, the notion's requirements will vary considerably from case to case. In determining whether or not a positive obligation exists, regard must be had to the fair balance that has to be struck between the general interests of the community and the interests of the individual, the search for which balance is inherent in the whole of the Convention.[34]

---

30 Feldman, 1997, p 267.
31 *Ibid*, p 270.
32 Pellegrino and Thomasma, 1988, pp 62–66.
33 See Art 8(2) of the ECHR.
34 *North West Lancashire HA v A, D & G* [1999] Lloyd's Rep Med 399, p 410.

It is suggested that the court would consider that a fair balance between the individual's rights and the community's interests would be achieved providing the State's provision of healthcare satisfied the requirements of Art 13 of the European Social Charter. This being the case, any demand for treatment over and above that allowed for by Art 13, would be covered by one of the grounds for derogation under Art 8 of the Convention. However, there are three Convention rights that may provide a stronger claim since they deny the State any grounds for derogation.

A specific right to life-saving treatment

The three Articles that may found a limited right to demand treatment are Arts 2, 3 and 14. Article 2 provides that:

> Everyone's right to life shall be protected by law.

Article 3 states:

> No one shall be subjected to torture or to inhuman or degrading treatment or punishment.

Article 14 acts to prevent a discriminatory application of the rights provided by the Convention. Thus, it must be used in conjunction with another Article to found a claim. It states:

> The enjoyment of the rights and freedoms set forth in this Convention shall be secured without discrimination on any ground such as sex, race, colour, language, religion, political or other opinion, national or social origin, association with a national minority, property, birth or other status.

It should be noted that the list of discriminatory grounds is not exhaustive and other grounds, such as age or disability would also fall within the umbrella of this provision. Thus, Opsahl suggests:

> Medical care, for example, is crucial, and in a modern society it is to some extent part of the protection 'by law'. If ... life-saving operations are available but a selection of cases must be made, one should not a priori deny that allegations of discrimination may have to be considered under Art 2 in conjunction with Art 14 of the Convention.[35]

In a similar vein, Beddard asks:

> ... questions arise in relation to the cost of medical care. There have been examples where a hospital authority, unable to afford kidney machines for all patients, has put an arbitrary upper age limit on their provision. Will a law which allows a health authority to save the life of one person, but refuse to do so for someone a year older, pass scrutiny under Art 2.[36]

---

35 Opsahl, 1993, p 212.
36 Beddard, 1993, p 78.

Although the right to life under Art 2 is most often seen as a negative liberty right, both the European Court of Human Rights (the Court) and the Commission have stated that it also has a positive aspect. Thus, in *Osman v UK*, the European Court noted that:

> ... the first sentence of Art 2(1) enjoins the state not only to refrain from the intentional and unlawful taking of life, but also to take appropriate steps to safeguard the lives of those within its jurisdiction.[37]

Regarding healthcare, the question of the State's obligation to provide free medical aid when an individual's life was at risk was raised in *X v Ireland*.[38] In *Association X v United Kingdom*, which concerned childhood vaccinations, the Commission stated that Art 2 required the State 'to take appropriate steps to safeguard life'.[39] The words adopted by the Commission, while not completely defining the extent of the State's obligations, suggest that the State's positive duty does not need to be exhaustive. Thus, the Commission – in *Association X v United Kingdom* – accepted that the State had satisfied its obligations under Art 2 even though other 'desirable precautionary measures' might have been taken.[40]

Another case that raised the State's positive obligations under Art 2 was *X v FRG*.[41] The issue before the court was whether force-feeding a prisoner breached Art 3. The Commission held that force-feeding 'does involve degrading elements which in certain circumstances may be regarded as prohibited by Art 3'. However, the Commission also argued that, under Art 2, the State was under an obligation to take 'active measure[s] to save lives when the authorities have taken the person in question into their custody'.[42] It concluded:

> The Commission is satisfied that the authorities acted solely in the best interests of the applicant when choosing between either respect for the applicant's will not to accept nourishment of any kind and thereby incur the risk that he might be subject to lasting injuries or even die, or to take action with a view to securing his survival although such action might infringe the applicant's human dignity.[43]

The rationale underlying this decision is that where the State incarcerates an individual such that they are no longer in a position to seek medical care without the State's assistance then the State has an obligation to provide that medical care. A wider interpretation of this argument might be that where the State has accepted responsibility for the individual then they have a positive

37 *Osman v UK*, App No 23452/94; (2000) 29 EHRR 245, p 305, para 115.
38 *X v Ireland*, App No 6839/74; (1976) 7 DR 78.
39 *Association X v UK*, App No 7154/75; (1979) 14 DR 31, p 32.
40 *Ibid*, p 34.
41 *X v FRG*, App No 1056/83; (1984) 7 EHRR 152.
42 *Ibid*, p 153.
43 *Ibid*, p 154.

obligation under Art 2 to protect that individual's life. Although the narrow interpretation of the case would only extend those obligations to situations where the individual is in the involuntary custody of the State, the wider interpretation might allow that the obligation exists when the individual is voluntarily in the State's care. Under this wider interpretation, the rationale can be broken down to two requirements: that the individual is in the State's care; and that they have no realistic opportunity of obtaining the necessary medical care without the State's assistance. Under these circumstances – which would include NHS in-patients and children in local authority care – the State would arguably have a positive obligation to provide assistance.

Limitations of Art 2

The State's positive obligations under Art 2 are not limitless. Two constraints may operate to restrict the individual's claim to a right to life-saving or life-preserving treatment. These constraints are where the treatment is not in the patient's best interests and where there are insufficient resources available.[44]

That resources would be accepted as a constraint is suggested by the European Court's judgment in *Osman v United Kingdom*. The Court stated:

> ... bearing in mind the difficulties involved in policing modern societies, the unpredictability of human conduct and the operational choices which must be made in terms of priorities and resources, such an obligation must be interpreted in a way which does not impose an impossible or disproportionate burden on the authorities.[45]

There is no reason why the same reasoning would not be applied to the State's obligation to provide medical assistance. Furthermore, the government's positive obligation is only to take 'appropriate steps' to protect life[46] and, in *Osman*, the European Court also stated that the authorities could satisfy their positive obligations under Art 2 if they 'do all that could be reasonably expected of them to avoid a real and immediate risk to life of which they have or ought to have knowledge'.[47]

It is also worth noting that the courts may draw a distinction between short term, immediately life-saving treatment and a sustained course of treatment aimed at prolonging life. Thus, McBride notes:

> There will be, at the very least, an obligation to provide the minimum medical treatment required to prevent someone from dying in an emergency situation

---

44 Feldman, 1993, p 91.
45 *Osman v UK*, App No 23452/94; (2000) 29 EHRR 245, p 305, para 116.
46 *Association X v UK*, App No 7154/75; (1979) 14 DR 31, p 32.
47 *Osman v UK*, App No 23452/94; (2000) 29 EHRR 245, p 305, para 116.

but a state could probably use cost to resist being expected to provide a course of treatment to ensure someone's long term survival.[48]

The constraint imposed by the best interests requirement is perhaps more contentious. The first difficulty is in deciding who determines what the patient's best interests are. It is suggested that the patient's views – or the parent's/relative's views where the patient is not competent – should, at the very least, be taken into account by the medical staff. To do otherwise would arguably breach Art 8.[49] However, given that the courts have traditionally relied strongly on the doctor's opinion as to the patient's best interests, it is likely that they will continue to do so under the HRA 1998. That this would be a legitimate approach is supported by the Commission's opinion in *Association X v United Kingdom*:

> The Commission considers that it is legitimate for the state to take the view that checks for contra-indications are matters best left to clinical judgment.[50]

It is suggested that the courts would be correct if they looked to medical opinion to determine the most appropriate medical treatment in respect of any particular health gain. Thus, it cannot be in the patient's best interests to be given a 'futile' treatment and the State is under no obligation to provide such a treatment.[51] The concept of futility, however, raises the second difficulty with the 'best interests' constraint, which is who determines what is an appropriate health gain.

While a lack of consensus persists as to the meaning of 'futility',[52] there is one contentious area that may be affected by the HRA 1998 – futility decision based on quality of life judgments. In *LCB v United Kingdom* the Commission stated:

> In order for the applicant to establish a violation of Arts 2 and 3 of the Convention, she must, at least, demonstrate that advice and information (pre-natally and post-natally) to the applicant's parents could have altered the fatal nature of her condition or the physical and consequent psychological impact of the disease.[53]

Thus, the Commission has recognised the concept of physiological futility and has rightly argued that there can be no right to such treatment. Brody has suggested an alternative definition of futility that: 'An intervention is futile if and only if it fails to promote any *reasonable purpose of treatment* in the patient.' This may be the case under several circumstances: (1) the probability of

---

48   McBride, 1999, HR/54.

49   Feldman, 1997, p 270.

50   *Association X v UK*, App No 7154/75; (1979) 14 DR 31, p 35.

51   See *LCB v UK* (1998) 27 EHRR 212.

52   Berger *et al*, 1998; Truog and Brett, 1992.

53   *LCB v UK* (1998) 27 EHRR 212, p 222.

benefit is unacceptably low; (2) the magnitude of benefit is unacceptably small; and (3) the harm is much too great relative to any benefit.[54] In determining whether a treatment has a 'reasonable purpose', judgments may be made that arguably breach Art 3 and/or Art 14.

The most problematic judgments are those based on assessments of the patient's 'quality of life'. The argument is as follows: the patient – usually severely disabled – has a life that the physician, as a fully able person, could never comprehend as having any value to him if he were in the patient's position. Since the doctor believes that he would not value such a life for himself, he argues that this means that the patient could not possibly gain any value from his life. It then follows that treatment which 'merely' maintains the patient's life in status quo could not be of any benefit to the patient and it is 'therefore' in the patient's 'best interests' not to be treated.

Ignoring the obvious non-sequiturs, this type of judgment may breach Art 3, which prohibits degrading, and inhuman treatment. This has been defined as 'that which grossly humiliates an individual before others or drives him to act against his will or conscience'[55] or as treatment which, 'lowers the individual in rank, position, reputation or character, whether in his own eyes or the eyes of other people'.[56] It is certainly arguable that deciding that a person's life is not worth saving 'lowers the individual in ... position'. To suggest that a fully able person's life is more valuable than the life of a severely disabled person is surely to 'lower' the position of that individual.

That the failure to provide medical care could constitute a breach of Art 3 was considered in *Hurtado v Switzerland*[57] where it was held that:

> Under Art 3 of the Convention the state has a specific positive obligation to protect the physical well-being of persons deprived of their liberty. The lack of adequate medical treatment in such a situation must be classified as inhuman.[58]

Since withholding life-saving or life-preserving treatment is an irremediable step, it is arguable that refusing to treat on the basis of a 'quality of life' judgment would achieve the degree of inhumanity required to constitute a breach of Art 3.[59] Similarly, to suggest that an able person should receive

---

54 Brody, 1992, p 177.

55 *Denmark, Norway, Sweden and The Netherlands v Greece* (1969) 12 Yearbook 186.

56 *East African Asians v UK*, App No 4403/70; (1981) 3 EHRR 76, pp 79–80.

57 *Hurtado v Switzerland*, Series A, No 280-A (1994).

58 *Ibid*, p 16.

59 The *obiter* comments of the Court of Appeal in *North West Lancashire HA v A, D & G* [1999] Lloyd's Rep Med 399, p 411, do not apply in this circumstance. In that case, Auld LJ stated that: 'It is plain, in my view, that Art 3 was not designed for circumstance of this sort of case where the challenge is as to a health authority's allocation of finite funds between competing demand.' First, the case was not one where the individuals' lives were at risk. Secondly, the health authority's decision was not, as in the *Glass* case, based on a quality of life decision. Third, the decision in *A, D & G* was concerned with the resource allocation for a treatment as a whole, rather than whether a treatment provided for other patients should also be provided to the patient in question, ie, it concerned macro-allocation not micro-allocation of resources.

treatment but the disabled person should not is to discriminate against the disabled person, which would breach Art 14. The only caveat to this is that it would be acceptable not to treat the disabled person if their disability rendered the treatment physiologically ineffective. Thus, not ventilating a patient in the terminal stages of lung cancer[60] may be acceptable but refusing a heart and lung transplant to a person with Down's syndrome might breach Art 14. [61]

DAVID GLASS AND THE HRA 1998

David Glass' illness provides a good example of a situation where the life-threatening illness must be distinguished from the underlying disability. The septicaemia that threatened David's life was incidental to his disability rather than a part of his disability. Since septicaemia is a potentially treatable condition – and David did get better when given antibiotics by his GP – it would not be physiologically futile to administer the appropriate antibiotics. Consider how the scenario is changed when David's place is taken by a 12 year old epileptic with no other disabilities. It is not contentious to suggest that physicians would not hesitate to give a 12 year old epileptic boy antibiotics if his life was threatened. Under those circumstances, the doctors would probably do whatever was necessary to preserve the child's life, including mechanical ventilation, inotropic support and dialysis. In David's case, however, they decided that his life was so devoid of value that he did not even warrant antibiotic treatment let alone any invasive therapy. This decision was based on David's underlying disability and not on the condition that required treatment. As such, it was discriminatory and could be a breach of Art 14, in conjunction with Arts 2 or 3 – as well as the domestic Disabilities Discrimination Act 1995. Furthermore, as discussed above, by deciding that David's life was less valuable than the life of an able bodied 12 year old, the physicians arguably breached Art 3 in its own right.

If the case had come before the High Court at a time when the HRA 1998 was in effect then the court would have had to consider that failing to provide treatment might breach the following human rights:

(a) David's right to life under Art 2;

(b) David's right not to be subjected to inhuman or degrading treatment under Art 3;

(c) David's right to respect for his private and family life under Art 8;

---

60 The person with the lung cancer is disabled by the cancer and ventilating the patient will not alter the outcome.

61 See the story of just such a case that happened in the USA recounted in Asch, 1998, p 81.

(d) David's right to protection of his rights under the Convention without discrimination under Art 14;

(e) the family's right – as indirect victims – not to be subjected to inhuman or degrading treatment under Art 3;[62] *and*

(f) the family's right to respect for family life under Art 8.[63]

The physicians would be unable to counter the claim by arguing that the treatment would be futile. Antibiotics are a recognised and appropriate treatment for septicaemia and it would be hard for the doctors to claim that they would be futile given that they would almost certainly treat an able bodied 12 year old with septicaemia. Furthermore, there was evidence that David responded with visible pleasure to hugs and cuddles and was not, therefore, in an equivalent position to a patient in the persistent vegetative state. Since it is impossibly hard for an able bodied person to appreciate what value David gets from his life, then surely we should accept the view of the person best placed to judge – which in this case is his mother – that it is in David's 'best interests' to be treated? Failure to give real weight to David's mother is prohibited by Art 8. The other possible limitation that might be raised is scarce resources. However, it is difficult to see this argument succeeding under the principle of proportionality since antibiotics are cheap and plentiful and David would still be taking up a hospital bed whether he was being treated or not.

As a counterclaim, the physicians may argue that directing them to provide treatment would either breach their own rights under the Convention or else would breach the integrity of the profession as a whole. Neither of these arguments should succeed. First, in making a treatment decision the physician is acting as the agent of a public body and, therefore, the Convention does not provide him with any protected rights relating to the decision.[64] Second, while defining what constitutes a breach of the medical profession's integrity may help to delimit the positive obligations that may reasonably be expected of the State, it is arguable that it would not breach the profession's integrity to accede to that request that lies within the scope of the acceptable goals of medicine. According to a special report, determined by an international consensus from groups of bioethicists, the four goals of medicine are:

(1) the prevention of disease and injury and the promotion and maintenance of health;

---

62 See Harris, O'Boyle and Warbrick, 1995, p 637; *Paton v UK* (1980) 3 EHRR 408.

63 Note that the non-consensual administration of morphine, which might have depressed David's respiration and hastened his death, could arguably be a breach of Art 2. However, this is a separate issue and involves the contentious doctrine of double effect. For further consideration, see Sapiro and Ungoed-Thomas, Chapter 17, below.

64 See *X v UK*, App No 10083/82; (1984) 6 EHRR 140, p 143. The Commission referred to the Commission's report in *Brüggemann and Scheuten v Germany*, App No 6959/75; (1981) 3 EHRR 244, paras 55–56 in support of this point.

(2) the relief of pain and suffering caused by maladies;

(3) the care and cure of those with a malady, and the care of those who cannot be cured; *and*

(4) the avoidance of premature death and the pursuit of a peaceful death.[65]

The report states that: 'In medicine's struggle against death, an appropriate aim first and foremost is to reduce premature death.'[66] It defines a premature death as:

> When a person dies before having had the opportunity to experience the main possibilities of a characteristically human life cycle ... [which includes] the chance ... to enter into close and loving relationships with others.[67]

Since David is capable of showing affection, he arguably has such a relationship with his mother and his death would be premature. Thus, acceding to his mother's request for the antibiotic treatment would hardly breach the integrity of the medical profession and the opposite may, in fact, be true.

These arguments suggest that a failure to provide David with antibiotics would breach the HRA 1998. Following an application to the court, the judge would have to issue a declaratory order stating that not treating would be unlawful. Although this would not direct a particular doctor to provide a particular treatment, it would imply that the doctor who is caring for David must either provide a reasonable treatment for the septicaemia or refer David to a physician who is willing and able to provide the treatment. Thus, although the court will not have directly ordered the treatment the effect will be the same as far as David is concerned.

CONCLUSION

The argument presented suggests that there may be occasions when the individual will be able to demand treatment as a right under the HRA 1998. These occasions will be limited to emergency life-saving care and to those where the individual has been discriminated against on some spurious or iniquitous ground such as disability or age. Decisions to withhold treatment made on abhorrent 'quality of life' grounds may also breach the Act. This is unlikely to affect decisions regarding patients in a persistent vegetative state since those patients do not have any interests and therefore it cannot be

---

65 Callahan, 1996, S9–S15.

66 *Ibid*, S13.

67 *Ibid*.

argued that providing treatment is in their best interests.[68] However, where there is evidence that the patient has interests, then 'quality of life' judgments that devalue their life may be unlawful. Thus, although the physician will still retain a large amount of clinical discretion, he will still have to provide a reasonable treatment for the relevant illness without regard to the patient's underlying disability. The only caveat is where the patient's disability will have a material effect on the likely success of the treatment.

This argument does of course depend on how the judges interpret the Convention rights under the HRA 1998. As McHarg suggests:

> ... perhaps the most central [question] is how British judges will respond to the interpretive challenges posed by broadly-drafted Convention rights and, in particular, the need to determine limits to those rights.[69]

Similarly, in a comment on rights in general, Ransom notes that: 'Supposedly fundamental rights are either too general to be effective as guarantees ... or too specific to retain their relevance.'[70] Thus, whether the theoretically limited right to treatment described becomes a reality depends on how the English judiciary interpret the Convention rights. Central to this is the question as to how the judges will resolve the tension between the individual rights and the judiciary's traditional deference to clinical discretion. It is suggested that a reasonable interpretation would support the argument made in this chapter that there are instances – where treatment has been withheld on discriminatory grounds that the judiciary has previously failed to condemn – that may be outlawed by the HRA 1998. Furthermore, it should also provide a greater force to the patient's claim and to the voices of his relatives. This should help to tip the balance away from the overly deferential attitude of the judiciary to medical opinion and, thus, should 'flesh out' the principles detailed by Lord Woolf. As a final caveat, however, the HRA 1998 should be seen as an instrument that, not only protects the individual from injustice, but also creates the duty that the individual will exercise his protected rights responsibly.[71] Thus, while demands for treatment that have been denied because of discrimination should be allowed, the courts are unlikely to look favourably on demands for expensive, esoteric treatment of doubtful or unproven efficacy.

---

68 See *Airedale NHS Trust v Bland* [1993] 1 All ER 821 and the High Court's recent decision in *NHS Trust A v Mrs M* and *NHS Trust B v Mrs H* [2000] EWHC 29, discussed in more detail by Sapiro and Ungoed-Thomas, Chapter 17, below.

69 McHarg, 1999, p 671.

70 Ransom, 1997, p 160.

71 See the Hon Sir John Laws, 1998, p 254; Beddard, 1999.

CHAPTER 7

ACCESS, PROCEDURE AND THE HUMAN RIGHTS ACT 1998 IN MEDICAL CASES

Charles Foster

INTRODUCTION

This chapter considers the effect which the Human Rights Act 1998 (HRA) will have on:

(a) the availability of funding for litigants in medical cases; and

(b) procedure in civil courts in medical cases; and

(c) procedure in other tribunals in which medical issues are debated.

In relation to (a) and (b) the position is easily summarised. It is most unlikely that the HRA will produce any significant change. The answer of any court to the suggestion that there is an obligation to provide funding is likely to be: 'No, there is no such obligation. We do much better than a number of countries bound by the European Convention who have not been criticised.' The answer of any English court to the suggestion that civil procedure falls foul of the HRA will be (and has been already): 'The Civil Procedure Rules make English law wholly compliant with the Act. The Act was in mind when the Rules were drafted and the Act has nothing to add to the Rules.'

There are three caveats to this general comment about civil procedure. The first relates to the law of limitation. It is possible that the very long limitation period enjoyed by minors, and/or the absence of a limitation period enjoyed by persons under a disability, will be found to fall foul of Art 6. The second relates to applications to strike out before there has been an airing of the facts. Again, such applications might sometimes be victims of Art 6. The third relates to giving medical treatment to persons under a legal disability. In *F v West Berkshire AHA* [1989] 2 All ER 545, *Bolam*[1] was controversially superimposed upon the best interests test such that the treatment will be lawful if a responsible body of medical opinion in the relevant speciality would have concluded that it is in the patient's best interests to receive it.

The main procedural effects of the HRA in medical cases will be:

(a) as an instrument for ensuring fair hearings in tribunals other than the civil courts, such as the NHS Tribunal, disciplinary tribunals such as the General Medical Council (GMC), the General Dental Council (GDC), the

---

1   *Bolam v Friern Hospital Management Committee* [1957] 1 WLR 582.

United Kingdom Central Council for Nursing, Midwifery and Health Visiting (UKCC) and trust and health authority domestic enquiries; and

(b) as a rhetorical device. For a long time, there will be judges who think that the HRA matters more than it in fact does, and will be scared more than the authorities indicate they should be by applications which mention Art 6.

Art 6 might have a lot of work to do in some English disciplinary tribunals. This chapter cannot and does not deal with all its implications there (for further details see Chapter 8), but concentrates on two aspects only: the right to a public hearing and the right to a hearing by an independent and impartial tribunal.

THE ANATOMY OF ART 6

General

The Act mainly affects procedure through Art 6. So it is necessary to dissect that Article. Article 6(1) provides that:

In the determination of his civil rights and obligations or of any criminal charge against him, everyone is entitled to a fair and public hearing within a reasonable time by an independent and impartial tribunal established by law ...

So it gives five rights, namely:

(a) A right to a hearing.

(b) A right to a fair hearing.

(c) A right to a public hearing.

(d) A right to a hearing within a reasonable time.

(e) A right to a hearing by an independent and impartial tribunal established by law.

Much of this chapter is structured around these headings.

The precondition to Art 6's relevance: 'In the determination of ... civil rights and obligations or of any criminal charge against [the applicant]'

Disciplinary proceedings

The wording of Art 6 implies that it will not necessarily extend to disciplinary proceedings and, indeed, it does not necessarily.[2] However, it is now

---

2   *Albert and Le Compte v Belgium* (1983) 5 EHRR 533, para 25.

established that the right to continue in professional practice (for example, as a doctor or a nurse) is a civil right. Art 6 therefore does apply to proceedings the outcome of which might be the loss of the right to practice.[3] If that right is not in jeopardy, Art 6 does not apply.[4]

It could be argued that proceedings which could, at worst, result in the restriction of a professional's right to practice rather than stopping him altogether do not fall within Art 6. An interesting illustrative case is the NHS Tribunal. This has the right to take away from a professional the right to practice within the NHS. It has no power to stop a professional doing private practice. Does Art 6 apply here? The position is not clear. Matters concerning public employment are not generally, in the unusual jurisprudence of Strasbourg, considered to concern 'civil rights'.[5]

However, public employees are frequent applicants to English employment tribunals and English courts are likely to say that the same set of standards should protect public employees there as protect private employees. An NHS tribunal has effectively the same power, so far as NHS employment is concerned, as an employment tribunal. Also, for most professionals affected by the decision of an NHS Tribunal, NHS work is the vast majority of their livelihood. For most of them, there will be little practical point in remaining on, for example, the Medical Register if NHS practice is impossible. So the NHS Tribunal's decision about their ability to continue in NHS practice is effectively determinative of their civil right to practice. It would be inconceivable that Art 6 would apply to NHS tribunal proceedings concerning a doctor with no, or little, private practice, but not to a doctor with a substantial private practice. Whether the same applies to disciplinary proceedings the possible outcome of which is the suspension of a professional's right to practice within a particular health authority or trust is more of a moot point. The employment tribunal analogy is likely to be found persuasive, having the effect of applying Art 6. And, if this is wrong, probably the court would decide that since, in practice, a decision of a domestic trust or health authority tribunal suspending a professional from practice with that trust or health authority might well have the effect of making the individual effectively unemployable elsewhere too, Art 6 should apply to the tribunal.

Does Art 6 apply to interim hearings?

The Article applies to the '*determination* of ... civil rights and obligations ...' (author's emphasis). Accordingly, it has been held that the Article does not

---

3   *Albert and Le Compte v Belgium* (1983) 5 EHRR 533, para 28; *Le Compte, Van Leuven and De Meyere v Belgium* (1981) 4 EHRR 1, para 48: *Wickramsinghe v UK* [1998] EHRLR 338; *X v UK* (1998) EHRR 480.

4   *X v UK* (1983) 6 EHRR; *Van Marle v The Netherlands* (1986) 8 EHRR 483.

5   *Kosiek v Germany* (1986) 9 EHRR 328; *Neigel v France* [1997] EHRLR 424; *Balfour v UK* [1997] EHRLR 665; *Huber v France* (1998) 26 EHRR 457; *Vogt v Germany* (1995) 21 EHRR 205.

apply to applications for interim relief,[6] or applications for leave to appeal.[7] However, sometimes the determination of preliminary issue will be decisive of the whole case or of entitlement to some remedy. Where this is the case, Art 6 will apply.[8] Article 6 has also been held to apply to cost proceedings and enforcement of judgment proceedings.[9]

THE RIGHT TO A HEARING

Does the right to a hearing mean that limitation periods are illegal?

English lawyers are fond of reciting the old wisdom that the defence of limitation bars the remedy, not the cause of action. However, effectively what they do is stop hearings. Is this a breach of Art 6?

The answer is clear: no. The Art 6 right to a hearing is not absolute. It is subject to limitations.[10] Some of the obvious limitations are imposed by Art 6 itself. Hearings have to be fair and to be held within a reasonable time. The court has said that time bars on actions will be acceptable provided it:

> ... is satisfied that the limitations applied do not restrict or reduce the access left to the individual in such a way or to such an extent that the very essence of the right is impaired. Furthermore, a limitation will not be compatible with Art 6(1) if it is does not pursue a legitimate aim and if there is not a reasonable relationship of proportionality between the means employed and the aim sought to be achieved ...[11]

The issue of limitation is considered in more detail below.

The effect of Art 6 on strike out applications

The argument under Art 6 that the strike out jurisdiction is illegal is based on the rather too obvious to be true contention that you cannot be said to have had a hearing, let alone a fair hearing, if the facts which underlie the case have never been rehearsed.

---

6   *X v UK* (1981) 24 DR 57; *Alsterland v Sweden* (1988) 56 DR 229 E Comm HR.

7   *Porter v UK* (1987) 54 DR 207 E Comm HR.

8   *Obermeier v Austria* (1990) 13 EHRR 290; *Silva Pontes v Portugal* (1994) 18 EHRR 156, para 33.

9   See, respectively, *Robins v UK* (1998) 26 EHRR 527, and *Hornsby v Greece* (1997) 24 EHRR 250.

10 See, eg, *Golder v UK* (1979–80) 1 EHRR 524.

11 *Stubbings et al v UK* (1997) 23 EHRR 213, p 233.

The assertion that striking out itself is unlawful is unsustainably wide. The court will certainly not let the HRA 1998 to be used as a crutch allowing obviously doomed cases to limp on, at colossal expense to everyone involved.

However, strike out applications based on some sort of policy based blanket immunity may be vulnerable to Art 6 challenge. In *Hill v Chief Constable of West Yorkshire*,[12] the House of Lords held that the police were immune to claims arising out of their activities in relation to the investigation or suppression of crime. That decision was challenged before the European Court of Human Rights (the Court) in *Osman v United Kingdom*.[13] The Court said that the blanket immunity was unlawful:

> ... the application of the [public policy immunity] rule in this manner without further enquiry into the existence of competing public interest considerations only serves to confer a blanket immunity on the police for their acts and omissions during the investigation and suppression of crime and amounts to an unjustifiable restriction on an applicant's right [under Art 6] to have a determination on the merits of his or her claim against the police in deserving cases ... it must be open to a domestic court to have regard to the presence of other public interest considerations which pull in the opposite direction to the application of the rule ...[14]

Osman has been rightly doused in academic and judicial obloquy.[15] Art 6 is to do with ensuring fair trial. It is essentially to do with procedure. It is illogical that a procedural provision should have the effect of changing the substantive law. But the courts seem determined to perpetuate the illogicality.[16] Although that is bad for logic, it might not be bad in practice.

Generally, Art 6 is an enemy of policy decisions. Policy underlies a lot of English law. If *Osman* is followed, there are, arguably, strong Art 6 objections to established principles such as the irrecoverability on grounds of proximity of damages for nervous shock for many classes of potential claimants, the bar by *res judicata* and other forms of estoppel on re-litigation, and expert immunity.

There are some early indications that, although they might not like the use of Art 6 language, the English courts have already adopted some of its distaste for policy based immunities.[17]

---

12 [1989] AC 53.

13 [1999] 1 FLR 193.

14 *Ibid*, p 232.

15 See, eg, *Barrett v Enfield LBC* [1999] 3 WLR 79.

16 See, eg, the decision of the Commission in *TP and KM v UK*, App No 28945/95, 26 May 1998 (*Re the Admissibility of an Application Re a Public Authority's Immunity to Negligence Actions Brought by Children*); 10 September 1999 (*Re Merits: Deciding for the Applicant*).

17 See, eg, *Waters v Commissioner of Police for the Metropolis* (2000) unreported, 27 July.

Article 6 could also be a valuable shield against legal conservatism and, ironically for a classical Romano-Germanic code, a positive encouragement to English common law judicial innovation; there will inevitably be much less suspicion of novel causes of action than there was under the old Rules of the Supreme Court. English courts have long recognised in theory that the boundaries of actionable breach of duty are pushed incrementally outwards,[18] but practice has often lagged a long way behind that theoretical recognition. Lots of imaginatively pleaded and worthy cases have been struck out by inflexible Masters who could find nothing in *Clerk & Lindsell* which completely described the cause of action being asserted. Article 6 will help such cases to survive until the facts behind them have been heard and, so, it will help to widen and refine and make more just the English law of negligence.

Medical treatment of persons under a legal disability

It often happens that someone under a legal disability (for example, a mentally handicapped adult), who is himself incapable of giving consent to medical treatment, requires treatment.

The treating clinicians have to decide whether the proposed treatment is in the best interests of the patient. Controversially, in *F v West Berkshire AHA* [1989] 2 All ER 545, *Bolam*[19] was applied in this context such that the treatment will be lawful if a responsible body of medical opinion in the relevant speciality would have concluded that it is in the patient's best interests to receive it.[20]

The application of the *Bolam* test leads to a number of doctors simply, and safely, making up their own minds about what amounts to the patient's best interests. Others, of course (and increasingly), cover their backs by asking the court for a declaration that the proposed treatment is in the patient's best interest. Article 6 provides a right of access to the court. It is arguable that this right of access is meaningless unless:

(a) in the case of persons under a disability there is a procedural requirement for the patient's best interest to be decided by the court; and

(b) once the case is before the court, that the court makes up its own mind about whether in fact the proposed treatment is in the patient's best interests (a question to which, precisely because it is a question of fact, the *Bolam* test is irrelevant).

If this analysis is right it is an interesting example of one way in which a procedural provision can force a change in the substantive law.

---

18 See, eg, *X v Bedfordshire CC* [1995] 2 AC 633.

19 *Bolam v Friern Hospital Management Committee* [1957] 1 WLR 582.

20 See, also, *Re SL* [2000] 2 FLR 452.

THE RIGHT TO A FAIR HEARING

Civil procedure generally

It is inconceivable that the English courts will hold that Art 6 requires more of them than the Civil Procedure Rules (CPR) do. The CPR were drafted with the Convention provisions in mind, and the Overriding Objective uses language which would gladden the heart of the European Court. It says:

> (1) [The CPR] are a new procedural code with the overriding objective of enabling the court to deal with cases justly.

Dealing with a case justly includes, so far as is practicable ensuring that the parties are on an equal footing; saving expense; dealing with the case in ways which are proportionate:

(i) to the amount of money involved;

(ii) to the importance of the case;

(iii)to the complexity of the issues; and

(iv)to the financial position of each party,

ensuring that it is dealt with expeditiously and fairly; *and* allotting to it an appropriate share of the court's resources, while taking into account the need to allot resources to other cases.[21]

That is a good, if rather tautological, gloss on the civil parts of Art 6. This is certainly the way that the English courts see it. In *Walker v Daniels*,[22] one party argued that the single expert provisions of the CPR fell foul of Art 6. He had the misfortune to be listed in front of Lord Woolf MR, the architect of the CPR. Lord Woolf gave him short shrift, saying:

> [If] the court is not going to be taken down blind alleys it is essential that counsel, and those who instruct counsel, take a responsible attitude as to when it is right to raise a HRA 1998 point ... Art 6 could not possibly have anything to add to the issue on this appeal. The provisions of the CPR 1998 ... make it clear that the obligation on the court is to deal with cases *justly* ... [emphasis in original].

The law of limitation

This topic is introduced above (see p 102). Article 6 comments implicitly on limitation periods by asserting both the right to a fair hearing and the right to a hearing within a reasonable time.

---

21 CPR, Pt 1.1.
22 [2000] UKHRR 648.

As noted above, the claimant's Art 6 right to a hearing may be in conflict with the defendant's Art 6 right to a fair hearing/a hearing within a reasonable time. As time passes, memories fade, witnesses disperse and die, and clinical practice changes so that it can be very difficult for courts to put themselves in the position, many years ago, of the doctor whose treatment is criticised. The Limitation Act 1980 exists to protect defendants against the prejudice which accrues with the passage of time. Its provisions are well known.

In cases involving personal injuries, the court has a discretion, under s 33 of the 1980 Act, to disapply the operation of the primary limitation period. There is some statutory guidance as to how this discretion should be exercised and there are lots of cases but, essentially, the court will weigh the prejudice which has resulted from the passage of time against the prejudice which will be caused if the action is declared to be statute barred, and will let the trial go ahead if, all things considered, it is just to let it go ahead. That sort of vague equitable exercise is just the sort of exercise which Art 6 loves. Section 33 is likely to survive.

More vulnerable are the long limitation periods which apply in the case of minors, and the fact that there is no limitation period at all where the claimant has, since the relevant accident, been under a legal disability.

These rules are well meaning. They are designed to protect vulnerable people from their own vulnerability. The rule about minors says that the right to sue lasts until three years after the beginning of the period (at age 18) when the person is presumed to able to consider himself whether he can and should exercise the right. Since it is presumed that a person under a perpetual disability will never be able properly to consider these things, time never starts to run against him. However, the rules ignore realities.

Often the parents of a child born with cerebral palsy will start investigating immediately what went wrong and, usually, although the child is of course the named claimant, the things which are sought in a clinical negligence action are things which benefit the parents just as much, if not more, than the child. At any rate, the parents and the child have a complete community of interest. Often the carers of an incompetent adult injured in a medical accident will start investigating immediately.

Why, in these circumstances, should a defendant not be able to say that a 21 year delay in the first case, or a (say) 40 year delay in the second case, both of which will have made it practically impossible to run a realistic defence, has deprived him of a right to a fair trial, and that the legislation which authorises those delays is contrary to Art 6?

This argument might find judicial favour. In *Stubbings v Webb*,[23] the court decided that limitation periods did have a legitimate place in litigation. They

---

23 [2000] UKHRR 648.

protected defendants against the need to fight ancient claims and they introduced some desirable certainty into the litigation process. Stubbings itself concerned a claim for trespass to the person. The trespass occurred during the applicant's childhood. The court expressed concern that, with a six year limitation period running from the applicant's 18th birthday, the defendant would be fighting a very elderly claim indeed.

Of course, there are difficulties in knocking down the legislation which deals with limitation periods in the case of minors and others under a disability. If you say that time starts to run against A when B, acting on A's behalf, has the actual or constructive knowledge which would, were it B's case, have set time running against B, then:

(a) in the case of actual knowledge, you penalise A for having alert and concerned carers; and

(b) in either case, absent some sort of immunity, you open up the possibility of an action by A against B for the value of A's lost claim – a possibility which has all sorts of objections against it, some of them based on limitation concerns.

However, arguably these sorts of concerns are not relevant to Art 6's (or any other of Convention Article). Article 6 exists to ensure a fair trial. If you delay too long, fair trial is impossible.

It will not be easy to challenge the English limitation rules. The courts have made it clear that they will be slow to criticise national limitation legislation. The rules about minors and persons under a disability certainly serve a function which it is easy to express in Art 6 terms, and a court considering their compliance with the Convention could well find that the English approach to ensuring access to the courts for these particularly vulnerable groups falls within the 'margin of appreciation'.

THE RIGHT TO A PUBLIC HEARING

The Art 6 provision

After providing generally for a public hearing,[24] Art 6 goes on:

Judgment shall be pronounced publicly but the press and public may be excluded from all or part of the trial in the interest of morals, public order or national security in a democratic society, where the interests of juveniles or the protection of the private life of the parties so require, or to the extent strictly necessary in the opinion of the court in special circumstances where publicity would prejudice the interests of justice.

24　See above, p 100.

Why the right is important

The right to a public hearing is a right to have a tribunal which is publicly accountable for its procedure and decisions. It protects against secret, and therefore arbitrary, decision making. It also has the effect of increasing (hopefully) public confidence in the tribunal.

An oral hearing is implicit

If a tribunal makes its decisions simply by reading documents silently to itself and then pronouncing judgment, no one will know the basis on which its decision is reached. In these circumstances the presence in the courtroom of the whole of Fleet Street watching the judges reading would not give the parties the protection which this part of Art 6 is designed to give.

At the level at which the civil rights are finally determined, therefore, the Art 6 requirement for a public hearing is implicitly a right to an oral hearing.[25]

Of course, many tribunals have effectively secret, non-oral, paper determinations of preliminary issues (such as whether there is a case to answer). Since these determinations do not finally decide any civil right, Art 6 does not apply to them.

Press access

The press are part of the public and, accordingly, should not generally be excluded,[26] but the obligation not to exclude does not imply an obligation to invite: nor is there any obligation to advertise a hearing.[27]

Permitted restrictions on the operation of the rule

Article 6 itself permits a number of restrictions (see Chapter 5). There is a lot of case law on how these caveats should be read. A lot of medical and related tribunals will deal with highly confidential material which affects the private lives of people involved in it (for example, patients). The phrase 'private life of the parties' has been construed widely to include the private life of people involved generally, rather than merely the parties to the litigation or the person whose conduct is being investigated. Thus, Art 6 will allow many, but not all, medical disciplinary proceedings to be held in private.[28]

---

25 *Fischer v Austria* (1995) 20 EHRR 349.
26 See *Axen v Germany* (1983) 6 EHRR 195.
27 *X v UK* (1979) 2 Digest 444 E Comm HR.
28 See *Guenoun v France* (1990) 66 DR 181 E Comm HR.

The accused can waive a right to have proceedings against him held in public if there is no compelling public interest in the proceedings being public.[29] That waiver can be implied, and may well be implied if there is a practice that proceedings are held in private unless the accused asks for a public hearing, and the accused, in fact, does not.[30] A practice of holding certain types of proceedings in private absent a specific request for a public hearing may well be lawful if, generally, the subject matter of such proceedings is such that it would fall within the Art 6 exceptions to the presumption of a public hearing.[31] This will be the case with many medical and related hearings.

The requirement for public pronouncement of the judgment

Article 6 makes this mandatory. Unlike the provisions for hearings, there are no circumstances under which judgment can be delivered privately. Of course, this does not make illegal the use of terms in the judgment which render anonymous parties who gave evidence privately.

The exact meaning of 'pronounced publicly' has yet to be worked out. The words of Art 6 imply an oral judgment, but handed down written judgments, provided that the text of such judgments is freely available, would certainly not be found to fall foul of the provisions. Likewise, if the people affected by a decision and interested in it would know that the text would be available on a particular website or noticeboard, publication there is likely to be found to be adequate.[32]

THE RIGHT TO A HEARING WITHIN A REASONABLE TIME

Time wasting trusts and health authorities: civil proceedings

In the past, it has been possible for health authorities and trusts, sued by privately funded individuals, to procrastinate by taking every conceivable interlocutory point and appealing everything: in effect, to abuse the rules of civil procedure in the hope that the financially exhausted claimant will give up. It has been suggested that Art 6's insistence on a hearing within a reasonable time is the remedy for that abuse.

---

29 See *Hakansson and Sturesson v Sweden* (1990) 13 EHRR 1; *Pauger v Austria,* 25 EHRR 105.
30 *Zumtobel v Austria* (1993) 17 EHRR 116.
31 *Schuler-Zgraggen v Switzerland* (1993) 16 EHRR 405.
32 See *Preto v Italy* (1983) 6 EHRR 182; *Axen v Germany* (1983) 6 EHRR 195.

Again, the advent of the CPR means that Art 6 will almost certainly never have to be invoked to stop these sort of games. The court's case management responsibility means that strict timetables will be set. Absurd interlocutory points are likely to be met with immediate orders for costs against the defendant. Article 6 really will do no more.

Other proceedings

In disciplinary proceedings, this part of Art 6 might have the effect of imposing a *de facto* limitation period. It is often very difficult (for all the reasons recited in almost every limitation argument in civil cases) to answer old allegations.

What is 'a reasonable time' will depend on all the circumstances. No useful general guidance can be given. The court has said (unsurprisingly and unnecessarily) that those circumstances include the complexity of the case,[33] the conduct of the applicant[34] and the conduct of the body bringing the proceedings.[35]

A plea that the delay has been caused by a huge workload and/or inadequate resources will not excuse,[36] unless the excessive workload has itself resulted from exceptional circumstances which have been addressed reasonably competently.[37] It would be interesting to see whether a court would regard as excusable the great delays in getting substantive hearings before the GMC, caused apparently by the wholly foreseeable increase in the number of complaints against doctors and the relatively small number of people available to sit on the Professional Conduct Committee.

RIGHT TO A HEARING BY AN INDEPENDENT AND IMPARTIAL TRIBUNAL ESTABLISHED BY LAW

Civil and criminal proceedings

There is nothing here of particular interest or relevance to healthcare law.

---

33 See *Andreucci v Italy*, Series A, No 228-G (1992) (number of witnesses relevant); *Wemhoff v Germany* (1968) 1 EHRR 55 (need to obtain expert evidence relevant); *Manieri v Italy*, Series A, No 229-D (1992) (intervention of other parties relevant).

34 *Eckle v Germany* (1982) 5 EHRR 1.

35 *Konig v Germany* (1978) 2 EHRR 170; *Eckle v Germany* (1982) 5 EHRR 1; *G v Italy*, Series A, No 228-F (1992).

36 *Muti v Italy*, Series A, No 281-C (1994).

37 *Bucholz v Germany* (1981) 3 EHRR 597.

Disciplinary proceedings

Independence

Lots of disciplinary tribunals in the healthcare world will have to be careful about this provision. There is a real danger in trust and health authority tribunals that the adjudicators are insufficiently distinct from the prosecutors. The UKCC's disciplinary machinery has recently been challenged on this basis in the Scottish courts. Judgment in this case is awaited.

Impartiality

There are two tests for impartiality; a subjective one and an objective one.[38] An applicant relying on the subjective test has to prove that the tribunal was in fact biased personally against him.[39] The objective test is much less demanding. An applicant relying on it must show that there is objectively justifiable doubt about the tribunal's impartiality.[40]

The medical world is a small world. It will often be difficult to obtain adjudicators who have no connection at all with the accused – a point relevant both to independence and impartiality. There will be plenty of opportunities for the constitution of tribunals to be questioned under the objective test, although the courts, acknowledging that it is desirable that medical personnel are tried by tribunals consisting *inter alia* of their peers, and recognising the difficulties associated with convening tribunals of appropriate professionals who have never heard of the accused, will be slow to find that doubt about impartiality is objectively justified.

Established by law

Most tribunals of relevance to the healthcare professions are creatures of statute, as are their rules of procedure. Simply to be set up by Parliament is not enough: the procedure must be regulated, too.[41] Occasionally, though, domestic enquiries which assume the power to dismiss (and therefore, *de facto* if not *de jure*, take away the right to practice) are convened by trusts or health authorities out of an excess of zeal or a hysterical fear of the press which have no statutory basis. These are vulnerable to Art 6 challenge.

---

38 See *Fey v Austria* (1993) 16 EHRR 387.
39 *Le Compte, Van Leuven and De Meyere v Belgium* (1981) 4 EHRR 1.
40 *Gautrin v France* (1998) 28 EHRR 196.
41 *Piersack v Belgium* (1986) B 47 23.

THE AVAILABILITY OF FUNDING

Many trust and health authority finance managers were enormously relieved to hear of the restrictions in the availability of public funding. There is no doubt that public funding was used in the past to fund laughably unarguable cases which, despite their inevitable failure, caused a lot of trouble and expense to defendants. Public funding remains available in many medical cases, but publicly funded clinical negligence cases have to be handled by solicitors with proven expertise in such cases, which is to the benefit both of claimants and defendants.

There is no point in having impressive assurances about the right to a hearing, and elaborate safeguards against unfairness at trial, if it is financially impossible to get to court. Article 6(3)(c) expressly confers a right to free legal assistance in criminal cases 'when the interests of justice so require' if the accused does not have the means to pay for it himself.

There is no similar general right to free legal assistance in civil cases. In relation to civil proceedings there is an obligation to make the courts (*inter alia* financially) accessible, but legal aid is not the only way to do this. In *Airey v Ireland*,[42] which concerned judicial separation proceedings, refusal of legal aid was said to deprive the applicant of her Art 6 rights: because of the complexity of the proceedings it was impracticable for her to present the case herself. If family rights or rights to liberty are directly at stake in the proceedings, the court will be more ready to say that there should be free legal help.[43] Almost certainly, the English legal aid regulations would be found to be invulnerable to Art 6 challenge. They were, after all, drafted with an eye to Art 6.

No public funding is available for disciplinary tribunals. Often, of course, the professional involved will obtain legal representation through a defence organisation or a union. Often, it will be a professional obligation to have the cover which entitles the practitioner to that representation (and the court would not be particularly sympathetic to a professional who was deprived of representation by his own failure to obey the disciplinary code). However, representation will not necessarily be available. Generally, though, the issues debated in such tribunals will, by definition, be easily comprehensible to, and easily managed by, the accused himself. This, combined with the relative affluence of most professionals will mean that Art 6 free representation points are unlikely to be taken successfully in relation to appearance before most disciplinary tribunals.

---

42   (1979) 2 EHRR 305.

43   See *Munro v UK* (1987) 52 DR 158; *Megyeri v Germany* (1992) 15 EHRR 584; *Aerts v Belgium* [1998] EHRLR 777.

CHAPTER 8

MEDICAL COMPLAINTS, DISCIPLINE AND THE HUMAN RIGHTS ACT 1998

Gerard Panting

INTRODUCTION

Medical practitioners are subject to numerous systems of accountability. One incident, clinical or otherwise, may give rise to: a complaint; disciplinary action by the employing authority; investigation by the Health Service Commissioner (the Ombudsman); a claim for compensation; an investigation by the GMC under one of its Fitness to Practise procedures; a criminal investigation and, in the event of a death, a Coroner's inquiry or, in Scotland, a Fatal Accident Inquiry by the Procurator Fiscal.

Even this list is not exhaustive. The Commission for Health Improvement created under the Health Act 1999 will investigate some adverse incidents in addition to conducting a rolling audit and there are tribunals with specific remits, such as the Home Office Tribunal, and recently a raft of public inquiries, for example, The Bristol Royal Infirmary Inquiry, the Ledward Inquiry and the forthcoming Shipman Inquiry. The professional consequences for the subject of these various procedures may be profound.

Article 6 of the European Convention on Human Rights (ECHR), concerning the right to a fair trial and enshrined in domestic law through the Human Rights Act (HRA) 1998, is clearly relevant to these issues. However, it has had little impact to date in terms of case law. In part, this may be because the HRA 1998 has only recently come into force and, in part, also because many rules governing these procedures have already been amended in the hope of forestalling many of the challenges which may be contemplated.

ARTICLE 6

Article 6(1) states that:

> In the determination of his civil rights and obligations or any criminal charge against him, everyone is entitled to a fair and public hearing within a reasonable time by an independent and impartial tribunal established by law. Judgment shall be pronounced publicly but the press and public may be excluded from all or part of the trial in the interests of morals, public order or national security in a democratic society where the interests of juveniles or the protection of the private life of the parties so require, or to the extent strictly

necessary in the opinion of the court in special circumstances where publicity would prejudice the interests of justice.

Articles 6(2) and (3) apply only to criminal charges setting out minimum guarantees, although the provisions of Art 6(3) may also appear minimum standards of fairness within disciplinary proceedings:

6.2 Everyone charged with a criminal offence shall be presumed innocent until proved guilty according to law.

6.3 Everyone charged with a criminal offence has the following minimum rights:

(a) to be informed promptly, in a language which he understands and in detail, of the nature and cause of the accusation against him;

(b) to have adequate time and facilities for the preparation of his defence;

(c) to defend himself in person or through legal assistance of his own choosing or, if he has not sufficient means to pay for legal assistance, to be given it free when the interests of justice so require;

(d) to examine or have examined witnesses against him and to obtain the attendance and examination of witnesses on his behalf under the same conditions as witnesses against him;

(e) to have the free assistance of an interpreter if he cannot understand or speak the language used in court.

The obvious beneficiaries of Art 6 in the medical context are doctors and other healthcare professionals but it is not beyond the bounds of possibility that the new provisions will be employed by complainants dissatisfied with the redress available through the NHS complaints procedure, a topic to which we will return at the end of this chapter.

But how might this Article be used to challenge the accountability procedures currently in place? The scope of Art 6 is limited to the relationship between individuals and public authorities which includes all NHS bodies, Government departments and the General Medical Council (GMC). The HRA 1998 may also have an impact in the private sector but, as yet, there is no developed body of jurisprudence in this country and anticipating how the courts may react is a matter of speculation. The following from Lord Woolf, when Master of the Rolls and prior to the introduction of the HRA 1998, illustrates how we can expect evolution rather than revolution in the English courts:

Quite apart from the fact that the HRA 1998 is not in force, if the court is not going to be taken down blind alleys it is essential that Counsel and those who instruct Counsel, take a responsible attitude as to when it is right to raise a Human Rights Act point ... Art 6 could not possibly have anything to add to the issue on this appeal ... When the 1998 Act becomes law, Counsel will need to show self-restraint if it is not to be discredited.[1]

---

1   *Walker v Daniels* [2000] UKHRR 648.

However, in *Stefan v GMC* [1999] Lloyd's Rep Med 90, the Privy Council, (Lords Slynn, Nicholls and Hoffman), again before the HRA 1998 came into effect, carefully considered the impact of the ECHR:

> Just because Parliament has ruled that some tribunals should be required to give reasons for their decisions, it does not follow that the common law is unable to impose a similar requirement upon other tribunals: *R v Civil Service Appeal Board ex p Cunningham* [1992] ICR 816.
>
> The trend of the law towards an increased recognition of a duty to give reasons was consistent with current developments towards increased openness in matters of government and administration, but the trend was proceeding on a case by case basis, and had not lost sight of the established common law position that there is no general duty to give reasons: *R v Royal Borough of Kensington and Chelsea ex p Grillo* [1996] 28 HLR 94.

The present case was not an appropriate opportunity to explore the possibility of a departure from that general rule. The passing of the HRA 1998 and the application of Art 6(1) of the Convention on Human Rights will require closer attention to be given to the duty to give reasons, at least in cases concerning a person's civil rights and obligations.

THE GMC

Introduction

One good example to examine the potential effects of Art 6 of the HRA 1998 is the GMC and its 'fitness to practise procedures'. The GMC is charged with regulating the medical profession and therefore has jurisdiction over all registered medical practitioners. Doctors whose fitness to practise is called into question may find themselves subject to investigation by the Council – the ultimate sanction for those who do not come up to the mark being removal from the Medical Register.

The GMC operates three fitness to practise procedures:

(a) conduct procedures;

(b) health procedures;

(c) performance procedures.

All complaints received by the GMC warranting further investigation are reviewed by members of Council termed 'screeners'. They decide if further action is required and, if so, which path that complaint should follow. Doctors are usually informed about complaints at an early stage and offered the chance to comment before the papers are reviewed by the screener.

Historically, only a minority of cases are pursued beyond the screening stage but in the wake of the *Toth*[2] case, in which the complainant challenged the screener's decision not to admit his complaint for further investigation, this is likely to change. The court ruled:

> The role of the screener was a narrow one; to filter from the formally correct complaints, not those which in his view ought not to proceed further, but those which he was satisfied (for some sufficient and substantial reason) need not proceed further. A complaint did not need to proceed where proceeding would serve no practical purpose. There might be an absence of need where there was nothing in law which amounted to a complaint; where formal verification was lacking; where the matters complained of could not amount to serious professional misconduct; where the complainant withdrew the complaint; or where the practitioner had already ceased to be registered.

Conduct procedures

Cases allocated to the conduct route are next considered by the Preliminary Proceedings Committee (PPC) which currently meets in private and usually considers cases on the papers alone.

The role of the Preliminary Proceedings Committee (PPC) was also discussed in *Toth*. The PPC's role is to decide whether the complaint 'ought to proceed'. This language must be read in the context of a scheme under which the complainant has no right to the practitioner's comments on the complaint or other material put before the PPC and a scheme of which the central feature is the investigation of complaints by the Professional Conduct Committee (PCC) before whom alone there is full disclosure of documents and evidence and a form of hearing where the complainant (and public) can see, and be reassured by seeing, the proper examination of the merits of the complaint. The PPC may examine whether the complaint has any real prospect of being established, may itself conduct an investigation into its prospects, and may refuse to refer it if satisfied that the real prospect is not present. But it must do so with the utmost caution, bearing in mind the one-sided nature of its procedures under the rules which provide that, whilst a practitioner is afforded access to the complaint and able to respond to it, the complainant has no right of access or to make an informed reply to that response and the limited material likely to be available before the PPC compared to that available before the PCC. It is not its role to resolve conflicts of evidence. There may be circumstances which entitle it to hold that the complaint should not proceed for other reasons, but the PPC must bear in mind its limited (filtering) role and must balance regard for the interests of the practitioner against the interests of the complainant and the public and the complainant,

---

2   *R v GMC ex p Toth* [2000] Lloyd's Rep Med 368; [2000] 1 WLR 2209; (2000) *The Times*, 29 June.

and bear in mind the need for the reassurance of the complainant and the public that complaints are fully and properly investigated and that there is no cover up. In the case of the PPC (as in the case of the screener), any doubt should be resolved in favour of the investigation proceeding.

In the exercise of their respective jurisdictions, the screener and PPC should be particularly slow in halting a complaint against a practitioner who continues to practise: as opposed to one who has since retired, for the paramount consideration must be the public's protection in respect of those continuing to practise; and they should at all times bear in mind the role of the Health Committee (HC) whenever questions arise of impairment of fitness to practise by reason of physical or mental condition.

The courts have also reviewed the action of the Preliminary Proceedings Committee in the case of *R v GMC ex p Richards* (2001) *The Times*, 24 January QBD Administrative Court (Sullivan J), 18 December, the decision of the PPC not to refer the case for full investigation by the PCC was quashed by the Divisional Court. There was a substantial conflict of evidence between complainant and defendant doctors and, whilst the court held that the PPC was entitled to form its own view on the accuracy of the medical records, further conflicting evidence from the deceased's family was also presented and the PPC was not in the position to resolve that conflict on the basis of documentary evidence alone. In this particular case, the court held that utmost caution should have been exercised as the decision reached by the PPC was contrary to a decision reached on the same facts by the Family Health Services Appeal Authority on the basis of a full hearing. Consequently, the decision was quashed and remitted to a freshly constituted PPC for reconsideration.

The PPC decides which cases should be referred on to the PCC. The PCC meets in public and conducts the hearing very much like a trial with both prosecution and defence represented by lawyers with evidence given on oath and, if necessary, witnesses compelled to attend by subpoena.

The PCC comprises medical and lay members. A legal assessor is also present throughout the public hearing and *in camera* deliberations to ensure that the Committee has access to appropriate legal advice. Most cases are concluded within a few days but some, like the Bristol and 'kidneys for sale' cases, last for weeks, interspersed by lengthy adjournments.

At the end of the hearing, the PCC considers first if the facts proved amount to serious professional misconduct and, if so, what sanctions should be applied. The options are:

(a) admonishment;

(b) conditions on the doctor's registration for up to three years;

(c) to suspend the doctor's name from the Medical Register for up to 12 months;

(d) to erase the doctor's name from the Medical Register now for a minimum period of five years.

The health procedures

Unlike the conduct procedures, the health and performance procedures are designed to be remedial although the prime objective is always to protect patients. Cases referred on for further investigation by the health screeners are dealt with relatively informally. The doctor is asked to undergo examination, usually by two doctors who then report their findings back to the Council. If necessary, the doctor will be asked to agree to the appointment of a medical supervisor who will report progress to the Council on a regular basis. Provided that the doctor agrees to co-operate and follows the various recommendations made (including medical treatment and restriction on medical practice) the case is unlikely to be referred to the HC.

Doctors who do not comply or default from supervision are referred to the HC which meets in private with the doctor present, together with appropriate legal representation. Article 6(1) expressly allows exclusion of the public from all or part of the trial where the interests of juveniles or the protection of the private lives of the parties so require.

The HC can impose conditions on the doctor's registration for up to three years and suspend a doctor from the Medical Register for up to 12 months.

Performance procedures

The performance procedures are designed to deal with doctors who display a pattern of seriously deficient performance. The performance procedures were established under the Medical (Professional Performance) Act 1995, establishing powers, through the Committee on Professional Performance (CPP), to suspend a doctor's registration or impose conditions on it in cases where the CPP found that the standard of professional performance had been seriously deficient.

Seriously deficient performance is not defined within the legislation but is defined within the GMC publication *When your Professional Performance is Questioned* (November 1997). It states:

> Seriously deficient performance is a new idea. We have defined it as a departure from good professional practice whether or not it is covered by specific GMC guidance, sufficiently serious to call into question a doctor's registration. This means that we will question your registration if we believe that you are repeatedly or persistently not meeting the professional standards appropriate to the work you are doing – especially if you might be putting patients at risk. This could include failure to follow the guidance in our booklet *Good Medical Practice*.

Where there is a suspicion that this is the case, doctors are invited to undergo an assessment by three assessors appointed by, but normally themselves members of, the Council – usually two doctors and one lay person. Prior to the assessment itself, doctors are asked to complete a portfolio setting out factual information about the doctor and his practice. The assessment is comprehensive and divided into two phases. The first lasts two or three days and includes interviews with the doctor, observing the doctor in practice, interviewing professional colleagues, examination of patient records and discussion based around particular cases. Phase 2, generally lasting one day, involves detailed assessment around simulated conditions. Following assessment, the assessors will submit a report to the Council's case co-ordinator with recommendations for the correction of identified deficiencies. If these are serious, the doctor will be invited to agree to a statement of requirements intended to correct specific problems. Once that action has been taken, the doctor will be reassessed in the same way.

If doctors do not agree to an assessment, the case is considered by the Assessment Review Committee whose function is to determine whether or not there are *prima facie* grounds for an assessment.

The CPP considers only those cases where the doctor has refused to co-operate or where appropriate improvement has not been made within the programme. The CPP may place conditions on the doctor's registration for up to three years, or suspend the doctor's registration for 12 months. Although the CPP cannot strike a doctor's name off the Register, it can suspend the doctor's name indefinitely once it has already been suspended for at least two years.

The performance procedures have been examined in one case before the Judicial Committee of the Privy Council in the case of *Krippendorf v GMC* [2000] PC (Lord Saville, Sir Ivor Richardson, Sir Christopher Slade), 24 November, (2000) TLR 29 November. Here, the Privy Council found that the report completed by the assessors and on which the PCC relied was flawed as a matter of law. The Board found:

> First, it demonstrated a basic error in the Panel's approach to their function, since, essentially, they had sought to assess her professional competence in a number of areas of work relating to what they perceived to be her job descriptions, and had thereby assessed her as incompetent, instead of assessing her professional performance by reference to the work she had actually been doing since 1997 ... Their Lordships do not go so far as to hold that in every case the complaint which triggers an assessment requires an investigation by the Panel and the CPP. On the facts of the present case, however, the complaints should in their Lordships' opinion have been investigated because nothing related more directly to the standard of the appellant's actual performance over the relevant period. The failure of both the Panel and the CPP to investigate the complaints reflects the erroneous concentration on her professional competence rather than her actual professional performance.

Secondly, ... the report on which the CPP so heavily relied was in their Lordships' opinion unfair to the appellant insofar as it relied on her answers given in the portfolio [when an assurance had previously been given that the portfolio did not constitute part of the assessment]. In the context of fairness, their Lordships add that, in their opinion, in the particular circumstances of this case, fairness demanded that the appellant should be given a proper opportunity to refute, if she could, the serious complaints which directly related to her professional performance and had led to the assessment.

Consequently, the appeal was allowed.

The rights of the complainant

The right to a fair trial does not apply to proceedings unless they are determinative of an individual's civil rights or obligations but, from the complainant's point of view, that may include cases at the screening and/or PPC phase as demonstrated by *Toth's* case which resulted in changes in procedure as the following extract shows.

> Under the Rules it is apparent that neither before the screener nor before the PPC is the complainant entitled to see the material made available to the screener or the PCC. But today with the imminent coming into force of the HRA 1998, the GMC properly acknowledges the responsibility that its practices and procedures should (so far as possible) be transparent and to this end it has decided to adopt a new form of practice as from 1 July 2000. This is set out in a letter dated the 19 June 2000 addressed to me by the GMC which (so far as material) reads as follows:
>
>> In relation to complaints received by the GMC after 1 July 2000, any material submitted by the doctor to the screener, before the screener makes his final decision under r 6, will be copied to the complainant, unless the screener considers that there are 'exceptional circumstances' which ought properly to preclude this.
>>
>> One such exceptional circumstance will be where disclosure could cause substantial harm to the doctor and/or to a third party, eg, by the disclosure of confidential medical material.
>>
>> When the screener considers that disclosure would involve 'substantial harm' he is not in an all or nothing situation. He has the discretion: (a) to allow disclosure if accompanied by a cross-undertaking; and/or (b) to allow, partial/edited disclosure.
>
> In anticipation of this change of practice the GMC has agreed ... that much of the documentation to be put before the new screener shall be disclosed to Mr Toth but an issue cannot be resolved by agreement, namely whether a confidentiality obligation can be imposed upon Mr Toth in respect of certain confidential medical material relating to Dr Jarman's health. It is incumbent on me to resolve this issue. It goes without saying that I am not concerned to

> consider whether, and if so how far, this material can be relevant to any
> decision to be made by the screener; it is not apparent to me that it is.

The judge quashed the decision of the screener and directed that the complaint proceeds before another screener and that that screener exercise his duties as having regard to the guidance set out in the judgment. Lightman J also held that the GMC is entitled to require the complainant to make an undertaking of confidentiality in respect of any confidential medical evidence adduced by the respondent doctor before the screener as a condition of supplying the same to him.

Separate administration of distinct phases of procedure

However, the duty to give reasons may itself give rise to unfairness if it carries with it bias against either party at the next stage of consideration. With this in mind, the GMC has now produced a memorandum of reasons for screeners to complete so that in referring cases forward to the PPC they do not set out their own opinions about the case which may colour the PPC's consideration.

Separation of prosecuting and adjudicating functions

The PPC, like the other fitness to practise committees are committees of the GMC. Their membership prior to 2001 has been drawn entirely from Council members. Their numbers have now been boosted by recruitment of non-Council members to serve on the PCC with plans to expand the scheme to cover other fitness to practise committees in due course. But these committees will remain committees of the GMC which therefore retains the role of prosecutor and adjudicator.

The GMC discussion paper on reform of governance canvasses views on separation of these functions. One view is that prosecuting complaints fits squarely with the role of setting the standards by which practitioners will be judged. Others argue that determining complaints is the proper function of the GMC and that investigation and prosecution should be undertaken by a separate body but, in any event, there is general agreement that the two functions should be separated. In the meantime, it will be interesting to see, given the public nature of this debate, if challenges to the GMC's procedures are mounted on grounds that the tribunal is not independent and impartial and therefore falls foul of Art 6(1) of the Convention. Pending reform of the GMC's governance, the executive within the Council have established separate teams within the Fitness to Practise Division to service the committees and process complaints.

Right of appeal

Article 6 provides the right to a fair trial; there is no right to an appeal process. But doctors found guilty of serious professional misconduct or whose registration has been adversely affected by decisions of the performance or health committees, do have a right of appeal to the Judicial Committee of the Privy Council. However, that right is limited to the following grounds: Procedural unfairness, illegality and a misunderstanding of the evidence by the Committee. In *Nwabueze v GMC* [2000] 1 WLR 1760; (2000) 56 BMLR 106; (2000) *The Times*, 11 April PC (Lord Hope, Sir Patrick Russell, Sir Andrew Leggatt), Dr Nwabueze appealed against a decision of the PCC of the GMC following allegations of sexual misconduct and dishonesty. During consideration of the case *in camera*, the legal assessor gave advice to the Committee which was repeated in the presence of the parties when the public were readmitted. Neither party was asked if they wished to make representations in relation to the advice of the legal assessor which was held to be a breach of the rules of natural justice and infringement under Art 6 of the ECHR.

In the same case, an example of procedural unfairness occurred in relation to allegations of bias. After the decision of the PCC was announced Dr Nwabueze came into possession of information which indicated that a lay member of the Committee had been biased by dint of undisclosed local connections with a practice where the appellant had worked as a trainee, her undisclosed office with a statutory body connected with nursing, midwifery and health visiting in Wales, and the manner of her questioning of the appellant when questions were put to him by members of the Committee at the end of his evidence. As a result, the case was remitted to the PCC differently constituted for reconsideration.

Rights of appeal are therefore limited and, although strictly beyond the scope of the HRA 1998 and disciplinary procedures, there is a question about what rights of appeal, if any, should exist. Should the grounds of appeal in a fitness to practise case be more limited than in other civil proceedings?

The Lord Chancellor has stated that the role of the Privy Council in GMC cases should be reviewed. If the appellate role is transferred to the High Court the opportunity to examine the grounds on which appeals may be lodged will also arise.

THE NHS COMPLAINTS PROCEDURE

Introduction

The 'new' NHS complaints procedure came into being on 1 April 1996 in the wake of the Wilson Report, *Being Heard*. The concept was to produce a system that was fair, accessible, speedy and free from bureaucracy. Most complaints, it was hoped, could be resolved at local level by the provider offering an explanation, where appropriate an apology and acting to rectify any faults which had come to light as a result of the complaint.

Local resolution

From 1 April 1996, all GP practices and NHS trusts must have in place their own complaints procedures with the emphasis on accessibility, informality, speed and fairness to all concerned.

Independent review

It is hoped that the vast majority of complaints will be amenable to local resolution but, if the complainant remains dissatisfied, he or she can ask for an independent review by the health authority. A non-executive director of the health authority (termed the convenor) will consider the request.

Eligibility for review

Before deciding whether or not to convene a review panel, the convenor must obtain a statement signed by the complainant setting out their remaining grievances and why they are dissatisfied with the outcome of local resolution. The convenor and a lay chairperson of the regional review panel will then consider whether any further action, short of establishing a panel, can be taken to satisfy the complainant; and whether all practical action has already been taken such that establishing a panel would add no further value to the process.

The convenor may refer the complaint back to the practice or to the health authority conciliation services, if it is considered that local resolution procedures have not been exhausted. If it is clear that everything that can be done has been done, the convenor may advise the complainant that no further action can be taken; or set up an independent review of the complaint.

If the complaint contains a clinical element, the convenor must take appropriate clinical advice before reaching a decision, but the final decision is for the convenor alone. Complainants denied an independent review will have a right of appeal to the ombudsman (Health Service Commissioner).

The review panel

The chair of the independent review panel has considerable discretion in deciding how best to investigate a particular case. There is no formal oral hearing with parties present. The panel will produce a report, copied to the complainant, the practice and the health authority reviewing the facts and, where necessary, making recommendations for remedial actions. The report will not make recommendations about disciplinary action; it will be for the health authority to decide whether or not any further action is necessary.

Acting as longstop to the NHS complaints procedure is the Health Service Commissioner or ombudsman whose jurisdiction includes investigation of clinical complaints as well as administrative matters within the NHS. Complainants refused independent review or who are dissatisfied with the outcome of a review panel may take their case to the ombudsman who will either decline to take any further action, direct that the health authority reconsider their position or assume responsibility for the investigation.

But if the Health Service Commissioner were to reject an application for further action, would the HRA 1998 provide a remedy? Adequate investigation of a *bona fide* complaint appears to qualify as a determination of an individual's civil rights. In the case of Toth, this point appears to have been anticipated (see above).

The complaints procedure is currently under review. The *NHS Plan*[3] said of it:

> Complaints are not always dealt with quickly with the resolution often taking months. The role of the independent convenor has been criticised and the overall complaints procedure is not seen as being independent or transparent. The NHS needs to find a better way of dealing with patients' concerns, preferably before they become official complaints. The NHS also needs to be seen to say sorry when things go wrong rather than taking a defensive attitude and to learn from complaints so that the same problems do not recur. The government is at present evaluating the complaints procedure, taking evidence from a wide range of sources. The government will act on the outcome of this evaluation and reform the complaints procedure to make it more independent and responsive to patients. Making the complaints procedure less adversarial should result in fewer clinical negligence claims against the NHS. We look to make further changes to the current system for clinical negligence.

Following the review of the NHS complaints system, radical overhaul seems almost inevitable. The new procedures will be drafted with a close eye on the HRA 1998 and its potential impact on the rights of complainants and respondent healthcare workers. The new system is likely to preserve the local procedure together with safeguards to ensure that unresolved complaints are admitted for further investigation, perhaps as of right.

---

3   DoH, 2000b.

Complaints requiring further investigation are likely to be considered by a panel truly independent of the trust or health authority involved, reflecting the requirement for an independent and impartial tribunal and incorporate procedures for testing the evidence given by both parties to the complaint. Whilst a public hearing would usually be out of the question, a system of public reporting and outcomes, much along the lines of the current ombudsman's reports, may well be a feature.

Another criticism of the current system is the delay in final resolution of cases which go to independent review. The requirement for a hearing within a reasonable time may, itself, also give rise to challenges if timetabling under the new system does not prove more efficient.

CONCLUSION

The HRA 1998 will doubtless be cited regularly in cases before the UK courts in future. But it remains to be seen what the extent of the impact will be.

CHAPTER 9

CONFIDENTIALITY, ACCESS TO HEALTH RECORDS AND THE HUMAN RIGHTS ACT 1998

David Stone

INTRODUCTION

In an interview with *The Times* newspaper in 1995, the American actor Robert Redford expressed nostalgia for the days when there was 'less information'. While his compatriot Bill Gates, the computer tycoon, might not share that view, few would disagree that advances in electronic communications over the last decade have brought with them – with a speed and to an extent perhaps not paralleled since the Renaissance – a huge increase in the range and volume of information to which we are now subjected. Just as the invention and spread of the printed word in the 15th century prompted challenges to many aspects of European culture, it is no exaggeration to say that modern society's development of the internet, the satellite and the mobile telephone as alternatives to traditional forms of communication presents important new legal and ethical issues which we may not yet be ready to resolve. Of these, perhaps the most important is that of privacy; how can we control access to and disclosure of the vast amount of confidential information now being generated and stored?

Nowhere is this issue more pressing than in the field of healthcare. Here, the confidentiality of information exchanged between doctor and patient has been recognised for centuries as a fundamental requirement of any civilised society. Yet even this principle faces challenges from several quarters: first, from the growth in the sheer volume of information now being generated and stored about every patient; secondly, from the constantly changing technology which enables that information to be stored, accessed and transmitted in an increasing number of ways; and thirdly, from the desire of government departments and healthcare organisations to monitor and evaluate that information more closely than ever before.

The coming into force of the Human Rights Act (HRA) 1998 in October 2000 was therefore timely. As the other chapters of this book make clear, the incorporation of the European Convention on Human Rights into English law signals a radical challenge by modern society to accepted legal principles. In particular, many commentators regard the 'right of privacy' in Art 8 as a powerful addition to the rather disorganised armoury of rights currently available to patients under English law. Others see it as no more than a deliberately restricted right that adds little to the existing regime of common law principles and data protection legislation. Article 8 states:

Right to respect for private and family life

1 Everyone has the right to respect for his private and family life, his home and his correspondence.

2 There shall be no interference by a public authority with the exercise of this right except such as is in accordance with the law and is necessary in a democratic society in the interests of national security, public safety, or the economic well-being of the country, for the prevention of disorder or crime, for the protection of health or morals, or for the protection of the rights and freedoms of others.

However, no proper analysis of Art 8 can be made without also analysing Art 10, which addresses the converse issue of freedom of information. Article 10 states:

Freedom of expression

1 Everyone has the right to freedom of expression. This right shall include freedom to hold opinions and to receive and impart information and ideas without interference by public authority and regardless of frontiers. This Article shall not prevent states from requiring the licensing of broadcasting, television or cinema enterprises.

2 The exercise of these freedoms, since it carries with it duties and responsibilities, may be subject to such formalities, conditions, restrictions or penalties as are prescribed by law and are necessary in a democratic society, in the interests of national security, territorial integrity or public safety, for the prevention of disorder or crime, for the protection of health or morals, for the protection of the reputation or rights of others, for preventing the disclosure of information received in confidence, or for maintaining the authority and impartiality of the judiciary.

In order to assess the likely impact of the HRA 1998 on the confidentiality and accessibility of patient records, this chapter will: first, analyse existing common law principles and related statutory provisions; secondly, examine the terms of the new Data Protection Act (DPA) 1998; and finally, discuss the extent to which, against this legal and technological background, the HRA 1998 is likely to affect the policy and practice of confidentiality in the NHS.

THE COMMON LAW OF CONFIDENTIALITY

Introduction

It is important to note from the outset that confidentiality is only one aspect of 'privacy'. It has frequently been pointed out, often in the course of formal inquiries into regulation of the press, that under English common law there is no specific right of privacy.[1] Those complaining of infringements of privacy have traditionally been forced to seek one or more of several unreliable remedies under a number of possible headings, such as trespass, defamation, nuisance, or breach of confidence.

One should also note that the law relating to the confidentiality of information has traditionally concerned itself not with the ownership of that information but with its disclosure or use. For example, the physical pages on which medical notes are recorded may be owned, for example, by the Department of Health (DoH); but it is the information comprising those notes which characterises them. Whereas 'knowledge' (for example, about a particular pharmaceutical process) may be owned and protected as 'intellectual property' (via contract, patent or copyright), it has long been assumed under common law that information is itself incapable of being owned or stolen.[2] Accordingly, the fact that a patient may, for example, have been treated for a communicable sexual disease is simply an empirical fact, incapable of ownership either by him or by those who treated him. It is the disclosure or non-disclosure of that information which attracts legal rights and duties.

Rights and duties

Those rights and duties are usually analysed as arising from the relationship between the confider and recipient of the information. In some cases, they may arise under a contract, for example, between an employer and employee. The principles applicable where there are no such contractual rights and obligations were summarised in *Coco v AN Clark (Engineers) Ltd*, a case about industrial secrets.[3] It was said that for there to be, in the absence of a contract, a breach of confidence, three elements must be present.

> First, the information itself ... must have the necessary quality of confidence about it. Secondly, that information must have been imparted in circumstances importing an obligation of confidence. Thirdly, there must be unauthorised use of that party to the detriment of the party communicating it.

In other words, the presence of these three factors creates a duty of confidence owed by the recipient to the confider, and a right enjoyed by the confider to enforce that duty, either by way of an injunction preventing disclosure of the confidential information or through damages for the detriment caused by disclosure. Although *Coco* was a commercial case, similar principles have been

---

1   *Kaye v Robertson* [1991] FSR 62, in which tabloid journalists photographed a television actor uninvited while he was recuperating in hospital.

2   *Oxford v Moss* (1979) 68 Cr App R 183.

3   *Coco v AN Clark (Engineers) Ltd* [1969] RPC 41.

applied to personal relationships;[4] press intrusion;[5] and to government servants' publication of official secrets.[6] Their applicability to the relationship between patients and healthcare professionals needs, perhaps, no explanation, and was confirmed in *W v Edgell*.[7]

Exceptions to the general rule

Yet, as we shall also see with Art 8 itself, the right of confidentiality is not absolute. To begin with, if it can be shown that the information is already in the public domain, for example, because the confider has already published it, the information will no longer have 'the necessary quality of confidence about it' and will therefore no longer attract the protection of the law. Alternatively, where, for example, obviously confidential information such as a diary is found in the street by a passer-by, it may be argued by reference to *Coco* that the recipient of the information is not bound by any duty of confidence because, first, there is no relationship with the confider, and secondly, the circumstances in which the information was received do not create or imply any duty of confidence. However, there is a contrary line of judicial reasoning. In the *Spycatcher* case,[8] Lord Goff attempted to define such circumstances more widely. In his view, even without a direct relationship between confider and recipient:

> ... a duty of confidence arises when confidential information comes to the knowledge of a person ... in circumstances where he has notice ... that the information is confidential, with the effect that it would be just in all the circumstances that he should be precluded from disclosing the information to others.

This is a broad interpretation of the circumstances in which a duty of confidentiality arises, and suggests a move away from a duty based on relationship, to a self-sufficient right based on the nature of the information. If this interpretation is correct (and it has been supported more recently by Mr Justice Laws),[9] it foreshadows the right expressed in Art 8.

Even in cases where a common law duty of confidentiality is agreed to exist, there may still be one or more of three possible defences to an allegation of breach of confidence. First, it may be that the confider, for example a patient, has consented to the disclosure of the information, either expressly or

---

4   Eg, the celebrated divorce case of *Argyll v Argyll* [1967] Ch 302.

5   Eg, the action against *The Mirror* newspaper by the late Princess of Wales in respect of photographs of her exercising in a gym. See, 'How the Snoop won the Photo Finish' (1995) *Sunday Times*, 12 February; and 'The Princess Wins her Prints' (1995) *The Independent*, 9 February.

6   As in the *Spycatcher* book case – *AG v Guardian Newspapers (No 2)* [1990] 1 AC 109.

7   *W v Edgell* [1990] 1 All ER 835.

8   *AG v Guardian Newspapers (No 2)* [1990] 1 AC 109.

9   *Hellewell v Chief Constable of Derbyshire* [1995] 4 All ER 473.

impliedly, for example, to the other healthcare professionals and managers involved in his treatment and care. In that case, the duty of confidence can be seen as waived or modified by the patient.

Secondly, it may be argued against the confider that disclosure is in the public interest. For example, it may be desirable that a blood sample taken from a motorist admitted to the Accident and Emergency Department after a road accident is passed on to the police investigating whether or not that motorist had committed a criminal offence by being drunk while driving. In that case, the right of the confider is not waived or modified but simply overridden. The principle of public interest was examined in *W v Edgell*,[10] where it was held that a doctor was justified on that ground in releasing to the proper authorities a medical report about the risks posed by the possible release of a schizophrenic patient who had been violent. In a more recent case,[11] it was held that the police were entitled in the public interest to release the contents of an interview with a nurse to the United Kingdom Central Council for Nursing, Midwifery and Health Visiting (UKCC), because that was the body required by statute to regulate the conduct of the nursing profession.

Thirdly, a breach of confidence may be excused because disclosure is expressly required by law, again overriding the confider's right of confidentiality. For example, a doctor has a statutory duty to report certain notifiable diseases under the Public Health (Control of Disease) Act 1984, and to report information about an abortion under the specific circumstances set out in the Abortion Regulations 1991. This exception to the usual principle of patient confidentiality is expressly recognised in the General Medical Council's (GMC) recently revised professional guidance.[12] Indeed, the GMC itself has surprisingly wide ranging statutory powers of its own under s 35A of the Medical Act 1983 to require disclosure of otherwise confidential information for the purposes of the Council or any of its committees.

So the common law duty of confidentiality is by no means absolute, and may be modified or overridden in a number of relatively familiar situations. However, one can see immediately that although such exceptions to the general rule may well be firmly established in English law, they involve precisely the type of encroachments against the individual that are likely to provoke challenge as infringements of, or as incompatible with, Art 8. We shall look at that possibility later in this chapter.

---

10 *W v Edgell* [1990] 1 All ER 835.

11 *Woolgar v Chief Constable of the Sussex Police* [1999] 3 All ER 604 CA.

12 GMC, 2000.

THE HEALTHCARE PROFESSIONS' VIEW

Traditional views

It is not surprising that confidentiality has always been recognised, from Hippocrates onwards, as fundamental to the relationship between patients and healthcare professionals. This is reflected very clearly in the guidance published by the various professions to their members, which usually contains a mixture of ethical, legal and practical advice. For example, the GMC's latest guidance[13] sets out, not only the principles of confidentiality which every doctor should bear in mind when receiving or communicating patient information, but also the practical safeguards to be employed. The UKCC's 1992 *Code of Professional Conduct* contains comparable guidance for nurses, midwives and health visitors.

The DoH has also long encouraged a wider appreciation of the need for the principle of confidentiality to be observed throughout the health service. For example, its own guidance[14] attempts to summarise the legal requirements as well as the practical difficulties likely to be routinely encountered not only by professionals but also by managers and non-professional staff.

Current practice

However, many observers would say that, at ground level, the rights and duties arising from patient confidentiality are honoured more in the breach than the observance. This may be because of a presumption that all patients impliedly consent to information about them being disseminated throughout the healthcare community. After all, in the normal course of treatment, there may be many people – clinicians in different specialities, nurses, laboratory technicians, hospital porters – to whom details of the patient's condition may have to be provided in order to enable effective treatment to be provided. Alternatively, the notion of confidentiality may not cross the minds of those involved in the patient's care, because it is genuinely believed that such dissemination, for example, for research or statistical purposes in connection with a national register for a particular medical condition, is always, in some undefined but incontrovertible way, for the public good and therefore 'in the public interest'.

The risk of routine disclosure of medical records without the patient's specific knowledge or express permission raises important issues for the related doctrine of consent to treatment. For example, should a patient's

---

13 GMC, 2000.
14 DoH, 1996a.

express consent for disclosure of clinical details to a specialist colleague at another hospital be sought at the outset of a particular treatment, perhaps on the initial consent form? If so, and it is refused, does the absence of consent prevent the doctor from providing that treatment? Such issues are discussed elsewhere in this book, but it is worth noting here that many problems of consent and disclosure have traditionally been overcome by the use of anonymisation of patient data.

Anonymisation of records

In 1997, the *Caldicott Report: On the Review of Patient-Identifiable Information*[15] made a number of detailed recommendations to the NHS on how to safeguard patient confidentiality through the anonymisation of the information being exchanged. The effect of anonymisation is likely to be scrutinised under the glare of Art 8. In the meantime, however, it was examined recently by the Court of Appeal in *R v Department of Health ex p Source Informatics Ltd* [2000] Lloyd's Rep 76. In this case, a company which collected prescription data for sale to pharmaceutical companies to assist their marketing analyses challenged the legality of DoH restrictions on anonymised prescribing information from GPs being passed on by pharmacists to the commercial sector. The judge at the first hearing said that when patients provided their GPs with information about their ailments, they did not impliedly consent to such data being disclosed for non-medical purposes, that is, to a medical data company. He held that even if the data were anonymised, such a disclosure amounted to a breach of confidence which could not be justified in the public interest.

The Court of Appeal disagreed. It reviewed the legal principles involved, and although it left uncertain many issues arising from patient confidentiality, it concluded that because anonymisation of the prescription forms removed the information capable of identifying the patient, it succeeded in removing the very data capable of making that information confidential to the patient. In other words, by reference to the *Coco v Clark* principles discussed on p 129, above, the remaining information no longer had the 'necessary quality of confidence about it'. It was a view shared by Lord Justice Bingham in *W v Edgell*,[16] although the DoH's guidance (DoH, 1996a) warns that removal of personal details may not be sufficient in itself to protect a patient's identity if, for example, he/she has a particularly rare condition.

---

15 DoH, 1997.
16 [1990] 1 All ER 835.

ACCESS TO HEALTH RECORDS

The context

The other side of the confidentiality coin is freedom of information. If the cloak of confidentiality is not to become a blanket of secrecy, any measures taken to protect information must include provisions to allow controlled access. For this reason, the right of privacy enshrined in Art 8 is conspicuously balanced by the right to freedom of expression and exchange of information contained in Art 10. Similarly, as most of the professional and DoH guidance recognises, the common law duty to keep patient information confidential is balanced by the right of the patient – and, in certain circumstances, others – to obtain access to that information.

Miscellaneous legislation

Leaving aside the question of contractual rights, which the parties to a contract (for example, for private healthcare) can agree between themselves, the right of access to confidential information is usually statutory. For example, in the context of litigation, the Supreme Court Act 1981 and the Civil Procedure Rules 1998 grant rights to litigants to see certain categories of otherwise confidential documents held by their opponents. Another example is the Access to Medical Reports Act 1988, which entitles individuals to see medical reports about them prepared by doctors for third parties such as employers or life assurance companies.

Common law

However, the common law also recognises that patients have a right of access to their medical records, quite apart from any contractual entitlement. This may, however, be restricted in the patient's best interests, that is, if to see the information would cause the patient undue distress. The issue was discussed in the case of *Martin*.[17] As one would expect from the analysis of common law principles above, the Court of Appeal considered the matter to involve not so much a right of the patient, as a duty owed to the patient by the doctor and the health authority to act in the patient's best interests.

---

17   *R v Mid Glamorgan Family Health Services ex p Martin* [1995] 1 All ER 356.

Access to Health Records Act 1990

In practice, the patient's right of access to medical records has for the last few years been controlled by the Access to Health Records Act 1990. This provided, in summary, that patients or persons authorised on their behalf could have access to health records held by, or on behalf of, health professionals. However, by defining the categories of entitlement to access, it reinforced the general rule of confidentiality, thereby reflecting both sides of the coin. It is significant that the Act was passed as a response to the decision of European Court of Human Rights (the Court) about Art 8 in the case of *Gaskin*.[18] In that case, Mr Gaskin wanted access to social services files about his childhood in care, for the purposes of a negligence action against the local council concerned. He was refused access on the grounds that the consent of the contributors to those records was necessary. The Court accepted that confidentiality of public records was important, but considered that the lack of any provision for an independent arbiter to review the question of disclosure in the absence of that consent was in breach of Mr Gaskin's right under Art 8 to respect for his private and family life.

The repercussions of the *Gaskin* case should not be underestimated. The Access to Health Records Act 1990 represented a significant response to the requirement for a statutory safeguard for patients' rights of access; and, although it has since been mostly repealed (except in relation to dead patients), its replacement, the DPA 1998, is now the dominant component of the existing framework of English law relating to the protection of, and access to, confidential information. The DPA 1998 is now the principal means by which the protection of, and access to, patient records is regulated, and we must therefore examine its main features.

THE DPA 1998

Background

The DPA came into force in March 2000. However, some of its provisions will be phased in gradually until 2007. It is important to understand its European context.

The implementation of its predecessor, the DPA 1984, was in response to a 1981 European treaty[19] and introduced into English law a new and detailed statutory framework governing the processing, storage and disclosure of information about individual citizens held on computer. At the time, the

---

18   *Gaskin v UK* (1989) 12 EHRR 36.
19   Treaty 108.

legislation was viewed by many as relatively marginal, affecting only the comparatively few areas of commercial and government activity in which computers were in everyday use. However, the arrival of a new European Union Directive in 1995[20] took matters further, addressing the new issues created by the enormous growth in the use and capabilities of computers in people's business and domestic lives. The Directive's object was partly to harmonise data protection law throughout the Community and thereby facilitate the free movement of data between Members States, but principally:

> ... to protect the fundamental rights and freedoms of natural persons, and in particular their right to privacy with respect to the processing of personal data.

It is in this Directive that we see the 'right to privacy' expressed not as a combination of duties and obligations arising from a relationship between confider and recipient, as understood by English common law before Spycatcher, but as a 'fundamental right' – a point dealt with below.

An outline of the Act

The DPA 1998 is the means by which the UK has implemented the Directive. It is a long and intricate piece of legislation, and we can do no more here than touch on some of the features most relevant to the management of health records.

From the definition of its key terms, it is clear from the outset that the DPA 1998 is designed to regulate virtually every aspect of activity in relation to the storage and use of personal information, in order to prevent damage or distress to individuals. In summary, it will generally be a criminal offence to store or use information about living individuals ('data subjects') unless the data controller is registered with the Data Protection Commissioner established by the Act to monitor and enforce compliance (s 17). Breach of the Act's provisions to provide the requisite information to data subjects may attract an enforcement notice by the Data Protection Commissioner; or an information notice, requiring confirmation of the nature and extent of the data held; or, in extreme cases, prosecution and fines for unlawful obtaining or selling of personal data.

Like its predecessor, the DPA 1998 is expressly based on eight Data Protection Principles against which the detailed provisions are to be interpreted. With regard to medical records, the core elements of the new principles may be summarised as follows:

(a) personal data must be processed 'fairly and lawfully' (see First Principle);

---

20 95/46/EC.

(b) data shall only be obtained for one or more specified and lawful purpose and shall not be used for another, incompatible purpose (see Second Principle);

(c) data must be accurate and kept up to date (see Fourth Principle);

(d) data must be kept safe and secure (see Seventh Principle).

Almost all medical records and almost every type of information contained in them are now covered by the DPA 1998. The 'personal data' referred to in the Act comprise not only information held on a computer, but also (unlike the 1984 Act) information on paper or in other forms that is recorded as part of a 'relevant filing system', that is, which is structured in such a way that details relating to a specific person are readily accessible, such as traditional medical records (s 1(1)). Even where the information is not part of a relevant filing system, it will still be caught by the Act if it forms part of 'an accessible record', a term which includes (*inter alia*) 'a health record' consisting of information about the individual's physical or mental health which 'has been made by or on behalf of a health professional in connection with the care of that individual' (ss 68–69).

'Personal data' are data which relate to a living individual (the 'data subject') who can be identified from those data either alone or in conjunction with other information held by the data controller (s 1(1)). This includes expressions of opinion or statements of intention in relation to that individual. A subsidiary category of information is defined as 'sensitive personal data', that is, relating to the subject's physical or mental health or condition or his sexual life (s 2). It is clear, therefore, that the DPA 1998 is intended to cover all medical records, a point emphasised by the fact that the Access to Health Records Act 1990 is expressly repealed except in respect of records relating to patients who have died.

Restrictions on processing data

The first main purpose of the DPA 1998 is to control the way in which such data are 'processed'. This is a comprehensive term covering almost every conceivable activity in relation to such information. Under s 1(1), 'processing' includes the, 'obtaining, recording or holding ... organisation, adaptation or alteration ... retrieval, consultation or use ... disclosure ... alignment, combination, blocking, erasure or destruction' of data.

A 'data processor' is anybody who does one of these things. It will therefore include hospital staff, GPs and their staff; while a 'data controller' is anybody who determines the purpose for which, or manner in which, the data are processed. This will include NHS organisations and GPs alike. Almost everyone who reads or uses patient records in any way – even putting copies in the post or reading them on screen – will be 'processing' data and will therefore be bound by the provisions of the DPA 1998. This will include not only professional staff but, for example, hospital managers and GP receptionists.

Within this framework, the primary legal obligation of data processors and controllers under the DPA 1998's 'First Data Protection Principle' is to process patient data 'fairly and lawfully'. Every question about the way in which information is treated must be tested against that principle. To be 'fair' the data must, in general terms, have been obtained from the patient honestly or in accordance with a legal obligation; the patient must have been told the purposes for which the information is to be processed; and the rules for providing access to the data subject must also have been observed (Sched 1, Pt 2).

The word 'lawfully' is not defined. However, it implies that the processing must not be in breach of any other existing legal restrictions, for example, the common law duty of confidence. This emphasises the point that the DPA 1998 does not replace the common law framework of confidentiality and access, but is an addition to it – albeit a dominant one.

Most importantly, it should be noted that, to be considered fair and lawful, the processing of patient records (as 'sensitive personal data') must meet at least one detailed specific criterion from Sched 2 and at least one from Sched 3. In summary, these are:

(a) that the patient has given 'explicit consent' to the processing ('explicit' is not defined, but Guidance from the Data Protection Commissioner suggests that it means that the patient's consent must be absolutely clear, that is, that it should cover the specific purpose of the processing); or

(b) that the processing is necessary for the purposes of exercising or performing a right or obligation imposed by law; or

(c) that it is necessary to protect the vital interests of the patient or another person where consent cannot be given by or on behalf of the patient, or where the data controller cannot reasonably be expected to obtain it or it has been unreasonably withheld; or

(d) that the information has already been deliberately made public by the patient; or

(e) that the processing is necessary for the purpose of actual or prospective legal proceedings, or for obtaining legal advice, or for the purpose of establishing, exercising or defending legal rights; or

(f) that it is necessary for the purposes of 'legitimate interests' pursued by the data controller or the third party to whom the data are to be disclosed, unless disclosure would be unwarranted because it would prejudice the data subject; or

(g) that it is necessary for the administration of justice, or for the exercise of statutory functions; or

(h) that it is necessary for medical purposes (including preventive medicine, diagnosis, research, care, treatment and management of healthcare services), and is carried out by a healthcare professional (as defined in s 69) or by a person who owes the patient an equivalent duty of confidentiality; or

(i) that it is authorised by an Order of the Secretary of State.

For the most part, the processing of patient records will be necessary for medical purposes (Sched 3, para 8), so one can avoid the need for consent in that way. However, one can see areas of uncertainty where important issues will arise. Some of these are discussed on p 143, below.

Providing access to data

In line with the Directive, the second main purpose of the DPA 1998 is to enable data subjects to discover what data are held about them and what they are being used for. Every individual (that is, competent adult, or, in the case of data about a child, the person with parental responsibility) is entitled to require the relevant data controller to confirm within 40 days of the request a description of the data being held about him/her; the purpose or purposes for which the data are intended to be processed; and any other information required in the particular circumstances to ensure that the processing is fair (s 7). Any such request by the patient must be in writing and accompanied by the statutory fee, unless the supply of the information would identify another individual without that person's consent, or a copy would be impossible or involve 'disproportionate effort' on the part of the data controller (s 8). Failure to comply with a proper request will attract enforcement or penal sanctions from the Data Protection Commissioner.

Exemptions

Just as the common law relating to confidentiality contains crucial exceptions to the general rules, the DPA 1998 similarly contains a number of exemptions from its general regime, some within the Act itself, others by way of Orders made by the Secretary of State under the Act. Within the context of medical records, these include an exemption from the general processing and subject access provisions where the data is processed for the prevention or detection of crime (for example, DNA or blood samples – see p 131, above) (s 29); or for research purposes (s 33). In addition, there is an exception which goes further than the 'best interests' exception in s 4 of the Access to Health Records Act 1990, but echoes s 5: namely, that patient records can be withheld from patients if the appropriate health professional involved considers that disclosure would be likely to cause serious harm to the physical or mental health or condition of the data subject or any other person.[21]

THE IMPACT OF THE HRA 1998

The new duty

As explained in more detail in the introduction to this book, s 6 of the HRA 1998 makes it unlawful for any public authority a duty to act in a way which is incompatible with the rights set out in the European Convention and listed in Sched 1 of the HRA 1998. The term 'public authority' will obviously include in this context all NHS organisations such as trusts and health authorities since they are bodies whose functions are of a public nature. However, it will also include organisations performing a public function, such as the UKCC and GMC, and is likely to include GPs and other health professionals to the extent that they are performing NHS functions.[22] Furthermore, it is important to note for the purposes of this discussion of confidentiality law that even in the context of private healthcare, professionals will not necessarily be exempt from the requirements of the HRA 1998. This is because as well as this 'vertical' application of the HRA 1998 direct to public authorities, there will also be a 'horizontal' application in the sense that the courts (as public authorities themselves) are obliged in every case to interpret common law in a way which is compatible with Convention rights. Furthermore, the courts are obliged by s 3 of the HRA 1998 to give effect to all legislation, so far as it is possible to do so, in a way which is compatible with Convention rights. This will mean that any ambiguities in legislative provisions, including, for example, under DPA 1998 will be resolved in accordance with Convention rights, an obvious advantage to litigants.[23]

The remedies

The HRA 1998 provides two alternative avenues for redress. Either the 'victim' of an abuse can bring a claim against the alleged offender, for example, for damages or an injunction, on the grounds that the offender has acted incompatibly with a Convention right and, therefore, unlawfully (s 7); or if the offender is excused by the provisions of the domestic legislation, the court can be asked to make an Order that the legislation is itself incompatible with the Convention (s 4) – and the relevant Secretary of State will then have

---

21 Data Protection (Subject Access Modification) (Health) Order 2000 SI 2000/413.
22 See the Lord Chancellor's comments during the House of Lords Committee Stage: 583 HL Official Report (5th series) col 811 (24 November 1997).
23 See Hunt, 1998.

the option (not the obligation) to ask Parliament to make an Order to remedy this defect (s 10).

Effect of Arts 8 and 10

We can see from this brief outline of the existing domestic law relating to confidentiality of and access to health records that the common law principles have been strengthened and extended by the highly detailed statutory framework of the DPA 1998. But is this new composite framework likely to be affected by Arts 8 and 10 of the European Convention which the HRA 1998 incorporated into English law on 2 October 2000? Will the present system for creating, storing, using and disclosing patient records be declared incompatible with the Convention, thereby rendering the activities of NHS organisations unlawful and open to judicial challenge?

The DPA 1998 itself offers some clues. First, it derives, as we have seen, from a European Directive whose linked objectives were the harmonisation of data protection law, the free movement of data between Member States, and the protection of the individual's 'right to privacy'. Until the HRA 1998, the notion of individuals having any 'fundamental rights' was foreign to English law. For centuries, accepted political and legal theory in the UK has been that individuals can do what they like unless specifically prevented, either by Parliament through statute, or by the courts through the application of the common law principles that have been gradually developed over the centuries. Accordingly, English common law contains, as we have seen, no specific right of privacy but a patchwork quilt of duties and obligations under the headings of, for example, trespass, defamation and – most notably – confidentiality. The effect of the DPA 1998 was to introduce into English law the European concept of a specific and fundamental right, in the sense recognised by Art 8, and a positive framework for protecting it, as required by the Court.[24] Consequently, it is unlikely that a court applying Art 8 under the HRA 1998 would find significant incompatibilities between it and the DPA 1998.

Secondly, although the DPA 1998 introduces a new and apparently comprehensive statutory regime for the protection of and access to personal data such as health records, it is important to note that it is an addition to, not a replacement for, the existing common law framework of confidentiality. For one thing, when the First Data Principle refers to 'lawful' processing, it is a reference to the legal context in which the Act should be read and operated; and for another, the common law will continue to govern data not covered by

---

24   *X and Y v The Netherlands* (1985) 8 EHRR 235 [93].

the DPA 1998, for example, information not contained in a s 68 'health record'. This is consistent with the aims of the HRA 1998, which does not replace all existing domestic law but simply requires the courts to interpret it afresh in the light of Convention rights. This may mean, as the Lord Chancellor said in the Parliamentary debate on the Human Rights Bill, that judges would deliver 'a law of privacy', but this would be simply a development of the common law.

Thirdly, the DPA 1998 attempts a balance between protection and access. This balance reflects not only the common law tension between the right of confidentiality, the right of access, and the public interest, but also the apparent conflict between Art 8's right of privacy and Art 10's right to receive and impart information. As we have seen from the text of the Articles above, both contain specific reservations allowing the State to limit these rights, and the intricate framework of the DPA 1998 and common law may be seen in this respect as entirely consistent with the scheme of the Convention. Certainly, it was argued by the British Government in the Earl Spencer case,[25] even without reference to the DPA 1998, that the common law remedies under breach of confidence, trespass, nuisance, etc, satisfied the balancing reservations of Arts 8 and 10.

Nevertheless, it is likely to be those reservations by which that framework will be judged. In approaching this task, the English courts will be obliged under the HRA 1998 to take into account previous decisions by the Court in Strasbourg in so far as they are in the opinion of the court relevant (s 2(1)). The 'Strasbourg case law' imports the requirement of proportionality whenever the domestic authorities or law permit restrictions on the exercise of the rights contained in Arts 8 and 10. Articles 8(2) and 10(2) both permit restrictions 'necessary in a democratic society'.

There are few European cases which offer solid precedent, but some do offer guidance. In respect of the patient's right of confidentiality, it was held in the case of Z v Finland,[26] for example, that the disclosure of a wife's HIV status during the trial of her husband for rape was considered to be a breach of her rights under Art 8. Although disclosure of this evidence had been necessary in the circumstances 'for the prevention of disorder or crime, for the protection of health or morals, or for the protection of the rights and freedoms of others' (echoing the public interest principle in W v Edgell),[27] it was not necessary for the trial court's judgment to identify the witnesses. This reinforces the Caldicott thesis (see p 133, above) that health records should be anonymised whenever possible.

---

25 Spencer v UK [1998] EHRLR 348. Here, failure by the applicant to even attempt redress in the domestic courts through breach of confidence, allowed the Commission to find the application inadmissible for failure to exhaust domestic remedies.

26 Z v Finland (1998) 25 EHRR 371.

27 W v Edgell [1990] 1 All ER 835.

With regard to the rights of patient to see their own records, the case of *Gaskin* is helpful (see p 135, above). In that case, the criticism was not so much of the decision to refuse the applicant access to the personal records about him, but of the absence of any specific system for handling such requests and dealing with appeals against refusal. As we have seen, it was that case which led to the creation of the system enshrined in the Access to Health Records Act 1990. It may well be argued in response to any future such challenge that the introduction of that Act and of its successor, the DPA 1998 – particularly the role of the Data Protection Commissioner in supervision and enforcement – is more than adequate to meet the compatibility and proportionality tests.

Similarly, the case of *McGinley*[28] considered an application by two ex-servicemen for disclosure of Government documents which contained information about the nuclear tests in the 1950s which they said had caused them health problems. The Court held that the question of access to documents relating to the danger to which the applicants had been exposed was sufficiently closely linked to their private and family lives to raise an issue under Art 8. Although the application failed for other reasons, it was held that in these circumstances Art 8 required an effective and accessible procedure to enable such persons to seek all relevant and appropriate information. In other words, a defence on the grounds of national security would not have succeeded. It is possible, therefore, that in certain circumstances, the comparable exemption in the DPA 1998 or under common law might be adjudged incompatible with the patient's rights under Arts 8 and 10.

These decisions suggest that any vulnerability to challenge by patients will lie in the exceptions to and exemptions from the general common law rules and the Data Protection Principles in the DPA 1998. The courts will be examining whether or not those exceptions and exemptions fall properly within the State interventions envisaged in Arts 8 and 10.

Potential problems

In practical terms, there are a wide range of every day situations in a hospital or surgery in which the legal rights and duties of NHS data controllers may not be clear – it is impossible in this chapter to cover every eventuality. However, one example would be where a trust has the opportunity to generate income by selling prescribing data to a data collection company. Will the court necessarily agree with the Court of Appeal's view in the *Source Informatics* case[29] that anonymisation is sufficient to dispel any common law

---

28 *McGinley and Egan v UK* (1998) 27 EHRR 1.

29 *R v DoH ex p Source Informatics Ltd* [2000] Lloyd's Rep 76.

duty of confidentiality? Or should the process of anonymising prescriptions be deemed 'processing' for the purposes of the DPA 1998, as the DoH seemed to be arguing in that case? If so, what would be the position if the patient had explicitly indicated his/her opposition to such a process? Would Art 8 enable a GP to rely on the legitimate interests exception under Sched 2 to the DPA 1998, where the sole purpose of the exercise was commercial and contractual?

Again, the issue of disclosing information capable of identifying the patient has caused difficulties. The increasing sophistication of information technology has facilitated the production of group studies and the creation of national databases to assist with the treatment and prevention of conditions such as cancer. However, with rare conditions such as CJD, the possibility of a patient being identified even by anonymised information can never be completely eliminated as the GMC's guidance[30] recognises. It is likely that where a legitimate public health purpose can be shown here (for example, under the Public Health (Control of Disease) Act 1984), the conditions of Art 8 will be adjudged to have been met. However, that is not to say that patients will not challenge the disclosure.

Another possible difficulty might arise from relying on an exemption under Scheds 2 and 3 of the DPA 1998 based on a legal obligation. For instance, under s 35A of the Medical Act 1983, the GMC is entitled to demand disclosure of information from any person in order to assist with the performance of the GMC's functions. But what if the patient is specifically asked first, for example, as a matter of courtesy, and explicitly refuses disclosure out of loyalty to the doctor: does the exemption available to the data controller override the patient's views, or would disclosure be unlawful in the terms of the First Data Protection Principle and Art 8?

Similarly, the Secretary of State is empowered by the DPA 1998 to make Orders in respect of disclosure in a variety of circumstances without the data subject's consent. For example, the Data Protection (Processing of Sensitive Personal Data) Order 2000[31] allows disclosure of patient records without consent for a range of purposes 'in the substantial public interest', including for the prevention and detection of crime or protecting the public against incompetence or misconduct. The Order falls squarely within Scheds 2 and 3 of the DPA 1998 allowing the disclosure of health records without the patient's consent; but will such blanket authorisations be considered consistent with the specific reservations set out in Art 8, or will patients be able to challenge them successfully as illegitimate encroachments on the basic principle of right to private and family life?

---

30 GMC, 2000.
31 SI 2000/417.

Comparable challenges may emerge to the restrictions on access. For example, a statutory instrument allows data controllers to withhold information from patients under the DPA 1998 if disclosure 'would be likely to cause serious harm to the physical or mental health or condition of the data subject or any other person' (see p 139 above).[32] This provision can no doubt be stoutly defended in principle, but a challenge by a patient claiming an infringement of his/her autonomous right to know the truth cannot be ruled out.

CONCLUSIONS

Overall, the field of confidentiality of and access to patient records is unlikely to prove immediately fertile for challenges under Arts 8 and 10. The DPA 1998 is a thoughtful and wide ranging addition to a well established set of common law principles, and represents a comprehensive enactment of the Directive. Accordingly, it is likely that the courts – which have already indicated in other contexts that their approach will be firmly rooted in the reality of existing legal principles – will regard the current composite framework as being broadly compatible with the Convention. One should, however, add three notes of caution.

First, although this chapter has dealt principally with the right of privacy in the limited sense of confidentiality of information, the scope of Art 8 is much wider. It has been widely interpreted to mean the individual's fundamental right of autonomy and self-determination, including the right 'to establish and develop relationships',[33] and the right to treatment for gender reassignment.[34] This concept of a fundamental right to make one's own decisions about oneself is inherent in the principles of consent to medical treatment, and has also been applied to Coke's *dictum* that 'a man's home is his castle', of which we were recently reminded in the context of a health authority promising a patient a home for life.[35] So, although the courts have already warned that they will not be impressed by far fetched claims[36] there is no doubt that they are obliged by the HRA 1998, and will be encouraged by the changing social and ethical climate, to approach the question of confidentiality in a new and radical way.

Secondly, the nature of modern healthcare means that confidential information about a patient can seldom be restricted to the traditional small circle of patient, immediate family, and the family doctor. We expect it –

---

32   Data Protection (Subject Access Modification) (Health) Order 2000 SI 2000/413.

33   *Niemetz v Germany* (1992) 16 EHRR 97.

34   *R v North West Lancashire HA ex p A and Others* [1999] LLR 399.

35   *R v North and East Devon HA ex p Coughlan* [1999] Lloyd's Rep 306.

36   *R v North West Lancashire HA ex p A and Others* [1999] LLR 399.

even require it – to be passed, quite legitimately and usefully, among many different professionals and managers. In cases involving community care, there will often be several different agencies involved, some from outside the NHS (see the Health and Social Care Act 2001, particularly s 60). In respect of conditions such as cancer or heart disease, there will also be national agencies set up to gather data from as many patients as possible. The whole issue of confidentiality, therefore, has for some time been moving away from the traditional question of whether or not patient records are to be disclosed to third parties, to the presumption that they will, and the consequent need for effective and consistently applied controls.

Thirdly, the starting point for this chapter was the proliferation of information as a result of advances in technology. There is no doubt that, for the NHS, the benefits of information technology are matched by the risks. Although it was only in October 2000, for example, that GPs were formally permitted to keep patient records on computer,[37] the vision set out in the DoH's information strategy, *Information for Health* (1998) and in *The NHS Plan* (2000) is of an NHS within the next few years where the whole community of GPs and hospitals will be linked electronically, allowing instant exchange of data, remote diagnosis and other forms of telemedicine, such as on-line prescribing; and where every patient will have an on-line electronic patient record (EPR) of their current in-patient treatment, a lifelong on-line electronic health record (EHR), and a 'smart card' to enable easier access to these records from anywhere in the country.

The dangers which this new technological landscape poses to security and confidentiality are obvious. The extent to which patients successfully challenge them as infringements of the human rights under Arts 8 and 10 will largely depend on the good sense of health professionals and managers, the effectiveness of the NHS Information Authority and the new National Confidentiality and Security Advisory Body in formulating and monitoring policy, and the practical implementation of the DPA 1998. It is too late for Robert Redford to turn back the clock or return the information revolution to Pandora's box; it is not too late for the NHS to reappraise its approach to confidential patient information and take the necessary steps to minimise the risks of breaching patients' human rights.

---

37   NHS (General Medical Services) Amendment (No 4) Regulations 2000 SI 2000/2383.

CHAPTER 10

VULNERABLE ADULTS – CONFIDENTIALITY AND INTER-DISCIPLINARY WORKING

Katherine S Williams and John Williams

INTRODUCTION

A dilemma facing those charged with law reform is the difficulty of striking a balance between the desire of society to intervene to protect vulnerable adults, and the danger that intervention will violate their human rights. Vulnerable adults need special consideration for a number of reasons. They are adults and, despite being vulnerable, often have legal capacity. Defining legal capacity is difficult, but it is important that professionals recognise that an individual may lack capacity in some areas, but have it in others. Unlike other adults, their vulnerability may mean that care is provided through intervention rather than choice. When possessing capacity, the vulnerable adult should be centrally involved in decisions on intervention and the provision of care. In addition, the care is more likely to include a number of professionals from different areas of health and social care, and from the statutory and independent sectors. They often work in an inter-disciplinary or multidisciplinary team where issues of confidentiality are particularly problematic and are tested to the limit. The placing of rights at the centre of decision making has increased the control of individuals over personal information, although making confidentiality more complex for the professionals. This chapter considers these problems, outlines the different approach of the new rights culture and assesses whether the new guidance provides adequate safeguards against abuse.

VULNERABLE ADULT

'Vulnerable adult' is a term that is increasingly recognised and used by medical and social work practitioners. Although not a precise term, it covers adults who may be considered exposed to a risk sufficient to necessitate some form of intervention. The risk may be of physical or sexual abuse by another, self-neglect, financial abuse or some other form of harm or injury linked to their vulnerability. At present, the law provides very little protection for vulnerable adults. Unlike incompetent children,[1] regard must be had to the right that adults have to autonomy. In identifying the threshold criteria for intervention in the lives of vulnerable adults, law must carefully balance the need, desire or duty to protect, with the right we all enjoy to make our own decisions (good or bad). This point was clearly reinforced in a medical context by the Court of Appeal in the case of *Re T (Adult: Refusal of Treatment).*[2] Lord Donaldson MR said:

> An adult patient who ... suffers from no mental incapacity has an absolute right to choose whether to consent to medical treatment, to refuse it or to choose one rather than another of the treatments being offered ... This right of choice is not limited to decisions which others may regard as sensible. It exists notwithstanding that the reasons for making the choice are rational, irrational, unknown or even non-existent.[3]

The threshold of intervention arising out of this judgment is that of incapacity. The 'capable' person may exercise autonomy (even if this leads to a 'foolish' or life threatening decision). However, for the incapacitated individual medical intervention without consent is possible if it is in the 'best interests' of the patient.[4] Fortunately, the courts have adopted a functional approach to determining a person's capacity rather than one based on status or ability to make rational decisions.[5] However, vulnerability and incapacity are not conterminous. A clear definition of 'vulnerable adult' is elusive. Section 80(6) of the Care Standards Act 2000 defines 'vulnerable adult' as:

> ... an adult to whom accommodation and nursing or personal care are provided in a care home;

> an adult to whom personal care is provided in their own home under arrangements made by a domiciliary carer; or

> an adult to whom prescribed services are provided by an independent hospital, independent clinic, independent medical agency or NHS body.

This is in the context of the Secretary of State being required under the provisions of the Act to keep a list of individuals who are unsuitable to work with vulnerable adults.[6] This definition, which concentrates on a person being

---

1   The House of Lords in *Gillick v West Norfolk and Wisbech AHA* [1986] AC 112 recognised that children can consent to any intervention which they have 'sufficient understanding and intelligence' to make a competent decision about. This can be done without the involvement of the parents. However, on the other hand, according to the Court of Appeal in *Re W (A Minor) (Medical Treatment)* [1993] Fam 64 and *Re R* [1991] 3 WLR 592 doctors can force an intervention on a competent minor. For further discussion and an analysis of whether the HRA 1998 will have an impact see Garwood-Gowers, Chapter 14.

2   [1992] 4 All ER 649.

3   *Ibid*, pp 652–53.

4   *Re F (Mental Patient: Sterilisation)* [1989] 2 All ER 545.

5   See Thorpe J in *Re C (Adult: Refusal of Medical Treatment)* [1994] 1 All ER 819 and the Court of Appeal in *Re MB* [1997] 2 FLR 426.

6   See s 70.

in receipt of a particular service, does not provide a comprehensive definition capable of being used as threshold criteria for interfering with basic rights. To move away from the consensual receipt of services to the 'power' of intervention requires a more robust definition that embraces the concept of 'risk'.

In its report *Mental Incapacity*, the Law Commission defined 'vulnerable person at risk' as including:

> ... any person aged 16 or over who (1) is or may be in need of community care services by reason of mental or other disability, age or illness and who (2) is or may be unable to take care of himself or herself, or unable to protect himself or herself against significant harm or serious exploitation.[7]

As a working definition, this is helpful, although it raises many subtle questions of interpretation. It establishes that vulnerability includes people lacking capacity, but is not restricted to that client group. The physically frail, the chronically sick and elderly people may (not must) fall within this definition. This definition is sufficiently broad to include social and financial, or other forms of vulnerability, though it is unclear how those who use it will interpret it. The definition has been adopted in the Department of Health guidance on the protection of vulnerable adults at risk, *No Secrets*.[8] The guidance for Wales, *In Safe Hands*, also adopts the same definition.[9]

Public authority

Under the Human Rights Act (HRA) 1998,[10] rights are to be given a new and more prominent position in the courts and in all official actions. For example, all legislation, new and old, must, as far as possible, be interpreted in a way that is compatible with European Convention on Human Rights (ECHR).[11] It does not incorporate the Convention into our law as such, but courts are obliged both to decide cases in line with its provisions and to consider Strasbourg case law,[12] unless they are prevented from doing so by primary legislation or provisions made under primary legislation.[13] This ensures a human rights perspective in all judicial decision making.

The main impact of the HRA 1998 is on 'public authorities'. It is now unlawful for a public authority to act in a way that is incompatible with a

---

7   Law Com 231 1995.

8   DoH, 1999b, paras 2.3–2.4.

9   Social Services Inspectorate for Wales, 1999; see para 7.2.

10 The Act came into force fully on 2 October 2000, but had previously been in force, in part at least, in Scotland and Wales.

11 HRA 1998, s 3.

12 *Ibid*, s 2(1).

13 *Ibid*, ss 3 and 6.

Convention right[14] (unless there is a clear statutory obligation to the contrary).[15] In the exercise of all functions, the Convention and its case law bind public authorities.[16] All public authorities have a positive obligation to ensure the effective protection of Convention rights. It is in this way that the HRA 1998 has its most profound effect. Unfortunately, the Act does not define with any great precision 'public authority', although it does give some indication of what is to be included. It expressly includes 'any person certain of whose functions are functions of a public nature'.[17] Clearly, a body that is a wholly public authority (such as the police, local education authorities, social services or probation) is within the definition. However, the definition will also include some bodies that exist in the independent sector. In talking about 'any person', the Act includes the independent sector when carrying out public functions. A similar problem arises with residential care homes and registered nursing homes. They may make provision for people who are funded by a public authority (a local authority or a health authority), and for those who are privately funded. Does this mean that they are not public authorities? Does the fact that they have to be registered under the Residential Homes Act 1984[18] bring them into the realms of public authority in all aspects of their activity? These are complex issues similar to those raised in cases of judicial review. The judiciary will need to identify the principles applicable in such cases; clarity at present is elusive.[19]

SHARING INFORMATION IN AN INTER-AGENCY SETTING

The White Paper, *Modernising Social Services*,[20] emphasised the importance of providing appropriate protection for children and vulnerable adults. In the Introduction, it states that:

---

14 *Ibid*, s 6(1).

15 The HRA 1998 preserves the supremacy of Parliament and, therefore, where applying an Act of Parliament would lead to a breach of human rights, everyone (including the courts) is bound to apply the Act and breach the right. However, where there are two possible interpretations of an Act of Parliament, one of which would respect human rights and the other which would not, then they must act in accordance with the interpretation which upholds the right, even if this may not have been intended by Parliament when they passed the legislation.

16 HRA 1998, s 7.

17 *Ibid*, s 6(3)(b).

18 To be replaced by the Care Standards Act 2000.

19 See Sherlock, 1998, pp 43–61.

20 Cm 4169 (1998), HMSO.

> Any decent society owes to every child a safe and secure upbringing, and to every elderly or disabled man or woman the right to live in dignity, free from fear of abuse. These duties must be given greater effect in future.[21]

In Safe Hands and *No Secrets*, provide guidance on how adult protection procedures can be implemented in Wales and England. They are designed to achieve a co-ordinated response by the various agencies (health, social services, police and housing) that may be called upon to respond to cases of abuse. Both documents define abuse as 'a violation of an individual's human and civil rights by any other person or persons'.[22]

An essential feature of both approaches is the need for different statutory agencies to work together. In part, this is a recognition that problems rarely come in self-contained compartments. They straddle a number of different statutory remits. Furthermore, attempts at distinguishing health and social care are often futile. Is it possible to determine whether a bath in the community is a health or social need?[23] The emphasis on inter-agency work reflects the success of this approach in child protection. The recently revised version of *Working Together*[24] highlights a number of benefits to this approach. These include 'sound decision making based on information sharing, thorough assessment, critical analysis and professional judgment'.[25] Although *Working Together* identifies the need for information sharing, it does not provide any clear guidance on when and how this should be done. It refers to comments by Butler-Sloss LJ in *Re G (A Minor)*:[26]

> The consequences of inter-agency co-operation is that there has to be free exchange of information between social workers and police officers engaged in an investigation ... The information obtained by social workers in the course of their duties is however confidential and covered by the umbrella of public interest immunity ... It can however be disclosed to fellow members of the child protection team engaged in the investigation of the possible abuse of the child concerned.

Three points need to be noted. First, any exchange of information protocols or policies in relation to child protection will be informed by the welfare principle.[27] Secondly, although the quotation refers to exchange of information between social workers and the police, it has wider implications for other professions including healthcare. Thirdly, children of 16 or 17 years,

---

21 *Ibid*, para 1.4.

22 See DoH, 1999b, para 2.6; and Social Services Inspectorate for Wales, 1999, para 7.4.

23 See generally, Pearson and Wistow, 1995, pp 208–09; and Challis and Henwood, 1994, pp 1496–99.

24 DoH, 1999c.

25 *Ibid*, para 9.7.

26 [1996] 2 All ER 65, p 68.

27 See Children Act 1989, s 1.

or those under 16 who are *Gillick* competent have the same right to confidentiality as any other adult.[28]

Working Together recognises the importance of sharing information, but emphasises the need to 'have regard to both common and statute law'.[29] At this point generalisation creeps in and little specific guidance is given. One criticism is that it leaves too much scope for individual agencies or professionals to rely on their own approach to sharing information, rather than tackle the issue in an integrated manner.[30]

Turning to the protection of vulnerable adults the position is more complex. *No Secrets* emphasises the importance of sharing information, but states that personal information can only be disclosed lawfully and fairly. Where information is obtained or held under a common law duty, it may only be disclosed with the individual's consent or where there is an overriding public interest or justification for doing so.[31] The guidance states that confidentiality policies should adhere to a number of principles:

(a) information will only be shared on a need to know basis;

(b) information will only be shared when it is in the best interests of service users;

(c) confidentiality must not be confused with secrecy;

(d) informed consent should be obtained, but if this is not possible and other vulnerable adults are at risk, it may be necessary to override it.[32]

This represents a standard way of addressing the issue of confidentiality and the sharing of information in an inter-disciplinary setting. However, it begs the question whether it provides adequate safeguards for the rights of those who may fall into the category of vulnerable adult.

RESOLVING THE DILEMMAS – CONFIDENTIALITY AND THE PUBLIC INTEREST EXCEPTION

Seeking to resolve those dilemmas by reference to the common law of confidentiality involves some difficult judgments as to what is in the public interest. Lord Goff in the *Guardian Newspapers* case stated that: 'Although the basis of the law's protection of confidence is that there is a public interest that confidences should be preserved and protected by the law, nevertheless that public interest may be outweighed by some other countervailing public

---

28 DoH, 1999c, para 7.32.

29 *Ibid*, para 7.28.

30 See Williams, 1992, pp 68–71.

31 DoH, 1999b, para 6.19.

32 *Ibid*, para 6.20.

interest which favours disclosure ...'[33] For the medical profession, the courts take note of the professional guidance issued by the General Medical Council (GMC) in deciding whether the counter public interest should prevail. The Courts in *R v Egdell*[34] (see below) and *X v Y*[35] had regard to the professional guidance issued by the GMC in deciding whether the public interest required a disclosure of otherwise confidential information.

Good Medical Practice, published by the GMC, requires, *inter alia*, doctors to respect patients' privacy and dignity and treat information about patients as confidential.[36] The specific guidance on confidentiality, *Confidentiality: Protecting and Providing Information*[37] lays down a number of guidelines. Patients have a right to expect that their doctors will hold information about them in confidence. Doctors should:

(a) Seek patients' consent to disclosure of information wherever possible, regardless of whether the patient can be identified from the disclosure.

(b) Anonymise data where unidentifiable data will serve the purpose.

(c) Keep disclosures to the minimum necessary.[38]

Doctors must justify their decisions in accordance with the GMC guidance and ensure that information on patients is effectively protected against improper disclosure.

Where patients have consented to treatment, express consent is not usually required before personal information is shared. Patients should be made aware that personal information might be shared within the healthcare team. It is important that patients understand what will be disclosed if it is thought necessary to share personal information with anyone in another organisation or agency. The wishes of any patient who objects must be respected, except where this would put others at risk of death or serious harm. Anybody to whom personal information is disclosed must be told that it is given to him or her in confidence and that they are bound by a duty of confidence. Where a patient cannot be informed about the sharing of information, for example, because of a medical emergency or the patient lacks capacity, relevant information should be passed to those providing medical care.[39]

If a doctor has considered all ways of obtaining consent, but is satisfied that it is not practicable, or the patient is incompetent or withholds consent, personal information may be disclosed in the public interest if the benefits to an individual or society of disclosure outweigh the public and the patient's

---

33 [1988] 3 All ER 545.

34 [1990] 2 WLR 471.

35 [1988] 2 All ER 648.

36 GMC, 1998.

37 GMC, 2000. Currently in the process of revision.

38 *Ibid*, para 11.

39 *Ibid*, paras 7–10.

interest in confidentiality. In such cases, doctors must weigh the possible harm (to the patient, and to the doctor/patient relationship in general) against the benefits likely to arise from disclosure. Ultimately, the courts determine the 'public interest'; but the GMC may also require a doctor to justify a disclosure if a complaint is made.[40]

This guidance is more detailed than previously and refers to the Data Protection Act 1998. Although it was produced in June 2000 (with a supplement in September 2000), there is no mention of the HRA 1998 or of the Convention. Interestingly, the 1998 publication *Good Medical Practice* (mentioned above) has a section concerning working in a multidisciplinary team, but this does not include guidance on confidentiality.

The extent to which this professional and government guidance enables practitioners to achieve consistency and fairness is debatable. Given the broad-brush approach of the existing law on confidentiality, it is difficult to anticipate how any individual practitioner would respond in any given situation. Professional judgment is an important feature. This was recognised by Bingham LJ in *Edgell*:

> ... it does not follow that the doctor's conclusion is irrelevant. In making its ruling the court will give such weight to the considered judgment of a professional man as seems in all the circumstances to be appropriate.[41]

It is inevitable that professional judgment will be relevant in decisions as to whether confidential information should be shared within an inter-disciplinary team. However, the question arises whether giving 'such weight' to the professional's judgment builds in sufficient safeguards for the individual. This is all the more significant, as we do not appear to be developing an inter-disciplinary or inter-professional approach to making such judgments. Every profession or agency involved in an inter-disciplinary team will undoubtedly sign up to the duty of confidentiality. However, they may have different views as to when disclosure is in the public interest. Thus, police, doctors, nurses and social workers will not necessarily agree on the appropriate responses in any given situation. Sharing a confidentiality within a group will subject it to the lowest common denominator in respect of a willingness to share that information with others. Three stages in the process can be identified:

Stage 1   Individual professional does not share confidentiality.

Stage 2   Individual professional sharing confidentiality with other professionals/team.

Stage 3   Professionals/team sharing collective confidentiality with outsiders.

---

40   GMC, 2000, para 14.

41   [1990] 2 WLR 471, p 490.

To illustrate the point, when a professional is given confidential information he or she has absolute control over that information and is able to make, 'a public interest professional judgment as to whether to share it or not' (Stage 1). Once he or she shares that information with the team, the control is lost. A Doctor may decide to report abuse to a social worker, but may have reservations about reporting the matter to the police. However, the social services department may have a policy of automatic referral. The Doctor can do little about it once it gets to Stage 2. The law, practice and procedure do not provide any certainty as to how far the confidence will travel once it gets to Stage 2. An inter-disciplinary understanding of confidentiality and, probably more importantly, the public interest exception, is lacking.

Our existing law of confidentiality tolerates this relatively casual approach to sharing information in inter-disciplinary teams. Public interest is an elusive concept and, if professionals and the courts take a paternalistic approach, it seems that protection will in most cases outweigh autonomy. The HRA 1998 requires a rethink of this approach. Relying on guidance that is vague and full of platitudes may not provide the certainty that the HRA 1998 demands.

THE IMPACT OF THE HRA 1998

Introducing the relevance of the HRA 1998

Section 6 of the HRA 1998 makes it unlawful for any public authority to act in a way that is incompatible with a Convention right. In its guidance to the HRA 1998, the Home Office identifies the essential obligations for public authorities. They are:

Respect for Convention rights should be at the heart of practice.

Consider how the relevant parts of the Act apply to all aspects of practice.

Be able to show that this has been done.

Be able to justify decisions in the context of the Convention rights.

Consider how, and the extent to which, the laws underpinning policies and procedures could help to do more to build a culture of rights and responsibilities.[42]

For those in public authorities working with vulnerable adults, one of the most relevant provisions of the Convention is Art 8(1) which states that:

Everyone has the right to respect for his private and family life, his home and his correspondence.

---

42   See, Home Office, 1999, para 40.

It is curious that neither *In Safe Hands*[43] nor *No Secrets*[44] specifically refers to Art 8 and the impact that it may have on sharing information. However, the revised *Working Together*[45] devotes two paragraphs to the Article. It recognises that disclosure of information without consent 'might give rise to an issue under Art 8'. Disclosure may be justified under Art 8(2), but it should be 'appropriate for the purpose and only to the extent necessary to achieve that purpose'.[46] *Working Together* is to be congratulated on making specific reference to Art 8; whether it provides practitioners with adequately focused guidance is debatable.

Article 8(2) defines the circumstances in which the rights may be interfered with by a public authority:

> There shall be no interference by a public authority with the exercise of this right except such as is in accordance with the law and is necessary in a democratic society in the interests of national security, public safety or the economic well-being of the country, for the prevention of disorder or crime, for the protection of health or morals, or for the protection of the rights and freedoms of others.

Starmer summarises the position as being that the right may be interfered with if:

> ... it is in accordance with the law,
>
> the aim of the restriction is legitimate, and
>
> the reason is necessary in a democratic society.[47]

As far as the exceptions are concerned, this is an exhaustive list. It is also to be narrowly construed and States are not allowed to extend interpretation of the provision beyond ordinary language.[48]

Article 8(1) refers to respect for private and family life. The Court has adopted a broad interpretation of private and family life. It includes not only the notion of the 'inner circle', but also 'to a certain degree the right to establish and develop relationships with human beings'.[49] Sexuality and relationships are within Art 8. The European Court of Human Rights found, in *Z v Finland*,[50] that the confidentiality of medical records fell within the ambit of private life. The question before the Court was whether the interference with that right under Finnish Law could be justified under Art 8(2). The applicant

---

43 Social Services Inspectorate for Wales, 1999.

44 DoH, 1999b.

45 DoH, 1999c.

46 *Ibid*, paras 7.34–5.

47 Starmer, 1999, para 4.56.

48 *Sunday Times v UK* (1979) 2 EHRR 245.

49 *Niemetz v Germany* (1992) 16 EHRR 97, para 29.

50 (1998) 25 EHRR 371. See, also, the European Commission in *Chare née Jullien v France* (1991) 71 DR 141.

complained that the Finnish law on disclosure of medical records in criminal proceedings was couched in 'dangerously' broad terms. The legislation could not be said to 'fulfil the requirements of precision and foreseeability flowing from the expression "in accordance with the law"'. On the facts of the case, the Court rejected the argument. However, in doing so it recognised that to comply with Art 8(2) the effects of any law seeking to interfere with the right must be foreseeable:

> The Court, however, sharing the views of the Commission and the Government, finds nothing to suggest that the effects of the relevant [domestic] law were *not sufficiently foreseeable for the purposes of the quality requirement which is implied by the expression 'in accordance with the law'* in para 2 of Art 8 (Art 8.2). (Emphasis added.)

Where State measures require the disclosure of confidential information without consent, they should be subjected to the scrutiny. The Court:

> ... will take into account that the protection of personal data, not least medical data, is of fundamental importance to a person's enjoyment of his or her right to respect for private and family life as guaranteed by Art 8 of the Convention (Art 8). Respecting the confidentiality of health data is a vital principle in the legal systems of all the Contracting Parties to the Convention. It is crucial not only to respect the sense of privacy of a patient but also to preserve his or her confidence in the medical profession and in the health services in general.[51]

If confidence in the profession is compromised, it will deter people from seeking assistance. However, as always, a broader public interest must be considered:

> At the same time, the Court accepts that the interests of a patient and the community as a whole in protecting the confidentiality of medical data may be outweighed by the interest in investigation and prosecution of crime and in the publicity of court proceedings (see, *mutatis mutandis*, Art 9 of the above mentioned 1981 Data Protection Convention), where such interests are shown to be of even greater importance.[52]

This envisages a balancing exercise similar to that propounded by Lord Goff in *Guardian Newspapers*. The principal difference between the two approaches is that the Court (and the courts of this country since the implementation of the HRA 1998) is concerned to ensure that law governs the exceptions, and that it does so with a considerable degree of certainty. The point was discussed in the cases of *Halford v United Kingdom*,[53] *Silver v United Kingdom*[54] and *Malone v United Kingdom*.[55] In *Halford*, the Court found that it was entitled to look at the quality of the law that sought to justify interference with Convention rights. It said:

---

51 *Z v Finland* (1997) 25 EHRR 371, para 95.

52 *Ibid*, para 97.

53 (1997) 24 EHRR 523.

54 (A/161) (1983) 5 EHRR 347.

55 (1984) 7 EHRR 14.

In terms of the quality of the law, the Commission notes that the law must be compatible with the rule of law in providing a measure of protection against arbitrary interferences by public authorities and, in this context, it must be accessible to the person concerned *who must moreover be able to foresee the consequences of the law for him.*[56]

In *Malone* the Court recognised that: 'The degree of precision required of the "law" in this connection will depend upon the particular subject matter.' The interception of communications, by its secretive nature, requires a considerable element of precision.[57]

Is existing law on information sharing Convention compliant?

Is it possible to say that any individual can foresee the consequences of the law as it applies to information sharing in an inter-disciplinary setting? A number of difficulties can be identified.

What is the proposed threshold for intervention?

In this context, intervention refers to the sharing of confidential information a *prima facie* breach of the individual's right to a private life and, if it results in the person's living arrangements being disrupted, their family life. The definition provided by the Law Commission defines 'vulnerable person at risk'. It does not, however, build in sufficient safeguards for compromising an individual's autonomy. Nor does it recognise that the right to private life remains the presumption. Therefore, information should not be shared merely because a person may be vulnerable, or because it might be convenient for the professionals or relatives. To rebut the presumption of confidentiality the State will need to rely on one of the Art 8(2) exceptions and meet the three criteria as summarised by Starmer.[58]

Do existing legal rules on sharing confidential information in an inter-disciplinary setting, and proposed reforms, satisfy the 'in accordance with the law' requirement in Art 8(2)?

The law on confidentiality is, in the main, a creature of common law.[59] As noted above the courts will have regard to the judgments of professionals and any guidance given by professional bodies. This provides us with the basic rules relating to confidentiality and the general principle that confidences may be shared, if to do so is in the public interest. So far so good. However,

---

56 (1997) 24 EHRR 523 and *Kruslin v France* (1990) 12 EHRR 547, paras 26–27. (Emphasis added.)

57 (1984) 7 EHRR 14.

58 Starmer, 1999, para 4.56.

59 See *Sunday Times v UK* (1979) 2 EHRR 245.

difficulties arise when trying to determine what is or is not in the public interest. Here the common law is supplemented by *In Safe Hands* and *No Secrets*. It is on the basis of these documents that professionals will decide whether information should be shared. Both documents must be considered, at best, as being soft law. The tone of both documents is that they seek to enable and facilitate the introduction of local procedures and protocols, rather than lay down specific criteria for intervention. The following extract from *No Secrets* illustrates the permissive nature of the document:

> The document gives guidance to local agencies who have a responsibility to investigate and take action when a vulnerable adult is believed to be suffering abuse. It offers a structure and content for the development of local inter-agency policies and procedures, which will be informed by good practice nationally and locally. Local operational guidance should be developed in all areas of the country by all the statutory, voluntary and private agencies that work with vulnerable adults working within the framework set by the Department of Health on joint working.[60]

In short, the documents are designed to provide broad guidance to statutory agencies and others on how vulnerable adult procedures should be developed, rather than provide clear guidance on when intervention is acceptable. It is a template rather than the actual rules of engagement.

Following on almost inevitably from this point, the guidance does not enable professionals and service users to foresee, with the required degree of certainty, the consequences of the law. It is accepted that absolute certainty is not required and that flexibility is necessary.[61] Thus, it is unnecessary to have a detailed set of criteria, but something more than reliance on the principles set out in para 6.20 of *No Secrets*[62] is required. These principles may be criticised for their generality. For example, to state that information should only be shared on a 'need to know' basis is meaningless. If a doctor knows the information, he or she has to make a judgment as to whether the social worker also needs to know. On what basis is such a judgment made? Indeed, it can be argued that we need to know everything in order that we can assess whether or not it is relevant to our purpose. Similarly, the reference to only sharing information if it is in the 'best interests' of the service user provides us with little guidance. In the case of incapacitated vulnerable adults the 'best interests' test may (but only may) be appropriate.[63] In the case of a person with capacity, but who is vulnerable and at risk, the 'best interests' is a dangerously vague test. To what extent would sharing confidential information be intruding on the autonomy of that individual to make foolish

---

60 DoH, 1999a, para 1.5.
61 *Wingrove v UK* (1997) 24 EHRR 1.
62 See earlier discussion, p 151.
63 See *Re F (Mental Patient: Sterilisation)* [1989] 2 All ER 545.

as well as wise decisions? Thus, an elderly person who is being mistreated by a family member may be vulnerable and at risk, and protecting him or her from abuse may be in his or her 'best interests'. Nevertheless, it may be argued that the information should remain confidential because that is a risk he or she is willing and able to undertake.[64] To justify sharing the information the professional should be required to identify something in addition to best interests, otherwise paternalism will rule and respect for autonomy will suffer.

Is there a legitimate purpose for sharing the confidential information?

This requirement is less problematic. Sharing confidential information about a vulnerable adult at risk within an inter-disciplinary setting may be legitimate for reasons of public safety, protection of health or morals, the prevention of disorder or crime, or the protection of rights of others.[65] However, these stated purposes are a reminder that no other reason may be used to justify violating the Art 8(1) right. Seeking to justify disclosure because it is 'agency policy' or it is 'the most efficient way of utilising adult protection resources' will be insufficient.

Is sharing the information 'necessary in a democratic society'?

The Court in *Sunday Times v United Kingdom*[66] (a case involving the Art 10 right to freedom of expression) stated:

> It is not sufficient that the interference belongs to that class of the exceptions listed in Art 10(2) which has been invoked; neither is it sufficient that the interference was imposed because its subject-matter fell within a particular category or was caught by a legal rule formulated in general or absolute terms: the Court has to be satisfied *that the interference was necessary having regard to the facts and circumstances prevailing in the specific case before it.*[67]

This has implications for the protection of vulnerable adults at risk. The decision to share confidential information must be informed by the individual circumstance of each case and not be the result of an indiscriminately applied policy. An integral part of the 'necessary in a democratic society' requirement is that the action must be proportionate to the aim pursued.[68] The legitimate interest of society to prevent abuse must be balanced against the importance

---

64 Subject to the Court's decision in *Laskey v UK* (1997) 24 EHRR 39.

65 The legitimate purpose needs to be clear, s 115 of the Crime and Disorder Act 1998 empowers health authorities to disclose information relevant for the purposes of the crime and disorder. This does not mean that confidence can be breached unless there is a need to do so, such as an individual poses a risk to him/herself or to others. Just because there is a law, does not release the burden of confidence.

66 (1979) 2 EHRR 245.

67 *Ibid*, para 65. Emphasis added.

68 *Handyside v UK* (1979–80) 1 EHRR 737.

of protecting the individual service user's human rights.[69] Blanket policies of disclosure are not acceptable – they cannot be couched in absolute terms.[70] The Government White Paper said:

> ... that even if a particular policy or action which interferes with a Convention right is aimed at pursuing a legitimate aim (for example, the prevention of crime) this will not justify the interference if the means used to achieve the aim are excessive in the circumstances. Any interference with a Convention right should be carefully designed to meet the objective in question and must not be arbitrary or unfair.

Again, it is doubtful whether the existing laws on confidentiality and information sharing, even when read in conjunction with the guidance, really satisfy the above requirements.

CONCLUSION

For those working with vulnerable adults, the implementation of the HRA 1998 will require a radical rethink of policies, practices and procedures. Lord Williams of Mostyn, the Minister of State at the Home office, described the impact of the HRA 1998 as follows:

> The Act changes the legal landscape. It doesn't herald a revolution, because it preserves the supremacy of Parliament and the separation of powers between the different branches of government. However, it does make everything look different. This is new law. The Convention rights are no longer in the background. They are centre stage [Lord Williams, 1999].

Health authorities, social services departments and individual professionals must be able to justify sharing confidential information in the context of the Convention rights and be able to demonstrate that they have considered the nature and limits of these rights.

In the context of 'vulnerable adults', it is insufficient for separate professional bodies to set out guidance rules to be followed by their members. Most work with 'vulnerable adults' takes place in an inter-agency team and, as illustrated above, it is in this environment that confidentiality is most at risk. One solution would be to withdraw from information sharing, but that removes a crucial ingredient of joint working. Lack of information sharing has

---

69 *Soering v UK* (1989) 11 EHRR 439.
70 *Open Door Counselling and Well Woman v Ireland* (1993) 15 EHRR 244.

been identified by a number of independent reports as being the cause of failures to meet the statutory requirements of 'vulnerable adults'. Inter-agency teams need to address this issue and do so with some degree of urgency. They need rules governing when information can be shared within the group and, more importantly, when it can be shared outside it. Relying on the concepts of the common law of confidentiality will no longer be adequate to meet the new expectations of the HRA 1998. However, too prescriptive an approach would clearly be undesirable, as it would fail to take account of the role of professional judgments in such a complex and diverse decision making process. It is clear that an appropriate balance has to be sought through detailed evaluation of, firstly, the dynamics of professional interaction in this area and, secondly, of each profession's thinking on confidentiality (or more precisely the exceptions to the duty of confidentiality). It is equally clear that this will be a difficult process. However, failure to achieve it will either destroy inter-agency work or will endanger the individual's right to privacy.

In *Artico v Italy*,[71] the Court noted that the Convention guarantees rights that are 'practical and effective' and not 'theoretical or illusory'. Furthermore, Art 8 imposes a positive obligation on the State to ensure that the rights are effectively protected. As the Court said in *X and Y v The Netherlands*:[72] 'These obligations may involve the adoption of measures designed to secure respect for private life.'[73] The case emphasises the importance of the protective duties of the State to ensure that the professionals and groups of professionals have, and abide by, policies that guarantee a private and family life for vulnerable adults and only tolerates clearly defined exceptions. In a post-devolution Britain, this may be harder to guarantee when several levels of government are involved. As noted, current law, guidance and practice falls far short of providing the appropriate level of protection. At the moment, both central government and public authorities are failing properly to protect the right of vulnerable adults to a private and family life.

---

71 (1981) 3 EHRR 1.
72 (1986) 8 EHRR 235.
73 *Ibid*, para 23.

THE IMPACT OF THE HUMAN RIGHTS ACT 1998 ON MENTAL HEALTH LAW AND PRACTICE: PART I

Laura Davidson

INTRODUCTION

The following two chapters will investigate the rights that may be affected by virtue of the suspected or actual presence of mental disorder in the context of the fact that the Human Rights Act (HRA) 1998 brings rights drawn from the European Convention on Human Rights (ECHR) into the fabric of English law.[1] The first chapter briefly introduces mental health issues in the context of the ECHR and then analyses Art 5(1) of the Convention. Under the HRA 1998, victims who allege a breach of their 'Convention rights' may gain remedy for this in the domestic courts, instead of having to travel to Strasbourg after exhausting local remedies. Section 2 of the HRA 1998 states that in interpreting whether or not these rights have been violated regard shall be had, where appropriate, to previous Convention jurisprudence, such as that of the European Court of Human Rights (the Court). Hence, case law is analysed in some detail. As the range of rights protected under the ECHR is too broad to hope to examine in any detailed way, what is provided is an overview of a variety of legal issues relating to mentally disordered adults which may be open to challenge under the 1998 Act.

MENTAL HEALTH RIGHTS AND THE MARGIN OF APPRECIATION

In the context of mental health, 'special procedural safeguards may prove called for in order to protect the interests of persons who, on account of their mental disabilities, are not fully capable of acting for themselves'.[2] Furthermore, 'the position of inferiority and powerlessness which is typical of patients confined in psychiatric hospitals calls for increased vigilance in reviewing whether the Convention has been complied with'.[3] Nonetheless,

---

1   These two chapters will examine the law of England and Wales, with reference to the law of Scotland or Northern Ireland where applicable.
2   *Winterwerp v The Netherlands* (1979) 2 EHRR 387.
3   *Herczegfalvy v Austria* (1992) 15 EHRR 437.

the European Court has allowed a broad 'margin of appreciation' to states on mental health issues. In this context, the doctrine's effect is that there will be in general a reinforcement of the decision of a national court, which will be departed from only where the existence of a mental disorder was not established by independent medical evidence, the type of disorder did not warrant confinement, or the grounds stated in the medical evidence for confinement no longer exist.[4] However, if admission is for 'emergency' purposes, the fact that no objective medical evidence has been relied on prior to detaining an individual need not violate the right to liberty for a period for as long as six weeks.[5] For example, no medical report is required prior to the removal of a person suspected of being mentally disordered to a place of safety by a police officer under s 136 of the Mental Health Act (MHA) 1983. As removal must be in the interests of the person concerned or for the protection of others, this would probably be viewed as an emergency and thus lawful.

It is likely, however, that the margin of appreciation doctrine cannot be relied upon by respondents in relation to human rights' issues in the domestic courts as it is a principle of public international law. This means that the English courts should be more ready to find a breach of Art 5 for reasons other than and in addition to all three of the requirements laid down in *Winterwerp* relevant in assessing the legality of the detention.

ARTICLE 5(1)

Everyone has the right to liberty and security of the person. No-one shall be deprived of his liberty save in the following cases and in accordance with a procedure prescribed by law:

(a) the lawful detention of a person after conviction by a competent court; ...

(e) the lawful detention of persons for the prevention of the spreading of infectious diseases, of persons of unsound mind, alcoholics or drug addicts or vagrants.

This Article has led to significant jurisprudence, having proved useful to those detained for mental disorder. The right to liberty and security of the person is not absolute, relevant exceptions for those detained as a result of mental disorder being found in Art 5(1)(a) and (e). The former permits the lawful detention of someone who is convicted of a criminal offence, and the latter, the lawful detention in a hospital, clinic, or 'other appropriate institution authorised for the purpose'[6] of someone of 'unsound mind'. It should be noted that 'unsoundness of mind' has not been defined, except that it must be a 'true mental disorder'.[7]

---

4   *Herczegfalvy v Austria* (1992) 15 EHRR 437.
5   As in *Winterwerp v The Netherlands* (1979) 2 EHRR 387.
6   *Ashingdane v UK* (1985) 7 EHRR 528.
7   *Winterwerp v The Netherlands* (1979) 2 EHRR 387.

Questions relating to the lawfulness of the detention (the 'deprivation of liberty') of a mentally disordered individual who is considered a dangerous risk to himself or to the safety of others will not arise until it is established that he has been detained. Where he is detained in a prison or remand centre as a result of a criminal charge or conviction, no dispute about whether or not the person is 'detained' will usually occur. However, presence in a mental institution does not necessarily mean that a person is 'detained' in law.

Is there a detention?

The ECHR jurisprudence makes it clear that in order to decide whether a 'detention' has occurred for the purposes of the Convention, a range of factors such as the nature, duration, effects and manner of execution of the penalty or measure should be considered.[8] In *Ashingdane*, the European Court held that the applicant had been 'detained' even when he was in an open ward. In domestic law, 'detention' in the context of mental health legislation has often included patients on leave,[9] not least because the definition of 'hospital' in the MHA 1983 includes houses in the community owned by NHS trusts. However, it seems that out-patient treatment in the community cannot amount to 'detention' under the ECHR, as in *W v Sweden*,[10] where the applicant before the Commission was subject to treatment in the community involving an obligation to take medication, with hospital treatment every second week.[11]

R v Bournewood Community and Mental Health NHS Trust ex p L[12] was a case concerned with the definition of a 'deprivation of liberty' under the English tort of false imprisonment. L was a profoundly learning-disabled man who had been conditionally discharged from hospital to the community with paid carers for three years. Following a tantrum when his carers (who could normally deal with him) could not be contacted, he was removed to hospital. As he lacked capacity, he was present there on an informal basis. Thus, it was not clear whether or not L had been 'detained' under English law. Under the

---

8   *Engel v The Netherlands* (1976) 1 EHRR 647.

9   *Safford v Safford* (1944). See, also, more recently, *Barker v Barking, Havering and Brentwood Community Healthcare NHS Trust and Dr Jason Taylor* [1999] Lloyd's Rep Med 101.

10 (1988) 59 DR 158.

11 Interestingly, although there is a duty on the local authority to provide ongoing services under s 117 of the MHA 1983 for all those previously subject to involuntary detention, as a conditional discharge will not amount to detention under the ECHR it would seem that charging for those services would not breach Art 5. However, since there is a statutory duty on the authority to provide services, it has been held that to charge for it would be contrary to domestic law and, thus, charging would be arbitrary and unlawful for the purposes of the Convention. See, further, *R v Richmond LBC ex p W* [2000] BLGR 318 QBD; *R v North and East Devon HA ex p Coughlan* [1999] BLGR 703.

12 [1998] 3 All ER 289.

ECHR, relevant factors when assessing this have been held to include the type and effects of the measure to which resort is had, its degree, intensity and duration, and the manner of its implementation.[13] It seems, then, that the fact that L's carers were denied access to him when he was removed to hospital in an emergency (clearly, an 'effect', adding to the intensity of the detention, and arguably also its manner) would be a relevant factor in the consideration of whether or not he was detained. In order to keep him compliant, L was given drugs in hospital. This was not usually necessary when he lived with his carers in the community as they were able to deal with his tantrums without providing him with medication. This must surely have added to the intensity of any deprivation. However, the House of Lords made no distinction between those who are not unwilling to enter a hospital, and those who have been rendered compliant through the use of (lawfully administered) sedative drugs. If a mentally incapacitated person is unable to communicate, a judgment of their 'willingness' is extremely difficult.

The House of Lords were split 3:2 on the issue of whether or not L was actually detained. Lord Goff claimed that detention was limited to the conveying of L in the ambulance and within the hospital. Lords Steyn and Nolan were firmly of the view that L was detained, but that this was lawful under the common law. Lord Steyn stated that the suggestion that L was free to leave (had he had the capacity to choose to do so) was 'a fairy tale'. L could not actually have acted on his right to liberty, as it was conceded that had he attempted to do so, he would have been prevented by formal admission under the MHA 1983. Unfortunately, the Lords avoided a final decision on whether or not L was 'detained', but the case has now gone to the European Court.

Is the detention lawful?

Once it is clear that there has been a deprivation of liberty, its legality must be tested. Any discretion exercised by the State must be sufficiently precise to provide 'adequate protection against arbitrary interference'.[14] For the law to be valid, then, it must be foreseeable (and, thus, non-arbitrary) in its motivation and effect.

Permitted exceptions

The most obvious breach of Art 5(1) as regards the detention of an individual will occur if the detention is not one that falls within one of the permitted

---

13 See *Guzzardi v Italy* (1980) 3 EHRR 333; *Ashingdane v UK* (1985) 7 EHRR 528; *Engel v The Netherlands* (1976) 1 EHRR 647.

14 *Gillow v UK* (1986) 11 EHRR 335.

exceptions under sub-paras (a) to (e). In general, this will not be the case with those with mental disorder, as either sub-para (a) relating to offenders or (e) in relation to those of unsound mind will apply. However, an apposite example of a possible breach of Art 5(1) on this ground can be found in detention under s 47 of the National Assistance Act 1948 governing the removal of persons in need of care and attention. Under the Act, a magistrates' court may make the order on application by a local authority for the removal of persons from their home on the grounds that they are suffering from a grave chronic disease, or, being aged, infirm or physically incapacitated, they are living in insanitary conditions and unable to look after themselves (and they are not receiving proper care and attention from another person). Their removal must be necessary in their own interests or for preventing injury to the health of, or serious nuisance to, other persons.[15] The most likely applicable exception is that of Art 5(1)(e), concerning 'the lawful detention of persons for the prevention of the spreading of infectious diseases, of persons of unsound mind, alcoholics or drug addicts or vagrants'. However, the person removed may not be infectious, mentally disordered, addicted to drugs or alcohol, or a 'vagrant'.[16] It is certainly arguable that removal and detention would not fall within this exception and the government is aware of the possible incompatibility of this legislation with the HRA 1998.[17]

Contrary to legal intention

A useful illustration of seeming arbitrariness in this context is provided again in *Bournewood*. After removal to the hospital's Accident and Emergency department, L was taken to the mental health behavioural unit where he was informally detained. L's carers were not allowed access to him as it was thought that he might become agitated and desire to leave with them. There was no right to appeal against the informal detention and refusal of access. It is arguable that the decision to detain informally rather than to use the powers to detain under the MHA 1983 was in order to avoid the statutory review procedures. This would be an arbitrary interference and, hence, unlawful.

The legality of detention will also depend on certain safeguards being in place. The MHA 1983 provides extensive powers to detain and treat mentally disordered individuals. In *Bournewood*, the House of Lords held that the

---

15 Similar powers are planned to enable the removal of a person from private property for assessment.

16 A vagrant is defined as a person with 'no fixed abode, no means of subsistence, and no regular trade or profession'; see, further, *De Wilde, Ooms and Versyp v The Netherlands* (1971) 1 EHRR 373.

17 See DoH Note: 'The Human Rights Act, s 47 of the National Assistance Act 1948, and s 1 of the National Assistance (Amendment) Act 1951', 16 August 2000.

actions of the doctor had been lawful on the basis of common law necessity.[18] Clearly, disregard for domestic law will almost certainly entail a breach of the ECHR[19] – but the common law is also part of that domestic law. If it is used to circumvent the purpose of the statutory provisions, however, there would be a breach of Art 5(1)(e). The purpose of the common law surely should be to provide a safety net to cover emergencies where those authorised to admit under the Act are not available. The use of statutory powers only as a last resort by those with powers to detain under the Act risks subverting the purpose of the statutory regime. In addition, depriving L of access to his carers was not necessary for, or proportional to, the protection of his health, but instead to prevent the necessity of resort to the admission provisions within the MHA 1983 should he have attempted to leave. Thus, the aim of the detention was unlawful.

Obviously, detention for assessment is for the purposes of diagnosis. Under the MHA 1983, assessment must take place within 28 days and, thereafter, the detainee must be released or detained under another section of the Act (generally, s 3 for treatment). In *R v Wilson ex p Williamson*,[20] it was held that the renewal of an assessment order made under s 2 of the MHA 1983 where a nearest relative refused permission to detain a patient for treatment under s 3 was unlawful. The correct procedure would have been to displace the nearest relative under s 29, and then to detain the patient under s 3. Section 2(4) specifically excluded the possibility of a further s 2 application being made whilst another s 2 order was 'alive'. Thus, the renewal of the first order under s 2 had subverted the purpose of the Act.

In *Anderson v The Scottish Ministers and Another*,[21] it was held that where a man was of unsound mind, it was not an abuse of his human rights to detain him in hospital on the ground that to do so was necessary to protect the public from serious harm, even where he had originally been detained on a different ground (albeit also related to mental disorder) which no longer applied. This appears to contradict the *dicta* in *Winterwerp* to the effect that the doctrine of the margin of appreciation is not so broad as to permit detention where the grounds stated in the medical evidence for confinement no longer exist. *Anderson* is also authority for the proposition that it would not be contrary to the HRA 1998 for the legislature to make a new law requiring the detention of such patients on the ground of necessity for the protection of the public from serious harm, even though this would negate the validity of an extremely good claim as regards the original detention. However, this would only be the

---

18 Despite various attempts to rely on the rights enshrined under the ECHR, the House of Lords did not deal with such issues. The case has now gone to the European Court, with the applicants alleging breaches of Arts 5 and 8.

19 *Winterwerp v The Netherlands* (1979) 2 EHRR 387.

20 [1996] COD 42.

21 Inner House, 16 June 2000.

case where the new law was deemed to be proportionate to its object of protecting the public. In applying the ECHR, a balance must be struck between the general interest of the community and the requirement to protect the individual's fundamental rights.[22] What might make such a situation unlawful would be the lack of a review in any new legislation.

The least restrictive environment

Where detention is disproportionate to its aim, it may be arbitrary.[23] This suggests that although the public is entitled to the protection of the state from those who are or are likely to be dangerous, a mentally disordered individual deprived of his liberty on the grounds of mental health should not be detained in an environment that is more restrictive than necessary to fulfil the objective of protection of himself and/or others. This principle is reflected within the MHA 1983 where an Approved Social Worker (ASW) making an application for admission under s 3 must decide under s 13(2) whether detention in a hospital is 'in all the circumstances of the case *the* most appropriate way of providing the care and medical treatment of which the patient stands in need'.[24] Thus, the ASW's role in any admission for treatment under s 3 is to safeguard the individual from being detained in hospital where a less restrictive measure would suffice.

Assessment in the community

Section 135 of the MHA 1983 concerns the removal of someone to a place of safety in the event of ill treatment, neglect, or lack of 'proper control', or if they are living alone and unable to care for themselves. An application may be made by an ASW to court for a police warrant to enable entry to premises in order to make an assessment and if necessary effect a removal of such a person. A police officer may also remove to a place of safety a person who is in a public place who appears to have a mental disorder and is in immediate need of care and control, under s 136 of the MHA 1983.[25] A place of safety may be a police station, hospital, mental nursing home or residential home for people with a mental disorder, residential home provided by the social services, or any suitable place where the occupier is willing to have that

---

22 See *Soering v UK* (1989) 11 EHRR 439.

23 See *Zamir v UK* (1983) 40 DR 42 and *Sunday Times v UK* (1979) 2 EHRR 245.

24 Emphasis added.

25 The government proposes to introduce new police powers to remove a person also from private property 'in an extreme emergency' (as yet undefined). The power is to be available on the advice of a senior experienced mental health practitioner that the person appears to be in immediate need of care and control, in order to prevent serious harm to himself or to other people. See DoH and Home Office White Paper, *Reforming the Mental Health Act*, December 2000, para 3.82.

person.[26] However, it is arguable that the use of police stations as the 'place of safety' under ss 135 and 136 of the MHA 1983 violates Art 5(1)(e) as it is a non-therapeutic setting and inappropriate for assessment[27] – particularly where there is a more suitable alternative (albeit perhaps more difficult to arrange).

Under the government's new proposals, the police will continue to have the power to remove a person from a public place to a place of safety for assessment for up to 72 hours. However, where a police cell is used as the place of safety, there will be a duty on the local hospital trust to arrange a preliminary examination within six hours if requested to do so by a Forensic Medical Examiner, or to transfer the person to hospital for examination during that period. In these circumstances, the powers appear to accord with Art 5 since the removal of the person can be categorised as an emergency, and the six hour time limit is a safeguard to ensure that the person will be transferred to a more appropriate setting if at all possible.

The recent joint Department of Health (DoH) and Home Office White Paper, *Reforming the Mental Health Act*[28] (the White Paper), claims that those patients considered to be a high risk of being dangerous will be subject to 'sufficiently flexible' care and treatment plans in order to provide for the immediate healthcare needs of individuals and to ensure that they are kept in the appropriate degree of security.[29] The fact that the importance of the least restrictive environment is being recognised by the government is to be welcomed. However, it is unclear whether or not community services will be provided for individuals diagnosed as having personality disorders at an early stage, which may prevent serious problems in the future. In addition, the government has proposed new powers for assessment of those within this group for a period totalling four months,[30] and it is submitted that this may be disproportionate where an individual is not dangerous either to self or others and could be adequately assessed in the community.

Hospitalisation

In *Ashingdane*, the applicant, an offender with paranoid schizophrenia, claimed a breach of Art 5(1)(e) since he was detained in the strict regime at Broadmoor for 19 months longer than his mental state required. However, his application failed. The Court held that (unlike Art 3) Art 5(1)(e) was unconcerned with the conditions of confinement. Nevertheless, in the earlier case of *Engel v The Netherlands* (relating to military conscripts), the Court had held that both the *effect* – in that case, the use of isolation – and the aims of the deprivation were pertinent in assessing whether or not there had been a

---

26   MHA 1983, s 135(6).

27   *Aerts v Belgium* [1998] EHRLR 777.

28   DoH, December 2000a.

29   *Ibid*, Executive Summary, Pt II, para 7.

30   See, further, below.

breach of Art 5. The effect of deprivation is surely inextricably bound up with issues such as the conditions of confinement.

In *Bournewood*, the effect that detention away from his carers had on L was manifested by an appearance of sadness; although he was incapable of expressing himself, he seemed withdrawn. It is arguable that this separation was detrimental to L's health and a breach of Art 5. However, in *Aerts v Belgium*,[31] the European Court refused to accept reports from both psychiatrists and the Mental Health Board as 'proof' that the applicant's detention in the particular conditions had been harmful to him. Nonetheless, the case is not necessarily a stumbling block to L's complaint of a breach of Art 5; it may be significant that *Aerts* was decided several years ago since the jurisprudence of the Court is intended to develop as society changes, in the same way as does the English common law. Although there may not yet be a positive right to the least restrictive environment, it is clear that L's carers were able to deal with his tantrums and it seems that they could have continued to look after him effectively in the community. In addition, they did not have to resort to drugs – a particular intrusion – to make him amenable. The case is now being taken to Strasbourg, but the margin of appreciation allowed to the State there may be sufficiently broad to allow the government to succeed in their argument that the aim of the detention was protection of health, which could only be effected if L was in hospital. Under the 1983 Act, a mental disorder must be of the kind or degree which warrants compulsory confinement. Clearly, a professional cannot be certain that this is the case until the person concerned has been assessed – but thereafter, the confinement must be necessary. It is likely that the European Court will not wish to assess whether or not L's condition was such that he required hospitalisation, and the doctor's assessment that this was necessary at the requisite time, regardless of any insistence otherwise by L's carers, will be accepted.

R v MHRT ex p Secretary of State[32] established that a Mental Health Review Tribunal's (MHRT) power to adjourn a case is limited to enabling it to better perform one of the functions under the Act. The Tribunal was unable to adjourn the hearing for the purpose of obtaining information about the possibility of a transfer to a less secure setting since it had no power to make a direction concerning the transfer of a restricted patient to another hospital. This appears to be arbitrary and may preclude the detention of a patient in the least restrictive environment appropriate to his condition, amounting to a breach of Art 5(1).[33]

---

31 [1998] EHRLR 777.

32 (2000) unreported, 15 December (CO/1928/2000).

33 See, also, *Stanley Johnson v UK* (1999) 27 EHRR 296, where the applicant had to wait three and a half years for a place in a hostel because the MHRT had no power to demand the provision of a such a place in fulfilment of a conditional discharge. This amounted to an indefinite deferral and a breach of Art 5(1).

In *Aerts v Belgium*[34] it was held that the detention of a person on the grounds of mental health would only be lawful for the purposes of Art 5(1)(e) if effected in an appropriate institution. To be appropriate, there must be a link between the aim of the detention and the conditions in which it takes place. The medical reports showed that because the prison was not an appropriate environment for the applicant, his detention there had been harmful, constituting a breach of Art 5. This appears to suggest that the European Court's jurisprudence has moved on since *Ashingdane*, in which the conditions of the detention – the strict regime – were irrelevant under Art 5, regardless of their detrimental effect on the applicant. It appears in the light of *Aerts* that the European Court would conclude on the same facts today that the detention was not lawful. Thus, conditions of detention would now seem to be relevant in assessing the legality of detention under Art 5.

In the current climate of scarcity of NHS resources, the non-availability of a hospital bed may result in a mentally disordered offender who requires treatment in hospital under s 37 of the MHA 1983 being sent instead to prison. This would seem to be a breach of Art 5, since the aim of the detention (treatment) would not be accomplished by imprisonment.[35] Applying this logic, any greater restriction of liberty than is clinically justified due to lack of resources would be a breach of Art 5. This might apply to a patient who is not released because there is an inadequate support structure available to him in the community.

In *H v MHRT for the North and East London Region*,[36] H received a hospital order with a restriction order on conviction for manslaughter in 1988. He applied to an MHRT for discharge in December 1999 at which two medical experts agreed that the treatment of his schizophrenia did not require high security conditions. The independent psychiatrist's view was that continued detention would be purely for confinement, and that any risk could be sufficiently reduced through the provision of aftercare. However, rather than discharging the applicant, the MHRT recommended his short term transfer to a medium secure unit, having judged that he was likely to omit to take medication on discharge, which might endanger others. The Tribunal was of the view that H could be gradually assimilated into hostel accommodation thereafter. On judicial review, it was held that an adjournment of a case may be for the sole purpose of enabling the MHRT to better perform one of the functions under the Act. Thus, as it does not have the power to make a direction concerning the transfer of a restricted patient to another hospital, it cannot adjourn the hearing to enable information to be provided to it about the possibility of such a transfer. In view of the increasing realisation that the environment must be appropriate for the patient for any deprivation of liberty to be lawful, it is arguable that the fact that MHRTs lack this power is a breach of Art 5.

---

34   [1998] EHRLR 777.

35   *Stanley Johnson v UK* (1999) 27 EHRR 296.

36   CO/2120/2000 (transcript: Smith Bernal) QBD and now (2001) *The Times*, 2 April; [2001] EWCA Civ 415 CA.

In *R v MHRT for the South Thames Region ex p Smith (Anthony David)*,[37] it was held that although latent, the nature of the applicant's paranoid schizophrenia was such that he should continue to be detained. Yet, if a condition of continued treatment in the community could be attached to a discharge, it seems unlawful to continue to detain him in hospital, which would be neither 'appropriate' nor 'necessary'. The continued detention of someone with no current symptoms appears to be contrary to Art 5 when there is a less restrictive alternative.

The recent White Paper sets out an intention to provide for the compulsory reviewable detention of those considered dangerous who have a diagnosis of personality disorder (described therein as 'dangerous severe personality disorder' (DSPD)). The creation of a separate institution has been proposed for this small number of individuals (estimated at 2,200 people) who are untreatable, and in these circumstances it is likely that a mentally disordered offender sentenced (if convicted) or removed to confinement (under civil powers) in such an institution would not have a valid complaint under Art 5. The government could argue that the aim of the new institution would be to contain those subject to the new order in order to protect the public. Indeed, each detainee is to have a care plan which will either 'give therapeutic benefit to the patient *or* ... manage behaviour associated with a mental disorder that might lead to serious harm to other people'.[38] It appears that the treatability requirement, under which those with psychopathic disorder or mental impairment may not be admitted to hospital for treatment unless it is 'likely to alleviate or prevent a deterioration' of their condition[39] is not to be retained in any new Mental Health Act. This requirement caused the loophole which has in the past led to the inability to detain untreatable personality disordered individuals.[40] Yet, the White Paper states that: 'Treatment will be designed both to manage the consequences of a mental disorder as well as to enable the individuals themselves to work towards successful re-integration into the community.' This seems to define management as treatment. It may be that the Government is simply being cautious in case the ECHR requires treatment to be provided for those in detention. However, the jurisprudence as it stands does not require this, and detention may be justified on the ground simply on the basis that it is necessary to protect the public.[41] Indeed, in *Anderson*, the court specifically rejected the argument that detention in a hospital, as opposed to prison, was

---

37 (1999) 47 BMLR 104 QBD.

38 Emphasis added; DoH, December 2000a, Executive Summary, Pt II, para 10.

39 Section 3(1)(2)(a), MHA 1983.

40 Despite the fact that the definition of treatment within the Act is exceptionally broad; under the MHA 1983, s 145(1), 'treatment' is defined as including 'nursing ... care, habilitation and rehabilitation under medical supervision'. See, also, Eastman and Peay, 1999, p 203; a tribunal hearing accepted a computer course to be 'treatment', justifying continued detention.

41 See *Guzzardi v Italy* (1980) 3 EHRR 333, and *Litwa v Poland* (2000) unreported, 4 April.

unlawful where there was no treatment available. It seems that under the ECHR a hospital offering a therapeutic environment is an appropriate place to detain people of unsound mind, regardless of whether or not they are treatable.[42]

It should be noted, however, that, although resources for purpose built institutions for those with DSPD have been allocated, they are unlikely to be in place by the time the proposed new legislation becomes law. The government envisages 'a programme of service development that will *begin* to provide the capacity and specialist approaches to treatment and assessment that this group needs'.[43] If those with DSPD are housed in prisons because the new institutions are yet to be completed, it is arguable that there will be a breach of Art 5 where the basis for detention does not stem from a criminal act (and, thus, where detention is based upon Art 5(1)(e) rather than Art 5(1)(a)).

Containment for the protection of the public

In *Reid v Secretary of State for Scotland*,[44] at first instance, the Scottish courts held that the term 'medical treatment' did not include preventive detention where the only purpose of the treatment was containment,[45] and that any treatment had to either alleviate or prevent a deterioration in a patient's condition. When the case reached the House of Lords,[46] however, it was emphasised that the treatability test was sufficiently wide to include things other than medication and psychiatric treatment. Thus, although the medical experts agreed that medical treatment was not likely to alleviate R's condition, R's anger management could be improved in the structured and controlled environment of the hospital, and so his condition was alleviated by the treatment he was receiving in hospital.

It is arguable that a transfer from prison to hospital at the end of a prison sentence breaches Art 5 since the purpose of the original detention (retribution) is not the same as the purpose of the transfer (nominally treatment; in reality, often mere incapacitation).[47] The only circumstance in which such a transfer would be lawful is where a prisoner happens to develop a mental disorder right at the end of his sentence – which must be rare.

---

42 See, *Ashingdane v UK* (1985) 7 EHRR 528 and *Aerts v Belgium* [1998] EHRLR 777.

43 Emphasis added; DoH, December 2000a, Executive Summary, Pt II, para 13. The government has pledged an additional £126 million over the next three years for the development of new specialist services; a welcome medium term commitment, but the time-scale of which will not provide immediate protection for the rights of those with DSPD.

44 1997 SLT 555 OH; see, also, the Court of Appeal decision, [1999] 2 AC 512.

45 Emphasis added; *R v Mersey MHRT ex p D* [1987] CLY 2420.

46 [1999] 2 AC 512 HL.

47 *R v Secretary of State for the Home Office ex p Gilkes; Aerts v Belgium* [1998] EHRLR 777.

Indeed, late transfers to hospital under s 47 of the MHA 1983 have been criticised for resulting in extremely lengthy undeserved, unjustifiable and unfair periods of custody.[48]

The government has indicated its intention to replace the MHRT with a new Mental Health Tribunal (or the court, in the case of mentally disordered offenders). This body is to have the power to make a care and treatment order[49] authorised in a care plan recommended by a clinical team. Such a care plan is intended to give therapeutic benefit to the patient or to manage behaviour associated with mental disorder that might lead to serious harm to the public. It is difficult to see how 'management' differs from mere containment. However, it does not appear to be arguable that, where a non-offender patient is not treatable, it would be contrary to Art 5 to detain him for purely management purposes, provided that the detention for the purposes of management is necessary to protect the public.[50] This is because the right to liberty under the ECHR is not absolute and community interests and individual rights must be balanced in its application.[51]

Currency of symptomology

On assessment

For detention for assessment under Art 5(1)(e) to be lawful, mental disorder must be at least suspected. In general, English law appears to comply with this requirement. Even within the criminal justice system there is a process prior to sentencing for ensuring medical assessment of those suspected or diagnosed with a mental disorder.[52] Under s 4(1) of the Criminal Justice Act (CJA) 1991 a pre-sentence report is required where a custodial sentence is contemplated, and the sentence is neither fixed by law nor a mandatory life sentence under s 2(2) of the Crime (Sentences) Act 1997. However, s 4(2) states that such a report is not essential 'if, in the circumstances of the case, the court is of the opinion that it is unnecessary to obtain a report'. If the lack of necessity is due to the fact that the court has already had evidence of a disorder provided to it, such as on a defence of insanity, this failure to require a report will not breach Art 5. However, if the failure to obtain a report is arbitrary, then there will be a violation.

---

48 See, eg, Grounds, 1990, pp 544–51.

49 The first two orders will be for up to six months each, with subsequent orders available for periods of up to 12 months; see DoH, December 2000a, Executive Summary, Pt I, para 11.

50 See *Guzzardi v Italy* (1980) 3 EHRR 333, and *Litwa v Poland* (2000) unreported, 4 April.

51 See *Soering v UK* (1989) 11 EHRR 439.

52 See, eg, MHA 1983, s 54 and Bail Act 1976, s 3(6A), as regards a charge of murder.

In its recent White Paper, the government has proposed the introduction of a power for all criminal courts to remand a person for assessment by specialist mental health services, either in hospital or in the community on bail, on the basis of a single medical opinion from an appropriately qualified doctor that a care and treatment order *may* be an appropriate disposal.[53] Compulsory treatment would not be permitted in the absence of a second medical opinion. Given that medical evidence is to be required, this legislation appears to comply with Art 5(1). However, the Home Secretary is to have a new power to direct a prisoner to undergo a specialist assessment for mental disorder in either a hospital or a special section of a prison. For this to comply with Art 5 of the ECHR, medical evidence would be required.[54]

At discharge

The legality of detention under Art 5(1)(e) will depend on the presence of mental disorder (the person must be of 'unsound mind'). Although the discharge criteria for those who have been detained under s 3 do not specifically include the treatability criterion which is a prerequisite of admission under that section,[55] it still appears in a less mandatory form. Thus, the tribunal need only 'have regard' to 'the likelihood of medical treatment alleviating or preventing a deterioration of the patient's condition' – albeit that consideration at least is mandatory.[56] Under the MHA 1983, discharge must be directed where an individual is not suffering from mental disorder 'of a nature or degree which makes it appropriate for him to be detained in hospital for medical treatment',[57] or that his own health or safety or the protection of others does not require that he receives treatment.[58] In *R v Canons Park MHRT ex p A*,[59] the Court of Appeal held by a majority that the discharge criteria in s 72 of the MHA 1983 did not mirror the treatability criterion in the admission criteria. However, perhaps surprisingly, this case was doubted in *ex p Smith (Anthony David)*,[60] and disapproved in *R v London South and South West Region MHRT ex p Moyle*.[61]

Reid[62] dealt with the procedure for discharge by a Scottish Sheriff (equivalent to the MHRT in England and Wales). It was held that the tribunal

---

53 Emphasis added.

54 *Winterwerp v The Netherlands* (1979) 2 EHRR 387.

55 For discussion on this point, see, further, *The Queen on the Application of H v MHRT, North and East London Region* (2000) unreported, 15 November QBD.

56 MHA 1983, s 72(2)(a).

57 *Ibid*, s 72(2)(b)(i).

58 *Ibid*, s 72(2)(b)(i).

59 [1995] QB 60.

60 (1998) unreported, 4 August; see, further, below.

61 [2000] Lloyd's Rep Med 143.

62 [1999] 2 AC 512.

must first decide whether the patient is mentally disordered at the time of the hearing. If it he is not, then he must be discharged. If he remains mentally disordered, its nature and degree must be identified, and the possibility of treatment for the disorder considered. Where the applicant has a psychopathic disorder or is mentally impaired (to a non-severe degree), the tribunal must consider whether such treatment is likely to alleviate or prevent a deterioration of the condition. If it is not likely to do so, then discharge must follow. However, if the tribunal is not certain as to whether or not the treatment would be unlikely to alleviate or prevent a deterioration of the condition, or if it is dealing with any other kind of mental disorder, it must contemplate whether the patient should receive the medical treatment whilst detained in hospital. This requires a consideration of the nature and degree (already identified) of the mental disorder. If, in all the circumstances (including the health and safety of the patient and the safety of others), the patient is not suffering from a mental disorder of a nature or degree which makes detention for medical treatment appropriate, then the patient must be discharged.[63] A regime of supervised care which had the effect of preventing a deterioration of a disorder, rather than the return of the disorder itself, *the symptoms*, could require continued hospitalisation.

It would seem that the 'uncertainty' consideration was included because of the lack of agreement in the psychiatric profession as to the treatability of psychopaths. In *Canons Park* the Divisional Court found at first instance that it was unlawful to continue to detain a psychopath who was deemed untreatable. However, this was overturned by the Court of Appeal, which held that although an automatic discharge must follow a finding that it was neither appropriate nor necessary to detain an individual for the safety of herself or others in hospital, medical treatment should be broadly construed. Thus, as was the case with A, a patient was not to be considered untreatable merely because she refused to co-operate with treatment (there, group therapy). Nonetheless, it is submitted that, where an individual is suffering from mental disorder which is not amenable to treatment, it cannot be 'appropriate for him to be detained in hospital *for medical treatment*',[64] no matter what the nature or degree of that disorder may be. Furthermore, it seems unfair that the applicant's detention could be justified on the basis of the need to protect the public, since whilst that may be true, the receipt of treatment will not reduce the risk he poses to the public, having no effect. Nevertheless, whilst this is a logical conclusion, the jurisprudence of the European Court has taken a pragmatic and narrow approach to this, and no breach is likely to be found, since the balance is likely to fall in favour of

---

63 In other words, if the tribunal is satisfied that the requirements of s 72(1)(b)(i) have been met, then it is not necessary for it to consider s 72(1)(b)(ii) and it should turn to s 73(1)(b).

64 Emphasis added; MHA 1983, s 72(2)(b)(i).

public protection.[65] It is important to reiterate that this is because the right to liberty under the ECHR is not absolute and it must be balanced against community interests and individual rights.

In *Moyle* (which followed *Reid*), it was held that the discharge criteria would be satisfied where a tribunal believed that there was no possibility of a patient failing to take medication in the community and a consequent relapse *in the near future*. While the criteria for admission and discharge were mirror images, the tribunal had to apply them in the context of a reversed burden of proof, and so an assessment of whether the admission criteria would be fulfilled was not strictly necessary. This is a complex test, and it should be noted that the reversal of the burden of proof may in certain circumstances itself breach the Convention.[66] There will always be a *possibility* of relapse, since patients no longer subject to compulsion may omit to take medication. The effect of this decision is that a person might be no longer suffering from a mental disorder requiring treatment in hospital, yet discharge could be refused by a tribunal on the basis of a possibility of future relapse. In view of the *Winterwerp* requirement that a government may not rely upon the margin of appreciation where the grounds stated in the medical evidence for confinement no longer exist, however, this appears to be a breach of Art 5. A recent declaration of incompatibility[67] means that Parliament must remedy this situation, and this it may do by introducing compulsory care and treatment orders as it intended, in which case the test in *ex p Moyle* could become redundant and a violation of Art 5 is less likely.

In *ex p Smith*, the court held that the phrase 'nature or degree' in s 72 of the MHA 1983 is disjunctive. This means that a mental disorder need have no current symptomology in order that there may be continued detention. If controlled by drugs, a person's mental disorder may not be of a *degree* to require detention, although its *nature* is such that without close monitoring, the degree of the disorder will worsen. This decision seems to be in breach of Art 5 since what is required under the ECHR is that a person detained should be suffering from a *current* mental disorder. If currency were not essential, a recent medical examination as required for detention in a non-emergency situation to be lawful under Art 5(1)(e)[68] would surely be superfluous.

There are various instances when the Home Office has the final say on whether or not a patient is discharged, such as with restricted patients. Under the current MHA 1983, discharge must be directed where an individual is not suffering from mental disorder 'of a nature or degree which makes it appropriate for him to be detained in hospital for medical treatment'. The

---

65 See *Guzzardi v Italy* (1980) 3 EHRR 333, *Litwa v Poland* (2000) unreported, 4 April and *Soering v UK* (1989) 11 EHRR 439.

66 See, eg, *Salabiaku v France* (1988) 13 EHRR 379. See, also, Foster, Chapter 7, above, and Davidson, Chapter 12, below.

67 See s 4 HRA 1998, and *R v MHRT, North and East London Region and Another ex p H* [2001] EWCA Civ 415; (2001) *The Times*, 2 April, discussed in Chapter 12, below.

68 *Winterwerp v The Netherlands* (1979) 2 EHRR 387.

Home Office is not in a position to assess this. Thus, continued detention must be on the basis that the Home Secretary considers it to be necessary for the patient's own health or safety, or for the protection of others. There must be evidence to support such an assessment, and in the absence of a medical report which says so, continued detention risks being arbitrary and in violation of the right to liberty. Where the Home Secretary refuses to release a patient contrary to medical opinion, this would seem to breach Art 5 since the purpose of the medical report is to justify the need for detention.

On recall

In relation to mentally disordered offenders, recall to prison following conviction for an imprisonable offence will not breach Art 5(1)(a).[69] This is because detention after recall is based on the original criminal conviction – a legitimate reason for detention. However, this may not be the case where the justification for the original detention from which a recall stems is unsoundness of mind under Art 5(1)(e). Either the Home Secretary or the MHRT may attach conditions to a discharge, but only in relation to a restricted patient.[70] As a restricted patient's original detention will have been based on Art 5(1)(a), the legality of recall on the basis of Art 5(1)(e) would be doubtful. An example might be where a prisoner is transferred from prison to hospital near the end of his sentence for the purposes of treatment, and hence the basis for his detention has changed. Interestingly, the DoH's view in 1993 was that a power to recall to hospital where a patient was refusing to accept supervision in the community would be incompatible with Art 5.[71] If this view is correct, it would seem unlikely that a refusal to release on the basis of possible future non-compliance with a requirement to take medication (as in *Ex p Moyle*) could lawfully found the basis of continued detention under the MHA 1983. The accuracy of risk assessment will not be improved by guesswork as to the likelihood or not of the cessation of medication at some uncertain point in the future.

Thus, it is more likely that the courts will consider recall in the absence of compliance with medication to be justified, providing that there is independent medical evidence of the presence of mental disorder which warrants detention. This would not be difficult to prove, since presumably knowledge of the cessation of medication would have been based initially on suspicion brought about by symptoms of mental disorder. To be lawful, any

---

69 *Van Droogenbroeck v Belgium* (1991) 13 EHRR 546 and *Weeks v UK* (1987) 10 EHRR 293.

70 MHA 1983, ss 42 and 73(2) respectively.

71 DoH's Internal Review, 'Legal powers on the care of the mentally ill', August 1993, p 7, in response to a proposal by the Royal College of Psychiatrists.

recall of a former patient could only result from a breach of the conditions of a conditional discharge.[72]

On the basis of *Ashingdane* and *W v Sweden*, conditional release does not amount to detention. It seems, then, that the government's new proposals for the availability of a care and treatment order in the community would not breach Art 5 of the ECHR, since the individual who is subject to it would not be detained. Forced medication would not be permissible under the new regime except in a clinical setting. Clearly, however, there would have to be a good reason for the recall of a patient to hospital.[73] Recall due to a breach of conditions would be in accordance with domestic law, although a recent medical assessment would be essential, and it will probably be essential for the patient to fulfil the requirements for admission under s 2 or 3 of the MHA 1983. The only justification for the recall of a former patient without first obtaining a medical report would be a genuine emergency situation.[74] In *K v United Kingdom*,[75] for example, in which a friendly settlement was reached, the Committee of Ministers found a breach of Arts 5(1) and (4) because the Home Secretary may recall a conditionally discharged restricted patient without obtaining a medical report.

---

72 If mental disorder is suspected, the proper procedure would be to admit the individual for a fresh assessment under the MHA 1983, s 2.

73 *Roux v UK* [1997] EHRLR 102.

74 As in *R v Bournewood Community and Mental Health NHS Trust ex p L* [1998] 3 All ER 289.

75 (1991) App No 11468/85, 15 April 1988.

CHAPTER 12

THE IMPACT OF THE HUMAN RIGHTS ACT 1998 ON MENTAL HEALTH LAW: PART II

Laura Davidson

INTRODUCTION

Chapter 11 discussed Art 5(1) of the European Convention on Human Rights (ECHR) in the context of the rights of those with mental disorder. This chapter will first discuss the right to review of detention under Art 5(4), then Arts 3 and 8, which may be applicable to those with mental disorder, will be examined in the context of the European Court of Human Rights (the Court) jurisprudence.[1]

ARTICLE 5(4)

Article 5(4) states that:

> Everyone who is deprived of his liberty by arrest or detention shall be entitled to take proceedings by which the lawfulness of his detention shall be decided speedily by a court and his release ordered if his detention is not lawful.

Under Art 5(4), a person who is deprived of his liberty is entitled to have the lawfulness of his detention tested and reviewed by a judicial body which has the power to enquire whether or not any reasons justifying the original detention continue to exist, and if not, to order his discharge. Where access to such a review is absent (rather than merely delayed) there will be a clear breach of Art 5(4). For example, under s 29(3)(c) of the Mental Health Act 1983 (MHA), a nearest relative who is unreasonably objecting to the compulsory admission of a patient may be displaced on an application to the County Court. However, if the Approved Social Worker (ASW) makes such an application, the patient will have no right to a review of detention during the necessary extended period prior to the hearing. Similarly, the absence of a right of appeal against an order under s 1 of the National Assistance Amendment Act 1951 breaches Art 5(4).

---

1   Other Articles may also be applicable, but will not be examined here; see, eg, Art 2 concerning the right to life, and Art 14, which is not a freestanding right, but concerns the right to non-discrimination. Art 6 is also very important for those who are charged with offences, but as it contains similar provisions to those safeguards guaranteed in Art 5, it will not be the subject of discussion.

The recent White Paper[2] includes a proposal for a new power for the Home Secretary to direct a prisoner to undergo a specialist assessment for mental disorder in either a hospital or a special section of a prison, under which there does not seem to be a right of appeal from his decision. Obviously, this has the potential for substantially increasing the length of time a prisoner may be incarcerated and, should no review be possible under the new legislation, this will breach Art 5(4).

Fairness

To comply with Art 5(4) the court must ensure that certain minimum procedural requirements are met. These are similar, though not identical, to the guarantees for a fair trial under Art 6.[3]

Independence of reviewing body

In order to comply with Art 5(4), a State must ensure that any review of detention is fair. This means that the reviewing court must both be independent of the executive (and impartial),[4] and have the power to order release. Interestingly, as current tribunal members are paid by the health authority, they may not be independent and impartial as required.[5] Indeed, the most important factor in an assessment of independence has been held to be that a decision making body should not lack security of tenure.[6] However, the government proposes the replacement of the Mental Health Review Tribunal (MHRT) by a Mental Health Tribunal which is to be independent.

The dual role of the medical member of the MHRT under r 11 of the MHRT rules has been criticised due to the fact that he has much influence, and is not subject to cross-examination. In *H v MHRT, North and East London Region*[7] it was submitted that tribunal medical members acted both as expert witness and decision maker and, thus, the reviewing body was not independent as required under Art 5(4). However, it was held that there was nothing unlawful about a tribunal system that was of an inquisitorial nature common in civil law States.[8] In any case, the government is likely to change the membership of the replacement tribunal system.

---

2   DoH, Cm 5016-I, and Home Office White Paper, December 2000a, Pt II, paras 4.11–4.14.
3   See, eg, *Toth v Austria* (1991) 14 EHRR 551.
4   See, eg, *Schiesser v Switzerland* (1979) 2 EHRR 417.
5   *Starrs v Ruxton* [2000] JC 208. See, also, *K v Austria*, Series A/255-B (1993).
6   *Starrs v Ruxton* [2000] JC 208, p 230. See, also, *R v Spear (John)* [2001] 2 WLR 1692.
7   (2000) unreported, 15 November QBD.
8   See, also, *Johnson v UK* (1997) EHRR 296.

Openness and equality of arms

A detainee must be given disclosure of all relevant evidence.[9] The MHRT may keep certain matters and reports on which they rely confidential on the basis that it would be harmful to the patient to disclose them.[10] However, this appears to breach the requirement under Art 5 that there be 'equality of arms'.[11] This has been defined as the necessity to ensure equal treatment, and to be adversarial in nature.[12] Thus, Crane J held in *H v MHRT, North and East London Region* that fairness and natural justice required that:

> ... if the medical member is taking into account or is drawing to the attention of other members, either evidence or his views as an expert, then the claimant and his advisors should be alerted to such evidence and such views in sufficient detail, and sufficiently early in the proceedings, to enable them to deal with them.

This openness would ensure equality of arms since the evidence relied upon by the medical member could be challenged by the applicant. It should be noted that it is also necessary in terms of equality of arms and the right to a fair hearing that legal representation should be available for tribunal hearings (in good time so as to allow for sufficient preparation before the hearing)[13] and legal aid should be available to those with insufficient means.[14] This is the case at present, and under the new proposals will continue to be the case for all those detained under compulsory powers. The government has also promised the creation of an independent specialist advocacy service, the Patient Advocacy Liaison Service. As regards permissible non-disclosure under r 12 of the MHRT Rules, which is for the purposes of protecting the welfare of the patient where necessary, there is no reason why there should not be disclosure to his legal representative.

Power to release

Article 5(4) has proved useful to mentally disordered patients in the past when it resulted in a change in the MHRT powers so that the tribunal itself

---

9 See *Lamy v Belgium* (1989) 11 EHRR 529 and *Weeks v UK* (1987) 10 EHRR 293. However, the Commission has observed that the disclosure requirements are less extensive under Art 5(4) than under Art 6; see *Rowe and Davies v UK*, App No 28901/95 (1998).

10 MHRT Rules, r 12.

11 Although some earlier cases seem to suggest that this principle, generally applied under Art 6, is not applicable to Art 5(4) (see, eg, *Neumeister v Austria* (1968) 1 EHRR 91 and *Matznetter v Austria* (1969) 1 EHRR 198), recent cases state otherwise; see, eg, *Sanchez-Reisse v Switzerland* (1986) 9 EHRR 71; *Lamy v Belgium* (1989) 11 EHRR 529; and *Toth v Austria* (1991) 14 EHRR 551.

12 See *Lamy v Belgium* (1989) 11 EHRR 529; *Toth v Austria* (1991) 14 EHRR 551.

13 See, eg, *Winterwerp v The Netherlands* (1979) 2 EHRR 387; *Megyeri v Germany* (1992) 15 EHRR 584.

14 *Zamir v UK* (1983) 40 DR 42.

could discharge a patient who no longer warranted detention.[15] However, there are numerous situations where the Home Secretary has the final say on release, which appears to be a clear breach of Art 5(4), particularly in view of the decision in *X v United Kingdom*[16] which indicated that a tribunal should have the power to review the Home Secretary's decision.

R v Bournewood Community and Mental Health NHS Trust ex p L[17] clarified that non-resisting patients who lack the capacity to consent to admission to hospital or to treatment cannot rely on any of the safeguards in the MHA 1983 such as the right to a review of their detention. Being informally detained, the applicant in *Bournewood* had no access to an MHRT,[18] and so had to resort to judicial review and habeas corpus proceedings in the High Court. This court did not have the power to discharge L (being unable to examine the merits), but could only remit the case to the decision making body (in this case the hospital). In any case, as Lord Nolan pointed out, if L was not detained, there was no legal ground under which the hospital could be called upon to justify their unwillingness to release him. This is because habeas corpus is only available if the person is detained. If, as it appears under the jurisprudence of the European Convention on Human Rights (ECHR),[19] L was in fact detained, the decision in *Bournewood* has resulted in a clear breach of Art 5(4); L had no effective right to a hearing on the legality of his detention by an independent body which could order his discharge.

The effectiveness of powers of discharge was examined in *Stanley Johnson v United Kingdom*.[20] The applicant had been subject to a hospital and restriction order, and was granted a conditional discharge on the basis that he was no longer suffering from a mental illness, but that if he were released without rehabilitation after almost five years in hospital he might have a relapse. However, he had to wait three and a half years after he was found to be no longer suffering from a mental illness before he was discharged, due to difficulties in locating a supervised hostel place that was required to fulfil his conditional discharge. The MHRT had no power to demand the provision of a place in a hostel and so discharge, conditional on such a requirement, in

---

15 Eg, *X v UK* (1981) 4 EHRR 188, the result of which s 73 of the MHA 1983 was enacted so that a tribunal could discharge a restricted patient itself.

16 (1981) 4 EHRR 188.

17 [1998] 3 All ER 289.

18 In the light of *Bournewood* [1998] 3 All ER 289, the government has proposed new safeguards for informally detained individuals, under which at any stage the patient or his representative may apply to the new tribunal either to challenge detention or in order to challenge the care and treatment plan drawn up and discussed with the clinical supervisor who will have consulted the patient's carers and close relatives and a person nominated by a social care representative in that regard. The tribunal is then to commission a report from the expert panel with possible proposed changes to the care plan. These safeguards are proportionate to the aim of detention and are likely to be in compliance with Art 5.

19 See Davidson, Chapter 11, above.

20 (1999) 27 EHRR 296.

essence amounted to an indefinite deferral, thereby breaching Art 5(1). The applicant also argued that this was contrary to Art 5(4) since an order for discharge on this basis was in fact 'toothless'. However, the Commission had considered that the applicant's complaint under Art 5(4) did not give rise to any separate issue, having regard to its finding under Art 5(1).

Similar considerations were the subject of R's complaints in *R v MHRT ex p Secretary of State*,[21] where it was established that a MHRT's power to adjourn a case was limited to enabling it to better perform one of the functions under the Act. The Tribunal was unable to adjourn the hearing for the purpose of obtaining information about the possibility of such a transfer since there was no power for it to make a direction concerning the transfer of a restricted patient to another hospital. This appears to be arbitrary and so under the ECHR it appears to breach Art 5. Nonetheless, the Court was of the view that there was no breach of Art 5(4) since any veto of a transfer by the Home Secretary could be challenged by judicial review. In fact, this safeguard is illusory since the Divisional Court has no power to order transfer, but only to remit the decision back to the Home Secretary.

The burden of proof

The exceptions available under Art 5(1) are indicative of the fact that the right to liberty and security of the person is not an absolute one. Where a right is not absolute, it is clearly for the State to justify any deprivation of liberty. It is logical, then, that the fact that a patient must justify his grounds for release (the reversal of the burden of proof in the MHA 1983 discharge criteria) will breach the Convention. To place the burden on the patient is unfair and too onerous,[22] and this was addressed in a recent landmark decision, *R v MHRT, North and East London Region and Another ex p H* concerning an appeal against a decision not to discharge a patient.[23] The case resulted in the first of the Court of Appeal's declarations[24] that a piece of domestic legislation is incompatible with the 1998 (HRA). The Court ruled that the discharge criteria requiring patients to prove their fitness for release under s 72 was incompatible with the HRA 1998. Instead, hospitals must show that a patient's detention should be continued. The government will have to amend the current MHA 1983 to comply with this ruling.

For the mentally disordered offender who is given a discretionary life sentence, there is a similar reversal of the burden of proof in s 34 of the Criminal Justice Act (CJA) 1991. The Parole Board cannot release a prisoner

---

21   (2000) unreported, 15 December (CO/1928/2000).

22   See, eg, *Salabiaku v France* (1988) 13 EHRR 379.

23   [2001] EWCA Civ 415; (2001) *The Times*, 2 April.

24   Under HRA 1998, s 4.

unless satisfied that it is no longer necessary for the protection of the public that he should be confined. This places the burden on the prisoner to prove that he is not dangerous. In addition, the courts have held that the Board must be satisfied that there is 'no more than a minimal risk' of re-offending.[25] However, the original preventive sentence was not imposed because the offender failed to satisfy the court that he did not present a more than minimal risk of re-offending, but because the court was positively satisfied that his detention was necessary to protect the public from serious harm. His continued detention, then, does not appear to be justified by reference to the objectives and criteria that governed the imposition of the original sentence. In order to justify continued detention, the danger to the public should be the same as that which was present and justified the preventive sentence.

However, reverse burdens of proof do not automatically breach rights provided that they are proportionate.[26]

RIGHT TO SPEEDY REVIEW OF LEGALITY OF DETENTION

The European Court has not precisely defined 'speedily' but has given some pointers in various cases. The Court of Appeal recently confirmed this approach, in *R (On the Application of C) v Mental Health Review Tribunal, London South and South West Region* ((2001) *The Times*, 3 July). Although the Mental Health Review Tribunal Rules (SI 1983/942) did not set a specific time limit within which an application for review had to be heard, a policy of hearing applications within eight weeks was in force. It was held that it would be arbitrary and therefore unlawful under the HRA 1998 for any specific time limit to apply to all cases where a more speedy review date would be reasonably practicable.

Review of detention under Art 5(1)(e)

Permitted period prior to review of detention for assessment

In *Bournewood*, the period of detention exceeded what could be considered reasonable if categorised as an emergency, and so it is submitted that he should have been admitted for treatment under s 3 of the MHA 1983 after initial assessment. An emergency situation will be one in which an individual's mental disorder will inevitably require assessment. In *E v Norway*,[27] it was held that there was a breach of Art 5(4) when a newly detained patient had to wait 55 days from application to a decision on the

---

25 *R v Secretary of State for the Home Department ex p Bradley* [1991] 1 WLR 134.
26 See, eg, *Salabiaku v France* (1988) 13 EHRR 379. See, also, Davidson, Chapter 11, above.
27 (1990) 17 EHRR 30.

legality of his detention. Under the MHA 1983, assessment must take place within 28 days, and thereafter the detainee must be released or detained under another section of the Act (generally s 3, for treatment). This appears to comply with Art 5(4).

The recent White Paper proposes that those with suspected dangerous severe personality disorder (DSPD) are to be subject to an initial period of assessment of up to 28 days in order to assess whether there is sufficient evidence of DSPD to justify a more intensive assessment (probably in a regional NHS secure facility).[28] There will be a right to a review of the detention at this point by the new independent decision making body, the Mental Health Tribunal, which is to replace the MHRT.[29] It will also be possible to request an expedited referral to a tribunal for review before the completion of 28 days. The tribunal may then authorise further detention for a period of intensive assessment for three months in a specialist DSPD unit.[30] It seems a fiction to refer to the period of three months as an 'assessment period', since the primary period of 28 days must have established that there is sufficient evidence of DSPD to classify the individual as appropriate for the specialist DSPD facility. Indeed, MIND is of the view that these 'extensive powers ... have more to do with dangerousness than with mental disorder'.[31] In view of the decision in *E v Norway*,[32] it is likely that this lengthy period of assessment would be in breach of Art 5(4), since it is an arbitrary timescale during which the detainee appears to have no right of review. *Koendjbiharie v The Netherlands* makes it clear that in relation to second or later applications, there will be a violation where a delay is of four months or longer.[33] However, as that case involved admission for treatment, rather than assessment, it cannot be authority to suggest that three months without a further review would not breach Art 5(4).

Also in its recent White Paper, the government has proposed the introduction of a power for all criminal courts to remand a person for assessment by specialist mental health services, either in hospital or in the community on bail, on the basis of a single medical opinion from an appropriately qualified doctor that a care and treatment order *may*[34] be an appropriate disposal. However, compulsory treatment would not be permitted in the absence of a second medical opinion. MIND has criticised the proposals because such a remand will be renewable at 28 day intervals for up

---

28 DoH, 2000a, Pt II, Chapter 4.

29 This new body will obtain advice from independent experts as well as taking evidence, where appropriate, from the clinical team, patients and their representatives, and other relevant agencies.

30 DoH, 2000a, White Paper, Pt II, para 6.42.

31 See MIND's comments on the White Paper, *Policy and Parliament Unit*, 8 January 2001.

32 (1990) 17 EHRR 30.

33 (1990) 13 EHRR 820.

34 Emphasis added.

to 12 months, yet 'even for personality disorder patients the specialist intensive assessment procedure is only envisaged as lasting three months'.[35] Clearly, assessment is not required for such a lengthy period, and once diagnosed, the individual should be sentenced appropriately or detained under the applicable civil provisions. If the legislation is enacted, a breach of Art 5(4) may be inevitable.

In *K v United Kingdom*,[36] a friendly settlement was reached, a condition of which was that the MHRT rules would be amended to introduce a fixed time limit of two months for the hearing to take place in the case of conditionally discharged restricted patients who have been recalled. Unfortunately, this has not been done and a challenge under the HRA 1998 would certainly succeed. Another area vulnerable to challenge is s 47 of the National Assistance Act 1948 governing the removal of persons in need of care and attention. Under this Act there is a right of review after six weeks, although the order lasts for up to three months, extendable by the court for further periods of up to three months. The period of six weeks may be considered too lengthy to comply with Art 5(4) since the original detention was clearly based on what could only be classified as an 'emergency'. In view of *E v Norway* and *Koendjbiharie v The Netherlands* this period may breach Art 5(4) of the ECHR in that access to review is insufficiently 'speedy'.

Permitted period prior to review of detention for treatment

An anomaly may be seen as regards those detained continuously under s 6 of the 1959 Mental Deficiency Act. Such patients have only a two year right to apply to a MHRT, unlike others who may apply annually.[37] Although this applies to very few patients now, it is almost certainly a breach of Art 5(4).

Review of detention under Art 5(1)(a)

For release

In *Weeks v UK*, the successful applicant was the subject of a discretionary life sentence and complained that he did not have access to a court with the necessary procedural safeguards that could order his release at the post-tariff stage of his sentence.

A similar and more recent case, *Curley v United Kingdom*,[38] concerned the delay of release of a convicted murderer held at Her Majesty's pleasure. The European Court held that on expiry of his tariff of eight years he was entitled

---

35 MIND's comments on the White Paper, *op cit*, fn 31, above.

36 App No 11468/85 (1991), 15 April 1988.

37 MHA 1983, Sched 5, para 33(2).

38 App No 32340/96, 28 March 2000; (2000) *The Times*, 5 April.

to have the lawfulness of his detention reviewed speedily in adversarial proceedings by a body which had the power to order his release if appropriate.[39] At his fifth review after the expiry of his tariff period of eight years, the Parole Board recommended that the applicant be given a provisional release date 12 months from the hearing, during which time he should spend six months in a category D open prison, followed by six months in a pre-release employment scheme hostel. This recommendation was not accepted by the Home Secretary, who directed the applicant's transfer to a category D prison with a direction that he was to have a further review in 12 months' time. The applicant's tariff expired in 1987 and he was not released until May 1997. In the intervening period he did not receive a meaningful review, as the Parole Board (even under interim arrangements put in place as a result of decisions by the European Court)[40] did not have the power to order his release. The Court concluded unanimously that there had been a breach of Art 5(4) of the ECHR.

There may also be a possible breach of Art 5(4) as regards an offender who is subject to a longer than normal sentence under s 2(2)(b) of the CJA 1991; a sentence which need not be divided into tariff (the part to be served under retribution) and prevention. There is no provision for early parole review by an independent body when the punitive period is over, or indeed mandatory release if the person is no longer a danger to others. Under s 33 of the CJA 1991, a prisoner may be released by the Parole Board after serving half of a short term sentence. However, a prisoner sentenced under s 2(2)(b) will not be entitled to review until he has served half of his sentence, not merely half of the *retributive* period of his sentence. This is unfair and arbitrary, and appears to be a breach of Art 5(4).

Delay of discharge after review

The offender in *Stanley Johnson v UK*[41] had to wait three and a half years for the supervised hostel place that was required to fulfil the conditional discharge ordered by the Tribunal. The MHRT had no power to demand a place in a hostel, and the resultant indefinite deferral breached Art 5(1). This also seems to be contrary to Art 5(4) since the deferral was not for a reasonable period of time, and the tribunal did not have the power to order that conditions be met either by a fixed date or at all.[42] However, the Art 5(4) point was held not to raise another issue in view of the breach of Art 5(1). The European Court made it clear that there is no duty upon a hospital to

---

39 See *Hussain v UK* (1996) 22 EHRR 1; *Singh v UK* (1967) 10 YB 478; *V v UK* and *T v UK* (1999) EHRR 121.

40 *Hussain v UK* (1996) 22 EHRR 1 and *Singh v UK* (1967) 10 YB 478.

41 [1999] 27 EHRR 296.

42 See, also, *R v MHRT and Others ex p Russell Hall* [1999] 2 All ER 132, which also discussed the problem of the lack of powers available to a tribunal to order conditions to be put in place, but this case was prior to the coming into force of the HRA 1998.

discharge a patient as soon as they are found to be no longer requiring treatment in hospital, and deferral with regard to a conditional discharge is permissible. However, it did not specify what period might amount to a 'reasonable' one.

It seems, then, that deferred conditional discharges for restricted patients under s 73(7) of the MHA 1983 may breach the Convention if the delay before arranging the requisite conditions (such as a place of residence in a hostel) is too lengthy. This would apply also to unrestricted patients whose release under s 72(3) is delayed. If the requisite conditions cannot be put in place in a reasonable time, the authorities would seem to have a duty under Art 5 to decide whether a detainee should be unconditionally discharged, or conditionally discharged on a different basis.

ARTICLE 3

Article 3 states:

No one shall be subjected to torture or to inhuman or degrading treatment or punishment.

Article 3 preserves the right to freedom from torture, inhuman or degrading punishment or treatment. The right under Art 3 is absolute and no derogation may be made from it. The abhorrence felt towards actions amounting to 'torture', however, means that a finding of such will only be upheld in the most serious situations and the European Court has always been reluctant to stigmatise a State by such a finding.

Perhaps surprisingly, the argument in *Aerts v Belgium*[43] that detention of a person on the grounds of mental health would only be lawful for the purposes of Art 5(1)(e) if effected in an *appropriate* institution did not succeed in the context of Art 3. The conditions of the applicant's detention and lack of medical or psychiatric attention had caused a deterioration of his mental health, and his psychiatrist and the Mental Health Board wrote reports stating that the applicant was being harmed by being detained in such conditions. The Commission had found that the State, by its omission, had caused the applicant to suffer treatment which in the circumstances had been inhuman, or at the very least degrading. Nonetheless, the Court disagreed; the ill-treatment suffered did not attain the minimum level of severity to fall within the scope of Art 3. Oddly, the Court was not satisfied that the independent reports 'proved' that there had been a deterioration in the applicant's state of mental health, which begs the question as to what evidence would have been acceptable as 'proof'; especially since the Court accepted that the applicant, being mentally ill, would be unlikely to be able to describe the effect the

---

43   [1998] EHRLR 777.

conditions had had on his health himself. It appears that where general conditions of confinement are unsatisfactory and the standard of care falls below the minimum level acceptable from an ethical and humanitarian point of view, this is not sufficient to prove a breach of Art 3.

Thus, until recently, no argument that the type of punishment or treatment given to an individual prisoner or patient was inhuman or degrading had succeeded.[44] Nonetheless, it seems that the European Court is becoming more open to arguments alleging breaches of Art 3.[45] This is because the ECHR is a 'living instrument'; under the principle of evolving interpretation, the older a decision, the less value it may have as a guide to construction. Furthermore, what is seen to be proportionate in a democratic society will inevitably vary over time. The ECHR is flexible in order to respond to cultural differences and changes in moral thinking. Thus, there now appears to be scope for saying that the place of detention (for example, a prison) is so inappropriate for a patient that it amounts to degrading punishment.

It should be noted that susceptibility to ill treatment 'depends on all the circumstances, such as the duration of the treatment, its physical or mental effects', and the age, sex, state of health or vulnerability of the victim.[46] Thus, whether ill treatment can amount to inhuman or degrading treatment may vary depending upon the particular person who is invoking the protection of Art 3. It follows, then, that the mentally disordered may be able to tolerate ill treatment less well than others, and so the test for degrading treatment should be lower.

This was expressly recognised in *Keenan v United Kingdom*,[47] in which the applicant's son was admitted to prison to serve a sentence of four months for assault on his girlfriend. He then assaulted two hospital officers, and was placed in a segregation unit. By way of punishment, his release from prison was delayed by 28 days, including seven extra days in segregation in the punishment block. He subsequently committed suicide. It was held that it should have been recognised that this punishment, imposed two weeks after the assault and nine days before his expected date of release, could have threatened his physical and moral resistance. This was incompatible with the standard of treatment required in relation to a mentally ill person. The Court noted that careful monitoring of Keenan, a known suicide risk, should have been carried out, particularly due to the fluctuating nature of the condition

---

44 In *Ireland v UK* (1978) 2 EHRR 25, it was agreed that torture constituted 'an aggravated and deliberate form of cruel, inhuman or degrading treatment or punishment' and degrading treatment will cause a victim fear, anguish and inferiority that humiliates and debases him, and may break his physical and moral resistance.

45 It is possible that the claim in *Ashingdane v UK* (1985) 7 EHRR 528 would have been more successful under Art 3.

46 *Ireland v UK* (1978) 2 EHRR 25; *Stanley Johnson v UK* (1999) 27 EHRR 296.

47 Application No 27229/95, 3 April 2001; (2001) *The Times*, 18 April ECtHR. The Court found no breach of Art 2 (relating to the right to life).

from which he suffered. 'Degrading' treatment within the meaning of Art 3 would adversely affect a person's personality such as to arouse feelings of fear, anguish and inferiority capable of humiliating or debasing them and possibly breaking their physical or moral resistance, or to drive them to act against their will or conscience.[48] The authorities had failed to carry out their obligation to protect the health of persons deprived of liberty; and a high standard of care was required with regard to the mentally ill who were likely to be less robust than others. In so much as the segregation unit was a more restrictive environment than was appropriate in the knowledge of the particular vulnerability of those with mental disorder and of the suicidal tendencies of the applicant's son, the case also appears to reinforce the argument that Art 3 includes a right to the least restrictive environment.

Necessary treatment

As a general rule, a measure which is a therapeutic *necessity* cannot be regarded as inhuman or degrading. The prolonged use of handcuffs and a security bed were used according to the psychiatric principles generally accepted at the time in *Herczegfalvy v Austria*,[49] and as medical necessity justified the patient's treatment, there had been no violation of Art 3. This appears to suggest that the positive right is merely a weaker duty on behalf of the treating doctors to act reasonably when deciding upon a patient's best interests. It should be noted, however, that long term seclusion is unlikely to be considered a therapeutic necessity, and it seems that this could amount to inhuman or degrading treatment.[50] In addition, there have been instances of treatment in hospitals within the UK which would amount to such treatment, such as the strapping of elderly psychiatric patients to a toilet whilst they were being fed in a hospital.[51]

Side-effects of medication

In *Grare v France*[52] it was held that Art 3 was not breached where compulsory medication with unpleasant side-effects was given to the applicant in the community. It is unlikely that medication lawfully prescribed would ever be found to breach Art 3. However, administering a medicine to a detained

---

48 See *Ireland v UK* (1972) 15 YB 76; *Stanley Johnson v UK* (1999) 27 EHRR 296.

49 (1992) 15 EHRR 437.

50 See, eg, *A v UK* (1998) 27 EHRR 611, where the repetition of beatings by a parent was a significant factor in a breach of Art 3.

51 See, further, the Commission for Health Improvements' Report regarding Garlands Hospital, Cumbria, *Investigation into the North Lakeland NHS Trust: Report to the Secretary of State for Health*, November 2000.

52 (1992) 15 EHRR CD 100.

patient that has more side-effects than an alternative, but is less costly, could amount to inhuman or degrading treatment.[53]

A failure to treat

In *Aerts v Belgium*,[54] the issue of the *omission* of treatment was considered in the context of Art 3. Throughout his detention, the applicant had not received any regular medical or psychiatric attention, causing a deterioration in his mental health. Reports from both psychiatrists and the Mental Health Board stated that detention in such conditions was harmful to the applicant. The Commission found a breach in that the omission was at the very least degrading, and the State did not contest that the general conditions had been unsatisfactory and the standard of care fell below the minimum level acceptable from an ethical and humanitarian point of view. Nevertheless, the European Court found no breach of Art 3 since there was no proof of a deterioration in the applicant's state of mental health caused by the living conditions. In view of the medical reports which appeared to say otherwise, the case is illustrative of the strictness of the test for a breach under this Article.

Length and severity of treatment

In addition to claiming breaches of Art 5, the applicant in *Stanley Johnson v UK* claimed a breach of Art 3. The Commission found no such breach because the level of ill treatment received – resulting from the length of time in detention (three and a half years when he was no longer suffering from mental disorder) – did not attain the requisite level of severity. The assessment of the minimum level of severity was relative, depending on all the circumstances of the case, such as the duration of the treatment, and its physical or mental effects. If not causing actual bodily harm, such treatment had to cause at least intense physical and mental suffering to amount to inhuman treatment. The Commission also reiterated the fact that Art 3 could not require a life sentence to be reviewed with a view to its remission or termination.

In *Curley v United Kingdom*,[55] the applicant succeeded in his claim that Art 5(4) had been breached. However, he also claimed that such a long period of detention (a tariff of eight years, followed by 10 more years in detention) in the absence of any proper or adequate procedure to decide upon his release

---

53   See *Herczegfalvy v Austria* (1992) 15 EHRR 437; *Grare v France* (1992) 15 EHRR CD 100.
54   [1998] EHRLR 777.
55   App No 32340/96, 28 March 2000; (2000) *The Times*, 5 April.

constituted inhuman or degrading punishment. The claim as regards Art 3 failed again, on the basis that the treatment was not considered to be sufficiently severe.

Disproportionality

In *Weeks v United Kingdom*,[56] the Commission had 'serious doubts' about the compatibility of Art 3 with a life sentence that was entirely disproportionate to the offence. This has serious implications for English sentencing. Where a mentally disordered offender does not fulfil the conditions required for a hospital order under s 37 of the MHA 1983 because he is not regarded as treatable, he is at a greater risk of being sentenced to very long periods of imprisonment than most other offenders. A sentence greater than that which is merited by the seriousness of the offence may be imposed by a court in order to protect the public.[57]

Under s 2(2)(b) of the CJA 1991, the court may pass a longer than normal sentence on someone convicted of a violent or sexual offence in order to protect the public from 'serious harm', and such sentences are often deemed appropriate for mentally disordered offenders.[58] Under s 1(2) of the CJA 1991,[59] a custodial sentence must only be imposed where an offence or 'the combination of the offence and one or more offences associated with it'[60] is so serious that only custody is justified, or, in relation to violent or sexual offences, where only custody would adequately protect the public from serious harm caused by him. Thus, in the case of violent or sexual offences, it is possible that the predicate offence is not very serious and entirely disproportionate to the crime. The law requires an assessment of possible future harm, and since risk assessment is notoriously inaccurate, this has the potential for unfairness. Detention will become arbitrary (and, thus, breach Art 5) if it ceases to serve the purpose of the original sentence. This surely has implications where the purpose of the original sentence was to protect the public from a dangerous offender, since dangerousness may wane over time. For this reason, in *Weeks* it was held that there must be periodic reviews where the original detention was based on dangerousness or mental instability.[61]

R v Hodgson[62] is the leading case on life sentences to protect the public which makes it clear that the offence on which such a sentence is based must

---

56 *Weeks v UK* (1987) 10 EHRR 293.

57 *R v Moore* (1986) 8 Cr App R(S) 376; *R v Zacharcko* [1988] Crim LR 546.

58 See, eg, *R v Lyons* [1993] 15 Cr App R(S) 460; *R v Fawcett (Lynne)* [1994] Crim LR(S) 704; *R v Etchells* [1996] 1 Cr App R(S) 163 CA.

59 As amended by the CJA 1993.

60 This means either sentenced for them at the same time, or convicted of them in same proceedings, or where a defendant asks for them to be taken into consideration (s 31(2)).

61 See, also, *Thynne, Wilson and Gunnell v UK* (1990) 13 EHRR 666.

62 (1967) 52 Cr App R 113.

be serious enough to require a very long period in custody.[63] Either the nature of the offence or the offender's history must show that the consequences to others, should he commit more offences, must be especially serious, or that he is a person of unstable character who is likely to commit offences in the future. This latter ground means that the mentally disordered offender is also more likely to receive a discretionary life sentence on the grounds of his 'instability of character'.[64]

Indeterminacy

It is not clear whether the indeterminate nature of a sentence could amount to a breach of Art 3. The American courts and the Privy Council have held that lengthy delays resulting in the uncertainty of time remaining before execution is in some cases so unfair that the death sentence should be commuted.[65] More recently, in *V v UK*[66] and *T v UK*[67] the European Court admitted that 'an unjustifiable and persistent failure to fix a tariff', particularly in relation to an offender who had been very young at the time of conviction, might give rise to a claim under Art 3. Rather than the length or lack of proportionality being the cause of the breach, it was the uncertainty over many years as to an offender's future which caused additional punishment in the form of psychological pressure that could amount to inhuman or degrading punishment or treatment.

ARTICLE 8(1)

Article 8(1) states:

> Everyone has the right to respect for his private and family life, his home and correspondence.

---

63 However, this is liberally interpreted by the courts; see *R v Blogg* (1981) 3 Cr App R(S) 114.

64 See, eg, *R v Hodgson* (1967) 52 Cr App R 113; *AG's Reference (No 34 of 1992)* (1993) 15 Cr App R(S) 167.

65 See, eg, *Pratt v AG for Jamaica* [1993] 4 All ER 769; a death sentence should be carried out as soon as possible after sentencing, allowing for appeal. See, also, *Guerra v Baptiste* [1996] 1 AC 397 where a delay of four and a half years from a receipt of death sentence for murder to the hearing of an appeal against conviction and sentence constituted cruel and unusual punishment contrary to the Constitution of Trinidad and Tobago. It was held that two years for the appellate process was the waiting maximum period in view of the inhumanity of prolonging the period of waiting on death row. See, also, *Soering v UK* (1989) 11 EHRR 439.

66 (1999) EHRR 121.

67 *Ibid*.

X v Iceland[68] established that Art 8 included 'the right to establish and to develop relationships with other human beings, especially in the emotional field for the development and fulfilment of one's own personality'. Any interference with such a right must be in accordance with the law, and necessary in a democratic society for the protection of (*inter alia*) public health.

Non-arbitrary interference

For the law to be valid, it must be foreseeable in its effects (in other words, not arbitrary); any discretion must be sufficiently precise to provide 'adequate protection against arbitrary interference'.[69] In *Bournewood*, L's carers were forbidden to see him as it was thought that he might become agitated and want to accompany them out of the hospital. There was no right to appeal against the informal detention and refusal of their access to him. It is arguable that the decision to detain informally rather than to use the MHA 1983 was in order to avoid the statutory review procedures. This appears to be an arbitrary interference. Furthermore, potentially not only L's right to family life under Art 8 was breached, but also his carers' rights. In this respect, however, it should be noted that L's carers would not have qualified as nearest relatives as they had not lived with him for the requisite five years. Nonetheless, it is clear from *X, Y and Z v UK*[70] that Art 8 rights are not limited to those who have formal family status under domestic law.

A friendly settlement based on respect for human rights[71] was struck in *JT v UK*[72] on the agreement of the UK to amend the MHA 1983 to enable patients to apply to the court to have the 'nearest relative' replaced on the basis of a reasonable objection to a certain person. The applicant was detained from 1984 until 1996 under s 3 of the Act. Various psychiatric and social work reports compiled during her detention outlined her difficult relationship with her mother and mentioned repeated allegations that she had been sexually abused by her stepfather. The applicant was aware that her mother and stepfather lived in the same house, despite their divorce in 1977, and, accordingly, she did not want her mother to know of her whereabouts. A report in 1993 referred to the applicant's desire, despite her mother's wish to remain so, to remove her mother from the position of nearest relative and to replace her with a particular social worker. However, the applicant was not able to do so under the requisite legislation, and so complained of a violation

---

68 (1976) 5 DR 85.
69 *Gillow v UK* (1986) 11 EHRR 335.
70 (1997) 24 EHRR 143. See, also, *Gaskin v UK* (1989) 12 EHRR 36.
71 As defined in the ECHR or its Protocols (Art 37(1) and r 62(3) of the Rules of Court).
72 App No 26494/95, 30 March 2000.

of Art 8 of the ECHR. Had there not been a friendly settlement, a finding of a breach of the Convention would have been almost certain.[73]

The government's recent White Paper favours replacing 'nearest relatives' with 'nominated persons', who are to be chosen by the social worker or equivalent person in consultation with the patient's relative or main carer.[74] Although recent advance Directives are to be taken into account, a patient will have no say in the nomination. This appears to be an arbitrary interference and a clear breach of Art 8. It is submitted that the new tribunal's power to appoint a different nominated person where it is impractical or inappropriate for the person nominated to act on the patient's behalf would be an insufficient safeguard to remedy the breach.

'Best interests'

It is clear that under Art 5(4) an individual seeking a review of his detention must be given access to all relevant evidence in the possession of the authorities.[75] In spite of this requirement, the MHRT may keep reports on which they rely confidential on the basis that it would be harmful to the patient to disclose them.[76] As mentioned in the previous chapter, this may breach Art 5 since there is an inequality of arms. In addition, the hospital may share this information on the patient with various relevant bodies. The government has indicated that it is committed to increasing this kind of information sharing, and intends to include in any new legislation a duty covering disclosure between health and social services and other agencies. Naturally, this is with the safety of both the patient and public in mind. To ensure compliance with the right of the patient to privacy and confidentiality under Arts 8(2) and 10(2), the White Paper suggests that the legitimacy of information sharing could be based upon a consideration of the best interests of the patient,[77] or in order to prevent a significant risk of serious harm to others.[78] The proposals may indeed reduce the risk of harm to both patient and the public, but it is important that there is strict adherence to the rules governing the sharing of such information.[79]

---

73 See, also, *FC v UK*, App No 37344/97, 30 March 1999.

74 DoH, 2000a, Pt I, para 2.23.

75 *Weeks v UK* (1987) 10 EHRR 293.

76 MHRT Rules, r 12.

77 For a helpful consideration of domestic law in this area, see *W v Egdell* [1990] 2 WLR 471. It should be noted that doctors and health authorities must also ensure their actions comply with the Data Protection Act 1998.

78 MIND suggests that the 'best interests' test is too broad; *op cit*, fn 31.

79 See, also, *Z v Finland* (1998) 25 EHRR 371.

Compulsory treatment in the community

Compulsory treatment and physical intervention have been held to violate Art 8, and thus it may be contrary to Art 8 to make discharge conditional on the taking of medication.[80] Thus, the government's proposed new community care and treatment orders have the potential for violating this Article.

ARTICLE 8(2)

Article 8(2) states:

> There shall be no interference by a public authority with the exercise of this right except such as is in accordance with the law and is necessary in a democratic society in the interests of national security, public safety or the economic well-being of the country, for the prevention of disorder or crime, for the protection of health or morals, or for the protection of the rights and freedoms of others.

The rights under Art 8 are not absolute, and interference with them may be justified on any of the grounds stated in Art 8(2). In general, the interference will only be justified if 'in accordance with the law', and if necessary in a democratic society, which means that there must be a 'pressing social need' for it.[81] These two requirements will not be met should the interference be disproportionate to its aim.[82] In relation to the mentally disordered, justifications tend to be on the bases of public safety, or for the protection of health. The protection of the rights and freedoms of others may also be relied upon by a State, as it is a broad 'catch-all' phrase.

The protection of public health

Article 8(2) provides, *inter alia*, that there may be interference with the right to private life 'for the protection of health' if the action being taken is 'such as is in accordance with the law and is necessary in a democratic society'. Detention under s 47 of the National Assistance Act 1948 and under ss 135 and 136 of the MHA 1983 permit a severe interference with a person's liberty. Nonetheless, it is likely that the European Court would consider that detention under these provisions are permitted 'for the protection of public health'.[83] However, it is arguable that the powers are not 'necessary' since

---

80 See, eg, *X v Austria* (1979) 18 DR 154; *Peters v The Netherlands* (1994) 77A DR 75.

81 *Handyside v UK* (1976) 1 EHRR 737; *Sunday Times v UK* (1979) 2 EHHR 245.

82 For a good example of disproportionality of justification, see *Niemetz v Germany* (1992) 16 EHRR 97.

83 ECHR, Art 8(2).

they are disproportionate to this aim, which could be achieved by a viable less restrictive alternative that would not interfere with the right to respect for privacy and family life under Art 8 of the ECHR. For example, there are alternative powers available in relation to the protection of public health, such as the Public Health (Control of Disease) Act 1984 governing infectious diseases, which enables the courts to order the medical examination and detention in hospital[84] of a person carrying,[85] or thought to have or to be carrying,[86] a notifiable disease.[87]

Any future community treatment order may also, perhaps, be justified if its purpose is to prevent a deterioration of a patient's health. The government's proposed new orders are intended to include specifications to prevent non-compliant patients from becoming a risk to themselves or others.[88] To avoid breaching Art 8, such orders must also be proportionate to the aim of protecting public health, and indeed it is not intended that patients be given medication forcibly, except in a clinical setting.[89] Furthermore, an order might avoid the additional restriction of liberty involved in hospital detention, and a patient subject to it 'need not suffer the possible distress of repeated unplanned admissions to acute wards'.[90]

Public safety

R v Secretary of State for Health ex p ML[91] involved restrictions on child visits to patients in high security hospitals who had committed murder, manslaughter, or certain sexual offences. It was held that unless the child was one of a permitted category, such restrictions were lawful and did not breach Art 8 of the ECHR. The relationship between an aunt or uncle and a nephew or niece did not automatically constitute family life within the meaning of Art 8, but

---

84 Public Health (Infectious Diseases) Regulations 1988 SI 1988/1546, reg 3, extends these powers to several other diseases. There is an appeal against the order to the Crown Court under Public Health (Control of Disease) Act 1984, s 67(2).

85 Public Health (Control of Disease) Act 1984, s 37.

86 *Ibid*, s 35.

87 Cholera, plague, relapsing fever, smallpox and typhus.

88 DoH, 2000a, Pt I, para 2.18.

89 It is unclear as to what might amount to a 'clinical setting'; it may be very broad. It should also be noted that consent to treatment in the community may well not be true consent, but consent for the purposes of avoiding the inevitable consequences of not giving consent – see DoH, 2000a, Executive Summary, Pt I, para 13: 'Steps will be specified in community orders to prevent patients, if they do not comply with their order, becoming a risk to themselves, their carers, or the public.' This can only mean compulsory admission.

90 *Ibid*.

91 [2001] 1 FLR 406.

was dependent on the facts of an individual case.[92] The onus of establishing family life, a flexible concept, was on the applicant. Where there were conflicting rights, there was necessarily a wider margin of appreciation for the Member State in interpreting how the provision of Art 8 should be applied. The ECHR required a balance to be struck between the rights of children and the rights of patients, and the directions relating to child visits were not disproportionate to the aim they sought to achieve, which was the protection of children.

CONCLUSION

There are numerous areas in the present MHA 1983 open to challenge under the HRA 1998. On the basis of the Home Office White Paper, it would seem that certain provisions of any new Act may conflict with the ECHR. What should be remembered, however, is that where legislation cannot be interpreted in a way which is compatible with the HRA 1998, a declaration of incompatibility will be made by the court. The White Paper, *Bringing Rights Home,* stated that the aim of bringing in Convention rights was 'straightforward'; to make rights 'more directly accessible', and 'to bring those rights home'.[93] Indeed, not only must all legislation carry a statement that it is compatible with the HRA 1998,[94] but the Preface to the White Paper specifically stated that introducing the HRA 1998 would eliminate the need to go to Strasbourg.[95] Should a Minister fail to amend the legislation in a reasonable time, it is arguable that this failure to act could be challenged under the HRA 1998 itself as being contrary to the intention of Parliament.

---

92 See, also, *Marckx v Belgium* (1979) 2 EHRR 300; *Keegan v Ireland* (1994) 18 EHRR 342; and *Boughanemi v France* (1996) 22 EHRR 228.

93 Home Office, 1997, para 1.19.

94 HRA 1998, s 19.

95 Except, of course, where the challenge is against a final appeal.

THE HUMAN RIGHTS ACT 1998 AND PRIVATE PROPERTY RIGHTS IN THE CONTEXT OF COMMUNITY CARE

Rod Edmunds and Teresa Sutton[1]

INTRODUCTION

Throughout the latter part of the 20th century closing asylums and hospitals has been a major component of successive governments' policy on community care,[2] both as it applies to people with mental health problems and also those with learning difficulties.[3] Recent political debate has highlighted perceived failings in the implementation and delivery of the policy.[4] Some have even suggested that the shift from institutions into the community may have gone too far.[5] All such differences of emphasis aside, commitment to the principle that people with mental health problems should as far as possible be cared for in home-like surroundings remains unchallenged. Self-evidently, the provision of appropriate housing has a pivotal role in the success of deinstitutionalisation.[6] Even those favouring future housing provision policy and practice (in Scotland) for people with learning disability being developed in a way that maximises opportunities for truly independent living in the community, concede:

> ... it may be appropriate to develop a local strategy that will include group homes for respite, transitional or permanent accommodation (if this is clearly based on need) and will be sustainable in the longer term.[7]

---

1   Our thanks to Charlotte Skeet for helpful comments. The usual caveats apply.

2   Although 'community care' and 'care in the community' are not defined in the National Health Service and Community Care Act 1990, s 46(3) refers to 'community care services'. For an excellent mental health law perspective see Bartlett and Sandland, 2000, Chapters 3 and 9.

3   For convenience, unless the contrary is specifically stated, subsequent references to 'people with mental health problems' are intended to apply equally to people with learning disabilities. Space does not allow consideration of how far there might be cause to distinguish between these two categories in the course of the legal arguments made.

4   For an overview of recent political developments and debate, see the House of Commons Select Committee on Health, 1999.

5   One recent illustration can be seen in Frank Dobson's proposal for a 'third way': DoH press notice 1998/311, 29 July 1998. See, also, his predecessor as Secretary of State for Health, Stephen Dorrell's comments, *Hansard*, HC, 20 February 1996, cols 175–77.

6   On the positive effect of community care on former patients, see Leff and Trieman, 2000.

7   Scottish Executive, 1999. See, also, Simons, 1999.

Reliance upon small group homes,[8] established and run by public bodies (such as mental health charities, housing trusts or health authorities), therefore looks set to continue. This raises the prospect that neighbourhood resistance will also continue. NIMBY (not in my back yard) anxieties may be expressed in terms of the impact the proposed group home is expected to have upon local amenities in terms of noise, parking, property values, anti-social behaviour and violence.[9] Any or all these fears may lack substance.[10] Opposition, perhaps shaped by media attention, may therefore be rooted in prejudice and perpetuate discrimination.

To prevent a group home from being set up, opponents may object to any necessary planning permission. Alternatively, or additionally, neighbours may invoke private rights provided by restrictive covenants. This chapter is concerned only with opposition through such private rights. It, first, illustrates the discriminatory effects covenants can have in English law. By depriving people with mental health problems of a home in the community, the neighbours are in effect interfering with other people's civil rights. Their actions also have the effect of undermining the delivery of care in the community. The chapter therefore seeks to analyse the extent to which the Human Rights Act 1998 (HRA) may prevent covenants being enforced in a bid to prevent the establishment of group homes. It is argued that the legislation holds no guarantee of protection for residents. Consequently, the chapter concludes by briefly identifying how American law may suggest ways in which the Disability Discrimination Act 1995 might be modified to more effectively protect the housing rights of people with mental disability.

OPPOSING COMMUNITY CARE:
THE ROLE OF COVENANTS

Introduction

As equitable property interests, freehold covenants have the potential to control land use long after either or both of the original parties have sold their land.[11] As such it has become clear over the last 10 or so years that commonly encountered restrictive covenants can effectively frustrate attempts to

---

8   See, further, Trieman, 1997.

9   For a valuable survey of the extent and nature of neighbourhood opposition, see Repper, 1997.

10 On the extensive literature, see Edmunds and Sutton, 2001. The preponderance casts doubt upon any negative impact, either in terms of depreciation in property values or because of the risk of violent behaviour.

11 For a comprehensive discussion of covenants, see generally, Newsom, 1998; and Harpum, 2000, Chapter 16.

establish group homes within the community. Earlier illustrations can be found in American jurisprudence.[12] It is not proposed to consider all the relevant English decisions here.[13] Rather, in order to demonstrate flaws inherent in the common law, we will first highlight some of the emergent general points in the body of case law. This is followed by a fuller analysis of two decisions, one (*Dr Barnardo's* case) decided before and the other (*Milbury*) after the shift to deinstitutionalisation. Overall, this survey will illustrate how, in deciding covenant disputes, English courts have been reluctant to invoke wider policy concerns about community care and the human rights of people with mental health problems who aspire to make their homes in ordinary houses in residential neighbourhoods. Revealing this anti-human rights tendency will also help to tease out some of the principal competing anxieties of those who use covenants to challenge the establishment of group home facilities.

English covenants cases and group homes: a general perspective

Covenant disputes are often adjudicated upon in one of two litigation contexts. The question may be posed in a dispute between the parties to the covenant concerning the construction of a covenant. A different route involves the group home provider making an application for the Lands Tribunal to use its statutory jurisdiction to discharge or modify of the terms of a covenant that would otherwise preclude the establishment of a group home.[14] Successful reliance on a covenant may lead to the award of an injunction. This can have a variety of devastating effects on the provision of a group home. It may result in delay, closure, or abandonment. At the very least, it may mean that the group home provider is forced to change the level of support offered.[15]

It is also important to appreciate that in cases where construction is an issue, opponents may succeed by invoking private covenants that seem to be couched in 'neutral' terms about who may occupy the property. Thus, the courts may determine as a matter of strict interpretation that the home is in breach of a covenant because it will constitute an 'annoyance' or 'nuisance' or 'detriment' to the objectors, or because it falls foul of a prohibition on using the land either for 'trade or business purposes' or other than as a 'private dwelling'. The problems this latter type of covenant can cause group homes

---

12 Many are considered by Brussack, 1981; Guernsey, 1984; and Hubbard, 1988.

13 The cases are fully surveyed by Edmunds and Sutton, 2001, pp 133–48.

14 Other possibilities include proceedings: (a) where though a covenant is breached an injunction is refused because the use is for the statutory purposes under the NHS and Community Care Act 1990 (see *Brown v Heathlands Mental Health Services Trust* [1996] 1 All ER 133); or (b) consequential compensation claims under the Compulsory Purchase Act 1965 (see *Richard and Others v Surrey Hampshire Borders NHS Trust*). See further, Edmunds and Sutton, 2001, pp 138–41; and Rutherford, 1996, pp 260–73.

15 See *National Schizophrenia Fellowship v Ribble Estates SA* [1994] 1 EGLR 181.

arose starkly in *C & G Homes v Secretary of State for Health*.[16] The reluctance of the Court of Appeal to allow the policy of resettling former mental patients into a supervised group home to influence their construction of the covenant's language is particularly noteworthy and regrettable. It confirms the suspicion that the judiciary prefer to isolate private property law rights from considerations that touch public policy and human rights. The decision begins to look all the more unsatisfactory when considered against the more recent decision in *Caradon DC v Paton*.[17] That case turns upon the interpretation of the words 'private dwelling' in a covenant imposed on a sale of former council house to its tenant under the Housing Act 1980. In awarding the Council an injunction to restrain the house from being used as a holiday home, the Court of Appeal emphasises the significance of the legislative context of the right to buy legislation, which is to protect amenity and preserve the local housing stock as 'homes'. Even though the Court in *Caradon* purportedly follows *C & G Homes*, there seems to be disparity between the two cases on the priority to be given to governmental policy when construing covenants.

To date, neither the English courts nor the Lands Tribunal have been faced with a covenant that explicitly purports to deny use of land as a group home or other facility for people with mental health problems or learning difficulties. It is to be hoped that there would be no judicial hesitation in striking such a covenant down, perhaps by dint of public policy. However, the position is far from certain which provides one reason for examining whether such a covenant might be successfully challenged for being in violation of the new human rights legislation.

Dr Barnardo's case[18]

Dr Barnardo's deals with a covenant imposed to preclude land being used for an institution of the kind group homes were introduced to replace. Dr Barnardo's applied to the Lands Tribunal for modification of the terms of a covenant, to facilitate their sale of a large building set in 54 acres. The Victorian covenant included a prohibition on the property being used 'as an asylum for the insane'. This, it was assumed for the purposes of the proceedings, would preclude the prospective purchasers, a Regional Hospital Board, from using property for the 'reception and care of mental defectives'. The tribunal refused the application deciding, *inter alia*, that the provision was not obsolete, because the intentions behind the restriction when it was imposed over half a century earlier were still justified.

---

16 [1991] Ch 365. For commentary, see Devonshire, 1991, pp 388–93; Edmunds, 1992, pp 343–49.

17 [2000] 3 EGLR 57.

18 *Re Dr Barnardo's Homes National Incorporated Association's Application* (1955) 7 P & CR 176. See Bynoe, Oliver and Barnes, 1991, p 26; and Gooding, 1994, pp 135–36.

It is of course important to remember that the decision precedes the shift towards deinstitutionalisation as part of any recognised governmental policy on community care. This may in some way help to explain why the validity of the covenant was not challenged directly. In this respect, the decision contains a candid and revealing aside on the propriety of this type of restriction:

> The very act of imposing such a covenant discloses the universal abhorrence felt by ordinary folk for the 'mental case' and while the revulsion may derive from ignorance and be justly stigmatised as prejudice it is not less poignant for being unjustified.[19]

With the advent of community care, some might contend that today there is an altered public perception.[20] Yet, reliance upon covenants in opposition to group homes is still a powerful indicator of discrimination and prejudice, even if it is less overtly acknowledged in cases since *Dr Barnardo's*. There are other reasons why it would be shortsighted to relegate this decision as an historical curiosity. For one thing the reasoning contains a striking confusion about how much weight should be placed upon objective evidence as distinct from unsubstantiated public fears. The Hospital Board argued that it intended to use the property to provide for the 'medium' of three grades of 'mental defective'. This meant that although the prospective occupants were fully developed adults physically, they 'would display an attitude to the conventions of society expected from the child of under 10 years of age'.[21] Nonetheless, the tribunal was more than satisfied to endorse the expert evidence that the residents posed no greater degree of danger, inconvenience or annoyance than would occur if the property was to be used as a children's home. Similarly, it recognised that once the institution became operational it was likely to gain local acceptance. To this extent the acceptance of objective medical evidence in the 1950s constitutes judicial enlightenment. Ultimately, however, the tribunal allows its endorsement of objective evidence to be overridden by one particular unsubstantiated fear. The application floundered essentially because it is accepted that local prejudice towards the establishment of a home for mental defectives would have an adverse impact on the marketability of the neighbouring property. Not a shred of evidence is offered to support the assertion. Similar contentions have surfaced in some recent group homes cases. It has been suggested that depreciation in the value of the objector's house is in breach of a covenant not to cause 'detriment'. Although the response has moved away from the automatic acceptance evident in *Dr Barnardo's*, regrettably the courts have not drawn upon objective evidence that robustly denies any possibility of such market depreciation.[22]

---

19 *Dr Barnardo's* (1955) 7 P & CR 176, p 180.
20 How much of a shift may depend upon a range of factors (in relation to people with learning disability, see Ritchie, 1999).
21 *Dr Barnardo's* (1955) 7 P & CR 176, p 177.
22 Compare the approach on this point in *C & G Homes v Secretary of State for Health* [1991] Ch 365 with *National Schizophrenia Fellowship v Ribble Estates SA* [1994] 1 EGLR 181, p 182.

Implicit in the reasoning is an apparent willingness to accept that covenants may in effect do more than offer protection against interference arising from how land is being occupied. It suggests that it is legitimate for the language of covenants to be invoked on the back of stereotypical view as to how people who are mentally ill or have learning difficulties behave, and the impact such occupant's presence may be assumed to have upon the amenity of the neighbourhood. Covenants may readily be seen as legitimate tools to prevent one resident on a housing estate from disturbing other resident's rights to own and enjoy neighbouring land. It is suggested that this should not automatically mean that a covenant should be available to regulate behaviour by a mentally disabled neighbour in circumstances where the same behaviour would have been tolerated if the neighbour were free from mental health problems or learning difficulties.

Re Milbury Care Services Limited's Application[23]

Some of the objections in *Milbury* were rooted in the consequences of using property as a residential care home, whilst others were more to do with anxieties linked to perceptions and prejudices about the occupiers. The applicant company had won a tender from Sandwell MBC to provide a staffed group home for five elderly residents with learning difficulties who were being returned from hospital to the community. In 1995, they acquired a three bedroom bungalow situated on the Grove Vale Estate, a 1960s development of 100 or so 'self-build' houses close to the M6. Along with all the properties on the estate, the bungalow was subject to covenants in the same terms, including one (in clause (g) of the conveyance) confining use as a 'private residence' and (in clause (h)) prohibiting anything that might be 'a damage, nuisance, disturbance or annoyance'. Before the home could be altered and opened, one of the neighbours succeeded in obtaining a declaration that use as a group home was in breach of clause (g). However, the proceedings were stayed pending the outcome of this application by Milbury to the Lands Tribunal. The home was therefore allowed to operate for the three or so years before the Lands Tribunal declined to discharge or modify the covenants in clause (g) on either of the grounds in (aa) and (c) of s 84(1) of the Law of Property Act 1925.[24]

The first point of interest for present purposes lies in the tribunal President's treatment of the objector's various complaints based on the way

---

23 1999/LP/78/95; transcript 30 April 1999.

24 '(aa) that ... the continued existence thereof would impede some reasonable user of the land for public or private purposes or, as the case may be, would unless modified impede such user'; '(c) that the proposed discharge or modification will not injure the persons entitled to the benefit of the restriction.'

the group home had been functioning. Happily, allegations of residents' gesticulating at the neighbours were considered to be 'minor,' and the presence of clinical waste in the home's wheelie bin a 'misconception'.[25] Other evidence relating to more tangible interference with neighbour's residential amenity was of more relevance. This evidence included the institutional appearance of the property, disturbance both from the operation of night staff and the volume of cars parked outside. Moreover, the President thought episodic shrieking by one elderly resident represented the potential disturbance the home might cause. Yet, this last point apart, none of the evidence was seen as being so significant in itself for it to be argued that the ability of clause (g) to prevent these things from happening could be said to deprive the objector of a practical benefit of substantial value or advantage. Rather, it was the uncertainty that the objector would be sufficiently protected from such 'annoyance' and 'disturbance' by clause (h) that seems to have clinched the Tribunal's refusal to find that this element of ground (aa) was satisfied in respect of clause (g):

> Were they left to rely on covenant (h) not only would the residents have to monitor and record instances of annoyance, but they would also embark on injunctive proceedings knowing there was a risk that, although to them the instances were extremely disturbing, a court might hold that the evidence failed to establish annoyance according to the objective standard to be applied (*Tod-Heatley v Benham* ...).[26] In this respect the ability to rely on covenant (g) to prevent the use is a practical benefit and one which is of substantial advantage to those residents affected or potentially affected by a disturbing business use.[27]

Whatever misgivings there might be with this reasoning and, in particular, the way it links separate covenants, it is striking that much of the emphasis is upon the adverse impact of the use of the property rather than the (actual or perceived) behavioural traits of the residents. Even the shrieking was found to 'go beyond the sort of disturbance from the ill or afflicted that neighbours in such area might reasonably be expected to tolerate'.[28] In these respects, ironically, it also seems that the fact that the home was allowed to operate before the hearing probably did it no favours.

A second strand in the reasoning is even more lamentable. Providing group homes for elderly people with special needs was recognised as being in accordance with community care policy statements of central government and at local level (in the Sandwell Unitary Development Plan 1995). Doubtless the applicant company thought in the light of the previous groundbreaking tribunal decision, *Re Lloyd's Application*,[29] this made their argument that the

---

25 1999/LP/78/95; transcript 30 April 1999, p 7.

26 (1880) 40 Ch D 80.

27 *Ibid*, p 14.

28 *Ibid*, p 9.

29 (1993) 66 P & CR 112.

group home was in the 'public interest' compelling. Regrettably, the President disagreed. He confined *Lloyd* to circumstances where there was evidence of a desperate need for a group home. Arguably, this is far too restrictive an interpretation of *Lloyd*. If correct, it also sets an unacceptably high and imprecise threshold for determining the 'public interest'. It seems to require establishing more than a concrete local authority policy in support of using residential homes as a group home. The evidence will have to show some shortage of appropriate accommodation in a particular area.

Analysis of the English case law to date demonstrates how the principles governing the construction, operation and modification of freehold covenants have singularly failed to accommodate the establishment of group homes. The courts have not felt willing or able to use these individual disputes to balance out the competing public and private rights.[30] Whatever the merits or demerits this stance may have had in the past, an important new question emerges. Will the judges be able to maintain their reticence in the light of the implementation of the HRA 1998?

APPLICATION OF THE HRA 1998

This section seeks to consider the potential for facilitating the provision of group homes for those with a mental disability using the HRA 1998. Chapter 1 of this book has set out the general tenets and requirements of the Act (including victim status) and has described the past application of the ECHR in Strasbourg.[31] In the context of this chapter, it is necessary to examine both the standard vertical application of the Act (governing relations between the State or other public bodies or bodies exercising a public function and individuals) and the possibility of a horizontal application (additionally, governing relations between private individuals and bodies). This section of the chapter will examine the usual vertical application of three relevant Articles using past decisions from the European Court of Human Rights (the Court) and Commission of Human Rights. In practice, these cases will in no way confine the application of the Act in the UK. It is open to the UK courts to use wider (but not narrower) interpretations of the Articles. Since a number of the group home cases do not involve a complaint by a 'victim' against a public authority the usefulness of the vertical application will be limited. Therefore the section then moves on to discuss in more detail the possibilities and uncertainties of a horizontal effect and the application of the Articles to

---

30 See, eg, *C & G Homes v Secretary of State for Health* [1991] Ch 365, pp 379 (Nourse LJ) and 387 (Lord Donaldson MR and Russell LJ).

31 For an overview of past applications of the ECHR in property law see Howell, 1999 and 2001 and Allen, 1999.

disputes involving private individuals. In some respects this division is artificial,[32] but it will provide a framework within which to discuss the variety of issues involved.

Article 14: prohibition of discrimination

Article 14 states that:

> The enjoyment of the rights and freedoms set forth in this Convention shall be secured without discrimination on any ground such as sex, race, colour, language, religion, political or other opinion, national or social origin, association with a national minority, property, birth or other status.

Article 14 encompasses the possibility of discrimination because of mental disability.[33] At a general level one of the most encouraging aspects of the Art 14 is the breadth and lack of limitations given to the definition of discrimination. This has been contrasted positively to comparable definitions of discrimination in domestic legislation.[34] In other quarters, the lack of assistance given to applicants with a disability by Art 14 in the past has been much criticised.[35] Article 14 is qualified in that it can only be used in conjunction with or respect to another right protected under the Convention or Protocols.[36] Recognition of the limitations of this approach has led to the signing of a new freestanding Protocol 12 to the European Convention on Human Rights (ECHR) prohibiting all forms of discrimination. This Protocol was signed by 25 Member States (excluding the UK) in November 2000.[37] In our current context, a claimant would argue that mental disability qualified as 'any other status' under Art 14. Then they would have to demonstrate that

---

32 Cooper's approach from the angle that 'the concepts of horizontal and vertical application should be considered as the two extremes on a continuum, with a variety of approaches in between' is helpful. Cooper, 2000, p 53.

33 The Explanatory Report to Protocol 12 (discussed below, fn 36) notes that the discriminatory grounds in the new provisions are the same as in Art 14 and observes that: 'This solution was considered preferable over others, such as expressly including certain additional non-discriminatory grounds (eg, physical or mental disability, sexual orientation or age), not because of a lack of awareness that such grounds have become particularly important in today's societies as compared with the time of drafting of Art 14 of the Convention, but because such inclusion was considered unnecessary from a legal point of view since the list of non-discriminatory grounds is not exhaustive, and because inclusion of any particular additional ground might give rise to unwarranted contrary interpretations as regards discrimination based on grounds not so included.'

34 Starmer, 1999, p 684; Coppell, 1999, p 170. See, further, below, p 211.

35 Quinn, 1999, p 296. *Botta v Italy* (1998) 26 EHRR 241.

36 Art 14 can, nevertheless, in theory be breached where there is in practice no actual breach of another substantive right. See Starmer, 1999, p 685 and Livingstone, 1997.

37 Press statement, Council of Europe Press Service, 4 November 2000. Protocol 12, Art 1: '1 The enjoyment of any right set forth by law shall be secured without discrimination on any ground such as sex, race, colour, language, religion, political or other opinion, national or social origin, association with a national minority, property, birth or other status. 2 No one shall be discriminated against by any public authority on any ground such as those mentioned in para 1.'

because of the mental disability there had been a difference in treatment by a public authority under the situations covered under Art 8 or Art 1 of the first Protocol or perhaps in this instance under Art 6 and the right to a fair trial.[38] It can be shown that the courts' past application of the rules relating to the interpretation and enforcement of freehold covenants has differed in cases dealing with homes for the mentally disabled.[39] Any difference in treatment must occur in the absence of any 'reasonable or objective justifications' and is subject to the normal prerequisites of proportionality. It is difficult to envisage any justification for any such different interpretation in the case of mental disability. However, the use of Art 14 will be limited by the fact that in practice the claimants (especially under Art 1 of the first Protocol) may well be the providers or owners of the group home rather than the disabled persons.

Article 1 of Protocol 1: protection

Article 1 of Protocol 1 states that:

> Every natural or legal person is entitled to the peaceful enjoyment of his possessions. No one shall be deprived of his possessions except in the public interest and subject to the conditions provided for by law and by the general principles of international law.

> The preceding provisions shall not, however, in any way impair the right of a State to enforce such laws as it deems necessary to control the use of property in accordance with the general interest or to secure the payment of taxes or other contributions or penalties.

In practice there have been relatively few successful cases under Art 1 of the First Protocol in Strasbourg. The Article basically gives a general guarantee of property rights[40] whilst recognising legitimate State interference in the form of certain deprivations and controls. Following decisions such as *Sporrong and Lonnroth v Sweden*[41] and *James v United Kingdom*,[42] the approach has been to consider whether the case falls within the 'deprivation' or control categories and then, if neither of the former apply, to consider the general guarantee. In all three situations State action can be justified under certain conditions some of which are expressly set out in the Article. In the group home situations it will be the health authority, the charity or other facility provider who will hold the freehold or long lease of the property in question. The persons

---

38 ECHR, Art 6 begins: 'In the determination of his civil rights and obligations or of any criminal charge against him, everyone is entitled to a fair and public hearing within a reasonable time by an independent and impartial tribunal established by law.' See, also, the discussion of s 6 below.

39 These cases have been discussed above, see pp 203–08.

40 *Marckx v Belgium* (1979) 2 EHRR 300, p 354, para 63.

41 (1982) 5 EHRR 35, p 50, para 61.

42 (1986) 8 EHRR 123, para 37.

occupying the home will have at most a short lease or more probably a mere licence. Freehold and leasehold interests qualify for protection under Art 1 (as do the actual freehold covenants in question).[43] A licence may be sufficient. Whilst a wide variety of interests have been regarded as possessions the situation with respect to licences in this context is unclear.[44] Even if a licence were to be enough, in most of these group home situations the dispute over the covenant occurs prior to the setting up of the home at which point there is a mere expectation of a right. Such expectations are insufficient for the purposes of the Article, which concerns actual rights, rather than the acquisition of future rights.[45] If a qualifying property right could be identified under the Article, the existence of a freehold covenant is likely to be regarded either as actually defining the limit of the property right in the first place or, in the absence of discrimination, as a legitimate control.[46] In the context of interpreting freehold covenants the recent decision in *Biggin Hill Airport Ltd v Bromley LBC*[47] may also prove relevant. Interpretation of clauses in a lease created prior to October 2000 were said to be unaffected by the 1998 Act. This principle could equally be applied to freehold covenants thereby limiting the scope of considerations in such applications.

One rare case concerning covenants reached the Commission in 1984. In *S v United Kingdom*[48] the applicant held covenants in the context of an Irish fee farm grant of freehold land at a perpetual rent. The covenants included restrictions on building and provided that the land should be used for recreation and sport. The land had been built on in ignorance of the covenants. When the parties were unable to agree on terms to waive the covenants an application was made to the Lands Tribunal for their discharge or modification.[49] That application was successful with a small sum of compensation awarded in respect of any reduction brought about in the original price of the land through their existence. The applicant challenged both the validity of the legislation interpreted by the Lands Tribunal and their findings. The application was brought within Art 1 of the First Protocol together with Art 14. The order of the Lands Tribunal was not recognised as a deprivation because the applicant continued to enjoy the rent and remaining covenants but it was recognised as a control. The existence of such a control was justifiable and in the context of the circumstances in which it arose it was regarded as a proportionate control. As the applicant could not show that she

---

43 *James v UK* (1986) 8 EHRR 123.
44 Grosz *et al*, 2000, p 338; and Howell, 1999, p 295.
45 *Marckx v Belgium* (1979) 2 EHRR 300, p 335.
46 *Iskon v UK* (1994) 76A D & R 90.
47 (2001) 98 LSG 42.
48 App No 10741/84 (1984), as discussed in Dawson, 1986.
49 The application was in respect to Art 5 of the Property (NI) Order SI 1978/459 (NI 4) which includes provisions equivalent to Law of Property Act 1925, s 84.

had been treated any differently to any other relevant category of persons no discrimination was recognised.

In this case it was possible to challenge the State because it was the UK through the Lands Tribunal who were exercising the control of the pre-existing possession, the covenant, and thereby the potential breach of the Convention right. In most of the group home situations under consideration in this chapter the provider of the group home will either be facing the enforcement of the benefit of another's covenant against them or applying themselves for the modification or discharge of a covenant. In either case it is arguable that the courts (including the Lands Tribunal) will have a duty to deal with the issue in accordance with the Act under s 6; and if they fail to do so that decision could be challenged. The debate over the existence and content of such a duty is discussed below.[50] In the instance of a new application to modify or discharge a covenant preventing the use of property as a group home there is additional scope. Section 3(1) of the Act provides that: 'So far as it is possible to do so, primary legislation and subordinate legislation must be read and given effect in a way which is compatible with the Convention rights.' Unlike the ordinary day to day rules concerning covenants, applications for the modification or discharge of covenants are governed by statute. In interpreting this legislation, s 84 of the Law of Property Act 1925, the Lands Tribunal will be bound to 'give effect' to the rights and if necessary build a new body of case law.[51] This could work both ways in group home covenant cases. Covenantees may seek additional protection as *per S v UK*. On the other hand it might allow a more generous interpretation of s 84 than has hitherto occurred in cases such as *Milbury*.

Article 8: the right to respect for private and family life

Article 8 states that:

(1) Everyone has the right to respect for his private and family life, his home and his correspondence.

(2) There shall be no interference by a public authority with the exercise of this right except such as is in accordance with the law and is necessary in a democratic society in the interests of national security, public safety or in the economic well-being of the country, for the prevention of disorder or crime, for the protection of health or morals, or for the protection of the rights and freedoms of others.

---

50 See p 216, below.

51 If such interpretations are impossible, courts are to alert Parliament if legislation is incompatible so it can be amended so as to conform to the Convention. Application of s 3 to the interpretation of the Limitation Act 1980 in the context of adverse possession was considered by the Court of Appeal in *JA Pye (Oxford) Ltd and Another v Graham and Another* [2001] 2 WLR 1293.

With Art 8 there is an important additional possibility of identifying positive duties. Article 8 is extensive, covering rights to private and family life and correspondence in addition to the home. As such, it has been frequently used by applicants and has been the source of much media speculation about domestic and privacy issues in the run up to the implementation of the HRA 1998. Its application to the group home situation raises interesting property questions. Historically, English property lawyers have not been inclined to attach any intrinsic value to a building simply because it is shown to be a home. Value is traditionally given to property rights. Once acquired, these rights are generally independent of the character of the use of the property in question although they may be readjusted in certain situations.[52] These property rights are protected by Art 1 of the First Protocol suggesting that Art 8 is intended to provide a different sort of protection.[53] It is arguable that it is independent of proprietary interest, resting on a mere question of fact of whether the applicant is actually living there.[54] As with Art 1 of the First Protocol it would not seem to apply, at least in the vertical application, to a prospective or past home,[55] but includes access to a current home.[56] These initial differences would appear to make Art 8 of more assistance in the group home situations under discussion. The interpretation of the 'right to respect' as involving a positive duty on the State to act in certain situations to ensure the provision or protection of rights in the Article is particularly helpful. For example, Art 8 has been found to be capable of requiring a State to act to protect an individual from persistent harassment in their home.[57] If there is the potential to identify a positive duty to act where one individual is failing to respect another's home, then Art 8 may have more to offer in a situation where a property owner or owners are trying to frustrate the use a group home by other individuals. Article 8(2), which sets out justifications for interference by public authorities, cannot be applied in positive duty situations. Nevertheless, a wide margin of appreciation has been allowed with the same mitigating effect.[58] Notwithstanding the number of failed applications resting on positive duties under Art 8, it has been questioned whether Art 8 might in certain circumstances oblige a State to make provision for homes for certain 'vulnerable individuals'. This suggestion is made on the basis of observations in the case of *Burton v UK* where the Commission rejected an application on the part of a seriously ill Romany gypsy to be

---

52 For discussion of the treatment of the 'family home' in English property law, see Dewar, 1998.
53 In practice applicants have frequently chosen to claim a breach of both Articles together.
54 *Mentes v Turkey* (1998) 26 EHRR 595. See, also, Grosz *et al*, 2000, p 272.
55 Grosz *et al*, 2000, p 272.
56 *Gillow v UK* (1989) 11 EHRR 335.
57 *Whiteside v UK* (1994) 76A DR 80.
58 Coppell, 1999, p 290.

placed in a home appropriate to her traditions.[59] Such an obligation would now seem much more unlikely given the recent European Court judgment in *Chapman v UK*.[60]

A *de facto* common law cause of action?[61]

The whole issue of positive duties under Art 8 is inextricably linked to (or indeed part of) one of the most significant debates that has been continuing over the HRA 1998. This debate concerns the impact of incorporation upon domestic private law. In the best traditions of the common law, we are in a period of uncertainty during which the final relationship between Convention rights and private law remains unclear. If an extensive horizontal effect flowing from the Act and progressing beyond the positive duties already discussed can be recognised, the rights have the potential to be utilised by a victim in any litigation before the courts, public or private. This would overcome some of the reservations expressed above about the practicalities of applications under the Act in group home situations based upon past applications before the European Court and Commission.

Professor Wade, one of the proponents of extensive horizontal application, sees 'the spirit of the Act' as allowing a citizen to expect 'his human rights will be respected by his neighbours as well as by his government'.[62] In our group home situations, we are quite literally asking for respect from the neighbours. Professor Wade's support for recognition of a horizontal effect is based upon two central points. Firstly, that as s 6(1) of the Act states that, 'It is unlawful for a public authority to act in a way which is incompatible with a Convention right', and s 6(2) includes courts and tribunals within the definition of public authority courts must take the Convention rights into account in all cases, public or private. Secondly, that the 'spirit of the Act' is such that rights

---

59 (1996) 22 EHRR CD 134. Starmer, 1999, pp 592–93. See, also, *Varey v UK*, App No 26662/95 where it was found that there had been a violation of Art 8 in circumstances where a gypsy family had already established their home.

60 App No 27238/95, Judgment 18 January 2001. The European Court considered four other cases at the same time: *Beard v UK*, App No 24882/94; *Coster v UK*, App No 24876/94; *Lee v UK*, App No 25289/94; and *Jane Smith v UK*, App No 25154/94. Whilst it was acknowledged that occupation on the part of the gypsy applicants was an inherent part of their identity and the government measures did interfere with the applicants' right to respect for private and family life, such actions were 'in accordance with the law' under Art 8(2). Most significantly, no duty to provide an appropriate number of suitable sites was recognised and it was specifically noted that no right to be provided with a home was recognised (para 99).

61 Cooper, 2000, p 69 describes a bold approach as being 'to argue that by accepting incorporation and the positive obligations that flow from it, that we have, in effect, created a de facto common law cause of action, or a constitutional tort, and that to argue otherwise is an unsustainable fiction'.

62 Wade, 2000, p 224.

included 'have a universal and fundamental character which ought, one might think, to be operative *erga omnes*'.[63] Taking the vertical approach, Lord Justice Buxton has argued that the Act 'does nothing to create private law rights' and that the courts should be free of such concerns and allowed to concentrate on applying the HRA 1998 'in the sphere of public law where it, and the ECHR, properly belong'.[64]

A variety of approaches have been adopted in other jurisdictions.[65] At its theoretical extreme a full direct horizontal approach could even allow new rights to be claimed in private law – new actions to be begun against private individuals on the basis of the Act. Such an approach could allow a resident to commence an action where the future of a home was being jeopardised by community reaction. However, the construction of the Act and the statements made during the passage of the bill suggest that the direct horizontal effect is so unlikely that it should be disregarded.[66] The most that it appears possible to even anticipate is that as and when a case of this nature reaches the courts (for example, an application in respect of such a covenant) the court will be under a duty to ensure that the law is compatible with the Convention rights (as discussed in the previous section) even though the case is one that concerns private litigation.[67] The facilitators of a group home could trigger the circumstances for such a consideration by making an application for the modification or discharge of the offending covenant. This approach has been represented as the 'stronger' model of the indirect horizontal effect. This possibility is by no means certain. Elsewhere it has been argued that because, *inter alia*, the rights are not actually formally incorporated they are limited to 'legal values and principles' within private litigation and that any s 6 duty upon the courts could frequently fall short of being a 'duty to intervene' in private cases. Furthermore, it is argued that such principles will be best applied where the elements of the common law action 'are inherently broad and open to a wide variety of interpretations'.[68] Such areas are far removed from those under discussion in this chapter. All these issues remain to be determined fully and it is probable that the detailed answers will become apparent over the coming years rather than months. It seems highly likely that there will be some form of indirect effect but the practical outworkings of that are unclear.

---

63 Wade, 2000.

64 Buxton, 2000, p 65. The most recent contribution to the debate, Bamforth, 2001, emphasises the role of s 3 of the HRA 1998 in the horizontal argument.

65 Cooper, 2000, p 64; Hunt, 1998, p 427.

66 Hunt, 1998; Phillipson, 1999.

67 Hunt, 1998, p 442.

68 Phillipson, 1999, pp 836–83.

Examples of early considerations since the coming into force of the HRA may be found in two[69] very different Court of Appeal cases, *Alliance and Leicester plc v Slayford*[70] and *Douglas v Hello! Ltd*.[71] The first case concerned a mortgagee pursuing a defaulting mortgagor on their personal covenant with a view to ultimate bankruptcy proceedings having failed to gain possession through the normal routes due to a spouse's overriding interest under the Land Registration Act 1925. The mortgagor and his wife argued, *inter alia*, that the long running proceedings were contrary to Art 6(1) concerning the provision of a fair and public hearing within a reasonable time. Direct application of the Article was ruled out as the bank is not a public authority. The court was prepared to assume (without actually deciding the point) that s 6 of the HRA 1998 required an indirect application through the duty of the court but found that nevertheless no breach was in existence.[72]

The second case, *Douglas v Hello! Ltd*, concerned a dispute between *Okay!* magazine and *Hello! Magazine* over photographs taken at the wedding of Michael Douglas and Catherine Zeta-Jones. This particular litigation dealt with the lifting of an injunction against the publication of photographs by *Hello!* On its specific facts, the judgment has much discussed implications for the law concerning privacy generally. It also contained some preliminary consideration of the application of the HRA 1998 between two private litigants. At a general level the decision indicates that there will be scope for an indirect horizontal application of the Act. Whilst expressing a reluctance to address the whole vertical/horizontal debate,[73] there was a clear willingness to have regard to the Act in the development of the common law. Lord Justice Sedley referred to the area of law under consideration as 'precisely the kind of incremental change for which the Act is designed; one which without undermining the measure of certainty which is necessary to all law gives substance and effect to s 6 ...'.[74]

The approach in these two Court of Appeal decisions is encouraging. Whatever ultimate resolution is reached, it is inevitable that the advent of the

---

69 *JA Pye (Oxford) Ltd and Another v Graham and Another* [2001] 2 WLR 1293 also acknowledged these issues. The Court of Appeal did not regard it as necessary to consider the 'very difficult and important questions' about the impact of s 6(1) on private law issues (Mummery LJ, para 42). As noted above (fn 51), s 3 (whilst not affecting the outcome of the case) was considered at length.

70 2000 WL 1480058.

71 [2001] 2 WLR 992.

72 Peter Gibson LJ, para 16.

73 Sedley LJ, para 128. Keene LJ, para 166: 'Since the coming into force of the HRA 1998, the courts as a public authority cannot act in a way which is incompatible with a Convention right: s 6(1). That arguably includes their activity in interpreting and developing the common law, even where no public authority is a party to the litigation. Whether this extends to creating a new cause of action between private persons and bodies is more controversial, since to do so would appear to circumvent the restrictions on proceedings contained in s 7(1) of the Act and on remedies in s 8(1).'

74 Sedley LJ, para 129.

HRA 1998 will bring about an additional general increased awareness of rights based approaches in modern property law. Prior to the Act, the Convention has already been influencing the development of the common law, although not in the areas we are discussing to any recognisable degree.[75] Without necessarily amounting to a 'magic carpet' or a 'knight in shining armour',[76] the impact of the Act will result in an increased judicial willingness to address human rights issues in property cases.[77] In group home situations this may allow more than the technical covenant issues to be discussed in conflicts where private individuals challenge the existence of homes or where applications for the discharge or modification of covenants are made. This would be an improvement on the position in recent years.

DISABILITY DISCRIMINATION AND COVENANTS

Introduction

For all its anti-discriminatory potential, on the analysis above, the HRA 1998 offers little immediate prospect of assisting group home residents who are faced with covenant based neighbour opposition. It is not the first domestic legal regime aimed at promoting the civil rights of the disabled. This section of the chapter explores the extent to which group homes may find protection through the Disability Discrimination Act 1995 (DDA).[78] Although heralded as a comprehensive measure, it is widely accepted that the DDA falls short, its provisions being flawed in a number of critical areas.[79] In 1997 the new Labour government, recognising the force of such criticisms, commissioned a review from the Disability Rights Task Force. In addition to paving the way

---

75 For a full discussion of the horizontal approach in respect to property law see Howell, 2001.

76 Cooke and Hayton, 2000, p 438, state that: 'It would be foolish to suggest that the Human Rights Act will ride like a knight in armour to the rescue at this point, but it may – given a creative approach by the judiciary – provide inspiration and a starting point.' They add (p 441) that, 'The European Convention on Human Rights is not a magic carpet to take us to an era of flexible and imaginative justice in land law. But it could be a starting point'.

77 The extent of any indirect effect or influence has also been discussed at length elsewhere and again expectations vary. Buxton, 2000, p 65 notes that, 'The Act, and unconnected developments in *Osman*, may have a more tangential effect on private law litigation, but the English judge will need to proceed with great caution in drawing such conclusions from the ECHR in all but the clearest cases'. Grosz, Beatson and Duffy, 2000, p 385 state that, 'in other situations there is likely to be a substantial indirect horizontal effect in the manner in which courts and tribunals dispose of proceedings between private parties'.

78 On the Act in general, see Doyle, 2000 and Gooding, 1996.

79 See, eg, Sayce, 2000, pp 179–80 and Gooding, 1996, pp 1–8.

for the creation of the Disability Rights Commission,[80] their Final Report, *From Exclusion to Inclusion*, notes that the DDA 1995:

> ... marked an important step forward in disabled people's rights. But there are gaps and weaknesses in the Act which mean that disabled people continue to be denied comprehensive and enforceable civil rights.[81]

Disposal of premises and the limited 'terms' of the DDA 1995

Part III of the DDA 1995 contains a range of provisions prohibiting discriminatory behaviour in selling or letting premises.[82] Apart from covering a vendor's refusal to sell, s 22(1)(a) prohibits discrimination against a disabled person 'in the terms on which he offers to dispose of those premises'.[83] In this context, discrimination occurs if there is, without justification, less favourable treatment for reasons that relate to disability.[84] Whilst the legislative language does not seem to have restrictive covenants expressly in mind, it is presumably open to argue that they are as much a 'term' of the disposal as one that requires a higher purchase price or deposit from the prospective purchaser.[85] On its face, the legislation may therefore seem to provide a valuable mechanism to protect group home residents from the operation of discriminatory covenants. However, a closer examination reveals a number of general and specific concerns about the efficacy of the legislation in this connection.

It is possible to identify a number of crucial gaps and weaknesses in Pt III that diminish its application to discriminatory covenants. Serious gaps are left by s 22(1)(a) in the extent to which it applies to covenants. For, although it may be argued that it is unlawful for the seller to impose a covenant that explicitly restricts the premises from becoming a group home, it is far more debatable whether the DDA 1995 prohibits a vendor from trying to include

---

80 See the Disability Rights Commission Act (DRCA) 1999; and Disability Rights Commission Act 1999 (Commencement No 1 and Transitional Provision) Order 1999 SI 1999/2210 and Disability Rights Commission Act 1999 (Commencement No 2 and Transitional Provision) Order 2000 SI 2000/880.

81 Disability Rights Task Force, 1999, Chapter 1, para 1.

82 Introduced on 2 December 1996. Although the scheme is broadly similar to equivalent provisions in the Sex Discrimination Act 1976 and the Race Relations Act 1976, there are significant differences; see Gooding, 1996, pp 4–5.

83 Private sales and sales of small dwellings are outwith the legislation; ss 22 and 23 of the DDA 1995, respectively.

84 DDA 1995, s 24(1).

85 Which are examples given in the Code of Practice (the Code), 1999, para 8.5. (This replaces and revises the original 1996 Code.) Although the Code neither creates legal duties nor is it authoritative on the law, compliance may assist in defending court proceedings, see para 1.4.

any covenant that is neutral on its face but has the same effect indirectly. Yet cases such as *Milbury* indicate how powerful the discriminatory potential covenants confining the use of the land to a private residence or those controlling annoyances can have. Part of the problem here lies in the relatively restrictive notion of discrimination contained in Pt III. Part III tackles direct discrimination. However, its does not unambiguously extend to indirect discrimination. Gooding has argued that indirect discrimination may to some extent be caught by the basic definition (wider than its counterparts in other domestic discrimination legislation) because it is amenable to a broad interpretation.[86] However, to date this optimistic assessment remains judicially untested. More specifically, Pt III of the DDA 1995 does not currently recognise a legal duty that the person disposing of premises must make 'reasonable adjustments' in terms of the transaction such as covenants.[87] Nor has this aspect of the legislation been subjected to judicial scrutiny. Even if a court can be persuaded to imply such a duty in respect of covenants proposed by the seller,[88] this may not be enough to ensure that neighbours are deprived of the ability to enforce pre-existing restrictive covenants. By focusing narrowly on the terms of the sale, the DDA leaves untouched those terms upon which the seller acquired the property. In this way, there is a further weakness in the reach of the law because it can have no impact upon troublesome pre-existing covenants.

The position of group homes is aggravated further because less favourable treatment relating to disability will not constitute unlawful discrimination if it falls within one of the statutory grounds of justification. One of the recognised conditions within this defence is that, '... the treatment is necessary in order not to endanger the health or safety of any person (which may include that of the disabled person)';[89] regrettably, it is the seller's perception at the time of the disposal that matters, although his or her opinion has to be reasonable in all the circumstances.[90] Such a subjectively orientated test raises the unedifying prospect of pleas of justification being based upon the perceived risks posed by people with mental health problems. This leaves unclear what weight might be given to expert evidence on the reality of risk.[91] The Task

---

86 Gooding, 1994, p 6.

87 The Task Force recommends that this omission should be rectified: Disability Rights Task Force, 1999, Chapter 6, para 41.

88 See Doyle, 2000, p 125.

89 DDA 1995, s 24(3)(a).

90 See the only reported case to date, *Rose v Bouchet* [1999] IRLR 463 considered by Lawson, 2000. See, also, Doyle, 2000, pp 125–26.

91 This parallels the similarly unsatisfactory way in which *Milbury* (1999/LP/78/95; transcript 30 April 1999) interprets the *Tod-Heatley v Benham's* test ((1880) 40 Ch D 80) for determining what is annoying use in breach of covenant, above, p 207. The Code strikes a positive note in para 8.33 by citing as unjustifiable a landlord who persists in the opinion that a tenant with AIDS is a risk when he or she has been provided with government literature to the contrary.

Force acknowledges that this feature of the justification defence may serve to endorse stereotypes and prejudice.[92] However, because of a dearth of case law, it only recommends that the Disability Rights Commission keeps the matter under review.

A final specific weakness lies both with the enforcement mechanisms and the remedies available where the terms of the sale are in breach of Pt III of the DDA 1995.[93] The establishment of the Disability Rights Commission, with a range of enforcement procedures at its disposal,[94] may have drawn some of the sting from the charge that the failure to provide an enforcement body was 'one of the greatest flaws in the DDA'.[95] However, for the purposes of Pt III of the DDA, litigation remains the ultimate means of redress for group residents. In such civil proceedings[96] the remedy provided by the statute is damages.[97] By virtue of s 25(2), the award may 'include compensation for injury to feelings whether or not they include compensation under any other head'. Even if an award of damages is augmented in this way, it is hardly the most apposite remedy for those deprived of an opportunity to live in a group home in the community.

The Disability Task Force rightly recognises how, 'living in suitable housing is as important to disabled people as everyone else in society'.[98] Disappointingly, its recommendations do not go anywhere near far enough to maximise the DDA's potential to outlaw covenants that enable NIMBY opposition to group homes. Reading the Task Force's Report it is difficult to escape the conclusion that it predominately focuses upon strengthening Pt III to remove discrimination experienced by people with physical disabilities. A similar impression is conveyed by the Code of Practice. This stands in contrast to the parliamentary recognition of the problems associated that NIMBY opposition to the provision of group housing in the community when the

---

92 When, in relation to the provision of services under Pt III, it observes: 'We considered whether this test was too subjective and placed too much emphasis on the service providers' opinion. We felt that legislation should not endorse stereotypes and prejudice. We concluded that there needed to be a defence for service providers acting in "good faith" and therefore their opinion should be considered, but not given undue weight.' Disability Rights Task Force, 1999, Chapter 6, para 19.

93 DDA 1995, ss 25–28 (as amended by the DRCA 1999, s 10).

94 Provided by the DRCA 1999 include: formal investigations (s 3); service of non-discrimination notices (s 4); and s 5 of the 1999 Act makes novel provision for an agreement in lieu of enforcement action; see generally, Doyle, 2000, Chapter 9.

95 Disability Rights Task Force, 1999, Chapter 1, para 4; and see Gooding, 1996, p 6.

96 In the county court in England and Wales: s 25(3) of the DDA 1995. In addition to providing assistance for the litigation (see the DRCA 1999, s 7), the Disability Rights Commission may make arrangements for the dispute to be the subject of 'conciliation services': DDA 1995, s 28(1) as substituted by s 10 of the 1999 Act.

97 Enforcement of court orders is a function of the Disability Rights Commission. See para 23(1) of Sched 3 to the Disability Rights Commission Act 1999.

98 Disability Rights Task Force, 1999, Chapter 2, para 10.

DDA was being enacted.[99] Overall, the DDA is in need of substantial reform if it is to promote the housing rights of people with mental health problems over and above the private property rights of neighbours. It is instructive to consider briefly how an appropriate direction for such reforms might be found in the experience of similar measures in the USA.

A fairer housing approach to discrimination?

Commentators have persuasively argued that the American anti-discrimination legislation provides a valuable model,[100] yet the DDA 1995 did not draw extensively upon it. From the perspective of group homes in the sphere of mental health, the Federal Fair Housing Amendments Act (FHAA) 1988 is of most relevance.[101] This legislation amended the Fair Housing Act of 1968 specifically in response, first, to the need to tackle housing discrimination arising from deinstitutionalisation of people with mental disability, and, second, to remedy the lack of enforcement powers in the original legislation.[102] Like the DDA, it renders unlawful, *inter alia*, discrimination in the sale of a dwelling to any buyer because of a handicap.[103] However, in stark contrast to the DDA, it is clear that, in addition to prohibiting the use of public measures such as statutes and zoning regulations,[104] the legislators explicitly intended the FHAA to be applicable to prevent housing discrimination through private property rights such as restrictive covenants.[105]

Under the FHAA, the Attorney General may sue neighbours who attempt to enforce covenants (for example, 'single-family' or 'residential use' covenants) in the State courts as a means of preventing the sale of houses to group home providers. Neighbours may be motivated by much the same anxieties as has surfaced in English cases such as *Milbury*. They may fear depreciation in the value of their property, cite increased traffic and noise from the property, and harbour notions about how people with mental

---

99 *Hansard*, HL, Vol 566, cols 271–74 (Lord Rix); and cols 969–72 (Lords Carter and Addington).

100 See Gooding, 1996, Chapter 1; Sayce, 2000, esp Chapters 8 and 9; and Bynoe *et al*, 1991.

101 Other important federal provisions include the Rehabilitation Act 1973, s 503 and the American Disabilities Act 1990, Title II.

102 See Kanter, 1994, pp 933–44.

103 42 USC, para 3604(f)(1) (1994).

104 On zoning regulations, see the landmark Supreme Court decision in *Cleburne Living Centre Inc v City of Cleburne* 437 US 432 (1985).

105 In the Report of the Judiciary Committee of the House of Representatives, 1998 (the Report), which accompanied the FHAA amendments it states (at p 2179): '... the Act is intended to prohibit the application of ... restrictive covenants ... that have the effect of limiting the ability of [handicapped] individuals to live in residences of their choice.' Some States have additional specific legislation to curb the extent to which covenants can be used to impede group homes, see Kanter, 1994, p 990.

problems pose a threat to their personal safety. However, it has been held that neighbours' attempts to enforce even what appears on its face to be a neutrally worded covenant is a violation of the FHAA.[106] There is currently no equivalent to such extensive legislative protection in English law. This American model graphically illustrates how the DDA might be amended to ensure that community care policy and the civil rights of mentally disabled people take precedence over private property rights.[107]

It is worth emphasising that the virtue in this American federal law does not simply reside in offering group homes greater protection through a tougher enforcement regime. What is equally crucial in these successful actions is the FHAA's broad approach to the concept of discrimination. In the FHAA discrimination has been interpreted to encompass and extend beyond direct discrimination of the kind provided for in Pt III of the DDA 1995. The FHAA also covers situations where there is a discriminatory impact and/or a failure to make reasonable accommodations.[108] This means that even if the language of a facially neutral covenant is not found to discriminate against a group home for people with a mental health problem intentionally, a court may still find that there is an FHAA violation under either or both of the other two heads.

An illustration of this broad notion of discrimination is provided in a Supreme Court of New Mexico decision, *Hill v Community of Damien of Molokia*.[109] In 1993, four neighbours sought an injunction to close a group home for people with AIDS on the basis that it violated the terms of a covenant that the land should only ever be used as a single family residence. They argued that the group home residents were not a family because they were unrelated. The Community of Damien of Molokia, the group home provider, successfully disputed this construction of the covenant on the basis that the group home offered an equivalent 'stability, permanency and functional lifestyle' to that found in a traditional family.[110]

---

106 See *US v Scott* 788 F Supp 1555 (D Kan 1992); and *US v Wagner* 940 F Supp 972 (ND Tex 1996). There are other cases where the courts have relied upon State laws to bar enforcement of restrictive covenants, see *Crane Neck Association v New York/Long Island County Services Group* 460 NE 2d 1336 (NY 1984). See, further, Flinn, 2000.

107 Kanter, 1994, p 990, suggests a simpler and even more direct approach: 'Incorporating a provision that explicitly bans restrictive covenants would preclude any questions of their validity and eliminate expensive and time consuming litigation that might otherwise be required to invalidate the covenant.'

108 Defined in para 3604(f)(1) of the FHAA as 'a refusal to make reasonable accommodations in rules, policies, practices or services, when such accommodations may be necessary to afford such persons equal opportunity to use and enjoy a dwelling'. There are statutory qualifications so that it is not reasonable (see para 3604(f)(3)(B)) 'if it would impose undue financial or administrative burdens on the defendant'.

109 911 P 2d 861 (NM 1996). See Kane, 1998.

110 Kane, 1998, p 599. Brussack 1981, Guernsey 1984 and Hubbard 1988, indicate that disputes turning upon the interpretation of covenants are not always resolved in favour of group homes, nor have American courts shown consistency in how to approach such issues.

The Community also sought an injunction against the neighbours on the basis that to allow enforcement of the covenant would amount to unlawful discrimination under the FHAA. The Supreme Court ruled that there was no evidence of direct discrimination. The neighbours were not intending to discriminate. They had not invoked the covenant because the residents of the group home were disabled. However, it was held that the neighbours' behaviour was discriminatory in two ways. First the court was satisfied that it had a discriminatory impact. By attempting to enforce the covenant to oppose a group home they were in effect denying housing to disabled people, when such people commonly had a need for such accommodation to aid their reintegration into the community. Secondly, it was decided that the neighbours had failed to make a reasonable accommodation: '... a reasonable accommodation would have been not to seek to enforce the covenant.'[111] It must be stressed that the American jurisprudence, whether arising from covenant disputes or anti-discrimination legislation such as the FHAA, does not always reflect a similar preference level for promoting deinstitutionalisation over private property rights.[112] It has even been argued that because *Hill* shows that the FHAA is failing 'to strike a meaningful balance of competing interests', integration of the disabled into the community is being unjustifiably privileged over the individual property owner's right to use covenants to protect their 'homes, lives, investments and dreams'.[113] If this is an accurate assessment of the position in America, the imbalance in English law is surely in the opposite direction. For, even considered in combination, it seems that the HRA 1998 and Pt III of the DDA 1995 can have minimal impact upon neighbours' rights to enforce private covenants to impede a group home for disabled people.

CONCLUSION

This chapter has focused on community care for those with mental health problems as one example of an area of healthcare provision which may be affected by the HRA 1998. The difficulties encountered in providing group homes in the community are widely recognised and the ongoing nature of NIMBY opposition has been demonstrated through both past and recent litigation. Unlike some of the other healthcare situations considered in this volume, the impact of the HRA 1998 on this area is most likely to be an

---

111 Kane, 1998, p 603. In 1999, a Republican Representative from New Orleans unsuccessfully attempted to introduce legislation designed to dilute the FHHA.

112 Examples include, *Mains Farm v Worthington* 854 P 2d 1072 (Wash 1993) and *Michigan Protection and Advocacy Service v Babin* 18 F 3d 337 (6th Cir 1994). Also see Flinn, 2000, p 1809.

113 Kane, 1998, p 619–20.

indirect one. Group home provision may benefit from the extra protection and respect afforded to both property rights and homes and the prohibition against discrimination. The most likely general way for this to make any meaningful difference to everyday care situations is through an increased willingness to address rights issues in property cases. More specifically it could occur through the operation of s 3 of the HRA 1998 in the context of applications to the Lands Tribunal to vary potentially difficult restrictive covenants under the Law of Property Act 1925 or through the possibility that s 6 will be interpreted to allow the Act to impact significantly upon litigation between private parties. Very early indications from the courts suggest a willingness to at least consider points taken under the HRA 1998 in the context of litigation not involving a public body. At the moment, all that the Act can offer is limited and very uncertain potential.

Precisely because doubts exist about the application of the new general human rights legislation, it becomes all the more significant to consider how robust the alternative specific domestic DDA 1995 is as a means of challenging covenants that are being used to perpetuate discrimination against group homes. The chapter has highlighted the inherent difficulties in applying the legislation to restrictive covenants in this context. Even the Disability Task Force discussion of future reform of the DDA 1995 has failed to consider fully the needs for housing on the part of those with mental health problems. In the light of what has been achieved through similar legislation in America, the current situation in relation to private property rights and the provision of group homes in the UK becomes even more disappointing. It can only be hoped that favourable interpretations of the new HRA 1998 and sympathetic reform of the DDA 1995 may lead to a gradual improvement in the current provision of group homes.

TIME FOR COMPETENT MINORS TO HAVE THE SAME RIGHT OF SELF-DETERMINATION AS COMPETENT ADULTS WITH RESPECT TO MEDICAL INTERVENTION?

Austen Garwood-Gowers

INTRODUCTION

Lord Scarman in *Sidaway v Bethlem Royal and Maudsley Hospital Governors* [1985] AC 871 suggested that: 'The existence of the patient's right to make his own decision ... may be seen as a basic human right protected by common law.'[1] Common law jurisdictions as a whole have long recognised that this right of self-determination is, as a general rule,[2] inviolable but often only for competent adults. For example, Cardozo J in *Schloendorff v Society of New York Hospital* 211 NY 125 (1914) states that:

> Every human being of *adult years* and sound mind has a right to determine what shall be done with his own body, and a surgeon who performs an operation without his patient's consent, commits an assault.[3]

Few would argue with the right of self-determination being denied on paternalistic grounds where a patient is incompetent but what grounds for denying the competent minor the general right?

DEVELOPMENTS IN ENGLISH MEDICAL LAW

The last decade saw some positive developments in English law with regard to the right to self-determination. Numerous forthright statements have been made in cases about the patient's right to refuse. *Re S (Adult: Refusal of Medical Treatment)* [1992] 4 All ER 671 rather controversially denied a competent woman the right to refuse a Caesarean section judged to be in the best interests of herself and her foetus. However, it was later overturned by the Court of Appeal in *Re MB (An Adult: Medical Treatment)* [1997] 2 FLR 426.

---

1   [1985] AC 871, p 882.
2   An exception is when the right is denied where necessary and proportional to the protection of the rights of others. However, beyond this any denial of the right is controversial.
3   211 NY 125 (1914), p 126. Emphasis added.

Despite these positive changes the right to self-determination continues to be denied to two classes of competent person in English medical law:

(a) the competent person defined as having a mental disorder – compulsory detention and treatment is possible here under the Mental Health Act 1983;

(b) the competent minor – by allowing a concurrent parental right of consent the questionable Court of Appeal precedents of *Re R (A Minor) (Wardship: Consent to Treatment)* [1991] 4 All ER 177 and *Re W (A Minor) (Medical Treatment)* [1992] 3 WLR 758 continue to deny competent minors the same degree of control over their own medical decisions as adults get.

Here after looking at the current law in detail, the case for using the HRA 1998 to shoot the *Re R* and *Re W* approach down will be examined.

THE LEGAL POSITION UNDER ENGLISH COMMON LAW

Parental objection to a minor undergoing a medical intervention has no legal force if the minor gives valid consent. The minor can give valid consent when competent to decide on the intervention at hand. Lord Scarman in the landmark House of Lords decision in *Gillick v West Norfolk and Wisbech AHA*[4] considered that a minor becomes competent once they:

> ... achieves a significant understanding and intelligence to enable him or her to understand fully what is proposed.[5]

This test has been accepted and applied in English law[6] and in several other jurisdictions.[7] As regards English law, Lord Scarman's speech seemed also to promote the notion that a minor would if competent also have a right to refuse treatment. In other words he seemed to be saying that competent minors like competent adults have a general legal right to self-determination with respect to medical intervention. However, subsequently, a number of English cases in the 1990s moved away from this position. Elliston[8] points out that a movement toward a more restrictive approach started with *Re E (A*

---

4   [1985] 3 All ER 402. Decision that a 14 year old girl had capacity to take the contraceptive pill. The girl did not want to take the contraceptive pill but her mother, being generally opposed to doctors prescribing contraception to minors, brought the case to establish certain points of law on the matter and with regard to a Department of Health circular relating to girls under 16 being prescribed the contraception.

5   See *ibid*, p 423j. For Lord Fraser's approach, see p 409d and e.

6   However, a modified approach is taken in cases where a minor has a mental disability (see *Re R (A Minor) (Wardship: Consent to Medical Treatment)* [1992] Fam 11).

7   Bainham, 1992, p 194.

8   Elliston, 1994, p 31.

Minor) (Wardship: Medical Treatment) [1993] 1 FLR 386[9] in which it was dubiously concluded that a 15 year old Jehovah's Witness minor was incompetent to refuse a blood transfusion. Subsequently, the Court of Appeal in *Re R (A Minor) (Wardship: Consent to Treatment)* [1991] 4 All ER 177 reached the even more strained conclusion that a 15 year old with fluctuating mental health was not competent to refuse anti-psychotic drug treatment in spite of the fact that she had clearly refused such treatment in lucid periods of remission where she met the *Gillick* test of competence. Lord Donaldson came to the perverse conclusion that:

> There is no suggestion that the extent of this competence can fluctuate upon a day to day or week to week basis.[10]

Having noted that the judges in the High Court and in *Re E* had treated *Gillick* as deciding that a *Gillick*-competent child has a right to refuse treatment his Lordship stated *obiter* that he felt this was 'in error' and that parents retained a concurrent power of consent until the minor reached majority, which he stated was 18 years old. Section 8(1) of the Family Law Reform Act 1969 (FLRA) appears to treat 16 and 17 year olds as adults for the purposes of medical treatment. It states that:

> The consent of a minor who has attained the age of 16 years to any surgical, medical or dental treatment which, in the absence of consent, would constitute a trespass to his person, shall be as effective as it would be if he were of full age and where a minor has by virtue of this section given an effective consent to any treatment it shall not be necessary to obtain any consent for it from parent or guardian.

However, s 8(3) of the FLRA 1969 states that:

> ... nothing in this section shall be construed as making ineffective any consent which would have been effective if this section had not been enacted.

Lord Donaldson argued that one of these effective consents was, under the common law, parental until majority and that hence whilst s 8(1) treated 16 and 17 year olds as adults for the purposes of agreeing to medical treatment but not for the purposes of refusing since a medical professional could rely on the consent of a parent alone irrespective of the objection of the minor. In *Re W (A Minor) (Medical Treatment)* [1992] 3 WLR 758, where treatment on a refusing 16 year old anorexic girl was authorised, his Lordship confirmed this view that concurrent rights of consent can exist even when the minor is competent. Referring to *Gillick* he stated:

> ... only Lord Scarman's speech is couched in terms which might suggest that the refusal of a child below the age of 16 to accept that medical treatment was determinative ... because there could never be concurrent rights to consent.[11]

---

9   Case actually heard in 1990.
10   [1991] 4 All ER 177, p 187.
11   [1993] 1 FLR 1, p 7.

Lord Donaldson then quoted the relevant passage of Lord Scarman's speech in *Gillick* which states that:

> ... the parental right to determine whether or not their minor child below the age of 16 will have medical treatment terminates if and when the child achieves a sufficient understanding and intelligence to enable him or her to understand fully what is proposed.[12]

His Lordship went on to make the dubious comment that, in the light of the different issue before the House in *Gillick*, Lord Scarman had meant no more, 'than that the *exclusive* rights of the parents to consent to treatment terminated'.[13] He was perhaps correct to add the caveat, 'though I may well be wrong'[14] given the rights based tenor of Lord Scarman's speech. Indeed, his Lordship's interpretation of Lord Scarman's speech seems perverse and perhaps even devious since Lord Scarman made no mention of concurrent rights of consent and rightly stated that:

> ... the underlying principle of the law was exposed by Blackstone and can be seen to have been acknowledged in the case law. It is that the parental right yields to the child's right to make his own decisions when he reaches a sufficient understanding and intelligence to be capable of making up his own mind on the matter requiring a decision.[15]

John Murphy in 'W(h)ither adolescent autonomy?'[16] is surely right to suggest that whilst *Gillick* had no clear ratio it clearly established an absolute right of self-determination on behalf of the intellectually mature minor where that child is in dispute with his or her parents. On this basis the approach in *Re R* and *Re W* may be bad law. Nonetheless, it has been applied on a number of occasions and is so well entrenched that, in the recent case of *Re M (Child: Refusal of Medical Treatment)*,[17] Johnson J in the Family Division of the High Court authorised a heart transplant to be carried out on a 15 and a half year old young woman against her wishes without feeling it was even necessary to determine whether or not she was competent to refuse.

Writing in 1995, Elliston suggested that Scotland was unlikely to adopt the same position as England.[18] In Scotland a '*Gillick*-like' test of competence is embodied in legislation – s 2(4) of the Age of Legal Capacity (Scotland) Act 1991 stating that a child under 16 has legal capacity to consent to medical treatment if 'he is capable of understanding the nature and possible consequences of the procedure of treatment'. Elliston's prediction initially

---

12 [1985] 3 All ER 402, p 423.
13 [1993] 1 FLR 1, p 7.
14 *Ibid.*
15 [1985] 1 AC 112, p 188.
16 [1992] Journal of Social Welfare and Family Law 539.
17 [1999] 2 FCR 29.
18 Elliston, 1994, p 49.

proved correct when the Sherriff's Court, in *Houston, Applicant*,[19] decided that the effect of this legislative provision was that under Scottish law the competent minor had a right to self-determination. However, more recently another Sherriff's Court decision has brought this position into question.

HOW MUCH DIFFERENCE DOES IT MAKE IN PRACTICE THAT A COMPETENT MINOR HAS NO RIGHT OF SELF-DETERMINATION?

Some sturdy statements have been made about the courts being more reluctant to go against the will of more mature minors. For instance, Balcombe LJ, in *Re W*,[20] stated that:

> Undoubtedly, the philosophy ... is that, as children approach the age of majority, they are increasingly able to take their own decisions concerning their medical treatment. In logic there can be no difference between an ability to consent to treatment and an ability to refuse treatment ... Accordingly, the older the child concerned the greater the weight the court should give to its wishes, certainly in the field of medical treatment.

However, such a statement is ultimately just making it clear that the correct application of paternalism requires a clear focus on the functional value of allowing people to make their own decisions. In other words it is about utilitarianism rather than standard bearing for fundamental rights. On these lines his Lordship went on to say:

> In a sense this is merely one aspect of the application of the test that the welfare of the child is the paramount consideration. It will normally be in the best interests of a child of sufficient age and understanding to make an informed decision that the court should respect its integrity as a human being and not lightly override its decision on such a personal matter as medical treatment, all the more so if that treatment is invasive ...

The question arises as to what circumstances, in practice, are the courts going against the will of more mature minors. Two years ago in an article in the Modern Law Review, Bridge suggested that cases of legal intervention prompted by the young person's refusal to accept treatment fell into one of two categories: '(1) the young person concerned has been mentally disturbed or mentally ill, thus, rendering the objection to treatment invalid; or (2) the refusal has been prompted by a religious belief which denounces the specific form of treatment.'[21] The first category, she suggests, involved persons who were incompetent – a controversial view given that the minor in *Re R* had periodic lucidity where objection to treatment was arguably competently

---

19   (1997) 5 Med LR 237.

20   [1992] 2 FCR 785, p 810; [1993] Fam 64, p 88.

21   Bridge, 1999, p 585.

expressed. As regards the latter, she suggests that belief, in its own right should not form part of the assessment of adolescent competence[22] which would mean treatment on some minors with strongly held religious beliefs will, as the law stands, occur in spite of a competent refusal. This is exactly what recently occurred in the High Court in *Re L (Medical Treatment: Gillick Competency)* [1998] 2 FLR 810 where a 14 year old Jehovah's Witness girl was refusing 'life saving' surgical intervention that included blood transfusions. Nonetheless, Bridge foresaw that treatment against the will of the competent minor might occur in circumstances other than where religious belief was at issue – she asked whether such minors would 'ever be able to make grave decisions that compromise their welfare'.[23] Indeed, such a conclusion was not just warranted on the grounds that the matter would be determined by best interest but consistent with Balcombe LJ's comments in *Re W* that:

> ... if the court's powers are to be meaningful, there must come a point at which the court, while not disregarding the child's wishes, can override them in the child's own best interests, objectively considered. Clearly such a point will have come if the child is seeking to refuse treatment in circumstances which will in all probability lead to the death of the child or to severe permanent injury.[24]

This is probably what has occurred in the recent decision of *Re M (Child: Refusal of Medical Treatment)*, though, as already noted, Johnson J in this case did not determine whether or not the minor refusing the heart transplant was competent. It is also entirely possible that physical force would be used under certain circumstances to secure treatment much as was authorised for use, if necessary, by the High Court with respect to a 16 year old incompetent minor in *Re C (Courts' Inherent Jurisdiction) (Child: Detention and Treatment)* (1998) 40 BMLR 31.

One of the problems comes in the fact that some interventions have the potential to prevent death or severe permanent injury but might be likely to do so for only a short span of time. In such an instance, the 'utilitarian value' of overriding the will of the competent minor is obviously reduced. A good example of this can be the receiving of a transplant which, as already noted, was the subject of *Re M (Child: Refusal of Medical Treatment)*. Johnson J in this case noted that the doctors had concluded the transplantation was the only course of action to save her life but the obvious limitation of this course of action was that she might die within days after the transplant and, even if this was averted, she would be likely to live only a short life with impaired quality of life (suppressed immune system, being on medication for the rest of her life, etc). The question is, even if the procedure was in her best interests, was it justifiable to override her wishes and, indeed, is it ever justifiable to override

---

22 Bridge, 1999, p 589.

23 *Ibid*, p 592.

24 *Ibid*.

the wishes of the competent minor, bearing in mind the fact that we never do this on paternalistic grounds to the competent adult?

The power to override the wishes of competent minors could potentially lead to some unedifying decisions. For example, Kennedy and Grubb note the disturbing possibility that doctors have a legal basis on which they could perform a sterilisation or abortion on a young competent woman without her consent.[25] Similarly disturbing is the fact that there might be a legal basis to force a competent minor to donate a tissue or organ. However, I have stated elsewhere[26] that the fact that consent exercised on behalf of a minor has to be exercised in his or her best interests would make forced minor living donation exceptional because in forcing the minor you dilute or counteract the psychological benefits that he or she must get from donation at a level outweighing the physical harm and jeopardy. So far in the US there have not been any cases where a minor has been forced to donate and much of the case law emphasises minor agreement as a necessity. In English law Lord Justice Balcombe in *Re W* stated *obiter dicta* that a competent minor could not be forced to donate and the case commentary in *Re Y* has even hypothesised that the court would, as a rule of thumb, look for agreement in bone marrow donation by an *'incompetent donor'*.[27]

CHALLENGING THE DENIAL OF SELF-DETERMINATION TO COMPETENT MINORS

It is somewhat surprising that in all these common law decisions that resulted in forcible intervention on competent minors, not one of the minors applied to get his or her case heard in Strasbourg under the European Convention on Human Rights (ECHR). Perhaps no one in the legal profession considered the arguments.

The arguments are of violations of Art 5, which protects the right to liberty and security, or Art 8, which includes the right to respect for private life. Alternatively, Art 14, a parasitic right which prohibits discrimination in the enjoyment of Convention rights, could have been used in combination with Art 5 or 8. In other words, the argument that forcing intervention on a competent minor, but not generally on the competent adult, amounts to age discrimination affecting the right to privacy or liberty and security.

Following the implementation of the HRA 1998, these arguments can now be used forcefully in the domestic courts. Under the HRA 1998, the English Courts have an obligation to act in a way which is consistent with Convention rights (s 3); this means bringing common law into line with Convention rights

---

25 Kennedy and Grubb, 1994, p 393.

26 Garwood-Gowers, 1999, p 134.

27 'Re Y Commentary' (1996) Med L Rev 205, p 207.

and interpreting legislation as far as possible, consistently with them. In general, in assessing whether violations of an Article have taken place, s 2 of the Act requires the English courts to take into account, in so far as they think they are relevant to the case at hand, judgments, decisions, declarations and advisory opinions of the European Court of Human Rights (the Court), opinion of the Commission given under a report adopted under Art 31 of the Convention, decisions of the Commission in connection with Arts 26 or 27(2) and decisions of the Committee of Ministers taken under Art 46 of the Convention.

Hence, in examining relevant 'Convention jurisprudence', we can build a picture not just of the likely response of the European Court if it were faced with a competent minor asserting a legal right but also the likely response of an English court faced with this issue once the HRA 1998 is in force.

LEGISLATION PRESENTS NO OBSTACLE

The main legislation relevant to the issue is the Children Act 1989 which if anything would lend support to the view that the competent minor should have a legal right of self-determination with respect to medical intervention. For example, under the Children Act 1989 a child who has sufficient understanding has a right to make an informed refusal to submit to a medical or psychiatric assessment or examination.[28] Meanwhile, as already stated, Lord Donaldson's judgment in *Re R* and *Re W* emphasised that parents had concurrent rights of consent with a competent minor on the basis of this being his view of the common law. He viewed s 8(3) of the FLRA 1969 as allowing the common law to stay in place but this in no sense meant that s 8(3) or any part of the FLRA 1969 demanded, expressly or even impliedly, that their should be concurrent parental rights of consent. Hence, there is no question that the HRA 1998, as well as the Convention itself, could be used as a basis for reinterpreting the legal position in *Re R* and *Re W* without coming into conflict with any express legislative provision.

RELEVANT GENERAL PRINCIPLES USED
IN INTERPRETING THE CONVENTION

The effectiveness principle

Underlying interpretation of all the Convention rights is the effectiveness principle which is to say that the Court is concerned with interpreting rights

---

28   See Children Act 1989, ss 43(8), 44(7) and Sched 3, paras 4(4) and 5(5).

in a manner which is practical and effective. One aspect of this is that the Court has stressed the importance of looking beyond appearances and formalities to the realities of the position of the individual. There is plenty of case law to illustrate the principle in action but this need not be elaborated upon here because its key application to the question of competent minors making medical decisions is obvious; it would simply mean that the Court would look beyond the technicalities of the current position under national law and examine the substance of arguments for and against affording the competent minor the same right as a competent adult to self-determination in medical matters.

Evolutive interpretation

The principle of evolutive interpretation is focused on the fact that the Convention standards change over time to reflect social changes. Hence, for example, while contemporary realities and attitudes in 1950 *might* make judicial corporal punishment of juvenile offenders in the Isle of Man 'acceptable', by the 1970s it was not 'acceptable' and infringed Art 3 in 1978 when considered by the Court in the *Tyrer* case.[29] The principle of evolutive interpretation shares some common ground with the English common law which has always sought to evolve over time in the light of social changes – the *Gillick* case being a classic example of this. However, the difference is that English law is certainly more heavily bound up with standing by cases already decided; though social changes can lead to a change in the law, they will only do so within the narrow confines that rules of precedent allow – under the ECHR, on the other hand, a general reverence for previous decisions of the Court would be unlikely to ever stand in the way of a new approach should this be demanded.

Proportionality

The interpretation of the Convention as a whole is heavily affected by the principle of proportionality, implying as it does the need to strike a proper balance between various competing interests. Deviation from rights and freedoms, where allowed, must not be excessive in relation to the legitimate needs and interests occasioning it such as the interests of the community. Proportionality is also infused into the structure of some of the Articles, a key example for the purpose of this paper being Art 8. A general statement to make at this point is that the case against competent minors having the same legal right of self-determination in respect of medical intervention as

---

29   (1978) 2 EHRR 1.

competent adults must be strong enough to provide sufficient justification for denial of such a right, raising as it does fundamental issues of liberty for the competent minor with violations of bodily integrity, security and personal privacy that are almost necessarily significant and at times severe, as in such cases where an intervention contravenes a strongly held structure of values and/or is of a serious nature in clinical terms and/or is of an unusually personal nature even by medical standards.

The margin of appreciation

The doctrine of the margin of appreciation is not relevant in interpreting the HRA 1998.[30]

The relevance of Art 3

Article 3, which protects the right to be free from degrading and inhuman treatment has been used in medical cases such as *X v Denmark* (1983) 32 DR 282. However, as Michalowski notes in the following chapter[31] subsequent case law has made it clear that, as a general rule, measures which, according to established medical principles, are of therapeutic necessity will not be regarded as inhuman or degrading. Indeed, one might go further and doubt whether a non-therapeutic intervention (such as living donation or non-therapeutic research) would be degrading if it was in the best interests of the person to undergo it. Of course, whether or not the person agrees to undergo a non-therapeutic intervention would be heavily influential in determining whether or not it was in their best interests and it might be argued that forcing such an intervention on, most especially a competent person, would, even if they were a minor, be sufficiently degrading to constitute a violation of Art 3.

IS DENYING THE COMPETENT MINOR THE RIGHT TO SELF-DETERMINATION WITH REGARD TO MEDICAL INTERVENTION: A VIOLATION OF ART 5?

Article 5 concerns the right to liberty and security of the person. It reads as follows:

---

30 See Chapter 1.
31 See p 244.

1   Everyone has the right to liberty and security of person. No one shall be deprived of his liberty save in the following cases and in accordance with a procedure prescribed by law:

   (a) the lawful detention of a person after conviction by a competent court;

   (b) the lawful arrest or detention of a person for non-compliance with the lawful order of a court or in order to secure the fulfilment of any obligation prescribed by law;

   (c) the lawful arrest or detention of a person effected for the purpose of bringing him before a competent legal authority on reasonable suspicion of having committed an offence or when it is reasonably considered necessary to prevent his committing an offence or fleeing after having done so;

   (d) the detention of a minor by lawful order for the purpose of educational supervision or his lawful detention for the purpose of bringing him before the competent legal authority;

   (e) the lawful detention of persons for the prevention of the spreading of infectious diseases, of persons of unsound mind, alcoholics or drug addicts or vagrants;

   (f) the lawful arrest or detention of a person to prevent his effecting an unauthorised entry into the country or of a person against whom action is being taken with a view to deportation or extradition.

2   Everyone who is arrested shall be informed promptly, in a language which he understands, of the reasons for his arrest and of any charge against him.

3   Everyone arrested or detained in accordance with the provisions of para 1(c) of this Article shall be brought promptly before a judge or other officer authorised by law to exercise judicial power and shall be entitled to trial within a reasonable time or to release pending trial. Release may be conditioned by guarantees to appear for trial.

4   Everyone who is deprived of his liberty by arrest or detention shall be entitled to take proceedings by which the lawfulness of his detention shall be decided speedily by a court and his release ordered if the detention is not lawful.

5   Everyone who has been the victim of arrest or detention in contravention of the provisions of this Article shall have an enforceable right to compensation.

Article 5 is primarily targeted at providing guarantees against arbitrary arrest and detention but its wider objective is to guarantee liberty and security as a whole. The security aspect of Art 5 is purely physical and would not cover areas like the right to life and peaceful protest which are dealt with by other Articles.[32] It also does not refer, for example, to mental, economic or social

---

32   In particular, Arts 2 and 10, respectively. See, further, Murdoch, 1993, p 495.

security – although such interests may be protected in relevant cases by other Articles such as Art 8. Notwithstanding the confusing language of the Commission, it is clear from the case law, as Murdoch points out, that liberty and security are not to be taken as individual concepts but examined in a unitary fashion.[33]

As regards competent minors making medical decisions, the absence of the legal right to self-determination most obviously violates physical liberty and security and so could be a matter for consideration under Art 5. Arguably, even if the intervention were just psychological (such as counselling) it could still be relevant to Art 5 because its use could be physically enforced (such as by locking a person in the room) or simply because the context of the absence of an enforceable right to refuse implies to the person that such force might be used. In *Nielson v Denmark*,[34] the European Commission and then the European Court were faced with a person complaining that his rights under the Convention had been violated when, as a 12 year old boy, he had been hospitalised for approximately six months in a State hospital psychiatric ward against his will but with the consent of his mother as the sole holder of parental rights. The complaint was framed under Art 5.

Of course, the substantive result in *Nielson* is also very much of interest here. Interestingly, the Commission felt that the rather limiting conditions in which the boy stayed in hospital must in principle be considered a deprivation of liberty and declared by 11:1 that there had been a violation of Art 5(1) and by 10:2 that there had also been a violation of Art 5(4).[35] However, the Court took a different approach saying that Art 5 was not applicable because it felt that 'the exercise of parental powers constitutes a fundamental element of family life'[36] that covered this situation because, 'he was still of an age at which it would be normal for a decision to be made by the parent even against the wishes of the child'[37] and the restrictions within hospital were made in good faith and were normal requirements for the care of a child of 12 years of age receiving treatment in hospital – even when these restrictions were imposed against his will.[38]

This type of approach subsequently also found favour in *Family T v Austria*[39] where the Commission decided that the placement of a child in a children's home by the social authorities did not constitute a deprivation of

---

33 1998, p 31.

34 (1988) 11 EHRR 175.

35 Report 12 March 1987, Series A, No 144, pp 38–43.

36 Citing *R v UK* (1988) 10 EHRR 74, para 64.

37 See particularly, (1988) 11 EHRR 175, para 72.

38 Judgment 28 November 1988, Series A, No 144, pp 24–26.

39 App No 14013/88, 14 December 1989; (1990) 64 DR 176.

liberty, because the upbringing of children may require certain restrictions on liberty. However, clearly, this does not justify extreme or unnecessary restrictions on the liberty of a minor. Hence, in the slightly earlier decision of *Boumar v Belgium*,[40] the Court concluded that Art 5(1) d did not preclude the placing of a child in an adult prison where there was supervised education but that, on the facts, the provision had been violated by the shuttling to and fro of a 16 year old boy between prison and other arrangements for a total of 119 days in a 291 day period. When it comes to medicine, there are clearly going to be interventions on a minor that violate Art 5. In this light, the Court in *Nielson* spoke of parental powers not being unlimited.[41] However, *Nielson* did not really define what these limits are – apart from the obvious one of control exercised in bad faith.

One of the criticisms that can be made of *Nielson* is that rather than basing their decision on competence the Court was focused on age, with the Court stating that, of course, this age based approach has echoes of English law before *Gillick*. Nonetheless, we should not read into this that the Court would view a competent minor as not having a legal right to self-determination. In all probability the 12 year old was incompetent in spite of the fact that the Commission described him as 'a normally developed 12 year old who was capable of understanding his situation and to express his opinion clearly'.[42] Accordingly, we can say that the Court might if faced with a competent minor decide that there is either a general right of self-determination or one that exists in all but exceptional circumstances such as where forced intervention is necessary as a life saving measure or at least to avert a prospectively grave impact on health. Even if *Nielson* is a reason for pessimism, it is now as old as the minor was in it and it might be argued that the evolutive principle would now come into play to result in a more forthright approach to the rights of the competent minor should the matter be considered by the Court under Art 5 in the near future. On the other hand, at least as far as the UK is concerned, many of the legislative and social policy shifts that occurred in favour of children's rights were in the 1980s along with *Gillick* – hence, it could be argued that little evolution has occurred in this area since *Nielson* was decided in 1988.

Furthermore, the Court's conservatism in accepting therapeutically necessary medical intervention as generally not a violation of Art 3 is likely to extend to Art 5. In *Guzzardi v Italy* (1980) 3 EHRR 33 the Court stated, in taking into account whether a 'deprivation of liberty' within the meaning of Art 5 has occurred, the starting point must be the claimant's 'concrete situation and

---

40   Judgment 28 November 1988, Series A, No 129; (1989) 11 EHRR 1.
41   Judgment 28 November 1988, Series A, No 144, pp 24–26.
42   (1988) 11 EHRR 175, para 71.

account must be taken of a whole range of criteria such as the type, duration, effects and manner of implementation of the measure in question'.[43] Force in medical intervention on a competent minor is, of course, normally shortlived and designed to protect the health of a person who is a member of a vulnerable class of people. These factors mitigate against Art 5 being successfully used. However, in *Guzzardi* the Court added that the 'difference between deprivation of and restriction upon liberty is nonetheless merely one of degree or intensity, and not one of nature or substance'.[44] This suggests the possibility that, at least in certain circumstances, forced medical intervention might amount to a violation. However, such circumstances might be restricted to where the intervention is not in the interests of the competent minor or is non-therapeutic in character In *Guzzardi*, it was noted that should Art 5 not be applicable because the degree and intensity of confinement is not sufficient to warrant its use, Art 2 of the Fourth Protocol to the ECHR, concerning freedom of movement, is an alternative.[45] Article 2 of the Fourth Protocol, has quite similar restrictions on its scope to Art 8 (as contained in Art 8(2) which is discussed next). However, Art 2 of Protocol 4 cannot be used by somebody making a claim under the HRA 1998 since it is not scheduled to the Act. Furthermore, it cannot be used by someone bringing a claim in the Court against the UK under the ECHR since the UK has not ratified it.

IS DENYING THE COMPETENT MINOR THE RIGHT TO SELF-DETERMINATION WITH REGARD TO MEDICAL INTERVENTION A VIOLATION OF ART 8?

The phrase an 'Englishman's home is his castle' reflects the notion of personal space being something sacred in English culture. Hence, it is not surprising that, as Coppell points out:

> The English law notion of private life tends to focus upon privacy in the sense of excluding the outside world from the individual's personal space.[46]

This kind of privacy is also the starting point of Art 8(1) which states that:

> ... everyone has the right to respect for his private life, his home and his correspondence.

Article 8(2) defines the limits of protection of this right stating that:

> ... there shall be no interference by a public authority with this right except such as in accordance with the law and is necessary in a democratic society in the interests of national security, public safety or the economic well-being of

---

43 (1980) 3 EHRR 33, para 92.
44 *Ibid*, para 93.
45 *Ibid*, para 92.
46 Coppell, 1999, p 281.

the country, for the prevention of crime and disorder, for the protection of health or morals, or for the protection of the rights and freedoms of others.

Complaints concerning medical treatment without consent are most likely to be examined in relation to Art 5. However, Art 8 does have a dimension of protecting physical integrity that can result in such claims being brought under it. Hence, in *X v Austria*, the obligation to take a blood test was held by the Commission to be covered by Art 8.[47] Indeed, the Commission stated that:

A compulsory medical intervention, even if it is of minor importance, must be considered as an interference with this right.[48]

The attempt to justify the denial of self-determination of competent minors in relation to medical treatment would shift the focus to Art 8(2) and specifically involve showing that it was a necessary interference to achieve its desired aim of protection of health. According to existing case law such 'necessity' appears to mean that it must be both intended to meet a 'pressing social need'[49] and its restrictive effects 'must be proportionate to the objective(s) which it seeks to achieve'.[50] Clearly where a patient is incompetent, justification for compulsory intervention can be found, as was the case in *Herczegfalvy*, where it was stated that Art 8 was generally not breached where intervention was a medical necessity.[51] It must at least be doubted whether a general denial of the right of self-determination of competent minors fulfils any notion of proportionality. However, it must, at best, be the case that only a more limited power of intervention against the will of the competent minor in cases of grave prospective health detriment can be justified as proportionate given the importance of the principle of self-determination and its recognition in the case of competent adults.

THE RELEVANCE OF ART 14 USED IN CONJUNCTION WITH ART 5 OR 8

Introduction

So far we may conclude that, if Arts 5 and 8 do permit restrictions on self-determination of the competent minor, these would at most involve cases where the prospective health detriment is grave. However, even such a more limited restriction might be in conflict with Art 14 since it involves an age based discrimination. Article 14 states that:

---

47 App No 8278/78; (1979) 18 D & R 154.

48 *Ibid*, p 156.

49 *Handyside v UK* (1976) 1 EHRR 737, pp 753–54.

50 Coppell, 1999, p 289.

51 Judgment 24 September 1992, Series A, No 244, p 26: adult psychiatric patient whose illness was regarded as rendering him entirely incapable of making decisions for himself.

> The enjoyment of the rights and freedoms set forth in this Convention shall be secured without discrimination on any ground such as sex, race, colour, language, religion, political or other opinion, national or social origin, association with a national minority, property, birth or other status.

In the *Spadeo and Scalabrino* case, the Court held that:

> Article 14 will be breached where, without objective and reasonable justification persons in 'relevantly' similar situations are treated differently. For a claim of violation of this Article to succeed, it has therefore to be established, *inter alia*, that the situation of the alleged victim can be considered similar to that of persons who have been better treated.[52]

A justification could only be objective and reasonable if it involved the pursuit of a legitimate aim with the value of achieving this aim being in proportion to the restriction on rights. Article 14 'has no independent existence' but is brought into play whenever the differential treatment of persons relates to a matter affecting one of the substantive rights. In this case, it is consequently a matter of examining Art 14 in conjunction with Art 5 and, alternatively, Art 8.

Article 14 with Art 5

In using Art 14 in conjunction with Art 5 it can be said that denying competent minors the legal right of self-determination with respect to medical intervention discriminates against them in terms of liberty and security. The focus would, thus, be on examining whether there was an objective and reasonable justification for such discrimination which must be doubted.

Article 14 with Art 8

Coppell points out that:

> Article 8 is frequently more potent where it can be coupled with a claim of discrimination under Art 14.[53]

These two Articles in combination with Art 14 were the subject of an age based issue in *Dudgeon v United Kingdom* [54] where a provision applying to Northern Ireland making buggery with persons under 21 illegal was found to be justified even though it was discriminatory in the sense that heterosexual intercourse, and indeed lesbian sexual activity, were only illegal with persons under 17. More recently, almost the same issue was raised in relation to UK mainland law in *Sutherland v United Kingdom* 24 EHRR CD 22–35. Here, the

---

52 Judgment 28 September 1995, Series A, No 315-B, p 28.

53 Coppell, 1999, p 288.

54 Judgment 22 October 1981, Series A, No 45.

relevant provisions made buggery illegal unless performed as a homosexual act in private between two persons of at least 18 years of age.[55] Contrastingly, the offence of indecent assault on a woman could only be committed for lack of age to consent where that woman was under 16 years of age.[56] The principle of evolutive interpretation was obviously at work in this case because the Commission declared the complaint admissible, concluding that there was no reasonable and objective justification for the discrimination. Coppell rightly notes that:

> ... once a state has taken a positive step to promote of protect private or family life, it must, in principles extend the benefits to all without discrimination.[57]

On a few occasions a State has been able to justify its discrimination but there has had to be sufficient rationale as there was, for example, in *Petrovic v Austria* which concerned a complaint that, although maternity leave payments were provided, paternity leave payments were not.[58] Here, it has to be asked what possible basis is it justifiable to treat one competent person any differently from another?

CONCLUSIONS

Recent decades have seen society place increased emphasis on the principle of autonomy in relation to minors. Many people now consider it to be a good thing to let minors participate in their own decisions as part of the maturation process. However, the theoretical or even legal possibility of participating in a decision is quite different from the legal right to control over one's decisions.

Three justifications can be found for denying the competent minor the right to be treated in the same fashion as the competent adult but all of them are flimsy. The *first* is that a child is somehow *per se* different for decision making purposes. Along these lines, Lowe and Juss suggest that, 'in the final analysis, a child is still only a child'.[59] However, it could equally be argued that an adult with the same level of competence as a competent child is in no different a position when it comes to making medical decisions and that, consequently, the two should not be treated differently in law and that to do so is a violation of Art 14. Teenage minors may typically have a different perception of risk to adults and less experience and ability in decision making but this can adequately be taken into account by the level at which the

---

55 Taking together the Sexual Offences Act 1956, s 12(1), and the Sexual Offences Act 1967, s 1, as amended in respect of reducing the age from 21 to 18 by The Criminal Justice and Public Order Act 1994.

56 Sexual Offences Act 1956, s 14(1).

57 Coppell, 1999, p 288.

58 [1998] EHRLR 487.

59 Lowe and Juss, 1993, p 865.

threshold of competency is set and more serious health decisions can, and already do, require correspondingly higher levels of maturity and understanding for competency to make. The *second* justification is that medical professionals deserve immunity from liability for going against the will of the competent minor where they get the consent of a parent. In *Re W*, Lord Donaldson seemed to reflect long held judicial concerns about making doctors too vulnerable to liability in using a military analogy that, in relying on the consent of either the parent or the *Gillick* competent minor, the medical professional would have a protective 'flak jacket' against liability in battery.[60] The reality is that such concerns would struggle to form a valid ground under a human rights analysis for denying competent minors the right of self-determination. It is not as if, after all, medical professionals get such protection when they violate the self-determination of the competent adult. The third, linked, justification revolves around the practical difficulties of making determinations concerning competency. However, as Elliston points out, 'while setting an arbitrary age for such reasons as ability to vote is acceptable, since the administrative difficulties involved in questioning every citizen in order to establish their competence for enfranchisement would be practically insurmountable, the same is not true where decisions about the management of the health of an individual are concerned. Here the individual's ability to make a decision can be scrutinised ...'.[61] Indeed, it can be seen that, in practice, medical professionals are already doing this all the time with adults. Surely the time is becoming ripe for competent minors to be afforded a legal right of self-determination with respect to medical intervention.

---

60 [1992] 3 WLR 758, p 767.
61 Elliston, 1994, p 42.

CHAPTER 15

YOUNG CHILDREN, BEST INTERESTS AND THE HUMAN RIGHTS ACT 1998

Sabine Michalowski

INTRODUCTION

Decisions regarding the medical treatment of young children sometimes raise difficult legal issues. Given that young children lack the capacity to give valid consent, the lawfulness of their medical treatment will usually depend on the consent of the child's parents. Treatment decisions on which the child's treating physician and parents agree may sometimes give rise to concern for the child's rights or welfare, for example, where there is an agreement to administer invasive high risk treatment. However, such cases will normally not come to the attention of the courts. Instead, the involvement of the courts will mainly be sought where medical practitioners and parents are in disagreement as to the right course of treatment for the child, or where the parents cannot agree on the treatment decision to be made. It is well established that in such cases the courts' decisions will be based on an assessment of the best interests of the child, an approach which reflects the paramount importance accorded to the welfare of the child under s 1(1) of the Children Act 1989.

The Human Rights Act 1998 (HRA) raises interesting questions for the future application of the best interests test in the context of medical treatment decisions on behalf of young children. According to s 6(1) and (3)(a) of the Act, courts as public authorities have to act in accordance with Convention rights. Consequently, the future of the best interests test depends on its compatibility with the European Convention on Human Rights (ECHR) and the HRA 1998.

RIGHTS-BASED APPROACH UNDER THE ECHR

Almost no case law of either the European Commission or the European Court of Human Rights (the Court) deals directly with healthcare decisions on behalf of young children. Accordingly, an assessment of the approach to be adopted under the ECHR will have to be based on general principles drawn from cases which discuss relevant aspects in different contexts.

Various Convention rights may be of relevance to the issue of treatment decisions on behalf of young children. Such decisions may, for example, raise questions regarding the patient's right to life under Art 2(1) of the ECHR. Not many right to life cases have been decided under the ECHR and there is no case law directly concerned with treatment decisions on behalf of young children. Under Art 2(1), States are prohibited actively to take the life of a citizen. In addition, the Commission suggested, in *Association X v UK*,[1] that States are under a positive obligation to take adequate measures to protect life, hinting that this might raise issues with respect to the adequacy of medical care. This could have an impact on decisions of health authorities not to provide costly life-saving treatment and, more generally, on decisions to withhold or withdraw life-saving treatment, so that the child's right to life must be considered whenever a decision is made not to provide life-saving medical treatment.

Another right that may have to be considered in the context of treatment decisions is the right to be free from degrading and inhuman treatment under Art 3. In *X v Denmark*,[2] the Commission argued that gynaecological treatment of an experimental nature could be sufficiently humiliating to amount to inhuman and degrading treatment contrary to Art 3. In *Herczegfalvy v Austria*,[3] this statement has been qualified by the declaration that in cases related to medical treatment, the established principles of medicine are normally decisive, so that, as a general rule, measures which, according to established medical principles, are of therapeutic necessity will not be regarded as inhuman and degrading. However, the Court must satisfy itself that the medical necessity has been convincingly shown to exist. The right under Art 3 can also be violated if no adequate medical treatment is provided. In *Hurtado v Switzerland*,[4] the Commission argued that the lack of medical treatment or serious delays in the provision of medical treatment to persons who are deprived of their liberty can amount to inhuman and degrading treatment, as the State is under a positive duty to 'adopt measures to safeguard the physical well-being of a person placed in the charge of the police, judicial or prison authorities'. However, it is not at all clear whether the same principles would be applied to patients who are not in State detention. In another rather exceptional case, the European Court has held that the removal from the UK to St Kitts of a resident from that island violated his right under Art 3. The applicant who had been detained in the UK, was dying from AIDS and had received medical and palliative care in the UK after having been released on bail from immigration detention. Given that the UK had assumed

---

1   App No 7154/75; (1978) 14 DR 31; see, also, *Commission v Germany*, App No 10565/83; (1984) 7 EHRR 152; *LCB v UK* (1998) 27 EHRR 212, para 36.

2   (1983) 32 DR 282.

3   Series A, No 242-B, (1992) para 82.

4   Series A, No 280-A (1994), para 74.

responsibility for his condition for several years, given that his removal would hasten his death and that the standard of medical care in St Kitts as well as the lack of personal support would subject him to acute mental and physical suffering, this amounted to inhuman treatment under Art 3.[5] If, in a given case, Art 3 is found to be applicable and the 'minimum severity threshold' is attained, this provides particularly strong protection, as this right is guaranteed without qualification.

A very important right in the context of treatment decisions on behalf of young children is the right to respect for private and family life under Art 8(1). As the right to respect for private life protects a person's physical and moral integrity, it would, for example, be violated if the individual were subjected to compulsory physical interventions and treatment.[6] However, it is not at all clear whether this right applies to incompetent patients. In *Herczegfalvy v Austria*,[7] a violation of a psychiatric patient's right under Art 8 has been rejected on the grounds that it had not been disproved that the hospital authorities were entitled to regard the applicant's illness as rendering him entirely incapable of taking decisions for himself. This has been understood to establish the general principle that medical treatment without the patient's consent does not amount to an interference with the right to private life under Art 8 where the individual is not competent to give valid consent.[8] However, this is an unsatisfactory interpretation of the scope of the right to private life, as the physical integrity of the most vulnerable individuals would then not receive any protection. Article 8(1) should, instead, be interpreted as protecting the individual against any interference with his/her private sphere, which includes the individual's body, rather than exclusively focusing on a protection of the patient's autonomy. This was recognised in the recent Court of Appeal case of *Re A (Children)* involving a decision on the lawfulness of an operation to separate Siamese twins. Brooke LJ stated that a baby's rights under Art 8(1) included the right not to be subjected to compulsory medical interference.[9] As Art 8(1) imposes a positive obligation on the State to respect the individual's private life,[10] Art 8(1) might also be used where non-life-saving treatment is withheld from a young child.

Both the parents and the child may try to rely on the right to family life under Art 8(1). The right to family life guarantees that the State does not interfere with parental decisions regarding the upbringing of their children.[11] Therefore, this right will normally be invaded when courts override the

---

5   *D v UK* (1997) 24 EHRR 423, para 53.

6   *X v Austria*, App No 8278/78; (1979) 18 DR 154.

7   Series A, No 242-B, para 86.

8   Lord Lester of Herne Hill and Pannick, 1999, pp 167–68.

9   *Re A (Children) (Conjoined Twins: Medical Treatment)* [2001] 1 FLR 1, p 98.

10 *Sheffield and Horsham v UK* (1998) 27 EHHR 163, para 52.

11 Henderson, 1998, p 220.

parents' views as to the medical treatment to be given to their children. However, this does not necessarily mean that the courts will have to accept all parental treatment decisions. Instead, cases in which courts override a parent's treatment decision on behalf of his/her child must be measured at the limitations contained in Art 8(2). To justify an interference with the parental right under Art 8(1), the courts will, thus, have to establish that the interference was in accordance with the law and pursued legitimate aims under Art 8(2), such as the protection of health or of the rights of third parties. This means that in the context of parental treatment decisions, State interference would be in compliance with Art 8(2) if it were aimed at protecting the health or other rights of the child. In addition, the infringement must have been necessary in a democratic society, which means that the interference must be proportionate to the objective pursued by the State measure.[12] This proportionality requirement may command a balancing of rights where the rights of the parents and the rights of the child are in conflict with each other. To that effect, the European Court has argued in *Johansen v Norway*,[13] a case in which a mother had been deprived of access to her child, that a fair balance had to be struck between the interests of the child and those of the parent. The Court then specified the operation of the balancing exercise as follows:

> The Court will attach particular importance to the best interests of the child, which, depending on their nature and seriousness, may override those of the parent. In particular ... the parent cannot be entitled under Art 8 of the Convention to have such measures taken as would harm the child's health and development.[14]

Applied to treatment decisions on behalf of young children, this decision seems to suggest that, on the balance, the parental right will be outweighed where the treatment decision was found to impair the child's health. Consequently, parental claims of a violation of their right under Art 8 will rarely be successful in this context. However, parents have the right to be sufficiently involved in the decision making process to be able to make their views known and to protect their interests.[15] Thus, while parents cannot necessarily determine the outcome of decisions taken on behalf of their children by local authorities or the courts, such decisions will violate the parents' right under Art 8(1) unless the parents were given the opportunity to be adequately involved in the decision making process.

Another question that may be of importance is that of the margin of appreciation given to the State when violating the right to family life of a

---

12 See *Handyside v UK* (1976) 1 EHRR 737; Wadham and Mountfield, 1999, pp 13–16.
13 (1996) 23 EHRR 33.
14 *Ibid*, para 78.
15 *R v UK*, Series A, No 121-C (1987), paras 68 and 69.

parent in order to promote the rights of a child.[16] Particularly in the context of determining what course to take in the interests of a child, the State will have to be given a broad margin of appreciation, as the determination of the child's interests will usually depend on an assessment of the relevance of the views of all parties involved in a case, and State authorities are in a much better position than the European Court to make such an evaluation. Thus, the European Commission of Human Rights has held, in *Peter Smallwood v UK*,[17] in the context of a decision to rescind parental responsibility, that it was within a State's margin of appreciation for its judicial authorities to conclude how to serve the children's best interests. However, a question remains as to how much, if any, significance the margin of appreciation will be given under the HRA 1998 itself.

In addition to the parents' right to family life, it must also be considered whether the child's right to family life can be concerned in the context of parental decisions. This could be the case if the child's right to family life were interpreted as including the right that important decisions on his/her behalf be taken by the parents and not the State.[18]

The right to freedom of religion under Art 9 may also sometimes play a role in cases of medical treatment. Again, both the parents and the child patient may want to rely on this right. The right to freedom of religion includes the parents' right to determine the child's religious upbringing and it may be argued that it extends to making treatment decisions based on their religious beliefs. It can also be argued that the child has the right to be brought up according to the parents' religious beliefs and to have treatment decisions made for him/her which conform with the parents' religious beliefs. The right under Art 9 can be restricted for the purpose of protecting the health or other rights of the child.

WELFARE PRINCIPLE VERSUS HUMAN RIGHTS

It has sometimes been argued that the HRA 1998 may have the effect of weakening, rather than increasing the protection of children's rights in English law. This assessment is based on several considerations. Under the HRA 1998, decisions on behalf of young children can no longer be based solely on a consideration of the child's best interests. Instead, the rights of parents may likewise be part of the equation, given that every State interference with parental decisions must be justified according to the

---

16 Wadham and Mountfield, 1999, p 16.

17 App No 29779/96; [1999] EHRLR 221, p 222.

18 This point will be discussed below, p 252.

standards of Art 8(2).[19] This is regarded by some as an inroad in the strong protection of children's rights under current English law. As English law has gradually shifted from the concept of parental rights to a concept of parental responsibilities which are to be exercised in accordance with the welfare of the child,[20] there is some concern that the HRA 1998 might reverse this trend to the benefit of the parents and to the detriment of the child.[21]

To decide whether these fears are justified, whether the current practice of English courts will have to change under the HRA 1998, and, if so, whether this will strengthen or weaken children's rights in the context of medical treatment decisions, a careful analysis of the English approach needs to be performed. As the best interests test has been developed by English courts in a long line of cases, its application and its future under the HRA 1998 can best be demonstrated by analysing relevant court decisions. English cases in this area fall into two different categories:

(a) there are cases in which the treating physicians decided to withhold treatment and the parents sought a court order that treatment should be given; and

(b) there are cases in which parents refused to give consent to life-saving treatment proposed by the treating physician and in which the treating physician or the local authority sought the authorisation of the court to administer such treatment against the parents' wishes.

Cases from both categories will be analysed in order to evaluate how the courts have assessed the best interests of the child and what changes, if any, might be necessary under the HRA 1998.

Parental requests to continue life-saving medical treatment

Cases may come to court in which physicians want to withhold or withdraw medical treatment, but in which parents are strongly opposed to such a course of action. One such case was that of *Re C (Medical Treatment)*.[22] In that case, a 16 month old baby suffered from spinal muscular atrophy, a fatal disease, and had been placed on a ventilator to support her breathing. Although she was conscious and able to recognise her parents, the treating physicians described her as being in a 'no chance' situation, meaning that her disease was so severe that life-sustaining treatment would simply delay death without significantly alleviating her suffering. They, accordingly, wished to withdraw ventilation

---

19 For a discussion of the differences between the current English approach and the approach to be adopted under the HRA 1998, see Fortin, 1999b, pp 251–52; and Herring, 1999a, pp 230–32.

20 *Gillick v West Norfolk and Wisbech AHA* [1986] AC 112, p 170, *per* Fraser LJ.

21 Fortin, 1999b, p 255.

22 [1998] 1 FLR 384.

and did not want to reinstate it in the highly likely event of a further respiratory relapse, as such treatment would not improve her quality of life and would subject her to further suffering without conferring any benefit. Her parents were orthodox Jews whose religion did not permit them to support a course of action which would shorten their daughter's life, even if that action was designed to relieve suffering. Stephen Brown P, when establishing the best interests of the child, held that given that there was no hope for C, it was in her best interests to prevent her from further suffering. Consequently, he thought that the course of action proposed by the treating physicians was in her best interests.[23] This application of the best interests test was based on the authority of *Re J (A Minor) (Wardship: Medical Treatment)*,[24] in which Lord Donaldson MR had decided that:

> There is without doubt a very strong presumption in favour of a course of action which will prolong life, but ... it is not irrebuttable ... Account has to be taken of the pain and suffering and quality of life which the child will experience if life is prolonged. Account has also to be taken of the pain and suffering involved in the proposed treatment itself ... In the end there will be cases in which the answer must be that it is not in the interests of the child to subject it to treatment which will cause increased suffering and produce no commensurate benefit, giving the fullest possible weight to the child's, and mankind's desire to survive.

Such decisions thus depend on a careful assessment of the quality of life of the child if kept alive. If medical treatment is painful and may even increase the patient's suffering, without at the same time benefiting the patient's health, the courts take the stance that it is in the best interests of a patient to be allowed to die. The court in *Re C* did not think that the parents' wishes should be determinative. Instead, the court focused on the medical evidence and dismissed the parents' view as dictated by religious beliefs which did not allow them to accept the clinical judgment. An additional aspect of the decision in *Re C* was the court's unwillingness, again supported by the Court of Appeal's decision in *Re J*, to make an order requiring physicians to undertake a course of action which was contrary to their clinical judgment.

Would this decision stand in the light of the HRA 1998? It could be argued that C has been denied the right to life under Art 2(1), as this Article might be read as giving patients the right to receive life prolonging medical treatment.[25] However, in so far as Art 2(1) is aimed at prohibiting the State from taking the life of an individual, it can hardly be argued that in a case in which the State sanctions a decision that medical treatment be withheld from

---

23 [1998] 1 FLR 384, pp 390–91.

24 [1991] 1 FLR 366, p 375.

25 Wright, 1998, p 302.

a dying child, the State is actively taking the life of the patient.[26] That Art 2(1) imposes upon the State an obligation to provide adequate healthcare to protect the lives of individuals may carry some weight where the treatment sought would potentially prolong the child's life.

Arguably, even in such a case, this obligation will not give parents the right to demand that the life of their young child be preserved at all costs, or to claim a particular form of treatment.[27] In respect of a child whose further treatment has been regarded as futile, or where further treatment will not promote the health of a dying child, while causing prolonged suffering, a claim based on a right to life prolonging treatment is particularly unlikely to succeed. It could be argued that invasive but futile medical treatment, or measures which merely prolong suffering, amount to degrading treatment and are therefore prohibited under Art 3, as they are not justified by medical necessity.

This raises the question of the relationship between the right to life and the right to be free from degrading and inhuman treatment, where these rights are in conflict. In *Commission v Germany*,[28] it has been decided that force-feeding of a prisoner did not violate the prisoner's right under Art 3, as it was carried out with a view to fulfilling the State's positive obligation to protect the prisoner's right to life under Art 2, was in the best interests of the prisoner and only administered during a relatively short period of time. While it could be inferred from this decision that, in case of a conflict between the rights in Arts 2 and 3, the right to life should always prevail, such a general conclusion is not convincing. The case was only concerned with the particular situation of a person who was in the custody of the State, and force-feeding can hardly be compared to the administration of invasive medical treatment that may prolong the patient's life without providing sufficient benefits to outweigh the patient's suffering. Instead, in cases of conflict, both rights must be weighed in each individual case and, while there may be a presumption in favour of preserving life, this can be rebutted if life-saving medical treatment subjects the patient to prolonged serious mental or physical suffering[29] without being justified by medical necessity.

So far, one English decision has addressed the question of the compatibility of its best interests analysis with the HRA 1998 in a case in which the treating physicians wanted to withhold a particular course of life-saving but invasive and painful treatment from a terminally ill child and where the parents were opposed to this clinical decision.[30] In that case, the

---

26 For a discussion of the impact of the HRA 1998 on the withdrawal of treatment from a patient in persistent vegetative state, see the recent decision of *NHS Trust A v M; NHS Trust B v H* [2001] 1 All ER 801, pp 803–10, *per* Dame Butler-Sloss P.

27 Fortin, 1999a, Chapter 11.

28 App No 10565/83; (1984) 7 EHRR 152.

29 Wright, 1998, p 302.

30 *A NHS Trust v D* [2000] 2 FCR 577.

court inferred from the European Court's decision in *D v UK*[31] that Art 3 guarantees a right to die in dignity and consequently felt that the decision to withhold intrusive and painful life prolonging treatment from a terminally ill child would be supported by reference to Art 3. The court ruled out a violation of the child's right to life under Art 2 on the grounds that the order the court was asked to make was in the best interests of the child. It is submitted that a reference to the best interests of the child is in itself not sufficient to exclude or justify a violation of the child's right to life. It seems more convincing to say that the child's right to life is outweighed by the child's right to be free from medical treatment that prolongs the child's suffering.

Coming back to the case of *Re C*, under the HRA 1998 the parents' rights to family life under Art 8(1), and to freedom of religion under Art 9(1) would equally have to be considered. However, given that both rights can be restricted to protect the health or other rights of the child, it is very unlikely that the parents' rights will ever prevail where it has been established that the protection of the rights of the child under Art 3 demands that medical treatment be withheld. This is in line with English decisions which take the parents' views into account, but override them where this is regarded necessary in order to protect the welfare of the child.[32] A violation of the parents' right under Art 8(1) will probably only be found where the parents were not adequately involved in the decision making process.

It can be seen that a dying child's right to life does not require health authorities to provide life prolonging treatment under all circumstances, that the parents do not have a right to demand such treatment, and that the child may even sometimes have the right that life-saving treatment not be administered. In this particular context, English courts already perform a very careful analysis of the interests concerned, and even though the rights-based approach slightly shifts the emphasis, no significant changes to the future application of the best interests test will be required. However, it should be noted that the courts' near blanket refusal to order life-saving treatment against the physician's clinical judgment may not necessarily be compatible with the HRA 1998, as it would mean that physicians are given the power to make life and death decisions without any possibility of judicial control. It can hardly be said that this gives adequate protection to the patient's right to life in all situations.

The thought expressed by the Court in *Herczegfalvy v Austria*,[33] in the context of an alleged breach of Art 3, that the court must control carefully

---

31   (1997) 24 EHRR 423.

32   See, eg, *A NHS Trust v D* [2000] 2 FCR 577.

33   Series A, No 242-B (1992), para 86.

whether there was a medical necessity could arguably be used to introduce a minimum standard of judicial control of medical decision making. For cases of a withdrawal of life-saving treatment this would mean that it is for the courts to control whether or not treatment was, in fact, futile or for other reasons unsuitable, even though it would be inappropriate to order that an individual physician administer medical treatment against his/her clinical judgment.

Parental refusal to consent to life-saving medical treatment

Sometimes parents may be opposed to life-saving treatment suggested by the physician for their child, and they may consequently refuse to give their consent to such treatment. In *Re T (Wardship: Medical Treatment)*,[34] a child was born with a life threatening liver defect. His parents were unmarried and both health professionals experienced in the care of children. The unanimous medical opinion was that the child should have a liver transplant. Without it, the child's life expectancy would be just over two years, while the chances of success of a liver transplant were regarded as good. The parents were strongly opposed to this treatment. They thought it was better for their son to have a short and peaceful life, than to be exposed to invasive surgery with all the risks and pain and suffering involved. The three consultants who gave evidence in court disagreed on whether or not they would perform the operation in the light of the mother's refusal to consent to it. One consultant decided to respect her refusal, as it seemed to be the well informed decision of a loving parent, and as the success of the treatment depended on the mother's support and devoted post-operative care. The two other consultants were prepared to operate without the mother's consent, but one of them was not sure of his team's support for such a course of action. The Court of Appeal argued that the outcome of the best interests test should not rely entirely on the clinical assessment of the likely success of the proposed treatment. Instead, the mother's concerns regarding the benefits of the major invasive surgery and the post-operative treatment, the risks involved, and the post-operative quality of life were important considerations when deciding which course to take in the best interests of the child. Waite LJ stressed that when balancing the risks and benefits of the proposed treatment, the attitude taken by a natural parent will be a highly relevant factor.[35] When determining how much weight should be given to the wishes of the parent, he argued that:

> It can only safely be said that there is a scale at one end of which lies the clear case where a parental opposition to medical intervention is prompted by scruple or dogma of a kind which is patently irreconcilable with principles of child health and welfare widely accepted by the generality of mankind; and

---

34 [1997] 1 FLR 502.
35 *Ibid*, p 513.

that at the other end lie highly problematic cases where there is genuine scope for a difference of view between parent and judge. In both situations it is the duty of the judge to allow the court's own opinion to prevail in the perceived paramount interests of the child concerned, but in cases at the latter end of the scale, there must be a likelihood (though never of course a certainty) that the greater the scope for genuine debate between one view and another the stronger will be the inclination of the court to be influenced by a reflection that in the last analysis the best interests of every child include an expectation that difficult decisions affecting the length and quality of its life will be taken for it by the parents to whom its care has been entrusted by nature.[36]

Waite LJ's statement seems to imply that the parental prerogative to make decisions on behalf of their children is not just a parental right, but is also guaranteed in the interest of the child. Butler-Sloss LJ went even further in arguing that the interests of parents and children can sometimes be so closely linked that they cannot be determined separately. According to her: 'This mother and this child are one for the purpose of this unusual case and the decision of the court to consent to the operation jointly affects the mother and son ... The welfare of this child depends on his mother.'[37] She gave a lot of consideration to the effect of the proposed treatment on the mother and came to the conclusion that:

> The welfare of the child is the paramount consideration and I recognise the 'very strong presumption in favour of a course of action which will prolong life' and the inevitable consequences for the child of not giving consent. But to prolong life ... is not the sole objective of the court and to require it at the expense of other considerations may not be in a child's best interests ... The prospect of forcing the devoted mother of this young baby to the consequences of this major invasive surgery lead me to the conclusion ... that it is not in the best interests of this child to give consent ... I believe that the best interests of the child require that his future treatment should be left in the hands of his devoted parents.[38]

Would the HRA 1998 have affected the outcome of this highly controversial decision?[39] Given the high rank of the child's right to life, it seems at first sight as if the fact that life-saving medical treatment was available, and that the members of the medical profession were willing to perform the operation and, indeed, highly recommended it, would in itself have been sufficient to justify treatment. However, such an analysis would be too simplistic. The treatment suggested here was of a highly invasive nature, involving many risks, not the least of which was that the operation, if unsuccessful, might have dramatically

---

36 *Ibid*, pp 513–14.

37 *Ibid*, p 510.

38 *Ibid*, p 512.

39 For a critical discussion of the case, see, eg, Bainham, pp 266–67; Fortin, 1998, pp 260–63; Fox and McHale, 1997; Michalowski, 1997; 'Is it in the best interests of a child to have a life-saving liver transplantation?': *Re T (Wardship: Medical Treatment)* (1997) 9 CFLQ 179.

shortened the life of the child. Thus, a careful risk assessment would have to take place to decide whether or not the operation protected, rather than endangered, the child's right to life. A more difficult question is that of whether considerations regarding the future quality of life of the child can be brought into the equation. It is submitted that for this purpose, use might be made of Art 3. The right under Art 3 is aimed at protecting human dignity and the right not to be subjected to severe and unnecessary suffering. The Court's decision in *Herczegfalvy v Austria*[40] may be interpreted as excluding any reliance on Art 3 in the case of *Re T*, given that the three consultants agreed that the liver transplantation was the only recommended treatment option and accorded with medical standards. However, in *Herczegfalvy v Austria*, the Court stressed that the question of medical necessity was subject to careful judicial scrutiny, which gives courts the possibility to control medical decisions at least to some extent. It could be argued that courts can do no more than decide whether there was a medical necessity, but cannot find a violation of Art 3 on the grounds that medically accepted treatment was unwarranted in the individual case. Given the overriding importance of human dignity, it is submitted that in cases of medically indicated life-saving treatment which carries with it high risks, and may impose on the patient severe pain, or a poor quality of life, these factors must be balanced by the courts, and that the medical decision should be subject to comprehensive judicial control. As such an assessment depends on the overall circumstances of each case, a careful analysis of all the factors of the individual case must be performed to decide whether or not medical treatment might amount to inhuman treatment. Only based on such a finding, complying with the high threshold of Art 3, can the right to life exceptionally be overridden. The decision in *Re T* does not comply with human rights standards because the Court did not examine all the relevant information necessary for a complete assessment of the risks and effects of the medical treatment.[41]

Another important question raised by *Re T* is that of the significance of the wishes of the parents. Under the HRA 1998, the different rights holders, that is the child and the mother, are separate individuals and therefore hold rights independent of each other. The Court's approach in *Re T* according to which the child and the mother were regarded as one for the determination of the child's best interests could, thus, only hold if it can be maintained that the child's right to family life under Art 8(1) corresponds with that of the mother, that is, that the child has the right that important treatment decisions will be made by his/her parents, and that the parents' wishes be respected. In *Re C (HIV Test)*,[42] a case in which the court had to decide whether or not to authorise the testing of a baby for HIV and where the parents were opposed

---

40 Series A, No 242-B (1992), para 82.
41 See the discussion by Michalowski, 1997.
42 [1999] 2 FLR 1004.

to the test, Wilson J seems to have interpreted Art 8(1) this way. From Waite LJ's holding in *Re T* that 'the best interests of every child include an expectation that difficult decisions affecting the length and quality of its life will be taken for it by the parent to whom its care has been entrusted by nature',[43] Wilson J inferred a 'rebuttable presumption that the united appraisal of both parents will be correct in identifying where the welfare of the child lies'. He went on to consider that:

> Under Art 8 of the European Convention ... the parents and the baby all have a right to respect of their family life; and it will be interesting to see, once the HRA 1998 is in force, whether that Article will require our inquiry into a child's welfare to be analysed in that way.[44]

It is submitted that this is not how the analysis will have to performed under the HRA 1998. First, the case of *Re C* not only affected the right to family life, but also the child's right to physical integrity, and possibly even the child's right to life, aspects which would certainly have to influence any analysis under the HRA. More importantly, it is very questionable whether Art 8(1) can be interpreted as giving the child the right that important decisions be made according to his or her parents' wishes.[45] If the HRA 1998 were to be interpreted the way suggested by Wilson J, the worry that it will promote parental rights at the expense of the rights of children[46] would be justified. However, while the European Court has long established that the right to family life includes the right of parents and children mutually to enjoy each other's company,[47] it is also clear that, for example, in the context of care proceedings, the rights of the parent and the rights of the child have been formulated independently and are frequently perceived to be in conflict with each other.[48] This clearly shows that the child's right under Art 8(1) does not include the right that important decisions be made by his/her parents. In addition, given that parents do not have the right to endanger the child's health,[49] it cannot be argued that the child has a right that decisions made by his/her parents which may be detrimental to his/her health be upheld.

What does this mean for the influence of parental views on treatment decisions regarding young children? The parents' wishes may be important for the court's evaluation of the rights of the child, particularly as to whether or not medical treatment may violate the child's right under Art 3. The question of whether or not treatment must be regarded as inhuman cannot

---

43 [1997] 1 FLR 502, p 514.

44 [1999] 2 FLR 1004, p 1013.

45 For a critical analysis of a similar approach under the Irish Constitution, see Duncan, 1993, pp 431–45.

46 Fortin, 1999a, p 354.

47 *Marckx v Belgium* (1979) 2 EHRR 300, para 31.

48 See, eg, *Johansen v Norway* (1996) 23 EHRR 33.

49 *Johansen v Norway* (1996) 23 EHRR 33, para 78.

exclusively be regarded as a medical question. Thus, parents may make essential contributions to the court's assessment of whether or not treatment should be regarded as inhuman or degrading in a given case. Accordingly, the Court of Appeal's holding in *Re T* that the views of parents may be highly relevant for the balancing process is compatible with the HRA 1998. However, it is not at all clear under which circumstances, if any, parental views of what is in their child's best interests can or should be decisive. English courts have consistently stressed that once the court is involved in the decision making process, it is not bound by the views of the parents.[50] On the other hand, Waite LJ argued in *Re T* that in cases which leave room for a genuine debate as to the right course of treatment, there will be a strong inclination to respect the parents' wishes. This does not cause any problems under the HRA 1998, as it will be impossible to find a violation of any right of the child if, for example, the risk benefit analysis does not point towards a particular course of treatment, or where the medical opinion is split as to the recommended course of treatment. More difficult to reconcile with the HRA 1998 is Waite LJ's holding in *Re T* that parents' views can easily be overridden where they contradict the principles of child health and welfare that are widely accepted by the generality of mankind and are prompted by scruple and dogma. Based on this, Butler-Sloss LJ asked in *Re C (HIV Test)*:[51]

> Can it be in the child's best interests for the parents to remain ignorant of their own child's state of health? You only have to ask that question for most people to say no. We are not talking about the rights of the parents, we are talking about the rights of the child ... The parents' views, which are not the views of the majority, cannot stand against the rights of the child to be properly cared for in every sense. This child has the right to have sensible and responsible people find out whether she is or is not HIV positive.[52]

While the child surely has a right to physical integrity, the protection of which may require that parental opposition to medical treatment be overridden, to invent a right of the child that parental views can be ignored whenever they deviate from the views of the majority can hardly survive a human rights analysis, given that human rights are mainly aimed at protecting minorities.

Where the parents' views are overridden by the court, they may allege a violation of their right to family life, but such a violation will always be justified where the parental decision would have endangered the child's right to life. The question of whether or not the mother was prepared to provide the necessary post-operative care would thus not be a consideration to outweigh the child's rights in this case. Accordingly, under the HRA 1998, the parents' wishes will only be of subordinate significance. By contrast, the current

---

50 See, eg, *Re T (Wardship: Medical Treatment)* [1997] 1 FLR 502, p 509, *per* Butler-Sloss LJ; *Re A (Conjoined Twins: Medical Treatment)* [2001] 1 FLR 1, p 51, *per* Ward LJ.

51 [1999] 2 FLR 1004.

52 *Ibid*, p 1021.

application of the best interests test in English law makes it possible to merge the child's interests with those of the mother.[53] It therefore seems fair to say that, at least in the context of medical treatment decisions, the danger that the child's position may be adversely affected by the significance accorded to the interests of parents, is greater under the best interests test than under a human rights approach where different rights of the child must be taken into account and the parental rights are subject to the child's right to health.

The analysis of the Court of Appeal's decision in *Re T* demonstrates that the best interests test is so vague that it allows the courts to reach a decision without having to perform a careful analysis of the different rights or interests of the child which may be affected by the outcome of the case. It is submitted that the HRA 1998 provides a better framework to resolve such cases in accordance with the welfare of the child, as it forces the courts to consider the different rights of the child, and limits the rights of parents to the right to be involved in the decision making process, and the right to make decisions on behalf of the child that will not violate the child's health or other rights.

CONCLUSION

It has been demonstrated that the HRA 1998 may require some important changes regarding the application of the best interests test in the context of medical treatment decisions on behalf of young children. While in cases where the withdrawal of life-saving treatment is at issue, courts perform a careful balancing of the interests involved when determining the best interests of the child, in other areas the best interests test seems to be applied rather intuitively.[54]

The lack of consistent criteria that need to be considered when applying the best interests test makes the outcome of the test seem arbitrary, and there is often no transparency as to the reasons on which the outcome is based. Indeed, the test is so vague that it can accommodate the interests of other interested parties to the detriment of the child whose best interests the court is asked to protect. The analysis of the Court of Appeal's decision in *Re T* proves this point. It is, thus, submitted that children's rights are not adequately protected by the application of the best interests test and the welfare principle.[55] This is where the HRA 1998 may prove to be a useful vehicle to promote children's rights. Under the Act, English courts will have to analyse the best interests of a young child in compliance with human rights principles,

---

53 For a critical assessment of the English approach, see, eg, Bainham, 1998, p 267; Fox and McHale, 1997, p 708; Herring, 1999b, p 95.

54 Kennedy, 1992, p 395.

55 See, also, Fortin, 1998, pp 251–52.

which means that in every given case, the courts will have to identify which rights of the child may be involved. More importantly, in many cases the courts will have to weigh competing interests either of the child and the parents, or competing interests of the child itself, such as, in some cases, the child's right to life versus the child's right to be free from degrading and inhuman treatment. It is certainly true that the rights conferred by the Convention and the HRA 1998 'lack the fine tuning'[56] necessary to deal adequately with disputes over the rights of a child, but they provide a rights-based framework which can be used for a promotion of children's rights.

The rights-based approach does not provide a set solution to every given problem and mainly identifies the competing rights of the child and of each parent, without necessarily giving clear indications as to how to weigh these conflicting rights.[57] However, this does not mean that the rights-based approach cannot provide useful guidance as to the content and outcome of the balancing process. In the context of treatment decisions on behalf of young children, it has, for example, been demonstrated that the rights of parents will almost always have to yield, as they can be disregarded to protect the child's health and other interests. At the same time, it is important that the rights of the parents be considered, and that a clear ranking of the rights of the child and the parents be established, as the courts may otherwise tend to give too much weight to parental interests, as in the case of *Re T*. However, the impact of the HRA 1998 largely depends on the approach adopted by the judiciary. In that respect, the references made to the HRA 1998 in *Re C (HIV Test)*,[58] *Re J (Specific Issue Orders: Muslim Upbringing and Circumcision)*,[59] *A NHS Trust v D*[60] and *Re A (Conjoined Twins: Medical Treatment)*[61] are not too promising. If the courts decide to focus their rights-based analysis on the rights of the parents, and widely to ignore the more directly affected rights of the child, as in *Re C (HIV Test)* and *Re J (Specific Issue Orders: Muslim Upbringing and Circumcision)*, or merely state that the principles of the HRA 1998 have not been violated by the court's analysis of the child's best interests, as in *NHS Trust v D* and *Re A*, the opportunities provided by the HRA 1998 will be lost.

---

56 Fortin, 1999b, p 255.
57 For a critique of the rights-based approach on these grounds, see Herring, 1999a.
58 [1999] 2 FLR 1004 Fam Div, p 1013, *per* Wilson J.
59 [1999] 2 FLR 678 Fam Div, p 701, *per* Wall J.
60 [2000] 2 FCR 577, *per* Cazalet J.
61 [2001] 1 FLR 1, p 61, *per* Ward LJ.

CHAPTER 16

PREGNANCY AND THE HUMAN RIGHTS ACT 1998

Marc Stauch

INTRODUCTION

By its nature, the condition of pregnancy has at its core two interlinked, but separate beings with potentially distinct interests, the pregnant woman and her foetus.[1] Hitherto the law in the UK relating to pregnancy, including the statutory provisions that govern its termination, has been notable for its refusal, where conflict between the two interests may arise, to ascribe rights to either party. Instead, in opting for an approach centred on the exercise by doctors of medical discretion, it has invoked a mainstream consensus that foetal death or injury is, on occasion, the regrettable but necessary price of preserving the well-being of the pregnant woman. The polarisation of the debate into opposing camps supporting, on the one hand, the woman's 'right to choose' and, on the other, the foetus' 'right to life' has largely been avoided.

Now, however, in the light of the explicit rights discourse of the European Convention on Human Rights (ECHR), the continued viability of this consensus-based approach must be open to question. This chapter will look in turn at two contrasting areas in which it is likely that the courts will have to adjudicate upon the potential conflict between the putative rights of the foetus and those of the pregnant woman.[2] In the first place, there is the abortion issue, in which the woman's desire to be rid of the foetus, and the prospective burdens of advanced pregnancy and motherhood, entails the death of the foetus – usually as a result of the intervention of a doctor. Secondly, there are cases of prenatal harm, where a child is born alive, but significantly disabled, as a result of some intentional act or omission on the part of the woman while pregnant. The, at first sight paradoxical, conclusion reached is that, whereas the incorporation of the ECHR could see a liberalisation of abortion law in the UK, that safeguarding foetuses from prenatal harm at the hands of their mothers may, conversely, need to become stricter.

---

1   Although the foetus is inside the pregnant woman and receives all of the nutrients necessary for its growth from her, the House of Lords acknowledged its separate biological status in *AG's Reference (No 3 of 1994)* [1998] AC 245.

2   The position of the potential father (whose lack of rights under the ECHR has long been established: see *Paton v UK* (1981) 3 EHRR 408) will not be discussed in this chapter.

ABORTION

The existing law on abortion in England and Wales[3] is contained in three separate statutes, the Offences Against the Person Act 1861, the Infant Life (Preservation) Act 1929 and the Abortion Act 1967. In the first place, s 58 of the 1861 Act makes it a criminal offence, punishable by life imprisonment, to 'procure the miscarriage of any woman'. Further, s 59 of the Act criminalises the supply of drugs or other instruments for use in the principal offence. Secondly, and because of doubts over the ability of the last provisions (given their requirement for a 'miscarriage'), to protect a foetus already in the course of its birth, Parliament subsequently enacted the 1929 Act.[4] Section 1(1) of this Act creates the offence of 'child destruction', again punishable by life imprisonment, which is committed by 'any person who, with intent to destroy the life of a child capable of being born alive, by any wilful act causes a child to die before it has an existence independent of its mother'.

Thirdly, however, and of greatest significance in reflecting the more liberal attitude towards abortion that currently prevails in our society, there is the Abortion Act 1967.[5] The effect of this last statute is to provide the doctor who terminates a pregnancy in certain specified circumstances (as well as the woman whose pregnancy is terminated) with a statutory immunity, that is, no offence will have been committed under the 1861 or 1929 Acts. In fact, s 1(1) of the 1967 Act[6] provides for four alternative grounds that may justify abortion, namely:

(a) that the pregnancy has not exceeded its 24th week and that the continuance of the pregnancy would involve risk, greater than if the pregnancy were terminated, of injury to the physical or mental health of the pregnant woman or any existing children of her family; or

(b) that the termination is necessary to prevent grave permanent injury to the physical or mental health of the pregnant woman; or

(c) that the continuance of the pregnancy would involve risk to the life of the pregnant woman, greater than if the pregnancy were terminated; or

(d) that there is a substantial risk that if the child were born it would suffer from such physical or mental abnormalities as to be seriously handicapped.

---

3   There is some divergence in the law on the subject found in both Scotland and Northern Ireland (see fns 4 and 5, below).

4   The provisions of the 1929 Act were enacted in Northern Ireland (by s 25 of the Criminal Justice (Northern Ireland) Act 1945), but never in Scotland.

5   The 1967 Act was not enacted in Northern Ireland, where the grounds for permissible termination remain governed by the common law: see Re K (A Minor) (Abortion) (1993) unreported NI Fam Div, applying R v Bourne [1939] KB 687.

6   As amended by s 37 of the Human Fertilisation and Embryology Act 1990. The four grounds are found in s 1(1)(a)–(d) of the Act.

The section leaves the decision as to which, if any, of the above grounds is satisfied in a particular case to two doctors, who must have formed their opinion 'in good faith'. Indeed, the 1967 Act may plausibly be perceived as defusing abortion as a contentious and highly divisive political issue through a process of 'medicalisation': the legitimacy of the procedure is no longer characterised as a moral matter, but a medical one within the competence of the doctors.[7]

How, then, is the bringing into English law of Convention rights likely to impinge upon the above, pragmatically inspired scheme? The natural view of abortion, once rights enter the equation, is of a contest between the 'right to life' of the foetus and the 'right to a private life' of the pregnant woman. As one would expect, both the right to life (Art 2) and the right to a private life (Art 8) feature in the abstract in the ECHR. However, as will become apparent, their concrete application to the abortion issue remains extremely uncertain.

Looking first at Art 2, *if it were* interpreted as extending protection to the foetus, this would provide a *prima facie* argument against the legitimacy of the present abortion regime in the UK.[8] Given that the abortion process involves the active and intentional termination of the foetus' life, it falls within the first paragraph of the Article, which provides that 'no one shall be intentionally deprived of life save in the execution of a sentence of a court ...'.[9] On the face of it, the Abortion Act 1967, which, as we have seen, permits such terminations to be lawfully carried out by doctors in various prescribed circumstances, would infringe such a right. It is true that, to the extent that a weak view is taken of the foetus' right to life (see below), grounds (b) and (c), allowing for termination in cases of conflict with the vital interests of the pregnant woman, are likely to remain justified.[10] But grounds (a) and (d), which contemplate abortion in circumstances of less serious conflict, would become less obviously supportable.

However, would an English court construe Art 2 as covering foetal life? The extant jurisprudence of Convention institutions, which would otherwise serve as a guide, has left this issue unresolved. In *Paton v UK*,[11] the Commission noted three views that could, theoretically, be taken of Art 2 as it relates to the foetus. The first is that the Article does not cover the foetus at all. The second is that it confers some kind of 'weak' right to life upon the foetus,

---

7 See Sheldon, 1997.

8 It would not conclude the issue, for, in so far as the foetus enjoyed such a right, it might still be held to give way, in cases of conflict, to the rights of the pregnant woman; see further, below.

9 The second paragraph of the Article, which allows States to use potentially lethal force necessary for the maintenance of law and order, would not appear to be relevant.

10 In the Republic of Ireland, where the right to life of the unborn is expressly protected by Art 40.3.3 of the Constitution, termination has been held permissible if there is a 'real and substantial risk' to the life of the mother: see *AG v X and Others* [1992] 1 IR 1.

11 *Paton v UK* (1981) 3 EHRR 408.

which readily gives way, at least in the earlier stages of pregnancy, in the face of the countervailing interests of the pregnant woman. Thirdly, the Article might confer a strong right to life upon it, equivalent in its protection to the right enjoyed by those who have already been born. The Commission rejected the third view, commenting that:

> The 'life' of the foetus is intimately connected with, and cannot be regarded in isolation from, the life of the pregnant woman. If Art 2 were held to cover the foetus and its protection were, in the absence of any express limitation, seen as absolute, an abortion would have to be considered as prohibited even where the continuance of the pregnancy would involve a serious risk to the life of the pregnant woman. This would mean that the 'unborn life' of the foetus would be regarded as being of higher value than the life of the pregnant woman.[12]

On the other hand, the Commission refrained from choosing between the first and second positions. Instead, as is apparent from subsequent rulings, both by it and the Court,[13] a margin of appreciation has been left to signatory States to decide for themselves whether the unborn enjoy the weak right (as opposed to no right) and, if so, at what stage of development.

In the light of the above, a court in this country will have the task of determining the issue by reference to relevant national jurisprudence, and taking account of current social attitudes. In this regard, it is submitted that the most likely outcome is that the first position will be endorsed. That is to say, no right to life of an individual under Art 2 will be recognised until the moment of birth.[14] This would be consistent with the longstanding refusal of the English courts to accord the foetus legal personality, lest it detract from the exercise of the pregnant woman's autonomy.[15] Such an approach would also avoid the need to investigate further the problematic concept of a 'weak right to life',[16] as well as how the content of such a right might vary with the foetus' gestational age.

Assuming that the English courts reject the idea of the foetus enjoying any protection under Art 2, it might be thought that the existing abortion law could remain in its present form. However, we have not as yet addressed the potential application of Art 8 of the ECHR, which protects a person's right to a 'private and family life' from State interference. In particular, is it the case that

---

12 *Paton v UK* (1981) 3 EHRR 408, para 19.

13 *H v Norway* (1990) App No 17004/90; (1992) 73 DR 155; *Open Door and Dublin Well Woman v Ireland* (1992) 15 EHRR 244 ECtHR.

14 This view of Art 2 has been taken by the Austrian Constitutional Court in applying the ECHR as part of its constitutional law: see Decision of October 11, 1974, Erk Slg No 7400, EuGRZ 1975, p 74.

15 *Paton v Trustees of BPAS* [1979] QB 276; *C v S* [1988] QB 135; *Re F (In Utero)* [1988] Fam 122. The fact that the foetus is at term will make no difference: *Re MB (An Adult: Medical Treatment)* [1997] 2 FCR 541; *St George's Healthcare NHS Trust v S* [1999] Fam 26.

16 It certainly seems odd that a right of such vital substantive import should be defeasible as soon as the competing (and generally non-vital) interests of another individual enter the picture.

a pregnant woman could argue that the current statutory regime does not accord adequate respect to her rights in this regard? If such an argument could be made out, a relaxation of the current English abortion law may be required.

Such a possibility may seem surprising, given that the UK[17] is widely perceived as already having more liberal laws on abortion than many other countries (including other ECHR signatory States). Moreover, following earlier Convention jurisprudence, it could be argued that such restrictions as exist would not in any event infringe the Art 8 rights of pregnant women. Specifically, in *Brüggemann and Scheuten v Germany*, the Commission held that, given the societal interest in reproduction, 'Art 8(1) cannot be interpreted as meaning that pregnancy and its termination are, as a principle, solely a matter of the private life of the mother'.[18] It followed that signatory States were entitled to impose legal restrictions on access to abortion, whose precise substance would generally be a matter within each State's margin of appreciation.

Nevertheless, as regards the particular case of the Abortion Act 1967, the difficulty is that, to the extent that it is a liberal measure, this is a product of the substantive grounds on which termination is permitted, particularly the relative lack of restriction placed upon later terminations.[19] By contrast, there are two features of the current scheme that make it, in procedural terms, potentially quite illiberal in its application. In the first place, nowhere is any right as such conferred upon the pregnant woman to the abortion. Rather, as previously noted, the decision whether one of the four grounds for termination is satisfied is one for the doctors. Secondly, the phrasing of the four grounds (a)–(d) is extremely vague, sketching only in barest outline the factors to which the doctors should have regard, and leaving the latter a vast discretion to interpret them as they see fit.[20] The unsurprising consequence of these two points is that women, in similar circumstances, may enjoy a very different likelihood of obtaining an abortion (at any rate on the NHS). In fact, there is ample evidence that doctors apply the Abortion Act divergently in different parts of the country.[21] It is submitted that such legislatively inspired arbitrariness is likely now to fall foul of the Human Rights Act 1998. In particular, pregnant women who are refused an NHS abortion might

---

17 Northern Ireland, where, as already noted, the Abortion Act 1967 does not apply, is excluded from this assessment.

18 (1981) 3 EHRR 408, para 61.

19 Under grounds (b)–(d) terminations may, in principle, be carried out until birth.

20 In *R v Smith* [1974] 1 All ER 376, Scarman LJ commented that 'a great social responsibility is firmly placed by the law on the shoulders of the medical profession'.

21 Sheldon, 1997, notes that, in 1995, 95% of abortions in North Tyneside took place on the NHS in contrast with only 43% in Solihull.

justifiably claim that they have suffered unlawful discrimination contrary to Art 14 of the ECHR (operating in conjunction with Art 8).[22]

The ground for termination under the 1967 Act that is perhaps most open to challenge in this regard is the so called 'social ground' under s 1(1)(a), with its wide injunction to doctors to consider if continued pregnancy poses a 'risk, greater than if the pregnancy were terminated, of injury to the physical or mental health of the pregnant woman or any existing children of her family'.[23] To the extent that the discriminatory potential of this provision may require future attention, two possibilities suggest themselves. On the one hand, detailed guidance might be issued to doctors as to the section's proper interpretation, in an attempt to secure greater consistency in its application.[24] Alternatively, the need for doctors to attest to the existence of a ground justifying termination could, in the case of an early abortion, simply be removed. Which option is chosen will largely be a political question. Nevertheless, the latter course, at least in respect of first trimester pregnancies, would probably be more straightforward administratively. Indeed, it may be doubted whether the 'social ground' could be more precisely formulated without divesting it of its present quasi-medical character entirely, in which case the justification for leaving its certification to doctors would in any event disappear. Such a development, allowing the pregnant woman to determine for herself whether her circumstances warrant a termination of an early pregnancy, would bring the UK law into line with that in many other signatory States, including France, Germany, and the countries of Benelux and Scandinavia.[25]

---

22 It does not follow that abortions need necessarily be NHS-funded, as Art 8 will not, in itself, support a claim right of this sort: see *Sheffield and Horsham v UK* (1998) 27 EHRR 163, and the comments of the English Court of Appeal in *North West Lancashire HA v A, D and G* [1999] Lloyd's Rep Med 399. Rather, the ground for challenge derives from the discrimination inherent in the current system (where essentially identical cases may be treated differently).

23 This ground presently mandates over 90% of the abortions that are carried out in Great Britain. Indeed, it is often argued that its terms already permit sympathetic doctors to acquiesce to 'abortion on demand'.

24 Outside the abortion context, the need for greater consistency across the country in terms of treatments available on the NHS led to the establishment, in 1999, of the National Institute of Clinical Excellence, with its task of disseminating guidance to health authorities on their funding obligations.

25 The woman is generally required to have counselling before reaching her decision. Most of the countries mentioned apply such a scheme until the end of the 12th week of pregnancy (the limit in France is 10 weeks, in Sweden 18 weeks and in Holland 20 weeks), after which doctors must certify some medical justification (broadly similar to those found in grounds (b)–(d) of the Abortion Act 1967). See, further, Rolston and Eggert, 1994.

PRENATAL HARM CASES

Moving beyond the abortion issue and onto cases of prenatal harm, what are the implications of the incorporation of the ECHR for the existing law here? It is clear enough, as an abstract proposition, that a person's interests may be adversely affected by things done to them while they were still a foetus. As Lord Hope commented in *AG's Reference (No 3 of 1994)*:[26]

> For the foetus, life lies in the future ... It is not sensible to say that it cannot ever be harmed, or that nothing can be done to it which can ever be dangerous. Once it is born it is exposed, like all living persons, to the risk of injury. It may also carry with it the effects of things done to it before birth which, after birth, may prove to be harmful.[27]

Domestic law currently protects the interest of the unborn child[28] by allowing an action to be maintained for prenatal injuries under the Civil Liability (Congenital Disabilities) Act 1976.[29] The Act operates through a scheme of derivative liability, giving the child, after it has been born, a right to sue insofar as a duty owed to one of its parents has been breached (and notwithstanding that the parent may not him- or herself have suffered tangible injury). In other words, the child is owed a duty of care prior to birth, albeit that its right to sue remains contingent upon its subsequent birth. Significantly, however, the 1976 Act does not (apart from in one limited case[30]) allow the child to sue its own mother in respect of prenatal injuries. The reason for this is based on public policy, in particular, the perceived undesirability of fracturing the mother-child bond by the prospect of litigation.

An interesting question, following the incorporation of the ECHR, is whether this regime will require extension so that the child has a general right to maintain an action against its mother for injuries arising from faulty behaviour on her part. Admittedly, at first sight, ECHR rights may not be thought to add a great deal to the law in this area. As noted previously, it is unlikely that the UK courts will hold that a foetus has any right to life under Art 2, such as would hamper the woman's ability to seek a termination. And if the pregnant woman can dispose of the foetus altogether, does it not follow that she remains free to injure it in non-fatal ways as well? Indeed, the

---

26 [1998] AC 245.

27 *Ibid*, p 271.

28 In this part of the chapter, the terminology of the 'unborn' or 'future' child is used interchangeably with that of 'the foetus', as the underlying assumption is that a child will subsequently be born.

29 Subsequently, in two consolidated appeals where the injuries in suit predated the enactment of the 1976 Act, the Court of Appeal held that an action also lay at common law: see *Burton v Islington HA* and *de Martell v Merton and Sutton HA* [1992] 3 All ER 833.

30 See s 2 of the Act, which provides that the child may sue its mother in respect of injuries caused by a road accident. The exception is based pragmatically on the existence of compulsory insurance.

pregnant woman's position, and her liberty to engage in the relevant harm causing conduct, seems to be secured by the existence of Art 8, securing respect for her private and family life.

Nevertheless, and here is the rub, might not the foetus be able to assert that it, too, has a right under Art 8 to a private and family life that requires protection? If so, interference with the pregnant woman's own Art 8 right may be justifiable under Art 8(2), which allows this insofar as it is necessary 'for the protection of the rights ... of others'. At first glance, such a possibility may seem far fetched. The temptation is to say that, because the events compromising its subsequent ability to exercise its Art 8 rights occur at a time when the putative right-holder is a foetus (lacking in legal personality), no violation of any right can have occurred. However, this begs the question. In particular, it should be recalled that by 'foetus' we here mean the future child who (it is being assumed) will be born alive, but disabled, as a result of its mother's conduct while pregnant. The real issue is whether, in order to vindicate the future right of a legal person, viz the damaged child, the courts should be prepared, where necessary, to protect its interests at the prenatal stage.[31]

There is a paradox here that merits close attention, namely that even if the foetus has no right to life (or only a 'weak' right readily sacrificed to the interests of the pregnant woman), it may yet enjoy the right, *in so far as it is born*, to be free of reasonably avoidable disability. At any rate this seems plausible where the disability in question would have the effect of seriously compromising its chances in life. As Feinberg has suggested,[32] the source of the paradox lies in the 'harm principle'.[33] A foetus that is aborted will *ex hypothesi* never become a future person possessing actual interests and, accordingly, no such interests are set back through a decision to terminate pregnancy. By contrast, as previously discussed, it is quite possible to harm (by setting back the actual future interests of) a foetus that is subsequently born disabled. The child, that the foetus has become, must now go through life with its capacity for flourishing as a human being diminished, relative to its hypothetical level had there been no prenatal damage.[34]

---

31 Previously, the UK courts have adverted to the foetus' lack of legal personality in disclaiming jurisdiction to intervene where the interests of an as yet unborn child are at stake: see *Re F (In Utero)* [1988] Fam 122 and *Re MB (An Adult: Medical Treatment)* [1997] 2 FCR 541. However, it is submitted that this 'legalistic' approach will no longer be sufficient.

32 Feinberg, 1984, pp 95–100.

33 That is, JS Mill's famous doctrine that social restraint may be justified only in so far as a person's conduct presents a risk of harm to others.

34 The action in such a case is founded on the allegation that, but for the defendant's negligence, the child would have been born free of disability and should not be confused with an action for 'wrongful life' where it could only ever have been born disabled or not at all. In *Reeve v UK* (1994) 79A D & R 147, the Commission upheld the validity of the English courts' refusal to provide a remedy in the latter type of case (based, *inter alia*, on the impossibility of valuing the child's claim: see *McKay v Essex AHA* [1982] QB 1166).

It is clear that Art 8 encompasses a right to physical integrity, and a fortiori will accord protection against serious disablement prejudicial to a person's chances in life generally.[35] Moreover, it is also well established that, in order to secure that Article right, a State may be required to intervene in purely 'horizontal' disputes (represented here by the conflict of interest between pregnant woman and future child).[36] Do such considerations mean that, in the wake of the incorporation of the ECHR, the mother's immunity from suit (save in road accident cases)[37] may no longer be sustainable?

As previously noted, the immunity currently given to the mother of the child under the Congenital Disabilities (Civil Liability) Act 1976 was based on the perceived undesirable social consequences (in terms of undermining family cohesion) of permitting such actions. In fact, the Law Commission had originally thought that a potential action should lie against the mother,[38] but, in the light of submissions made to it by the Bar Council and the President of the Family Division,[39] later changed its mind. In its report[40] (which formed the basis for the 1976 Act) it had the following to say on the matter:

> There is a wide range of rash conduct during pregnancy by which a mother may cause injury to her unborn child, either by failing to heed medical advice or by herself taking unjustified risks of physical injury ... We now think that we underestimated the number of different ways in which it might be alleged that a mother's negligence caused her child's disability and the extent to which actions or threats of action might be used in matrimonial disputes. We have therefore concluded that legislation should not permit a right of action by a child against its own mother for prenatal injury resulting from the mother's negligence in the prenatal regime.[41]

This may seem to have much to commend it as a general rule of thumb,[42] but its absolute character is arguably out of temper with the need to balance individual rights (requiring the individual circumstances of a particular case to be investigated) that is central to the ECHR. Indeed, it is clear from other contexts, that 'blanket' type immunities, whereby the status of a putative defendant precludes it from being sued (without any enquiry into the nature

---

35 See Feldman, 1997 and, also, the decision of the Court in *Botta v Italy* (1998) 26 EHRR 241.

36 *Marckx v Belgium* (1979) 2 EHRR 300; *X and Y v The Netherlands* (1985) 8 EHRR 235.

37 See fn 30, above.

38 See its Working Paper No 47 (1973).

39 The Bar Council pointed out the added tension that would be introduced into the already stressful relationship of mother and disabled child, as well as the evidential difficulties inherent in such claims. The President (Sir George Baker P) raised concerns about the increased potential for marital conflict.

40 Law Commission, 1974.

41 *Ibid*, para 58.

42 Although it seems hard to square with the absence of any similar immunity enjoyed by the father.

of its fault and the harm thereby caused) will be held to violate a claimant's right to a fair hearing in the determination of its civil rights.[43]

Assuming that the general possibility of a child suing its mother for prenatal injury will now have to be recognised, there is a further, and critical, question that needs to be addressed. In particular, would any such action in any event have to await *the birth* of the damaged child, or could the promotion of the child's Art 8 rights support, and perhaps require, legal intervention to control the pregnant woman's conduct at the prenatal stage? Up until now, the system of protection from prenatal injury found in the Congenital Disabilities (Civil Liability) Act 1976 has operated purely by way of compensation *ex post facto* for injuries already suffered. No pre-emptive action, seeking injunctive relief in circumstances where injury to an unborn child is threatened, but has yet to materialise, has ever been brought under the statute. The reason for this seems largely to do with the rarity of a practical scenario arising (involving a defendant other than the child's mother)[44] where there will be an opportunity to pre-empt the harm in this way.

However, in so far as the defendant is the child's mother (which, it is being assumed, will now be a general possibility), opportunities for prenatal intervention to minimise the potential future harm to a child who is currently a foetus might arise in a range of situations. In particular, where it is known that some ongoing conduct by the pregnant woman (such as drug abuse) poses a serious risk to the well being of the future child, intervention may well constitute the most effective means of securing its Art 8 rights. By comparison, monetary compensation after the event may provide scant satisfaction.[45]

Of course, it might be argued that (apart from prenatal intervention) another means of more effectively protecting the rights of the future child exists, namely *criminal* sanctions against women who wilfully cause prenatal damage to their children. However, leaving aside the, in itself, highly contentious nature of such a response,[46] it is submitted that it would remain inadequate from the point of view of protecting the rights of a particular unborn child known to be at threat. It is as though the police, knowing of A's imminent intention to kill B, could let him do so and assert that B's rights were, nevertheless, sufficiently protected by the fact that A will now be liable to imprisonment.[47]

---

43 Under Art 6 of the ECHR, as established in *Osman v UK* [1999] 1 FLR 193.

44 Equally, the one possible action against the mother under the 1976 Act as it stands, viz in a road accident case, goes to past negligent conduct on her part.

45 Serious permanent disability in life can be classified as a 'incompensable' wrong, in that it is not something that, *ex ante*, a person would wish to trade for any amount of money: see Thomson, 1986, p 157.

46 See, further, Robertson, 1994, pp 180ff.

47 Cf *Osman v UK* [1999] 1 FLR 193.

Nevertheless, allowing that the State may, in principle, be required to intervene prenatally in order to secure the rights of the child to be against the threat posed by the conduct of its mother, a formidable practical difficulty remains. How, if such intervention occurs, can adequate safeguards be put in place so as to protect the freedom and dignity of the pregnant woman? Certainly, the potential for coercive restraint to be applied against the latter provokes instinctive disquiet. As Robertson comments, 'In the worst case scenario, special pregnancy police will be commissioned to monitor women for pregnancies, and then surveil their behavior ... Margaret Atwood's *The Handmaid's Tale*, a chilling novel of women forced to serve the needs of a repressive dictatorship, starts sounding much less fanciful than it appears to be ...'.[48]

In fact, though, it is suggested that an immediate basis for limiting prenatal intervention can be derived from the underlying nature of the harm principle (which, it will be recalled, provided the original argument for acting on the foetus' behalf at all). In particular, that principle has never been interpreted as imposing positive obligations upon a person to act (or permit themselves to be acted upon) to save another person from harm. To the contrary, the common law has evinced a longstanding repugnance at the prospect of treating one person merely as a means to another's benefit.[49] Rather, the harm principle contemplates a more limited negative duty to *forbear* from conduct that will cause unjustified harm.

Applying this to the case of pregnant women and their unborn children, two types of scenario should be kept firmly distinct. In the first place, the pregnant woman may be actively engaging in some positive conduct that poses a risk to her unborn child, for example, drug or alcohol abuse. Secondly, she may passively decline medical intervention necessary for the well being of the foetus, for example, she refuses her consent to a Caesarean section required to prevent the foetus suffering brain damage in the course of birth.

As regards the latter situation, where the vindication of rights of the child to be would require forcible, invasive treatment of the pregnant woman, the common law has recently confirmed, in unequivocal terms, that she has an absolute right to refuse such treatment.[50] The incorporation of the ECHR into English law is extremely unlikely to affect this principle. Indeed, in so far as

---

48 See Robertson, 1994, p 184.

49 The refusal of the common law to treat a person merely as a means to another's ends lies behind the well known decision in *McFall v Shimp* (1978) 10 Pa D & C (3d) 90, in which an American court refused to grant an order compelling a man to donate bone marrow to save the life of his cousin. Although the courts have not as yet been faced with a case where the putative donor and donee stand in a parent-child relationship, it is likely that the result would be the same.

50 *Re MB (An Adult: Medical Treatment)* [1997] 2 FCR 541; *St George's Healthcare NHS Trust v S* [1999] Fam 26.

the treatment were given, it would seem certain to infringe a number of the woman's own Convention rights, including Arts 3[51] and 8.

However, what of the other type of case where active conduct on the part of the pregnant woman threatens serious and lasting injury to the child to be? Though rare, an example of such a scenario is provided by the case of *Winnipeg Child and Family Services (Northwest Area) v G (DF)*, which recently came before the Supreme Court of Canada.[52] There the social services sought an order allowing them to place in protective custody a pregnant woman, who was addicted to glue-sniffing, and who had had two children previously, born with serious disability as a consequence of her inhalation of glue fumes while pregnant. Ultimately, the majority of the Supreme Court declined to grant the order, citing policy concerns of a consequentialist nature, in particular, the fear of frightening vulnerable women off antenatal care in the future, if they knew they were at risk of coercive measures restricting their behaviour.

In the light of an assertion of Art 8 rights enjoyed by the child to be, it may well be doubted now whether an English court could afford to take such a non-interventionist approach. Must a particular, identifiable child to be really be condemned to a future life of serious disability because of worries about the net effect of the decision on other hypothetical cases of varying closeness? It is arguably precisely one of the functions of the ECHR to forestall the sacrifice of a clear individual interest to amorphous collective concerns.

Nevertheless, to the extent that State intervention may be mandated in such a case, there is a need for clear principles to be articulated to prevent excessive restrictions upon the pregnant woman's autonomy. It would undoubtedly be disproportionate to countenance intervention in every case where active conduct by the pregnant woman threatens harm to her foetus.[53] Indeed, such an order of response would be impossible to achieve without the spectre of the 'pregnancy police' alluded to by Robertson. Instead, intervention should be reserved for the very clearest cases of serious and imminent risk to the child to be. Moreover, even then it ought to be regarded as the option of last resort, to be used only once attempts based on persuasion have failed to curtail the pregnant woman's harmful activity. In the *Winnipeg* case itself, the minority,[54] who would have granted the restraining order, suggested that four conditions should be satisfied: first, the woman must have decided to carry the child to term; secondly, proof must be presented to a civil standard that the abusive activity will cause harm to the foetus; thirdly, the

---

51 Protecting a person against 'inhuman or degrading treatment'.

52 [1997] 2 SCR 925.

53 ECHR, Art 8(2) (on which, as previously noted, derogation from the Art 8(1) rights of the pregnant woman is here based) requires that any interference with those rights should satisfy the proportionality test: see, eg, *Dudgeon v UK* (1981) 4 EHRR 149.

54 Major and Sopinka JJ.

remedy (that is, the degree of coercive restraint applied to the woman) must be the least intrusive option; and, finally, the process must be procedurally fair.

In the above circumstances, it is submitted that intervention would reflect the State's obligation to safeguard the Convention rights of the future child, while remaining consistent with the rights of the pregnant woman.

CHAPTER 17

EUTHANASIA AND THE HUMAN RIGHTS ACT 1998

Jeff Sapiro and Angie Ungoed-Thomas

INTRODUCTION

Euthanasia can be defined as the process whereby human life is ended by another in order to avoid the distressing effects of an illness. It may be voluntary in the sense that the person killed either requests death or agrees to it, or it may be involuntary in that the person killed either objects or is incapable of expressing an opinion either way and has not given consent in the past.[1]

There is a further distinction between active and passive euthanasia. Active euthanasia refers to the process whereby death is brought about by a positive act directed towards that end. The act must be accompanied by an intention on the part of the actor that death shall result and this intention must be the predominant one rather than a secondary or oblique intention. Passive euthanasia, by contrast, occurs where the doctor or other person responsible for the welfare of the person refrains from performing a particular act, with the specific intention that the patient should die as a result.[2] In effect, this amounts to death by omission.

This chapter will firstly address the present legal position in England and in other notable jurisdictions concerning the doctor's duty to protect, preserve and prolong life, and the circumstances in which the doctor can be absolved of these duties. Secondly, it will address the compatibility of domestic law with the Human Rights Act (HRA) 1998 with particular reference to Arts 2, 3, 8 and 10 as laid out in Sched 1 of the Act. The HRA 1998 is likely to be the main focus for reform in the coming years given the marked reluctance of the UK government to take a lead in this controversial area of medical law and ethics.[3]

---

1   Kennedy and Grubb, 1998, p 844.
2   *Ibid*, p 845.
3   See, eg, the House of Lords Select Committee on Medical Ethics, 1994.

CURRENT LAW AND MERCY KILLING

English law

The deliberate withholding or withdrawing of life prolonging medical treatment so as to hasten a patient's death is considered a 'passive' intervention, and can in certain circumstances be lawfully done. In contrast, an 'active' intervention, such as the killing of a patient through the deliberate administration of a drug given with the purpose of causing the patient's death, is treated by the law as murder, even when carried out at the request of the patient.

In *R v Cox* (1992) 12 BMLR 38, a patient suffering from the terminal stages of rheumatoid arthritis was given an intravenous injection of the lethal substance potassium chloride. The patient's pain was beyond the control of analgesic drugs and Dr Cox had acted in response to the patient's pleading to be put out of her misery.

Despite the fact that the doctor had acted out of compassion for the patient's extreme suffering, he was found guilty of attempted murder.[4] Since the injection had been given for the primary purpose of killing the patient, the crime had been committed, notwithstanding the wishes of the patient or her family.

The House of Lords in *Airedale NHS Trust v Bland* [1993] 1 All ER 821 confirmed that such active interventions designed to bring about death were unlawful. Lord Goff stated:

> ... it is not lawful for a doctor to administer a drug to his patient to bring about his death, even though that course is prompted by a humanitarian desire to end his suffering, however great that suffering may be ... Euthanasia is not lawful at common law.[5]

Thus, a doctor who intentionally causes the death of his patient commits the offence irrespective of the severity of the patient's suffering, the compassionate motives of the doctor or the patient's consent. It was, however, recognised that the legal distinction between discontinuation of treatment and active measures to bring about death might seem ethically suspect. Lord Browne-Wilkinson asked:

> How can it be lawful to allow a patient to die slowly, though painlessly over a period of weeks from lack of food but unlawful to produce his immediate death by a lethal injection, thereby saving his family from yet another ordeal to add to the tragedy that has already struck them?[6]

---

4   The charge of attempted murder was chosen, since the cremation of the patient's body made proof of causation of death difficult.

5   *Airedale NHS Trust v Bland* [1993] 1 All ER 821, p 867.

6   *Ibid*, p 884.

Although acknowledging that the ethical distinction between passive and active courses of action were 'for all relevant purposes indistinguishable'[7] the judges regarded any reform of the law to be a matter for Parliament.

The House of Lords Select Committee on Medical Ethics considered reform of the law. It recommended that there should be no change in the law to permit euthanasia, and it also rejected any distinction between murder and 'mercy killing'.[8]

Other jurisdictions

With the exception of The Netherlands, the law in other countries prohibits the killing of a person at their request. For example, killing upon request is specifically prohibited under German law and, in France, the killing of a person at their request is homicide.

In the US, the State of Oregon has legalised physician-assisted suicide through its Death With Dignity Act 1994. However, the ending of a patient's life by 'lethal injection, mercy killing or active euthanasia' is not permitted in the legislation.[9]

The Northern Territory of Australia passed the Rights of the Terminally Ill Act in 1995. In doing so it went further than the Oregon legislation in that it provided for the legalisation not only of assisted suicide, but also the administration to a patient of a lethal substance by a doctor. The Act, thus, created an exception to the crime of homicide contained in the Northern Territories Criminal Code. However, the Act remained in force for only a short period, being effectively repealed when the Federal Parliament passed the Euthanasia Laws Act 1996. The lives of four people were brought to an end under the provisions of the Act.

In The Netherlands, Art 293 of the Dutch Criminal Code explicitly prohibits the killing of a person at his request. However, the Dutch courts have held that Art 40 of the same Code provides a physician with a defence of justification due to necessity.[10] Subsequent secondary legislation enacted by the Dutch government in 1994 brought in new regulations relating to the reporting procedures required by doctors carrying out active voluntary

---

7   *Airedale NHS Trust v Bland* [1993] 1 All ER 821, p 885, *per* Lord Mustill.

8   House of Lords Select Committee on Medical Ethics, 1994, paras 237 and 260.

9   Oregon Death with Dignity Act 1994, s 3.14.

10 The Dutch Supreme Court held in the case of *Alkmaar*, Nederlands Jurisprudentie 1985, No 106 Supreme Court, 27 November 1984 that this defence could be invoked on the basis of the concept of *'noodtoestand'* (necessity and conflict of duty). Where a doctor is faced with a patient who depends on him and who is suffering unbearably and hopelessly, the doctor's duty to help that patient by ending his life can outweigh the requirements of the Criminal Code where the patient's death is the only means to end the suffering.

euthanasia.[11] No change was made to the substantive law, so that Art 293 was left unamended.[12] The questions to be answered under the reporting procedures had a strong resemblance to guidelines already issued by the Royal Dutch Medical Society.[13]

Most recently, in November 2000 the lower house of the Dutch Parliament passed a Bill to legalise euthanasia. It was ratified by the upper house and is now an Act (April 2001). The Act sets out the criteria required for the performance of lawful euthanasia: the adult patient must be in intolerable pain, and face a future of unremitting and unbearable suffering; there must be a voluntary, well considered and persistent requests to die from the patient who must be of sound mind and must be aware of the medical options; there must be no reasonable alternative solution to the patient's situation; and the patient's life must be ended in a medically appropriate manner. The Act also allows a patient to make a prior written request for euthanasia. Regional committees set up in 1997 will continue to review whether the criteria have been met, and will be empowered to report any suspicious cases to the State prosecution service.

CURRENT LAW AND ASSISTED SUICIDE

English law

In England, s 2(1) of the Suicide Act 1961 creates the offence of aiding, abetting, counselling or procuring the suicide or the attempted suicide of another. In *AG v Able* [1984] 1 All ER 277 members of the Voluntary Euthanasia Society were prosecuted for the distribution of a suicide manual. It was held that an offence would be committed if a defendant distributed the manual with the intention that it be used by someone contemplating suicide and that they intended the contents of the manual to assist that person; that they knew that a recipient of the manual planned to use it to commit suicide;

---

11 Bill 22572 amended the Burial Act 1991, changing the regulations relating to the dissemination of forms on which euthanasia is reported. An new appendix to the Burial Act introduced a list of questions to be answered by a doctor when reporting a case of active voluntary euthanasia or assisted suicide. The doctor's answers determine whether '*noodtoestand*' applies to protect the doctor from what would otherwise be illegal euthanasia. The questions require information about voluntariness, a persistent desire for death, unbearable suffering, and hopelessness of the prognosis.

12 Otlowski, 1997, p 443, cites as a principal criticism of these amendments that, 'it is illogical and contradictory to have under one Act a law which unequivocally prohibits active voluntary euthanasia (Art 293 of the Penal Code) and at the same time, to amend other legislation in a way which appears to condone the practice'.

13 Belian, 1996, p 272 notes that: 'By accepting the [Royal Dutch Medical Society's] guidelines as its own, the Hague court essentially delegated the task of policing and judging euthanasia law to the group primarily responsible for violating the law.'

and that that person was actually assisted by the publication to take or attempt to take their own life.

The application of this case to a doctor-patient situation is discussed by Otlowski, who points out that a doctor's conduct could attract liability for procuring or counselling suicide where, for example, the doctor provides a patient with information and advice regarding the toxicity and lethal dosage of drugs.[14] Whether or not the doctor's behaviour constitutes either assisted suicide or else active voluntary euthanasia amounting to murder is likely to depend on the degree of the doctor's involvement. Otlowski suggests that 'active assistance in suicide amounts to murder if death occurs as a result of an overt act of the assistant'. On the other hand, mere 'participation in the events leading up to the commission of the final overt act, such as providing the means for bringing about death for the patient's own use' would contravene the provisions of the 1961 Act.[15] In *R v Chard* (1993) *The Times*, 23 September, the judge directed the jury to bring back a not guilty verdict for a defendant who had provided paracetamol tablets on request to a person wanting to commit suicide. It was held that providing the deceased with the tablets had merely afforded an option to commit suicide, and that this fell short of criminal behaviour. Kennedy and Grubb conclude that in assisted suicide cases, much will turn on the jury's view of the facts and the leniency of the directions to the jury.[16] The House of Lords Select Committee's rejection of calls for reform in this area of law was supported by the Government, which saw no basis for permitting assisted suicide.[17] There are no signs that this situation is likely to change.

Other jurisdictions

In the USA, most States prohibit assisted suicide, although there have been few prosecutions under those statutes which criminalise such assistance.[18] The US Supreme Court held in *Washington v Glucksberg* 521 US 702 (1997) that State laws criminalising assisted suicide were constitutional, and that there was no due process right to enlist the aid of healthcare professionals to help end one's life and in *Vacco v Quill* 117 S Ct 2293 (1997) US Sup Ct it was held that the prohibition of assisted suicide did not violate the Equal Protection Clause of the 14th Amendment.

Oregon is the only US State to have passed legislation to legalise doctor-assisted suicide. The Death with Dignity Act 1994 permits a competent

---

14 Otlowski, 1997, p 60.

15 *Ibid*, p 61.

16 Kennedy and Grubb, 2000, p 1920.

17 House of Lords Select Committee on Medical Ethics, 1994.

18 See Smith, 1989.

terminally ill adult to obtain a prescription for a lethal dose of medication from a doctor. Safeguards contained in the statute include the requirement for repeated and verified oral and written requests, informed decision making and psychological consultation.[19] Assisted suicide is unlawful in Canada under s 241 of the Criminal Code. In *Rodriguez v AG of British Columbia* (1993) 82 BCLR (2d) 273 Can Sup Ct, it was held by a slim majority that, although the prohibition against assisting suicide did offend the applicant's right to liberty and security under the Canadian Charter of Rights and Freedoms, the infringement was not contrary to the principles of fundamental justice.

In Australia, assisted suicide is an offence in all States following the demise of the Rights of the Terminally Ill Act 1995, which was overruled by the Federal Government through the Euthanasia Laws Act 1997.

In European countries, there is considerable variation in the legal provisions related to assisted suicide. In Denmark, assisted suicide is unlawful, while in France, there is no formal prohibition.[20] In Germany, it is not a crime to assist suicide where the person being assisted is capable of exercising control over their actions and making a voluntary choice. The situation here, though, is complicated by the fact that a doctor may be criminally liable for not providing help for a person who has attempted suicide.[21] However, the duty of a doctor has been held to be limited where a patient 'experiences his life as a burden and wants to be freed from it'.[22]

It is not an offence to aid and abet suicide according to Belgian law. However, it is generally accepted that anyone failing to provide help to safeguard life following a suicide attempt could be infringing Art 422 of the Criminal code, although there are no examples of this in the jurisprudence.

In The Netherlands, the decriminalisation of assisted suicide has been formalised by the new legislation (see above).

CURRENT LAW AND PASSIVE EUTHANASIA

The legal distinction of active and passive euthanasia

English criminal law draws a clear distinction between acts which cause death, and omissions that bring about death. Lord Mustill, in *Airedale NHS Trust v Bland* [1993] 1 All ER 821, made this distinction clear when he stated:

---

19 For criticisms of the statutory safeguards, see Capron, 1996.

20 Law No 87-1133 of 31 December 1987 prohibits the encouragement of suicide, but does not prohibit aiding suicide.

21 The *Wittig* case (1984) G Sup Ct.

22 The *Hackethal* case (1988) G Sup Ct. See Nys, 1999, p 208 for a general review of European provisions.

If an act resulting in death is done without lawful excuse and with the intent to kill it is murder. But an omission to act, with the same result and with the same intent is in general no offence at all.

He went on, however, to say:

There is one important general exception at common law, namely, that a person may be criminally liable for the consequences of an omission if he stands in such a relationship to the victim that he is under a duty to act.

Death and the withdrawal of treatment

Although there is a strong presumption that doctors should take all steps to preserve life, this presumption holds true only if there is a life to be preserved. Thus, where it is clear that the patient is dead, as in the brainstem dead person, withdrawing treatment is not unlawful.[23] This is one area where the lawfulness of withdrawal is well established. There needs to be a clear distinction between who or what caused the brain stem death in the first place that then led to the withdrawal of ventilation which led to 'death', that is, cessation of biological activity.[24] Other jurisdictions have confirmed this view,[25] with the possible exception of Belgium.[26]

Self-determination and the competent person's right to refuse treatment even if this will lead to death

It is clear that preserving life is not an absolute obligation.[27] In common law jurisdictions generally, a competent adult has an unassailable right to refuse treatment, even where this will lead to their death.[28] In English law, respect for the principle of self-determination is so great that it even extends to allowing a competent pregnant woman to refuse treatment when this may lead to the death of her unborn child.[29] Lord Goff summed up the present legal position regarding the competent person's right to self-determination and the sanctity of life when he stated that, 'the principle of sanctity of human life must yield to the principle of self-determination'.[30] A substantial body of

---

23 *Re A* [1992] 3 Med LR 303.

24 *R v Malcherek; R v Steel* [1981] 2 All ER 422.

25 See *Smith v Smith* (1958) 317 SW 2d (275) Sup Ct Ark; *Finlayson v HM Advocate* [1979] JC 33; *R v Kitching and Adams* [1976] 6 WWR 697 (Manitoba).

26 Grubb *et al*, 1998, p 190.

27 See Taylor LJ in *Re J (A Minor) (Wardship: Medical Treatment)* [1990] 3 All ER 930; and Lord Goff in *Airedale v Bland* [1993] 1 All ER 821.

28 See *Re T (Adult: Refusal of Treatment)* [1992] 4 All ER 649; *Airedale NHS Trust v Bland* [1993] 1 All ER 821; *Re C (Adult: Refusal of Treatment)* [1994] 1 All ER 819.

29 *St George's Healthcare Trust v S* [1998] 3 All ER 673 CA.

30 *Airedale NHS Trust v Bland* [1993] 1 All ER 821.

case law exists in other jurisdictions in which the courts have sought to balance the right to self-determination against other interests of the State.[31]

Thus, where a competent patient refuses treatment, the doctor is absolved of his duty to preserve that life. The doctor may also lawfully withhold or withdraw treatment (passive euthanasia) where to do so gives effect to a competent patient's wishes. Where such wishes are expressed by a competent patient prior to their becoming incompetent, their wishes will still prevail. In *Airedale NHS Trust v Bland* [1993] 1 All ER 821, Lord Goff recognised the validity of advance statements when he stated that, 'the same principle [of self-determination] applies where the patient's refusal to give consent has been expressed at an earlier date ...'.[32]

The incompetent patient and passive euthanasia

In the USA, attempts to respect the principle of self-determination where a person is incompetent have given rise to the common law and statutory use of the principle of substituted judgment.[33] For example, in *In the Matter of Claire Conroy* 486 A 2d 1209 (1985) NJ Sup Ct it was held that, in the absence of advance wishes or clear and convincing evidence of prior wishes, the goal of decision making for non-competent patients should be the decision that the patient would have made if competent. However, substituted judgment is rejected as an approach in its own right under English law. Medical intervention can only be performed on an incompetent adult under English law if it is justified under the doctrine of necessity which, according to the House of Lords in *Re F*,[34] means showing that it is necessary to intervene to protect the best interests of the patient. What the patient might or would have done if competent is only relevant in as much as following the patient's possible or likely desires or wishes will, all other things being equal, be in the patient's best interests.

Usually, there is no difficulty in using the best interests test to justify treatment to enable an incompetent patient to recover from a life threatening condition that may be potentially curable. The court will generally authorise treatment in such circumstances even in the face of opposition from the patient's parents, the family or from the doctor.[35] However, justifying the use of the best interests test in relation to withholding or withdrawal of treatment

---

31 See, eg, *Schloendorff v Society of New York Hospital* 105 NE 92 (1914), *per* Cardozo J; and *Nancy B v Hotel Dieu de Quebec* (1992) 86 DLR (4th) 385 (Can).

32 *Airedale NHS Trust v Bland* [1993] 1 All ER 821, p 866

33 See, eg, *Re Quinlan* (1976) 70 NJ 10; 355 A 2d 647; and the Patient Self-Determination Act 1990.

34 *Re F (Mental Patient: Sterilisation)* [1990] 2 AC 1.

35 *Re T (A Minor) (Wardship: Medical Treatment)* [1997] 1 All ER 906.

that will lead to death is more problematic. Patients whose welfare and interests have received the attention of the courts can be categorised as follows:

(a) Patients (usually the new-born and infants) who suffer from extremely severe anatomical abnormality or physiological disturbance such that even medical care, although providing immediate correction to the defect, will not provide for a measurable prolongation of life. The doctor decides that it is no longer in the best interests of the patient to provide or continue to provide treatment or care that has the effect of artificially prolonging life.

(b) Patients such as those in a persistent vegetative state (PVS), where life sustaining treatment is of no benefit to the patient in that the chances of improvement are, in the opinion of the medical experts, virtually non-existent. The doctor decides that it is no longer in the patient's best interest to continue to provide treatment or care which has no benefit to the patient.

Best interests and quality of life

In relation to the first category, Lord Donaldson in *Re J (A Minor) (Wardship: Medical Treatment)* [1990] 3 All ER 930 pointed out that, although there is a balancing act to be performed, it is not so much balancing life against death, but rather a marginally longer life with pain, against a marginally shorter life free from pain and the ending of that life with dignity.[36] This was the approach taken in *Re B (A Minor) (Wardship: Medical Treatment)* [1981] 1 WLR 1421 CA, where the court authorised treatment for a Down's Syndrome child who was not dying and had a life span of 20–30 years. In *Re J*, termination of treatment was authorised because life was intolerable and so full of pain and suffering, and in *Re C (A Minor) (Wardship: Medical Treatment)* [1989] 2 All ER 782 CA because the neonate had multiple severe handicaps, was said to be dying and the prognosis was one of hopelessness.

Although these decisions might superficially appear relatively clear-cut, there is a danger that less severely handicapped patients could be denied life preserving treatment on the basis of inappropriate 'quality of life' decisions. In *Re C (A Baby)* (1996) 32 BMLR 44, authorisation for withdrawal of treatment was given where there were 'glimmerings of awareness', coupled with pain. Yet when authorising treatment withdrawal in *Bland*, Lord Mustill observed that, 'this is not to say I would reach the same conclusion in less extreme cases, where the glimmering of awareness may give the patient an interest which cannot be regarded as null'.[37]

---

36 *Re J (A Minor) (Wardship: Medical Treatment)* [1990] 3 All ER 930, p 935.
37 *Airedale NHS Trust v Bland* [1993] 1 All ER 821, p 896.

Furthermore, Kennedy strongly criticises the lack of guidance from the courts and argues that 'where a life is at stake ... the court has an obligation to provide, and those caring for children and their advisers have a right to obtain, a degree of guidance as to the factors which are relevant in reaching [a] conclusion'.[38] Kennedy's criticism comes in light of the decision in *Re C (A Minor) (Medical Treatment)* [1998] Lloyd's Rep Med 1 Fam Div, where the quality of life of was determined by some much criticised criteria issued by the Royal College of Paediatrics and Child Health. In this case, Sir Stephen Brown accepted the criterion of 'no chance' as a basis for his decision.

The problem with quality of life decisions is further exacerbated when courts move away from the paramountcy of the individual's interests to other factors. For example, in *Re D* (1997) 41 BMLR 81, authorisation was given for the withholding of dialysis for an adult patient who refused to co-operate, on the basis that to give the treatment would be impracticable (the patient would have had to be anaesthetised before each treatment session). And, in *Re T (A Minor) (Wardship: Medical Treatment)* (1996) 35 BMLR 63 CA, Butler-Sloss LJ held that the question of best interests should take account of the consequences of a mother's lack of total commitment to the life saving treatment proposed for her child. Thus, although courts have made strong statements regarding the sanctity of life, there is undoubtedly a readiness to extend the criteria that render non-treatment lawful on the basis of the quality of life.

Best interests and the duty of a doctor to continue or discontinue treatment

We now come to a group of patients who, by the nature of their medical problems, are neither dying nor suffering. Such patients may, for example, be in a permanent vegetative state. Here, decisions based on best interest are particularly problematic, since the patient is permanently insensate, and therefore not suffering either physically or mentally. Life preserving measures could keep the patient alive in this condition for many years.

Causing death by withdrawing treatment from a patient will constitute a criminal offence if that withdrawal is interpreted as a failure to perform one's duty.[39] The question of whether withdrawal in the case of a permanently insensate patient is a failure to perform one's clinical duty was addressed by the House of Lords in *Airedale NHS Trust v Bland*. The court held that the correct question to ask was not whether it was in Anthony Bland's best interest to die, but rather whether it was in his best interest to continue to receive treatment. The test could be applied negatively: where treatment was futile, any continued intervention would not be in the best interest of the

---

38 Kennedy, 1998, p 101.

39 See *R v Gibbins and Proctor* (1918) 13 Cr App Rep 134 (a murder charge); and *R v Stone* [1977] 2 All ER 341; [1977] QB 354 (a manslaughter charge).

patient. Discontinuation of treatment by the doctor would then not be in breach of a duty and, thus, could not amount to the crime of murder. Indeed, it was argued that to continue to treat in this situation would constitute battery since it constituted a physical touching of an incompetent that was not in his best interests. For the judges, *Bland* was a relatively clear case. It was suggested *obiter dicta* that where the position was less certain medical professionals should be given some leeway – only being liable if their decision did not stand up to the '*Bolam*' test in terms of its reasonableness.

The principles enunciated in *Bland* have been applied in several subsequent English cases.[40] As regards other jurisdictions, the legal reasoning may differ from country to country, but by and large, the outcomes have been the same. For example, in the Scottish case of *Law Hospital NHS Trust v Lord Advocate* (1996) 39 BMLR 166, the court arrived at the same result, but differed in their approach and reasoning. The outcome was the same in the Irish case, *In the Matter of a Ward of Court* [1995] 2 IRLM 401 Ir Sup Ct, even though the patient was 'very nearly PVS' and also in a German case (BGH 1 St R 357 BGB) where the patient was 'close to PVS'. Interestingly, in the New Zealand case of *Auckland AHB v AG* [1993] 1 NZLR 235 the patient was not in PVS, but was suffering from an extreme case of Guillain-Barre syndrome. However, the reasoning for treatment withdrawal was very similar to that used in *Bland*, and was cited with approval in *Bland* by Lords Goff and Mustill. It was held that the doctor was absolved of his duty to continue treatment as there was no medical justification for its continuation.

Grubb *et al* provide a convenient summary of the legal position in other jurisdictions and note that none of the participating countries in their study had specific legislation related to PVS.[41] In Europe, most countries (the UK being an exception) have written constitutions which are applicable to patients in PVS, but practical application varies from country to country. The jurisdiction with most of the well established common law judgments related to incompetent patients is the US, where the courts first examined many of the most profound and difficult cases.[42] Nonetheless, this area of law continues to be developed.

---

40 Eg, in *Frenchay Healthcare Trust v S* (1994) 17 BMLR 156 CA where the patient's feeding tube had become dislodged; in *Re G (Persistent Vegetative State)* [1995] 2 FCR 46 Fam Div despite the dissenting views of the mother; and in *Swindon and Marlborough NHS Trust v S* [1995] 3 Med LR 84 where the patient was being treated at home. Even in a case like *Re H (Adult: Incompetent)* (1997) 38 BMLR 11 Fam Div which did not fully satisfy the conditions laid out by the Royal College of Physicians for diagnosis of PVS, declarations were granted allowing discontinuation of treatment. In the two recent cases of *NHS Trust A v Mrs M* and *NHS Trust B v Mrs H* (1999) *The Times*, 29 November, Dame Butler-Sloss confirmed that the decision in *Bland* is still good law, and entirely in accordance with Convention case law.

41 Grubb *et al*, 1998, pp 161–90.

42 See, eg, *Re Quinlan* 355 A 2d 647 (1976); 70 NJ 10 (1976); and *Cruzan v Director, Missouri Department of Health* 497 US 261 (1990) US Sup Ct.

Kennedy and Grubb,[43] in the conclusion to their commentary on the *Bland* case in 1993, point out that the law relating to the incompetent at the end of life is less than satisfactory. It is doubtful that the law is much clearer in 2001!

THE HRA 1998 AND EUTHANASIA

In this part of the chapter, we will consider how the HRA 1998 might affect the current legal position whereby some forms of passive euthanasia are lawful but active euthanasia remains unlawful. We will discuss the established principles which forbid a doctor from intentional killing but authorise the withdrawal or withholding of treatment in the patient's best interest. We will suggest that the interplay between different Articles of the HRA 1998 (for the purposes of this chapter, Arts 2, 3 8 and 10) will be of fundamental importance, since the observance of rights and duties under one Article may involve infringement of rights under other Articles. For example, there might be limitations on the State's duty to protect life under Art 2 due to its concurrent duty under Art 3 not to impose inhuman or degrading treatments.

Article 2

Clayton and Tomlinson[44] point out that Art 2 of the European Convention on Human Rights (ECHR) which protects the right to life involves a 'negative' right preventing the intentional killing of individuals except in strictly defined circumstances and a positive obligation upon the State to take positive 'life preserving' steps.[45]

The European Court of Human Rights (the Court) stated this in *LCB v UK* (1998) 27 EHRR 212:

> ... Art 2(1) enjoins the state not only to refrain from the intentional and unlawful taking of life, but also to take appropriate steps to safeguard the lives of those within its jurisdiction.[46]

At first glance, this right would appear to be at variance with the concept of euthanasia which, in its voluntary form, seeks to give individuals control over

---

43 Kennedy and Grubb, 1993, p 369.

44 2000, p 343.

45 See, eg, *Stewart v UK*, App No 10044/82; 7 EHRR 457. Public policy considerations may require that public duties to the community as a whole do not apply toward individual members of the public: See *Hill v Chief Constable of West Yorkshire* [1989] AC 53 and also *Re HIV Haemophiliac Litigation* (1990) 140 NLJ 1349, *per* Bingham LJ.

46 (1998) 27 EHRR 212, para 36.

the time and manner of their own death. However, Strasbourg jurisprudence and judgments in the English courts show that the right to life is not an absolute one.[47] Article 2(2) provides exceptions to this right. Euthanasia is not one of the exceptions. However, a closer examination of the case law is required in order to determine if, or under what circumstances euthanasia will violate the Article.

The prevention of intentional killing – active euthanasia and Art 2

Some attempts have been made to clarify the extent of this obligation to prevent intentional killing. Nys argues that Art 2 does not place a State under an obligation to protect life in all circumstances.[48] But it is clear that this would depend on the facts of each case. For example, in *Osman v UK* (1998) 5 BHRC 293, it was noted that the authorities could satisfy their obligations by doing, 'all that could reasonably be expected of them to avoid a real and immediate risk to life of which they have or ought to have knowledge'.[49] In *LCB v UK* (1998) 27 EHRR 212, it was held that the court's task was to determine whether the State did all that could have been required of it to prevent the applicant's life from being avoidably put at risk.[50] The information available to the State regarding risks associated with irradiation was, in this case, insufficient to impose a duty to warn of a risk to life, although the court recognised that a right to life did require a State 'to take appropriate steps to safeguard life'.[51]

Walker LJ in the case of *Re A (Children) (Conjoined Twins: Medical Treatment)* [2000] 1 FLR 1, considered the applicability of Art 2 of the ECHR to baby M (the weaker of two conjoined twins). He confirmed that the positive obligation in Art 2(1) – that everyone's right to life shall be protected by law – was a weak obligation, and applied only to cases where the purpose of the prohibited action was to cause death. He held that no prohibitions were to be imported other than those found in the common law of England. In this case, M's death would not be the purpose or intention of the proposed surgery to separate the twins; her death would result because her body, on its own, was not and never had been viable. However, as Garwood-Gowers has pointed out, this is inconsistent with the definition of intention for the purposes of murder formulated in *Woollin* which covered acts foreseen as having the inevitable consequence of causing death.[52]

---

47 See Lord Keith in *Airedale NHS Trust v Bland* [1993] 1 All ER 821.

48 Nys, 1999, p 216.

49 *Osman v UK* (1998) 5 BHRC 293, para 116.

50 *LCB v UK* (1998) 27 EHRR 212, para 36.

51 *Ibid.*

52 Garwood-Gowers, 2001.

More specific guidance on the extent of the duty under Art 2 was provided in *Barrett v UK* (1997) 23 EHRR CD 185, where the Commission indicated that the responsibility of the State was twofold. Firstly, in the formulation of measures designed to secure the protection of life, including an effective procedure for investigating the circumstances of any loss of life, and, secondly, in the implementation of those measures. It is arguable that by making euthanasia unlawful, the State will be carrying out its obligation to take adequate measures to protect life by preventing intentional killing.

It might also be argued that if it is the right to life that it is being protected, then there are only two ways in which euthanasia could be permitted: (a) if the right that is protected is waived by the patient; or (b) if the right to life also encompasses a right to die. If the right to life does confer a choice to waive the right, this will impose a negative correlative duty – the duty of others not to interfere with this choice. On this view, if the choice is made to waive the right to life, the State would then be absolved of its obligation to protect that life.

Active euthanasia and Art 2's interplay with Arts 8 and 10

It can already be seen, under English law and, indeed, in most jurisdictions that the idea of the State being absolved of its duty to protect life is present when the principle of self-determination comes into play with regard to a competent person being entitled to refuse medical intervention when such refusal will bring about their own death.[53] Furthermore, it is arguable that the decriminalisation of the act of committing or attempting suicide under the Suicide Act 1961 is partially a recognition that choice extends to determining whether one wants to continue living. These principles have resonance with the privacy aspect of Art 8 of the ECHR – the right to respect for private and family life which as Nys states is 'most clearly concerned with individual choices as to bodily autonomy'.[54]

Art 8 is primarily a negative undertaking (*Marckx v Belgium* (1979) 2 EHRR 300), but it may impose positive obligations 'inherent in an effective respect for family life' (*Abdulaziz v United Kingdom* (1985) 7 EHRR 471). In *X v Austria*, App No 8278/78; (1979) 18 DR 154, the Commission held that medical intervention against the will of the patient, even of minimal importance, violates Art 8(1) and accordingly has to be justified under Art 8(2) in order for the Article as a whole not to be violated.

One important question is whether the right to privacy under Art 8 extends to those who request assistance from a third party in bringing about their own death. As stated earlier, in English law, aiding and abetting suicide remains a crime under s 2 of the Suicide Act 1961 and is, thus, treated

---

53 See, eg, *Re T (Adult) (Refusal of Treatment)* [1992] 4 All ER 649 and *Nancy B v Hotel Dieu de Quebec* (1992) 86 DLR (4th) 385.

54 Nys, 1999, p 209.

differently from suicide itself. The European Commission in *R v UK* (1983) 33 DR 270 considered whether this prohibition violated the right to privacy under Art 8. It was argued before the Commission that offering assistance to those wishing to commit suicide fell within the domain of private life, and that the applicant's conviction by the national court had therefore constituted a breach of his rights under Art 8. The Commission, however, held that aiding and abetting suicide did not come within the sphere of private life given protection under Art 8. It held that the acts of aiding and abetting suicide are excluded from the concept of privacy by virtue of their trespass on the public interest in protecting life as reflected in the criminal law provisions of the Suicide Act 1961. Similar reasoning was used by the European Court in *Laskey, Jaggard and Brown v UK* (1997) 24 EHRR 39, where it was held that the UK's margin of appreciation entitled them to regulate, through the operation of the criminal law, activities which involved the infliction of physical harm, albeit that the harm inflicted was consented to by the participants.[55]

Although the acts of aiding and abetting suicide were held not to come within the sphere of private life given protection under Art 8, the claim by the applicants in *R v UK* might have been successful if it had been pursued under Art 10. It could have been argued that the applicant's conviction for dissemination of advice regarding suicide constituted unwarranted State interference with their right to freedom of expression under Art 10. In *Open Door Counselling and Dublin Well Woman v Ireland* (1992) 18 BMLR 1 ECtHR a Supreme Court injunction had restrained the applicants from imparting information designed to assist pregnant women travelling abroad for abortions. The applicants alleged that this was a breach of their right to freedom of expression. The European Court held that the restraint imposed on the applicants was disproportionate to the aims being pursued by the State, and that there had been a violation of Art 10. However, it is doubtful whether the Irish case would have a significant bearing on any future application similar in its facts to *R v UK*, App No 25949/94; (1983) 33 DR 270. In the *Open Door* case, the court did not feel it necessary to decide whether the phrase 'rights of others' in Art 10(2) extended to the unborn – it left open the question of the status of the foetus. On the other hand, it is almost certain that a State interfering with Art 10 by prohibiting assisted suicide would seek to justify this under Art 10(2) as necessary for the protection of the rights of others – or indeed, protection of health or morals. Such an argument would have a high chance of success.

This issue of whether individuals have the right to assisted suicide was addressed on somewhat different grounds in a case brought before the Commission by a Spanish applicant who was tetraplegic (App No 25949/94). It was argued by the applicant that Art 2 encompassed a right to die, since the right to life involved the right to control that life, and included also the right of

---

55   See Coppell, 1999, p 297.

control over the time of one's death. The implications of the case are not clear since it was ruled inadmissible due to a failure to exhaust domestic remedies.

A further approach that might come to be successful is for a person who wants assistance, or believes they may do so in the future, to argue that the prohibition of assistance violates their right to privacy. In *R v UK*, the Commission recognised that Art 8 would come into play in these circumstances though they did not give a determination on whether it would be violated since the point was not of direct relevance to the facts of the application (it having being made by those offering assistance). The success of this approach would depend on whether the State could establish that it had a legitimate aim for its interference with a person's right to a private life and that the action taken was necessary to protect that aim. Even where there is a legitimate aim which justifies interference, the State will have to show that the action that it takes is actually necessary to protect that aim.[56] As earlier noted, the legitimate justifications are set out in Art 8(2). Those most obviously pertinent to assisted suicide are the 'protection of health or morals' and the 'protection of the rights and freedom of others'. A State will be able to prevent a claim to the right of assisted suicide being successful if it can show that it has a legitimate aim in criminalising assisted suicide; that the interference is necessary to realise that aim; and that the interference is proportionate to the aim pursued.

The above discussion relates to the issue of assisted suicide, where the person seeking assistance is competent, and is seeking control over the time and place of their death. The fact that the patient plays an active part in bringing about his own death may make it easier to ascertain that the patient's decision and behaviour are genuinely voluntary. The courts, however, may not view acts of mercy killing undertaken with patient agreement in the same way, since in these cases the doctor alone carries out the act of killing.

The position in relation to mercy killing is addressed in the Euthanasia Bill recently passed by the lower house of the Dutch parliament and expected to become law in 2001. The Dutch position is based on the argument that although Art 2 does impose a duty to protect life, the duty is only concerned with the protection of an individual from unwanted infringement of their life by third parties. The Explanatory Memorandum to the Bill states that, 'bearing in mind that euthanasia demands an express request from the person involved, and that it is his own life, a regulation of euthanasia is not in breach of Art 2 of the ECHR'.[57] So, it would appear that the Dutch position on the right to self-determination goes beyond the mere right to refuse treatment. It also recognises a right to request death.

---

56 See *Open Door Counselling and Dublin Well Woman Clinic v Ireland* (1992) 15 EHRR 244 where it was held that there was a legitimate aim which justified interference, but that the ban imposed by the State was not necessary to protect that aim.

57 See (1998) 5 European Journal of Health Law 301.

The question is, if there is a right to die can it be argued that there is also a legal right for a person to act as the agent of a person's will in killing them? Otlowski, however, rightly argues that a right to self-determination does not necessarily imply a legal right to request death, and therefore does not entail a legal duty to assist. In her model, there is no duty to assist because a person has only a 'liberty to choose' rather than a right.[58] However, a more straightforward interpretation is to say that this, as with many rights, doesn't mean that others have anything other than a negative obligation to avoid interference with this right.

Even if a claim could be brought under Art 8 that private life includes the right to assistance, it is inconceivable that this right would extend to a right to force others, such as doctors, to assist since this would conflict rather fundamentally with a number of rights held by those others. We can note here not just other Articles, such as Art 9, but also the inbuilt limitations of Art 8 itself – in the form of Art 8(2), which states that interference with the right to respect for private and family life can be justified where the legitimate aim is to protect the rights and freedoms of others. For a medical professional, the question of assistance would be a matter for individual conscience, just as abortion is.

It remains to be tested whether the right to die under the Dutch statute is compatible with the right to life under the Convention. This will only be tested if and when a 'victim' makes a claim for the right to die. It could not be tested by a 'victim' claiming that the right to life is being infringed by the decriminalisation of euthanasia since such a decriminalisation has no actual adverse impact on his or her right to life and as such he or she is not a victim. Under the Convention, the applicant must satisfy the test for 'sufficient interest'.[59] It will be possible for pressure groups in Holland to test the Dutch position, if they can show sufficient interest. In the UK, however, s 7(3) of the HRA 1998 alters the sufficient interest test so that an applicant will be taken to have sufficient interest in relation to the alleged breach 'only if he is, or would be, a victim of that act'. This will prevent public interest groups from bringing cases under the HRA 1998, but it will not exclude individuals who are seeking a right to die, and of course these individuals might also happen to be a member of a pressure group.

The UK has made it quite clear that it has no plans to legalise or decriminalise active euthanasia.[60] But if the Dutch position is held to be compatible with the Convention rights, it is arguable that an individual seeking the right to die in the UK could make a claim under the HRA 1998.

---

58   Otlowski, 1997, p 202.
59   See *Paton v UK* (1980) 19 DR 244, and *Open Door Counselling and Dublin Well Woman v Ireland* (1992) 15 EHRR 244.
60   See, eg, Lord Chancellor, 1999.

We have, however, shown previously that the State is allowed a margin of appreciation which affords it a degree of discretion when deciding whether its actions are reconcilable with its obligations. According to Coppell, the margin of appreciation can be equated with a 'test of justiciability, an enquiry into how well placed is the court to second-guess judgments made at a national level'.[61] He suggests that the margin of appreciation will be narrow where judgments relate to universal values understood and upheld by the Convention. In such cases, the European Court will be well placed to intervene but in cases where the subject matter is of a moral nature, with different States holding widely differing opinions, the margin of appreciation will be greater, and the European Court will be less likely to interfere. As yet no case concerning the right to euthanasia has been heard by the European Court, and we have seen that even where there was an opportunity to give a definitive judgment, the court has left the issue open.[62]

Blake argues that the weight given by the courts to the margin of appreciation will be influenced by the existing consensus among the European States.[63] She suggests that the case of *Dudgeon v UK* (1982) 4 EHRR 149 illustrates this relationship. In *Dudgeon*, Art 8 was extended to give rights to homosexuals in Northern Ireland at a time when this jurisdiction was one of the few in the Council of Europe which still had in place laws prohibiting homosexuality. Blake surmises that, since there is no discernible tendency among Member States toward the legalisation of assisted suicide, a generous margin of appreciation is likely to be allowed to States when they assess the necessity for interference.

Of course to what extent, if at all, the margin of appreciation will apply in domestic cases where the HRA 1998 is being considered is debatable. Nonetheless, the overwhelming consensus against the legalisation and decriminalisation of active euthanasia, both within Europe and beyond, is bound to be something of a disincentive to domestic judges holding that the UK's present legal position on active euthanasia is inconsistent with the Act.

Passive euthanasia and the duty to preserve life

The carrying out of passive euthanasia can infringe the obligation to preserve life. There has only been one case brought under the Convention that was specifically related to passive euthanasia – *Widmer v Switzerland*, App No 20527/92 (1993). The case was held inadmissible by the Commission on the grounds that the Swiss Government had in place adequate measures to protect life. However, because the facts of the application did not reveal the medical treatment or the circumstances of treatment withdrawal, the

---

61 Coppell, 1999, p 165.
62 See *R v UK*, App No 25949/94; (1983) 33 DR 270.
63 Blake, 1997, pp 312–13.

judgment does not provide much guidance on the implications for English cases involving withdrawal of treatment.

However, several cases do consider issues which are of relevance to the extent of the duty to preserve life. In *X v Germany* (1984) 7 EHRR 152, for example, the Commission argued that under Art 2, the State was under an obligation to take 'active measures to save lives when the authorities have taken the person in question into their custody'.[64]

Passive euthanasia and the interplay between Arts 2 and 3

The problem about taking active measures to protect life under Art 2 is that the treatment imposed on a patient could cause mental or physical suffering. This could then be held to be inhuman and degrading, and therefore a breach of Art 3. The question the Commission had to address in *X v Germany* was whether the forced feeding of a prisoner breached Art 3. An important point to note regarding Art 3 is that it involves an absolute prohibition, unlike the right to life under Art 2 where exceptions are allowed. Where an absolute duty has to be balanced against one which has exceptions, it might be supposed that the absolute duty would prevail. In decisions where Art 3 has not prevailed, the reasoning behind the decision needs to be explored carefully.

In *Ireland v UK* (1978) 2 EHRR 25 the activities prohibited by Art 3 were stated to be:

(a) torture – deliberate inhuman treatment causing very serious and cruel suffering;

(b) inhuman treatment – treatment that causes intense physical and mental suffering;

(c) degrading treatment – treatment that arouses in the victim a feeling of fear, anguish and inferiority capable of humiliating and debasing the victim and possibly breaking his or her physical and moral resistance.[65]

According to Clayton and Tomlinson,[66] Art 3 provides protection from only the most serious ill treatment. Consequently, for example, as Thorold suggests, the threshold for inhuman or degrading treatment set by the European Commission and Court has been high enough to make it likely that 'well regulated and monitored mental health practice, even when the extremes of treatment are used, will rarely if ever breach Art 3'.[67] What, however, is clear, is that the assessment of this minimum is relative: it

---

64 *X v Germany* (1984) 7 EHRR 152, p 153.
65 *Ireland v UK* (1978) 2 EHRR 25, para 167.
66 Clayton and Tomlinson, 2000, p 387.
67 Thorold, 1996, p 620.

depends on all the circumstances, such as the nature of the treatment, its duration, its physical and mental effects and, in some cases, the sex, age and state of health of the victim.[68] It also would vary over time since, as noted in *Selmouni v France* (2000) 29 EHRR 403, the Convention is a 'living instrument which must be interpreted in the light of present day conditions'. Acts which were classified in a particular way in the past could be classified differently in future in the light of 'the increasingly high standard being required in the area of the protection of human rights'.[69]

Clearly, the greater the stringency in the classification of what constitutes inhuman and degrading treatment, the wider the range of medical interventions which will potentially fall foul of Art 3. In *X v Germany*, the court held that the treatment imposed on a prisoner (forced feeding) did involve degrading elements which could, in some circumstances, be regarded as prohibited under Art 3. Nonetheless, they considered that, due to the short period of time in which the treatment was carried out, the applicant was not subjected to more constraint than was necessary. More recently, in *Herczegfalvy v Austria* (1992) 15 EHRR 437, the European Court held that treatment could also be enforced 'to preserve the physical and mental health of the patients who are entirely incapable of deciding for themselves'.[70]

These decisions seem to suggest that where a patient is incompetent and in the 'custody of the state', and where a conflict has arisen between Arts 2 and 3, the balancing exercise will be resolved by the European Court in favour of Art 2. However, in both cases, there is a presumption that forced treatment would be of benefit to the patient and that best interests are equated with preserving life.

If the decisions in *X v Germany* and *Herczegfalvy v Austria* were held to be applicable to neonates and those with permanent vegetative states discussed earlier in this chapter, then withholding and withdrawing treatment would be incompatible with the European decisions above, since the English cases have been decided in favour of allowing such patients to die. However, this seems unlikely: in *X v Germany*, the Commission stated that it was satisfied that 'the authorities acted solely in the best interest of the applicant' and this seems to suggest that where it can be shown that treatment would be futile, as was the case under English law in *Bland*, such treatment would not be in the best interest of the patient and, thus, withdrawal of treatment would be justified. The concept of futility was recognised in the case of *LCB v UK* (1998) 27 EHRR 212. The court held that in order to establish a breach of Arts 2 and 3, the applicant had to demonstrate that the action in question was capable of altering the fatal nature of the applicant's condition. Futility of treatment

---

68   See *A v UK* (1998) 27 EHRR 611, para 20.

69   *Selmouni v France* (2000) 29 EHRR 403, para 101.

70   (1992) 15 EHRR 437, para 82.

could, thus, be a justification for withdrawal of that treatment. However, there is something of a twist when considering whether Art 3 applies to PVS patients. In the post-HRA 1998 implementation High Court case of *NHS Trust A v Mrs M* and *NHS Trust B v Mrs H* [2000] EWHC 29, Dame Butler-Sloss suggested that:

> Article 3 requires the victim to be aware of inhuman and degrading treatment which he or she is experiencing or at least to be in a state of physical or mental suffering. An insensate patient suffering from permanent vegetative state has no feeling and no comprehension of the treatment accorded to him or her. Art 3 does not in my judgment apply to these two cases.[71]

Contrastingly, neonate patients can be in a state of physical or mental suffering. On this premise, treatment could justifiably be withdrawn if there are grounds to show that any continuation of treatment would be a breach of Art 3. However, in withdrawing treatment from this group of patients, there can be a problem of suffering between the time of withdrawal of treatment and the subsequent death of the patient. This period could itself constitute inhuman treatment since it has been held by the European Court that the lack of proper medical care for a serious illness can constitute inhuman treatment.[72] If the withholding of treatment can be interpreted as such a deprivation, then it is conceivable that non-treatment in order to allow death could be a violation of both Arts 2 and 3.

Passive euthanasia and the interplay between Arts 2 and 8

Where the relatives of a patient object to the treatment proposals, it might be possible for them to make a claim under Art 8 on the basis that the treatment decision (for example, to withdraw treatment) is an interference with the right to private and family life of the relatives.

Interestingly, the Commission in the *Widmer* case did not address the applicant's second complaint – that a breach of Art 8 had occurred.[73] In *NHS Trust A v Mrs M* and *NHS Trust B v Mrs H*, Dame Butler-Sloss suggested that the wishes and feelings of the patient's family could be relevant, but that those wishes and feelings could not outweigh any positive obligation on the State to maintain the patient's life. The question of whether the wishes and feelings of the patient's relatives would be similarly outweighed in relation to a decision to withdraw a patient's treatment was not addressed but it is likely that the conclusions would be similar.

---

71   *NHS Trust A v Mrs M* and *NHS Trust B v Mrs H* [2000] EWHC 29, para 49.

72   See, eg, *Hurtado v Switzerland* (1994) Series A, No 280-A; and *D v UK* (1997) 24 EHRR 423.

73   *Widmer v Switzerland*, App No 20527/92 (1993).

CONCLUSION

Cases heard in Strasbourg could have clearly defined the position of the Convention as regards euthanasia, but have largely failed to do so. Dame Butler-Sloss in the High Court has uncontroversially argued that the analysis set out in *Bland* is consistent with the Convention.[74] However, problems still exist in identifying the scope of medical duty with regard to passive euthanasia, both generally and possibly in the light of the HRA 1998. Moreover, the extent to which English law will prove compatible with the HRA 1998 when it comes to medically-assisted death remains uncertain.

---

74 *NHS Trust A v M* and *NHS Trust B v H* (2000) *The Times,* 29 November, *per* Butler-Sloss LJ.

CHAPTER 18

EXTRACTION AND USE OF BODY MATERIALS FOR TRANSPLANTATION AND RESEARCH PURPOSES: THE IMPACT OF THE HUMAN RIGHTS ACT 1998

Austen Garwood-Gowers

INTRODUCTION

Many UK hospitals have been implicated in recent scandals involving such activities as: retention for research purposes of body materials of deceased persons taken without either a valid consent or first checking with the relatives; taking far more materials than a consent allowed; disposal of deceased persons without checking first with their relatives; undignified disposal of deceased persons, including disposal of dead babies in clinical waste bags;[1] and selling the thymus glands of young children, removed in operations for heart conditions, to pharmaceutical companies, without consent (albeit the commercial exploitation of such body materials being mitigated by the fact that the unit price typically gained for such glands was so low that it might not have done more than cover the paperwork).[2]

So far, in relation to these activities there have been two major inquiries (at Bristol Royal Infirmary and Alder Hey hospitals), a unique Chief Medical Officer's Summit where the issues were aired in public,[3] a Department of Health Report entitled *Consent to Organ and Tissue Retention at Post-Mortem Examination and Disposal of Human Materials*[4] and various other governmental responses.[5]

The scale of these events has been shocking. However, the existence of controversy in extraction and use of body materials for transplantation and/or research purposes is nothing new. Many of the controversies have hinged on an age old ethical tension between rights and extreme visions of utilitarianism and deontology which allow for the violation of rights on grounds of collective benefit stemming from procuring more materials. The

---

1   These practices were discussed at the Chief Medical Officer's Summit, 2001, The Queen Elizabeth II Conference Centre, London, and noted within the Evidence Documentation.

2   This practice occurred at Alder Hey hospital.

3   Chief Medical Officer's Summit, 2001.

4   Elam, 2000.

5   The Scottish Health Minister, for instance, has stated that: 'Alder Hey must be a watershed for the NHS.' (Scottish Executive, 2001.)

controversies have spanned three classes of person: the living, the 'nearly dead' and the dead.

EXTRACTION AND USE OF BODY
MATERIALS FROM A LIVING PERSON

Can a competent person be forced to donate?

Not all utilitarians are of the view that violating rights is acceptable. JS Mill was a utilitarian but asserted that:

> ... the sole end for which mankind are warranted, individually or collectively, in interfering with the liberty of action of any of their number is self-protection.[6]

Equally, a common utilitarian perspective is that rights must be respected in order to have a society within which what is most useful is given a chance to flourish and many deontologists support the protection of rights as necessary to the cultivation of a decent society. However, both the extreme utilitarian and deontologist might argue otherwise.

In living donation, this argument could take the form of suggesting that taking materials from a living person without consent for the benefit of another or society at large is legitimate if the prospective harm caused to the donor is small and is exceeded by the prospective benefit to others from doing so. It must be dubious whether a person being sacrificed on the altar of utility in this fashion can ever actually be useful because of the ethical damage it does. Nonetheless, remarkably, it is an argument that has been legally tested in the US case of *McFall v Shimp* (1978) 10 Pa D & C (3d) 90 Ct Comm Pl, Pa. Here Robert McFall, an aplastic anaemia sufferer, asked the Civil Division of the Allegheny County Court to force David Shimp, his cousin, to undertake tests and, if suitable, ultimately donate bone marrow. The plaintiff recognised that this would infringe the right to bodily security of the defendant but noted that this was the only means available to save life. Flaherty J denied the plaintiff's claim in fierce terms:

> Our society, contrary to many other, has as its first principle, the respect for the individual, and that society and government exist to protect the individual from being invaded and hurt by another ... For our law to compel the defendant to submit to an intrusion of his body would change every concept and principle upon which our society is founded. To do so would defeat the sanctity of the individual, and would impose a rule which would know no limits, and one could not imagine where the line would be drawn ... For a society, which respects the rights of one individual, to sink its teeth into the

---

6   Mill, 1982, p 68.

jugular vein or neck of one of its members and suck its sustenance for *another* member, is revolting to our hard-wrought concepts of jurisprudence. Forcible extraction of living body tissue causes revulsion to the judicial mind. Such would raise the spectre of the swastika and the Inquisition, reminiscent of the horrors this portends.

This statement alludes to three core objections to violating the principle of self-determination:

(a) it interferes with rights;

(b) it is contrary to principle (deontological argument); and

(c) it has deleterious consequences for the fabric of society because once you place utility above rights you, ironically, end up with a society that is anti-utilitarian – it collapses in on itself because of its lack of definitive principle and respect for rights.

These same three arguments would undoubtedly also have applied if the proposed intervention had been for research purposes. Indeed, all three arguments are the sometimes stated and sometimes unstated foundation of respect for self-determination in medical law in common law jurisdictions that a competent adult has a legal right to self-determination with respect to medical intervention. Clearly, in this area resort to the Articles of the European Convention on Human Rights (ECHR) which would protect self-determination – namely the right to liberty and security (Art 5) and the right to a private life (part of Art 8)[7] – is superfluous.

Incompetent adult and incompetent minors as prospective living donors

The best interests test will not be successfully challenged

The incompetent adult can obviously not give consent on his or her own behalf and interestingly English common law does not provide a mechanism for someone to consent on their behalf either. Intervention can take place under the doctrine of necessity. The House of Lords, in *Re F (Mental Patient; Sterilisation)* [1990] 2 AC 1 HL, stated that an intervention will be regarded as a necessity for an incompetent adult where it is necessary to undertake it in order to protect that adult's best interests. Since it originates in common law, this test can be 'overturned' by a court under the Human Rights Act (HRA) 1998. The best interests test is also used when making decisions on behalf of minors but here it has a statutory basis (s 1(1) of the Children Act 1989).[8]

---

7   For a detailed explanation of the relevance of these Articles to self-determination in the field of medical intervention, see Garwood-Gowers, Chapter 14, above.

8   Children Act 1989, s1(1) states that: 'When a court determines any question with respect to – (a) the upbringing of a child; or (b) the administration of a child's property or the application of any income arising from it, the child's welfare shall be the court's paramount consideration.' Welfare is synonymous with best interests.

Consequently, it could not be overturned by the domestic courts. However, a declaration of incompatibility could be issued by the courts leaving it for Parliament to decide whether or not to take action, or alternatively a case could be taken to Strasbourg after exhausting domestic remedies.[9]

A challenge would be most likely to come under Art 5 and/or Art 8 which protect, respectively, the right to liberty and security and the right to a private and family life. However, it seems unlikely that the Courts would have much truck with an argument that the best interests test should be dispensed with either for incompetent adults or minors.[10] Both Articles contain within them the concept of proportionality whereby it can be argued that the restriction on rights posed by having a decision made on one's behalf is justifiable if one is not competent and the decision is made to protect one's best interests. Under Art 5, the argument would be made that the restriction on rights that the best interests test presents is justifiable as necessary and proportionate to the defence of the health interests of the incompetent. There have been a number of decisions made under the ECHR where minors have used Art 5 to challenge restrictions on their liberty. *Nielson v Denmark*[11] involved fairly strong restrictions on liberty for approximately six months within a State hospital psychiatric ward but a violation was not found. In *Family T v Austria*,[12] the Commission stated that restrictions could be justified in the upbringing of a child provided they were not extreme of unnecessary. Though a violation was found in *Boumar v Belgium*,[13] it was because of the severity of the restrictions imposed. The whole tenor of these cases is to suggest that restrictions are only a violation where they are reasonable. Clearly, any restriction that supported the best interests of an incompetent minor, or for that matter an incompetent adult, would be classified as reasonable. A case which more explicitly supports this point of view by analogy is *Herczegfalvy v Austria*[14] where it was stated that as a general rule, a measure which is performed on an incompetent adult as a matter of therapeutic *necessity* cannot be regarded as inhuman or degrading treatment under Art 3. Under Art 8, compulsory intervention by a medical professional upon a competent person has in the past been considered a violation even where it is of a minor nature such as a blood test.[15] However, a medical professional acting in the best interests of the incompetent adult or incompetent minor would again be able to justify a restriction. Article 8(2), which lists permissible restrictions, would be used to this end. Here, under Art 8(2) intervention would be justified as 'necessary in a democratic society ... for the protection of health'.

---

9 For more detailed elucidation of these points, see Garwood-Gowers and Tingle, Chapter 1, above.

10 The position of the competent minor is considered below.

11 (1988) 11 EHRR 175.

12 App No 14013/88, 14 December 1989; (1990) 64 DR 176.

13 (1989) 11 EHRR 1.

14 (1992) 15 EHRR 437.

15 See *X v Austria*, App No 8278/78; (1979) 18 D & R 154.

This discussion is not to say that Convention rights will have no impact when assessing the question of best interests. Michalowski has already argued convincingly in Chapter 15 that Convention rights will be a guide to interpreting what is in the best interests of a minor and there is no reason to think that the same will not be the case with incompetent adults.

Best interests, living donation and human rights

Living donation or non-therapeutic research will be in the best interests of the incompetent person where (s)he has the prospect of gaining psychological benefit from the intervention to a degree outweighing the prospective physical and psychological detriment it engenders. Most of the detriment here consists of physical harm and risk to the incompetent posed by donating the material.

This psychological benefit can take two forms. Firstly, the benefit of helping others – 'altruistic giving' as it is often termed. Secondly, in the case of giving materials for a transplant to a specific person who is significant, the benefit of having that bond secured – particularly where it is under serious jeopardy as would be the case if the incompetent person's material was the only suitable material available and that without using it the prospective recipient's life or well-being would be in serious jeopardy.

This approach has been witnessed in action in the courts in a number of instances involving the proposed donation of body materials by minors or incompetent adults. One of the earliest of the numerous US decisions on this issue was *Strunk v Strunk* 445 SW 2d 145 (Ky 1969) where the Kentucky Court of Appeals authorised, by a 4:3 majority, the removal of a kidney from an incompetent adult with limited understanding for the purposes of transplantation into his older brother. Two of the dissenters reached their decision on the basis of the evidence of benefit to the incompetent being insufficient. A third – Judge Samuel Steinfield – felt that consent was the only justification for organ donation and stated rather ominously:

> Apparently because of my indelible recollection of a government which to the shame of its citizens embarked upon a programme of genocide and experimentation with human bodies I have been more troubled in reaching a decision in this case than in any other.[16]

The danger of which this reminds us is of utilitarianism dressing up as best interests. Doubtless aware of the potential criticism in most cases judges have been at pains to examine the issue of benefit to the incompetent adult prospective donor closely. This is even so in the case of bone marrow donation which is prospectively less harmful and risky than the donation of a

---

16   445 SW 2d 145 (Ky 1969), p 149.

kidney.[17] Nonetheless, in some cases the evidence is a little on the fragile side. For example, in the English High Court decision of *Re Y* [1996] Med L Rev 204–07, Mr Justice Connell in authorising donation of bone marrow by an incompetent adult stated that, by donating, the incompetent would have not just the gratitude of her family but would have visits to her institution by her mother maintained at the same level whereas death of her sister – the prospective recipient – would result in their reduction because her sister had a child which the mother would have to look after. One would have thought that the mother would have been able to get respite care for this purpose.

Incompetent minors have become living donors of tissues or organs more frequently than incompetent adults. Occasionally, the claimed psychological benefits for donation have been brought into question by the tender age of a donor. For instance, in the US case of *Cayouette v Mathieu* [1987] RJQ 2230 Sup Ct donation of bone marrow by a five year old to his brother was authorised and in *Hart v Brown* 289 2 Ad 386 (1972) a minor of just under eight donated a kidney to his twin brother.

In these cases, the primary justification for donation is really the avoidance of the psychological harm that might be engendered to the prospective minor donor if the prospective recipient's health was jeopardised or life lost. This is particularly so, for example, in some cases of siblings – especially where they are twins. However, it would also presuppose that there are no other viable alternatives to protect the life or health of the prospective recipient which, in the case of kidney failure, isn't always so. However, to allay the suspicions of those who might worry that donation is somehow always found to be in the best interests of an incompetent minor it is important to state that in some cases authorisation of a proposed donation has been denied. For example, in the US case of *Camitta v Fager*, Eq No 73-171 (Mass, 5 September 1973), the minor had a mental state characterised as a combination of mild retardation and schizophrenia and authorisation was denied because it was doubtful that the minor would gain psychological benefit from it.

For reasons already stated, it is unlikely that the HRA 1998 could be used to challenge the 'best interest' authorisation of donations by incompetent minors or incompetent adults. However, the presence of the Act, and particularly Arts 5 and 8, does bolster the view that the authorisation must be carefully considered and reasonably based. Forcing an incompetent minor or adult to donate would seem to be 'off limits' in as much as it is not really a reasonable restriction on liberty given that the intervention concerned is of a non-therapeutic nature. In addition, force would probably nullify the possibility of the minor gaining psychologically from the donation and, hence,

---

17 Blood donation, for example, would normally be less risky than either. For a review of the detriment in donating organs, see Garwood-Gowers, 1999 (Chapters 2 and 6 particularly).

bring into question whether it was, in fact, in the incompetent's best interests. Some reference here could also be made to the fact that some transplant legislation protects the minor from forced donation of body material. For example, laws in Belgium, Colombia, Portugal, Slovenia, Sweden and The Netherlands.[18]

The competent minor

Minors can consent to medical intervention, even in the face of parental objection, when they have sufficient maturity and understanding to make the decision at hand (see *Gillick*). The age of majority for non-therapeutic interventions is 18 rather than 16[19] and, in general, it is likely that only older minors are likely to have sufficient maturity to undertake some non-therapeutic interventions, particularly those involving more complexity and prospective detriment such as living organ donation.[20]

As discussed in Chapter 14, the decisions in *Re W* and *Re R* mean that a person with parental authority can give valid consent on behalf of the minor resulting in the possibility of the competent minor having treatment forced upon him or her. It has been argued in that chapter that the competent minor will probably be able to challenge this violation of the right to self-determination under the HRA 1998 as a violation of the right to liberty and security under Art 5 and/or the right to a private life under Art 8. Even more potently, the competent minor would be able to argue discrimination has occurred in that the self-determination of competent adults is respected and, thus, they are treated differently. This would almost certainly amount to violating Art 14 in conjunction with either Art 5 or 8.

NON-CONSENSUAL ACTIVITY IN RELATION TO BODY MATERIALS IMMEDIATELY PRIOR TO DEATH

Non-consensual use of elective ventilation

The Royal Devon and Exeter Hospital was the first British hospital to develop a protocol for elective ventilation (EV).[21] This involved, with relatives' consent, transferring patients in deep irreversible coma and believed to be dying imminently of intracranial haemorrhage to intensive care, so that

---

18 See, further, Garwood-Gowers, 1999, pp 134–35.

19 See *Re W (A Minor) (Medical Treatment)* [1992] 3 WLR 758.

20 Rather pessimistically Lord Donaldson in *Re W* (*ibid*, p 767f) doubted whether a minor would ever be competent to consent to living donation of an organ.

21 Feest, 1990, pp 1133–35.

artificial ventilation could be commenced immediately respiratory arrest occurred and until brain stem death tests could be satisfied. The purpose of this action was not to benefit patients. It was to chill their organs in anticipation of their potential use for transplantation purposes following death. The result, in terms of organ procurement, was evaluated as a 50% increase over a four year period.[22] Although the number of donors used was not statistically significant[23] it is fair to say that:

> Elective ventilation has provided initial evidence of a substantial impact on donation rates; implementation of this procedure is recommended if legal and ethical questions relating to the interests of the potential donor can be resolved.[24]

Legally getting relative agreement was not significant. As earlier discussed, under English law no one can give valid consent on behalf of the incompetent adult. The incompetent adult can only be medically 'intervened on' under special legislative provisions, such as the Mental Health Act 1983, or under the common law doctrine of necessity where the intervention is necessary to protect his or her best interests. EV is, normally at least, not a procedure that could be justified as in the best interest of the incompetent adult. It does not constitute a valid treatment; merely a futile prolongation of life for the benefit of others. As well as being futile, it contains potential dangers including the possibility that it might increase the number of patients in a persistent vegetative state (PVS).

Since EV is not in the best interests of incompetent patients, it will be a legal trespass upon them unless they have made a valid advance directive allowing it.[25] EV was abandoned as a practice after the Health Departments of England and Wales issued guidelines noting the legal problems in October 1994.[26] However, there has been a call from the British Transplant Society for permissive legislation in this area.[27] Concerns about PVS ought to mean that this call should be rejected, but if EV is used again this should only be where the patient has consented to it through a valid advance directive. Otherwise, EV would clearly conflict with both a patient's right to liberty and security under Art 5 and the right to a private life as protected by Art 8. The arguments against there being a violation of these Articles would be that the restriction

---

22 New *et al*, 1994, p 55.

23 Routh, 1992, pp 60–61.

24 New *et al*, 1994, p 8.

25 Under the common law, advance agreement and refusal of medical intervention can be valid provided that the patient was competent when making the agreement, acting voluntarily and intended the directive to apply to the particular context at hand (see, particularly, *Airedale NHS Trust v Bland* [1993] AC 789, p 857, *per* Lord Keith).

26 Somerville, 1993. PIVOT (the potential of elective ventilation for organ transplantation) study was proposed to examine issues in EV but was abandoned due to the questionable legality of EV. (See New *et al*, 1994, p 56.)

27 British Transplant Society, 1995, p 32.

involved is justified in the interests of procuring extra organs. Article 5 would consider this argument within the general issue of proportionality and under Article 8 it would be considered within Art 8(2) which allows restriction 'necessary in a democratic society' for a number of purposes, including 'protection of health' and 'protection of the rights and freedoms of others'. However, it is difficult to see violating the freedom of the incompetent to gain protection from being justifiable when it is neither in his or her best interests or justified by reference to an advance directive. The European Convention on Human Rights and Biomedicine has no direct legal force in the UK but it will be relied on in future European Court of Human Rights (the Court) decisions and these decisions in turn will be taken into account, where appropriate by the domestic courts in interpreting the HRA 1998. It would support this conclusion through Art 2 which states that:

> The interests and welfare of the human being shall prevail over the sole interest of society or science.

As a final point, it can be argued that if EV creates a significant danger of PVS it might also constitute inhuman or degrading treatment under Art 3.[28]

Non-consensual use of non-heart beating donors

Traditionally, death was defined in terms of cessation of cardiovascular function, that is, the person had no pulse, was not breathing etc. This is obviously an obsolete test now. Brain stem death is the minimum standard of death that the courts will accept (see *Re A* [1992] 3 Med LR 303 Fam Div). This approach is consistent with practice and/or law in most other countries across the world. The definition used, in practice, is that put forward in 1976 in Guidelines issued by the Medical Royal Colleges, (1976) 2 BMJ 1187, which is based on irreversible loss of brain stem function – which indicates loss of possibility of awareness and of possibility for spontaneous reflexes such as respiration.

Ninety-nine per cent of cadaveric kidneys come from donors whose hearts are beating but are brain stem dead.[29] However, similar graft survival results can be obtained from using donors whose hearts have stopped but who have not yet reached brain stem death.[30] Some transplant centres are utilising non-heart beating donors (NHBDs) extensively with the effect of increasing their cadaveric procurement by between 25 and 40%[31] and, occasionally, upwards

---

28 For further discussion of Art 3, see MacLean, Chapter 6.

29 Cho *et al*, 1998, pp 221–25.

30 *Ibid*.

31 Schlumpf *et al*, 1996, p 107; Kootstra *et al*, 1991, pp 910–11; and Daeman's more recent study at Kootstra's Maastricht centre which indicated that a non-heart beating programme contributes 40% (Daeman, 1996, pp 105–06).

of this.[32] As David Price highlights in his article 'Organ transplant initiatives: the twilight zone',[33] there are two methods used to procure organs from NHBDs:

(a) the insertion of a catheter method – here the dying person has a catheter inserted in them to chill the organs *in situ* until relatives become available to offer consent or refusal upon death;

(b) the 'Pittsburgh Protocol' method – here patients with profound brain damage are, after two minutes of 'irreversible' loss of brain function, removed from ventilatory support with their advance consent in a directive, or the consent there and then of their relatives, and then, when they die, their organs are removed.

Both of these procedures are driven by the utility of gaining organs and both involve an intervention on an incompetent person which is not in their best interests. There are serious ethical and legal concerns about using both methods. With the Pittsburgh Protocol method there are two main problems. Firstly, there is a question about how irreversible is irreversible. Obviously, in a legal sense being 'nearly dead' is not the same as being dead – deriving extra organs may be all well and good but if the legal tests of death exist for a reason they should be upheld, and any determination of whether they are too strict or not, obviously, should be made independently of the pragmatic, utilitarian considerations of securing more organs. Secondly, when the method is used with the consent of the relatives, without a valid advance directive from the patient, it violates his/her right of self-determination since it is not in his/her best interests. The insertion of a catheter method would also have this problem unless backed by a valid advance directive. There are no signs of legislation being passed in the UK to permit these practices in the absence of a valid advance directive. Such legislation could come into conflict with the right to liberty and security under Art 5 and the right to a private life under Art 8 and, as with legislation permitting non-consensual EV, would almost certainly constitute a violation of these Articles.

REMOVING BODY MATERIALS AFTER DEATH FOR TRANSPLANTATION AND/OR RESEARCH PURPOSES

The context

Many body materials are needed for medical research and transplantation purposes. There is a shortage of suitable organs for transplantation in most countries. The quality of life of persons is diminished by having to wait for

---

32 Cho *et al*, 1998, pp 221–25.
33 1997, pp 170–75.

significant periods of time for organ transplants. In a considerable number of cases, people die because an organ does not turn up on time or are excluded from receiving a transplant because of the stringent manner in which many waiting lists have been deliberately drawn up as a means of ensuring that these 'limited resources' are put to best use.

There are varying reasons for shortages and various potential solutions.[34] The non-controversial solutions range from concentrating more on prevention and holistic treatment to better ICU bed provision, better transplant co-ordination. The not very controversial solutions include increasing the use of living donation of kidneys and, more arguably, liver segment and lung lobe. However, more controversial means of increasing supply from deceased persons continue to be suggested, including the development of a 'presumed consent' system of organ procurement.

A 'presumed consent' system, often called an 'opting out' system, involves taking the body materials of a dead person automatically where no objection has been expressed. The purest of such systems is in Austria, where the legally sanctioned and often used practice is to conscript the organs of the deceased *unless* (s)he had specifically objected to this outcome when alive.[35] A more common approach as a matter of law[36] or practice[37] is to ask the relatives of the person wherever practicable and allow them to prevent the organs being extracted, at the very least if the deceased didn't express a clear wish to donate whilst alive. Many countries reject presumed consent in as much as they will not take materials without an agreement but presume consent in relation to the deceased in as much as the agreement can come solely from his or her relatives. Such an approach is called 'broad opting in'.[38] The UK is often viewed as having a 'broad opting in' system but, in fact, the Human Tissue Act 1961 allows for the removal of the deceased's materials without the agreement of anyone. As we shall see, under s 1 of the Act, removal can simply take place wherever 'such reasonable inquiry as may be practicable' fails to come up with an unwithdrawn objection from the deceased or surviving relatives. This is a significant 'presumed consent' element. However, some within and outside the medical profession advocate UK law going further. To this end, earlier this year Kenneth Clarke[39] presented a private member's bill to Parliament entitled 'The Transplant of Human Organs Bill' which would amend s 1 of the Human Tissue Act 1961. This Bill is supported by the British Medical Association[40] which has argued for some

---

34 See, further, Garwood-Gowers, 1999, Chapter 1.

35 Conference of European Health Ministers, 1987.

36 Including France (see Hors, 1992) and Spain (see Matesanz and Miranda, 1992).

37 Eg, Greece, Italy and Spain.

38 Countries with broad opting-in include the Eire, USA, Holland, Germany, Canada, New Zealand and Australia.

39 17 January 2001.

years that such legislation is warranted on utilitarian ground as a device to increase the procurement of body materials from deceased persons for research and, especially, transplantation purposes.

However, there is a battle over the future of public policy in this area. Recent scandals have led to calls for legislation better to guard the principle of consent, and these have gained widespread support within the medical profession, including from the Chief Medical Officer, Liam Donaldson. Clearly, there is some need to go back to basic ethical and rights principles to assess current law and the possibilities for reform in this area.

Current English law

Section 1(1) of the Human Tissue Act 1961 states that removal of body materials for medical purposes must be based on the consent of the person now deceased, 'either in writing or orally in the presence of two or more witnesses during his last illness'. In addition, there must be consent of the person lawfully in possession of the body after death – which under s 1(7) would probably be the hospital where death occurs. However, s 1(2) allows the person lawfully in possession of the body after death to authorise the deceased's materials to be removed for medical purposes if, 'having made such reasonable inquiry as may be practicable', he has no reason to believe that the deceased:

(a) hadn't expressed an unwithdrawn objection; and that

(b) the surviving spouse or any surviving relative doesn't object.

In effect, this legislation allows violation of the notion of the living persons right to determine what happens to their bodily material upon death in two senses:

(a) there is a presumed consent aspect to the law in that where practicable inquiry has failed to come up with an objection from the deceased it is possible to remove his or her body materials provided that a spouse or surviving relative does not object;

(b) the law allows the wishes of the deceased to donate materials to be overridden by objections from relatives.

Clearly, in addition to this problem are the practices which have been occurring in many hospitals which go beyond the authority of the Act. These include:

---

40   BMA press release, 17 January 2001.

(a) removing organs from children with known relatives (usually including parents) without making 'reasonable enquiry as may be practicable' to ensure that these relatives do not object;[41] *and*

(b) exceeding the scope of what the relatives have agreed to such as removing more organs than was agreed to, using them for a purpose inconsistent with the agreement or disposing of them (or the whole body) inconsistent with the agreement.

However, the question of what one can do when the authority of the Act is exceeded is, according to Kennedy and Grubb, 'the most neglected'.[42] Kennedy and Grubb note the possibilities of both criminal and civil liability.[43]

With regard to criminal liability, Skegg's article, 'Liability for the unauthorized removal of cadaveric transplant material',[44] includes promising discussion of the offence of preventing lawful disposal of the body.[45] This would probably be committed where the whole body was retained or unlawfully disposed of but not where only internal organs were retained, at least if the body was still recognisable. Another possibility is the common law crime of disobedience of a statute. However, the continued existence of this crime has been doubted in *R v Horseferry Road Justices ex p Independent Broadcasting Authority* [1987] QB 54, [1986] 2 All ER 666 which added that if the crime does continue to exist at all it certainly does not apply to the Human Tissue Act 1961.[46]

With regard to tortious liability, Skegg suggested in 1974 that there are no torts applicable to unauthorised interference with a corpse. One of the possibilities he examines is liability to relatives for negligently caused psychiatric injury stemming from unauthorised extraction, use or disposal of body materials of their loved one. However, Kennedy and Grubb note that the relatives would be secondary victims and would not have sufficient proximity under the *McLoughlin/Alcock* rules to establish liability.[47] An additional possibility he rightly regards as hopeful is the intentional and unauthorised interference with the right to possession of a corpse of the person under the

---

41 The exact meaning of making 'such reasonable enquiries as may be practicable' is the subject of debate – see the contrasting views of Skegg, 1976, p 197 and Dworkin, 1970. However, this need not concern us here in so far as their have been many instances of relatives being clearly 'on hand' to hospital staff but whose views were not enquired of.

42 Kennedy and Grubb, 2000, p 1845.

43 *Ibid*, pp 1845–48.

44 Skegg, 1974, p 53.

45 *R v Young* (1784) 4 Wentworth's System of Pleading 219. There is also a narrower statutory crime of wilfully obstructing a burial; s 7 of the Burial Laws Amendment Act 1880.

46 Human Tissue Act 1961, s 1(8) of which states that 'nothing in this section shall be construed as rendering unlawful any dealing with, or with any part of, the body of a deceased person which is lawful apart from this Act'.

47 Kennedy and Grubb, 2000, p 1849.

duty to dispose of it.[48] Kennedy and Grubb are pessimistic about the possibility of liability in tort. However, they did not consider the possibility of tort evolving through use of the HRA 1998.

A relative using the HRA 1998 in relation to actions unauthorised by the Human Tissue Act 1961

Relatives of the deceased looking to bring a case for unauthorised interference with the corpse would be able to use the privacy and family life dimensions of Art 8 of the ECHR, as protected in domestic law under the HRA. This right must include within it the notion of family autonomy. The rights of the deceased if competent whilst alive should trump those of living relatives, but when a person died incompetent as an adult or minor it would seem to be a legitimate element of family life that their next of kin should, as a general rule, have control over disposal of the body.

Article 8(2) includes the statement that restrictions on the right to private and family life must be:

> ... necessary in a democratic society in the interests of national security, public safety or the economic well-being of the country, for the prevention of disorder or crime, for the protection of health or morals, or for the protection of the rights and freedoms of others.

It is highly doubtful that utilitarian desire by the medical profession for body materials for research or transplantation purposes would justify unauthorised extraction of them. It is also difficult to find justification under Art 8(2) for irreverent disposal of material in clinical waste bags unless there was some special public health issue at stake in a specific case. In these kinds of circumstances, a violation of Art 8 seems almost certain. The relative would be able to use such a violation in one of two ways:

(a) to result in existing law being reinterpreted in such a way as to become consistent with Art 8 so that the violation is eliminated. Under s 6 of the HRA, the courts will be acting unlawfully unless they interpret common law in a manner consistent with 'Convention rights';

(b) to claim against the relevant hospital directly under s 6 for being a public authority acting unlawfully by breaching a Convention right.

Remedies would be available under ss 7 and 8 of the HRA 1998.

---

48 See, eg, *R v Fox* (1841) 2 QB 246 and, for an example of successful recovery, the Canadian case of *Edmonds v Armstrong Funeral Home Ltd* (1931) 1 DLR 676, where a doctor had made an unauthorised post-mortem examination of a corpse.

Action on behalf of the deceased under the HRA 1998

Action on behalf of the deceased is not possible because only victims can use the HRA 1998. However, the notion of family life under Art 8 ought to provide an opportunity for a close relative to take action as a closely associated person who might be classed as a victim in his or her own right if extraction, use or disposal of the deceased's body materials is taking place in a manner contrary to rights. Clearly, the action taken would need to be unauthorised under the Human Tissue Act 1961 for a claim of violation of Art 8 to be successful. If the complained of behaviour violated Art 8 but was authorised under the Human Tissue Act 1961 the domestic courts could only issue a declaration of incompatibility. This, in turn, would place political pressure upon government to change the law. Failing such a change occurring, upon exhaustion of domestic remedies, a claim could of course be brought before the European Court itself under the Convention.

The 'potential deceased', whilst alive, arguing incompatibility of the Human Tissue Act 1961 with Convention rights

In anticipation of dying at some point, it is conceivable that a living person could argue that s 1 of the Human Tissue Act 1961 conflicts with their right to liberty and security under Art 5 and right to private and family life under Art 8. The conflict would exist because the Act conflicts with the right of a person to determine what happens to their bodily material upon death in two aforementioned respects:

(a) the presumed consent element – logically the right to choose must include the right to not have to make a choice; and

(b) the fact that where the deceased has not given consent materials can be taken if relatives, having been consulted where reasonably practicable, express no objection. This is just another version of presumed consent as far as the deceased is concerned unless (s)he died as a minor in which case consent of a parent would be a legitimate approach.

The fact that the complaint is about what might happen in the future is not necessarily a problem in that the Convention, specifically Art 8, has already been used by a person complaining that a law restricts the exercise of their future choices.[49] If a violation was found, the domestic courts would issue a declaration of incompatibility (the living person might also argue his case at Strasbourg before the European Court). However, aforementioned restrictions on the Convention rights within Arts 5 and 8 might defeat such a claim. The essence of the State's argument is likely to be that there are many laws on the

---

49 Hence, in *Sutherland v UK* (1997) 24 EHRR CD 22, a law restricting a young person from engaging in homosexual activity in private when he was at an age where the restriction wouldn't apply to heterosexual activity, was held to be a violation of Art 14 in conjunction with Art 8.

continent which contain a presumed consent element and that such an element is necessary in the interests of a democratic society for the protection of health via the benefits that can occur in terms of increased body materials for research and transplantation purposes. The arguments against this would be twofold:

(a) that gains in body materials are uncertain. Surveys typically show that around half of the public oppose presumed consent[50] so there is a danger that it would alienate a significant section of the public to introduce it and have counterproductive consequences for procurement. Recent body materials scandals have increased this danger;

(b) that a utilitarian need for organs doesn't suddenly make it acceptable to desecrate a dead person's body and use it for transplantation simply because they have failed to object to this when they are alive. There is no such thing as 'presumed consent' in philosophical or legal terms; consent is either implicit or explicit or it doesn't exist at all. In addition, in practical terms one cannot imply consent simply from absence of refusal since studies have shown that there is a large percentage of people who do not consider themselves to be organ donors. At the extreme, studies in the USA[51] and Holland[52] indicate only 36% and 38% of people respectively claim to be potential organ donors. The powerful analogy would be with a will; if we respect the living person's right to dispose of their personal property more or less as they please after death, then why shouldn't the same apply to their bodily 'property' which is, after all, in some senses more intimate.

It is difficult to assess how the courts would react to these arguments. At the end of the day, the idea that Arts 5 and 8 would be violated by introducing a greater presumed consent element to legislation may be rejected on the basis of a limited view of people's rights to determine what happens to their body materials upon death.

The Pennings system of organ procurement

An alternative approach to 'presumed consent' is to force people to express a view. For example, G Pennings has come up with a system of 'confirmed opinion and forced commitment'[53] under which, rather like registering for voting, all persons would have to register their wishes regarding disposal of

---

50 See New *et al*, 1994, p 43.
51 Kittur *et al*, 1991, pp 1441–43.
52 Kokkedee, 1992, pp 177–82.
53 In Englert, 1995, Chapter 22.

their body after death, but as well as registering 'yes' or 'no' they could register 'cannot answer the question'. This violates rights less but still places utility above them.

The contention might be rightly made that one should perform certain duties to others within society if one is to reap the benefits but, the action consistent with rights that follows this is not to force an act, but to withdraw the benefits of organ transplantation from those competent adults who do not make a positive choice to bequeath organs within a reasonable period of time.

RETHINKING ATTITUDES TOWARDS RIGHTS

The preceding analysis suggests the need to rethink attitudes towards consent in relation to removal, use and disposal of body materials. The social construction of Western societies reflects a tension between the Marxian notion of 'from each according to his ability, to each according to his need' and the Lockean notion that the State exists for our benefit and has no right to govern – only such licence as given by the consent of the people and needing to respect man's inalienable, God given, rights to 'life, liberty and estate'.[54] Today one of the central ways in which this tension 'plays out' is in the dilemma over how much it is legitimate to invade a person's property rights in the form of taxation in order to provide for 'social goods' ranging from transport and defence to healthcare and education. These tensions are also reflected in the treatment of healthcare issues under the ECHR where, for example, the right to life has being taking on an increasingly 'positive' character in the sense of expectations being placed on the State to provide life maintaining treatment.[55]

The balance that must be struck in this area of financial obligations placed on the populus is a matter of debate. However, there is a powerful argument to suggest that the imposition of other obligations should be avoided. 'Forcing' the public into activities like registering to vote, undertake national service (or a substitute) or giving up legitimate control over body materials whilst dead or live should be off limits. A system of procuring body materials based on self-determination is critical from a rights perspective. It may also, paradoxically, be the best way to protect utilitarian objectives since it avoids the significant dangers to procurement posed by potential alienation of a large proportion of the public under a 'consent violating' approach. In any case, if, from a utilitarian perspective, we want a decent society there is a need to question whether violating self-determination in such a fundamental area of bodily control is consistent with this.

---

54 Locke, 1925.
55 See, further, Maclean, Chapter 6, above.

A final point needs to be made about the role of the relatives of deceased persons. Clearly, this should not interfere with the self-determination of the deceased. However, relatives ought to have a significant input where their loved one has died incompetent, whether as a minor or adult. The law ought to be amended to make the consent – and not simply absence of objection – of the next of kin essential as a general rule under these circumstances. Some clear form of civil and criminal liability ought to ensue in the event that a medical professional fails to gain such consent. The civil law of trespass to the person ought to act as a model here with consent being treated as real only where it is voluntarily given by a competent person who has the authority to consent and is informed in broad terms of the nature and purpose of the proposed intervention[56] on the deceased. Withholding information in bad faith and acts of fraud and deception should, as in trespass to the person, be regarded as invalidating the consent.

---

56 See Bristow J in *Chatterton v Gerson* [1981] QB 432, p 442G. This approach is also common to other jurisdictions, eg, Canada (see *Reibl v Hughes* (1980) 114 DLR (3d) 646 Sup Ct of Canada).

CHAPTER 19

MEDICAL RESEARCH, CONSENT AND THE EUROPEAN CONVENTION ON HUMAN RIGHTS AND BIOMEDICINE

Aurora Plomer

INTRODUCTION

Medical law was still described only a decade ago as a 'comparatively young subject'.[1] It is also a subject which is constantly forced into reactive mode by the speed of technological change in the biomedical sciences. Against this background, the potential impact of the Human Rights Act (HRA) 1998 on healthcare law is likely to remain a matter of speculation for the foreseeable future. The challenges posed by scientific developments in science and biomedicine will ensure that ethical and legal principles are regularly revisited, refined or rewritten anew. In particular, biomedical research has provided the focus of increased regulatory activity at European and international level.[2] Most notably, the Council of Europe's Convention on Human Rights and Biomedicine (ECHRB) contains a lengthy chapter on scientific research with a view to protecting the rights of human participants in medical experiments. This paper discusses the potential impact of the ECHRB on domestic law in the field of medical research. The first part of the paper analyses the legal force of the biomedicine Convention and its relation to the HRA 1998.

LEGAL FORCE AND SCOPE OF PROTECTION

The ECHRB was opened for signature and ratification in Oviedo in 1997. The UK was a party to the negotiations which preceded the adoption of the ECHRB by the Council of Europe, but has not yet signed and *a fortiori* ratified it. What's more, even if the UK had ratified the biomedicine Convention, its practical impact would, in any event, appear to be considerably limited by the fact that there is no individual right of petition. Individuals, who feel that they have suffered a violation of the rights protected by the Convention on biomedicine, have no right to petition and obtain a remedy from the European

---

1   Kennedy and Grubb, 1994.
2   Clinical Trials Directive (OJ C306, 18.10.97); *ICH Guidelines for Good Clinical Practice* (1996). See, also, Sprumont, 1999.

Court of Human Rights (the Court). Instead, the European Court may give an advisory opinion on legal questions concerning the interpretation of the present biomedicine Convention, but only at the request of the *government* of a party to the ECHRB (Art 29).[3] This seems to rule out petitions from domestic courts in proceedings against the State from individuals seeking to rely on the biomedicine Convention. So at first sight, the ECHRB would appear to be of dubious practical interest to lawyers interested in the impact of the HRA 1998 on domestic health law.

Notwithstanding these limitations, the rights protected by the biomedicine Convention could nevertheless still be indirectly enforceable in two ways. First, in specific contexts, such as the regulation of clinical trials on pharmaceutical products, the ECHRB could acquire indirect legal force through its express endorsement by the European Union in a Directive such as the 1999 proposed Clinical Trials Directive (OJ C161, 8.6.99, p 5). The Clinical Trials Directive is designed to give legal force to principles and guidelines of good clinical practice to protect trial subjects in the conduct all clinical trials designed to develop medicinal or pharmaceutical products (Art 1(1) and (4)). If adopted, the Directive would confer indirect legal force on the ECHRB as the UK would have to apply the Directive in a manner which is consistent with the principles contained in the ECHRB and endorsed in the Preamble to the Directive.

Secondly, and more generally, the biomedicine Convention could in theory be invoked by individuals who are seeking to assert one or several of the rights contained in the main Treaty – such as the right to life, respect for family life or privacy. The Explanatory Report to the ECHRB (Strasbourg, 1997) expressly canvasses such a possibility in a note to Art 29. Article 29 details the rules on interpretation of the ECHRB:

> This Convention does not itself give individuals a right to bring proceedings before the European Court of Human Rights. However, facts which are an infringement of the rights contained in this Convention may be considered in proceedings under the European Convention on Human Rights, if they also constitute a violation of one of the rights contained in the latter Convention [Note 165].[4]

For instance, on the facts of *Gold v Haringey HA*,[5] Ms Gold could not bring an action against the UK in the European Court against breach of Art 5 of the ECHRB which states that: 'An intervention in the health field may only be

---

3 'The European Court of Human Rights may give, without direct reference to any specific proceedings pending in a court, advisory opinions on legal questions concerning the interpretation of the present Convention at the request of: 'The Government of a Party, after having informed the other parties; the Committee set up by Art 32, with membership restricted to the Representatives of the Parties to this Convention, by a decision adopted by a two-thirds majority of votes cast.'

4 Council of Europe, Explanatory Report to the ECHRB, Strasbourg, 1987.

5 [1987] 2 All ER 888, considered in more detail on p 321.

carried out after the person concerned has given free and informed consent to it. This person shall beforehand be given appropriate information as to the purpose and nature of the intervention as well as on its consequences and risks.' However, Ms Gold could, for instance, allege breach of Art 8 of the ECHR which protects the individual's right to respect for his private and family life.

The European Court has held that the concept of 'private life' covers the physical and moral integrity of the person, including his or her sexual life.[6] An alternative might be to invoke Art 10, which protects the individual's right to freedom of expression, including the right to receive information. Although Art 10 has traditionally been invoked to challenge State restrictions on acts of expression,[7] the nature of the right protected is arguably broad enough to encompass the individual's right to receive information which he or she requires to exercise fundamental choices affecting his or her mental and physical health or well-being. In *Open Door Counselling and Dublin Well Woman v Ireland*,[8] the European Court held that an injunction restraining the provision of information concerning abortion services outside the Irish Republic was in breach of Art 10 of the ECHR, because it interfered with a pregnant woman's right to receive information which may be crucial to a woman's health and well-being. Arguably, the rationale for the right protected by Art 10 is that freedom of expression and access to information is not only necessary in a democratic society but it is also required for the protection of the individual's emotional and intellectual development.[9] By implication, information which the individual requires to make informed decisions affecting his health and well-being can no more be arbitrarily or unnecessarily restricted than information required by individuals to exercise their right to hold government to account. In this way, informed consent can be interpreted as a necessary aspect of the democratic principle, or the individual's 'right to know'.[10] The English common law rule which requires doctors only to give information which it is the practice of other responsible doctors to disclose[11] arguably falls short of the protection required by Art 10. Assuming, then, that Arts 8 or 10 might be at issue for the reasons suggested, the crucial question would become whether the European Court could rely on Art 5 of the ECHRB to determine the scope of application of Arts 8 or 10 of the main treaty. The answer would seem to be that it could.

---

6   *X and Y v The Netherlands* (1986) 8 EHRR 235.

7   Eg, *The Observer and Guardian v UK* (1992) 14 EHRR 153.

8   (1992) 15 EHRR 244.

9   *Handyside v UK* (1979–80) 1 EHRR 737. This theme is taken up in Scanlon, 1972.

10 As eloquently endorsed by Lord Scarman, 1984.

11 See below, p 317.

The rights protected by the ECHR are very general and broad. Their precise scope of application is left to be determined by the European Court. The Court has considerable discretion to determine the specific nature and scope of the rights protected.[12] The principles of interpretation applied by the Court follow the general rules of international law on the interpretation of treaties contained in Arts 31 to 33 of the Vienna Convention on the Law of Treaties of 23 May 1969.[13] Article 31(1) of the Vienna Convention directs the Court to interpret a treaty in its context and in the light of its object and purpose. Article 31(3) specifies that there shall be taken into account, together with the context:

(a) any subsequent agreement between the parties regarding the interpretation of the treaty or the application of its provisions; and

(b) any subsequent practice in the application of the treaty which establishes the agreement of the parties regarding its interpretation ...

The biomedicine Convention is not strictly an agreement regarding the interpretation or application of the main ECHR under 3(a). However, the object of the ECHRB, as indicated by its Preamble, is to give a specific application in the field of biomedicine to the general rights contained in the European Convention for the Protection of Human Rights and Fundamental Freedoms (ECHR) 4 November 1950. On this basis, once a majority of members of the Council of Europe have signed and/or ratified the ECHRB, the European Court could conceivably construe such widespread and formal endorsement as a practice which establishes the agreement of the parties on the interpretation of the main Treaty in the field of biomedicine. In this manner, the specific rules contained in the Convention on biomedicine to protect patient's rights on matters such as consent, research, genetic information, etc, could in due course, guide the interpretation of the European Court in cases where the Court has to determine the specific application in a biomedical context of one the Articles in the ECHR.

The majority of Members of the Council of Europe have already signed the Convention on biomedicine.[14] Only a minority have ratified so far. However, since the procedure for ratification varies under domestic law and tends to be lengthy and drawn out, it should only be a matter of time before a majority of Members conclude ratification. In such an event, the conclusion of the above argument is that the UK could in theory find itself indirectly in breach of the provisions contained in the Convention on biomedicine. This could happen even if at that point in time the UK has still neither signed nor ratified.

---

12 Van Dijk and Van Hoof, 1998.

13 The Court endorsed these principles in the *Golder v UK* case, Judgment 21 February 1975, Series A, No 18, para 29; (1979–80) 1 EHRR 524, notwithstanding that the Vienna Convention was not yet in force at the time.

14 See Zilgalvis, Chapter 3, above.

There is a parallel here between the scenario just explored under Art 31(3)(b) of the Vienna Convention and the European Court's application of Art 31(3)(a) in cases where the individual applicant has alleged a violation of a Protocol which had not been ratified by the offending State. In such cases, the State often seeks to argue that the whole matter is governed by the Protocol. However, in the *Abdulaziz* case,[15] the applicant was able to rely on Art 8 on an issue concerning the UK immigration legislation, even though the UK is not a party to the Fourth Protocol. On this basis, it seems that the potential legal impact of the ECHRB on the jurisprudence of the European Court could be considerably greater than anticipated. The HRA 1998 directs UK courts to determine cases relating to the Convention in the light of the jurisprudence of the European Court. The Convention on biomedicine might, thus, gradually reshape domestic law.

THE MORAL AND POLITICAL CHALLENGE

Scientific research is required in order to uncover the causes of ill health or to discover new ways of treating or alleviating pain or illness. The international consensus is that the main purpose of medical research is, 'to improve diagnostic, therapeutic and prophylactic procedures and the understanding of the aetiology and pathogenesis of disease'.[16] Early modern theories on the purpose and limits of medical research, envisaged medical research to be conducted only on human subjects who could directly or personally derive a benefit from the research. Any benefits conferred on others were justified on the grounds that they were incidental to the benefit conferred on the participating individual: 'The principle of medical and surgical morality, therefore, consists in never performing on man an experiment which might be harmful to him to any extent, even though the result might be highly advantageous to science, that is, to the health of others. However, performing experiments and operations exclusively from the point of view of the patient's own advantage does not prevent their turning out profitably to science.'[17]

---

15   *Abdulaziz, Cabales and Balkandali v UK*, Judgment 28 May 1985, Series A, No 94; (1985) 7 EHRR 471. In the *Rasmussen* case, the applicant was able to rely on Art 8 in a case concerning paternity issues even though Denmark was not a party to the Seventh Protocol which sets out the Rights of parents in relation to their children (*Rasmussen v Denmark*, Judgment of 28 November 1984, Series A, No 87; (1985) 7 EHRR 372. Similarly, in the *Guzzardi* case, the applicant was able to rely on Art 5 in a matter concerning the rights of free movement contained in the Fourth Protocol which had not been recognised by Italy (*Guzzardi v Italy* (1980) 3 EHRR 333).

16   Declaration of Helsinki (revised 2000), Introduction.

17   Bernard, 1865.

By the time the Declaration of Helsinki was revised in 1975, the climate of opinion had changed and non-therapeutic biomedical research involving human subjects was considered acceptable providing that the subject was a volunteer who had consented.[18] Furthermore, the 1975 revision of the Declaration expressly stipulated that the experimental design should not be related to the patient's illness[19] thereby excluding the possibility that a volunteer who consented to participate in non-therapeutic research could do so in contemplation of deriving a potential benefit at some unspecified time in the future.

As regards human subjects who lacked the capacity to consent, the 1975 revision of the Declaration was ambiguous. Whilst not expressly prohibiting non-therapeutic research on those lacking the capacity to consent, the Declaration was, nevertheless, silent on the conditions, if any, under which such participants could be volunteered by others. Indeed, it is possible to interpret the omission as a tacit assumption that non-therapeutic research on the mentally incapacitated was considered unacceptable. Since such research cannot directly benefit the participating subject and in addition may expose him or her to risks of harm, it is plain that the purpose of the research is to benefit society rather than the individual participant. The Declaration of Helsinki makes clear that the guiding principle in the conduct of non-therapeutic research should be that, 'the interest of science and society should never take precedence over considerations related to the well-being of the subject'.[20] The Declaration's early ambiguity if not contradiction highlights the moral and political dilemmas which confronted the Council of Europe's drafting of the guiding principles for the conduct of medical research today.

On the one hand, it may be argued that individuals have a moral duty to act for the benefit of others. The obligation to benefit, it is said, is based on reciprocity: 'All our obligations to do good to society seem to imply something reciprocal. I receive the benefits of society, and therefore ought to promote its interests.'[21] In practical terms, adherence to the view that individuals are under a moral obligation to act for the benefit of others may require that in certain circumstances social welfare should trump individual autonomy.

An alternative view is that there is no moral duty to act so as to confer a benefit on others, or at any rate if there is such a duty it is a weak moral duty. The contrast here is between the negative duty captured in the Hippocratic oath 'at least do no harm' and a positive duty to act so as to benefit others.

---

18 Declaration of Helsinki (revised 1975), Chapter III, Art 2.

19 'The subjects should be volunteers – either healthy persons or patients for whom the experimental design is not related to the patient's illness.' Declaration of Helsinki, Chapter III, Art 2.

20 Declaration of Helsinki (revised 1975), Chapter III, Art 4. The principle has been retained in the 2000 revision (Introduction, p 5).

21 Hume, 1985.

According to the German philosopher Immanuel Kant, the latter may be morally laudable but only the former is morally obligatory. Kant's theory is founded on the primacy of respect for the individual's autonomy. In Kantian theory, autonomy is the basis of human dignity.[22] On this view, the deontological requirement that the individual's capacity to make autonomous (and rational) choices should be respected, carries with it the normative implication that collective and societal interests should be morally subordinate to the individual's exercise of his free and autonomous choices which in turn confer on the individual human dignity.

From a political perspective, Kant's ethical and meta-ethical theory is conceptually most congruent with liberal, rights-based political theories, which favour institutional arrangements which prioritise individual liberty over collective welfare. Such theories typically favour negative over positive formulations of rights.[23] In political terms, the imposition of positive moral obligations on individuals to act for the benefit of others has the potential to translate into the exercise of State power to coerce the individual to participate in medical research intended to confer collective benefits on society but not on the individual himself. The potential for abuse is well documented, from medical experiments conducted by the Nazis, to radiation experiments conducted for defence purposes, as late as the 1970s, by far less likely political regimes.[24] The moral and political challenge for the Council of Europe's ECHRB in the area of medical research has therefore been to reconcile the legitimate aims of science to advance the interests of society, with respect for the individual's right to autonomy and self-determination. How far does the ECHRB succeed in so doing? How does the ECHRB compare to domestic law?

THE ECHRB

Object and purpose

The purpose of the Convention on Biomedicine as stated in Chapter I is to 'protect the dignity and identity of all human beings and guarantee everyone, without discrimination, respect for their integrity and other rights and fundamental freedoms with regard to the application of biology and medicine' (I.1). The ECHRB asserts the primacy of the human being (Art 2) and like its predecessor, the Declaration of Helsinki, the Biomedicine Convention expressly endorses the principle that the interests and welfare of the human being shall prevail over the sole interest of society or science (Art 3). The other two basic objects of the ECHRB are to protect the

22 Kant, 1875.
23 Waldron, 1993.
24 See ACHRE, 1996. And for further discussion, Plomer, 2001.

individual's right *to equitable access to healthcare* and the requirement that any intervention in the health field, including research, must be carried out in accordance with relevant *professional obligations and standards*.

Substantive provisions

Chapters II to VII contain substantive detailed provisions on:

(a) consent (Chapter II);

(b) private life and right to information (Chapter III);

(c) human genome (Chapter IV);

(d) scientific research (Chapter V);

(e) organ and tissue removal from living donors for transplantation purposes (Chapter VI);

(f) prohibition of financial gain and disposal of a part of the human body (Chapter VII).

The rights detailed under the various Articles may be limited or restricted by the State, but only as prescribed by law and necessary in a democratic society in the interest of public safety, for the prevention of crime, for the protection of public health or for the protection and freedoms of others (Chapter IX, Art 26) except for Arts 11, 13, 14, 16, 17, 19, 20 and 21 which admit of no exception.

Medical interventions

General rule on consent

The ECHRB requires that in respect of individuals who are able to consent:

An intervention in the health field may only be carried out after the person concerned has given free and informed consent to it.

This person shall beforehand be given appropriate information as to the purpose and nature of the intervention as well on its consequences and risks.

The person concerned may freely withdraw consent at any time [Art 5].[25]

Article 5 thus clearly and expressly espouses the doctrine that consent should be informed in order to be legally effective. By contrast, English courts have expressly and unequivocally rejected the American doctrine of informed

---

25 According to the Explanatory Report, Art 2 'affirms the primacy of the human being over the sole interest of science or society. Priority is given to the former, which must in principle take precedence over the latter in the event of a conflict between them'.

consent and have favoured instead the view that the nature of the information to be disclosed to a patient, and the risks attending the proposed intervention should be judged by the professional legal standard set in *Bolam*.[26] The *Bolam*[27] rule is that a doctor does not act negligently if he acts in accordance with a practice accepted at the time as proper by a responsible body of medical opinion.

The *Bolam* test was endorsed by the House of Lords in *Sidaway* and applied in *Gold v Haringey*,[28] where the plaintiff was sterilised so as to avert any further pregnancies. The consultant obstetrician did not inform Ms Gold that the operation carried a risk of reversal. Ms Gold fell pregnant and was unable to recover damages. The Court of Appeal held that the obstetrician had not acted negligently as it was not standard practice at the time for patients to be informed that the operation might fail. The beginning of a judicial retreat from *Bolam* was initiated in *Bolitho*[29] where the House of Lords held that the court is not bound to hold that a defendant doctor escapes liability for negligent treatment or diagnosis just because he leads evidence from a number of experts who are genuinely of opinion that the defendant's treatment or diagnosis accorded with sound medical practice. The court has to be satisfied that the expert's opinion is capable of withstanding logical analysis. However, Lord Browne-Wilkinson expressly left open the question of whether the 'logical analysis' test applied to questions of disclosure of information and risks: 'I am not considering here questions of disclosure of risks.'[30] Although, there have been some decisions in the lower courts which have endorsed a more pro-patient oriented approach,[31] as English law currently stands, the *Bolam* test continues to apply in respect of disclosure of information and risks.

Does the *Bolam* standard meet the requirements of Art 5 that the patient's consent be *informed* and appropriate risks be disclosed to him or her? The question raises difficult issues about the extent to which the European Court would be prepared to interfere with professional judgment. It is to be expected that the Court will give a certain margin of appreciation to professionals. The Explanatory Report admits that much in its lengthy elaboration of Art 4 on professional standards. The notes acknowledge that 'the content of professional standards, obligations and rules of conduct is not identical in all countries' (note 31) and that 'it is accepted that professional

---

26 *Sidaway v Bethlem Royal and Maudsley Hospital Governors* [1985] AC 871.

27 *Bolam* [1957] 2 All ER 118.

28 *Gold v Haringey HA* [1987] 2 All ER 888.

29 *Bolitho v City and Hackney HA* [1998] AC 232.

30 *Ibid*, p 243.

31 *Smith v Tunbridge Wells HA* [1994] 5 Med LR 334; *Pearce v United Bristol Healthcare NHS Trust* [1999] PIQR 53.

standards do not necessarily prescribe one line of action as being the only one possible: recognised medical practice may, indeed, allow several possible forms of intervention, thus leaving some freedom of choice as to methods and techniques' (note 32).

This suggests that, if Ms Gold had suffered from clinical depression or some other recognised clinical condition which, in the view of some doctors but not others, would have caused her to be unnecessarily alarmed by a frank discussion of the risks attending the operation, then her doctor might have successfully pleaded that disclosure was not appropriate and there was no breach of Art 5. However, the explanatory notes in no way suggest that the question of what counts as an appropriate level of disclosure should be determined primarily by reference to the practice or standards of the medical profession. To do so would make the patient's right relative to the doctors' practice when the biomedicine Convention presupposes precisely the opposite and simply begs the question of why the standards of practice and ethics of the medical profession should play such a decisive role. As Lord Scarman's analysis of the doctrine of informed consent recognised in his dissenting judgment in *Sidaway*, the doctor's duty arises from his patient's rights. The English judicial doctrine of consent has so far failed to recognise clearly the primacy of the patient's rights.[32]

The House of Lords retreat in *Bolitho* is a belated and welcome departure from judicial deference to medical opinion. However, *Bolitho* needs to be clearly extended to disclosure of information and risks. It has been suggested that Lord Browne-Wilkinson's qualified comment in *Bolitho* could be read as a tacit acknowledgement that lower courts in recent years have already began the process of retreat from *Bolam* and returned to a more patient-oriented approach which was in any case already discernable in the original judgment of McNair J.[33] If that was the view alluded to by Lord Browne-Wilkinson's qualified comment, then it needs to be stated expressly and clearly. Until then, the natural reading of the case is that the court has reserved its judgment on the extension of the *Bolitho* test to matters other than diagnosis and treatment and, in particular, to disclosure of information. Furthermore, the suggestion that common law rules, and the original formulation of *Bolam* in particular, had all along contained within themselves the requisite elements to protect the individual's right to receive adequate information on the basis of which to consent to treatment, appears to overlook the conceptual limitations of common law rules *against* constitutionally entrenched rights.

A revised and more patient-oriented reading of *Bolam* no more guarantees protection of the individual's right to determine whether or not to undergo treatment on the basis of an informed decision based on relevant and

---

32 See Kennedy, 1998.

33 Brazier and Miola, 2000.

necessary information, than the English courts' recognition of the right of every individual to say or write what she pleases. To quote Dicey, it is 'essentially false' to say that 'the right to the free expression of opinion ... is a fundamental doctrine of the law of England'.[34] Or, in the words of Brennan J, the 'fragility' of the common law 'right' is in part due to the absence of a constitutionally entrenched right to freedom of expression/access to information.[35] Similarly, it is arguable that the fragility of the *Bolam* test in protecting the patient's rights to self-determination has been in part due to the absence of a constitutionally entrenched right to informed consent.

The contrast between England and the USA, where the doctrine of informed consent originated, is instructive. As commentators have noted, it is no accident that the doctrine of informed consent was developed in a society whose 'explicit constitutional commitment to democratic ideals was to be reflected in a continuing distrust of paternalism, whether as exercised by government officials or professional grounds, and a correspondingly strong conviction that the "right to know" and formal accountability are integral to the democratic process'.[36] Article 5 of the ECHRB now provides a legal vehicle by which to ensure that any residual paternalism and deference to the medical profession by English courts can be replaced by a clear and explicit judicial recognition of the primacy of the patient's 'right to know' when the 'logical analysis test' is expressly extended to disclosure of information.

Persons unable to consent

When the individual lacks the capacity to consent, then medical intervention may only be carried out:

> ... for the person's direct benefit (except in two circumstances covered by Arts 17 and 20 discussed below) [Art 6(1)].
>
> ... in the case of a minor who lacks the capacity to consent ... with the authorisation of a representative or an authority or person or body provided by law ... [Art 6(2)]
>
> ... the conditions and information referred to in Art 5 apply [Art 6(4) and (5)].

The meaning of the word 'intervention' is not restricted to 'medical treatment' and includes medical research. The Explanatory Report stresses that 'one of the important fields of application of this principle concerns research'.[37] However, the Biomedicine Convention also contains additional specific rules on research.

---

34 Dicey, 1959, p 239.
35 *Nationwide News Pty Ltd v Wills* (1992) 177 CLR 1 FC 92/032.
36 Teff, 1985.
37 Explanatory Report, note 21.

Research

Form of Consent – In respect of research, the general consent requirement in Art 5 is strengthened in Art 16 by the requirement that: '... the necessary consent as provided for under Art 5 has been given expressly, specifically and is documented.' (Article 16(v).) The Explanatory Report explains that 'specific' consent is to be understood as meaning consent which is given to one particular intervention carried out in the framework of research (para 102). In addition, the project must have been approved by a competent body after independent assessment of its scientific merit and multidisciplinary review of its ethical acceptability (Art 16(iii)).

The consent must be specific and in writing (Art 17(1)(iv)). The ECHRB, thus, appears to draws a distinction between consent which is documented (general rule on consent to research, Art 16) and consent given in writing (rule applicable to person's lacking capacity to consent to research, Art 17). However, the distinction is obscured by the Explanatory Report, which explains the need for general strengthened consent requirements in respect of research (Art 16). The Report states that: 'In the sphere of research, implicit consent is insufficient. For this reason the Art 16 requires not only the person's free and informed consent, but their express, specific and written consent [para 102].' Article 17 is then explained as strengthening the protection of persons unable to consent, 'by the requirement that the necessary authorisation ... be given specifically and in writing' (para 105).

The difference in wording could be significant for the UK. There is at present no legal requirement in English law that prior specific consent be given *in writing* by a subject participating in a trial.[38] Hence, in respect of persons who have the requisite capacity to consent, the UK's position would be compliant with the biomedicine Convention if, contrary to the Explanatory Report, the different wording of Arts 16 and 17 is to be read as signifying the possibility that consent need not be given in writing, providing it is evidenced in other ways.

As regards the consent requirements in respect of persons who lack the capacity to consent, the UK's position is potentially more problematic. A distinction here needs to be drawn between children and adults who lack the capacity to consent.

---

38 The rules of Research Ethics Committees (RECs) and Multi-Centre Research Ethics Committees (MRECs) do require that consent be given in writing, but the rules are administrative and have no statutory basis. See, also, Multi-Centre Research Ethics Committees: Statement of compliance with international committee on harmonisation/good clinical practice (ICH), guidelines for the conduct of trials involving the participation of human subjects, November 1997.

Children

There is currently no general legislation in the UK regulating the conduct of medical research on human subjects, whether the individuals involved are adults or children. There are no reported cases either. The legal obligations of researchers and rights of child participants have to be surmised from general statutes such as the Children Act 1989 and well established common law principles in medical law. If the child is below the statutory age of consent or lacks the mental capacity to consent, then the common law requires that consent be given, instead, by someone who has legal authority to consent on behalf of the child (for example, the father) and failing this from the Family Division of the High Court which has the power to make decisions concerning the child, including decisions in an emergency. In the famous words of Lord Donaldson:

> It is trite law that, in general, a doctor is not entitled to treat a patient without the consent of someone who is authorised to give that consent [*Re R (A Minor) (Wardship: Medical Treatment)*) [1992] 1 FLR 190, p 196].

Children who are 16 or over have been conferred statutory authority to consent to medical treatment in the Family Law Reform Act 1969 (s 8) although the courts have since ruled that this authority does not extend to refusal of treatment, particularly life saving treatment.[39] Further, in the celebrated case of *Gillick v West Norfolk and Wisbech AHA*,[40] the House of Lords ruled that a child who is under 16 may be able to give valid consent to treatment if she has the mental capacity to understand the nature and effects of the proposed treatment (*Gillick*-competent). If the child is under 16 and not *Gillick*-competent, consent must be obtained from someone who has legal authority to give that consent under the Children Act 1989.

In short, in respect of children who lack the capacity to consent, English law has developed a set of common law principles and statutory rules to protect the child through the requirement that consent be obtained from those who have the authority to do so. This is not to say that the application of these rules to specific cases by English courts is free from controversy, and is otherwise compliant with Human Rights law. By contrast, the position of mentally incapacitated adults in English law is potentially more problematic.

Adults who lack the capacity to consent

The position of adults who lack the mental capacity to consent to a medical intervention is determined by the common law. In the case of *F v West Berkshire AHA* [1989] 2 All ER 545, the House of Lords had to consider whether a surgical sterilisation could be lawfully performed on mentally

---

39 *Re R* [1991] 4 All ER 177 and *Re W (A Minor) (Medical Treatment)* [1992] 4 All ER 627.
40 [1985] 3 All ER 402.

handicapped woman who was 36 years old at the time of the hearing, but who had the mental capacity of a child of four or five. The court had been asked by the applicant health authority to authorise the operation. In a landmark ruling, the House of Lords determined that it lacked the power to consent to (or refuse) the operation on behalf of the mentally handicapped woman. The *parens patriae* jurisdiction which enabled the court to make decisions on behalf of the mentally handicapped had been abolished by the Mental Health Act 1983 and a legal lacuna had inadvertently been created in respect of decision making procedures concerning medical interventions. In the view of the House of Lords, the position in English law is that no one, not even the court, has legal authority to consent or refuse treatment on behalf of an adult who lacks the mental capacity to consent. As a result of this extraordinary legal lacuna, the legal protection given to the mentally incapacitated by English law has been described by the Law Commission as 'a far cry from what the UN declaration identifies as the "right to a qualified guardian"' (para 2.26).

F v West Berkshire gave rise to several reports on mental incapacity from the Law Commission, culminating in a Final Report in 1995 recommending statutory changes to the present law, including a requirement that decisions made on behalf of the mentally incapacitated should have a clear legal basis extending to court approval in cases of certain treatments (that is, sterilisation, abortion and bone marrow donation). Instead of legislation, the Final Report was followed by another Consultation Paper,[41] Green Paper and Final Report conceding a clear need for reform of the law.[42] However, in the absence of legislation, there seems little doubt that English law currently fails to provide the protection required for mentally incapacitated adults under Arts 6 and 17 of the ECHRB, which respectively require approval for medical interventions to be given by a legal representative, specifically and in writing in the case of research.

In addition, the absence of a legal procedure in English law to enable a guardian, representative or the court itself to consent to medical interventions on behalf of a mentally incapacitated adult could potentially constitute a violation of Arts 6 and 14 of the ECHR, respectively. Article 6 entitles each individual to a 'fair and public hearing' and more generally the right to real and effective access to a court. As English law currently stands, in the event of a dispute as to whether a mentally incapacitated adult should participate in a medical research trial, the court could not hear the views of the individual's legal guardian or representative since there are no procedures for the appointment of a legal representative in respect of medical interventions. Neither could the court itself consent or refuse on behalf of the individual concerned. English law, thus, appears to discriminate against a group of

---

41 Lord Chancellor, 1997.
42 Lord Chancellor, 1999.

individuals who are already in a vulnerable position and in need of enhanced rather than reduced protection. By failing to secure the right to a legal representative or guardian in respect of decisions concerning medical interventions on mentally incapacitated adults, English law is also arguably in breach of Art 14 of the ECHR which prohibits discrimination on any ground including birth or other status.

In addition, medical interventions or research of an invasive nature such as sterilisations, which are conducted without the requisite authorisation, could potentially amount to a violation of Art 3 which forbids 'torture or inhuman or degrading treatment'.

Non-therapeutic research

Exceptionally, Art 16(ii) sanctions the conduct of non-therapeutic research on human subjects, including the mentally incapacitated. The ECHRB does not use the words 'therapeutic' and 'non-therapeutic' but distinguishes instead between research which has the potential to produce results of *real* and *direct* benefits to the participant (Art 17(1)(ii)) from research which has:

> ... the aim of contributing, through significant improvement in the scientific understanding of the individual's condition, disease or disorder, to the ultimate attainment of results capable of conferring benefit to the person concerned or to other persons in the same age category or afflicted with the same disease or disorder or having the same condition [Art 17(2)(i)].

Such research is subject to the further condition that it:

> ... entails only minimal risk and burden for the individual concerned [Art 17(2)(ii)].

Where the 1975 revision of Declaration of Helsinki was ambiguous, the ECHRB, thus, expressly permits non-therapeutic research on human subjects, whether they have the capacity to consent or not. Further, in contrast to the Declaration which stipulated that the experimental research must not be related to the patient's illness (Chapter 3, Art 2), the Convention on biomedicine takes the opposite stance in requiring that the research should aim to obtain results which are ultimately capable of conferring a benefit on the participant subject, or others afflicted with the same disease or disorder. The ECHRB seems right and, indeed, the latest revision of the Declaration of Helsinki (October 2000) has been brought into line with the ECHRB in this respect.[43]

---

43   The Declaration of Helsinki (October 2000) now provides that: 'Medical research is only justified if there is a reasonable likelihood that the populations in which the research is carried out stand to benefit from the results of the research [Art 19].' In the case of groups who are not mentally competent to give consent: 'These groups should not be included in research unless the research is necessary to promote the health of the population represented and this research cannot instead be performed on legally competent persons [Art 24].'

In the case of the mentally competent, political (and moral) legitimacy may be conferred on the conduct of non-therapeutic research through the requirement that prior informed consent be obtained from the participating individual and the further limitations concerning risk and prior approval by an independent multidisciplinary ethics committee. It could plausibly be argued that, if a mentally competent and appropriately informed individual chooses to run the risks to participate in research from which he does not stand to derive any direct benefit, it is simply his right to do so. The ECHRB gives the competent individual the option to exercise his choice, both whether to consent and refuse to participate in non-therapeutic research.

However, the same argument cannot apply to the mentally incapacitated whom, by definition, lack the capacity to exercise a choice. The ECHRB allows others to volunteer the mentally incapacitated to participate in research from which they will not derive any direct benefit and which might expose them to burden and risks, albeit minimal (Art 17(2)(ii)). In those circumstances, it could be argued that such research is morally objectionable because it involves using human beings as a mere means to an end. The requirement imposed by the ECHRB that the research should have the aim of contributing to the attainment of results capable of conferring a benefit on the individual could be seen as going some way towards defusing the objection. However, in practice, much would depend on the precise interpretation and application of the conditions imported by the biomedicine Convention. On a wide construction, the ECHRB could be read as providing insufficient protection for the mentally incapacitated. Much depends on what is to count as 'minimal risks' and how loosely the requirement that the research aims to ultimately confer some benefit on the individual is interpreted. The default institutional safeguard is approval by a multidisciplinary research ethics committees, but in order to work effectively to protect research subjects these require standardised and sufficiently specific guidelines and norms.

Finally, the ECHRB raises further difficult questions about the nature and purpose of proxy consent and the extent to which a guardian or representative could or should have legal authority to make decisions on behalf of the mentally incapacitated guided by considerations other than the welfare or best interests of the individual concerned. In the case of children, for instance, the United Nations Convention on the Rights of the Child (1989) envisages that:

> In all actions concerning children, whether undertaken by public or private social welfare institutions, courts of law, administrative authorities or legislative bodies, *the best interests of the child shall be the primary consideration* [Art 3].

It is not immediately clear how it could be in the best interests of a child to be volunteered as a participant in research which will expose her to risks and from which it is not anticipated that she will derive any real or direct benefit. Indeed, it is not difficult to imagine circumstances in which participation in such research could potentially involve a violation of Art 3 of the United Nations Convention on the Rights of the Child.

The potential difficulties can be gauged by comparing the position in English law. The Council of Europe's Explanatory Report on the ECHRB gives as an example of a procedure involving minimal risk, the taking of a single blood sample from a child. However, it has been suggested that common law principles developed by Canadian courts, and similar to the English principles in *Re F*, may not sanction venepuncture for blood testing, as the procedure itself may carry more than minimal risks in children and even when the risks are minimal, the procedure cannot be described as beneficial when undertaken to conduct research alone, such as to establish typologies or a normal range in a control group.[44] On this view, the common law position is that blood may lawfully be drawn by venepuncture from a small child for a legitimate diagnostic, therapeutic or monitoring purpose, such as establishing whether the child suffers from leukaemia, but it cannot be drawn purely for the purpose of discovering the causes or improving the treatment of leukaemia in children as suggested by the Explanatory Report on the biomedicine Convention (Art 17, note 113b) unless the drawing of the blood is incidental or additional to the taking of the main sample for diagnostic or therapeutic purposes. Alternatively, it has been suggested that English law may accept a more relaxed test of whether the proposed research is *not against* the child's interests, instead of showing that the proposed research will directly benefit the child.[45] Such a relaxation would at least begin to address the concerns expressed by the Council of Europe that legal restrictions on research based on 'potential direct benefit' test would make paediatric research such as prophylaxis through vaccination, dietary measures or preventive treatments whose effectiveness requires evaluation, impossible in the future.[46] It would also begin to address the charge that the legal prohibition of non-therapeutic research on children constitutes an injustice to the child.[47] However, the difficulty lies in ensuring that the law offers adequate protection to the child, whilst facilitating the advancement of scientific knowledge from which the child himself or herself may indirectly benefit in the future.

---

44 Dickens, 1998. See, also, Plomer, 2000.
45 Kennedy and Grubb, 1994, pp 256–58, 1061–65; 1998, pp 728ff.
46 Explanatory Report, para 112.
47 Dickens, 1998.

Hence, it has been argued that the proposed relaxation should be subject to two further provisos. First that the research be approved by a REC and second that there should be 'strict limits' to that for which the parent may volunteer the child.[48] The first condition that the research be approved by a REC is not currently a requirement of English law, although it is found in the ECHRB (Art 16(iii)). The second stipulation that there should be 'strict' limits on that to which the parents may consent invites further elaboration and clarification. Should the limits depend on the nature of the research (that is, collection of data, observation versus invasive procedures) and/or on the degree of discomfort, pain, etc? Pending the elaboration of the research protocol, the biomedicine Convention may be charged with offering too weak or insufficient protection to the mentally incapacitated. By contrast, although the legal principles applicable to medical research are still a matter of speculation, it is thought that the extension of the 'best interests' test to research would be overprotective and restrictive. In theory, the 'best interests' principle should provide greater protection for subjects who are volunteered as participants in non-therapeutic research but at the cost of stifling research from which the individual might ultimately benefit. In practice, in the field of medical intervention, the application of the best interests principle by the courts has been questionable.[49]

---

48 Kennedy and Grubb, 1998, p 730.
49 See, for instance, *Re Y (Mental Incapacity: Bone Marrow Transplant)* [1997] 2 WLR 556.

CHAPTER 20

THE EUROPEAN CONVENTION ON BIOMEDICINE AND THE HUMAN RIGHTS ACT 1998: GRASPING THE NETTLE OF BIOMEDICINE?

Melanie Latham and Siobhan Leonard

INTRODUCTION

On the threshold of the new millennium, the average European is conversant with the concept of human rights and, more often than not, able to specify the most basic of these. This has been due largely to mass media coverage of human rights issues as well as the groundbreaking efforts of individuals, non-governmental organisations, States and international organisations working in this sphere during the past 50 years. At an international level, the most prominent intergovernmental institution responsible for safeguarding human rights across Europe is the Council of Europe.[1] Through the promulgation of various Conventions protective of human rights, it has proven itself to be in the global vanguard in this area.

Initially, the Council sought to protect the most basic and commonly accepted rights, such as the right to life and the right to be free from torture, or inhuman and degrading treatment, as enshrined in the European Convention on Human Rights (ECHR).[2] In common with the European Union (EU), it has begun to concern itself with newly emergent issues in the spheres of biotechnology and biomedicine.[3] Biotechnology concerns research involving living organisms that might have industrial or commercial potential. Biomedicine more usually refers to new medical techniques involving the human body and body parts. Ethical or bioethical issues arise from both.

This chapter seeks to explore the regulation of bioethical issues in Europe. It questions whether the attempts made by the EU and the Council of Europe

---

1   As of July 2001, there are 43 Members of the Council of Europe.

2   ECHR, Arts 2 and 3 respectively.

3   In 1991, the Council of Ministers, one of the main political institutions within the Council of Europe, instructed the Council of Europe Steering Committee on Bioethics (CDBI) 'to prepare, in close co-operation with the Steering Committee for Human Rights (CDDH) and the European Health Committee (CDSP) ... A framework Convention, open to non-Member States, setting out common general standards for the protection of the human person in the context of the biomedical sciences and Protocols to this Convention, relating to in a preliminary phase: organ transplants and the use of substances of human origin and medical research on the human being'. (Council of Europe: Explanatory Report 'To the Convention for the Protection of Human Rights and Dignity of the Human Being with regard to the application of Biology and Medicine: Convention on Human Rights and Biomedicine' DIR/JUR (97) 1, para 4.)

are sufficient in the context of human rights and bioethics. In particular, it considers whether the situation has been improved by the new European Convention for the Protection of Human Rights and Dignity of the Human Being with regard to the application of Biology and Medicine known commonly as the European Convention on Human Rights and Biomedicine (ECHRB[4]). It chiefly considers how the ECHRB will affect individuals living within the UK in view of the fact that the Human Rights Act (HRA) 1998 does not directly address bioethical issues. In this new instrument on biomedicine, then, we ask whether the Council of Europe has found a suitable method of taking up a nettle that other institutions have been less willing to grasp, and if so, how enforcement has been facilitated.

BIOETHICS AS A GLOBAL DEBATE

Biotechnology as a growth industry

Biotechnology has now begun to play an increasingly important part in the worlds of medicine, health and ethics. The superpowers of the USA, Japan and Europe are currently battling for economic control of a vast new market covering vaccines, gene therapy, drug delivery systems, diagnostics, agriculture, food processing, and the creation of organic fuels. In 1994, accountants Ernst and Young estimated that European biotechnology would exceed turnover of over $94 billion by the year 2000 and would create around two million jobs.[5]

Patients in advanced societies are themselves beginning to demand that the State provide them with the benefits of progress in medicine as a basic social right.[6]

Biotechnology, bioethics and regulation

Biology and medicine have a direct impact on human beings, posing questions that concern us all, as individuals and as a society. Ethical issues in medicine cover a wide variety of issues including the doctor-patient relationship, and the allocation of limited healthcare resources.

The ethical implications of biotechnology are numerous, wide ranging and strike at the very heart of humanity and civilisation. Scientific and medical research, particularly genetic research, and the application of those

---

4   Council of Europe, Strasbourg, DIR/JUR (96) 14. The Convention was opened for signature on 4 April 1997.

5   Rogers and Durand de Bousingen, 1995, p 91.

6   Vuckovic and Nichter, 1997.

technologies, threaten human dignity and human rights. They involve, inter alia, issues of informed consent, patient control, commercialisation, experimentation, confidentiality and safety. Discrimination by insurers, or indeed by health providers, might result from the detection of genetic disease in patients. Sex selection of human embryos involved in gene therapy raises questions of gender discrimination. Experimental research on the unconscious, the child or the foetus challenges accepted rights in relation to inhuman or degrading treatment of the patient. Such rights might also be in question in relation to the commercialisation of human body parts as a result of organ donation, or the patenting of genetic information.

Bioethics can provide fundamental, universal and democratic principles to supplant the competing demands and values of the market, which ignore their social consequences. This area also offers matter for national and international reflection and a platform for debate. This can help regulators to respond to the diverse demands of society whilst safeguarding the human rights of their populations.[7] Such rights need to be protected and enforced where necessary. After all, bioethical problems know no territorial boundaries.[8] Yet, until recently, scientific researchers and medical practitioners had been left very much to regulate themselves free from strict safeguards in relation to relevant ethical issues. Many States where biomedical practices are carried out still have little or no legal regulation in place of treatment given. The health of patients undergoing biomedical treatments would be safeguarded if there were regulation of, for example, the qualifications of medical personnel; the testing of gametes or donors for all known transmissible diseases, including HIV and the human variation of Creuzfeldt-Jacob disease; the availability of counselling; and the proper use of informed consent to treatment.[9]

EUROPE'S RESPONSE

Biotechnology, bioethics and the EU

All Europeans have an interest in the economic growth of the biotechnology industry. The pertinent ethical issues are similar in most European countries. Arguably, this places obligations on bodies representing European society to regulate cross-nationally. As will become apparent, the Council of Europe has made progress in establishing minimum European standards in bioethical

---

7 For further background information on this issue, see Riis, 1993.

8 Arguably, this makes harmonisation desirable across Europe, from service provision to recognition of medical qualifications, and access to treatments, in order to safeguard the health of those seeking treatments across Europe (see Nielsen, 1996).

9 For example, Belgium, Ireland, Italy and the US. See Nielsen, 1996, for a comparative assessment of regulation of assisted conception in Europe.

research and development via the Convention on Biomedicine. The EU, for its part, has been concerned traditionally with establishing and enforcing obligations of a primarily economic nature, and has consequently given health and related social issues a lower priority. Its efforts to promote bioethical standards have been quite cautious thus far, chiefly because of the understandable reluctance of Member States to yield further sovereign power to this supranational organisation in a field traditionally thought to lie within the sphere of national competence. As Weatherill has stated:

> The treaty does not explicitly share out or set boundaries between the competences of the Community and the Member States [and] offers no statement of the consequences for national competence of Community competence in a particular field.[10]

Consequently, the EU has only just begun to become directly involved in promulgating a health policy during the last decade, although arguably it already came within its sphere of competence indirectly on both economic and social grounds. For example, the free movement of medicines across Europe serves the economic interests of industry. This then impinges on the social policy of the EU as it broadens patient choice and necessitates commonly agreed safety and quality standards for patient care.[11] However, EU health policy is only in its infancy and Member States wish to retain a high level of autonomy in relation to health matters, particularly in the areas of healthcare systems and resource allocation.[12]

In an attempt to provide a harmonious and ethical EU policy response to biotechnology, former European Commission President Jacques Delors created a nine member consultative group of eminent bioethical advisors, the Biotechnology Co-ordination Committee (GAEIB), in 1992. The group's main task has been:

> ... identifying and defining ethical questions raised by biotechnology and with providing an evaluation of ethical aspects arising from the activities of the Community in this area and of studying the potential impact for society and individuals of such activities.[13]

Thus far, the group has issued opinions concerning, *inter alia*, the use of bovine somatropin, products derived from human blood or human plasma, legal protection for biotechnological inventions, transgenic animals and gene therapy.[14] However, this Committee only has an advisory role – it cannot

10 Weatherill, 1994.

11 Roscamm Abbing, 1997.

12 The Treaty of Amsterdam sees the virtual overhaul of the EU's pre-existing policy on public health, and gives the Council wider decision making powers in this area. It still affirms the sovereign interests of States in this field, in that it claims 'to fully respect the responsibility of the Member States for the organisation and delivery of health services and medical care'. See Craig and De Búrca, 1998, p 37.

13 European Commission press release IP/94/153.

14 Cf Riis, 1993.

make recommendations or instigate policy. These shortcomings illustrate the difficulties faced in attempting to secure the proper regulation of bioethical issues in the EU. The lack of consensus nationally and in political European institutions such as the European Parliament has left a legal and regulatory hiatus within the biotechnological sphere. The political implications of specifying coherent guidelines in the area of bioethics have proved problematic and have contributed to an unwillingness of bodies such as the European Commission to deal with the problem directly. Nonetheless, most of the ethical questions raised by biotechnology require serious consideration. Their widespread effect predisposes some pan-European organisation to instigate some form of universal regulation that reflects common European values.

In July 1994, William Hunter, Director of the Public Health Division (DG5) described how the normal consultation procedures within the EU institutions such as the economic and social committee were being followed in relation to public health, with a list of priorities emerging. For each priority a programme was being drawn up and a committee appointed to advise on each proposal.[15] In January 1995, the then European Social Affairs Commissioner, Padraig Flynn, gave a speech in London on the issue of European health policy. He spoke of the necessity for the EU to address the broader issues of health, such as European co-operation on disease prevention and the socio-economic determinants of health, rather than involvement solely in the financial organisation of health services.[16] In May 1995, the European Commission produced its first comprehensive annual report on the health implications of all areas of EU activity, the Report on Integration of Health Protection Requirements in Community Policies.[17] This was followed in 1997 by changes occasioned by the Amsterdam Treaty, which amended and renumbered the title on Public Health, originally introduced by the Treaty on European Union, Art G, para 38.

Article 152(1) of Title XII of the treaty as amended, stresses, inter alia, that the activities of the Community in the field of public health will 'complement national policies' (our emphasis), and provides in para 4 for the further adoption of 'measures setting high quality and safety of organs and substances of human origin, blood and blood derivatives'. It also goes on to state under Art 176, that 'these measures shall not prevent any Member State from maintaining or introducing more stringent protective measures', in line with similar developments in the field of environmental protection, for example. This amendment appears to both formally recognise the need for some advancement in the evolution of a coherent EU health policy, giving a mandate to the Community to develop the policy in close co-operation with

---

15 Richards and Smith, 1994.
16 Nicolaou, 1995.
17 COM (95) 196 final, 26 May 1995, (1995) 311 British Medical Journal, 29 July, p 282.

the Member States, while at the same time respecting the differing approaches of the various Member States toward biomedical issues. This emphasis on the development of a common health policy through co-operation and the adoption of complementary measures, suggest that Member States are to be actively encouraged to participate in the process and that the EU is mindful of Member States' reticence to surrender sovereignty on this issue. Such an approach is reminiscent of its early forays into environmental protection, where initial developments were criticised as being too technical and regulatory and, thus, not encouraging of fiscal or other initiatives which could further develop policy.[18] Could the same be said of present health policy initiatives?

Just as the development of health policy has been coveted by States, biotechnology and associated ethical solutions have often been felt by European Member States to fall within sovereign territory. To date, bioethical issues have been dealt with largely through national responses such as guidelines, commissions of inquiry, ethics committees, and in a minority of cases, by statute.[19] European societies are by their nature pluralistic so that these questions tend to be tackled only after a fine-tuning of the power balance, which differs from State to State. Forces in conflict include political parties, the medical profession, the media, and religious groups including the Roman Catholic Church.[20]

This disparity of reaction and lack of consensus is apparent both within European nations and the institutions that purport to represent them. Debates on ethical issues have been rather heated. In the European Parliament, for example, it has been nigh on impossible to achieve a consensus of opinion on bioethical issues.[21] This has resulted in EU institutions concentrating mainly on the strictly technical issues associated with biotechnology rather than the philosophical and political aspects, on account of the many possible ethical implications of the adoption of standards or regulations in the field of research, health or biotechnology. The EU itself is committed to securing 'respect for human rights and fundamental freedoms' and also purports to respect fundamental rights by the ECHR, as these form part of the general principles of law protected and enforced by the EU.[22] Any State breach of technical measures adopted in furtherance of the aims of Art 152 could

---

18 Hughes, 1996.

19 Eg, in the area of embryo regulation, Italy has no regulating statute, whereas the UK regulates embryo research under the Human Fertilisation and Embryology Act 1990. See Goldbeck-Wood, 1996, p 512.

20 Cf Riis, 1993.

21 Rogers and Durand de Bousingen, 1995, p 208.

22 See TEU, Art 6(1) and (2).

potentially have serious ramifications for that State if an individual's fundamental rights were breached thereby.[23]

The Council of Europe and the bioethics issue

The idea of international organisations finding common solutions to ethical and human rights problems is by no means new. Take for example the ECHR, which has been an invaluable tool for both individuals and States in challenging the conflicting laws, policies or practices of contracting States.

Indeed, the Council of Europe appears to have had more success in this field.

It has now seized the initiative in the field of biomedicine, publishing the ECHRB in December 1996, an instrument with potentially far reaching powers, that individuals can utilise to protect their rights where these are infringed by medicine or the biotechnology industry.

In summary, the Biomedicine Convention requires that its signatories ensure provision of the following basic standards in their own countries:

(a) equitable access to healthcare (Art 3);

(b) free and informed consent by patients before any medical intervention on their person (Art 5);

(c) no discrimination on grounds of genetic heritage (Art 11);

(d) human genome modification for diagnostic or therapeutic purposes only and no germ line genetic modification (Art 13);

(e) no sex selection unless this is on the grounds of a threat of the transmission of a serious sex related hereditary disease (Art 14);

(f) a limitation on research on the human embryo (Art 18);

(g) no financial gain from the human body and its parts (Art 21);

(h) a system of adequate compensation for undue damage after a medical intervention (Art 24).

The ECHRB itself makes some important additions to the existing, protected body of human rights and fundamental freedoms, and the full title of the Convention emphasises this nexus. The Preamble makes explicit reference to the notion of human rights protection, declaring that those drafting the instrument are, *inter alia*:

> ... conscious of the accelerating developments in biology and medicine; convinced of the need to respect the human being both as an individual and as a member of the human species and [recognise] the importance of ensuring the

---

23 The most likely way in which this would arise would be on the issue of enforcement proceedings under Art 226 or, on a request for a preliminary ruling from a national court with jurisdiction on the matter, under Art 234, where such an issue was canvassed successfully.

dignity of the human being; conscious that the misuse of biology and medicine may lead to acts endangering human dignity.

The ECHRB – mechanisms for enforcement

The new Convention is one of a number of recent additions to the Council of Europe's burgeoning portfolio of human rights instruments. The ECHR was meant to provide as complete a list of agreed, legally binding, civil and political rights as was then possible and a proper institutional procedure for their enforcement. On the other hand, other subsidiary Conventions have a narrower, more focused remit and obligations arising thereunder are scrutinised in differing ways.

The means of enforcement of these Conventions differ according to the levels of both political goodwill and controversy surrounding their inception. By way of example, the European Social Charter ensures the observation of legal obligations by way of a reporting system that has been roundly criticised for effectively enabling contracting parties to police themselves.

The Torture Convention 1987[24] has established a more rigorous enforcement machine, setting up a Committee comprised of independent scrutineers, the Committee for the Prevention of Torture. Committee members are experts in their field, empowered, *inter alia*, to visit sites where Convention breaches have allegedly occurred or are occurring, to discuss violations and report on them accordingly. Although normally confidential, these reports may be published and States publicly embarrassed in order to effect the required changes.[25] How then do the enforcement provisions of the new instrument compare?

As with the ECHR, Art 1 of the ECHRB states that, 'each party to this Convention shall take in its internal law the necessary measures to give effect to the provisions of this Convention'. This is also reflected in Chapter VIII of the ECHRB, which details the enforcement mechanisms supporting the main provisions. Article 23 places the onus for protecting Convention rights on the parties themselves who are obliged, 'to provide for the possibility of judicial action to prevent or put a stop to [unlawful] infringements of the principles set forth in the Convention', whether these are pre-existing, or merely threatened.

---

24 European Convention for the Prevention of Torture and Inhuman or Degrading Treatment or Punishment.

25 This strategy has successfully identified Turkey as one of the worst offenders on Europe's fringes. For further details, see Public Statement on Turkey, adopted 15 December 1992: (1993) 14 HRLJ 49, and Second Public Statement on Turkey (1997) 18 HRLJ 294.

The ECHRB is legally binding on all States which ratify it and entered into force on 1 December 1999, for the first five States who have done so.[26] The discretion enjoyed by each ratifying State, has been viewed by the Council of Europe as one of the principal strengths of the system, and was purposely introduced so that States could choose the solutions best suited to their constitutional requirements and the convictions of national public opinion.[27] The ECHRB also attempts to ensure that appropriate sanctions are applied by Member States in the event of infringement[28] and that parties to the Convention provide for the possibility of rapid judicial action to prevent or put a stop to infringement of the Convention's principles.[29]

This enforcement mechanism emphasises the discretionary nature of the instrument, and is indicative of the cautious approach adopted by the Council of Europe toward what is still a difficult area within which to obtain pan-European agreement. The potential difficulty inherent in enforcing a system operating on a discretionary basis is that it could run contrary to the interests of individual complainants. However, in permitting Member States this measure of national control as regards implementation, common principles could be introduced, divergences between the future laws of Member States could be avoided and harmonisation made more probable.[30]

The Role of the European Court of Human Rights in enforcing the ECHRB

The Council of Europe wishes to retain control over Conventions for which it has ultimate responsibility, and the ECHRB is no different in this respect. The European Court of Human Rights (the Court) may have a role to play where bioethical issues are raised under the new Convention either through the provision of advisory opinions by request, or the investigation of complaints where an allegation is made of a breach of one or more provisions of the ECHR.

Advisory opinions

As is the case under Art 47 of the ECHR, Art 29 of the ECHRB enables the European Court to give Advisory Opinions, on legal questions concerning the interpretation of the Convention. However, it can do so only in abstract, at the

---

26 These are Denmark, Greece, San Marino, Slovakia and Slovenia. Spain, which ratified in 1999 has also been subject to the Convention from 1 January 2000.

27 Group of Advisors to the European Commission, 1996, p 11.

28 ECHRB, Arts 24 and 25.

29 *Ibid*, Arts 124 and 126.

30 Council of Europe, 1989, p 13.

request of a government of a State which is party to the Biomedicine Convention and ongoing court proceedings must not be referred to directly in the request. Under the Second Protocol of the statute of the Council of Europe, the conditions for obtaining advisory opinions from the Court are framed so restrictively that this has limited its usefulness as a legal or political remedy. In fact, this form of redress, such as it is, has never been used to date, so it is a matter of some conjecture as to whether it will be of any practical use in the context of the present text.

More significantly, aggrieved individuals are unable to access the Court using this mechanism, this leaves them with only one option, the possibility of court action. Again, they cannot use breach of the ECHRB to found an action in itself, as the complaint under the Convention on biomedicine must also fall within the parameters of the ECHR, for this option to be a viable one.

Taking a case to Strasbourg

The ECHRB is deficient in terms of giving individuals the remedy of seising the court directly when breaches occur, thus, encouraging them to rely heavily on the enforcement mechanisms provided by the ECHR. Whilst this is far from ideal, it should be borne in mind that the ECHRB represents a significant compromise between 'progressive' States seeking to forge minimal pan–European standards in this area and more 'cautious' nations that have had substantial moral and political difficulty in accepting it in its entirety. When then might the Court come to deal with complaints that straddle both Conventions? There have been a number of occasions when the Court has either directly dealt with, or at least touched upon, issues which might now find greater expression and protection under the ECHRB.

There are numerous examples to be found across the ECHR. A case in point is the thorny issue of consent, now dealt with at some length by the ECHRB under Art 5. Previously, it was considered under a number of provisions under the ECHR, specifically Arts 2 and 3, namely the right to life and freedom from torture, inhuman and degrading treatment, and even occasionally under Art 8, the privacy provision. Various medical practices such as abortion and euthanasia, have been touched upon under Art 2. In relation to the former, examples of case law where consent, or rather the lack of it, has been raised unsuccessfully in the context of the male partner objecting to an abortion before the European Commission on Human Rights, include *X v UK* and *H v Norway*.[31]

As regards euthanasia, this has been considered to date in one instance only, namely in the case of *Widmer v Switzerland*, where euthanasia by

---

31 App No 8416/78; (1980) 19 DR 244; No 17004/90 (1992) unreported.

omission, or passive euthanasia, was considered by the Commission.[32] Would the position of any of the applicants in these cases be strengthened by combining Art 2 of the ECHR and Art 5 of the ECHRB? In the abortion cases, the answer would have to be no, as both cases ultimately failed to surmount basic requirements as regards *locus standi*. On the other hand, the euthanasia debate has been little explored by the Strasbourg organs and, more significantly, the medical treatment in question is so detrimental to the health of the individual concerned, that it would seem unlikely to assist anyone campaigning on that front.[33]

The question of consent in relation to the enforced medical treatment of prisoners, detainees and medical patients, has traditionally proved to be a fertile ground for at least minimal consideration of bioethical issues under the ECHR.[34] The case of *Herczegfalvy*[35] arguably combines an analysis of these three forms of vulnerability. The applicant was a hunger-striking prisoner who had been diagnosed as suffering from mental illness. He was fed and medicated forcibly by the authorities while in detention. Although the Court did not uphold his claim that this treatment was contrary to Art 3, it did sound a note of caution to all contracting States with regard to the treatment of individuals in a position of weakness as regards State interference:

> The Court considers that the position of inferiority and powerlessness which is typical of patients confined in psychiatric hospitals calls for increased vigilance in reviewing whether the Convention has been complied with ... [though] as a general rule, a measure which is a therapeutic necessity cannot be regarded as inhuman or degrading.[36]

The question then arises as to whether a susceptible patient's position could be enhanced through reliance on Art 3 of the ECHR and on the ECHRB?[37] The answer is that it most probably would. Whereas Art 8 ECHRB provides for emergency intervention, Art 7 specifically prevents State interference in all situations except where *serious* harm might otherwise befall a patient. Routine forcible medication would not be covered, due to the insertion into the ECHRB of a set of safeguards protecting the vulnerable and contained in Arts 6

---

32   App No 20527/92 (1993), unreported; 244 (1992) Com Rep, para 254.

33   For further discussion of euthanasia in relation to the ECHR and the HRA 1998, see Sapiro and Ungoed-Thomas, Chapter 17, above.

34   For further discussion on the implications of such treatment by the State as regards its obligations to preserve life under Art 2, see Harris, O'Boyle and Warbrick, 1995, pp 72–73.

35   *Herczegfalvy v Austria* (1993) 15 EHRR 437.

36   *Ibid*, para 82, p 484.

37   For further discussion of mental health law and human rights, see Davidson, Chapters 11 and 12, above.

and 16.[38] The legal burden of proving the *sufficiency* of harm rests with the State and now has a clear statutory footing.

Other current areas of ethical controversy which could have clear implications as regards Art 2 of the ECHR, but which have not so far been considered under the ECHR, include embryonic and foetal research, which is now the subject of regulation under the ECHRB,[39] and 'maternal responsibility' during pregnancy, which is not.[40]

This may also be linked to Arts 8 and 12 of the ECHR, which provide respectively for the right to respect for one's family and private life, and the right to marry and to found a family. On this point, the well publicised *Blood* case[41] might have raised issues in that arena in relation to a plethora of rights specifically protected by the ECHR, such as the right to life, respect for family and private life, and the right to marry and found a family.[42]

Blood concerned a wife's right to access to her dead husband's sperm, taken from him whilst he was in a comatose state, and then stored at a licensed clinic. The relevant UK statute, the Human Fertilisation and Embryology Act 1990, prevented Mrs Blood from gaining access to the sperm in the absence of the donor's express consent, but the situation was resolved domestically without recourse to the European Court. Pragmatically, the Court of Appeal upheld the clinic's statutory objections to treating her. However, in doing so, it declared that its refusal to release the sperm to a Belgian clinic where Mrs Blood might be treated, ran contrary to her right to receive medical services abroad, as protected by the European Community Treaty.[43] If this case had reached the European Court when the ECHRB was in operation, it might have specifically addressed not only the above issues raised under the ECHR, but also some of the attendant ethical implications involving Art 5 of the ECHRB, which is concerned expressly with consent. The UK in its defence could have relied upon the husband's failure to provide 'free and informed consent' as required under Art 5, to the procedure leading to the removal of his sperm in the first place.

The above examples provide a snapshot of the potential for further exploration of current areas of biomedical controversy, but what of the practical possibility of using the system to bring a court action successfully?

---

38   Eg, Art 6(3) provides that the State may only intervene where the adult concerned is, *inter alia*, mentally disabled, when 'the authorisation of his or her representative or an authority or a person or body provided by the law' is obtained.

39   ECHRB, Art 18. See McColgan, 2000.

40   For further discussion of beginning of life issues in relation to human rights, see Stauch, Chapter 16, above.

41   *R v Human Fertilisation and Embryology Authority ex p Blood* [1997] 2 FLR 742 QBD and CA.

42   ECHR, Arts 2, 8 and 12 respectively.

43   Based on Arts 49 and 50.

USING THE ECHRB IN THE UK

There are important limits to the ability of the new Convention on Biomedicine to protect rights in the field of biotechnology. The principal constraint is the large amount of residual discretionary power enjoyed by each ratifying State. This has been purposely built into the instrument in order to accommodate the wishes of those States wishing to retain tighter measures of control at national level in what has proven to be a highly controversial area, while at the same time establishing acceptable minimum standards in Europe.

The other clear restriction on the instrument's utility is the fact that, where a State fails to adhere to its obligations, the enforcement procedure established by the ECHR may only be utilised where the infringement in question simultaneously breaches the ECHR itself. The ECHRB will also inevitably suffer from the other inherent flaws of the Strasbourg system. One such weakness is that the Council of Europe does not insist that the ECHR, although now widely ratified, necessarily needs to be incorporated. This gives rise to the age old problem concerning the status of the ECHR within national legal systems.[44]

The Council of Europe like any other international organisation responsible for developing global or regional standards, is unable to insist upon incorporation into domestic legal systems. Here, the UK Parliament, albeit belatedly in comparison with other European States, has incorporated the bulk of rights protected under the ECHR and confers on those provisions binding legal effect, where previously they had enjoyed only persuasive moral authority in the domestic forum. How then does an aggrieved individual living in Britain utilise this system to ensure his or her views are fully aired in court?

---

44 For monist States with a written constitution, all instruments of international law automatically become part of the law of that State, once the instrument in question has been ratified. However, even where this is the case, the level of protection accorded still differs from State to State, in order to accommodate the unique legislative heritage of each contracting party. For example, in Germany, the ECHR has the status of ordinary domestic law and, in Austria, of constitutional law. In France, the ECHR has a status that is higher than ordinary legislation but lower than the Constitution. On the other hand, the UK as a dualist State having an unwritten constitution, does not treat international law, whether ratified or not, as constituting part of national law, until that law is incorporated into domestic law by an enabling statute.

THE HRA 1998

An individual's liberty and attendant rights and freedoms are clearly better protected when substantive rights guaranteed by international Conventions are enforceable in national courts. Unfortunately, the Convention on biomedicine has not yet been ratified in the UK. This lack of recognition by the UK has resulted in a series of potential problems for any individual seeking to find redress in a court in the UK.

Past British governments have argued that the rights guaranteed by the ECHR are already protected in domestic law by a combination of rights and remedies.[45] Unfortunately, this attitude has traditionally meant that when domestic law falls short of the requirements of the ECHR, and an issue cannot be resolved at domestic level by national courts, the result has been a virtual stampede of individuals taking their complaints to Strasbourg.[46] This unsatisfactory situation has largely been remedied by the HRA 1998 which came into force on 2 October 2000. The new statute is useful to the present discussion insofar as it incorporates most, but not all, of the provisions of the ECHR. It represents a loose translation of the majority of obligations accepted by ratifying States under the ECHR, excepting Art 13, which guarantees the individual a right to an effective remedy in a domestic context.[47] The UK is alone in this omission and has been condemned because of it, insofar as it places the UK courts in the invidious position of being able to find in favour of complainants where breaches occur, but unable to afford redress, if domestic statutes do not permit this. Some individuals will still, therefore, have to consider taking the time consuming and frequently costly, Strasbourg route, when failing to achieve satisfaction before national courts.

These criticisms apart, can the Act play any part in securing the rights of individuals rights under the ECHRB? The answer to this is a qualified 'yes'. As previously discussed, the ECHR will be of use to an individual claiming violation of a provision of both the ECHRB and the ECHR itself, but will not be of use where the alleged violation is simply of the former Convention alone. In such a case, the individual concerned will have to rely on national remedies decided upon at the discretion of the State concerned. In any domestic case where alleged breaches of the ECHR occur, then, to quote John

---

45 This view is based upon the views of Dicey, 1959, and are discussed at some length by Puddephat, 1999.

46 Indeed, during the period 1 January to 31 December 1998, 290 provisional files were opened, detailing complaints against the UK and 588 applications were pending as of 1 January 1999. This gives the UK one of the highest rates of complaint, although other States such as Italy, France and Germany had higher levels of complaint during that period. (Source: ECHR website: www.dhcour.coe.fr.)

47 Puddephat, 1997.

Wadham, 'the interpretive obligation [on national courts] does not create free standing rights'. Although this statement could be viewed with some degree of pessimism, he does, however, go on to affirm that:

> ... in cases between private individuals as well as those between an individual and the state, a United Kingdom court (as a public authority) will be obliged to act in a way which is compatible with the Convention, by interpreting statute and common law consistently with it wherever possible, and by exercising judicial discretion compatibly with it.[48]

Nonetheless, it would be beneficial if the UK Government would consider the future ratification of the ECHRB and incorporation of some of the basic rights it safeguards, in order to maximise the level of protection afforded to individuals in this country in the area of biomedicine and biotechnology.

CONCLUSIONS

Biotechnology continues to be a rapidly expanding economic sector of particular importance within Europe, and brings in its wake enormous social and human challenges. Scientific research and medical practice have, thus far, been able to develop in many European States without effective State regulation or debate. National governments and institutions, such as the EU, have been unwilling or unable to tackle the issue of biotechnology as a result of a number of political, economic and social reasons.

As evidenced above, both the compliance system envisaged by the ECHRB and the Council of Europe's own enforcement systems, have several inherent shortcomings. In spite of these, the ECHRB provides much needed parameters in an area of increasing concern from a global human rights perspective. The Council of Europe is a democratic, intergovernmental body and its political and judicial institutions possess a wealth of theoretical and practical experience in the continual evolution of a canon of human rights law of universal significance. The new regulatory framework has much potential. It can assist those European decision makers who are its signatories in safeguarding their citizens' human rights in the area of health and biotechnology. It can also initiate debate on the wide range of ethical issues biotechnology gives rise to, thus, helping to engender appropriate national policy and law based on the common values espoused by the Biomedicine Convention.

The Council of Europe has gone some way to grasping the nettle that is biomedicine. It is to be hoped that contracting parties to the ECHRB may be relied upon to demonstrate at least the same degree of tenacity where enforcement is concerned. Likewise, until such time as the HRA 1998 fully

---

48   Wadham, 1999, p 33.

incorporates the ECHRB, then those living in the UK seeking to protect rights raised by biotechnology and biomedicine will need to be creative in their pursuit of an effective remedy in the European Court.

THE HUMAN RIGHTS ACT 1998

1998 Chapter 42 – continued

An Act to give further effect to rights and freedoms guaranteed under the European Convention on Human Rights; to make provision with respect to holders of certain judicial offices who become judges of the European Court of Human Rights; and for connected purposes.

[9th November 1998]

BE IT ENACTED by the Queen's most Excellent Majesty, by and with the advice and consent of the Lords Spiritual and Temporal, and Commons, in this present Parliament assembled, and by the authority of the same, as follows:–

Introduction

The Convention Rights

1.– (1) In this Act 'the Convention rights' means the rights and fundamental freedoms set out in –

(a) Articles 2 to 12 and 14 of the Convention,

(b) Articles 1 to 3 of the First Protocol, and

(c) Articles 1 and 2 of the Sixth Protocol as read with Articles 16 to 18 of the Convention.

(2) Those Articles are to have effect for the purposes of this Act subject to any designated derogation or reservation (as to which see sections 14 and 15).

(3) The Articles are set out in Schedule 1.

(4) The Secretary of State may by order make such amendments to this Act as he considers appropriate to reflect the effect, in relation to the United Kingdom, of a protocol.

(5) In subsection (4) 'protocol' means a protocol to the Convention –

(a) which the United Kingdom has ratified; or

(b) which the United Kingdom has signed with a view to ratification.

(6) No amendment may be made by an order under subsection (4) so as to come into force before the protocol concerned is in force in relation to the United Kingdom.

Interpretation of Convention rights

2.– (1) A court or tribunal determining a question which has arisen in connection with a Convention right must take into account any –

(a) judgment, decision, declaration or advisory opinion of the European Court of Human Rights,

(b) opinion of the Commission given in a report adopted under Article 31 of the Convention,

(c) decision of the Commission in connection with Article 26 or 27(2) of the Convention, or

(d) decision of the Committee of Ministers taken under Article 46 of the Convention, whenever made or given, so far as, in the opinion of the court or tribunal, it is relevant to the proceedings in which that question has arisen.

(2) Evidence of any judgment, decision, declaration or opinion of which account may have to be taken under this section is to be given in proceedings before any court or tribunal in such manner as may be provided by rules.

(3) In this section 'rules' means rules of court or, in the case of proceedings before a tribunal, rules made for the purposes of this section –

(a) by the Lord Chancellor or the Secretary of State, in relation to any proceedings outside Scotland;

(b) by the Secretary of State, in relation to proceedings in Scotland; or

(c) by a Northern Ireland department, in relation to proceedings before a tribunal in Northern Ireland –

(i) which deals with transferred matters; and

(ii) for which no rules made under paragraph (a) are in force.

Legislation

Interpretation of legislation

3.– (1) So far as it is possible to do so, primary legislation and subordinate legislation must be read and given effect in a way which is compatible with the Convention rights.

(2) This section –

(a) applies to primary legislation and subordinate legislation whenever enacted;

(b) does not affect the validity, continuing operation or enforcement of any incompatible primary legislation; and

(c) does not affect the validity, continuing operation or enforcement of any incompatible subordinate legislation if (disregarding any possibility of revocation) primary legislation prevents removal of the incompatibility.

Declaration of incompatibility

4.– (1) Subsection (2) applies in any proceedings in which a court determines whether a provision of primary legislation is compatible with a Convention right.

(2) If the court is satisfied that the provision is incompatible with a Convention right, it may make a declaration of that incompatibility.

(3) Subsection (4) applies in any proceedings in which a court determines whether a provision of subordinate legislation, made in the exercise of a power conferred by primary legislation, is compatible with a Convention right.

(4) If the court is satisfied –

(a) that the provision is incompatible with a Convention right, and

(b) that (disregarding any possibility of revocation) the primary legislation concerned prevents removal of the incompatibility, it may make a declaration of that incompatibility.

(5) In this section 'court' means –

(a) the House of Lords;

(b) the Judicial Committee of the Privy Council;

(c) the Courts-Martial Appeal Court;

(d) in Scotland, the High Court of Justiciary sitting otherwise than as a trial court or the Court of Session;

(e) in England and Wales or Northern Ireland, the High Court or the Court of Appeal.

(6) A declaration under this section ('a declaration of incompatibility') –

(a) does not affect the validity, continuing operation or enforcement of the provision in respect of which it is given; and

(b) is not binding on the parties to the proceedings in which it is made. Right of Crown to intervene.

5.– (1) Where a court is considering whether to make a declaration of incompatibility, the Crown is entitled to notice in accordance with rules of court.

(2) In any case to which subsection (1) applies –

(a) a Minister of the Crown (or a person nominated by him),

(b) a member of the Scottish Executive,

(c) a Northern Ireland Minister,

(d) a Northern Ireland department,

is entitled, on giving notice in accordance with rules of court, to be joined as a party to the proceedings.

(3) Notice under subsection (2) may be given at any time during the proceedings.

(4) A person who has been made a party to criminal proceedings (other than in Scotland) as the result of a notice under subsection (2) may, with leave, appeal to the House of Lords against any declaration of incompatibility made in the proceedings.

(5) In subsection (4) –

'criminal proceedings' includes all proceedings before the Courts-Martial Appeal Court; and

'leave' means leave granted by the court making the declaration of incompatibility or by the House of Lords.

Public Authorities

Acts of public authorities

6.– (1) It is unlawful for a public authority to act in a way which is incompatible with a Convention right.

(2) Subsection (1) does not apply to an act if –

(a) as the result of one or more provisions of primary legislation, the authority could not have acted differently; or

(b) in the case of one or more provisions of, or made under, primary legislation which cannot be read or given effect in a way which is compatible with the Convention rights, the authority was acting so as to give effect to or enforce those provisions.

(3) In this section 'public authority' includes –

(a) a court or tribunal, and

(b) any person certain of whose functions are functions of a public nature but does not include either House of Parliament or a person exercising functions in connection with proceedings in Parliament.

(4) In subsection (3) 'Parliament' does not include the House of Lords in its judicial capacity.

(5) In relation to a particular act, a person is not a public authority by virtue only of subsection (3)(b) if the nature of the act is private.

(6) 'An act' includes a failure to act but does not include a failure to –

(a) introduce in, or lay before, Parliament a proposal for legislation; or

(b) make any primary legislation or remedial order.

Proceedings

7.– (1) A person who claims that a public authority has acted (or proposes to act) in a way which is made unlawful by section 6(1) may –

(a) bring proceedings against the authority under this Act in the appropriate court or tribunal, or

(b) rely on the Convention right or rights concerned in any legal proceedings, but only if he is (or would be) a victim of the unlawful act.

(2) In subsection (1)(a) 'appropriate court or tribunal' means such court or tribunal as may be determined in accordance with rules; and proceedings against an authority include a counterclaim or similar proceeding.

(3) If the proceedings are brought on an application for judicial review, the applicant is to be taken to have a sufficient interest in relation to the unlawful act only if he is, or would be, a victim of that act.

(4) If the proceedings are made by way of a petition for judicial review in Scotland, the applicant shall be taken to have title and interest to sue in relation to the unlawful act only if he is, or would be, a victim of that act.

(5) Proceedings under subsection (1)(a) must be brought before the end of –

(a) the period of one year beginning with the date on which the act complained of took place; or

(b) such longer period as the court or tribunal considers equitable having regard to all the circumstances, but that is subject to any rule imposing a stricter time limit in relation to the procedure in question.

(6) In subsection (1)(b) 'legal proceedings' includes –

(a) proceedings brought by or at the instigation of a public authority; and

(b) an appeal against the decision of a court or tribunal.

(7) For the purposes of this section, a person is a victim of an unlawful act only if he would be a victim for the purposes of Article 34 of the Convention if proceedings were brought in the European Court of Human Rights in respect of that act.

(8) Nothing in this Act creates a criminal offence.

(9) In this section 'rules' means –

(a) in relation to proceedings before a court or tribunal outside Scotland, rules made by the Lord Chancellor or the Secretary of State for the purposes of this section or rules of court,

(b) in relation to proceedings before a court or tribunal in Scotland, rules made by the Secretary of State for those purposes,

(c) in relation to proceedings before a tribunal in Northern Ireland –

(i) which deals with transferred matters; and

(ii) for which no rules made under paragraph (a) are in force, rules made by a Northern Ireland department for those purposes, and includes provision made by order under section 1 of the Courts and Legal Services Act 1990.

(10) In making rules, regard must be had to section 9.

(11) The Minister who has power to make rules in relation to a particular tribunal may, to the extent he considers it necessary to ensure that the

tribunal can provide an appropriate remedy in relation to an act (or proposed act) of a public authority which is (or would be) unlawful as a result of section 6(1), by order add to –

(a) the relief or remedies which the tribunal may grant; or

(b) the grounds on which it may grant any of them.

(12) An order made under subsection (11) may contain such incidental, supplemental, consequential or transitional provision as the Minister making it considers appropriate

(13) 'The Minister' includes the Northern Ireland department concerned.

Judicial remedies

8.– (1) In relation to any act (or proposed act) of a public authority which the court finds is (or would be) unlawful, it may grant such relief or remedy, or make such order, within its powers as it considers just and appropriate.

(2) But damages may be awarded only by a court which has power to award damages, or to order the payment of compensation, in civil proceedings.

(3) No award of damages is to be made unless, taking account of all the circumstances of the case, including –

(a) any other relief or remedy granted, or order made, in relation to the act in question (by that or any other court), and

(b) the consequences of any decision (of that or any other court) in respect of that act, the court is satisfied that the award is necessary to afford just satisfaction to the person in whose favour it is made.

(4) In determining –

(a) whether to award damages, or

(b) the amount of an award,

the court must take into account the principles applied by the European Court of Human Rights in relation to the award of compensation under Article 41 of the Convention.

(5) A public authority against which damages are awarded is to be treated –

(a) in Scotland, for the purposes of section 3 of the Law Reform (Miscellaneous Provisions) (Scotland) Act 1940 as if the award were made in an action of damages in which the authority has been found liable in respect of loss or damage to the person to whom the award is made;

(b) for the purposes of the Civil Liability (Contribution) Act 1978 as liable in respect of damage suffered by the person to whom the award is made.

(6) In this section –

'court' includes a tribunal;

'damages' means damages for an unlawful act of a public authority; and

'unlawful' means unlawful under section 6(1).

Judicial acts

9.– (1) Proceedings under section 7(1)(a) in respect of a judicial act may be brought only –

(a) by exercising a right of appeal;

(b) on an application (in Scotland a petition) for judicial review; or

(c) in such other forum as may be prescribed by rules.

(2) That does not affect any rule of law which prevents a court from being the subject of judicial review.

(3) In proceedings under this Act in respect of a judicial act done in good faith, damages may not be awarded otherwise than to compensate a person to the extent required by Article 5(5) of the Convention.

(4) An award of damages permitted by subsection (3) is to be made against the Crown; but no award may be made unless the appropriate person, if not a party to the proceedings, is joined.

(5) In this section –

'appropriate person' means the Minister responsible for the court concerned, or a person or government department nominated by him;

'court' includes a tribunal;

'judge' includes a member of a tribunal, a justice of the peace and a clerk or other officer entitled to exercise the jurisdiction of a court;

'judicial act' means a judicial act of a court and includes an act done on the instructions, or on behalf, of a judge; and

'rules' has the same meaning as in section 7(9).

Remedial action

Power to take remedial action

10.– (1) This section applies if –

(a) a provision of legislation has been declared under section 4 to be incompatible with a Convention right and, if an appeal lies –

(i) all persons who may appeal have stated in writing that they do not intend to do so;

(ii) the time for bringing an appeal has expired and no appeal has been brought within that time; or

(iii) an appeal brought within that time has been determined or abandoned; or

(b) it appears to a Minister of the Crown or Her Majesty in Council that, having regard to a finding of the European Court of Human Rights made after the coming into force of this section in proceedings against the United Kingdom, a provision of legislation is incompatible with an obligation of the United Kingdom arising from the Convention.

(2) If a Minister of the Crown considers that there are compelling reasons for proceeding under this section, he may by order make such amendments to the legislation as he considers necessary to remove the incompatibility.

(3) If, in the case of subordinate legislation, a Minister of the Crown considers –

(a) that it is necessary to amend the primary legislation under which the subordinate legislation in question was made, in order to enable the incompatibility to be removed, and

(b) that there are compelling reasons for proceeding under this section, he may by order make such amendments to the primary legislation as he considers necessary.

(4) This section also applies where the provision in question is in subordinate legislation and has been quashed, or declared invalid, by reason of incompatibility with a Convention right and the Minister proposes to proceed under paragraph 2(b) of Schedule 2.

(5) If the legislation is an Order in Council, the power conferred by subsection (2) or (3) is exercisable by Her Majesty in Council.

(6) In this section 'legislation' does not include a Measure of the Church Assembly or of the General Synod of the Church of England.

(7) Schedule 2 makes further provision about remedial orders.

Other rights and proceedings

Safeguard for existing human rights

11.– A person's reliance on a Convention right does not restrict –

(a) any other right or freedom conferred on him by or under any law having effect in any part of the United Kingdom; or

(b) his right to make any claim or bring any proceedings which he could make or bring apart from sections 7 to 9.

Freedom of expression

12.– (1) This section applies if a court is considering whether to grant any relief which, if granted, might affect the exercise of the Convention right to freedom of expression.

(2) If the person against whom the application for relief is made ('the respondent') is neither present nor represented, no such relief is to be granted unless the court is satisfied –

(a) that the applicant has taken all practicable steps to notify the respondent; or

(b) that there are compelling reasons why the respondent should not be notified.

(3) No such relief is to be granted so as to restrain publication before trial unless the court is satisfied that the applicant is likely to establish that publication should not be allowed.

(4) The court must have particular regard to the importance of the Convention right to freedom of expression and, where the proceedings relate to material which the respondent claims, or which appears to the court, to be journalistic, literary or artistic material (or to conduct connected with such material), to –

    (a) the extent to which –

        (i) the material has, or is about to, become available to the public; or

        (ii) it is, or would be, in the public interest for the material to be published;

    (b) any relevant privacy code.

(5) In this section –

'court' includes a tribunal; and

'relief' includes any remedy or order (other than in criminal proceedings).

Freedom of thought, conscience and religion

13.– (1) If a court's determination of any question arising under this Act might affect the exercise by a religious organisation (itself or its members collectively) of the Convention right to freedom of thought, conscience and religion, it must have particular regard to the importance of that right.

(2) In this section 'court' includes a tribunal.

Derogations and reservations

Derogations

14.– (1) In this Act 'designated derogation' means –

    (a) the United Kingdom's derogation from Article 5(3) of the Convention; and

    (b) any derogation by the United Kingdom from an Article of the Convention, or of any protocol to the Convention, which is designated for the purposes of this Act in an order made by the Secretary of State.

(2) The derogation referred to in subsection (1)(a) is set out in Part I of Schedule 3.

(3) If a designated derogation is amended or replaced it ceases to be a designated derogation.

(4) But subsection (3) does not prevent the Secretary of State from exercising his power under subsection (1)(b) to make a fresh designation order in respect of the Article concerned.

(5) The Secretary of State must by order make such amendments to Schedule 3 as he considers appropriate to reflect –

(a) any designation order; or

(b) the effect of subsection (3).

(6) A designation order may be made in anticipation of the making by the United Kingdom of a proposed derogation.

Reservations

15.– (1) In this Act 'designated reservation' means –

(a) the United Kingdom's reservation to Article 2 of the First Protocol to the Convention; and

(b) any other reservation by the United Kingdom to an Article of the Convention, or of any protocol to the Convention, which is designated for the purposes of this Act in an order made by the Secretary of State.

(2) The text of the reservation referred to in subsection (1)(a) is set out in Part II of Schedule 3.

(3) If a designated reservation is withdrawn wholly or in part it ceases to be a designated reservation.

(4) But subsection (3) does not prevent the Secretary of State from exercising his power under subsection (1)(b) to make a fresh designation order in respect of the Article concerned.

(5) The Secretary of State must by order make such amendments to this Act as he considers appropriate to reflect –

(a) any designation order; or

(b) the effect of subsection (3).

Period for which designated derogations have effect

16.– (1) If it has not already been withdrawn by the United Kingdom, a designated derogation ceases to have effect for the purposes of this Act –

(a) in the case of the derogation referred to in section 14(1)(a), at the end of the period of five years beginning with the date on which section 1(2) came into force;

(b) in the case of any other derogation, at the end of the period of five years beginning with the date on which the order designating it was made.

(2) At any time before the period –

(a) fixed by subsection (1)(a) or (b), or

(b) extended by an order under this subsection, comes to an end, the Secretary of State may by order extend it by a further period of five years.

(3) An order under section 14(1)(b) ceases to have effect at the end of the period for consideration, unless a resolution has been passed by each House approving the order.

(4) Subsection (3) does not affect –

(a) anything done in reliance on the order; or

(b) the power to make a fresh order under section 14(1)(b).

(5) In subsection (3) 'period for consideration' means the period of forty days beginning with the day on which the order was made.

(6) In calculating the period for consideration, no account is to be taken of any time during which –

(a) Parliament is dissolved or prorogued; or

(b) both Houses are adjourned for more than four days.

(7) If a designated derogation is withdrawn by the United Kingdom, the Secretary of State must by order make such amendments to this Act as he considers are required to reflect that withdrawal.

Periodic review of designated reservations

17.– (1) The appropriate Minister must review the designated reservation referred to in section 15(1)(a) –

(a) before the end of the period of five years beginning with the date on which section 1(2) came into force; and

(b) if that designation is still in force, before the end of the period of five years beginning with the date on which the last report relating to it was laid under subsection (3).

(2) The appropriate Minister must review each of the other designated reservations (if any) –

(a) before the end of the period of five years beginning with the date on which the order designating the reservation first came into force; and

(b) if the designation is still in force, before the end of the period of five years beginning with the date on which the last report relating to it was laid under subsection (3).

(3) The Minister conducting a review under this section must prepare a report on the result of the review and lay a copy of it before each House of Parliament.

Judges of the European Court of Human Rights

Appointment to European Court of Human Rights

18.– (1) In this section 'judicial office' means the office of –

(a) Lord Justice of Appeal, Justice of the High Court or Circuit judge, in England and Wales;

(b) judge of the Court of Session or sheriff, in Scotland;

    (c) Lord Justice of Appeal, judge of the High Court or county court judge, in Northern Ireland.

(2) The holder of a judicial office may become a judge of the European Court of Human Rights ('the Court') without being required to relinquish his office.

(3) But he is not required to perform the duties of his judicial office while he is a judge of the Court.

(4) In respect of any period during which he is a judge of the Court –

    (a) a Lord Justice of Appeal or Justice of the High Court is not to count as a judge of the relevant court for the purposes of section 2(1) or 4(1) of the Supreme Court Act 1981 (maximum number of judges) nor as a judge of the Supreme Court for the purposes of section 12(1) to (6) of that Act (salaries etc);

    (b) a judge of the Court of Session is not to count as a judge of that court for the purposes of section 1(1) of the Court of Session Act 1988 (maximum number of judges) or of section 9(1)(c) of the Administration of Justice Act 1973 ('the 1973 Act') (salaries etc);

    (c) a Lord Justice of Appeal or judge of the High Court in Northern Ireland is not to count as a judge of the relevant court for the purposes of section 2(1) or 3(1) of the Judicature (Northern Ireland) Act 1978 (maximum number of judges) nor as a judge of the Supreme Court of Northern Ireland for the purposes of section 9(1)(d) of the 1973 Act (salaries etc);

    (d) a Circuit judge is not to count as such for the purposes of section 18 of the Courts Act 1971 (salaries etc);

    (e) a sheriff is not to count as such for the purposes of section 14 of the Sheriff Courts (Scotland) Act 1907 (salaries etc);

    (f) a county court judge of Northern Ireland is not to count as such for the purposes of section 106 of the County Courts Act Northern Ireland) 1959 (salaries etc).

(5) If a sheriff principal is appointed a judge of the Court, section 11(1) of the Sheriff Courts (Scotland) Act 1971 (temporary appointment of sheriff principal) applies, while he holds that appointment, as if his office is vacant.

(6) Schedule 4 makes provision about judicial pensions in relation to the holder of a judicial office who serves as a judge of the Court.

(7) The Lord Chancellor or the Secretary of State may by order make such transitional provision (including, in particular, provision for a temporary increase in the maximum number of judges) as he considers appropriate in relation to any holder of a judicial office who has completed his service as a judge of the Court.

Parliamentary procedure

Statements of compatibility

19.– (1) A Minister of the Crown in charge of a Bill in either House of Parliament must, before Second Reading of the Bill –

(a) make a statement to the effect that in his view the provisions of the Bill are compatible with the Convention rights ('a statement of compatibility'); or

(b) make a statement to the effect that although he is unable to make a statement of compatibility the government nevertheless wishes the House to proceed with the Bill.

(2) The statement must be in writing and be published in such manner as the Minister making it considers appropriate.

Supplemental Orders etc under this Act

20.– (1) Any power of a Minister of the Crown to make an order under this Act is exercisable by statutory instrument.

(2) The power of the Lord Chancellor or the Secretary of State to make rules (other than rules of court) under section 2(3) or 7(9) is exercisable by statutory instrument.

(3) Any statutory instrument made under section 14, 15 or 16(7) must be laid before Parliament.

(4) No order may be made by the Lord Chancellor or the Secretary of State under section 1(4), 7(11) or 16(2) unless a draft of the order has been laid before, and approved by, each House of Parliament.

(5) Any statutory instrument made under section 18(7) or Schedule 4, or to which subsection (2) applies, shall be subject to annulment in pursuance of a resolution of either House of Parliament.

(6) The power of a Northern Ireland department to make –

(a) rules under section 2(3)(c) or 7(9)(c), or

(b) an order under section 7(11),

is exercisable by statutory rule for the purposes of the Statutory Rules (Northern Ireland) Order 1979.

(7) Any rules made under section 2(3)(c) or 7(9)(c) shall be subject to negative resolution; and section 41(6) of the Interpretation Act (Northern Ireland) 1954 (meaning of 'subject to negative resolution') shall apply as if the power to make the rules were conferred by an Act of the Northern Ireland Assembly.

(8) No order may be made by a Northern Ireland department under section 7(11) unless a draft of the order has been laid before, and approved by, the Northern Ireland Assembly.

Interpretation, etc

21.–(1) In this Act –

'amend' includes repeal and apply (with or without modifications);

'the appropriate Minister' means the Minister of the Crown having charge of the appropriate authorised government department (within the meaning of the Crown Proceedings Act 1947);

'the Commission' means the European Commission of Human Rights;

'the Convention' means the Convention for the Protection of Human Rights and Fundamental Freedoms, agreed by the Council of Europe at Rome on 4th November 1950 as it has effect for the time being in relation to the United Kingdom;

'declaration of incompatibility' means a declaration under section 4;

'Minister of the Crown' has the same meaning as in the Ministers of the Crown Act 1975;

'Northern Ireland Minister' includes the First Minister and the deputy First Minister in Northern Ireland;

'primary legislation' means any –

(a) public general Act;

(b) local and personal Act;

(c) private Act;

(d) Measure of the Church Assembly;

(e) Measure of the General Synod of the Church of England;

(f) Order in Council –

(i) made in exercise of Her Majesty's Royal Prerogative;

(ii) made under section 38(1)(a) of the Northern Ireland Constitution Act 1973 or the corresponding provision of the Northern Ireland Act 1998; or

(iii) amending an Act of a kind mentioned in paragraph (a), (b) or (c); and includes an order or other instrument made under primary legislation (otherwise than by the National Assembly for Wales, a member of the Scottish Executive, a Northern Ireland Minister or a Northern Ireland department) to the extent to which it operates to bring one or more provisions of that legislation into force or amends any primary legislation;

'the First Protocol' means the protocol to the Convention agreed at Paris on 20th March 1952;

'the Sixth Protocol' means the protocol to the Convention agreed at Strasbourg on 28th April 1983;

'the Eleventh Protocol' means the protocol to the Convention (restructuring the control machinery established by the Convention) agreed at Strasbourg on 11th May 1994;

'remedial order' means an order under section 10;

'subordinate legislation' means any –

(a) Order in Council other than one –

    (i) made in exercise of Her Majesty's Royal Prerogative;

    (ii) made under section 38(1)(a) of the Northern Ireland Constitution Act 1973 or the corresponding provision of the Northern Ireland Act 1998; or

    (iii) amending an Act of a kind mentioned in the definition of primary legislation;

(b) Act of the Scottish Parliament;

(c) Act of the Parliament of Northern Ireland;

(d) Measure of the Assembly established under section 1 of the Northern Ireland Assembly Act 1973;

(e) Act of the Northern Ireland Assembly;

(f) order, rules, regulations, scheme, warrant, bylaw or other instrument made under primary legislation (except to the extent to which it operates to bring one or more provisions of that legislation into force or amends any primary legislation);

(g) order, rules, regulations, scheme, warrant, bylaw or other instrument made under legislation mentioned in paragraph (b), (c), (d) or (e) or made under an Order in Council applying only to Northern Ireland;

(h) order, rules, regulations, scheme, warrant, bylaw or other instrument made by a member of the Scottish Executive, a Northern Ireland Minister or a Northern Ireland department in exercise of prerogative or other executive functions of Her Majesty which are exercisable by such a person on behalf of Her Majesty;

'transferred matters' has the same meaning as in the Northern Ireland Act 1998; and

'tribunal' means any tribunal in which legal proceedings may be brought.

(2) The references in paragraphs (b) and (c) of section 2(1) to Articles are to Articles of the Convention as they had effect immediately before the coming into force of the Eleventh Protocol.

(3) The reference in paragraph (d) of section 2(1) to Article 46 includes a reference to Articles 32 and 54 of the Convention as they had effect immediately before the coming into force of the Eleventh Protocol.

(4) The references in section 2(1) to a report or decision of the Commission or a decision of the Committee of Ministers include references to a report or decision made as provided by paragraphs 3, 4 and 6 of Article 5 of the Eleventh Protocol (transitional provisions).

(5) Any liability under the Army Act 1955, the Air Force Act 1955 or the Naval Discipline Act 1957 to suffer death for an offence is replaced by a liability to imprisonment for life or any less punishment authorised by those Acts; and those Acts shall accordingly have effect with the necessary modifications.

Short title, commencement, application and extent

22.– (1) This Act may be cited as the Human Rights Act 1998.

(2) Sections 18, 20 and 21(5) and this section come into force on the passing of this Act.

(3) The other provisions of this Act come into force on such day as the Secretary of State may by order appoint; and different days may be appointed for different purposes.

(4) Paragraph (b) of subsection (1) of section 7 applies to proceedings brought by or at the instigation of a public authority whenever the act in question took place; but otherwise that subsection does not apply to an act taking place before the coming into force of that section.

(5) This Act binds the Crown.

(6) This Act extends to Northern Ireland.

(7) Section 21(5), so far as it relates to any provision contained in the Army Act 1955, the Air Force Act 1955 or the Naval Discipline Act 1957, extends to any place to which that provision extends.

SCHEDULES

Schedule 1

THE ARTICLES

PART I

THE CONVENTION RIGHTS AND FREEDOMS

ARTICLE 2

RIGHT TO LIFE

1.– Everyone's right to life shall be protected by law. No one shall be deprived of his life intentionally save in the execution of a sentence of a court following his conviction of a crime for which this penalty is provided by law.

2.– Deprivation of life shall not be regarded as inflicted in contravention of this Article when it results from the use of force which is no more than absolutely necessary:

(a) in defence of any person from unlawful violence;

(b) in order to effect a lawful arrest or to prevent the escape of a person lawfully detained;

(c) in action lawfully taken for the purpose of quelling a riot or insurrection.

ARTICLE 3

PROHIBITION OF TORTURE

No one shall be subjected to torture or to inhuman or degrading treatment or punishment.

ARTICLE 4

PROHIBITION OF SLAVERY AND FORCED LABOUR

1.– No one shall be held in slavery or servitude.

2.– No one shall be required to perform forced or compulsory labour.

3.– For the purpose of this Article the term 'forced or compulsory labour' shall not include:

    (a) any work required to be done in the ordinary course of detention imposed according to the provisions of Article 5 of this Convention or during conditional release from such detention;

    (b) any service of a military character or, in case of conscientious objectors in countries where they are recognised, service exacted instead of compulsory military service;

    (c) any service exacted in case of an emergency or calamity threatening the life or well-being of the community;

    (d) any work or service which forms part of normal civic obligations.

ARTICLE 5

RIGHT TO LIBERTY AND SECURITY

1.– Everyone has the right to liberty and security of person. No one shall be deprived of his liberty save in the following cases and in accordance with a procedure prescribed by law:

    (a) the lawful detention of a person after conviction by a competent court;

    (b) the lawful arrest or detention of a person for non-compliance with the lawful order of a court or in order to secure the fulfilment of any obligation prescribed by law;

    (c) the lawful arrest or detention of a person effected for the purpose of bringing him before the competent legal authority on reasonable suspicion of having committed an offence or when it is reasonably considered necessary to prevent his committing an offence or fleeing after having done so;

    (d) the detention of a minor by lawful order for the purpose of educational supervision or his lawful detention for the purpose of bringing him before the competent legal authority;

    (e) the lawful detention of persons for the prevention of the spreading of infectious diseases, of persons of unsound mind, alcoholics or drug addicts or vagrants;

(f) the lawful arrest or detention of a person to prevent his effecting an unauthorised entry into the country or of a person against whom action is being taken with a view to deportation or extradition.

2.– Everyone who is arrested shall be informed promptly, in a language which he understands, of the reasons for his arrest and of any charge against him.

3.– Everyone arrested or detained in accordance with the provisions of paragraph 1(c) of this Article shall be brought promptly before a judge or other officer authorised by law to exercise judicial power and shall be entitled to trial within a reasonable time or to release pending trial. Release may be conditioned by guarantees to appear for trial.

4.– Everyone who is deprived of his liberty by arrest or detention shall be entitled to take proceedings by which the lawfulness of his detention shall be decided speedily by a court and his release ordered if the detention is not lawful.

5.– Everyone who has been the victim of arrest or detention in contravention of the provisions of this Article shall have an enforceable right to compensation.

ARTICLE 6

RIGHT TO A FAIR TRIAL

1.– In the determination of his civil rights and obligations or of any criminal charge against him, everyone is entitled to a fair and public hearing within a reasonable time by an independent and impartial tribunal established by law. Judgment shall be pronounced publicly but the press and public may be excluded from all or part of the trial in the interest of morals, public order or national security in a democratic society, where the interests of juveniles or the protection of the private life of the parties so require, or to the extent strictly necessary in the opinion of the court in special circumstances where publicity would prejudice the interests of justice.

2.– Everyone charged with a criminal offence shall be presumed innocent until proved guilty according to law.

3.– Everyone charged with a criminal offence has the following minimum rights:

(a) to be informed promptly, in a language which he understands and in detail, of the nature and cause of the accusation against him;

(b) to have adequate time and facilities for the preparation of his defence;

(c) to defend himself in person or through legal assistance of his own choosing or, if he has not sufficient means to pay for legal assistance, to be given it free when the interests of justice so require;

(d) to examine or have examined witnesses against him and to obtain the attendance and examination of witnesses on his behalf under the same conditions as witnesses against him;

(e) to have the free assistance of an interpreter if he cannot understand or speak the language used in court.

ARTICLE 7

NO PUNISHMENT WITHOUT LAW

1.– No one shall be held guilty of any criminal offence on account of any act or omission which did not constitute a criminal offence under national or international law at the time when it was committed. Nor shall a heavier penalty be imposed than the one that was applicable at the time the criminal offence was committed.

2.– This Article shall not prejudice the trial and punishment of any person for any act or omission which, at the time when it was committed, was criminal according to the general principles of law recognised by civilised nations.

ARTICLE 8

RIGHT TO RESPECT FOR PRIVATE AND FAMILY LIFE

1.– Everyone has the right to respect for his private and family life, his home and his correspondence.

2.– There shall be no interference by a public authority with the exercise of this right except such as is in accordance with the law and is necessary in a democratic society in the interests of national security, public safety or the economic well-being of the country, for the prevention of disorder or crime, for the protection of health or morals, or for the protection of the rights and freedoms of others.

ARTICLE 9

FREEDOM OF THOUGHT, CONSCIENCE AND RELIGION

1.– Everyone has the right to freedom of thought, conscience and religion; this right includes freedom to change his religion or belief and freedom, either alone or in community with others and in public or private, to manifest his religion or belief, in worship, teaching, practice and observance.

2.– Freedom to manifest one's religion or beliefs shall be subject only to such limitations as are prescribed by law and are necessary in a democratic society in the interests of public safety, for the protection of public order, health or morals, or for the protection of the rights and freedoms of others.

ARTICLE 10

FREEDOM OF EXPRESSION

1.– Everyone has the right to freedom of expression. This right shall include freedom to hold opinions and to receive and impart information and ideas without interference by public authority and regardless of frontiers. This Article shall not prevent States from requiring the licensing of broadcasting, television or cinema enterprises.

2.– The exercise of these freedoms, since it carries with it duties and responsibilities, may be subject to such formalities, conditions, restrictions or penalties as are prescribed by law and are necessary in a democratic society, in the interests of national security, territorial integrity or public safety, for the prevention of disorder or crime, for the protection of health or morals, for the protection of the reputation or rights of others, for preventing the disclosure of information received in confidence, or for maintaining the authority and impartiality of the judiciary.

ARTICLE 11

FREEDOM OF ASSEMBLY AND ASSOCIATION

1.– Everyone has the right to freedom of peaceful assembly and to freedom of association with others, including the right to form and to join trade unions for the protection of his interests.

2.– No restrictions shall be placed on the exercise of these rights other than such as are prescribed by law and are necessary in a democratic society in the interests of national security or public safety, for the prevention of disorder or crime, for the protection of health or morals or for the protection of the rights and freedoms of others. This Article shall not prevent the imposition of lawful restrictions on the exercise of these rights by members of the armed forces, of the police or of the administration of the State.

ARTICLE 12

RIGHT TO MARRY

Men and women of marriageable age have the right to marry and to found a family, according to the national laws governing the exercise of this right.

ARTICLE 14

PROHIBITION OF DISCRIMINATION

The enjoyment of the rights and freedoms set forth in this Convention shall be secured without discrimination on any ground such as sex, race, colour, language, religion, political or other opinion, national or social origin, association with a national minority, property, birth or other status.

ARTICLE 16

RESTRICTIONS ON POLITICAL ACTIVITY OF ALIENS

Nothing in Articles 10, 11 and 14 shall be regarded as preventing the High Contracting Parties from imposing restrictions on the political activity of aliens.

ARTICLE 17

PROHIBITION OF ABUSE OF RIGHTS

Nothing in this Convention may be interpreted as implying for any State, group or person any right to engage in any activity or perform any act aimed at the destruction of any of the rights and freedoms set forth herein or at their limitation to a greater extent than is provided for in the Convention.

ARTICLE 18

LIMITATION ON USE OF RESTRICTIONS ON RIGHTS

The restrictions permitted under this Convention to the said rights and freedoms shall not be applied for any purpose other than those for which they have been prescribed.

PART II

THE FIRST PROTOCOL

ARTICLE 1

PROTECTION OF PROPERTY

Every natural or legal person is entitled to the peaceful enjoyment of his possessions. No one shall be deprived of his possessions except in the public interest and subject to the conditions provided for by law and by the general principles of international law.

The preceding provisions shall not, however, in any way impair the right of a State to enforce such laws as it deems necessary to control the use of property in accordance with the general interest or to secure the payment of taxes or other contributions or penalties.

ARTICLE 2

RIGHT TO EDUCATION

No person shall be denied the right to education. In the exercise of any functions which it assumes in relation to education and to teaching, the State shall respect the right of parents to ensure such education and teaching in conformity with their own religious and philosophical convictions.

ARTICLE 3

RIGHT TO FREE ELECTIONS

The High Contracting Parties undertake to hold free elections at reasonable intervals by secret ballot, under conditions which will ensure the free expression of the opinion of the people in the choice of the legislature.

PART III

THE SIXTH PROTOCOL

ARTICLE 1

ABOLITION OF THE DEATH PENALTY

The death penalty shall be abolished. No one shall be condemned to such penalty or executed.

ARTICLE 2

DEATH PENALTY IN TIME OF WAR

A State may make provision in its law for the death penalty in respect of acts committed in time of war or of imminent threat of war; such penalty shall be applied only in the instances laid down in the law and in accordance with its provisions. The State shall communicate to the Secretary General of the Council of Europe the relevant provisions of that law.

Schedule 2

REMEDIAL ORDERS

Orders

1.– (1) A remedial order may –

    (a) contain such incidental, supplemental, consequential or transitional provision as the person making it considers appropriate;

    (b) be made so as to have effect from a date earlier than that on which it is made;

    (c) make provision for the delegation of specific functions;

    (d) make different provision for different cases.

  (2) The power conferred by sub-paragraph (1)(a) includes –

    (a) power to amend primary legislation (including primary legislation other than that which contains the incompatible provision); and

    (b) power to amend or revoke subordinate legislation (including subordinate legislation other than that which contains the incompatible provision).

  (3) A remedial order may be made so as to have the same extent as the legislation which it affects.

  (4) No person is to be guilty of an offence solely as a result of the retrospective effect of a remedial order.

Procedure

2.– No remedial order may be made unless –

    (a) a draft of the order has been approved by a resolution of each House of Parliament made after the end of the period of 60 days beginning with the day on which the draft was laid; or

    (b) it is declared in the order that it appears to the person making it that, because of the urgency of the matter, it is necessary to make the order without a draft being so approved.

Orders laid in draft

3.– (1) No draft may be laid under paragraph 2(a) unless –

    (a) the person proposing to make the order has laid before Parliament a document which contains a draft of the proposed order and the required information; and

    (b) the period of 60 days, beginning with the day on which the document required by this sub-paragraph was laid, has ended.

  (2) If representations have been made during that period, the draft laid under paragraph 2(a) must be accompanied by a statement containing –

    (a) a summary of the representations; and

    (b) if, as a result of the representations, the proposed order has been changed, details of the changes.

Urgent cases

4.– (1) If a remedial order ('the original order') is made without being approved in draft, the person making it must lay it before Parliament, accompanied by the required information, after it is made.

  (2) If representations have been made during the period of 60 days beginning with the day on which the original order was made, the person making it must (after the end of that period) lay before Parliament a statement containing –

    (a) a summary of the representations; and

    (b) if, as a result of the representations, he considers it appropriate to make changes to the original order, details of the changes.

  (3) If sub-paragraph (2)(b) applies, the person making the statement must –

    (a) make a further remedial order replacing the original order; and

    (b) lay the replacement order before Parliament.

  (4) If, at the end of the period of 120 days beginning with the day on which the original order was made, a resolution has not been passed by each House approving the original or replacement order, the order ceases to have effect (but without that affecting anything previously done under either order or the power to make a fresh remedial order).

Definitions

5.– In this Schedule –

'representations' means representations about a remedial order (or proposed remedial order) made to the person making (or proposing to make) it and includes any relevant Parliamentary report or resolution; and

'required information' means –

    (a) an explanation of the incompatibility which the order (or proposed order) seeks to remove, including particulars of the relevant declaration, finding or order; and

(b) a statement of the reasons for proceeding under section 10 and for making an order in those terms.

Calculating periods

6.– In calculating any period for the purposes of this Schedule, no account is to be taken of any time during which –

(a) Parliament is dissolved or prorogued; or

(b) both Houses are adjourned for more than four days.

Schedule 3

DEROGATION AND RESERVATION

PART I

DEROGATION

The 1988 notification

The United Kingdom Permanent Representative to the Council of Europe presents his compliments to the Secretary General of the Council, and has the honour to convey the following information in order to ensure compliance with the obligations of Her Majesty's Government in the United Kingdom under Article 15(3) of the Convention for the Protection of Human Rights and Fundamental Freedoms signed at Rome on 4 November 1950.

There have been in the United Kingdom in recent years campaigns of organised terrorism connected with the affairs of Northern Ireland which have manifested themselves in activities which have included repeated murder, attempted murder, maiming, intimidation and violent civil disturbance and in bombing and fire raising which have resulted in death, injury and widespread destruction of property. As a result, a public emergency within the meaning of Article 15(1) of the Convention exists in the United Kingdom. The Government found it necessary in 1974 to introduce and since then, in cases concerning persons reasonably suspected of involvement in terrorism connected with the affairs of Northern Ireland, or of certain offences under the legislation, who have been detained for 48 hours, to exercise powers enabling further detention without charge, for periods of up to five days, on the authority of the Secretary of State. These powers are at present to be found in Section 12 of the Prevention of Terrorism (Temporary Provisions) Act 1984.

Article 9 of the Prevention of Terrorism (Supplemental Temporary Provisions) Order 1984 and Article 10 of the Prevention of Terrorism (Supplemental Temporary Provisions) (Northern Ireland) Order 1984.

Section 12 of the Prevention of Terrorism (Temporary Provisions) Act 1984 provides for a person whom a constable has arrested on reasonable grounds of suspecting him to be guilty of an offence under Section 1, 9 or 10 of the Act, or to be or to have been involved in terrorism connected with the affairs of Northern Ireland, to be detained in right of the arrest for up to 48 hours and thereafter, where the Secretary of State extends the detention period, for up to a further five days.

Section 12 substantially re-enacted Section 12 of the Prevention of Terrorism (Temporary Provisions) Act 1976 which, in turn, substantially re-enacted Section 7 of the Prevention of Terrorism (Temporary Provisions) Act 1974.

Article 10 of the Prevention of Terrorism (Supplemental Temporary Provisions) (Northern Ireland) Order 1984 (SI 1984/417) and Article 9 of the Prevention of Terrorism (Supplemental Temporary Provisions) Order 1984 (SI 1984/418) were both made under Sections 13 and 14 of and Schedule 3 to the 1984 Act and substantially re-enacted powers of detention in Orders made under the 1974 and 1976 Acts. A person who is being examined under Article 4 of either Order on his arrival in, or on seeking to leave, Northern Ireland or Great Britain for the purpose of determining whether he is or has been involved in terrorism connected with the affairs of Northern Ireland, or whether there are grounds for suspecting that he has committed an offence under Section 9 of the 1984 Act, may be detained under Article 9 or 10, as appropriate, pending the conclusion of his examination. The period of this examination may exceed 12 hours if an examining officer has reasonable grounds for suspecting him to be or to have been involved in acts of terrorism connected with the affairs of Northern Ireland.

Where such a person is detained under the said Article 9 or 10 he may be detained for up to 48 hours on the authority of an examining officer and thereafter, where the Secretary of State extends the detention period, for up to a further five days.

In its judgment of 29 November 1988 in the Case of Brogan and Others, the European Court of Human Rights held that there had been a violation of Article 5(3) in respect of each of the applicants, all of whom had been detained under Section 12 of the 1984 Act. The Court held that even the shortest of the four periods of detention concerned, namely four days and six hours, fell outside the constraints as to time permitted by the first part of Article 5(3). In addition, the Court held that there had been a violation of Article 5(5) in the case of each applicant.

Following this judgment, the Secretary of State for the Home Department informed Parliament on 6 December 1988 that, against the background of the terrorist campaign, and the over-riding need to bring terrorists to justice, the Government did not believe that the maximum period of detention should be reduced. He informed Parliament that the Government were examining the matter with a view to responding to the judgment. On 22 December 1988, the Secretary of State further informed Parliament that it remained the Government's wish, if it could be achieved, to find a judicial process under which extended detention might be reviewed and where appropriate authorised by a judge or other judicial officer. But a further period of reflection and consultation was necessary before the Government could bring forward a firm and final view.

Since the judgment of 29 November 1988 as well as previously, the Government have found it necessary to continue to exercise, in relation to terrorism connected with the affairs of Northern Ireland, the powers described above enabling further detention without charge for periods of up to 5 days, on the authority of the Secretary of State, to the extent strictly required by the exigencies of the situation to enable necessary enquiries and investigations properly to be completed in order to decide whether criminal proceedings should be instituted. To the extent that the exercise of these powers may be inconsistent with the obligations imposed by the Convention the Government has availed itself of the right of derogation conferred by Article 15(1) of the Convention and will continue to do so until further notice.

Dated 23 December 1988.

The 1989 notification

The United Kingdom Permanent Representative to the Council of Europe presents his compliments to the Secretary General of the Council, and has the honour to convey the following information. In his communication to the Secretary General of 23 December 1988, reference was made to the introduction and exercise of certain powers under section 12 of the Prevention of Terrorism (Temporary Provisions) Act 1984, Article 9 of the Prevention of Terrorism (Supplemental Temporary Provisions) Order 1984 and Article 10 of the Prevention of Terrorism (Supplemental Temporary Provisions) (Northern Ireland) Order 1984.

These provisions have been replaced by section 14 of and paragraph 6 of Schedule 5 to the Prevention of Terrorism (Temporary Provisions) Act 1989, which make comparable provision. They came into force on 22 March 1989. A copy of these provisions is enclosed.

The United Kingdom Permanent Representative avails himself of this opportunity to renew to the Secretary General the assurance of his highest consideration.

23 March 1989.

PART II

RESERVATION

At the time of signing the present (First) Protocol, I declare that, in view of certain provisions of the Education Acts in the United Kingdom, the principle affirmed in the second sentence of Article 2 is accepted by the United Kingdom only so far as it is compatible with the provision of efficient instruction and training, and the avoidance of unreasonable public expenditure.

Dated 20 March 1952.

Made by the United Kingdom Permanent Representative to the Council of Europe.

Schedule 4

JUDICIAL PENSIONS

Duty to make orders about pensions

1.– (1) The appropriate Minister must by order make provision with respect to pensions payable to or in respect of any holder of a judicial office who serves as an ECHR judge.

(2) A pensions order must include such provision as the Minister making it considers is necessary to secure that –

(a) an ECHR judge who was, immediately before his appointment as an ECHR judge, a member of a judicial pension scheme is entitled to remain as a member of that scheme;

(b) the terms on which he remains a member of the scheme are those which would have been applicable had he not been appointed as an ECHR judge; and

(c) entitlement to benefits payable in accordance with the scheme continues to be determined as if, while serving as an ECHR judge, his salary was that which would (but for section 18(4)) have been payable to him in respect of his continuing service as the holder of his judicial office.

Contributions

2.– A pensions order may, in particular, make provision –

(a) for any contributions which are payable by a person who remains a member of a scheme as a result of the order, and which would otherwise be payable by deduction from his salary, to be made otherwise than by deduction from his salary as an ECHR judge; and

(b) for such contributions to be collected in such manner as may be determined by the administrators of the scheme.

Amendments of other enactments

3.– A pensions order may amend any provision of, or made under, a pensions Act in such manner and to such extent as the Minister making the order considers necessary or expedient to ensure the proper administration of any scheme to which it relates.

Definitions

4.– In this Schedule –

'appropriate Minister' means –

(a) in relation to any judicial office whose jurisdiction is exercisable exclusively in relation to Scotland, the Secretary of State; and

(b) otherwise, the Lord Chancellor;

'ECHR judge' means the holder of a judicial office who is serving as a judge of the Court;

'judicial pension scheme' means a scheme established by and in accordance with a pensions Act;

'pensions Act' means –

(a) the County Courts Act (Northern Ireland) 1959;

(b) the Sheriffs' Pensions (Scotland) Act 1961;

(c) the Judicial Pensions Act 1981; or

(d) the Judicial Pensions and Retirement Act 1993; and

'pensions order' means an order made under paragraph 1.

CONVENTION FOR THE PROTECTION OF HUMAN RIGHTS AND DIGNITY OF THE HUMAN BEING WITH REGARD TO THE APPLICATION OF BIOLOGY AND MEDICINE: CONVENTION ON HUMAN RIGHTS AND BIOMEDICINE

Oviedo, 4.IV.1997

Protocol to the Convention (ETS 168)

Preamble

The member States of the Council of Europe, the other States and the European Community, signatories hereto,

Bearing in mind the Universal Declaration of Human Rights proclaimed by the General Assembly of the United Nations on 10 December 1948;

Bearing in mind the Convention for the Protection of Human Rights and Fundamental Freedoms of 4 November 1950;

Bearing in mind the European Social Charter of 18 October 1961;

Bearing in mind the International Covenant on Civil and Political Rights and the International Covenant on Economic, Social and Cultural Rights of 16 December 1966;

Bearing in mind the Convention for the Protection of Individuals with regard to Automatic Processing of Personal Data of 28 January 1981;

Bearing also in mind the Convention on the Rights of the Child of 20 November 1989;

Considering that the aim of the Council of Europe is the achievement of a greater unity between its members and that one of the methods by which that aim is to be pursued is the maintenance and further realisation of human rights and fundamental freedoms;

Conscious of the accelerating developments in biology and medicine;

Convinced of the need to respect the human being both as an individual and as a member of the human species and recognising the importance of ensuring the dignity of the human being;

Conscious that the misuse of biology and medicine may lead to acts endangering human dignity;

Affirming that progress in biology and medicine should be used for the benefit of present and future generations;

Stressing the need for international co-operation so that all humanity may enjoy the benefits of biology and medicine;

Recognising the importance of promoting a public debate on the questions posed by the application of biology and medicine and the responses to be given thereto;

Wishing to remind all members of society of their rights and responsibilities;

Taking account of the work of the Parliamentary Assembly in this field, including Recommendation 1160 (1991) on the preparation of a convention on bioethics;

Resolving to take such measures as are necessary to safeguard human dignity and the fundamental rights and freedoms of the individual with regard to the application of biology and medicine.

Have agreed as follows:

Chapter I – General provisions

Article 1 – Purpose and object

Parties to this Convention shall protect the dignity and identity of all human beings and guarantee everyone, without discrimination, respect for their integrity and other rights and fundamental freedoms with regard to the application of biology and medicine.

Each Party shall take in its internal law the necessary measures to give effect to the provisions of this Convention.

Article 2 – Primacy of the human being

The interests and welfare of the human being shall prevail over the sole interest of society or science.

Article 3 – Equitable access to health care

Parties, taking into account health needs and available resources, shall take appropriate measures with a view to providing, within their jurisdiction, equitable access to health care of appropriate quality.

Article 4 – Professional standards

Any intervention in the health field, including research, must be carried out in accordance with relevant professional obligations and standards.

Chapter II – Consent

Article 5 – General rule

An intervention in the health field may only be carried out after the person concerned has given free and informed consent to it.

This person shall beforehand be given appropriate information as to the purpose and nature of the intervention as well as on its consequences and risks.

The person concerned may freely withdraw consent at any time.

Article 6 – Protection of persons not able to consent

1. Subject to Articles 17 and 20 below, an intervention may only be carried out on a person who does not have the capacity to consent, for his or her direct benefit.

2. Where, according to law, a minor does not have the capacity to consent to an intervention, the intervention may only be carried out with the authorisation of his or her representative or an authority or a person or body provided for by law. The opinion of the minor shall be taken into consideration as an increasingly determining factor in proportion to his or her age and degree of maturity.

3. Where, according to law, an adult does not have the capacity to consent to an intervention because of a mental disability, a disease or for similar reasons, the intervention may only be carried out with the authorisation of his or her representative or an authority or a person or body provided for by law. The individual concerned shall as far as possible take part in the authorisation procedure.

4. The representative, the authority, the person or the body mentioned in paragraphs 2 and 3 above shall be given, under the same conditions, the information referred to in Article 5.

5. The authorisation referred to in paragraphs 2 and 3 above may be withdrawn at any time in the best interests of the person concerned.

Article 7 – Protection of persons who have a mental disorder

Subject to protective conditions prescribed by law, including supervisory, control and appeal procedures, a person who has a mental disorder of a serious nature may be subjected, without his or her consent, to an intervention aimed at treating his or her mental disorder only where, without such treatment, serious harm is likely to result to his or her health.

Article 8 – Emergency situation

When because of an emergency situation the appropriate consent cannot be obtained, any medically necessary intervention may be carried out immediately for the benefit of the health of the individual concerned.

Article 9 – Previously expressed wishes

The previously expressed wishes relating to a medical intervention by a patient who is not, at the time of the intervention, in a state to express his or her wishes shall be taken into account.

Chapter III – Private life and right to information

Article 10 – Private life and right to information

1. Everyone has the right to respect for private life in relation to information about his or her health.

2. Everyone is entitled to know any information collected about his or her health. However, the wishes of individuals not to be so informed shall be observed.

3. In exceptional cases, restrictions may be placed by law on the exercise of the rights contained in paragraph 2 in the interests of the patient.

Chapter IV – Human genome

Article 11 – Non-discrimination

Any form of discrimination against a person on grounds of his or her genetic heritage is prohibited.

Article 12 – Predictive genetic tests

Tests which are predictive of genetic diseases or which serve either to identify the subject as a carrier of a gene responsible for a disease or to detect a genetic predisposition or susceptibility to a disease may be performed only for health purposes or for scientific research linked to health purposes, and subject to appropriate genetic counselling.

Article 13 – Interventions on the human genome

An intervention seeking to modify the human genome may only be undertaken for preventive, diagnostic or therapeutic purposes and only if its aim is not to introduce any modification in the genome of any descendants.

Article 14 – Non-selection of sex

The use of techniques of medically assisted procreation shall not be allowed for the purpose of choosing a future child's sex, except where serious hereditary sex-related disease is to be avoided.

Chapter V – Scientific research

Article 15 – General rule

Scientific research in the field of biology and medicine shall be carried out freely, subject to the provisions of this Convention and the other legal provisions ensuring the protection of the human being.

Article 16 – Protection of persons undergoing research

Research on a person may only be undertaken if all the following conditions are met:

i.   there is no alternative of comparable effectiveness to research on humans;

ii. the risks which may be incurred by that person are not disproportionate to the potential benefits of the research;

iii. the research project has been approved by the competent body after independent examination of its scientific merit, including assessment of the importance of the aim of the research, and multidisciplinary review of its ethical acceptability;

iv. the persons undergoing research have been informed of their rights and the safeguards prescribed by law for their protection;

v. the necessary consent as provided for under Article 5 has been given expressly, specifically and is documented. Such consent may be freely withdrawn at any time.

Article 17 – Protection of persons not able to consent to research

1. Research on a person without the capacity to consent as stipulated in Article 5 may be undertaken only if all the following conditions are met:

    i. the conditions laid down in Article 16, sub-paragraphs i to iv, are fulfilled;

    ii. the results of the research have the potential to produce real and direct benefit to his or her health;

    iii. research of comparable effectiveness cannot be carried out on individuals capable of giving consent;

    iv. the necessary authorisation provided for under Article 6 has been given specifically and in writing; and

    v. the person concerned does not object.

2. Exceptionally and under the protective conditions prescribed by law, where the research has not the potential to produce results of direct benefit to the health of the person concerned, such research may be authorised subject to the conditions laid down in paragraph 1, sub-paragraphs i, iii, iv and v above, and to the following additional conditions:

    i. the research has the aim of contributing, through significant improvement in the scientific understanding of the individual's condition, disease or disorder, to the ultimate attainment of results capable of conferring benefit to the person concerned or to other persons in the same age category or afflicted with the same disease or disorder or having the same condition;

    ii. the research entails only minimal risk and minimal burden for the individual concerned.

Article 18 – Research on embryos in vitro

1. Where the law allows research on embryos in vitro, it shall ensure adequate protection of the embryo.

2. The creation of human embryos for research purposes is prohibited.

Chapter VI – Organ and tissue removal from living donors for transplantation purposes

Article 19 – General rule

1. Removal of organs or tissue from a living person for transplantation purposes may be carried out solely for the therapeutic benefit of the recipient and where there is no suitable organ or tissue available from a deceased person and no other alternative therapeutic method of comparable effectiveness.

2. The necessary consent as provided for under Article 5 must have been given expressly and specifically either in written form or before an official body.

Article 20 – Protection of persons not able to consent to organ removal

1. No organ or tissue removal may be carried out on a person who does not have the capacity to consent under Article 5.

2. Exceptionally and under the protective conditions prescribed by law, the removal of regenerative tissue from a person who does not have the capacity to consent may be authorised provided the following conditions are met:

    i.   there is no compatible donor available who has the capacity to consent;

    ii. the recipient is a brother or sister of the donor;

    iii. the donation must have the potential to be life-saving for the recipient;

    iv. the authorisation provided for under paragraphs 2 and 3 of Article 6 has been given specifically and in writing, in accordance with the law and with the approval of the competent body;

    v.   the potential donor concerned does not object.

Chapter VII – Prohibition of financial gain and disposal of a part of the human body

Article 21 – Prohibition of financial gain

The human body and its parts shall not, as such, give rise to financial gain.

Article 22 – Disposal of a removed part of the human body

When in the course of an intervention any part of a human body is removed, it may be stored and used for a purpose other than that for which it was removed, only if this is done in conformity with appropriate information and consent procedures.

Chapter VIII – Infringements of the provisions of the Convention

Article 23 – Infringement of the rights or principles

The Parties shall provide appropriate judicial protection to prevent or to put a stop to an unlawful infringement of the rights and principles set forth in this Convention at short notice.

Article 24 – Compensation for undue damage

The person who has suffered undue damage resulting from an intervention is entitled to fair compensation according to the conditions and procedures prescribed by law.

Article 25 – Sanctions

Parties shall provide for appropriate sanctions to be applied in the event of infringement of the provisions contained in this Convention.

Chapter IX – Relation between this Convention and other provisions

Article 26 – Restrictions on the exercise of the rights

1. No restrictions shall be placed on the exercise of the rights and protective provisions contained in this Convention other than such as are prescribed by law and are necessary in a democratic society in the interest of public safety, for the prevention of crime, for the protection of public health or for the protection of the rights and freedoms of others.

2. The restrictions contemplated in the preceding paragraph may not be placed on Articles 11, 13, 14, 16, 17, 19, 20 and 21.

Article 27 – Wider protection

None of the provisions of this Convention shall be interpreted as limiting or otherwise affecting the possibility for a Party to grant a wider measure of protection with regard to the application of biology and medicine than is stipulated in this Convention.

Chapter X – Public debate

Article 28 – Public debate

Parties to this Convention shall see to it that the fundamental questions raised by the developments of biology and medicine are the subject of appropriate public discussion in the light, in particular, of relevant medical, social, economic, ethical and legal implications, and that their possible application is made the subject of appropriate consultation.

Chapter XI – Interpretation and follow-up of the Convention

Article 29 – Interpretation of the Convention

The European Court of Human Rights may give, without direct reference to any specific proceedings pending in a court, advisory opinions on legal questions concerning the interpretation of the present Convention at the request of: the Government of a Party, after having informed the other Parties; the Committee set up by Article 32, with membership restricted to the Representatives of the Parties to this Convention, by a decision adopted by a two-thirds majority of votes cast.

Article 30 – Reports on the application of the Convention

On receipt of a request from the Secretary General of the Council of Europe any Party shall furnish an explanation of the manner in which its internal law ensures the effective implementation of any of the provisions of the Convention.

Chapter XII – Protocols

Article 31 – Protocols

Protocols may be concluded in pursuance of Article 32, with a view to developing, in specific fields, the principles contained in this Convention.

The Protocols shall be open for signature by Signatories of the Convention. They shall be subject to ratification, acceptance or approval. A Signatory may not ratify, accept or approve Protocols without previously or simultaneously ratifying accepting or approving the Convention.

Chapter XIII – Amendments to the Convention

Article 32 – Amendments to the Convention

1. The tasks assigned to 'the Committee' in the present article and in Article 29 shall be carried out by the Steering Committee on Bioethics (CDBI), or by any other committee designated to do so by the Committee of Ministers.

2. Without prejudice to the specific provisions of Article 29, each member State of the Council of Europe, as well as each Party to the present Convention which is not a member of the Council of Europe, may be represented and have one vote in the Committee when the Committee carries out the tasks assigned to it by the present Convention.

3. Any State referred to in Article 33 or invited to accede to the Convention in accordance with the provisions of Article 34 which is not Party to this Convention may be represented on the Committee by an observer. If the European Community is not a Party it may be represented on the Committee by an observer.

4. In order to monitor scientific developments, the present Convention shall be examined within the Committee no later than five years from its entry into force and thereafter at such intervals as the Committee may determine.

5. Any proposal for an amendment to this Convention, and any proposal for a Protocol or for an amendment to a Protocol, presented by a Party, the Committee or the Committee of Ministers shall be communicated to the Secretary General of the Council of Europe and forwarded by him to the member States of the Council of Europe, to the European Community, to any Signatory, to any Party, to any State invited to sign this Convention in accordance with the provisions of Article 33 and to any State invited to accede to it in accordance with the provisions of Article 34.

6. The Committee shall examine the proposal not earlier than two months after it has been forwarded by the Secretary General in accordance with paragraph 5. The Committee shall submit the text adopted by a two-thirds

majority of the votes cast to the Committee of Ministers for approval. After its approval, this text shall be forwarded to the Parties for ratification, acceptance or approval.

7. Any amendment shall enter into force, in respect of those Parties which have accepted it, on the first day of the month following the expiration of a period of one month after the date on which five Parties, including at least four member States of the Council of Europe, have informed the Secretary General that they have accepted it. In respect of any Party which subsequently accepts it, the amendment shall enter into force on the first day of the month following the expiration of a period of one month after the date on which that Party has informed the Secretary General of its acceptance.

Chapter XIV – Final clauses

Article 33 – Signature, ratification and entry into force

1. This Convention shall be open for signature by the member States of the Council of Europe, the non-member States which have participated in its elaboration and by the European Community.

2. This Convention is subject to ratification, acceptance or approval. Instruments of ratification, acceptance or approval shall be deposited with the Secretary General of the Council of Europe.

3. This Convention shall enter into force on the first day of the month following the expiration of a period of three months after the date on which five States, including at least four member States of the Council of Europe, have expressed their consent to be bound by the Convention in accordance with the provisions of paragraph 2 of the present article.

4. In respect of any Signatory which subsequently expresses its consent to be bound by it, the Convention shall enter into force on the first day of the month following the expiration of a period of three months after the date of the deposit of its instrument of ratification, acceptance or approval.

Article 34 – Non-member States

1. After the entry into force of this Convention, the Committee of Ministers of the Council of Europe may, after consultation of the Parties, invite any non-member State of the Council of Europe to accede to this Convention by a decision taken by the majority provided for in Article 20, paragraph d, of the Statute of the Council of Europe, and by the unanimous vote of the representatives of the Contracting States entitled to sit on the Committee of Ministers.

2. In respect of any acceding State, the Convention shall enter into force on the first day of the month following the expiration of a period of three months after the date of deposit of the instrument of accession with the Secretary General of the Council of Europe.

Article 35 – Territories

1. Any Signatory may, at the time of signature or when depositing its instrument of ratification, acceptance or approval, specify the territory or territories to which this Convention shall apply. Any other State may formulate the same declaration when depositing its instrument of accession.

2. Any Party may, at any later date, by a declaration addressed to the Secretary General of the Council of Europe, extend the application of this Convention to any other territory specified in the declaration and for whose international relations it is responsible or on whose behalf it is authorised to give undertakings. In respect of such territory the Convention shall enter into force on the first day of the month following the expiration of a period of three months after the date of receipt of such declaration by the Secretary General.

3. Any declaration made under the two preceding paragraphs may, in respect of any territory specified in such declaration, be withdrawn by a notification addressed to the Secretary General. The withdrawal shall become effective on the first day of the month following the expiration of a period of three months after the date of receipt of such notification by the Secretary General.

Article 36 – Reservations

1. Any State and the European Community may, when signing this Convention or when depositing the instrument of ratification, acceptance, approval or accession, make a reservation in respect of any particular provision of the Convention to the extent that any law then in force in its territory is not in conformity with the provision. Reservations of a general character shall not be permitted under this article.

2. Any reservation made under this article shall contain a brief statement of the relevant law.

3. Any Party which extends the application of this Convention to a territory mentioned in the declaration referred to in Article 35, paragraph 2, may, in respect of the territory concerned, make a reservation in accordance with the provisions of the preceding paragraphs.

4. Any Party which has made the reservation mentioned in this article may withdraw it by means of a declaration addressed to the Secretary General of the Council of Europe. The withdrawal shall become effective on the first day of the month following the expiration of a period of one month after the date of its receipt by the Secretary General.

Article 37 – Denunciation

1. Any Party may at any time denounce this Convention by means of a notification addressed to the Secretary General of the Council of Europe.

2. Such denunciation shall become effective on the first day of the month following the expiration of a period of three months after the date of receipt of the notification by the Secretary General.

Article 38 – Notifications

The Secretary General of the Council of Europe shall notify the member States of the Council, the European Community, any Signatory, any Party and any other State which has been invited to accede to this Convention of:

a.   any signature;

b.   the deposit of any instrument of ratification, acceptance, approval or accession;

c.   any date of entry into force of this Convention in accordance with Articles 33 or 34;

d.   any amendment or Protocol adopted in accordance with Article 32, and the date on which such an amendment or Protocol enters into force;

e.   any declaration made under the provisions of Article 35;

f.   any reservation and withdrawal of reservation made in pursuance of the provisions of Article 36;

g.   any other act, notification or communication relating to this Convention.

In witness whereof the undersigned, being duly authorised thereto, have signed this Convention.

Done at Oviedo (Asturias), this 4th day of April 1997, in English and French, both texts being equally authentic, in a single copy which shall be deposited in the archives of the Council of Europe. The Secretary General of the Council of Europe shall transmit certified copies to each member State of the Council of Europe, to the European Community, to the non-member States which have participated in the elaboration of this Convention, and to any State invited to accede to this Convention.

BIBLIOGRAPHY

Advisory Committee on Human Radiation Experiments, *Final Report of the Advisory Committee on Human Radiation Experiments*, 1996, New York: OUP

Allen, T, 'The Human Rights Act (UK) and property law', in McLean, J (ed), *Property and the Constitution*, 1999, Oxford: Hart, pp 64–87

Asch, A, 'Distracted by disability' (1998) 7 Cambridge Quarterly of Healthcare Ethics 77

Bainham, A, *Children – The Modern Law*, 2nd edn, 1998, Bristol: Jordan

Bainham, A, 'The judge and the competent minor' (1992) 108 LQR 194

Bamforth, M, 'The true "horizontal effect" of the Human Rights Act 1998' (2001) 117 LQR 34

Bartlett, P and Sandland, R, *Mental Health Law Policy and Practice*, 2000, London: Blackstone, Chapters 3 and 9

Beddard, R, 'Duties of individuals under international and regional human rights instruments' (1999) 3 International Journal of Human Rights 30

Beddard, R, *Human Rights and Europe*, 1993, Cambridge: Grotius

Belian, J, 'Deference to doctors in Dutch euthanasia law' (1996) 10 Emory International Law Review 255–96

Berger, JT, Rosner, F, Potash, J, Kark, P, Farnsworth, P and Bennett, AJ, 'Medical futility: towards consensus on disagreement' (1998) 10 HEC 102

Bernard, C, *An Introduction to the Study of Experimental Medicine*, 1865, Greene, H (trans), reprinted in Hume, D, 'Of suicide', in Miller, E (ed), *Essays Moral, Political and Literary*, 1985, Indianapolis, IN: Liberty Classics

Blake M, 'Physician-assisted suicide: a criminal offence or a patient's right?' (1997) 5(3) Med LR 312–13

Brazier, M, *Street on Tort*, 10th edn, 1999, London: Butterworths

Brazier, M and Miola, J, 'Bye-bye *Bolam*: a medical litigation revolution' (2000) 8 Med L Rev 85

Bridge, C, 'Religious beliefs and teenage refusal of medical treatment' (1999) 62 MLR 585–604

Brody, H, *The Healer's Power*, 1992, New Haven: Yale UP

Brussack, RD, 'Group homes, families and meaning in the law of subdivision covenants' (1981) 16 Georgia Law Review 33

British Transplant Society, *Report of the BTS Working Party on Organ Transplantation*, 1995, London: BTS

Buxton, R, 'The Human Rights Act and private law' (2000) 116 LQR 48

Bynoe, I, Oliver, M and Barnes, C, *Equal Rights for Disabled People – The Case for a New Law*, 1991, London: Institute for Public Policy Research

Callahan, D, 'The goals of medicine: setting new priorities' (1996) 26 Hastings Center Report (Special Supplement) S1, S9–S15

Capron, A, 'Legalising physician-aided death' (1996) 5(1) Cambridge Quarterly of Healthcare Ethics 10

Challis, L and Henwood, M, 'Equity in the NHS: equity in community care' (1994) 308 BMJ 1496–99

Chief Medical Officer's Summit, Evidence Documentation, Thursday 11 January 2001 (BMA Press Release, 17 January 2001), The Queen Elizabeth II Conference Centre, London

Cho, J *et al*, 'Transplantation of kidneys from donors whose hearts have stopped beating' (1998) 338 (4) New Engl J Med 221–5

Clayton, R and Tomlinson, H, *The Law of Human Rights*, 2000, Oxford: OUP

Code of Practice: *Rights of Access: Goods, Facilities, Services and Premises, Disability Discrimination Act*, 1999, London: HMSO

Commission for Health Improvement, *Report to the Secretary of State for Health, Report regarding Garlands Hospital, Cumbria*, Investigation into the North Lakeland NHS Trust, November 2000, London: HMSO

Conference of European Health Ministers, *Current Legislation in Council of Europe Member States and Finland and Results of European Co-operation*, 1987, Strasbourg: Council of Europe

Constitution Unit, *Human Rights Legislation*, 1996, London: Constitution Unit

Cooke, E and Hayton, D, 'Land law and trusts', in Hayton, D (ed), *Law's Future(s): British Legal Developments in the 21st Century*, 2000, Oxford: Hart, p 433

Cooke of Thorndon (Lord), 'The British embracement of human rights' [1999] EHRLR 243

Cooper, J, 'Horizontality: the application of human rights standards in private disputes', in English, E and Havers, P (eds), *An Introduction to Human Rights and the Common Law*, 2000, Oxford: Hart, pp 53–69

Coppell, J, *The Human Rights Act 1998: Enforcing the European Convention in the Domestic Courts*, 1999, Chichester: John Wiley

Council of Europe, *European Convention on Human Rights and Biomedicine*, 1997, Oviedo: Council of Europe

Council of Europe, *Human Artificial Procreation*, 1989, Strasbourg: Council of Europe

Council of Europe, *The Protocol on the Prohibition of Cloning Human Beings*, 1988, Paris: Council of Europe

Council of Europe, Document DIR/JUR (98) 7, para 3

Craig, P and De Búrca, G, *EU Law, Text, Cases and Materials*, 2nd edn, 1998, Oxford: OUP

Daeman, JHC, 'Non heart-beating donor program contributes 40% of kidneys for transplantation' (1996) 28(1) Trans Proc 105–06

Dawson, N, 'Restrictive covenants and human rights' [1986] Conv 124

Department of Health, *Reforming the Mental Health Act*, Cm 5016-I and 5016-II, 2000a (December), London: Stationery Office

Department of Health, *The NHS Plan: A Plan for Investment, A Plan for Reform* Cm 4818-I, 2000b, London: Stationery Office

Department of Health, *No Secrets: The Protection of Vulnerable Adults*, 1999a, London: DoH

Department of Health, *Working Together to Safeguard Children: A Guide to Inter-Agency Working to Safeguard and Promote the Welfare of Children*, 1999b, London: DoH

Department of Health, *Information for Health*, 1998, London: HMSO

Department of Health, *The Caldicott Committee Report on the Review of Patient Identifiable Information*, 1997, London: DoH

Department of Health, *The Protection and Use of Patient Information*, 1996, London: HMSO

Department of Health, *Changing Childbirth*, 1993, London: HMSO

Department of Health/King's Fund, *A New Bond of Trust Between Patients and the NHS*, 2001, Department of Health Press Release 2001/0057, 29 January, London: DoH

Devonshire, P, 'Restrictive covenants and private dwelling-house' [1991] Conv 388

Dewar, J, 'Land and the family home', in Bright, S and Dewar, J (eds), *Land Law Themes and Perspectives*, 1998 Oxford: OUP, pp 327–55

Dicey, AV, 'On the matter of civil liberties', in *Introduction to the Study of the Law of the Constitution*, 10th edn, 1959, London: Macmillan

Dickens, B, 'The legal challenge of health research involving children' (1998) 6 Health Law Journal 131–48

Disability Rights Task Force, *From Exclusion to Inclusion: A Report of the Disability Rights Task Force on Civil Rights for Disabled People*, 1999, London: Disability Rights Task Force

Doyle, BJ, *Disability Discrimination: Law and Practice*, 3rd edn, 2000, London: Jordans

Duncan, W, 'The constitutional protection of parental rights', in Eekelaar, J and Sarcevic, P (eds), *Parenthood in Modern Society*, 1993, Dordrecht: Martinus Nijhoff, pp 431–45

Dworkin, G, 'The law relating to organ transplantation in England' (1970) 33 MLR 353

Dworkin, R, *Life's Dominion: An Argument about Abortion and Euthanasia*, 1993, London: HarperCollins

Dyer, C, 'Mother loses court battle on right to life' (1999) *The Guardian*, 23 April, p 9

Eastman, N and Peay, J, *Law Without Enforcement*, 1999, Oxford: Hart

Edmunds, R, 'Community care and private dwellings' (1992) 3 Journal of Forensic Psychiatry 343

Edmunds, R and Sutton, T, 'Who's afraid of the neighbours?', in Cooke, EJ (ed), *Modern Studies in Property Law*, 2001, Oxford: Hart, Vol 1: Property 2000, pp 133–48

Elam, G, *Consent to Organ and Tissue Retention at Post-Mortem Examination and Disposal of Human Materials*, Qualitative Social Policy Research, Ref P2010, 2000 (December), London: DoH

Elliston, S, 'If you know what's good for you: refusal of consent to medical treatment by children', in McLean, S, *Contemporary Issues in Law, Medicine and Ethics*, 1994, Aldershot: Dartmouth, pp 29–57

Englert, Y, *Organ and Tissue Transplantation in the European Union: Managements of Difficulties and Health Risks linked to Donors*, 1995, Dordrecht: Martinus Nijhoff

Feest, T *et al*, 'Protocol for increasing organ donation after cerebrovascular deaths in a district general hospital' (1990) 335 Lancet 1133–35

Feinberg, J, *Harm to Others*, 1984, Oxford: OUP

Feldman, D, 'Human dignity as a legal value – Part I' [1999] PL 682

Feldman, D, 'The developing scope of Art 8 of the European Convention on Human Rights' [1997] EHRLR 265

Feldman, D, *Civil Liberties and Human Rights in England and Wales*, 1993, Oxford: Clarendon

Fennell, P, 'Withdrawal of life sustaining treatment for child without parental consent' (2000) 8 Med L Rev 125

Flinn, HM, 'The necessary application of the contract clause to cases involving restrictive covenants and group family day care homes' (2000) 27 Fordham Urb LJ 1793

Fortin, J, 'Rights brought home for children' (1999a) 62 MLR 354–70

Fortin, J, 'The HRA's impact on litigation involving children and their families' (1999b) 11 CFLQ 237–55

Fortin, J, *Children's Rights and the Developing Law*, 1998, London: Butterworths

Fox, M and McHale, J, 'In whose best interests?' (1997) 60 MLR 700

Garwood-Gowers, A, 'There's something wrong about killing Mary', unpublished Middlesex University Business School Research Paper, 16 January 2001

Garwood-Gowers, A, *Living Donor Organ Transplantation: Key Legal and Ethical Issues*, 1999, Aldershot: Ashgate

General Medical Council, *Confidentiality: Protecting and Providing Information*, June 2000, London: GMC (updated September 2000)

General Medical Council, *Good Medical Practice*, July 1998, London: GMC

Gillon, R, *Philosophical Medical Ethics*, 1986, Oxford: OUP

Goldbeck-Wood, S, 'Europe is divided on embryo regulation' (1996) 313 BMJ 512

Gooding, C, *Blackstone's Guide to the Disability Discrimination Act 1995*, 1996, London: Blackstone

Gooding, C, *Disabling Laws, Enabling Acts: Disability Rights in Britain and America*, 1994, London: Pluto

Grosz, S, Beatson, B and Duffy, P, *Human Rights: The 1998 Act and the European Convention*, 2000, London: Sweet & Maxwell

Group of Advisors to the European Commission, *On the Ethical Implications of Biotechnology*, 1996, European Commission

Grounds, A, 'The transfer of sentenced prisoners to hospital 1960–1983: a study in one special hospital' (1991) 31 Br J Crim 54–71

Grounds, A, 'Transfers of sentenced prisoners to hospital' [1990] Crim LR 544

Grubb, A, '*Re Y* commentary' (1996) 4 Med L Rev 205–07

Grubb, A *et al*, 'Reporting on the persistent vegetative state in Europe' [1998] 6(2) Med LR 161–90

Guernsey, TF, 'The mentally retarded and private restrictive covenants' (1984) 25 William and Mary Law Review 421

Harpum, C, *Megarry and Wade's Law of Real Property*, 6th edn, 2000, London: Sweet & Maxwell, Chapter 16

Harris, DJ, O'Boyle, M and Warbrick, C, *Law of the European Convention on Human Rights*, 1995, London: Butterworths

Health Service Ombudsman for England, *Annual Report 1999–00*, Third Report for Session 1990–2000, 2000, London: Stationery Office (see www.ombudsman.org.uk)

Henderson, J, 'Family and child law', in Baker, C (ed), *Human Rights Act 1998: A Practitioner's Guide*, 1998, London: Sweet & Maxwell, pp 217–58

Herring, J, 'The Human Rights Act and the welfare principle in family law – conflicting or complementary?' (1999a) 11 CFLQ 223–35

Herring, J, 'The welfare principle and the rights of parents', in Bainham, A, Day Sclater, S, Richards, M (eds), *What is a Parent? A Socio-Legal Analysis*, 1999b, Oxford: Hart

Home Office, *Human Rights Act: Core Guidance for Public Authorities: A New Era of Rights and Responsibilities*, 1999, London: HMSO

Home Office, *Modernising Social Services*, White Paper, Cm 4169, 1998, London: HMSO

Home Office, *Bringing Rights Home*, White Paper, Cm 3782, 1997, London: HMSO

Home Office, *Rights Brought Home: The Human Rights Bill*, Cm 3782, October 1997

Hors, J *et al*, 'France Transplant', in Matesanz, R *et al* (eds) (1992) 4 Transplant, produced with the Council of Europe, Paris

House of Commons Select Committee on Health, *Provision of NHS Mental Health*, Fourth Report, HC 373-I, 1999

House of Lords Select Committee on Medical Ethics, HL Paper 21, Session 1993–94, Cm 2553, 1994, London: HMSO

Howell, J, 'The Human Rights Act 1998: the "horizontal effect" on land law', in Cooke, EJ (ed), *Modern Studies in Property Law*, 2001, Oxford: Hart, Vol 1: Property 2000, pp 149–60

Howell, J, 'Land and human rights' [1999] Conv 287

Hubbard, D, 'Group homes and restrictive covenants' (1988) 57 UMKC Law Review 135

Hughes, D, *Environmental Law*, 3rd edn, 1996, London: Butterworths

Hume, D, 'Of suicide', in Miller, E (ed), *Essays Moral, Political and Literary*, 1985, Indianapolis, IN: Liberty Classics

Hunt, M, 'The horizontal effect of the Human Rights Act 1998' [1998] PL 423

International Conference on Harmonisation of the Technical Requirements for the Registration of Pharmaceuticals for Human Use, *ICH Harmonised Tripartite Guidelines for Good Clinical Practice*, 2nd edn, 1997, Richmond: Brookwood Medical

Irvine of Lairg (Lord), 'The development of human rights in Britain under an Incorporated Convention on Human Rights' [1998] PL 221

Judiciary Committee of the House of Representatives, *Report*, 1998 HR Rep No 711, 100th Cong, 2d Sess 18 (1988) (reprinted in 1988 USCCAN 2173)

Kane, BA, '*Hill v Community of Damien of Molokai* and the character of the community: social policy, group residences and real covenants' (1998) 102 Dick L Rev 595

Kant, I, *Fundamental Principles of the Metaphysics of Morals*, Abbott, TK (trans), 1875, New York: Prometheus

Kanter, AS, 'A home of one's own: the fair Housing Amendments Act of 1988 and Housing Discrimination against people with mental disabilities' (1994) 43 Am UL Rev 925

Kapteyn, P and VerLoren van Themaat, P, *Introduction to the Law of the European Communities*, 2nd edn, 1989, The Hague: Kluwer

Kennedy, I, 'Commentary': *Re C (A Minor) (Medical Treatment)* (1998) 6(1) Med LR 100–03

Kennedy, I, *Treat Me Right*, 1992, Oxford: OUP

Kennedy, I and Grubb, A, *Medical Law*, 3rd edn, 2000, Butterworths: London

Kennedy, I and Grubb, A (eds), *Principles of Medical Law*, 1998, Oxford: OUP

Kennedy, I and Grubb, A, *Medical Law: Text with Materials*, 2nd edn, 1994, London: Butterworths

Kennedy, I and Grubb, A, 'A commentary; withdrawal of artificial nutrition: incompetent adult' (1993) 1(3) Med LR 369

Kittur, DS *et al*, 'Incentives for organ donation' (1991) 338 Lancet 1441–43

Kokkedee, W, 'Kidney procurement policies in the Eurotransplant region: "Opting in" versus "Opting out"' (1992) 352 Social Science and Medicine 177–82

Kootstra, G *et al*, 'Twenty per cent more kidneys through a non-heart beating programme' (1991) 23 Trans Proc 910–11

Law Commission, *Mental Incapacity*, 1995, Law Com 231

Law Commission, *Injuries to Unborn Children*, Cmnd 5709, 1974, Law Com 60

Law Commission, *Injuries to Unborn Children*, Working Paper No 47, 1973

Laws, J (Sir), 'The limitations of human rights' [1998] PL 254

Lawson, A, 'Selling, letting and managing premises: new rights for disabled people?' [2000] Conv 128

Leff, J and Trieman, N, 'Long-stay patients discharged from psychiatric hospitals' (2000) 176 British Journal of Psychiatry 217

Livingstone, S, 'Article 14 and the prevention of discrimination in the European Convention on Human Rights' [1997] 1 EHRLR 25

Locke, J, 'Of civil government, two treatises', in Locke, J, *Of Civil Government*, Carpenter, WS (ed), 1925, London: Dent, Everyman's Library, Vol 2, p 159

Lord Chancellor, *Making Decisions: The Government's Proposals for Making Decisions on Behalf of Mentally Incapacitated Adults*, Cm 4465, Final Report, 1999, London: HMSO

Lord Chancellor, *Making Decisions*, Consultation Paper, 1997, London: HMSO

Lester of Herne Hill (Lord) and Pannick, D (eds), *Human Rights Law and Practice*, 1999, London: Butterworths

Loucaides, L, 'Personality and privacy under the European Convention on Human Rights' (1990) 61 BYIL 175, p 175

Lowe, N and Juss, S, 'Medical treatment – pragmatism and the search for principle' (1993) 56 MLR 865

Macdonald, R St J, 'The margin of appreciation in the jurisprudence of the European Court of Human Rights', in *International Law at the Time of its Codification, Essays in Honour of Judge Robert Ago*, 1987, pp 187–208

Matesanz, R and Miranda, B, 'Organizacion Nacional de Transplantes', in Matesanz, R *et al* (eds) (1992) 4 Transplant, produced with the Council of Europe, Paris

McBride, J, 'Protecting life: a positive obligation to help' (1999) 24 EL Rev Human Rights Survey HR/43

McColgan, A, *Women Under the Law: The False Promise of Human Rights*, 2000, Harlow: Longman

McHarg, A, 'Reconciling human rights and the public interest: conceptual problems and doctrinal uncertainty in the jurisprudence of the European Court of Human Rights' (1999) 62 MLR 671

Medical Royal Colleges, 'Medical Royal Colleges Guidelines' (1976) 2 BMJ 1187

Michalowski, S, 'Is it in the best interests of a child to have a life-saving liver transplantation?: *Re T (Wardship: Medical Treatment)*' (1997) 9 CFLQ 179

Mill, JS, *On Liberty*, 1982, London/Harmondsworth: Penguin

Moon, G, 'The draft Discrimination Protocol to the European Convention on Human Rights: a progress report' [2000] 1 EHRLR 49

Murdoch, J, 'Survey of recent case law under Article 5 ECHR' (1998) 23 EL Rev 31–48

Murdoch, J, 'Safeguarding the liberty of the person: recent Strasbourg jurisprudence' (1993) 42 ICLQ 494

Murphy, J, 'W(h)ither adolescent autonomy?' (1992) Journal of Social Welfare and Family Law 539

National Audit Office, *NHS (England) Summarised Accounts 1998–99*, 2000, Press Notice 24/00, HC 356, 1999/2000, 5 April
(full report: www.nao.gov.uk/pn/9900356.htm)

New, B, Solomon, M, Dingwall, R and McHale, J, *A Question of Give and Take: Improving the Supply of Donor Organs for Transplantation*, King's Fund Research Report, 18, 1994, King's Fund Institute

Newsom, GL, *Preston and Newsom's Restrictive Covenants Affecting Freehold Land*, 9th edn, 1998, London: Sweet & Maxwell

National Health Service Litigation Authority, 'Human Rights – special edition' (2000) 19 NHSLA Review (summer), London: NHSLA

Nicolaou, D, 'Towards a European Health Policy?' (1995) Echo European News, January

Nielsen, L, 'Procreative tourism, genetic testing and the law', in Lowe, N and Douglas, G (eds), *Families across Frontiers*, 1996, Dordrecht: Kluwer

Nys, H, 'Physician involvement in a patient's death: a continental perspective' (1999) 7 (Summer) Med L Rev 208

O'Sullivan, D, 'The allocation of scarce resources and the right to life under the European Convention on Human Rights' [1998] PL 389

Opsahl, T, 'The right to life', in Macdonald, R St J, Matscher, F and Petzold, H (eds), *The European System for the Protection of Human Rights*, 1993, Dordrecht: Kluwer, p 207

Otlowski, M, *Voluntary Euthanasia and the Common Law*, 1997, Oxford: Clarendon

Park, GR *et al*, 'Organ donation' (1993) 306 BMJ 145 (letters)

Pearson, M and Wistow, G, 'The boundary between health care and social care' (1995) 311 BMJ 208–09

Pellegrino, ED and Thomasma, DC, *For the Patient's Good: The Restoration of Beneficence in Health Care*, 1988, New York: OUP

Phillimore Committee, *Report of the Committee on the Contempt of Court*, Cmnd 5794, 1974

Phillipson, G, 'The Human Rights Act "horizontal effect" and the common law: a bang or a whimper?' (1999) 62 MLR 824

Plomer, A, 'Principles underlying the conduct of research in Europe: international bioethics or moral bankruptcy?', in Megone, A and Mason, J (eds), *Euricon*, 2001, Aldershot: Ashgate

Plomer, A, 'Participation of children in clinical trials: UK, European and international legal perspectives on consent' (2000) 5 Medical Law International 1–24

Polakiewicz, J, *Treaty-Making in the Council of Europe*, 1999, Strasbourg: Council of Europe

Price, DPT, 'Organ transplant initiatives: the twilight zone' (1997) 23 J Med Eth 170–75

Puddephat, A, 'Incorporating the European Convention on Human Rights', in Hegarty, A and Leonard, S (eds), *Human Rights: An Agenda for the 21st Century*, 1999, London: Cavendish Publishing, pp 326–28

Quinn, G, 'Human rights and people with disabilities', in Alston, P (ed), *The EU and Human Rights*, 1999, Oxford: OUP, pp 281–326

Ransom, JS, *The Politics of Subjectivity: Foucault's Discipline*, 1997, Durham: Duke UP

Rayner, M, 'European Union policy and health' (1995) 311 (7014) BMJ 1180–81

Reid (Lord), 'The judge as law maker' (1972) XII Journal of the SPTL 22

Reiser, SJ, Dyck, AJ and Curran, WJ, *Ethics in Medicine*, 1977, Cambridge, Mass: MIT Press, pp 137–39

Repper, J, *Tall Stories from the Back Yard: A Survey of 'Nimby' Opposition to Community Mental Health Facilities, Experienced by Key Service Providers in England and Wales*, 1997, London: MIND

Richards, T and Smith, R, 'How should European health policy develop? A discussion' (1994) 309 BMJ 117

Riis, P, 'Medical ethics in the European Community' (1993) 19 Journal of Medical Ethics 7–12

Ritchie, P, *Public Attitudes to People with a Learning Disability and How to Influence Them*, 1999, Scottish Human Services Report

Robertson, J, *Children of Choice*, 1994, New Jersey: Princeton UP

Rogers, A and Durand de Bousingen, D, *The European Biotech '94 Report*, 1995, Ernst and Young (summarised in (1994) Chemistry in Britain (July), p 545)

Rolston, B and Eggert, A (eds), *Abortion in the New Europe*, 1994, London: Greenwood

Roscamm Abbing, HD, (1997) 3(1) Eurohealth (spring) 14–15

Routh, G, 'Elective ventilation for organ donation – the case against' (1992) 8 Care of the Critically Ill 60–61

Royal Commission, *The Report of the Royal Commission on the Law Relating to Mental Illness and Mental Deficiency*, Cmnd 169, 1957, London: HMSO

Rutherford, L, 'Community care and injurious affection' [1996] Conv 260

Sayce, L, *From Psychiatric Patient to Citizen: Overcoming Discrimination and Social Exclusion*, 2000, London: Macmillan

Scanlon, 'A theory of freedom of expression' (1972) 1 Philosophy and Public Affairs 204

Scarman (Lord), *The Right to Know*, 1984, Granada Guildhall Lecture

Schlumpf, R *et al*, 'Transplantation of kidneys from non-heart-beating donors: protocol, cardiac death diagnosis and results' (1996) 28(1) Trans Proc

Scottish Executive, 'Deacon promises new measures to improve consent in NHS', SEO 178/2001

Scottish Executive, *What are the Housing Solutions for the Future*, 1999, Review of Services for People with a Learning Disability (www.scotland.gov.uk/ldsr/housing_solutions.pdf)

Sheldon, S, *Beyond Control: Medical Power and Abortion Law*, 1997, London: Pluto

Sherlock, A, 'The applicability of the United Kingdom's Human Rights Bill: identifying public functions' [1998] 4 EPL 43–61

Simons, K, *The View from Arthur's Seat: A Literature Review of Housing and Support Options Beyond Scotland*, 1999, Scottish Executive

Singh, R, Hunt, M and Demetriou, M, 'Is there a role for the "margin of appreciation" in national law' [1999] EHRLR 15–22, p 15

Skegg, P, 'Human Tissue Act 1961' (1976) Med Sci Law 197

Skegg, P, 'Liability for the unauthorized removal of cadaveric transplant material' (1974) 14 Med Sci Law 53

Smith, C, 'Disabling autonomy: the role of government, the law and the family' (1997) 24 JLS 421

Smith, G, *Final Choices: Autonomy in Health Care Decisions*, 1989, Springfield: Thomas

Social Services Inspectorate for Wales, *In Safe Hands: The Implementation of Adult Protection Procedures in Wales*, 1999, Social Services Inspectorate for Wales

Somerville, A, *Medical Ethics Today: Its Practice and Philosophy*, 1993, London: BMA

Sprumont, D, 'Legal protection of human research subjects in Europe' (1999) 6 European Journal of Health Law 25–43

Starmer, K, *European Human Rights Law*, 1999, London: Legal Action Group

Supperstone, M and Coppell, J, 'Judicial review after the Human Rights Act' [1999] EHRLR 301

Teff, H, 'Consent to medical procedures' (1985) 1 LQR 443

Teitgen, PH, *Collected Edition of the Travaux Préparatoires*, 1975, The Hague: Martinus Nijhoff, Vol 1

Thomson, JJ, *Rights, Restitution and Risk*, 1986, Cambridge, Mass: Harvard UP

Thorold, O, 'The implications of the European Convention on Human Rights for United Kingdom mental health legislation' [1996] 6 EHRLR 619–36

Trieman, N, 'Residential care for the mentally ill in the community', in Leff, JP (ed), *Care in the Community: Illusion or Reality*, 1997, London: John Wiley

Truog, RD and Brett, AS, 'The problem with futility' (1992) 326 New Eng J of Med 1560

United Kingdom Central Council for Nursing, Midwifery and Health Visiting, *UKCC Code of Professional Conduct*, 1992, London: UKCC

United Nations, *United Nations Convention on the Rights of the Child*, CRC C SR, 1989

Van Dijk, P and Van Hoof, GJH, *Theory and Practice of the European Convention on Human Rights*, 1998, The Hague: Kluwer

Vuckovic, N and Nichter, M, 'Changing patterns of pharmaceutical practice in the United States' (1997) 44(9) Social Science and Medicine 1285–302

Wade, H, 'Horizons of horizontality' (2000) 116 LQR 217

Wadham, J and Mountfield, H, *Blackstone's Guide to the Human Rights Act 1998*, 1999, London: Blackstone

Waldron, J, *Liberal Rights*, 1993, Cambridge: CUP

Weatherill, S, 'Beyond pre-emption? Shared competence and constitutional change in the European Community', in O'Keeffe, D and Twomey, PM, (eds), *Legal Issues of the Maastricht Treaty*, 1994, Chichester: Chancery Law

Williams (Lord), 'The HRA 1998', speech at the College of Law, 28 January 1999, Chancery Lane

Williams, J, 'Working together II' (1992) 4 Child Law 68–71

Wright, T, 'Health', in Baker, C (ed), *Human Rights Act 1998: A Practitioner's Guide*, 1998, London: Sweet & Maxwell, pp 295–310

INDEX

A

Abortion Act 1967 260
Ad Hoc Committee of Experts
  on Bioethics
  See Steering Committee on Bioethics
Assisted reproduction
  designing babies 74–76
  fertility treatment 61
  regulation by HFEA 75–76
Assisted suicide
  See, also, Euthanasia
  non-UK law 277–78
  UK law 276–77
Autonomy and dignity
  bioethics .76–80
  definition .67–68
  designing babies 74–76
  expensive medical
    treatment 69–74
  legal regime .68

B

Best interests
  euthanasia 281–84
  living donor 297–301
Bioethics
  access to treatment 69–70, 72–74
  autonomy and
    dignity 67–68, 76–78
  biotechnology 332–33
  Council of Europe 337–38
  degrading treatment 70–72
  designing babies 74–76
  ECHRB provisions 338–42
  European Court of
    Human Rights 339–42
  European Union 333–37
  medical research 317–19
  respect for private life 72–74
  right to life 70
Biomaterials
  See Donor; Transplantation material

Biomedical research
  See Research; ECHRB
Biotechnology
  bioethics 332–33,
                                                337–38
  Council of Europe 337–38
  European Court of
    Human Rights 339–42
  European Union 333–37
  Human Rights Act 1998 343–45
  industry .332–33
  regulation 331–32
  UK law 343
Body material
  See Donor; Transplantation material
Bolam test, legal disability 104

C

CAHBI (Ad Hoc Committee of
  Experts on Bioethics)
  See Steering Committee on Bioethics
Care in the community
  See Community care
CDBI
  See Steering Committee on Bioethics
Children
  See, also, Competent minors;
    Incompetent persons
  best interests 243–258, 297–99
  confidentiality 150–51
  conjoined twins 58
  consent for medical
    interventions 325
  David Glass case 82–84, 94–96
  designing babies 74–76
  ECHR 243–47
  Human Rights
    Act 1998 243–58
  life-saving treatment 248–57
  living donors 297–301
  medical research 325
  parental consent 243–47,
                                                252–57, 325

pregnancy 259–71
treatment rights 82–84, 94–96
welfare principle 247–57
Civil procedure
fair hearings 105–07
medical cases 99–100
Clinical negligence
See Medical complaints
Cloning, protocol
on prohibition 44–45
Common law
access to health records 134
competent minors 226–29
confidentiality 128–31
consent 59
European Convention . . .13–15, 21–29
present position 21–29
private property 214–16
quality of life 58–59
right to life 58–59
right to treatment 84–87
Community care of
mentally disordered
covenants 202–03, 217–22
discrimination 217–22
Dr Barnardo's 204–06
fairer housing 221–23
group homes 203–04
Human Rights
Act 1998 208–17
opposition to 202–08
residential homes 206–08
Competent minors, self-determination
See, also, Incompetent persons
common law 226–29
Convention rights 233–34
denial of 231–32, 235–39
ECHR provisions 234–41
effectiveness principle 233
evolutive interpretation 233
Gillick-competent 325

legislation 225–32
margin of appreciation 234
medical intervention 301
proportionality 233–34
rights of self-determination 225–29
Competent person
tissue donor 296–97
Complaints
See Medical complaints
Compulsory treatment
of mental disorders 198
Confidentiality
See, also, Data protection; Information
access to records 134–35
common law 128–31
Data Protection Act 1998 135–40
ECHR provisions 141–45
freedom of expression 128
health professionals 132–33
Human Rights
Act 1988 . . . . .140–45, 155–61
patient records,
anonymity 133
private life 127–28
rights and duties 129–30
sharing of
information 150–52, 158–61
vulnerable adults 147–55
Conjoined twins 58
Consent
biomedical
interventions 37–39
ECHR provisions 59
experimental treatment 61, 324
life-saving treatment 248–57
medical
interventions 301–04, 320–23
medical research 324–25
non-consensual
treatment .61

non-therapeutic
   research 327–30
parental 248–57, 325
tissue donation 301–04
unable to consent 323–27
Council of Europe bioethics
   and biotechnology 337–38
   ECHR 32
   ECHRB 32
Covenants
   community care 202–08
   disability discrimination 217–23

D

Damages for clinical negligence 66
Data protection
   See, also, Confidentiality;
      Data Protection Act 1998
   ECHR, Art 10 141–43
   ECHR, Art 8 141–45
   Human Rights Act 1998 140–45
   patient confidentiality 135–40
   potential problems 143–44
   processing restrictions 137–39
Data Protection Act 1998
   See, also, Confidentiality;
      Data protection
   access to data 139
   exemptions 139–40
   outline 136–37
David Glass
   Human Rights Act 94–96
   right to treatment 82–84
DDA
   See Disability Discrimination Act
Deceased,
   use of body tissues 308–10
   See, also, Donor
Degrading treatment,
   ECHR, Art 3 51–52

De-institutionalisation
   See Community care
Designing babies
   See Assisted reproduction
Detention of
   mentally disordered
   assessments 169–70, 175–80,
              186–88
   definition 165–66
   discharge 176–78, 189–90
   for treatment 188–89
   hospitalisation 170–74
   lawfulness 166–69, 186
   least restrictive
      environment 169–75
   period of 186–88
   protection of public 174–75
   recall to 179–80
   release 188–89
   review under
      Art 5(1) 186–90
Dignity and autonomy
   definitions 67–68
   designing babies 74–76
   expensive medical
      treatment 69–74
   litigating bioethics 76–80
Disability Discrimination
   Act 1995 217–23
Discharge, mental disorders 176–78,
              189–90
Disciplinary proceedings,
   medical cases 100–01, 111
Discrimination prohibition
   action for
      non-discrimination 62
   community care 209–10
   ECHR, Art 14 ....54, 209–10
   group homes 217–18
   mental disorders 209–10, 217–18

Disposal of premises,
   disability discrimination 218–21
Disproportionality
   See Proportionality
Donor
   See, also, Living donor;
     Transplantation material
   body materials 43–44, 296–301,
                     310–11
   competency 296–97
   elective ventilation 301–03
   forced to donate 296–97
   Human Tissue
     Act 1961 308–10
   non-heart beating 303–04
   organ procurement 43–44, 310–11
   Pennings system 310–11
DPA
   See Data Protection Act 1998
Dr Barnardo's,
   community care 204–06
Drug side-effects in
   mentally disabled 192–93

E
ECHR
   See European Convention on
     Human Rights
ECHRB
   See European Convention on
     Human Rights and Biomedicine
Elective ventilation of
   potential donor 301–03
Electronic health record
   See Health records
Embryo
   See Pregnancy; Genetics
Emergency treatment
   See Life-saving treatment
Ethics
   See Bioethics

European Convention for the
   Protection of Human Rights
   and Fundamental Freedoms 35
European Convention
   on Human Rights
   biomedicine 31–47
   claims by patients in
     respect of healthcare 55–66
   common law 13–15
   Council of Europe 32
   delays in litigation 5, 61
   jurisprudence 15–21
   non-consensual and
     experimental treatment 61
   young children 243–47
European Convention on
   Human Rights, Art 2
   access to treatment 69, 70
   euthanasia 284–94
   lack of NHS resources 64
   life-saving treatment 89–94
   life-threatening conditions 55–59
   right to information 61
   right to treatment 91–94
   right to life 50–51
European Convention on
   Human Rights, Art 3
   access to medical care 70–72
   degrading treatment 51–52
   expensive treatment 69
   lack of NHS resources 64–65
   life-saving treatment 89–91
   mental disorders 190–95
   passive euthanasia 291–93
   quality of treatment 60
   self-determination 234
European Convention on
   Human Rights, Art 5
   competent minors 235–38
   liberty and security 52
   public protection 174–75

European Convention on
   Human Rights, Art 5(1)
   burden of proof,
     mental disability 185–86
   detention of mentally
     disordered 164, 166–67,
                            186–90
   hospitalisation of
     mentally disordered 170–74
   symptoms of mental
     disorders 175–80
European Convention on
   Human Rights, Art 6
   medical complaints 113–14
   public hearings 107–09
   relevance .100–02
   restrictions 108–09
European Convention on
   Human Rights, Art 6(1)
   action in respect of delays 62
   Convention rights 52–53
   provisions 100
European Convention on
   Human Rights, Art 8
   active euthanasia 286–90, 293
   assisted fertilisation 76
   competent minors 238–39
   Convention rights 53–54
   damages awards 66
   data protection 127–28
   expensive treatment 69–70
   patient confidentiality 141–43
   residential property 60, 212–14
European Convention on
   Human Rights, Art 8(1)
   access to medical care 72–74
   vulnerable adults 155–61
European Convention on
   Human Rights, Art 8(2)
   right to treatment 88–89
   vulnerable adults 155–61

European Convention on
   Human Rights, Art 9 54
European Convention on
   Human Rights, Art 10
   active euthanasia 286–90
   data protection 127–28
   patient confidentiality 141–43
European Convention on
   Human Rights, Art 12
   basic rights .54
   fertility treatment 61
European Convention on
   Human Rights, Art 14
   competent minors 239–41
   discrimination 54
   life-saving treatment 89
   mental health law 209–10
   non-discriminatory
     healthcare .62
European Convention on Human
   Rights and Biomedicine
   Art 1 36–37
   Art 2 37
   Art 4 37
   Arts 5–9 37–39
   Art 10 40
   Arts 11–13 42–43
   Arts 15–18 40–42
   Arts 21–22 43–44
   biotechnology and
     bioethics 44–47, 332–37, 343
   consent for medical
     interventions 37–39, 320–30
   Council of Europe 32, 337–38
   development 33–34
   discrimination 42–43
   enforcement 338–39
   European Court of
     Human Rights 339–42
   European Union 333–37
   genetics 42–43

human cloning 44–47
Human Rights Act 1998 343–45
human rights
    provisions 35, 36, 320
living donors 43–44
morality and politics 317–19
object and purpose 33–34, 36–37,
                                    319–20
primacy of the
    human being 37
private life and
    information 40
professional standards 37
research 40–42, 313–17
scope of protection 313–17
Steering Committee
    on Bioethics 33–34
United Kingdom 343
European Court of
Human Rights 339–42
European Social Charter 87–89
European Union,
    bioethics .333–37
Euthanasia
    active euthanasia 278–79, 285–90
    assisted suicide 276–78
    duty of physician 282–84
    duty to preserve life 290–91
    ECHR, Art 2 284–94
    ECHR, Art 8 . . . . .286–90, 293
    ECHR, Art 10 286–90
    English law 274–75
    general 273
    incompetent patient 280–82
    non-UK law 275–76
    passive euthanasia 278–84, 290–93
    self-determination 279–80
    withdrawal of
        treatment 279
EV
    See Elective ventilation

Evolutive interpretation,
    self-determination 233

F
Fair hearings, right to 105–07
Fairness, mental health
    law, ECHR 182–85
Family life, respect for 212–14
Federal Fair Housing
    Amendments Act 221–23
Fertility treatment,
    ECHR, Art 12 61
FHAA
    See Federal Fair Housing
        Amendments Act
Foetus
    See Pregnancy
Funding availability,
    medical cases 112

G
General Dental Council 99–100
General Medical Council
    conduct procedures 116–18
    ECHR, Art 6 113–15
    health procedures 118
    performance
        procedures 118–20
    procedural rules 99–100, 115–22
    prosecution and
        adjudication 121
    right of appeal 122
    rights of complainants 120–21
Genetics
    See, also, Research
    designing babies 74–76
    ECHRB, Arts 11–13 42–43
    human cloning 44–47
Gillick-competent,
    child consent 325

Glass, David
  See David Glass
GMC
  See General Medical Council

H

Health authorities
  See, also, NHS
  ECHR 50–54
  review of complaint 123
  statutory duty 49– 50
  time-wasting
    before hearings 109–10
  vulnerable adults 149–50
Health protection,
  ECHRB, Art 2 37
Health records
  access to 134–35, 141–43
  anonymisation 133
  common law .132
  Data Protection Act 1998 139–40
  Health Records
    Act 1990 135
  Human Rights Act 1998 140–45
Healthcare law,
  Human Rights Act 1998 7–11
Healthcare resources,
  lack of as defence 62–66
Hearings
  civil procedure 107
  criminal proceedings 110–11
  ECHR, Art 6 . . . . .101–02, 107–09
  fair hearing 105–07
  health authorities 109–10
  impartial tribunals 110–11
  law of limitation 105–08
  limitation periods 102, 109–10
  medical complaints 102–11
  oral hearing .108
  press access .108
  public hearing 107–09
  strike out applications 102–04

HFEA
  See Human Fertilisation and
    Embryology Authority
Hospitalisation,
  mental disorders 170–74
Housing, mental disorders 221–23
HRA
  See Human Rights Act 1998
Human cloning,
  protocol on prohibition 44–45
Human Fertilisation and
  Embryology Authority 75–76
Human Rights Act 1998
  assessment of impact 9–11
  biotechnology and
    bioethics 343–45
  common law rules 13–15
  compensation .6
  cultural awareness 6–8
  ECHR, Art 2 . . . . .50–51, 57–58
  ECHR jurisprudence 15–21
  European Convention 13–15
  healthcare law 21–29
  interpretation
    by courts .3–4
  mental health law 163–80, 208–17
  number of cases
    brought to court 5
  parliamentary effects 4–5
  private property rights 210
  protected rights 6
  quality of life 58–59
  right to life 50–51, 55–59
  right to treatment 94–96
  time delays 5
  UK constitution 1–7, 57–58
  vulnerable adults 155–62
Human Tissue Act 1961
  action for deceased 309
  potential deceased 309–10
  relatives of deceased 308

I

Impartiality, disciplinary
  proceedings 111
Incompetent persons
  euthanasia 280–82
  living donor 297–301
  mentally disabled 104
  minors 297–99
  patient consent 297–99, 323,
                              325–27
Independent review
  mental health 182
  NHS complaints 123
Indeterminacy, mental
  disability 195
Information
  See, also, Confidentiality
  access 127–28
  action to obtain 61
  confidentiality 130–31
  sharing 150–52
Informed consent
  See Consent
Inhuman treatment,
  medical intervention 70–72
Intentional killing,
  prevention of 285–86
Inter-agency working,
  vulnerable adults 150–52
Interim hearings,
  medical complaints 101–02

J

Judgment,
  public pronouncements 109

L

Law of limitation,
  rights in medical cases 105–07
Learning disability
  See Mental disorder

Least restrictive environment,
  mental disorder 169–75
Legal disability,
  medical intervention 104
Liberty and security, ECHR 52
Life-saving treatment
  action to obtain 59
  lack of NHS resources 64
  rights to 89–91
  young children 248–57
Life-threatening conditions
  claims in respect of 55–62
  protection under ECHR,
    Art 2 59
Limitation periods
  hearings in medical cases 102
  review of detention,
    mental disability 186–88
  rights to hearing 102, 105,
                                  109
Living donor
  See, also Donor; Transplantation
    material
  competent person 296–97
  extraction of body
    materials 296–301
  incompetent person 297–301
  non-consensual activity 301–03
  transplantation material 43–44

M

Margin of appreciation
  competent minors 234
  mental health rights 163–65
Marriage, under ECHR 54
Media, access to hearings 108
Medical complaints
  appeal 122
  conduct procedures 116–18
  disciplinary proceedings 100–01
  ECHR, Art 6 101–02,
                              107, 113–15

fair hearing 105–07
General Medical
    Council 113, 115–22
health procedures 118
independent tribunal 111
interim hearing 101–02
negligence 66
NHS procedure 122–25
performance procedures 118–20
public hearing 107–09
right to hearing 102–11
rights of complaint 120–21
time to hearing 109–10
Medical confidentiality
    See Confidentiality
Medical consent
    See Consent
Medical ethics
    See Bioethics
Medical Professional
    Performance Act 1995 118
Medical records
    See Health records
Medical research
    See Research
Medical treatment
    See Treatment
Mental disorders
    assessment 169–70
    best interests 197
    Bolam test 104
    burden of proof 185–86
    community care 169–70, 198,
        201–23
    compulsory
        treatment 198
    detention 165–69, 174–75,
        86–89
    discharge 176–79, 189–90
    discrimination 209–10
    disproportionality 194–95
    drug side-effects 192–93

ECHR, Art 3 190–95
ECHR, Art 8(1) 195–98
ECHR, Art 8(2) 198–200
ECHR, actions and
    provisions 62, 190–200
failure to treat 193
fairness 182–84
hospitalisation 170–74
Human Rights Act 1998 163–80,
        208–17
indeterminacy 195
power to release 183–85
private property rights 221–23
protection of public 174–75,
        198–200
review of detention 182
symptoms 169–70,
        175–80
treatment 104, 192–94, 198
Mental health law
    See Mental disorders
Mercy killing
    See Euthanasia
Minors
    See Children

N
National Health Service
    See, also, Health Authorities
    complaints procedure 122–25
    economics of resources 65–66
    lack of resources as defence 62–66
    life-threatening conditions 55–62
    resource allocation 49–66
    statutory duty 49–50
    time to action 62
Negligence
    See Medical complaints
NHBD
    See Non-heart beating donor
NHS
    See National Health Service

Non-consensual
    medical treatment 61
Non-heart beating donor 303–04

O

Oral hearing, medical cases 108
Organ donation
    See Donor; Transplantation material

P

Parliament and human
    rights issues 3–5
Patient confidentiality
    See Confidentiality
Patient consent
    See Consent
Patient records
    See Health records
Pennings system of
    organ procurement 310–11
Personal injury cases,
    damages 66
Physician assisted suicide
    See Euthanasia
Potential deceased,
    use of body tissues 308–10
Pregnancy
    abortion 260–64
    genetic testing 42–43
    Human Rights Act 1998 259
    prenatal harm 265–71
Prenatal harm
    See Pregnancy
Press, access to hearings 108
Primacy of the human being,
    ECHRB 37
Private life, respect for
    access to treatment 72–74
    mental disability 212–14
    right to information 40
Private property rights
    common law 214–16

community care 202–17
covenants 202–08
disability discrimination 209–10,
                       217–23
disposal of premises 218–21
fairer housing 221–23
Human Rights Act 1998 208–14
Professional complaints,
    See Medical complaints
Professional standards
    biomedical disciplines 37
    physician performance 118–19, 121
Proportionality
    self-determination
        by minors 233–34
    sentence in
        mental disorder 194–95
Public authorities
    provisions for
        vulnerable adults 149–50
    time-wasting 109–10
Public health authorities
    See Health authorities
Public hearing, rights in
    medical cases 107–09
Public interests
    announcements of
        judgments 109
    confidentiality exceptions 152–55
Public protection
    detention of mentally
        disordered 174–75
    ECHR, Art 8(2) 198–200
    health and safety 199–200

Q

Quality of life
    common law 58–59
    ECHR, Art 2 57–59
    euthanasia 281–84

R

Religion, freedom of thought 54
Reproductive technology
   See Assisted reproduction
Research
   children 325
   consent .320–26
   ECHRB 42–43, 313–20
   extraction of
      body materials 304–11
   genetics 42–43
   medical interventions 320–30
   morality and politics 317–19
   non-therapeutic 327–30
   persons unable
      to consent 323, 325–26
   protection 313–17
Residential homes
   action to preserve 60
   community care 202–08
Reviews
   detention of
      mentally disordered 186–90
   ECHR, Art 5(4) 182
   medical complaints 123–25
Right of appeal,
   General Medical Council 122
Right to hearings
   limitation periods 102, 105, 109
   medical cases 102–11
   strike out applications 102–04
Right to information
   ECHR, Art 2 .61
   private life 40
Right to life
   access to treatment 70
   common law 58–59
   ECHR, Art 2 50–51
   life-threatening conditions 55–60
   quality of life 58–59
Right to treatment 70, 72–74, 81–97

S

Self-determination
   See, also, Competent minor
   Convention rights 233–34
   ECHR, Art 3 234
   ECHR, Art 14 239–41
   English medical law 225–26
   medical intervention 235–38
   refusal of treatment 279–80
Siamese twins .58
Side-effects, drugs 192–93
Social services
   mental disorders 169–70
   vulnerable adults 150–52
Standards of care
   See Professional standards
Statutory duties,
   public health authorities 49–50
Steering Committee
   on Bioethics 33–34
Strike out applications,
   ECHR Article 6 102–04
Suicide
   See Euthanasia

T

Time limitations
   See Limitation periods
Time-wasting by
   public authorities 109–10
Tissue donation
   See Donor; Transplantation material
Torture, provisions of ECHR 51–52
Transplantation material
   ECHRB, Arts 21–22 43–44
   extraction after death 304–11
   Human Tissue
      Act 1961 308–10
   living donors 43–44, 295–301
   non-consensual
      activity 301–04

non-heart beating
    donors 303–04
organ procurement 43–44, 310–11
Treatment of patients
    children 235–39, 248–52
    common law 84–87
    community care 198
    compulsory 198
    David Glass case 82–84, 94–96
    discontinuation 282–84
    ECHR, Art 2 91–94
    ECHR, Art 3 .... 60, 192–94
    euthanasia 279–80, 282–84
    expensive treatment 69–70
    experimental 61, 69–70
    HRA 1998 81–82
    life-saving 89–91
    mental disorders 104, 188,
                   192–94, 198
    non-consensual 61, 69–70
    non-emergency 64–65
    quality of 60
    refusal 252–57, 279–80
    rights to 70, 72–74,
                   81–97
    Woolf reforms 83–87
Tribunals
    impartial 110–11
    medical cases 99–100
    oral hearing 108
    right to hearing 111

U

UKCC
    See UK Central Council for Nursing,
    Midwifery and Health Visiting

Unborn child
    See Pregnancy
United Kingdom law
    assisted suicide 276–77
    biotechnology regulations 343
    HRA 1998 .... 1–7, 57–58
UK Central Council
    for Nursing, Midwifery
    and Health Visiting 99–100

V

Vulnerable adults
    See, also, Mental disorders
    confidentiality 152–55
    definition 147–49
    information sharing 150–52
    public authorities 149–50

W

Welfare principle, young
    children
    human rights 247–57
    life-saving treatment 248–57
    parent refusal for
        treatment 252–57
    parent requests for
        treatment 248–52
Woolf reforms, medical
    treatment under HRA 1998 83–87

Y

Young children, best interests
    under HRA 1998 247–57